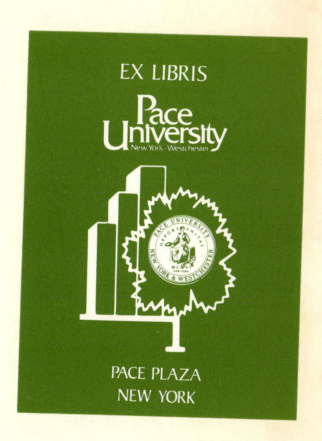

IRON AND STEEL
IN THE GERMAN INFLATION
1916–1923

GERALD D. FELDMAN

Iron and Steel in the German Inflation 1916-1923

PRINCETON UNIVERSITY PRESS

PRINCETON, NEW JERSEY

Library of Congress Cataloging in Publication Data
will be found on the last printed page of this book

Publication of this book has been aided by the Whitney Darrow
Publication Reserve Fund of Princeton University Press

Printed in the United States of America
by Princeton University Press
Princeton, New Jersey

TO PHILIPPA

Er drohte mit dem Austritt. Ein Kampf zwischen Eisen
und Kohle schien bevorzustehen, obwohl es ganz sicher war,
dass er niemals ausgetragen werden konnte, denn da es
unter den Grossen keinen gab, der nur auf *einem* dieser
Flügel stand, hätte jeder sich selbst bekriegen müssen.
Aber wie stets im industriellen Leben, so waren auch
diesmal nicht die Kampfresultate, sondern die blossen
Kampfmomente das Wesentliche—so wie es Wirtz in seinen
guten Zeiten gesagt hatte: Der Sieg des einen und die
Niederlage des anderen ist nur eine Beigabe zu den
industriellen Kämpfen, ausschlaggebendes Ziel ist allein
der Ausbau von Kampfstellungen. . . . Es kommt weniger
darauf an, dass man einen Kampf bis zum Ende durchficht,
als darauf dass man in Bereitschaft ist.

—Erik Reger, *Union der Festen Hand. Roman
einer Entwicklung* (Berlin, 1946), p. 393.

CONTENTS

CONTENTS

LIST OF TABLES

PREFACE

I did not intend to write this book when I began my researches into the socioeconomic history of the German inflation, but like many unplanned creations, its birth is no accident. My original intention was to write a study of industry, labor, and the state in the early Weimar Republic (1918–1923) as a sequel to my earlier study, *Army, Industry and Labor in Germany, 1914–1918* (Princeton, 1966). I was deflected from this original goal, which has now been broadened into a plan to write a social history of the German inflation, that is, a study of the effects of the inflation on all the significant socioeconomic groups and institutions of German society, for two reasons.

First, I discovered the enormous difficulties involved in attempting a relatively general study in a largely uncharted area of historical research. Although historians continuously and religiously pay tribute to the importance of the protracted German inflation of 1916–1923, the major studies focusing on the inflation have, until recently, all been undertaken by economists who paid little or no attention to the concurrent political, social, institutional, sociopsychological, and ideological developments. Thus, I found myself overwhelmed by the sheer difficulties of putting so complex a story together, and I came to the conclusion that the writing of a "preliminary study" of a significant segment of the larger theme might be a useful way of developing the foundations of a broader investigation. Second, I found that I had gathered a disproportionately large amount of what I believed to be highly significant primary source material on the German iron and steel industry during the period of inflation, which at once threatened to make a more general study list very heavily to one side and also required separate treatment because it had reached the point of forming an important story unto itself.

The origins of this book explain certain intentional limitations·on its scope of discussion which might appear disturbing to those acquainted with the period and its problems. The coal problem, so central to the economic and political issues of the period as well as to the special problems of the iron and steel industry and so intrinsically interesting because energy crises are no longer simply subjects of historical curiosity, is relatively neglected in this book. This problem, like the momentous social questions involving wages and working hours, come in for somewhat detailed treatment only in the final chapters. Were I to have treated these major issues in detail in this study, I believe that I would have distorted its purposes. These problems will be treated more fully in the general work I intend to write, and such explorations of them as appear here form points of intersection between the two works.

The purposes of this study are more than instrumental, however, and I believe that my work makes some contribution to certain basic problems of modern German and modern European history. On the most fundamental level, it is a study in business history, an examination of how the leaders of one of Germany's most important and powerful industries conducted business during seven years of inflation and political and social unrest, and of how this group emerged from this protracted crisis in a position of greater power and security than it merited for either economic or political reasons. Second, it is meant to be a contribution to the general history of the Weimar Republic. Until recently the culture and the politics of the Weimar Republic have been narrowly conceived and treated in too much isolation, because historians share Ernst Troeltsch's distaste for the "Americanization" of German life reflected in the Weimar Republic and find the traditional heroes of culture and politics more congenial. In the long run, however, history should not be written to taste, and the reality of heavy industry's enormous role in the culture and politics of Weimar Germany must find its rightful place in its history just as it found its place in the caricatures of Grosz, the articles of "Morus" in the *Weltbühne*, in the funding of Oswald Spengler, the *Süddeutsche Monatshefte,* and the Ufa, and in the desperate efforts of Stresemann to free himself and his party from the constraints that accompanied industrialist money.

A fundamental assumption underlying this study, however, is that the role of industry in the politics and culture of the Weimar Republic or in the politics and culture of any other place and time cannot really be understood in terms of politics and culture alone. To argue that the business of businessmen is business, not politics, and that their political engagement is almost invariably a function of their socioeconomic concerns is to make a methodological rather than a rhetorical point. The ideas and actions of Hugo Stinnes, the problems of export controls and vertical concentration, and the fundamental issues of producer-consumer relations are issues as central to the history of the Weimar Republic as those traditionally studied, because they explain by and large the actions of industrialists on the broader cultural and political stage and because they directly affected the lives of millions of people. Indeed, insofar as they constitute a part of the general history of what historians have increasingly come to recognize as the most fundamental and irreversible of all developments of the modern age, the process of industrialization, they are worthy of study for their own sake. Finally, at a time when "political economy" is being rediscovered, and the problems of relations among producers, consumers, and governmental authorities have taken on a new urgency, a study such as this one may have a certain contemporary pertinence.

My scholarly endeavors over the past decade, of which this book is the most substantial product to date, as well as my continuing work on the problems of the German inflation, have depended upon generous institutional support and personal assistance. Fellowships from the American Council of Learned Societies, the Humanities Research Fellowship Program of the University of California, and the John Simon Guggenheim Memorial Foundation, and grants from the Social Science Research Council and from the University of California at Berkeley's Committee on Research and its Institute of International Studies made it possible for me to investigate rather than to experience the ravages of inflation and stagflation. From the very inception of my work, I have received extraordinary tangible and moral encouragement from the Institute of International Studies of the University of California at Berkeley, for which I am extremely grateful.

This study is based largely upon archival materials and could not have been written without the access to materials afforded me by the various industrial concerns and organizations in the Federal Republic and by the public archives of the Federal Republic and the German Democratic Republic. I am deeply appreciative of the opportunity to work in these archives and particularly for the unrestrained and unrestricted use I have been able to make of the materials from private industrial archives. While I cannot mention all those who assisted me in so many ways, I wish to express special thanks to Count von Zedtwitz-Arnim of Fredrich Krupp, AG, Erich Warburg and Dr. Curt Duisberg for permission to use the papers in their charge. I also wish to thank Dr. Gertrud Milkereit of Thyssen, Dr. Manfred Pohl of the Deutsche Bank, Manfred Hanke of the Industrieinstitut in Cologne, Bergassessor Hans-Günther Conrad of the Bergbau Archiv und Museum in Bochum, Frau Denkinger of the MAN Augsburg, Dr. S. von Weiher of the Werner-von-Siemens-Institut, Dr. Helmut Lötzke, Director of the Deutsches Zentralarchiv Potsdam, and Dr. Thomas Trumpp of the Bundesarchiv Koblenz for their special efforts on my behalf. The late Dr. Harald Jaeger of the Bavarian State Archives and the late Dr. Gerhard Enders of the DZA Potsdam not only made major contributions to my work but enriched my visits to Munich and Potsdam with a hospitality and warmth I shall always remember. Frau Dr. Hedwig Behrens, the *doyenne* of German business archivists, disregarded the privileges of her well-earned retirement and underwent numerous inconveniences to place important collections at my disposal. For these sacrifices as well as for her splendid hospitality, I thank her sincerely. My debt to the

Historical Archive of the Gutehoffnungshütte, AG and to its head, Herr Bodo Herzog, should be apparent on most of the pages of this book. I thank him both for the most important research experience of my career and for one of the most pleasant.

In my research and writing, I have had the benefit of valuable information and advice from friends and colleagues. Henry Turner and Hans Mommsen were extremely helpful to my research, while Carl-Ludwig Holtfrerich, Jürgen Kocka, Arno J. Mayer, Walter McDougall, Ulrich Nocken, William N. Parker, Irwin Scheiner and Peter-Christian Witt read various parts of the manuscript and made helpful suggestions for improvement. Hans Rosenberg has not only made useful suggestions but, far more importantly, has remained a constant source of encouragement, inspiration and friendship during my years at Berkeley. I have also learned much from the work of Wolfgang Sauer and my conversations with him. I wish to express particular thanks to Heinrich Winkler for his exceptionally helpful reading of the manuscript and to Charles Maier for the time and energy he devoted to my manuscript and for his continuously valuable advice. Responsibility for all deficiencies in this study, of course, rests solely with myself.

Were it not for the help of talented and dedicated assistants, the completion of this study would have taken much longer than it has. Alan Kovan, Jeffrey Diefendorf and Pamela Munro assisted me during early stages of my research, while Cornelius Gispen was extraordinarily helpful during early stages of the writing. Irmgard Steinisch assisted me during the bulk of the time spent in the organization and composition of this study, and she did so with intelligence, imagination and sensitivity. I am extremely grateful to her, as I am to Heidrun Homburg for her splendid work in the final stages of this study and to Andreas Kunz.

I wish to express a special word of gratitude to Mrs. Cleo Stoker of the Institute of International Studies for her constant attention to my scholarly well-being and to the members of her staff, Bojana Ristich and Graeme Elberg, who typed the manuscript so quickly and so well.

It has always been a pleasure to work with the Princeton University Press, and Mr. Lewis Bateman has made this even more the case.

Finally, I wish to express my appreciation to my wife, Philippa, to whom this book is dedicated, and to my children, Deborah and Aaron, for their continued devotion to me despite the peculiar preoccupations reflected by this book.

Berkeley, California G. D. F.
April 1976

ABBREVIATIONS

ADGB	Allgemeiner Deutscher Gewerkschaftsbund General Confederation of German Trade Unions
AG	Aktiengesellschaft
AEG	Allgemeine Elektrizitätsgesellschaft
Arbeno	Arbeitgeberverband für den Bezirk der Nordwest- lichen Gruppe des Vereins deutscher Eisen- und Stahlindustrieller Employer Organization of the Northwest Group of the Association of German Iron and Steel Industrialists
ATH	August Thyssen Hütte
AVI	Arbeitsgemeinschaft der Eisenverarbeitenden Industrie Working Community of the Iron Finishing Industry
BA	Bundesarchiv Koblenz
BayHStA	Bayrisches Hauptstaatsarchiv
DEMAG	Deutsche Maschinenfabrik AG
Deutsch-Lux	Deutsch-Luxemburgische Bergwerks- und Hütten AG
DINTA	Deutsches Institut für technische Arbeitsschulung Institute for Technical Labor Training
DMV	Deutscher Metallarbeiterverband (Socialist) Metal Workers Union
DNVP	Deutsch-nationale Volkspartei German National People's Party
DVP	Deutsche Volkspartei German People's Party
DZA	Deutsches Zentralarchiv Potsdam
EWB	Eisenwirtschaftsbund Iron Trades Federation
GBAG	Gelsenkirchener Bergwerks AG
GHH	Gutehoffnungshütte AG
GmbH	Gesellschaft mit beschränkter Haftung Limited Liability Company

GM	Gold Mark
HA/GHH	Historisches Archiv der Gutehoffnungshütte
HANOMAG	Hannoversche Maschinenbau AG
IG	Interessengemeinschaft Community of Interest
IRMA	International Rail Manufacturers Association
IWK	Internationale Wissenschaftliche Korrespondenz zur Geschichte der deutschen Arbeiterbewegung
kgl.	königlich royal
KRA	Kriegsrohstoffabteilung Raw Materials Section
KrAMü	Kriegsarchiv München
Krupp WA	Krupp Werksarchiv
Langnamverein	Verein zur Wahrung der gemeinsamen wirtschaftlichen Interessen in Rheinland und Westfalen Association to Protect the Common Economic Interests of Rhineland-Westphalia
M	Mark
MAN	Maschinenfabrik Augsburg-Nürnberg AG
Northwest Group	Northwest Group of the Association of German Iron and Steel Industrialists
PM	Paper Mark
RAM	Reichsarbeitsministerium Reich Labor Ministry
RdI	Reichsverband der Deutschen Industrie Reich Association of German Industry
RFM	Reichsfinanzministerium Reich Finance Ministry
Rheinstahl	Rheinische Stahlwerke
RSchA	Reichsschatzamt Reich Treasury Office
RWA	Reichswirtschaftsamt Reich Economics Office
RWM	Reichswirtschaftsministerium Reich Economics Ministry
RWE	Rheinisch-Westfälisches Elektrizitätswerk AG

RWR	Reichswirtschaftsrat Reich Economics Council
SAA	Siemens Archiv Akten
SPD	Sozialdemokratische Partei Deutschlands Social Democratic Party
SRSU	Siemens-Rhein-Elbe-Schuckert Union
SSW	Siemens-Schuckert Werke
VDA	Vereinigung der Deutschen Arbeitgeberverbände Association of German Employer Organizations
VdE	Verein Deutscher Eisenhüttenleute Association of German Foundry Engineers
VDMA	Verein Deutscher Maschinenbauanstalten Association of German Machine Builders
VdESI	Verein Deutscher Eisen- und Stahlindustrieller Association of German Iron and Steel Industrialists
Vestag	Vereinigte Stahlwerke AG United Steelworks
ZAG	Zentralarbeitsgemeinschaft der gewerblichen und industriellen Arbeitgeber und Arbeitnehmer Deutschlands Central Working Community of the German Commercial and Industrial Employers and Employees
Zechenverband	Mine Owners Association
Zendei	Zentralverband der deutschen Elektrotechnischen Industrie Central Association of the German Electrotechnical Industry

IRON AND STEEL
IN THE GERMAN INFLATION
1916–1923

INTRODUCTION

THE RATIONALE FOR THIS STUDY AND SOME
METHODOLOGICAL CONSIDERATIONS

The German inflation of 1916–1923 was a trauma that the German people have found hard to forget and historians have found difficult to assess. As a consequence, there has been a strong convergence between the popular image of the inflation and the one presented by historians. Both have stressed the horrendous hyperinflation of 1923, that spectacular dénouement of a protracted period of inflation and instability. They have conjured up the familiar but always mysterious personage of Hugo Stinnes to serve as the archetype of inflationary profiteers, and the socioeconomic history of the inflation has been conceived largely in terms of his ilk reaping unwarranted gains while working-class wives rolled wheelbarrows filled with paper money to the bread lines and a "middle class" of savers and pensioners suffered the "ruin" that made them susceptible to fascism.[1]

To be sure, historians have realized that the inflation began in 1916 when government expenditure outstripped income from the domestic loans used to finance the war and the government failed, both then and subsequently, to remedy the situation through appropriate taxation and monetary policies. Similarly, historians conversant with the period normally recognize that the hyperinflation began in the last months of 1922 and thus antedated the Ruhr occupation and passive resistance.[2] The implication of much of the better historical literature on the period is that the inflation was not a natural disaster, that the dikes guarding against the flood had frequently been dismantled and that many had deliberately not been put up, that the looters had often been tolerated and even encouraged, and that no precise accounting

[1] See, for example, the useful little collection of primary and secondary sources by Fritz Ringer, *The German Inflation of 1923* (Problems in European History: A Documentary Collection) (New York, London, Toronto, 1969). The very title is illustrative of the point being made here, as is the collection itself. Contemporary texts and general surveys tend to treat the inflation similarly, as, for example, Hajo Holborn, *A History of Modern Germany 1840–1945* (New York, 1969), pp. 595–601, and Koppel Pinson, *Modern Germany. Its History and Civilization*, 2nd ed. (New York, 1966), pp. 446–447.

[2] Economic historians have made the most of these points, as, for example, Gustav Stolper, Karl Häuser, Knut Borchardt, *The German Economy. 1870 to the Present* (London, 1967), pp. 53–60, 74–89. A similar approach has been taken by some general historians, e.g., Holborn, *A History of Modern Germany.*

3

has ever been made of actual damage suffered and no reasonably acceptable demonstration attempted of the long-term consequences. There is no adequate history of the German inflation, a situation that ceases to be surprising when one considers that, until recently, historians of Germany have tended to concentrate on political and intellectual history and have neglected socioeconomic development. Furthermore, there can be no adequate history of the inflation until some progress has been made in attending to the host of problems and issues raised for the historian by the protracted inflation and peculiar socioeconomic developments of the 1916–1923 period.[3]

Not surprisingly, the signposts for such investigation have been provided by the economists, who have long been intrigued by the theoretical and practical conclusions that might be drawn from the study of the most extreme inflation ever to engulf an advanced industrial society. Unfortunately, the richness of the problems raised by the inflation has not always been complemented by the statistical material necessary to deal with them in a reasonably conclusive way, and the fact that the years 1914–1923 usually constitute a great gap in the time series on which economists depend, has made it more possible than usual to employ available data to argue differing points of view. Although the historian is far less equipped than the economist to decide most of the issues in debate among the economists, there is much that he can learn from the fact that there is a debate, and there are considerations and dimensions that he can add that might contribute to interdisciplinary discussion as well as raise the level of analysis in both fields.[4]

In contrast to historians, who generally condemn the inflation for its allegedly untoward political and social consequences, economists have been divided in their evaluation of the inflation because they have recognized the fact that the postwar German inflation enabled Germany to maintain a high level of employment, enjoy great export advantages, and reconstruct her industrial plant while the victors of World War I

[3] That progress is being made is demonstrated by Peter-Christian Witt, "Finanzpolitik und sozialer Wandel in Krieg und Inflation 1918–1924," in Hans Mommsen, Dietmar Petzina, and Bernd Weisbrod, eds., *Industrielles System und politische Entwicklung in der Weimarer Republik. Verhandlungen des Internationalen Symposiums in Bochum von 12.–17. Juni 1973* (Düsseldorf, 1974) (hereinafter cited as *Industrielles System*), pp. 395–425.

[4] The gaps in the time series are amply demonstrated in Walther G. Hoffmann, *Das Wachstum der Deutschen Wirtschaft seit der Mitte des 19. Jahrhunderts* (Berlin, Heidelberg, New York, 1965). For excellent surveys of the present state of the discussion among economists along with many penetrating insights, see Peter Czada, "Grosse Inflation und Wirtschaftswachstum," *Industrielles System*, pp. 386–394, and "Ursachen und Folgen der grossen Inflation," in Harold Winkel, ed., *Finanz- und Wirtschaftspolitische Fragen der Zwischenkriegszeit* (Schriften des Vereins für Sozialpolitik, Vol. 73) (Berlin, 1973), pp. 9–43.

enjoyed a brief postwar boom only in 1919 and early 1920 and then suffered from a severe depression and high unemployment in 1920–1922. Where economists have disagreed has been in their evaluation of the German boom. Costantino Bresciani-Turroni, in his classic study, asserted that the inflation produced economic "distortions" by encouraging wasteful investment and purely quantitative expansion. Frank D. Graham took a more sanguine posture and argued that the currency depreciation was "far from being an unmixed curse" because German domestic production was greater in 1920–1922 than it would have been under more stable economic conditions. More recently, the Scandinavian economists Karsten Laursen and Jørgen Pedersen have contended that the German industrial plant and capital base were qualitatively improved during the inflation and that the inflationary policies pursued by the government and the various economic interest groups, although certainly not creating ideal economic conditions, did permit Germany to enjoy a postwar recovery and full employment denied those countries pursuing a deflationary course during the same period.[5] Was the inflation a curse, a mixed curse, or a mixed blessing? A definite consensus has thus far eluded the economists and may continue to do so because of inadequate data and methodological differences, but it is a question the historian cannot evade in his own confrontation with the German inflation. Although the sociopolitical gains or losses accruing from the inflation necessarily weigh more heavily for the historian than they do for the economist in considering the consequences of the inflation, the sociopolitical balance sheet cannot be torn out and viewed in isolation from the economic ledger in which it is bound.

The structural changes that have taken place and continue to take place in the economic development of advanced industrial societies appear to have a certain independence of events of such monumental import to the historian as world wars, domestic political turbulence, and radical changes of political regime. Looking at the time series for the German case, economic historians have convincingly argued that "German industry has developed in the 'long run' according to the laws which apparently inhere in modern economies, and that the general and the typical break through more strongly than the special instances in which an attempt is made to impose political decisions upon the

[5] Costantino Bresciani-Turroni, *The Economics of Inflation. A Study of Currency Depreciation in Post-War Germany, 1914–1923* (London, 1968), esp. pp. 372–374 and 398–404. (The work was originally published in 1937, and the author had been an Italian representative on the Reparations Commission after World War I.) Frank D. Graham, *Exchange, Prices, and Production in Hyper-Inflation: Germany 1920–1923* (Princeton, 1930), esp. pp. 317–320; Karsten Laursen and Jørgen Pedersen, *The German Inflation 1918–1923* (Amsterdam, 1964), esp. pp. 123–127.

economic process."[6] One does not have to be an economic determinist to recognize that economic development and conditions provide parameters within which political action, social development, and intellectual life take place and that a historical understanding of any period must take account of the interconnection between economic and other structures. Recent research in nineteenth-century German history has demonstrated how close attention to the phases of industrial development, to so-called long waves and trend periods, and to business cycles make sociopolitical and cultural developments more intelligible.[7] Certainly the sociopolitical history of the twentieth century is even less separable from its economic history than that of the nineteenth, but unfortunately twentieth-century economic history is far harder to organize than that of the preceding century. David Landes has noted: "The twentieth century by contrast is a confusion of emergencies, disasters, improvisations, and artificial expedients. One passes in a few weeks of 1914 from a quiet stream, as it were, to white water."[8]

If the historian is not to be overwhelmed by the "exogenous" factors that have made this century so chaotic, then he must be aware of the "laws which apparently inhere in modern economies." Nevertheless, the context must not be so "long run" as to obliterate the significance of the short run and the "exogenous" on which the historian usually rivets his attention. Modest theoretical and conceptual frameworks would seem more appropriate than grander ones. The applicability of long waves and trend periods to the twentieth century is even more disputed than it is for its predecessor, and it is difficult enough to fit so limited and turbulent a phenomenon as the German inflation of 1916–1923 into the modest framework of the business cycle without attempting to relate it to more elaborate cyclical models.[9] Nevertheless, the long run must not be forgotten. In understanding the behavior of economic and political leaders in the postwar decades, there is much to be gained from realizing that the period 1817–1896 was one characterized by relatively uninterrupted deflation combined with enormous

[6] Wolfram Fischer and Peter Czada, "Wandlungen in der deutschen Industriestruktur im 20. Jahrhundert," in Gerhard A. Ritter, ed., Entstehung und Wandel der modernen Gesellschaft. Festschrift für Hans Rosenberg zum 65. Geburtstag (Berlin, 1970), p. 117.

[7] See, especially, Hans Rosenberg, Grosse Depression und Bismarckzeit. Wirtschaftsablauf, Gesellschaft und Politik in Mitteleuropa (Berlin, 1967).

[8] David Landes, The Unbound Prometheus. Technological Change and Industrial Development in Western Europe from 1750 to the Present (Cambridge, 1969), p. 359.

[9] Joseph Schumpeter, Business Cycles, 2 vols. (New York and London, 1939), II, p. 692ff.; Gustav Clausing, Die wirtschaftlichen Wechsellagen von 1919 bis 1932 (Jena, 1933), p. 49ff.

6

economic expansion.[10] As will be shown, the habits of mind, the intellectual presuppositions, and the practical actions of German businessmen and officials compelled to deal with the wartime and postwar inflation were informed by the nineteenth-century experience and the expectations that came with it. The presumption of deflation and continued expansion generally persisted throughout the inflation and provided the context within which policy was made.

As suggested above, the significance of the inflation and, indeed, of the entire history of the Weimar Republic, tends to be lost when placed in the context of the secular growth of the German economy. This is not the case when one places them in the context of economic growth in the interwar period. The economist Ingvar Svennilson has shown that the interwar period was one of relative stagnation, that is, of reduced output, in the European economy.[11] The economic context within which the tragedy of the Weimar Republic was played out deserves greater attention from historians if for no other reason than because it indicates certain general limitations on the capacity of the Republic to master its particular problems and inhibits speculative fantasizing about unhistorical alternatives.[12] At the same time, recognition of the interwar stagnation also serves to give more precise formulation to the earlier discussed problem of evaluating the consequences of the inflation. It is possible to argue that the economic development of Germany during the inflation either spared that country some of the symptoms of stagnation experienced by the other European nations or that it simply put off the day of reckoning and intensified later difficulties by multiplying and exacerbating the structural problems that characterized the stagnation. Both points may be and have been argued as economists have considered the structural problems of the German economy, the relative development of "new" and "old" industries, the balance of producer and consumer industries, and other questions of concern to students of economic growth.[13] In any case, the work of economists taking the view "that economic growth over a period must

---

[10] Landes, *Unbound Prometheus*, pp. 233–234.

[11] Ingvar Svennilson, *Growth and Stagnation of the European Economy* (Geneva, 1954), esp. p. 41ff.

[12] Dietmar Petzina and Werner Abelshauser, "Zum Problem der relativen Stagnation der deutschen Wirtschaft in den zwanziger Jahren," *Industrielles System*, pp. 57–76; and Wolfram Fischer, "Die Weimarer Republik unter den weltwirtschaftlichen Bedingungen der Zwischenkriegszeit," *ibid.*, pp. 26–50.

[13] Czada, "Grosse Inflation und Wirtschaftswachstum," in *ibid.*, pp. 391–392. See also the important work of Rolf Wagenführ, *Die Industriewirtschaft. Entwicklungstendenzen der deutschen und internationalen Industrieproduktion 1860 bis 1932* (*Vierteljahrshefte zur Konjunkturforschung*, Sonderheft 31) (Berlin, 1933), p. 20ff.

be regarded as a process in which each new step is determined by the steps preceding it"[14] is most pertinent to the interests of the historian, not merely because of the obvious analogy to the historical method, but also because it provides the best framework within which to analyze the impact of "exogenous" political and institutional influences on economic decision making.

However endogenous the character of secular economic development may be, it is also true that the tempo of such development, and the manner and conditions under which it takes place, are increasingly determined by "exogenous" influences. Hence the distinction between endogenous and exogenous influences is often artificial and misleading. Whatever the variations in the industrial development of the advanced industrial nations of the West and however different the role played by the state in their industrialization, there has been a high degree of convergence among them in this century in at least two respects.[15] On the one hand, industry everywhere has become more "collectivist" in character. Monopolistic or oligopolistic organization of many of the most important areas of production has become commonplace, and the industrial world has been increasingly dominated by cartels, trusts, and conglomerates. These developments have been promoted by the effort to reduce the impact of economic crises through self-help, by scientific and technological advances and the need for ever larger capital resources to apply them, by the interests and ambitions of the businessmen involved, and by varying degrees of government encouragement. The capitalist economies have long ceased to function in accordance with the classical and neoclassical models that have been used to explain and legitimize their existence, and industrial organizations have increasingly found it necessary to seek the support of the state and of "public opinion" to maintain and develop their interests. Modern industry, therefore, has not only become "collectivist" in its approach to production and the market but also in its sociopolitical activity. If their

[14] Svennilson, *Growth and Stagnation*, pp. 3–4. He goes on to point out that: "If a different attitude is adopted, if, for example, the successive stages in the development of an economy were regarded as a series of causally unconnected equilibria, that would certainly involve an entirely different approach. It would then be possible to explain the changes over a period of twenty years by a close examination of all the circumstances at the beginning and at the end of that period. But it is obviously impossible to use this much simpler method if the various changes in the intervening years are regarded as affecting one another in a chain of cause and effect, and thus as affecting also the final result of the end of the longer period."

[15] For a fuller discussion of the tendencies discussed below as well as the extensive literature, see Heinrich Winkler, ed., *Organisierter Kapitalismus. Voraussetzungen und Anfänge* (Kritische Studien zur Geschichtswissenschaft, Vol. 9) (Göttingen, 1974), esp. pp. 9–57.

origins lie in the nineteenth century, the interest group and the lobby have nevertheless truly blossomed in the twentieth century as a consequence of advanced industrialization and the growth and complexity of private economic power.

On the other hand, the state has everywhere played a greater role in economic life. The preparation and conduct of major wars have served as the catalysts of this process, but it is obvious that the growth of private economic power, the recognition that the state could itself take action to relieve and mitigate the effect of economic crises, and the intensified demand by large segments of the population for an increasing measure of social security in the broadest sense, have all served to increase the functions of the state. World War I is generally considered to be the great watershed in this development, albeit a watershed that was often ignored by contemporaries in their yearning for a return to the past and that is frequently exaggerated by present-day analysts who underestimate the extent to which its lessons were rejected in the interwar period. Yet, World War I did point the way to a quantitative and qualitative change in the state's socioeconomic role. Whatever the prewar precedents, and there were many, the state assumed a much more direct function in economic life as the major consumer of industrial production, regulator of production and distribution, and mediator or arbiter of socioeconomic conflict. The points of contact and interdependence between the public and private sectors suddenly increased beyond what anyone could have imagined as a consequence of these new functions and because of the state's dependence on the private sector for the organizational apparatus and expertise needed to fulfill them. The practice of subcontracting public functions to private organizations had begun along with the effort to implement government regulation through industrial self-administration. However great the retreat from war economics after 1918, the precedents had been established and were to be reemployed with increasing frequency in later years. Consequently, the potential conflict between public and private power has been made all the more complicated by their frequent intermingling.

These phenomena have encouraged a revival of interest in political economy, strictly speaking. Just as the great depression of the 1930s drove economists to a preoccupation with cyclical theory, and the problems of underdevelopment promoted the investigation of economic growth and development in the 1950s and 1960s, so the contemporary problems of economic management—persistent international monetary problems coupled with seemingly uncontrollable inflation, the emergence of the multinational corporation, the development of regional economic groupings, raw materials and ecological problems—have called into question tried formulas of economic theory and raised interest in defining the actual operation of political and private power in the economic realm and in the possibilities of economic planning so that blatant dysfunctionalities and irrationalities might become intelligible and avoidable. The complexity of contemporary socioeconomic and political life, however, has made it extraordinarily difficult to develop concepts and theories adequate to organize and analyze the available information and to point toward clear and promising lines of investigation.[16]

The search for adequate theories and concepts and the problematic nature of those available present a particularly inviting situation for the historian, whose critical empiricism has the function of testing existing theories and concepts, but also the constructive task of providing the factual and analytical data on which old theories and concepts may be refined and new hypotheses developed. The value of historical research for such purposes has already been made abundantly evident in the discussion of economic growth, where overly schematic theories have given way to more viable ones thanks to the work of economic historians. Similarly, conceptualization about the political economy of twentieth-century capitalist societies could certainly benefit from more empirical investigation about how businessmen and bureaucrats have actually interacted among themselves and with one another, of how industrial concentration and organization of various types have actually taken place, of why certain decisions were taken rather than others, and of how much "organization" there actually has been under capitalism as well as of what such "organization" has really meant. Furthermore, under the impress of the growing demand for accountability and growing concern with the legitimation of existing institutions and structures, historical investigation of concrete developments may help to provide a more realistic understanding of how socioeconomic decisions and actions have actually been undertaken and thereby assist in the definition of sensible expectations and criteria for evaluation.

This study of the German iron and steel industry in the inflation is meant to serve as a modest contribution to such goals and, hopefully, as an encouragement to further investigations along similar lines. It seeks to explain in concrete terms how the businessmen in this industry

[16] For discussions of the problems of theoretical and conceptual development, see Eike Hennig, "Materialien zur Diskussion der Monopolgruppentheorie," *Neue politische Literatur*, 18, April–June 1973, pp. 170–193; Winkler, *Organisierter Kapitalismus*, pp. 9–35, 150–154, 195–213; *Industrielles System*, pp. 955–956; and Claus Offe, *Strukturprobleme des kapitalistischen Staates* (Frankfurt a.M., 1973).

10

managed their enterprises, their relations with the customers in the
iron and steel consuming industries, and their relations with state and
society during almost a decade of war, revolution, and inflation. There
are good reasons for singling this industry out for investigation. Before
the war, it was the most blossoming, powerful and expansive branch
of the older "heavy" industries, and it exhibited considerably more
dynamism than the extractive industries, especially the coal industry,
over which it tended to exercise an increasing measure of domination.
David Landes has pointed out that, of all the old industries, "iron and
steel was the only one of the branches that had made the Industrial
Revolution to have a second youth,"[17] in the decades before World
War I thanks to great technological breakthroughs, the opening up of
new ore fields, and the highly favorable pattern of demand. Although
Germany's assumption of her status as Europe's leading industrial
power deserves measurement in more ways than one, and particularly
in the newer areas of electrotechnical and chemical production, her
prewar overtaking of Great Britain in iron and steel production has
often been used by scholars and laymen as both the actual and symbolic evidence for this triumph.[18] As the most technically advanced,
highly concentrated, and best organized of all the prewar European
iron and steel industries, it appeared paradigmatic of the peculiar
characteristics that were identified with German economic and political
power. It was no accident that the iron tariff of 1879 and its successors
constituted the cornerstone of the Empire's commitment to the "protection of the national labor" through industrial protectionism and the
most tangible expression of heavy industry's political influence in
Berlin.[19]

What also makes this industry so particularly suitable for examination during the years under consideration was that it stood so centrally
in the matrix of the structural, economic, social, and political transformations of the postwar period. The war heightened the industry's
importance by increasing the demand for iron and steel while creating
conditions harmful to production and requiring government support
and regulation as well as an intensification of industrial organization.
The iron and steel industry was the industry that suffered most from
the energy crisis, the coal shortage, of the wartime and early postwar
years. It was the industry that suffered most from the ravages of the
Versailles Peace Treaty, which tore away Lorraine, Luxemburg, and
portions of Upper Silesia and denied Germany the Saar for fifteen

[17] Landes, *Unbound Prometheus*, p. 460.
[18] For example, see Stolper, *German Economy*, pp. 24–25.
[19] See Rosenberg, *Grosse Depression*, p. 154ff.

11

years. As a result, Germany lost 43.5% of her pig iron capacity and 38.3% of her steel capacity.[20] It was generally accepted that the enormity of the iron and steel industry's losses gave it exceptional claims in the economic reconstruction, claims yet increased by the fact that this industry was compelled to make some of the most significant concessions to labor during the Revolution by accepting the eight-hour day and was particularly threatened by the tariff provisions of the Versailles Treaty. It was the industry hardest hit by the war and the peace.

Paradoxically, however, therein lay its strength during the inflation. It stood at the forefront of German industry's use of the inflationary pressures and incentives to rebuild its plant and recapture its markets. Because of its basic importance to the economy as a whole, its pricing policies were of central concern in the efforts to control the inflation and harmonize the relations between producers and consumers. The iron and steel industry thus became a major focus of the questions concerning the degree to which primary producers should be permitted to take advantage of raw materials shortages and inflation and disregard the interests of their customers in other industrial sectors, and the extent to which the state should and could regulate interindustrial relations. It also became the test case of the capacity and power of the state to define and achieve ends consonant with the best interests of the industry and the economy as a whole, just as it became the test case of an industry's willingness and ability to accomplish these goals on its own. Despite numerous setbacks and difficulties, the basic story to be told here is one of success for the iron and steel industry, success in rebuilding its plant through a ruthless pricing policy and use of the inflation to promote vertical concentration, success in eliminating or evading government controls, and, in the end, success in nullifying some of the most important social gains of the German Revolution of 1918.

No less paradoxical than the strength the iron and steel industry garnered from its weaknesses as a consequence of the war and revolution, however, was the fact that this very strength served to intensify the endogenous weaknesses of the industry and heighten its vulnerability to the relative stagnation of the interwar years. Already suffering a relative stagnation in technological development and demand in comparison to the newer chemical and electrotechnical industries, the post-inflationary iron and steel industry faced an extremely abrupt reckoning with the structural problems that had been veiled by the prewar prosperity and the inflationary reconstruction. Once the veil was lifted

[20] Landes, *Unbound Prometheus*, p. 462ff.

12

by the stabilization, the "brutal"[21] contrast with prewar conditions and the expectations that had been carried over from happier times produced not only economic, but also social and political problems of major proportions for the Weimar Republic. Yet it did not abate, but rather intensified the claims of this industry on the nation and the notorious, if often exaggerated and improperly depicted, political power that heavy industry exercised to 1933. For these reasons, its successes in the years of inflation constitute an important case study of the way in which the exercise of private economic power is accomplished as well as a means by which the historian may come to grips with some of the fundamental issues and developments of the German inflation itself.

IRON AND STEEL IN THE GERMAN PREWAR ECONOMY

The Great Concerns and Their Leaders

The outbreak of World War I marked the end of a long period of sustained growth for the German iron and steel industry. Germany stood second only to the United States in crude steel production, accounting for one-fourth of the world's production. In 1913, Imperial Germany, inclusive of Luxemburg, which formed part of the German customs area, produced 19,309,000 tons of pig iron and 18,935,000 tons of crude steel, whereas the United Kingdom produced 10,482,000 tons of pig iron and 7,787,000 tons of crude steel during that same year. The most important industrial area for Germany's iron and steel production was the Rhenish-Westphalian region, which produced 42% of the pig iron and 53% of the crude steel in 1913, but the regional concentration in the West of Germany is better expressed when account is taken of the German Lorraine, which had important interconnections with the Ruhr before the war. The two regions combined accounted for 61% of German pig iron and 65% of her crude steel production in 1913. The overwhelming preponderance of the Ruhr-Lorraine regions over the other significant producing areas of the Siegerland, the Saar and Silesia, is closely tied to the fundamental sources of Germany's triumphant history in prewar iron and steel production.[22]

[21] *Ibid.*, p. 459. See also Svennilson, *Growth and Stagnation*, p. 120ff.; and Norman Pounds and William N. Parker, *Coal and Steel in Western Europe. The Influence of Resources and Techniques on Production* (Bloomington, 1957), pp. 250–253.

[22] Paul Wiel, *Wirtschaftsgeschichte des Ruhrgebiets. Tatsachen und Zahlen* (Essen, 1970), pp. 226–227 and 238. Frederic Benham, whose total figures vary slightly from those of Wiel, and whose figures do not include Luxemburg, gives

13

Raw materials and technological development were the primary initial bases of success, and they went hand in hand with one another in creating the expansion of heavy industry.[23] The foundation of the Ruhr's extraordinary position in the industrial history of the West was its exceptional supply of anthracite coal highly suitable for coking, an advantage that enabled iron producers to go over to the coke-blast furnace in the 1850s. Large-scale steel production in Germany, however, was retarded until the invention of the Thomas process for the production of basic steel in 1879. In contrast to England, with its ample supply of nonphosphoric ores suitable for the production of acid steel in the unmodified Bessemer converter, Germany was not blessed with a satisfactory ore supply. The Ruhr was poor in ore, and the ores of the Siegerland region were expensive and presented special problems. It was the Thomas process that made it possible for Germany to make use of the great supplies of phosphoric minette ore in Lorraine and to import phosphoric ores from Sweden, Spain, and Morocco. During the ensuing decades, German industry employed this process, as well as the Siemens-Martin open-hearth process (1864), which utilized scrap and pig iron to produce a higher quality steel more easily controlled as to specifications than Thomas steel, to undertake the mass production of steel that gave it continental leadership.

The annexation of Lorraine in 1871, therefore, yielded unanticipated benefits in the form of the minette ore fields and encouraged a high degree of fruitful interchange and some division of labor between the Ruhr and Lorraine. The Lorraine received coal from the Ruhr and returned ores, and there was thus some transport benefit through the return haul. Also, there was some tendency for the production of pig iron and other of the industry's cruder products to concentrate in Lor-

---

the following breakdown of production in the chief producing areas in *The Iron and Steel Industry of Germany, France, Belgium, Luxemburg and the Saar* (London, 1934), p. 18:

Output of Germany in 1913
(in thousands of tons)

	Pig Iron	Steel
Germany (1922 frontiers)	10,904	12,182
Polish Upper Silesia	625	1,050
Lorraine	3,864	2,286
Saar	1,371	2,080
Totals	16,674	17,598

[23] The discussions of the role of raw materials and technology in this section follow closely the discussions given in Landes, *Unbound Prometheus*, pp. 215–219, 249–269; Pounds and Parker, *Coal and Steel*, pp. 262–271. See also Emil Schrödter, "25 Jahre deutsche Eisenindustrie," *Stahl und Eisen*, 24, May 1, 1904, pp. 490–500.

raine, whereas the production of more advanced products centered in the Ruhr, where there was a supply of high-quality labor and also proximity to the finishing industries. Nevertheless, it is misleading to overstate the interdependence of the two regions or to suggest that there was a true "Ruhr-Lorraine system,"[24] a matter of importance to the historian because of the claims of German annexationists during the war as well as of critics of the Versailles Treaty after 1918. The Lorraine was dependent on the Ruhr for more than half of its coke supply, but the Ruhr in 1914 took only 24% of its iron ore from Lorraine and Luxemburg. The Ruhr was far more heavily dependent on Sweden and Spain, whose ores had a higher iron content, and it was favorably located to receive shipments of these ores thanks to the Rhine River. Lastly, the actual share of pig iron production in Lorraine and Luxemburg sent to the Ruhr before the war was diminishing, not increasing.

Thus, the reality was that the two regions were competitive, except for the Lorraine's dependence on Ruhr coke, and that the basic advantages lay with the Ruhr thanks to its coal supply, superb location from a transportation point of view, and ready supplies of cheap scrap that permitted an employment of the open-hearth process not equally possible in Lorraine. The Ruhr had the strength and flexibility to survive without Lorraine. What is more to the point in considering the prewar period is that the Lorraine constituted an integral part of the German economy, that German interests in the region were expanding, and that some of the great German concerns, like Klöckner and Stumm, were centered in the Southwest, or, like Thyssen and Stinnes' Deutsch-Luxemburg concern, had built large new modern plants in Lorraine before the war.

Insofar as organizational factors played a major role in the strength of the industry, as they most certainly did, they lay not in regional integration, but rather in the development of large capacities and the advancement of vertical and horizontal integration. Although technological developments after 1880 were not as spectacular as those that had preceded, they favored increases in the scale of production and integration of the various stages of production. Engineering improvements, the employment of electricity, advances in fuel utilization and economy permitting sophisticated interchanges of gases and employment of fuels, all favored the large-scale "mixed" or integrated concerns

[24] As does Guy Greer in *The Ruhr-Lorraine Industrial Problem. A Study of the Economic Inter-Dependence of the Two Regions and their Relation to the Reparation Question* (New York, 1925), pp. 18ff and 68ff. My discussion is based on the more convincing analyses of Pounds and Parker, *Coal and Steel*, pp. 287–293, and William N. Parker, "Coal and Steel Output Movements in Western Europe," *Explorations in Entrepreneurial History*, 9, April 1957, pp. 214–230, esp. pp. 225–227.

that came to dominate the industry. There were great economic and technological advantages to combining ore fields, coal mines, cokeries, blast furnaces, steel plants, and rolling mills. On the one hand, there were the benefits of greater self-sufficiency that came with the control of the primary raw materials, and, as shall be discussed later, these were increased by the cartelization process. A more diversified production also gave the great concerns the advantage of being able to compensate for losses in one sphere of production through profits in another. On the other hand, large-scale operation and integration made it possible to link a number of coal mines to large-scale coking facilities and, thanks to the invention of the mixer (1874) and its implementation, to coordinate blast-furnace, converter or open-hearth, and rolling operations in such a way that as much as possible was produced in "one heat."

By 1914, 21% of the production of the Rhenish-Westphalian coal mining industry was being produced by the "mixed works" of the iron and steel industry.[25] It is a measure of the degree of concentration in the industry that in 1904, when the most important of the industry's cartel organizations, the Steel Works Association (*Stahlwerksverband*) was founded, its members, the number of which varied between 27 and 31 and all of whom were "mixed"—that is, integrated firms and concerns—produced 73.45% of all German steel production sent to market. The percentage was 81.71% in 1911.[26] The "outsiders" in 1904 were largely the "pure" rolling mills (*reine Walzwerke*), most of whom were to be absorbed or to go out of business in the coming decade, and certain open-hearth producers in the Siegerland, who were able to prosper in the shadow of the Steel Works Association because of the specialized nature of their production and certain locational advantages. Even these facts however, do not do full justice to the importance of the largest integrated firms and concerns. A better measure of their domination is provided by their cartel quotas in the Steel Works Association as shown in Table 1, which includes only the major Ruhr mills and excludes such important producers as the Saar concerns of Stumm and Röchling. Yet to measure their strength thus is still to omit as much as it is to tell. It excludes ore, coal and coke, and by-product production, not to mention pig iron production and the large amounts of crude and semifinished steel consumed by the concerns themselves in the production of rolled and more finished products and

[25] Wiel, *Wirtschaftsgeschichte*, p. 213. See also the basic study by H. G. Heymann, *Die gemischten Werke im deutschen Grosseisengewerbe* (Stuttgart and Berlin, 1904).

[26] H. Bogner, *Die Wandlungen in der Organisation der deutschen Stahlindustrie und ihre Ursachen*, diss. Phil. (Heidelberg, 1929), p. 17.

TABLE 1

The Participation of the Ruhr Mills in the Steel Works Association
(Measured in thousands of tons and percentages)

	1904		1905		1907	
	Thousand Tons	Percent	Thousand Tons	Percent	Thousand Tons	Percent
Thyssen	694	9.3	704	8.7	974	8.2
Gutehoffnungshütte	408	5.5	408	5.0	585	4.9
Hörde	425	5.7	424	5.2	—	—
Rheinstahl	385	5.2	385	4.7	489	4.1
Krupp	456	6.1	456	5.6	977	8.2
Bochumer Verein	306	4.1	306	3.8	336	2.8
Phoenix	—	—	515	6.4	1130[a]	9.5
Hoesch	321	4.3	321	4.0	455	3.8
Total	2995	40.2	3519	43.4	4946	44.3

[a] Inclusive of Hörde.

Source: Wilhelm Treue, Die Feuer verlöschen nie. August Thyssen-Hütte 1890–1926 (Düsseldorf and Vienna, 1966), p. 144. The 1912 statistics have been left out because they do not include all steel production.

the manufacture of machinery. Also, it does not take into account transport and marketing operations.

In 1913, Thyssen, to take an outstanding but representative example, fully owned nine coal mines in the Ruhr along with mine construction facilities; ore fields in Lorraine, Normandy, and on the Lahn; a limestone quarry and cement plant in Rüdersorf and another cement plant in Hagedingen; iron and steel works in Bruckhausen and Dinslaken (Gewerkschaft Deutscher Kaiser), Mülheim/Ruhr, Meiderich, Hagendingen (Lorraine), and Reisholz (central Germany); a major machine building plant in Mülheim/Ruhr; a coal marketing firm with branches in Bruckhausen, Mannheim, Strasbourg, Paris, Naples, Oran, Suez, and Genoa; four iron and steel marketing firms, the branches of which were to be found in Berlin, Stettin, Duisburg, Ludwigshaven, Königsberg, and Buenos Aires; three transportation enterprises that included a transport operation in Rotterdam, a fleet of five high seas freighters, and port facilities in Mannheim and Strasbourg; and the waterworks of the Gewerkschaft Deutscher Kaiser in Bruckhausen. At the same time, the Thyssen concern participated in the ownership of a coal mining company in the Ruhr and in the Saar and in a tar plant; ore fields in Tschiaturi and Nikolajeff (Russia); a limestone and dolomite works; and steel plants in Krefeld, Oberbilk, and Caen (Normandy).[27]

[27] Wilhelm Treue, Die Feuer verlöschen nie. August Thyssen-Hütte 1890–1926 (Düsseldorf and Vienna, 1966), pp. 156–157.

Like Thyssen, the great concerns were all highly complex, far-flung enterprises.[28] Although they produced many of the same things, by and large, it is important to recognize that they were also individually unique in major aspects of their production programs and emphases. They had all integrated backwards by one means or another into ore and coal mining and into coke production, and they were all heavily engaged in the production of pig iron and crude steel as well as the more finished foundry and rolled products. However, the vertical expansion of Phoenix and Rheinstahl, in contrast to Thyssen and Hoesch, did not extend forward to machine construction before the war, and the vertical expansion of the latter concerns into finishing and manufacturing was in no way as extensive as that of Krupp and the Gutehoffnungshütte. Although a giant producer of primary products, Krupp was Germany's most important private producer of artillery, had become a major manufacturer of machines through its takeover of the Grusonwerke in Magdeburg in 1893 and, after taking over the Maschinenbau AG Germania in Kiel in 1902, entered the field of shipbuilding and the large-scale construction of steam engines, steam turbines, and diesel motors. The less mammoth but venerable Gutehoffnungshütte (GHH) in Oberhausen had long produced steam machines and boilers at its plants in nearby Sterkrade and ships for inland waterways at its yards in Walsum. During the prewar period, there was a clear thrust on the part of the major concerns in the direction of finishing and the manufacture of large machines because their profitability was higher than the cruder products. Thus, whatever the individuality of the concerns, it is also possible to note common patterns of expansion. What does make the individuality of the concerns important, despite their propensity to copy one another in order to remain competitive, is that it exercised an important influence on their policies and business styles and helps to explain differences of opinion over cartel and syndicate pricing policies as well as over those organizations themselves.

Policies and business styles, however, were also strongly influenced by the history and traditions of the concerns and their ownership and financing. The beginnings of the GHH could be traced back to 1741 and those of Krupp to 1811. They were both family concerns, the GHH being largely in the possession of the Haniel family, and the identification with a family was a characteristic they shared with Thyssen, Hoesch, Stumm, and Röchling and various Upper Silesian enterprises. In this respect they were different from more impersonal corporations

[28] This discussion is based largely on the wealth of material scattered throughout Arnold Tross' invaluable *Der Aufbau der Eisen und eisenverarbeitenden Industrie-Konzerne Deutschlands* (Berlin, 1923). The expansion of the Ruhr concerns may also be followed chronologically in Wiel, *Wirtschaftsgeschichte*, pp. 245–273.

like Phoenix and Rheinstahl. As is well known, banks played a major role in the development of German heavy industry, and this encouraged a measure of depersonalization of the enterprises and dispersion of ownership. Few concerns were as autonomous as the GHH, which seems to have maintained almost total independence of the banks thanks to the capacity and willingness of the Haniel family to supply its capital requirements. The great Upper Silesian firms were largely family financed as well. During the initial period of expansion, banks often played the major role in the founding of concerns, as in the case of the Gelsenkirchener Bergwerke AG (GBAG), and strongly influenced their policies directly through their positions on the supervisory boards (*Aufsichtsräte*) and indirectly through various forms of encouragement and pressure. The boards of directors (*Vorstände*) of the concerns necessarily heeded the will of the supervisory boards, because the dispersion of stock was not very great in German industry and general stockholder meetings counted for even less than they do in the United States.[29]

In the decades before the war, two tendencies were in evidence with regard to the financing of heavy industry. First, such financing tended to be undertaken by consortia rather than by individual banks because the capital requirements had become so great. Second, the financial strength and power of the concerns had increased to the point where not only were the banks wooing them rather than the reverse, but also the concerns themselves had greatly improved their capacity for self-financing by the storing up of silent reserves and cautious dividend policies carried to the point where 20–25% of their expansion was self-capitalized. To be sure, industrialists chaffed a bit under their continued dependence on banks, but the evidence militates against all notions of a domination by "finance capital" in the years before the war. The trend was precisely in the opposite direction.[30] Krupp ruled in Essen, Haniel in Oberhausen, and Thyssen in Bruckhausen. Although August Thyssen needed large amounts of outside money just before the war to

[29] See Jürgen Kocka, *Unternehmer in der deutschen Industrialisierung* (Göttingen, 1975), p. 100ff. On the relationship between banking and industry, see O. Jeidels, *Das Verhältnis der deutschen Grossbanken zur Industrie mit besonderer Berücksichtigung der Eisenindustrie* (Leipzig, 1905); E. Riesser, *Die deutschen Grossbanken und Ihre Konzentration* (Jena, 1910); M. Gehr, *Das Verhältnis zwischen Banken und Industrie in Deutschland seit der Mitte des 19. Jahrhunderts*, diss. Phil. (Stuttgart, 1959); W. Hagemann, *Das Verhältnis der deutschen Grossbanken zur Industrie* (Berlin, 1931), esp. pp. 18ff. and 86ff.

[30] See Walther G. Hoffmann, "Die unverteilten Gewinne der Aktiengesellschaften in Deutschland 1871–1957. Trend, Konjunkturverlauf und branchenmässige Unterschiede," *Zeitschrift für die gesamte Staatswissenschaft*, 115, 1959, pp. 271–291.

finance the construction of the new works at Hagendingen, more than half of his capital resources in 1913, 126,890,000 out of 249,920,000 marks, were his own.[31] Indeed, the size of the great concerns encouraged investment because their very enormity made a return likely and failure difficult to imagine. At the same time, industrialists like Thyssen and Hugo Stinnes recognized that if their debts were sufficiently high, then they could have as much if not more of a hold on their creditors as the latter had on them.[32]

The very size and complexity of concerns set increasing limits on the possibilities of personal management and promoted the separation of ownership from control, but it is important not to exaggerate these well-known phenomena when considering the German iron and steel industry.[33] Strong personal rule or surveillance from the top continued before the war and during the period discussed in this study, whether it was exercised by the family ownership, as in the case of Gustav Krupp von Bohlen und Halbach (1870–1943), who exercised a personal surveillance over his directors in matters of basic policy and never allowed his leading director, even one so domineering as Alfred Hugenberg (1865–1951), who held the position from 1907 to 1918, to be more than a *primus inter pares* among the directors,[34] or whether it was exercised by founder entrepreneurs, like August Thyssen (1842–1926),[35] or by general directors, like Paul Reusch (1868–1956) of the GHH, who had and deserved the complete confidence of the Haniel family.[36] Also, an important role was played by new men in the industry, like Peter Klöckner (1863–1940), the son of a shipyard owner, who had begun his career in the iron merchant firm of Carl Spaeter and then became an industrialist in 1900 when he assumed leadership and controlling interest in the Lothringer Hütten und Bergwerksverein.[37] Another new man in the industry who entered from a similar background was the "merchant from Mülheim," as he chose to style himself, Hugo Stinnes

[31] Treue, *August Thyssen-Hütte*, pp. 150–155.

[32] Herbert von Beckerath, *Grossindustrie und Gesellschaftsordnung. Industrielle und Politische Dynamik* (Tübingen and Zürich, 1954), pp. 18–19.

[33] The same is true of other industries and large concerns, as has been shown by Jürgen Kocka in his important study, *Unternehmensverwaltung und Angestelltenschaft am Beispiel Siemens 1847–1914. Zum Verhältnis von Kapitalismus und Bürokratie in der deutschen Industrialisierung* (Stuttgart, 1969), esp. pp. 233ff. and 429ff.

[34] See the revealing material in Ernst Schröder, *Otto Wiedfeldt. Eine Biographie* (Beiträge zur Geschichte von Stadt und Stift Essen, Vol. 80), p. 94.

[35] Treue, *August Thyssen-Hütte*, p. 246ff.

[36] Erich Maschke, *Es entsteht ein Konzern. Paul Reusch und die GHH* (Tübingen, 1969), pp. 230–231.

[37] Jakob Reichert, "Peter Klöckner," in *Rheinisch-Westfälische Wirtschaftsbiographien* (Münster i.W., 1960), pp. 85–104.

(1870–1924). He was the son of a Rhine shipowner, who founded a coal trading firm in 1893 and then moved into the iron and steel industry after 1900 when he created and developed the Deutsch-Luxemburg (Deutsch-Lux) concern.[38] Klöckner and Stinnes played a very direct role in management, and thus maintained a strong connection between ownership and control. Only within this context can one say that they were to depend very heavily on the directors who conducted the day-to-day operations of their concerns and, as the relationship between Hugo Stinnes and the general director of Deutsch-Lux after 1915, Albert Vögler (1877–1945), or Karl Haniel and Paul Reusch will show, general directors or prominent directors could and did play an increasingly important and independent role in the development of general policy and, in their turn, became dependent on the industrial bureaucracy below them for day-to-day operations.

The importance of the great general directors who stood at the summit of this growing bureaucracy of "leading employees" (*leitende Angestellte*), i.e., directors and officials (*Beamte*) in the great concerns was already in evidence before the turn of the century in the persons of Emil Kirdorf (1847–1938) of the Gelsenkirchener Bergwerke (GBAG) and Wilhelm Beukenberg (1858–1923) of Phoenix. The son of an unsuccessful textile manufacturer, Kirdorf left textiles and entered the coal industry in 1871 at the lowest level of administration, where he learned the trade and proved his abilities despite the insensitive and humiliating manner in which the owners of those days handled their "employees." In 1873 he entered the GBAG, which he was to direct for 53 years, and not only built up the concern into Germany's greatest prewar coal producer, but also played a leading role in the founding of the Rhenish-Westphalian Coal Syndicate in 1893. Then, in 1902–1903, in close collaboration with his brother Adolph (1845–1923), the general director of the Aachener Hüttenvereins, and in keen competition with Thyssen and Stinnes, who sought to gain an interest in the GBAG for their own purposes, he guided the GBAG's expansion into iron and steel. Although his career and activity was closer to that of Thyssen and Stinnes in many respects than it was to the more typical general director, Kirdorf always considered himself the "responsible administrator of the property of others" rather than an owner-entrepreneur, like the founders of the GBAG and his first masters, Friedrich Grillo and Adolph von Hansemann. The latter men were also the

---

[38] There is a large and controversial literature on Stinnes, ranging from the adulatory work of Gert von Klass, *Hugo Stinnes* (Tübingen, 1958), which must be treated with great caution, to the penetrating but impressionistic essay by Felix Pinner (Frank Fassland) in *Deutsche Wirtschaftsführer* (Berlin, 1924), pp. 11–32. Hopefully this study will contribute something to an understanding of his activities.

founders of the Disconto-Gesellschaft, and the otherwise cantankerous Kirdorf not only generally accepted his dependence on the banks as a fact of life, but also worked very harmoniously with the president of his supervisory board during the period covered by this study, Arthur Salomonsohn of the same bank.[39]

If Kirdorf stands out as the archetype of what the great *Generaldirektor* and concern builder was and could be, he was nevertheless a very unique personality who bridged the transition from the German industrial revolution to its period of advanced industrialization. Beukenberg, despite his age, is more typical in training and career pattern of the group of top executives who reached the height of their careers before the war and dominated heavy industry during the Weimar Republic. Born in the Ruhr in 1858, he attended Gymnasium and then did two years of practical work in state plants and machine works before attending the famous Technische Hochschule in Berlin. In 1888, he passed the government examination in machine construction (*Regierungsbaumeister des Maschinenfachs*) and took over the leadership of the construction and machine plants of the Dortmund-Gronau-Emscheder Railroad Co. He became a director in 1895, but left in 1903 when it passed under state control to become general director of the Hoerder Bergwerks- und Hüttenvereins, which merged with Phoenix in 1906. Until his retirement in 1922, Beukenberg directed the affairs of this important producer, and "technical progress and careful accounting were the most distinguishing marks of his activity." Not only did Beukenberg serve Phoenix directly, however, but he also served his concern and industry indirectly through his membership on various government commissions dealing with freight rates and other transportation problems, matters of no small moment to heavy industry, and played a prominent role in the major cartels and syndicates as well as on the boards of various institutes and technical schools devoted to the advancement of knowledge and the training of personnel needed by industry.[40]

In all these characteristics, Beukenberg was more or less at one with the group of younger top executives who had reached the summit of their careers before 1918 and became the model group for future gen-

[39] Helmut Böhme, "Emil Kirdorf, Überlegungen zu einer Unternehmerbiographie," *Tradition. Zeitschrift für Firmen Geschichte und Unternehmerbiographie,* 13, December 1968, pp. 282–300.

[40] Stahl und Eisen, 43:2, August 16, 1923, pp. 1092–1093. The obituaries in this journal are often an excellent source of information on important industrialists. Another useful source in addition to the others cited here is Georg Wenzel, *Deutsche Wirtschaftsführer. Lebensgänge Deutscher Wirtschaftspersönlichkeiten. Ein Nachschlagebuch über 1300 Wirtschaftspersönlichkeiten unserer Zeit* (Hamburg, Berlin, Leipzig, 1929).

erations of German managers. Most of them were in their forties during the war, came of solid but by no means wealthy middle-class backgrounds, had technical, commercial, or legal training, and combined these special skills with the kind of administrative ability and dedication that earned them the recognition and authority necessary for the rapid rise to leading positions. Albert Vögler, for example, became general director of Deutsch-Lux in 1915 at the age of 38. The son of a factory manager in Essen, he attended the more modern Realgymnasium and then went to the Technische Hochschule in Karlsruhe. After working as an engineer for a machine plant in Herne and at a large iron works, the Georgs-Marienhütte in Osnabrück, he was hired by the Dortmunder Union as a director in 1906. When Deutsch-Lux took over the Union in 1910, Stinnes made Vögler a member of the board of directors and increasingly his most trusted manager. Vögler was indeed an extraordinary individual, who combined a genuine interest in technology and science with a keen business sense and remarkable organizational and administrative abilities.[41]

Paul Reusch, although certainly not uninterested in technological and scientific matters, was above all a shrewd businessman and exceptional organizer and leader. Unlike most of the leading Ruhr managers, Reusch came from South Germany and was the son of a Württemberg mining official. He attended the Technische Hochschule in Stuttgart, and then went to work for iron and steel concerns in Budapest and Wittkowitz (Moravia) before taking employment at the Friedrich-Wilhelms-Hütte, a Deutsch-Lux holding. In 1905, he became a member of the GHH's board of directors and took over the general directorship in 1908 at the age of 40. Temperamental and stubborn, when it suited his purposes, Reusch was to become a commanding and respected figure in the industry for the strength of his views and the vigor with which he presented them. His personality comes fully to the fore in his correspondence, which, in its frankness and clarity, reflected his penchant for laconic commentary and forceful command. Yet he could also be very skillful in negotiation, knew how to distribute responsibility and gain sincere loyalty from his subordinates, and was well suited to become an imposing, albeit, at times, somewhat extremist representative and spokesman for the industry as a whole.[42]

Although a technical background was often an essential component

[41] On Vögler, see Gert von Klass, *Albert Vögler. Einer der Grossen des Reviers* (Tübingen, 1957) and *Nekrologe aus dem Rheinisch-Westfälischen Industriegebiet. Jahrgang 1939–1951* (Schriften der Volks- und Betriebswirtschaftlichen Vereinigung im Rheinisch-Westfälischen Industriegebiet) (Düsseldorf, 1955), pp. 121–123.

[42] Maschke, *Konzern*, p. 32ff.

of a successful career in the prewar iron and steel industry, an industry that in the German case prided itself on the assiduous promotion and utilization of every technical development possible, important posts were increasingly being assumed by men with legal and governmental backgrounds. Concern building was a legal, financial, and administrative matter after all, and lawyers were often more suited to direct industrial bureaucracies than technicians and they were often more skillful in dealing with government agencies and handling marketing problems as well. A good example was Johann Hasslacher (1869–1940), who became general director of Rheinstahl in 1910. He was the son of a Saar mining official, but he went to a classical Gymnasium and received a law degree at Bonn, after which he continued to work in the legal field until 1896, when he went to work as a legal expert and then director at the GBAG. Rheinstahl employed him because of his legal skills, negotiating ability, and understanding of commercial and marketing problems. In these characteristics he was similar to other important directors with a legal background, such as Heinrich Vielhaber (1868–1940) of Krupp, Oscar Sempell (1876–1942) of Deutsch-Lux, and Gustav Dechamps (1878–1942) of the Rombacher Hütte. A background in marketing and finance, as in the case of August Thyssen's important director and adviser, Carl Rabes (1871–1942), could also be the source of a rapid rise and a splendid career in a major heavy industrial concern.[43]

These, then, were the types of men who presided over growing industrial bureaucracies of directors, plant managers, and technical and commercial staffs and who gave orders to the once independent firm owners or managers who often remained with their works after, for reasons of interest or necessity, they had entered into a community of interest (*Interessengemeinschaft*) or had fully merged with a larger concern. Historians frequently draw a useful analogy between industrial bureaucratization in the late nineteenth and early twentieth centuries and the earlier bureaucratization of the state. Just as kings and princes came to view themselves as the "first servants of the state," so some owners came to view themselves as servants of their enterprises, which took on an "objective existence" and had "objective necessities" of their own. The general directors and their colleagues were like ministers,

---

[43] For the biographies of these industrialists, in order of mention, see *Nekrologe*, pp. 30–31, 41–42, 71–72, 63–65, 69–70. On the social and educational backgrounds of the managerial group, see Heinz Sachtler, *Wandlungen des industriellen Unternehmers in Deutschland seit Beginn des 19. Jahrhunderts. Ein Versuch zur Typologie des Unternehmers*, diss. Phil. (Halle, 1938), p. 40ff. Although his methodology presents problems, his conclusion that an increasing number of the group came from upper-class backgrounds and had traditional academic training is quite likely to be correct.

24

who could be hired and fired at will and whose existence was necessitated as much by the uncertain quality of the owner's heirs as by the complexity of the enterprise itself. As in the case of the state, so in the case of the concerns the tension between the continued effort at personal rule by the owner and the progress of bureaucratized management was being decided painfully but fatefully in favor of the latter.[44] Also quite in keeping with the analogy, however, was that the general directors and their colleagues were something more than "employees" and were not without direct financial interest or family interest in their positions. They received high salaries and other emoluments, often owned some stock themselves, and were appointed to boards of supervisors of firms belonging to the concern as well as to supervisory boards of firms in which they might have an interest and that might have a desire to gain the benefit of their advice and support. They were also well on the road to establishing dynasties of general directors. Director and later General Director Fritz Springorum (1886–1942) of Hoesch certainly owed something to the fact that his father, Friedrich, had been general director of Hoesch, and Ernst Poensgen (1871–1949) of Phoenix certainly had a head start in industry because he had inherited his family's pipe and rolling works. These had been merged with Phoenix in 1910, and the latter gave him a concern directorship at that time.[45] Similarly, Paul Reusch was to see his son Hermann assume his old position after World War II. All this is not to say that Fritz Springorum, Ernst Poensgen, and Hermann Reusch were not extremely able men. The evidence seems to demonstrate that they were and that Fritz Thyssen (1871–1951) was also an able successor to his father.[46] However, it must be emphasized that the leading directors of the industrial concerns constituted a developing managerial elite filled with personal and social ambition as well as talent and energy.

Like the founding generation of German heavy industry, the general directors were seeking to make a respected place for themselves in German society, and they faced many of the same difficulties and employed many of the same solutions. The "feudalization" of the great early industrialists, their quest for titles, and their building of castles and villas are well known and amply illustrated by Krupp and Stumm.[47] However, the social ambiguity of the new managerial group was even

[44] See the excellent discussion in Kocka, *Unternehmensverwaltung*, p. 547ff. The analogies with the development discussed in Hans Rosenberg, *Bureaucracy, Aristocracy, and Autocracy. The Prussian Experience 1660–1815* (Cambridge, Mass., 1958) are quite striking.

[45] *Nekrologe*, pp. 172–174, 72–73.

[46] *Ibid.*, pp. 234–236.

[47] Friedrich Zunkel, *Der Rheinisch-Westfälische Unternehmer, 1834–1879* (Cologne, 1962), pp. 93–132, 246–253.

greater than that of the earlier generation of owner-entrepreneurs because they were only "employees" and, it was argued, did not bear the
risks and sense of responsibility of the founders. They, therefore, had
the double burden of proving themselves within their own environment
and capturing the coveted titles and acceptance in the upper echelons of
German society that they naturally desired. Although many could take
pride in their titles as Royal Commercial Councilors (*Kgl. Kommer-
zienräte*), their reserve officer status, and, as in the case of Kirdorf and
Reusch, their respective estates "Streithof" and "Katharinenhof," they
were still men who had guaranteed entrée to the best hotels but not
to the best salons. At the same time, however, they were a group increasingly conscious of their own worth and accomplishments, with a
profound sense of "calling," a growing conviction that they were the
bearers of the nation's economic future, and a certain disdain for privy
councilors in Berlin, who had the illusion that an economy could be
run from the "green table," and professors who fantasized that socioeconomic problems could be solved on the basis of economic theory
rather than the hard realities of economic life. The idea that the separation of ownership from control meant that industry was falling into the
hands of a less responsible generation was nonsensical. If anything, the
sense of responsibility of the general directors for the property placed
in their charge was heightened by their sense of calling and desire to
prove themselves as a new elite directly responsible for thousands of
workers and massive economic units vital to the economy as a whole.[48]

It has been argued that the coming of the general directors marked
a decline in the vitality of entrepreneurship and the willingness to take
risks demonstrated by the founding generation in German heavy industry.[49] It seems significant that so successful a general director as Paul

[48] The importance of the group discussed here as a new elite inspiring even the
present-day generation of German managers should not be forgotten, because
there is almost complete continuity between the group directing German industry
in 1914 and in the Weimar Republic. See Wolfgang Zapf, *Wandlungen der
deutschen Elite. Ein Zirkulationsmodell deutscher Führungsgruppen 1919–1961*
(Munich, 1965), pp. 236–237. On the ideology and problems of German executives,
see Heinz Hartmann, *Authority and Organization in German Management* (Princeton, 1959), pp. 16–50. There is a fine discussion in Kocka, *Unternehmer in der
deutschen Industrialisierung*, pp. 215–223. See also Kurt Wiedenfeld, *Das Persönliche im modernen Unternehmertum*, 2nd ed. (Munich, 1920). In his *Unternehmensverwaltung*, pp. 556–559, Kocka makes the excellent point that the
Weberian model of bureaucratization as a means of domination (*Herrschaft*) is
particularly in need of modification when applied to industrial bureaucratization,
where the well-being and profitability of the firm imposes a testable standard of
performance in the legitimation of organizational change.

[49] For a discussion of the literature on this and related problems, see Wolfgang
Zorn, "Typen und Entwicklungskräfte deutschen Unternehmertums im 19. Jahr-

Reusch was to be so taken with the gloomy prognostications of Oswald Spengler.[50] The Faustian spirit that had typified the industrial revolution and the readiness to bear risks and losses became, it would seem, increasingly tempered by a sense that dikes had to be constructed to preserve what had been accomplished. The most famous of these dikes, of course, were the cartels and syndicates, and it has been claimed that just as concern building undermined the role of the individual in industry and forced the entrepreneur to give way to the manager, so the cartels destroyed the willingness to take risks and expand. Such arguments are more nostalgic than illuminating, however, and they distract from an actual consideration of the role of personalities and economic organizations in advanced stages of industrial development and promote an understatement and an underestimation of dynamic qualities that have shifted their focus rather than been eliminated.

Cartels, Syndicates, and Trade Associations

To be sure, the original purpose of the cartels was a defensive one and had the reduction of risk through the prevention of cutthroat competition as its object. They were almost invariably formed to deal with crises, and although the first cartel-like agreements in the iron industry can be dated back to 1844–1845, it is no accident that cartels proliferated during the downswing of 1873–1896. During this period, they represented a more sophisticated industrialist response to the downturns in the business cycle and the periodic capital shortages and inventory crises by which they had long been plagued. Initially, they had treated such crises fatalistically, as products of "times" that were always "changing," an attitude that suggests that a sense of helplessness in the face of crises constituted an important component of the "willingness" to take risks in earlier entrepreneurial generations. Much of this attitude persisted later on and provided an undercurrent of pessimism that is to be found even in the most expansionist and optimistic of periods among the Ruhr industrialists. Yet there was a growing sophistication about crises and a sense that something could be done about them. First, an effort was made to explain them by specific causes, such as the drop in demand in a particular market, a tariff

---

hundert," *Vierteljahrschrift fur Sozial- und Wirtschaftsgeschichte*, 44, March 1957, pp. 57–77. A good illustration of the pessimistic point of view is Joseph Schumpeter, "Der Unternehmer in der Volkswirtschaft von Heute," in Bernhard Harms, ed., *Strukturwandlungen der deutschen Wirtschaft*, 2 vols. (Berlin, 1928), I, pp. 295–312.

[50] Bodo Herzog, "Die Freundschaft zwischen Oswald Spengler und Paul Reusch," in Anton Koktanek, ed., *Spengler-Studien. Festgabe für Manfred Schröter zum 85. Geburtstag* (Munich, 1965), pp. 77–97.

increase somewhere, or the emergence of new competition. With the crisis of 1873, however, there developed a more general sense that there were deeper economic causes underlying the crises and that their impact could and should be mitigated or reduced through collective policies and actions. Increased sophistication of perception was accompanied by increased sophistication of reaction. The "classic" capitalistic responses to crises that took the form of wage reductions, dismissals of workers, reductions of investment and production, and price reductions were never totally abandoned, but they were superseded to an increasing extent by efforts at a more countercyclical approach in the form of demands for state contracts and credits, tax and freight rate reductions, and tariffs. Although the state did help sporadically with such measures, it never developed a real countercyclical policy of its own, and industrialists turned to self-help through the creation of cartels to stabilize prices and regulate production and of syndicates, which had the added function of marketing the regulated products. Although cartel agreements were binding in public law, it must be recognized that most of the cartels of the 1873–1896 period in heavy industry were notoriously unstable short-term affairs and were undermined by both their members and outsiders.[51]

What these experiences in cartelization did create, however, was a growing appreciation of the value of organization and some understanding of how they might be made to work more effectively. The high fixed costs in heavy industry created a combined need for high productivity to reduce costs and stabilize prices that would ensure a return (*Rentabilität*). The iron tariff of 1879 made such organization seem all the more imperative, because mechanisms were needed to ensure that industry would gain from the tariff on the domestic market while being able to enjoy the favorable export market as well. Given the increasing similarity in production methods and costs structures on, at least, the basic products of the industry by the turn of the century, serious competition would only have dissipated the advantages of the tariff and of higher production. In short, price stability in certain areas of production seemed more profitable than competition. Although the early cartels were true "children of distress" (*Kinder der Not*) and although the initial deliberations leading to the great cartels and syndicates of the industry had begun in times of depression, many of the

---

[51] Wolfram Fischer, "Konjunkturen und Krisen im Ruhrgebiet seit 1840 und die wirtschaftspolitische Willensbildung der Unternehmer," in *Wirtschaft und Gesellschaft im Zeitalter der Industrialisierung. Aufsätze, Studien, Vorträge* (Göttingen, 1972), pp. 179–193; Rosenberg, *Grosse Depression*, p. 268ff.; Veit Holzschuher, *Soziale und ökonomische Hintergründe der Kartellbewegung*, diss. Phil. (Erlangen, 1962), p. 49ff.

important ones were actually formed in more prosperous years and reflected a sustained effort to eliminate short-term speculative fluctuations in prices and introduce stability in pricing in both good and bad times for certain products through regulation of production and prices, common marketing arrangements, and regional allocation of orders to save on transport cost.

To a considerable degree, the cartels and syndicates were successful in stabilizing prices, but it would be mistaken to conceptualize their operation in static rather than in dynamic terms.[52] There is good reason to argue that the cartels, despite intentions to the contrary, accelerated tendencies toward vertical integration and promoted the destabilization of the industry by encouraging overproduction. The first tendency was already evident when the Rhenish-Westphalian Coal Syndicate was founded in 1893. The actual as well as potential increase in coal prices encouraged the backward integration of the iron and steel producers already in progress. They now had added reason to assure themselves a cheaper coal supply through the acquisition of coal mines and through the exercise of the self-consumption rights (*Selbstverbraucherrechte*) allowed syndicate members, that is, their right to produce and utilize coal over and above their quotas. The iron and steel cartels and syndicates, by contrast, promoted both backward integration, in the case of pig iron, and forward integration by stimulating heightened productive efforts in the less cartelized or uncartelized finished products. Why this was the case is best understood from an analysis of the major cartels in the industry during the prewar period.

The most basic and well organized of these in the last years before the war was the Pig Iron Syndicate (*Roheisenverband*) which, after its reorganization in 1910, encompassed all pig iron producers. Sales were made through the syndicate, which had the form of a limited-liability corporation (*GmbH*) composed of its members. Voting rights on quota allocation and prices as well as other important questions were vested in the membership in accordance with their quotas, but the quotas did not include pig iron produced and employed by the members for their own use. The successful organization of this area of

[52] The approach taken here is very close to that of Erich Maschke in his important *Grundzüge der deutschen Kartellgeschichte bis 1914* (Dortmund, 1964) and is also in conformity with the discussions in Pounds and Parker, *Coal and Steel*, p. 315ff., and D. L. Burn, *The Economic History of Steelmaking* (Cambridge, 1940), pp. 275–285. The literature on cartels and other forms of industrial concentration is quite large, but special note should be taken of Robert Liefmann, *Cartels, Concerns and Trusts* (London, 1932), Hermann Levy, *Industrial Germany. A Study of Its Monopoly Organizations and Their Control by the State* (Cambridge, 1935), and Herbert von Beckerath, *Modern Industrial Organization. An Economic Interpretation* (New York and London, 1933).

production had been a long time in coming. Initial efforts had been regional in nature and, although the organization of the Rhenish-Westphalian Pig Iron Syndicate in 1896 was a major breakthrough, it had a troubled history and suffered dissolution along with all but the Upper Silesian Pig Iron Syndicate in 1908. In that year, a bad one on the pig-iron market, the organizations were unable to withstand the pressures of English competition and the competition of German producers who refused to submit to cartelization, especially the Eisenwerk Kraft in Stettin. Significantly, the years 1910–1912 were good ones on the pig iron market, and this reduced the quarrels over quotas that made organization so difficult. No less significantly, however, the lead was taken by a "rump syndicate" of the six major Rhenish-Westphalian mixed works, which demonstrated its predominance by gradually persuading the other works and regional groupings to join in a common organization. Yet another indication of the predominance of these works was the unrestricted self-consumption right included in the new contract. The mixed works were in a position either to supply less than their allotted quotas when the market was good so as to utilize their pig iron for more lucrative steel production or to make maximum use of their quotas in bad years when they felt happy to sell anything. Although this placed some extra burdens on the smaller works, there can be no question about the fact that the Pig Iron Syndicate did produce a high degree of price stability in both good and bad years. In the good year of 1912, German prices varied only 4.03% while English and American prices varied 25.75% and 26.32%, respectively.[53]

The effort to attain such success, assuming one regards it as such from a general economic perspective, was necessarily more troubled and complicated in steel because more products were involved and the range of cartelization as one moved from cruder to more finished products was always a major question. The great breakthrough came in 1904 with the founding of the Steel Works Association, an effort by the mixed works to put an end to "unhealthy competition" and ensure reasonable returns through the stabilization of prices and production. As the case of pig iron demonstrated, syndicalization is easiest in the case of cruder, more uniform products, which permit sale through a central agency. It is much more difficult where specifications or profiles vary and questions of quality become involved. Consequently, the Steel Works Association created two categories of products. The crude A products consisted of semifinished steel (*Halbzeug*—ingots, slabs, billets, sheet bars, broad tool steel), railroad material (*Eisenbahnober-*

[53] Arthur Klotzbach, *Der Roheisen-Verband. Ein geschichtlicher Rückblick auf die Zusammenschlussbestrebungen in der deutschen Hochofen-Industrie* (Düsseldorf, 1926); Willi Tübben, *Die nationale und internationale Verbandspolitik der Schwerindustrie vor und nach dem Kriege*, diss. Phil. (Heidelberg, 1930), p. 23ff.

bau—rails, spikes, joint bars, and fish plates), and structural steel (*Form-eisen*—girders and universal steel). These products were uniform and easily marketed through a central agency—that is, syndicalized—and an agreement was made to set up quotas and market them through the Steel Works Association. The more finished B products—merchant bars (*Stabeisen*), rolled wire (*Walzdraht*), steel plate (*Blech*), pipes (*Röhren*), and cast and forged pieces (*Guss- und Schmiedstücke*)—were not dealt with in the same way. They were not syndicalized, the marketing remaining in the hands of the individual concerns, but quotas were placed on production. At the same time, A and B products consumed by the works themselves were not included in the quota restrictions.

The Steel Works Association proved effective in maintaining stable price levels for the A products and in strengthening Germany's position in the formation of certain international agreements among steel producers, particularly the Girder Agreement with the Belgian and French producers in 1904 and the International Rail Manufacturers Association (IRMA) of the same year. It gave producers a stronger hand in dealing with the associations of iron and steel merchants, because the Steel Works Association could offer rebates to merchants who were cooperative. It also proved effective in helping Germany to meet the challenge of international competition, such like that presented by the United States Steel Corporation, the giant trust founded in 1901 and bringing together a large number of steel producers, in part with the object of permitting the United States to compete effectively on world markets now that the domestic market was no longer consuming all its production. Between 1904 and 1911–1912, the amount of production sold by the Association abroad increased from 28.1% to 39.7%. Although this involved a considerable amount of dumping in that export prices were always lower than domestic prices, it also reflected an extremely aggressive marketing operation abroad by the Association. There is no evidence that the domestic market was being deprived by the quest for foreign markets. In 1906–1908, for example, when domestic demand was very high, exports by the Association dropped to 18.4%. Furthermore, the Association gave rebates to manufacturers employing iron and steel for the purpose of exporting manufactured products (*Ausfuhrvergütungen*).[54]

These undeniable successes, however, must be set against the very real difficulties and dysfunctionalities of the Steel Works Association which plagued it from the moment of its birth and persisted throughout its existence. It was meant to serve as an all-encompassing organization that would include all the production of the industry and would absorb preexisting cartels already formed. When compared to the organ-

[54] *Ibid.*, p. 34ff.

izational situation of other steel producing nations at the time, then, it certainly must be celebrated (or deplored) as the quintessence of cartelization. Nevertheless, by 1912 it had really failed of this purpose of all-inclusiveness, just as it had failed in its proclaimed intention of promoting stabilization in the industry and acting as an instrument for the encouragement of rationalization through the limitation of excess capacity and the placing of a premium on efficiency. To begin with, long-term intentions are not easily realized by three-year contracts. The Steel Works Association, quite in keeping with the past cartel traditions, was based on a short contract, and this meant that there was a periodic, regularly scheduled struggle for quotas for which the members had to prepare. Because power in the cartels was measured in terms of the quotas, this was in itself an encouragement to expand in order to demonstrate that old quotas were too low. To this incentive to expand was added that of a still unsatiated foreign market.[55]

In this context, the full syndicalization of the A products only encouraged the integrated works to take advantage of their self-consumption rights in the A products to produce more B products. On the one hand, production quotas on the B products in the Steel Works Association were looser than for the A products. On the other hand, there was the good export market. The end result was a strong incentive to produce more of everything. At cartel renewal time, the entire complex of circumstances provided splendid reasons for adjusting quotas to the latest increases in capacity, as was done in the 1907 renewal. The most important consequence was an enormous increase of B product production and sale. In 1911–1912, the sale of A products was only 32.24% above 1905–1906, but that of B products was 106% more, and the sale of the most important of the latter, merchant bars, had increased 124.10%. The undeniable stabilization of prices in the A products and of the amounts thrown on to the market had encouraged a dramatic expansion—probably an overexpansion—of production in the more finished B products, which had become a safety valve (*Sicherheitsventil*) for the mixed works seeking to exploit their capacities and increase profitability.[56]

Syndicalization of the B products had been the stated goal of the Association when the production quotas were set up in 1904, but consistent discussion of the subject since that time had led to consistent

---

[55] See the excellent discussion in H. R. Todsal, "The German Steel Syndicate," *Quarterly Journal of Economics*, 32, 1917, pp. 259–306. Also, see Bogner, *Wandlungen*, pp. 5–28; G. Embscher, *Periodische Wandlungen im Zusammenschluss der deutschen Industrie*, diss. Phil. (Dessau, 1928), pp. 30–72.

[56] Bogner, *Wandlungen*, p. 73, and Todsal, in *Quarterly Journal of Economics*, 32, pp. 289–299.

failure. Indeed, an increasing number of producers were anxious to eliminate even the production quotas after 1907, and the concerns gave implicit recognition to the instability of the Association by developing their marketing organizations and forming close connections with iron merchant firms not only to satisfy immediate needs but also in anticipation of the Steel Works Association's demise.[57] The atmosphere surrounding the renewal of the Association in May 1912 was extraordinarily tense, and although it appears to have been standard procedure for holdouts to play "*va banque* with the nerves of the participants in the negotiations," the fears of a "collapse comparable to an economic Jena" certainly were quite real.[58] In fact, it could be argued that the compromises made in order to extend the life of the Association another five years had only served to undermine it still further, and whatever the successful battle for renewal might be called, it certainly was no economic Leipzig.

In the discussions, Adolph Kirdorf argued in vain that the "elimination of B-quotas will be a regression to the old conditions, and a Steel Works Association without B-quotas will no longer be a Steel Works Association."[59] He was outvoted, however, by colleagues such as August Thyssen, who demanded either the syndicalization of the B products or the termination of all restraints on their production, and by those who considered the whole effort to organize the B products in any manner hopeless or undesirable. There was also a last minute battle over the apportionment of the A quotas. Although it would appear that no one, not even Hugo Stinnes, whose resistance to a diminution of his monopoly in production of the so-called Grey girders actually brought the negotiations beyond the twelfth hour, was willing to take responsibility for breaking up the Association in 1912, its future seemed far from rosy. Thyssen, without whom the Association could not have survived, was bitter over the concessions made to Stinnes, and was to be successful in winning similar rights for himself in court. He was also profoundly dissatisfied with his quota in A products, which he felt insufficient in the light of his increased capacity thanks to the new plants in Hagendingen. In the last analysis, however, the jockeying over the A product quotas was not the main issue, but rather the fact that, by 1912, less than one-third of the industry's production was encompassed by the Steel Works Association in any form because of the decartelization of the B products. The famed Association had become a "torso."[60] (See Table 2.)

[57] *Ibid.*, pp. 270–271.

[58] *Stahl und Eisen*, 32, May 9, 1912, p. 769.

[59] Steel Works Association negotiations, April 19, 1912, HA/GHH, N. 3000030/16.

[60] Negotiations of April 30–May 1, 1912, *ibid.*, and Bogner, *Wandlungen*, p. 72.

TABLE 2

The Participation Quotas in the Steel Works Association in 1912–1913
(Measured in tons and percentages)

Concern	Semifinished Steel		Railroad Material		Structural Steel		Totals	
	Tons	Percent	Tons	Percent	Tons	Percent	Tons	Percent
Gelsenkirchener Bergwerks-AG	66,675	5.0241	74,297	2.9919	134,532	5.5277	275,504	4.4122
Hoesch	—	—	84,611	3.4072	86,379	3.5492	170,990	2.7384
Deutscher Kaiser, Thyssen & Co.	18,420	1.3880	179,837	7.2420	157,338	6.4648	355,595	5.6948
Gutehoffnungshütte	30,481	2.2968	184,169	7.4164	66,911	2.7493	281,561	4.5092
Stahlwerk Haspe	13,000	0.9796	—	—	42,883	1.7620	55,883	0.8950
Phoenix	134,396	10.1269	214,896	8.6538	111,162	4.5675	460,454	7.3742
Rheinstahl	77,030	5.8043	157,372	6.3333	37,108	1.5247	271,410	4.3466
Krupp	198,945	14.9908	252,995	10.1880	73,887	3.0359	525,827	8.4211
Deutsch-Lux	104,132	7.8465	221,452	8.9178	244,179	10.0329	569,763	9.1247
Bochumer Verein	50,651	3.8166	152,852	6.1553	2,000	0.0822	205,503	3.2911
v. d. Zypen-Wissen	7,403	0.5578	5,999	0.2416	25,953	1.0664	39,355	0.6303
Georgs-Marienhütte	500	0.0377	90,000	3.6243	—	—	90,500	1.4494
Peiner Walzwerk	—	—	6,776	0.2729	201,510	8.2797	208,286	3.3357
Burbach-Eich-Düdelingen	184,000	13.8647	124,635	5.0190	212,839	8.7452	521,474	8.3514
Röchling	18,324	1.3807	74,696	3.0080	168,849	6.9377	261,869	4.1938
Stumm	38,676	2.9143	93,950	3.7833	130,242	5.3514	262,868	4.2098
Dillinger Hüttenwerke	42,760	3.2220	61,249	2.4665	—	—	104,009	1.6657
de Wendel & Co.	12,000	0.9042	130,700	5.2632	203,500	8.3615	346,200	5.5444
Rombacher Hüttenwerke	176,505	13.2999	67,292	2.7098	104,675	4.3009	348,472	5.5808
Lothr. Hüttenverein Aumetz-Friede	98,853	7.4487	54,906	2.2110	93,512	3.8423	247,271	3.9600

S.-A. d'Ougrée-Marihaye, Rodingen	48,225	3.6338	—	—	65,000	2.6707	113,225	1.8133
Maximilianshütte	5,000	0.3768	73,748	2.9698	98,746	4.0573	177,494	2.8426
Sächsische Gussstahlfabrik, Döhlen	1,138	0.0858	25,500	1.0269	—	—	26,638	0.4266
Königs- und Laurahütte	—	—	60,660	2.4428	34,000	1.3970	94,660	1.5160
Oberschles. Eisenbahn-Bedarfs-AG ⎫								
Kattowitzer AG ⎬	—	—	90,769	3.6552	138,571	5.6937	229,340	3.6729
Oberschles. Eisen-Industrie								
Bismarckhütte ⎭								
	1,327,114	100.00	2,483,261	100.00	2,433,776	100.00	6,244,151	100.00

Source: Willi Tübben, *Die nationale und internationale Verbandspolitik der Schwerindustrie vor und nach dem Kriege,* diss. Phil. (Würzburg, 1930), p. 38.

The motives of industrialists in cartel discussions concerning quotas and prices are difficult to analyze because they were a compound of short-term considerations of advantage, long-term calculations, personal beliefs and styles of operation, and functional responsibilities.[61] Naturally, a good deal of bluffing also went on at these meetings, but the profounder tendencies deserve some attention. The business managers (*Geschäftsführer*) and directors of the cartels and syndicates had an obvious stake in their existence in many cases, and an influential syndicate manager, such as the marketing director of the Steel Works Association, Carl Gerwin, could be counted on in his commitment to strengthening the Association. This was not because such men could not gain employment elsewhere. Theodor Müller (1869–1940), the general director of the Stumm concern since 1907, began his career as an "association man" (*Verbandsmann*) in various cartels and remained a passionate supporter and organizer of cartels and syndicates throughout his career. In this he was very similar to Bruno Bruhn and Arthur Klotzbach, both of Krupp and both enthusiastic leaders of the Pig Iron Syndicate.[62] The supporters of the cartels were convinced that, at best, they ensured the economic soundness of the industry and, at worst, they were better than chaos. They were reluctant to test them too severely, and although some industrialists felt that the Steel Works Association should fulfill its function of trying to rationalize the industry, Adolf Kirdorf warned against discussions of the closing of inefficient plants and the distribution of production according to profiles and types on the grounds that such discussions of rationalization would be "endless" and destructive. Such attitudes could only strengthen the impatience of critics such as Stinnes, who argued in 1910 that "It is absolutely necessary to have a period without syndicates, because otherwise we can never have healthy conditions. There are altogether too many works which do not have any right to exist; only free competition can create complete clarity in this regard."[63] This attitude seems

---

[61] For a suggestive discussion, see William Parker, "Entrepreneurship, Industrial Organization and Economic Growth: A German Example," *Journal of Economic History*, 14, 1954, pp. 380–400, in which the author correctly warns against "obtaining a study of economic growth that reduces itself to a matter of price relationships and the biographies of industrial titans" (p. 381) and demonstrates that industrialists in the Coal Syndicate did not maximize certain potential monopolistic advantages for a variety of complex reasons.

[62] On Müller, see *Nekrologe*, pp. 36–38. On Gerwin (b. 1869), Bruhn (b. 1872), and Klotzbach (b. 1877), see Wenzel, *Wirtschaftsführer*, pp. 722, 326, 1171.

[63] Report of Director von Bodenhausen of Krupp on discussions of March 21, 1910, Krupp WA E 81. The hope that the Steel Works Association would rationalize the industry was clearly expressed in 1904 by Dr. Emil Schröter, Business Manager of the Association of German Foundry Engineers: "In view of our present production and market conditions it is doubtless the immediate task of the existing

similar to that of the other dynamic concern builder, August Thyssen, who argued as early as 1905 that "the time of syndicates is actually past and we must move on to the time of trusts."[64] Thyssen, however, may have shared something of Kirdorf's view that Stinnes was a brash and irresponsible young man who did not know what he was doing. In 1912 Thyssen supported the renewal of the Steel Works Association and the syndicalization of the B products, in part because his own position was so strong that this would have given him advantages, in part because he was pessimistic about the future of the market and thought that final solution of syndicalization of the A products better than nothing at all.[65] In any case, these discussions demonstrate the complex considerations and motives underlying the compromises finally worked out.

They also expose the underlying structural tendencies and problems of the industry and illuminate the efforts of its leaders to deal with the complex and contradictory characteristics of the institutions they had created. The major prewar cartels in and of themselves were neither a consequence nor a cause of any loss of industrialist initiative. They were institutions arising from the very condition of the industry itself as it existed in Germany, and the industrialists were often caught between their cartels and their concerns. The basic tendency of the most dynamic industrialists was to favor the latter if and when a choice had to be made: "The giants of Rhenish heavy industry do not hide the fact that the market security given them by the cartels is not worth being restrained in their own potential for development, and they are only to be had for rigid syndicates to the extent that a wide gate is left open to them through which their independence of the syndicate permits them again to expand their production beyond its existing limits in accordance with their own judgment."[66]

Yet many of these same industrialists were also increasingly aware of the fact that the industry as a whole had problems that neither cartels nor individualistic concern expansion were solving but that both may have been making worse. The consciousness of the need for rationalization that periodically received overt expression, as shown above, was highly significant. A technically minded industrialist such as Albert

---

works to operate much more intensively than expansively. They should say that through mutual understanding and skillful division of the various products among one another, large, and by no means insignificant, savings can be made through technical improvements," *Stahl und Eisen,* 24, May 1, 1904, p. 500.

[64] Quoted in Maschke, *Grundzüge,* p. 32.

[65] Bodenhausen report, March 21, 1910, Krupp WA IV E 81, and Treue, *August Thyssen-Hütte,* pp. 142–143.

[66] Kurt Wiedenfeld, *Ein Jahrhundert rheinischer Montan-Industrie, 1815–1915* (Bonn, 1916), p. 145.

Vögler was keenly aware that there had been a relative absence of significant scientific and technical breakthroughs in the industry during the decade before the war. This important symptom of the retardation of industrial growth in an aging industry was not the only one being experienced by its leaders.[67] There were also the increasing intensity of international competition, the foreboding about a relative stagnation of demand, and the growing awareness of the fact that the value of its exports was declining relative to machine construction industry exports. There was concern that rising fixed costs could no longer be matched by equivalent increases in returns from sales and that every new financial burden of a social nature was disproportionately hurtful. Clearly this was an undercurrent before the war, albeit one that could rise very suddenly to the surface in a bad year such as 1913. In short, the industry suffered from particular endogenous problems which were raising serious questions about its structure and organization and whose solution was inhibited by certain internal and external constraints.

The appeal of trustification, for example, was limited by cultural and sociopolitical considerations. There was a strong feeling that "Germany is not the U.S.A." and that "the personal element and the historical background, family possession and tradition"[68] militated against a complete trustification of the industry even if not against the creation of giant concerns. Although the domination of independent firms by the concerns through the creation of "communities of interest" (*Interessengemeinschaften*—IG) that preserved the formal existence of the absorbed unit was often employed for financial and strategic reasons and was frequently little more than a stepping stone to complete fusion, the IG was also employed to spare the firms involved the total loss of identity. The term IG encompassed every form of contractural relationship among firms and concerns to pool profits or collaborate organizationally and technically that stopped short of fusion. There was a prejudice against "trustification" in the sense of a rigorous amalgamation of the members of an oligopolistic industry, be it through fusion or the instrument of a holding company, that would deprive them of all autonomy. The official organs of the industry themselves took the position that rationalization through trustification was "out of the question" and furthermore "undesirable" because of such "unhappy accompanying phenomena as overcapitalization, the high profits coming from

[67] See Vögler's memorandum of July 1919 in HA/GHH, N. 3000030/12. For the general theoretical problem, see Simon Kuznets, "Retardation of Economic Growth," *Journal of Economic and Business History*, 1, August 1929, pp. 534–600, esp. p. 547.

[68] Quoted in Fritz Blaich, *Kartell- und Monopolpolitik im kaiserlichen Deutschland* (Düsseldorf, 1973), p. 153.

its establishment, as well as the ruthless large-scale shutting down of plants and worker dismissals" that would follow in its wake. Consequently, the cartel seemed to be the "only means to give a certain stability to our iron industry which is dependent upon the changes of the world market as well as the domestic market." To be sure, cartels were not cures for everything. They could only mitigate the ebb and flow of the business cycle, which is "almost as unstoppable as the operation of a law of nature,"[69] and then only insofar as the cartels were of sufficient size and organizational strength. The dilemma of how the industry was supposed to maintain such cartels while it systematically undermined them remained unanswered, and the tension between cartel and concern building and the problem of rationalization constituted the legacies of the prewar period rather than the products of the war and its aftermath. So, too, was the fatalistic and resigned ideology and economic philosophy with which such problems were treated.

The heavy industrialists looked askance at all notions of state interference in the way they ran their industries, but they did expect and receive a considerable amount of state support. The prewar Reich and the Prussian state had been most supportive of both vertical and horizontal combination before the war through a combination of minimal interference and general encouragement. Germany's political leadership seemed to accept the claim of the industrialists that the concerns and cartels were acting in the national interest, that the pricing policies of the cartels followed the "middle line," and that they promoted stability and helped to maintain high employment. This attitude was reinforced by the prominent national economists of the period, who warned the government against heeding Reichstag complaints about the cartels and passing hasty legislation that might prove more harmful than helpful, and it was sanctioned by the famous Reichsgericht decision of 1897 confirming cartel agreements as binding in law. Although the government and particularly the military procurement agencies did take certain immediate actions to counter harmful cartel abuses, the aggregate effect of state action and inaction with regard to cartels was supportive.[70] Although the primary consumers of cartelized products initially did look to the Reichstag and state for help, they increasingly came to feel that they did best by settling interindustrial differences within

[69] Verein Deutscher Eisenhüttenleute, *Gemeinfassliche Darstellung des Eisenhüttenwesens* (Düsseldorf, 1918), pp. 292–293.

[70] Blaich, *Kartell- und Monopolpolitik*, pp. 293–295. The major opposition to cartels came from the Reichstag, and although the government could not ignore this pressure and did conduct investigations and introduce a cartel register, it is impossible to speak of a very active government policy against cartel abuses in the prewar period. See also E. R. Huber, *Deutsche Verfassungsgeschichte seit 1789*, 4 vols. (Stuttgart, 1963ff.), IV, p. 1110ff.

industry itself and passing the additional costs on to the final consumer in the form of higher prices. "Production policy," not "consumption policy," to use a favorite distinction of the Ruhr industrialists, ruled in Berlin, and there was much to learn from the fate of the pure rolling mills. The latter had asked the government to create a large state-owned steel plant to supply the rolling mills with cheap steel in 1904 and again in 1908–1909 in an attempt to break the power of the Steel Works Association, and the government had responded by refusing to protect them in any way from the Association's discriminatory practices and by indicating that the inefficiency of the pure rolling mills in comparison with the integrated works made the former unworthy of protection.[71] Indeed, in contrast to what used to be called the Anglo-Saxon countries, government interference in Germany with regard to cartels is less to be viewed from the perspective of prevention of abuses and weakening of the organizations than from the perspective of government promotion of syndicalization as an instrument of a national economic policy. There is no overt evidence in the lengthy secret negotiations among the Steel Works Association members in 1912 that anxiety over state action played any prominent role in the decision to prolong the Association, but the industrialists certainly must have been aware that the breakdown of the Association could have political as well as economic consequences. The Potash Law (*Kaligesetz*) of 1910 was proof of a government disposition to compulsory syndicalization in any industry where competition threatened to waste the national resources. It was surely this precedent that was in the mind of the *Stahl und Eisen* editorialist of 1912 when he praised the leadership of the Steel Works Association for its success in getting the organization renewed without "legislative assistance."[72]

Heavy industry, of course, would have opposed such government interference in the self-government (*Selbstverwaltung*) of its affairs. It prized its independence, insisted that it was fully and solely capable of operating its industries, and had long been accustomed to a very high degree of freedom in return for its backing of the authoritarian, pseudoparliamentary political system of the prewar Reich. As is well known, the nineteenth-century Prussian state had effectively bribed the Rhenish-Westphalian industrialists into the surrender of most of their liberal bourgeois principles after 1848 by permitting and encouraging the pursuit of industrial expansion and a retreat from politics. The ef-

[71] The government declared that "The plant combinations are the result of technical progress and are absolutely necessary for a rationalization of production; the pure rolling mills have only their backwardness to thank for their difficult situation," quoted in Bogner, *Wandlungen*, p. 19.

[72] *Stahl und Eisen*, 32, May 9, 1912, p. 769.

fort had been successful. Insofar as heavy industry returned to national politics after the founding of the Reich, it did so as the ally of the Prussian Junkers, an alliance formed in the tariff legislation after 1879, recemented by the Junker support for naval building and industrialist support for agricultural tariffs after 1900, and periodically rewelded in the anxious defence of the obnoxious but advantageous three-class voting system in Prussia and against the rising tide of liberal and Socialist criticism of the existing order. Economically, the alliance was one of producers against consumers, and it was based on an ideology of the "protection of the national labor" (*Schutz der nationalen Arbeit*) and of the "productive estates" (*schaffenden Stände*) against democracy and socialism. Before the war, it was heavily laden with nationalist, pan-German, and imperialist sentiment at once sincerely felt and designed to rally a mass base from the heterogeneous middle strata of society in support of the conservative order and against the growing strength of the Socialists and the trade unions.[73]

Heavy industry stood at the forefront of the resistance to unionization. It was famous for its patriarchalism, and it was true that certain concerns such as Krupp continued the employment of their workers in hard times and provided important welfare benefits. It was also famous for its harsh discipline, black lists, and long working hours. The continuously operating plants of the iron and steel industry worked on a two-shift system, and the workers spent twelve hours a day at the plants. They worked ten hours at heavy manual labor, often subjected to high heat and dust, and received two hours of pauses. The six-day work week was punctuated every two weeks by the infamous twenty-four-hour shift (*Wechselschicht*) on Sunday when the workers changed their shift. Obviously, this was a far cry from the eight-hour day called for by the unions, but the employers claimed that this was the only way in which they could maintain high employment and the necessary profitability (*Rentabilität*) of the industry. The German heavy industrialists were not alone in such practices, of course, and even their demand to remain "masters in their own house" (*Herr-im-Hause-Standpunkt*) was not unique. Nevertheless, it may be argued that the authoritarian ideology of the German heavy industrialists was more heavily pronounced than those of their counterparts elsewhere, and that there was a stronger identification of their authority with that of the state and of factory discipline with the discipline of prewar Germany's most honored institution, the army.[74]

[73] There is a big literature, but a good summary discussion with stimulating analysis is provided by Wolfram Fischer, "Staatsverwaltung und Interessenverbände im Deutschen Reich 1871–1914," in *Wirtschaft und Gesellschaft*, pp. 194–223.

[74] Otto Neuloh, *Die deutsche Betriebsverfassung und ihre Sozialformen bis zur*

Before the war, the industrialists had increasing cause to be concerned with the, to them, weakening of the authority of the state that was reflected in the growing power of the Reichstag, the increased militance of organized labor, and the tendency of bureaucrats in Berlin to pay heed to these forces and to the criticisms and proposals of academic social reformers and critics of heavy industry. The efforts by the Reichstag to use the Potash Law to impose various progressive labor measures in that industry, and the record of government interference on behalf of the coal miners, showed that industrial self-government could not be taken for granted. The case of the potash industry demonstrated that industrial self-government could cut two ways and that industry could be organized in order to achieve goals it did not itself desire. In encouraging the industrialists to keep out of "high" politics and to concentrate on their own affairs, the political leadership of Prussia and Germany had trained them to think in narrow terms beginning with their own self-interest and always returning to it. It was no accident that they were most directly active politically on the local level and provincial level and least responsible on the national level, and it was also no accident that as the rulers of miniature "states within the state,"[75] huge concerns employing thousands of workers for whom they had responsibility, that they had little tolerance for outside interference but were blindly insistent that their wishes had to be met. The instruments for the protection of their autonomy and the presentation of their wishes and demands were the interest groups, and the weakness of parliamentary institutions in so highly advanced an industrial society as Germany encouraged the development of interest groups and a very exaggerated form of interest group politics in which heavy industry had particularly distinguished itself.

The strength of the trade associations, interest group organizations, and employer organizations of the iron and steel industry as well as its domination of important national, industrial, and employer organiza-

---

Mitbestimmung (Tübingen, 1956), p. 108ff.; Christian Helfer, "Über militärische Einflüsse auf die industrielle Entwicklung in Deutschland," *Schmollers Jahrbuch für Gesetzgebung, Verwaltung und Wirtschaft*, 83, 1963, pp. 597–609; Hans Jaeger, *Unternehmer in der deutschen Politik* (1890–1918) (Bonner Historische Forschungen, Vol. 30) (Bonn, 1967), p. 90ff. Two important recent investigations of industrial labor relations in the prewar period are Elaine Glovka Spencer, "West German Coal, Iron and Steel Industrialists as Employers, 1896–1914," Ph.D. Diss. (Berkeley, 1970), and Klaus Saul, *Staat, Industrie, Arbeiterbewegung im Kaiserreich. Zur Innen- und Sozialpolitik des Wilhelminischen Deutschland 1903–1914* (Düsseldorf, 1974).

[75] Ferdinand Graf von Degenfeld-Schonberg, "Die Unternehmerpersönlichkeit in der modernen Volkswirtschaft," *Schmollers Jahrbuch für Gesetzgebung, Verwaltung und Volkswirtschaft im Deutschen Reich*, 55, 1929, pp. 55–75, esp. p. 58.

iron and steel producers and the electrotechnical Siemens-Schuckert concern. The Southern and Central German Groups were composed almost entirely of machine construction works. There was, therefore, a certain ambivalence in the character and functions of the VdESI. On the one hand, it was an organization for the adjustment of those interregional and interindustrial differences necessary for the prevention of open conflict within industry and for the formulation of common policies. On the other hand, it was an organization dominated by the iron and steel producers, particularly those in the Northwest Group. The latter paid 13,862 marks membership dues in 1910, followed by the Southwest Group, which paid 6,516 marks. This is not a very subtle measure of power, but the VdESI's consistent support of the policies of the iron and steel producers both before and after the war makes it very meaningful.[77]

Naturally, it took considerable effort on the part of the VdESI's management to implement this producer power with a minimum of friction. The VdESI's chairman from 1909 to 1929, Wilhelm Meyer of the Ilsede Hütte in Peine, Hannover (Northern Group), seems to have exercised considerable skill in these respects, but the day-to-day operation of the organization in the period covered by this study was the responsibility of its business manager, Jakob Reichert (1885–1948). Reichert was only 28 years old when he took this position in 1913, and he was to retain it as the VdESI underwent various organizational changes, until 1945. The son of a posting house keeper in Baden, he attended a humanistic Gymnasium in Wertheim and then studied law and economics at Berlin, Heidelberg, Munich, and Rostock, finally receiving his doctorate from Heidelberg in 1908. The very bright and ambitious young Reichert then headed for the Ruhr, where from 1908 to 1912 he served as a consulting staff member and then a syndic of the Duisburg Chamber of Commerce. Paul Reusch was impressed with him, and it was Reusch who recommended his appointment to the VdESI. The choice was an excellent one. Reichert was an extremely energetic and resourceful man who commanded and manipulated technical detail with great rapidity and skill, was a forceful but subtle negotiator who understood the interests of those with whom he dealt, and who rapidly developed the fine art of expanding his own powers as far as he could with the understanding of how to beat a hasty and self-preserving retreat when strongly challenged. He was a reliable and dedicated servant of heavy industrial interests throughout his career, and

[77] On the VdESI, see Clemens Klein's unpublished "Geschichte des Vereins Deutscher Eisen- und Stahlindustrieller (1874–1924)," in BA R 13 I/12-13, and Helmut Kaelble, *Industrielle Interessenpolitik in der Wilhelminischen Gesellschaft. Centralverband deutscher Industrieller 1895–1914* (Berlin, 1967), pp. 127–128.

the consummate trade association manager as demonstrated by his survival in office until 1945.[78]

As noted earlier, the power of the producers within the VdESI and their strength within industry as a whole, as well as the ease with which they organized and controlled organizations, was a reflection of the limited size of their group, the large size of their concerns, and their strong geographical concentration. To these factors might also be added a certain homogeneity of approach and mind created by the fact that they were all in the business of mass producing fairly uniform primary products in plants where fixed costs were quite high and the labor force was largely unskilled. The conditions under which their primary consumers in the manufacturing industries operated were very different. A neat distinction between the iron and steel producers and the finishing and manufacturing industrialists is never entirely possible. Rolling mills and foundries may be identified now with one group, now with another depending on what is being produced and for whom it is intended. Also, certain of the great concerns were deeply involved in the manufacture of machines. Nevertheless, differentiation is possible, although some of the distinctions were more important for the period under discussion than they are today. In any case, certain characteristics of the machine construction and electrotechnical industries were markedly different from those of the iron and steel industry.[79]

In manufacturing, and particularly in machine construction, heterogeneity rather than homogeneity was the rule. Firms were spread all over the country and size varied considerably, but optimum plant size was generally much smaller than in heavy industry. Normally, labor costs rather than fixed costs played the greatest role in determining prices for the highly differentiated production of these industries, and they were largely dependent on skilled labor. Cost calculations were very difficult because these industries manufactured complex products that often involved months or even years to complete. The development of uniform standards, viable costing techniques, reasonable contract terms and provisions, and industry-wide policies in general was, therefore, most difficult. There were, of course, exceptions to many of these generalizations. The machine construction industry could boast such giants as the Maschinenfabrik Augsburg-Nürnberg (MAN), directed by the Bavarian industrialist Anton von Rieppel (1852–1926), the Borsig Werke in Berlin directed by Ernst von Borsig (1869–1933), and the Deutsche Maschinenfabrik AG (DEMAG), led by Wolfgang Reuter (1866–1947). The electrotechnical industry was dominated by two

[78] *Nekrologe*, pp. 158–159.

[79] In this discussion, I follow closely the valuable analysis of Wiskott, *Eisenschaffende und eisenverarbeitende Industrie*, pp. 5–58.

giants, Siemens & Halske, led by Carl Friedrich von Siemens (1872–1941), and the Allgemeine Elektrizitäts-Gesellschaft (AEG), led by Walther Rathenau (1867–1922). Cartelization had been fairly successful in the locomotive building industry, and regional groups of a reasonably homogeneous character, such as the iron wares industry (*Kleineisenindustrie*) in the Bergisches Land could organize fairly effectively.

Yet heterogeneity and disunity were dominating characteristics. Although the manufacturers of products employing iron and steel were often worried and irritated by the power of heavy industry, frightened by its expansion into their spheres through vertical concentration, irritated by high prices and the iron tariff, annoyed by late deliveries and exploitative contract provisions that were a consequence of their dependence on the primary producers for raw materials, they found it very difficult to respond in an organized manner.[80] Although it was ritualistic but by no means invalid to point out that primary producers and manufacturers needed one another and were dependent ultimately on their mutual prosperity, the former ensuring that the latter would have the raw materials they needed and serving as a major purchaser of machines and electrical equipment, the latter producing Germany's most valuable exports because of the refined technology and skilled labor that went into its products, there was a growing sense before the war that the subordinate position of the manufacturers was unwarranted in terms of the numbers of workers employed in the two types of industries and the increasing importance of manufactured exports relative to that of the iron and steel industry.

It was fully in keeping with the above-described conditions, however, that the leading trade association of heavy industry's primary consumers formed before the war, the Association of German Machine Builders (*Verein deutscher Maschinenbauanstalten*—VDMA), was founded in 1892 in close collaboration with the iron industry and had its base of operations in Düsseldorf. To be sure, the founding twenty-seven firms that had set up the organization were from the Rhenish-Westphalian region, and their object was to procure better payment and delivery conditions from the mines and steel mills they supplied with machinery. Yet the first Business Manager of the VDMA was Dr.-Ing. Emil Schrödter, who held the same position in the Association of German Foundry Engineers (*Verein deutscher Eisenhüttenleute*), the impressive organization that was devoted to the industry's technical and scientific problems and that produced its splendid and exceptionally

---

[80] This is not to say that they did not try. See the pioneering work of Helga Nussbaum, *Unternehmer gegen Monopole. Über Struktur und Aktionen antimonopolistischer bürgerlicher Gruppen zu Beginn des 20. Jahrhunderts* (Berlin, 1966), esp. pp. 54–98.

informative trade journal, *Stahl und Eisen*. The initial appeal of the VDMA was not very great because it was viewed as a creature of the iron industry. Gradually, however, it demonstrated a high degree of fruitful acivity and increasing independence.[81]

This was particularly the case after the business management was taken over by Friedrich Frölich (b. 1872) who held the position from 1910 to 1924. An engineer trained at the Technische Hochschule in Hannover, he had practical experience working at the GHH and a Berlin machine works as well as extensive experience in the United States. He thus had a good background for an industry in which complex engineering problems were combined with patent and license questions and important foreign marketing operations. Frölich made a great effort to increase the VDMA's membership. When he took office, the firms belonging to the VDMA employed only 142,000 of the 400,000 workers in the industry. On January 1, 1914, the VDMA had 246 member firms with 189,000 workers. More important, the VDMA encouraged the formation of trade associations for the various branches of the industry, although the VDMA often found it difficult to persuade the groups belonging to it to keep it abreast of their various activities and support a coordinated policy.[82]

In general, the members of the industry became increasingly grateful to the VDMA for its informative publications, its hard work in representing the industry's interests with both the government and heavy industry, and its growing militance. It should not be thought, however, that the VDMA's prewar development was accomplished in conflict with heavy industry. Industrialists closely connected with heavy industry, such as Kurt Sorge (1855–1928) of the Krupp-Gruson Werke and Ernst von Borsig, were prominent members. Paul Reusch was an enthusiastic prewar member, and he encouraged the development of trade associations in the various branches of the industry. Furthermore, the export rebates granted to manufacturers by the Pig Iron Syndicate, which amounted to 4.75M per ton, and by the Steel Works Association, which amounted to 10–12.50M per ton in November 1914, were restricted to firms that were members of trade associations that could vouch for the fact that the iron and steel were actually employed in manufacture for export. Heavy industry, therefore, played a major role in the organization of its primary consumers.[83]

[81] See the unpublished history of the VDMA in the VDMA Archiv, "Der Deutsche Maschinenbau 1890–1923," and Otto Polysius, *Verbandsbestrebungen im Deutschen Maschinenbau*, diss. Phil. (Dessau, 1921).

[82] "Deutscher Maschinenbau," pp. 149–151. On Frölich, see Wenzel, *Wirtschaftsführer*, p. 670.

[83] Polysius, *Verbandsbestrebungen*, p. 82, and Deutscher Maschinenbau," p. 160ff.

Yet there were plenty of conflicts that proved the VDMA's worth as a counterforce to heavy industry. The VDMA fought to increase the export rebates and strongly opposed the periodic Steel Works Association threats to drop them altogether. It opposed the latter's discriminatory practice of giving rebates only to manufacturers who dealt exclusively with Association members. In retrospect, however, perhaps the most important sign of the VDMA's growing independence of heavy industry was its decision to move its headquarters from Düsseldorf to Berlin. Most of the membership still came from Rhineland-Westphalia and there was some fear that the organization would not take as strong a stand in its dealings with the government if it became subjected to "Berlin influences." In 1913, however, the move to Berlin was decided, and it took place in October 1914. The basic questions pertaining to foreign trade and other important economic issues were being decided in Berlin, itself a center of the manufacturing industry, and the conclusion was reached that Berlin was where the VDMA belonged rather than in the shadow of heavy industry's imposing headquarters in Düsseldorf, the Stahlhof.[84]

The move was symptomatic of a general change in the locus of interest group action in socioeconomic activity before the war as the central government of the Reich increasingly overrode the state governments in importance and the Reichstag played a more important role. This constituted something of a problem for heavy industry, which was regionally based and even somewhat provincial in outlook. The interest-group organizations on which heavy industry relied were located in the Ruhr. In addition to the chambers of commerce in cities such as Duisburg and Essen, over which heavy industry had great influence, it controlled the activities of the so-called Langnamverein (Long-Name Association), originally known as the Association to Protect the Common Economic Interests in Rhineland and Westphalia (1871), whose leading personnel were practically identical with those of the Northwest Group of the VdESI. In the years before the war, the regionally based organizations of heavy industry found it more and more necessary to mobilize the Berlin-based "peak organization" (*Spitzenverband*) meant to organize German industry as a totality, the Central Association of German Industrialists (*Centralverband deutscher Industrieller*), which had been founded in large measure under heavy industrial auspices in 1876. Heavy industry dominated the Central Association, but its policies met with considerable opposition within the organization as well as from the competing Federation of German Industrialists (*Bund der Industriellen*), founded in 1895 to represent the lighter and new industries. Similarly, in its efforts to fight the

[84] *Ibid.*, p. 149ff.

48

challenges of organized labor and other groups opposed to heavy industry's labor and social policies, its men in Berlin had to work harder mobilizing the central employer organizations located there, just as it had to expend greater funds and effort to secure the election of Reichstag deputies friendly to heavy industrial interests. It was easier to reign in Düsseldorf than in Berlin, and the growing importance of the capital constituted a great problem for the iron and steel men.[85]

As always, it is as important not to read too much of the future into the past as it is to recognize that much of the future is written in the past. The German iron and steel industry, whatever its structural and organizational problems, its changing position relative to other industries, the increasing challenges to its authority within German industry, the political and social changes in Germany that were shaking the presuppositions on which its policies rested, appeared as strong as ever in 1914. The prestige and domination of heavy industry was backed by a long history of success as well as of all the advantages that come with years of assiduous devotion to the accretion of strength and power. It was led by an energetic group of resourceful men who were self-confident in their convictions and almost blindly dedicated to their enterprises. These were invaluable points of departure in dealing with the structural problems confronting them, but this was to be all the more the case where normal development and adjustments were to become impossible because of "exogenous" factors that were to turn the functions of their organizations upside down in many instances, deal significant blows to the economic bases of their strength, and give their opponents and critics new and more potent weapons and arguments with which to resist and attack. The war wrought a revolution in their circumstances, as did ensuing developments, and, in a time of such rapid change, the capacity of the iron and steel industrialists to employ the favorable points of departure inherited from the prewar period becomes an important measure of the degree of continuity between Imperial Germany and the Weimar Republic.

[85] These tendencies are discussed, and somewhat exaggerated, in Kaelble, *Industrielle Interessenpolitik*. Demonstrative of the interrelationships in the pre-1914 period as well as of the political involvement of these organizations are the persons of Wilhelm Beumer and Henry Axel Bueck. The former was business manager of the Langnamverein and Northwest Group as well as member of the Executive Committee of the Central Association of German Industrialists and a deputy in the Prussian Lower House and Reichstag. The latter was business manager of the VdESI and Central Association of German Industrialists and a member of the Prussian Lower House.

CHAPTER ONE

The Dilemmas of Industrial Self-Government, September 1916–July 1919

World War I revolutionized the relationship between industry and government in Germany. Whatever their distaste for the republican regime that succeeded the monarchy after the Revolution of November 9, 1918, businessmen were aware of the fact that the "revolution" in industry-state relations had taken place during the war and recognized the significant continuity in the economic problems and practices of the wartime and postwar periods.[1] The Weimar Republic took up economically where the previous regime had left off. The wartime experience, therefore, is not so much background for this study as its logical point of departure, nor is the end of the war by any means the real end of a phase. The developments between the Revolution of November 9 and the German signature of the Treaty of Versailles on June 28, 1919, completed a stage in the relationships among iron and steel producers, their primary consumers, and the state that had originated in the final years of the war. From the perspective of this study, as well as from the viewpoint of a host of other socioeconomic problems, the years 1914–1919, and more especially the period between the launching of the Hindenburg Program for the production of weapons and munitions in September 1916 and the coming into force of the Versailles Treaty, may be treated as a unit.

In its general economic characteristics, this was a period of falling production, high demand, increasing costs, and rising prices in which the market conditions of the iron and steel industry were transformed and the well-being and autonomy of the industry were severely threatened. The decline in coal, pig iron, and crude steel production all follow a similar pattern (Table 3), as do the increasing costs of the raw materials used in iron and steel production and the prices of iron and steel themselves (Table 4). There was a decrease in production during the first two years of the war that was primarily a consequence of the drafting of large numbers of miners and workers into the army. Costs and prices rose as a result of the combination of increased fixed costs arising from insufficient employment of plant facilities and high demand. Following the battle of the Somme in the summer of 1916 and

[1] See, for example, the speech by General Director Paul Silverberg of the lignite industry of October 12, 1922, BA, Nachlass Silverberg, Nr. 2, Bl. 5.

TABLE 3

Coal, Pig Iron, and Crude Steel Production in Germany, 1913–1919
(In thousands of tons)

Year	Coal	Pig Iron	Crude Steel
1913	190,109	19,309	17,148[a]
1914	161,385	14,390	15,620
1915	146,868	11,529	13,288
1916	159,170	13,314	16,183
1917	167,747	13,142	15,288
1918	160,822	11,755	13,871
1919	115,707	6,284	7,021

[a] Excluding Luxemburg.

Source: Paul Wiel, *Wirtschaftsgeschichte des Ruhrgebietes. Tatsachen und Zahlen* (Essen, 1970), pp. 127, 227, 238.

TABLE 4

Average Prices and Percentage of Price Increases of the Most Important Raw Materials and Iron and Steel Products, 1914–1919
(1914 = 100)

		1914	1915	1916	1917	1918	1919
Coke	M	17.00	16.50	19.00	27.80	35.40	92.70
	%	100	97	101	163	208	545
Siderite	M	19.00	22.50	25.50	33.60	41.30	91.80
	%	100	118	134	176	217	483
Hematite	M	11.75	12.90	15.80	25.00	25.00	45.50
	%	100	109	134	212	212	387
Lorraine	Fr.	4.40	4.40	4.75	5.50	6.75	—
minette	%	100	100	107	125	153	—
Hematite	M	25.00	111.00	145.00	202.00	222.00	544.00
pig iron	%	100	130	170	237	261	640
German	M	77.95	91.00	109.50	132.50	162.50	490.50
foundry pig iron	%	100	117	140	170	209	620
Blooms	M	95.50	111.80	114.50	182.50	192.50	660.00
	%	100	106	125	190	200	690
Girders	M	111.50	125.00	150.00	210.00	220.00	642.00
	%	100	112	143	197	198	575
Merchant	M	95.00	125.00	170.00	217.50	235.00	665.00
bars	%	100	131	178	238	247	700
Heavy	M	102.00	136.00	180.00	242.00	275.00	722.00
plate	%	100	133	176	237	269	707
Sheet	M	135.00	170.00	290.00	325.00	325.00	1150.00
steel	%	100	125	215	240	248	851

Source: Alfons Schlaghecke, *Die Preissteigerung, Absatzorganisation und Bewirtschaftung des Eisens 1914–1920*, diss. Phil. (Giessen, 1920), p. 67.

the appointment of Hindenburg and Ludendorff to the Supreme Command on August 31, however, the military authorities reversed the fairly conservative procurement policies they had followed prior to that time, embarked on the so-called Hindenburg Program, and released thousands of miners and workers from the army to meet the staggering production demands of a nation committed to "total war." The production increases of 1916–1917 reflect this abandonment of the illusion that the war would be short in favor of the illusion that Germany could sustain a battle of production against a vastly superior enemy coalition and realize her immoderate war aims. The sharp increase in costs and prices reflect this high demand as well as the government's willingness to provide maximum incentives to producers.[2]

By 1917–1918, Germany's incapacity to sustain the production increases triggered by the Hindenburg Program was clear in all areas of production. Uneconomic exploitation of coal mines combined with an inefficient labor supply aggravated the already serious coal shortage and undermined the productive efforts of an iron and steel industry handicapped by its own labor shortages and raw materials difficulties. In the competition between factory and front for labor, the latter's needs once again became dominant, only now as a matter of necessity as well as policy. As in the prewar economic competition among nations, so in the wartime battle of production steel became the measure of Germany's strength. In the end, the Hindenburg Program had to be cut back because Germany could not produce the amounts of steel it required, a situation that reflected the ultimate strain on her total resources in 1918. If the rate of price increases on primary products slowed down in 1917–1918, this was largely a consequence of governmental action. When the military collapse came, price controls were lifted along with most of the already badly shaken economic and political restraints on wage demands. The result was the catastrophic decline in production arising out of the defeat and unrest of 1919 along with an accompanying massive increase in costs and prices.[3]

Needless to say, the severity of the German wartime and postwar inflation was closely bound up with the conditions described above. Indeed, after 1916 Germany suffered in varying degrees from all three

[2] The Hindenburg Program and its consequences are discussed in Gerald D. Feldman, *Army, Industry and Labor in Germany, 1914–1918* (Princeton, 1966), pp. 149ff., 253ff., 493ff.

[3] On economic conditions in 1919, see Hans Schieck, *Der Kampf um die deutsche Wirtschaftspolitik nach dem Novemberumsturz 1918*, diss. Phil. (Heidelberg, 1958), p. 7ff.

of the basic aspects of inflation.[4] First, the government financed the war and demobilization by increasing the amount of money in circulation rather than by seeking to correct its budget deficit through the heavy taxation of profits as well as other taxation methods. The fateful step toward reliance on the printing press had been taken in the opening days of the war, when the government suspended the conversion of notes into gold and permitted the Reichsbank to discount short-term treasury notes (*Reichsschatzwechsel*). While thus formally retaining the regulation that Reichsbank notes had to be covered at least one-third in gold and two-thirds in commercial bills (*Handelswechsel*), the Reich had effectively placed treasury notes on a par with commercial bills and removed important restrictions on the use of the printing press to cover its expenditures. Until 1916 the increased costs of the war were covered by the domestic loans on which the government relied to finance it. When these no longer sufficed, however, the government proved unwilling and unable to offend the most powerful classes in society by imposing an effective system of taxation, and the war profits, turnover, and coal taxes imposed in 1916–1917 proved insufficient. The floating debt of the Reich rose from 300 million marks in July 1914 to 55.2 billion marks in December 1918.[5] Second, just as the government had been unable to control war profits, so was it unable to control the rapid rise of wages after the launching of the Hindenburg Program. Although real wages declined, the paper wages of male workers in the war industries increased 152% between 1914 and 1918—that is, before the massive increases of the revolutionary period.[6] Finally, there was a third aspect of inflation that was less apparent during this period, and this was the depreciation of the value of the mark abroad due to the adverse balance of payments. Just as price controls and other regulatory measures obscured the domestic inflation during the war, so the closure of the stock exchange and ban on quotations from foreign exchanges veiled the deterioration of the value of the mark abroad.[7] Government officials were fully

[4] Here I follow W. Arthur Lewis, *Economic Survey, 1919–1939* (New York and Evanston, 1969), pp. 23–24.

[5] See Konrad Roesler, *Die Finanzpolitik des Deutschen Reiches im Ersten Weltkrieg* (Untersuchungen über das Spar-, Giro-, und Kreditwesen. Schriften des Instituts für das Spar-, Giro-, und Kreditwesen an der Universität Bonn, Vol. 37) (Berlin, 1967); Stolper, *German Economy*, p. 54ff.; Bresciani-Turroni, *Economics of Inflation*, pp. 25–28; P. Barrett Whale, *Joint Stock Banking in Germany. A Study of German Credit Banks Before and After the War* (London, 1930), p. 185ff.

[6] Feldman, *Army*, pp. 471–472.

[7] Stolper, *German Economy*, p. 60.

aware of the decline in the value of the mark on foreign exchanges during the war, as were iron and steel industrialists. The latter purchased 17,005,428 tons of Swedish iron ore between 1915 and 1918. At the government's request, these purchases were made on credits supplied by Swedish banks repayable in kronen after the war because the German authorities did not want to increase the depreciation of the mark by having the industrialists send out large sums of German currency. The industrialists were happy to comply because they, like the German authorities, anticipated victory, an improvement in the exchange rate after the war, and a great exchange profit. Like the war itself, it was a giant speculation, and it was just as unprofitable (Table 5).[8]

In the last analysis, however, this was one of the very few unprofitable speculations the iron and steel producers were to make and, as shall be shown, it provided yet another reason for them to challenge the authority of the government. As indicated above, the imposition of government controls on prices played a significant role in the war, and it is patently obvious that the high demand and resulting scarcities required government intervention in production and allocation as well. The efficacy of government controls, however, rests on its authority, and the latter depends in turn on the degree to which the government is able to enforce its will and convince its people that it is competent in its decisions and fair in their implementation. When the Imperial Government suspended the various Reichsbank coverage requirements in July 1914 and thereby gave effective expression to the power of the state and the primacy of its interests over economic considerations, no one could imagine that the consequence of these actions would become the measure of the government's impotence. Yet this is precisely what happened by 1918 because of the failure of the government to manage the economy effectively during the war. The loss of governmental authority because of its failures in wartime politics and economics unleashed a bitter and protracted battle between industry and government over the extent and nature of economic controls and the role and character of industrial self-government. The conflict began during the war and continued into the Weimar Republic, and, like the economic problems arising from the war, provides an important element of continuity during a period of traumatic change.

[8] Alfons Schlaghecke, *Die Preissteigerung, Absatzorganisation, und Bewirtschaftung des Eisens 1914–1920*, diss. Phil. (Giessen, 1920). The entire question will be dealt with in detail in this and the following chapter.

TABLE 5

The Price of Swedish Iron Ore in Kronen, the Exchange Rate of the German Mark
in Kronen, the Price and Percentage Price Increase of Swedish Iron Ore in Marks,
1914–1919

	Swedish Kronen Price	Cost of 100 Swedish Kronen in Marks	Cost of 1 Ton of Swedish Ore in Marks	Percent of Increase in Marks
1914	17	112	17.92	100
1915	18	—	—	191.60
April 30, 1916	—	159.75	39.33–51.12	—
December 31, 1916	—	171.75	42.93–54.96	—
1916	25–32	—	—	283.30
January 2, 1917	—	171.75	45.74	—
September 1, 1917	—	238.25	58.56	—
November 1, 1917	—	255.75	63.93	—
1917	25	—	—	533.30
July 1, 1918	—	182.75	45.68	—
December 28, 1918	—	244.25	61.06	—
1918	25	—	—	466.60
January 15, 1919	—	240.75	45.74	—
March 12, 1919	—	285.75	54.29	—
June 19, 1919	—	386.00	73.34	—
August 8, 1919	—	470.00	89.30	—
September 11, 1919	—	595.00	113.05	—
September 13, 1919	—	336.00	120.84	—
September 16, 1919	—	719.00	136.61	—
October 30, 1919	—	699.00	132.81	—
November 29, 1919	—	951.75	188.83	—
December 6, 1919	—	1039.25	197.41	—
1919	19	—	—	900.00

Source: Alfons Schlaghecke, *Die Preissteigerung, Absatzorganisation und Bewirtschaftung des Eisens 1914–1920*, diss. Phil. (Giessen, 1920) pp. 30–31.

CARTELS AND SYNDICATES BETWEEN
COMPULSION AND UNCERTAINTY

The wartime organization of the iron and steel industry developed slowly and painfully. During the first two years of the war there was constant squabbling between the industrialists and the military authorities, and, although relations between heavy industry and the General Staff were to improve after August 1916, it cannot be said that the relationship with the military bureaucracy in Berlin was particularly sparkling throughout the war. Although industrialists ad-

mired Prussian militarism from afar, they found it much less enchant-
ing when they were greeted by a gruff "what d'you want?" in response
to the polite "good morning" with which they greeted the officer-in-
charge at a military bureau.[9] Underlying such social tension, however,
was the growing contempt businessmen felt for the rigidity, ignorance, and technical incompetence they found in military circles. After
the war, it was not uncommon for industrialists to blame the loss of
the war in large part on the economic and technical backwardness of
the military. On the other side, military men were naturally distrustful
of men engaged in the unheroic occupation of business, and although
prepared to accord high production of weapons and munitions grudging respect, they could not help suspecting business of profiteering
from what they viewed as the noblest of human occupations. More
immediately, the two sides fought because they were engaged in
different enterprises with different rationalities. The industrialists
complained that the army had taken their best workers, that their costs
were being increased by the underemployment of their plants through
inefficient and erratic procurement policies, that they were being
denied an adequate profit by the War Ministry's efforts to reduce
prices and prevent exports, and that the military's efforts to pacify
and win over the workers were promoting unwanted unionization and
high wages. The War Ministry, for its part, insisted on giving priority
to the war effort over maximum utilization of plant facilities and also
felt called upon to win over those social groups previously uninte-
grated into the state.[10]

Despite the complaining of the businessmen, however, the extent of
government interference before the summer of 1916 was quite minimal. The War Ministry sought to influence the utilization of labor
and pricing policies through the granting of war contracts on special
terms, but there was no direct control over prices and very little direct
control over distribution. Mounting iron and steel prices alarmed not
only government officials and Reichstag deputies but also some of the
industrialists themselves. Paul Reusch of the GHH, a man who was
quite old fashioned in his sociopolitical views and hardly backward
when it came to making a profit for his concern, was incensed at the
profiteering of some of his colleagues, correctly feared that the manufacturing customers of the steel industry would follow the lead in
immoderately increasing prices, and instructed the GHH's representative to the Steel Works Association to vote against price increases

[9] Director Wedemeyer of the GHH to Dr. Hellmich of the Association of German
Engineers, January 6, 1919, HA/GHH, Nr. 3001008/6.
[10] Feldman, *Army*, chap. I.

because Reusch wanted no "responsibility for the consequences of a pricing policy such as the one conducted recently by short-sighted industrialists."[11]

From the standpoint of the war effort, the failures of industrial self-government in the area of supply were even more serious than the abuses in pricing. With one important exception, the government had refrained from organizing the distribution of iron and steel production. The demand for pig iron had been so great and so competitive that the Raw Materials Section (*Kriegsrohstoffabteilung*—KRA) of the Prussian War Ministry found it necessary to appoint a commissar to the Pig Iron Syndicate to oversee distribution in accordance with priority lists sent out by the ministry's Pig Iron Distribution Bureau. The arrangement seems to have been desired by both sides, and the industrialists surely were well satisfied with the personage appointed as commissar, Florian Klöckner, the brother of Peter Klöckner.[12] As was to be demonstrated time and again, however, control of pig iron distribution was relatively easy because the syndicate rigidly controlled marketing. The same was not true of the A and B products, where sales were made by the syndicates and the firms and where independent merchants had considerable freedom. In 1916 the Steel Works Association had a very difficult time supplying its customers with material necessary for war production. In October, for example, although obligated to supply 60,000 tons monthly in semis, it could not supply even half that amount. The reason was that its members were evading their obligations to the Steel Works Association in order to fill lucrative contracts, some of a nonmilitary nature, or to supply iron merchants with whom they wished to maintain connection.

Syndicate obligations could be evaded in a variety of ways. One was to take advantage of the Steel Works Association contract provision permitting producers to sell semis of special quality directly at a higher price than that set by the Association. It was virtually impossible to distinguish between those firms keeping to the spirit as well as the letter of this contract provision and those who were employing "every conceivable quality designation" to make a higher profit. Similarly, there was no way of preventing a major producer from deciding "to hold back temporarily with the sale of iron bars and only to give out small quantities at high prices" because costs were going up and the going prices seemed insufficiently rewarding.[13]

[11] Reusch to H. Boecker, May 18, 1916, HA/GHH, Nr. 300193003/3.

[12] Klotzbach, *Roheisen-Verband*, p. 219ff.

[13] Steel Works Association meeting, October 4, 1916, HA/GHH, Nr. 3000030/10.

Only the most flagrant and visible abuses could receive attention within the organs of industrial self-government. When the Phoenix concern not only failed to supply its quota of production to the Rolled Wire Syndicate but also tried to purchase material from other firms in the Steel Works Association, it was called to order by the latter's chairman, Louis Röchling, who reminded Phoenix of its "patriotic duties" and informed the concern that the other concerns were not prepared to act as supply depots for Phoenix so that the latter could maintain its connections with the iron merchants.[14] Similarly, although it was understandable that firms wished to export in order to benefit from the high prices they could impose on the neutrals, such exports became distressing when they deprived the war effort of needed material, and they became truly alarming when some of the material inadvertently ended up in enemy hands. Even so enthusiastic and indiscriminate a defender of high war profits and other dubious industrial practices as Jakob Reichert, felt impelled to warn his colleagues that "day after day large quantities of German iron are sent from Switzerland to France and Italy" and that this was "something to think about." Apparently, however, Reichert did not want the War Ministry to think too much about the problem, because he and some of his colleagues were telling the ministry that its concern was partially "unfounded" and partially "exaggerated."[15] Such cases cast serious doubt on the claims of Reichert and his colleagues that industrial self-government was sufficient to ensure industrial responsibility in the military emergency. Similarly, there was very good evidence that the actual creation of industrial self-government, even where it was clearly to industry's advantage, could not always proceed without government intervention.

Because it was hard to police exports, it was industry that frequently called upon the government to impose controls and compel industrialists to eliminate competition abroad so as to maximize profits and the procurement of foreign exchange. In peacetime, exports had been a dire necessity, involving severe competition in the effort to dispose of inventories and had often been characterized by dumping. The war turned the export of iron and steel into a remarkably profitable luxury, profitable because the neutrals, having either no steel industry of their own or extremely inadequate ones, were in desperate need of iron and steel, a luxury because excessive exports could deprive the army of vitally needed matériel. The temptation to export was increased enormously after mid-1915, when Great Britain cut off her iron and steel exports to neutrals, and the latter seemed willing to pay any price for

---

[14] Rolled Cable Cartel meeting, October 4, 1916, *ibid.*, Nr. 3000034/21.
[15] July 1916 VdESI Executive Directors meeting, BA, R 13 I/149.

the German products. The situation placed a premium on organization. On the one hand, iron and steel exporters could best profit if they formed export syndicates and thereby controlled the export price at a high level instead of competing with one another to the advantage of buyers. On the other hand, the government, and especially the Reichsbank, were anxious to improve the German balance of payments and to secure foreign exchange.[16] As so often happened, however, a great producer felt it more advantageous to maintain a free hand and resisted the efforts of his colleagues to organize for the benefit of all. When Reusch and Röchling proposed the creation of a syndicate for merchant bars at the end of 1915, Hugo Stinnes refused to commit Deutsch-Lux. Instead of despairing, however, Reusch contacted friends in the Reich Office of the Interior, and Stinnes was soon invited to Berlin for a discussion with government and Reichsbank officials. Reusch was not averse to using government pressure if Stinnes would not cooperate. When Stinnes remained resistant the government banned the export of merchant bars, as it had already banned the export of certain strategic materials, until the industrialists organized a compulsory export syndicate.[17] On January 6, 1916, the export of merchant bars and other major A and B products was formally banned, and a series of export syndicates were set up within the Steel Works Association. Following a practice already begun in 1914, industrial self-government in the iron and steel industry was centralized in a new Central Bureau for Export Permits for Iron and Steel Products (*Zentralstelle der Ausfuhrbewilligungen für Eisen- und Stahlerzeugnisse*) under the leadership of Reichert and attached to the VdESI. Its task was to assist in the implementation of government export quotas and ensure that iron and steel were exported only at syndicate prices. In effect, it provided the government with the expert advice necessary to determine these prices. The new bureau enormously enhanced the activities of the VdESI and increased the powers of Reichert because it gave the trade association important official functions.

The export of iron and steel flourished at a rate of 250,000 tons a month through the first half of 1916, at enormous profit to those engaged in the business. Much of this profit was owed to the government's export bans, which constituted the foundations on which the powers of the various export syndicates rested. Yet the industrialists were outraged at the idea that their high export profit should be taxed in any way, and they only gave way to the government's demand for a very moderate export levy (*Ausfuhrabgabe*) because they feared that

[16] Feldman, *Army*, pp. 157–158; *Stahl und Eisen*, 39, June 6, 1919, pp. 627–632; VdE, *Gemeinfassliche Darstellung*, pp. 310–312.

[17] Reusch to Röchling, December 29, 1915, HA/GHH, Nr. 300193221.

the government would bring the matter to the Reichstag where demands had been raised for appropriation of 75% of the export profit instead of the 5–7% arranged between the industrialists and the treasury.[18]

These simple and pleasant solutions to the export question broke down in the summer of 1916, when the great munitions crisis provoked by the Battle of the Somme made it impossible to continue exports at a high level. In mid-July the industrialists voluntarily suspended exports, an action made all the more necessary by the preference for exports shown by some firms. Exports in limited quantities were soon resumed because of neutral threats to cut off important raw materials and German need for foreign exchange. From this point onward, however, exporting became a Kafkaesque, albeit profitable activity in which a multitude of military and semi-official "self-governing" industrial agencies controlled exports in accordance with a complex and ever-changing series of regulations. The character and tone of state-industry relations in the area of exports was changed. A governmentally sanctioned and protected industrial self-government in the field of exports gave way to a government-imposed and controlled organization of exports employing businessmen and their self-governing organizations as its agents. These controls were all the more onerous because they were largely devised and implemented by the military authorities.[19]

The development of export controls with its dual object of protecting domestic supply and reaping profits from sales paid for in foreign exchange remained one of the most important issues in industry-state relations throughout the inflation. At the same time, the pattern of industry-government interaction in this area reflected a larger pattern of relations. Could effective industrial self-government be created and maintained under conditions of national emergency and chronic economic difficulty? Was it possible to employ the powers of the government and work with the government and still maintain industrial self-government? The answer to these questions depended in large measure on the extent to which each side could satisfy the other's demands for efficiency. The industrialists expected the government to be firm, effective, and well organized but not to interfere substantively with the

---

[18] VdESI circular of June 23, 1916, *ibid.*, Nr. 30019322/7. Reichstag deputies, particularly the influential Centrist Matthias Erzberger, later severely attacked the government's policy. See Friedrich Zunkel, *Industrie und Staatssozialismus. Der Kampf um die Wirtschaftsordnung in Deutschland 1914–1918* (Düsseldorf, 1974), p. 25n–32.

[19] See Julius Hirsch, *Der moderne Handel, seine Organisation und Formen und die staatliche Binnenhandelspolitik. Grundriss der Sozialökonomik V. Abteilung. Handel, Transportwesen. Bankwesen.* II Teil., 2nd ed. (Tübingen, 1925), p. 173ff.

independence or the profitability of their industry. The military and civilian authorities expected a satisfactory level of quality production at reasonable prices and distribution in the best interests of the nation.

In the summer of 1916 it became clear that the resources of both government and industry would have to be employed more fully in the service of the economic war effort. The iron and steel industrialists took advantage of the munitions crisis to attack the "planlessness" and inefficiency of the War Ministry, to hold it responsible for the crisis, and to demand a reorganization along lines that typified the industrialist conception of proper government-industry coordination. They proposed the creation of a new authority with a high-ranking officer at its head to ensure the coordination of procurement, and they suggested that this officer be supplied with a "top-flight personage" from industry to assist in establishing collaboration with industry. The industrialists made it clear that they wanted a strong agency with "appropriate power," that would not "slow up the conduct of business," but would collaborate with industry.[20]

This was neither the first time nor the last that the industrialists called for the creation of a "dictatorial" military agency under its influence that would bypass or subordinate existing agencies. Yet industry's wishes were best realized when they had powerful support in government circles, and after the assumption of the Supreme Command by Hindenburg and Ludendorff at the end of August 1916, there was a real "honeymoon" between army and industry. The new military leaders introduced a massive munitions program which promised maximum utilization of plant facilities, and they shared the industrialists' contempt for the War Ministry. On November 1, the government centered economic mobilization in the Prussian War Office, a new agency put under the leadership of General Wilhelm Groener. Dr. Kurt Sorge, General Director of the Krupp-Gruson Works in Magdeburg, was appointed Chief of Groener's Technical Staff and was duly congratulated by his industrialist colleagues, who hoped that "you . . . will work in the sense of the industrialists, particularly the iron and steel industrialists."[21] At the same time, the industrialists did their share to organize the war economy more efficiently by founding the German Steel Federation (*Deutscher Stahlbund*) on October 4, 1916, an organization encompassing all the iron and steel producers as well as their organizations and designed to organize the procurement of previously nonsyndicalized products. The producers pledged themselves to supply

[20] See the important memorandum of the VdE, August 23, 1916, HA/GHH, Nr. 30019326/29. For a general discussion, see Feldman, *Army*, chap. III.

[21] Reichert to Sorge, November 18, 1916, BA, R 13 I/88.

the demands of the war effort as fully and as quickly as possible and to defer all other orders until military requirements were met.[22]

It did not take long for the new War Office to prove as "bureaucratic" as the War Ministry and for the good intentions of the producers to founder on the realities of wartime economics. The allocation of iron and steel and its distribution were placed under rigorous and strict control by the Raw Materials Section. The leader of this agency, Lieutenant-Colonel Josef Koeth, was very friendly to industry, and industrialists could hardly complain about the staffing of the leading positions in the Iron Section of Koeth's agency because they were given to General Director Burgers of the Gelsenkirchener Bergwerks AG, Florian Klöckner, Director Gerwin of the Steel Works Association, and Director Fischer of the Diskonto-Gesellschaft. Nevertheless, these friendly officials could not spare their industrialist colleagues from the nightmare of guidelines, priority lists, and endless forms that accompanied wartime controls. Nor could they prevent the War Office from insisting on the creation of price ceilings for all iron and steel products between February and June 1917, although here again controls were implemented in collaboration with the industrialists because the price ceilings were determined initially by the Steel Federation and then negotiated with the War Office.[23]

Still, the industrialists found it difficult to behave as well as they had promised to behave in October 1916. In April 1917 the shortage of semis had become so serious that leaders of the Steel Works Association spoke of the "bankruptcy" of their organization because of its inability to meet its delivery obligations. They contemplated asking the government for a 40–50 mark delivery premium per ton in order to inspire producers, but recognized that this would call into question their claims that it was the steel shortage alone that was responsible for the supply problem.[24] As 1917 wore on, public outrage over rising prices and high dividends further tarnished the public image of the industry. The government and the army could not overlook entirely the state of either public finances or public opinion, and although proponents of truly strong measures such as General Groener, who advocated control over profits, could be eliminated from high office,

[22] "They take on the obligation to employ all the resources at their disposal to support the German Steel Federation in its task of mediating the most rapid delivery of all rolled products made of iron and steel needed by the military authorities and, in all cases where it is required, to hold back on all other deliveries. . . ." Quoted in Schlaghecke, *Bewirtschaftung des Eisens*, p. 75.

[23] *Ibid.*, pp. 74–82, and Alfred Müller, *Die deutsche Rohstoffbewirtschaftung im Dienste des deutschen Monopolkapitals* (Berlin, 1955), p. 17ff.

[24] Steel Works Association meeting, April 13, 1917, HA/GHH, Nr. 3000030/11.

as he was in August 1917, it was less easy to forget the friendly advice of Colonel Koeth "that in his view . . . it is in the interests of the iron industry to have negative balances."[25] Koeth refused to grant price increases on most iron products after the summer of 1917, and although rising material and labor costs made it possible for the industrialists to argue convincingly that they were losing money on the A products and even some of the B products, the mildness of their complaints suggests that Koeth's argument had made a deep impression on them.[26]

Needless to say, the iron and steel industry had not decided to operate at a loss for the duration. For one thing, it is very misleading to confuse the official prices with those actually paid. One of the consequences of the shortages, decreased productivity, increased costs, and a mountain of regulations that characterized the controlled economy (*Zwangswirtschaft*) was a significant decline in business morals. Price ceilings could be and were evaded in a variety of ways. As noted earlier, firms commonly took advantage of the excessively high price allowed for higher quality Siemens-Martin steel both to make an excess profit on such steel and to make what might be termed a super profit by selling regular steel under quality labels.[27] It should be clear, however, that the customer as well as the buyer was cheating, because customers were so desperate to get iron and steel that they were prepared to pay higher prices for what they knew were standard-quality goods. Another technique employed by firms was to take advantage of the higher price allowed iron merchants, which was approximately 80 marks per ton in 1918. A number of industrial firms already owned or bought up iron trading firms, just as in the notorious case of the Cologne iron merchant Otto Wolff (1881–1940), merchants invested in industry. In either case, the producers involved replied to requests from customers with this type of answer: ". . . yes, you can have iron at the price ceiling with a delivery time of eight to ten months, but perhaps my iron trading company has iron in stock that costs 80 marks per ton more. Perhaps you could discuss it with them."[28]

It would be primitive to think that the substance of industry's profits depended on such devices, however, or that the government was will-

[25] Reported by Röchling at a meeting on January 24, 1918, *ibid.*, Nr. 3000030/11. On Groener's program and his dismissal, see Feldman, *Army*, p. 373ff.

[26] See the various Steel Federation meetings of 1918 in HA/GHH, Nr. 3000030/11 and Schlaghecke, *Bewirtschaftung des Eisens*, p. 32ff.

[27] Steel Works Association meeting, November 21, 1918, HA/GHH, Nr. 3000030/11.

[28] Robert Liefmann, *Die Kartelle in und nach dem Kriege* (Berlin, 1918), p. 24. On Otto Wolff, see Pinner, *Wirtschaftsführer*, pp. 40–47, and Walther Hermann's biographical essay in *Rheinisch-Westfälische Wirtschaftsbiographien*, Vol. 8 (Münster, 1962), pp. 123–156.

ing to endanger productivity by effectively reducing profits through price ceilings. The great concerns may not have been making a profit on some of their iron and steel production, but their coal mines were doing rather well.[29] Profitability was found above all at the other end of the heavy industrial spectrum—that is, in the more finished and higher quality products. The iron and steel producers were well aware that Koeth was not out to ruin them, and that when he insisted that they sell merchant bars at a loss in 1918 it was because he was allowing them a high profit on steel for shells (*Geschossstahl*).[30] Compulsory syndicalization and price ceilings thus accelerated the prewar tendency toward seeking profitability in the more finished products.

One of the great transformations wrought by the war was that the state was now directly and openly concerned with the preservation and operation of cartels and syndicates. As Reichert noted, "Previously the chief thing was the price battles within the syndicates; today the chief thing is the price conflict between syndicates and the government."[31] This, however, was an understandable wartime situation and would presumably be temporary. It became much more alarming, however, in the context of the increasing discussion in governmental and private circles about maintaining syndicates as a means of exercising control over the economy and taxing industry more effectively and efficiently after the war. Were such ideas to become reality, then the days of autonomous decision making about the renewal of syndicates and cartels would be over, and the government would preempt what had previously been an independent area of entrepreneurial perogative.[32]

During the war, cartels and syndicates lost their traditional functions of limiting output and keeping prices stable. Shortages and high demand placed a premium on maximum production and ensured high prices. Debates about the renewal of these organizations, therefore, were based largely on past experiences and speculations about the future rather than immediate conditions, and this complicated efforts to come to concrete decisions. Although the Steel Works Association was not scheduled for renewal until 1917, there was continuous discussion of the renewal problem and particularly of the syndicalization

[29] Steel Works Association meeting, January 24, 1918, HA/GHH, Nr. 3000030/11, where it was noted "that at least there is still a profit in coal while money has to be placed on the A products . . . all along the line."

[30] As noted by Peter Klöckner at a meeting of November 21, 1918, *ibid.* Also, see Zunkel, *Industrie*, pp. 26–27.

[31] VdESI Executive Directors meeting, June 21, 1917, BA, R 131/151.

[32] See Herbert von Beckerath, *Kräfte, Ziele und Gestaltungen in der deutschen Industrie* (Jena, 1922) for an excellent discussion of these problems, and Zunkel, *Industrie*, pp. 98–99.

of the B products.[33] The war eliminated the immediate urgency of the question, but there was a strong sense in industrial circles that the war provided the proper atmosphere and opportunity to cut through old conflicts and organize effectively. Ironically, one of the motives for the desire to undertake a more thoroughgoing syndicalization of the iron and steel industry in wartime was that the Rhenish-Westphalian Coal Syndicate seemed to be falling apart because of conflicts between the integrated works and the pure mines, and its dissolution threatened to raise the cost of steel and reduce profitability unless the B products were syndicalized. A further increase in costs was anticipated as a consequence of the changed political situation within Germany since August 1914. The Social Democrats had supported the war effort, and this was bound to improve the bargaining position of the workers when it came to wages and social legislation. Louis Röchling pointed out that "the iron industry [would] have to pay the most, and the increase of costs could make the maintenance of its productivity and continued existence impossible without stringently organized associations."[34]

Lastly, the German iron industry was bound to face greater competition abroad after the war. Theodor Müller of Stumm was convinced that the "economic war [would] outlast this one"[35] and that cooperation within the German iron and steel industry was imperative. Hasslacher of Rheinstahl thought that the steel industry had every reason to be "ashamed" of the way its various members had competed with one another abroad and warned that they would all be demanding increased quotas after the war because of the higher production costs. In his view, the war was an opportunity to set up quotas and organizations that would ensure the industry's stability and competitiveness after the war was over.

On January 20, 1915, the iron and steel industrialists had set up a committee with Müller as chairman to deal with the syndicalization problem. Six months later, however, Müller had little progress to report. To be sure, there was a general willingness to join in a German Steel Federation that "would only fulfill goals of a general nature, that is, not concern itself with the sale of any products, which would be left to the sales syndicates,"[36] but there was strong disagreement the moment there was concrete discussion of the quotas on which syndicates would be based. Thyssen was proving particularly difficult because he resented his compromise of 1912 in accepting only half of the 200,000-ton quota for his new plant in Hagendingen that he had

---

[33] For these discussions, see HA/GHH, Nr. 3000035/1.
[34] Steel Works Association meeting, January 20, 1915, *ibid.*
[35] Report by T. Müller of May 1915, *Ibid.*, Nr. 3000035/0.
[36] *Ibid.*

been counting on. He had made the compromise in anticipation of good sales abroad by the Steel Works Association, but now the war was destroying "the valuable international connections that had contributed at least to an improvement in the world market prices of A-products. . . ."[37]

It was in the midst of such traditional disagreements that the steel industrialists suddenly found that the government was not inclined to stand aside and see the syndicates disappear. On July 12, 1915, the government issued a decree empowering the states of the Empire to syndicalize the coal industry for the purpose of controlling prices, production, and distribution if the industry did not "voluntarily" syndicalize itself. On January 1, 1916, the Rhenish-Westphalian Coal Syndicate temporarily extended its own existence until March 31 and then managed to negotiate a new five-year agreement on October 14, 1916.[38] The lesson for iron and steel was quite clear. Although the government certainly was gratified by the creation of the Steel Federation on October 4, 1916, in connection with the Hindenburg Program, it was really nothing more than the industrialists were planning to do anyway. It was an organization that had the function of further syndicalizing and cartelizing the industry. Clearly, the government was not prepared to tolerate the dissolution of the Steel Works Association at the end of June 1917, and the members of the industry recognized this by renewing the organization temporarily while they worked at the negotiation of a new and more long-lasting contract. Whether or not they could succeed as well as the coal industry, however, was quite another matter.

The question of renewing the Steel Works Association and expanding it to include the B products, as was demanded by the government, was steadily debated among the industrialists during the last two years of the war.[39] Thyssen took a position similar to the one he had taken in 1912, namely, that the B products had to be syndicalized or the entire discussion was worthless, and he had no intention of "staying in the Steel Works Association in its present form for a moment longer than the present situation requires."[40] This view was shared by Vögler, who regarded the existing Steel Works Association as "a structure of the

[37] Bogner, *Wandlungen*, pp. 27–28, and Gewerkschaft Deutscher Kaiser to the Steel Works Association, December 16, 1916, HA/GHH, Nr. 3000030/10.

[38] Archibald H. Stockder, *History of the Trade Associations of the German Coal Industry Under Private and State Control* (New York, 1924), pp. 112–118.

[39] See the debates between February 1917 and June 1918 in HA/GHH, Nr. 3000035/2. Also, see Zunkel, *Industrie*, pp. 104–105, 150n2.

[40] Gewerkschaft Deutscher Kaiser to the Steel Works Association, December 16, 1916, *ibid.*, Nr. 3000030/10. In this note, Thyssen refused to consider renewing the Steel Works Association for more than one year at a time.

most miserable sort."[41] Röchling was convinced that they had to conclude a long-term agreement that would prevent government action.
He and his allies continually brought back tales of woe following their
meetings with military and civilian officials in Berlin. The government,
they told their colleagues, was going to take 30% of their profits, maintain price ceilings after the war, continue the export levy (*Ausfuhrabgabe*)—"The people in Berlin are convinced that we can bear *everything.* . . ."[42] They were particularly alarmed at the possibility that the
government might turn to the Reichstag, as it had at the time of the
syndicalization of the potash industry in 1910, and that then the Reichstag would use the opportunity, as it had used the attempt at compulsory civilian mobilization in the Auxiliary Service Law of December
5, 1916, to impose all kinds of social legislation on industry.[43] Röchling warned that "We should voluntarily join together in our own most
basic interest and not await pressure from above." Peter Klöckner was
not so sure. Although he admitted that the government at the moment
was completely under the influence of the "consumer point of view"
and "hates us like the plague," he felt that this might change. Just as
Vögler thought that the government could not force the industrialists
to maintain syndicates that were not viable, so Klöckner believed that
the complexities of forming syndicates were so great "that the Reich
government cannot in any way master them."[44]

Certainly, industrialists showed neither the ability nor the general
disposition to set up new syndicates. Although supporters of a long-
term contract such as Müller of Stumm and the business manager of
the Pipe Syndicate, Berthold Nothmann, developed simple and then
increasingly complex schemes to create a long-term syndicate, they
constantly encountered one type of objection or another.[45] If one tried,
as did Müller, to set up a simple formula allowing the works to choose
their best twelve months between 1912 and 1914 as the basis for a
quota, then one ran into protests from colleagues such as Bruhn of
Krupp, who reminded everyone of Krupp's great expansion during the
war. Before the war, Krupp's crude steel production was 1.6 million
tons. Under government pressure, the firm had increased its capacity
by 800,000 tons. Bruhn pointed out to his colleagues that the plants
were too new to have been amortized during the war and bluntly

[41] Vögler to Carl Duisberg, October 8, 1917, Werksarchiv Bayer-Leverkusen,
Autographensammlung Duisberg.

[42] Meeting of July 16, 1917, HA/GHH, Nr. 3000035/2.

[43] On the Auxiliary Service Law, see Feldman, *Army*, chap. IV.

[44] Meeting, April 6, 1917, and May 15, 1918, in HA/GHH, Nr. 3000035/2.

[45] Meetings of April 6 and July 16–19, 1917, in *ibid.*, and Bogner, *Wandlungen*,
p. 30.

threatened that Krupp would seek government support for its claims if necessary.[46] Twenty-one of the works had similar claims, either on the basis of plans made before the war or on the basis of wartime construction. More complicated schemes designed to accommodate such considerations inevitably proved less feasible than the simpler ones because they introduced new inequities and were often simply nonsensical.

The dilemma was that no one knew what the shape of economic life would be like after the war. Those like Röchling, who were sincerely anxious to create a syndicate for a long period, were willing to take the risk that some of the calculations on which the quotas would be based would be mistaken. For him, organization was the thing of paramount importance because the Steel Works Association had secured such good prices for its products before the war. Vögler was less certain. In his view, the concerns had done better on the export market themselves, and if they had not sold as much as the Steel Works Association, they had received a better price. Röchling admitted that this might be true, and he was certain that demand for iron and steel would be high. However, he did not think that the money would be available to pay high prices either in Germany or anywhere else. He felt that the war had "thrown Europe back in its development one hundred years," that the standard of living would decline after the war, and that plants opened during the war would have to be shut down.[47] Clearly, Röchling did not think that the achievement of a German victory and German war aims would ensure that country's postwar prosperity, or at least the prosperity of his industry. Although some industrialists felt that they could not plan for the future and enter long-term syndicates until they knew if Germany was going to gain the rich French ore fields of Briey-Longwy, others felt that this mattered little in comparison to a secure supply of the scrap and pig iron needed for the greatly expanding open-hearth capacity.[48] The end result of all these long-term speculations and calculations as well as the immediate jockeying for advantage, however, was to kill all proposals for a long-term renewal of the Steel Works Association. The question of whether or not the wartime organization of the industry would have any lasting effects and whether the government would compel syndicalization in peace, as it had in war, remained completely open.

[46] Meetings of April 6, 1917, and May 15, 1918, HA/GHH, Nr. 3000035/2.

[47] Meetings of August 20, 1917, and February 27, 1918, *ibid.*

[48] Discussion of these plans to annex Briey-Longwy are scattered throughout Hans Gatzke, *Germany's Drive to the West. A Study of German War Aims During the First World War* (Baltimore, 1950), and Fritz Fischer, *Griff nach der Weltmacht* (Düsseldorf, 1961). The plans were maintained as late as September 1918, see Zunkel, *Industrie*, pp. 161–162.

Furthermore, as before the war, vertical organization continued, and trustification appeared as an alternative to syndicalization. The coal shortage that developed in 1916–1917 encouraged mixed concerns such as Krupp, the Rheinstahl, and Hoesch to increase their holdings in the mining industry, but the most significant form of vertical expansion was in the direction of finishing and manufacturing. Heavy industry's substantial war profits and its desire to evade taxation by "trying everything possible to use this money in such a manner that it will be untaxable" made it possible for the large iron producing concerns to make substantial inroads into the shipbuilding and mechanical engineering industries.[49] This trend toward finishing, however, was also carried on in the belief that it was essential if heavy industry was to maintain its position in the postwar economic competition. Other countries had either expanded their iron and steel production capacities during the war or, as in the case of India, developed such a capacity for the first time. In the view of many industrialists, this meant that heavy industry had to develop a more secure domestic market for its cruder products and seek profit on the world market with quality products and finished goods. In 1918, for example, General Directors Reusch and Vögler emphasized this point to the leading stockholders of their respective concerns. Reusch argued that the GHH would lose its old markets in England and in the English colonies and that profitability had to be sought through "the attachment of manufacturing industries and the development of our own finishing plants,"[50] while Vögler catalogued Deutsch-Lux aspirations in finishing, the automotive and airplane industries.

At the same time as individual concerns were expanding their holdings in raw materials and finishing, however, some of their leaders were contemplating rationalization through large-scale fusion within heavy industry itself. Sometime during the war, General Director Beukenberg of the Phoenix concern suggested to Vögler that the Phoenix and Deutsch-Lux concerns unite in an *Interessengemeinschaft*. This proposal easily suggested a parallel to the massive process of

[49] Report of Director Arndt von Holtzendorff of the Hamburg-America Line, September 26, 1917, Berichte Holtzendorff, Rep. 300. Reichsinstitut für Geschichte des neuen Deutschland, Hauptarchiv Berlin-Dahlem. On the expansion into shipbuilding, see Günther Leckebusch, *Die Beziehungen der deutschen Seeschiffswerften zur Eisenindustrie an der Ruhr in der Zeit von 1850 bis 1930* (Schriften zur Rheinisch-Westfälischen Wirtschaftsgeschichte, Vol. 8) (Cologne, 1963), p. 101ff.; see also the detailed information in Tross, *Aufbau*, and the concentrated surveys in Wiel, *Wirtschaftsgeschichte*, p. 245ff., and Georg Embacher, *Periodische Wandlungen im Zusammenschluss der deutschen Industrie*, diss. Phil. (Dessau, 1928), pp. 81–84.

[50] Mashke, *Konzern*, p. 110, and Friedrich-Wilhelms-Hütte Archiv, Nr. 123/19.

concentration that had taken place in the chemical industry under the leadership of Carl Duisberg. There, too, fusion had begun before the war with the formation of an *Interessengemeinschaft* among a few producers, and this was followed by a substantial expansion of the number of members in 1915. Vögler was very impressed with Duisberg's achievement, just as he was very depressed by the inadequacies of the Steel Works Association as reflected in its failure to carry out the rationalization it promised to promote in its charter.[51] Stinnes learned of Beukenberg's idea through Vögler, but it was not until October 1918 that Stinnes pursued it in a serious manner. By then the war was clearly lost, and Stinnes was anxious to increase the coal base of the Deutsch-Lux concern by a fusion with Emil Kirdorf's Gelsenkirchener Bergwerke. In a letter to Kirdorf, Stinnes mentioned Beukenberg's idea, pointed out that a "triple alliance" of Deutsch-Lux, Phoenix, and Gelsenkirchener Bergwerke would "with its strength and many-sidedness be up to coping with every storm of the postwar period,"[52] and informed Kirdorf that he had asked Vögler to pursue the idea. This Vögler did in a memorandum that was to move the process of steel trustification a major step forward. In October 1918, however, this memorandum, the revised version of which will be dealt with later, had a very tentative quality because the case for trustification was presented as an alternative to the apparent inability of the members of the Steel Works Association and the other cartels to come to a viable long-term agreement.[53] Thus, at the conclusion of the war, the organizational problems of the industry were more serious than ever.

IRON AND STEEL PRODUCERS AND THEIR INDUSTRIAL CONSUMERS BETWEEN CONFLICT AND COOPERATION

In War

As iron and steel producers looked toward an uncertain postwar future, they faced not only the problems created by a government more inclined than ever before to interfere in economic affairs and a militant, organized labor movement whose power had been enhanced by the war, but also the potential difficulties of dealing with customers who had attained a higher level of organization thanks to the war economy. The machine builders could hardly have moved

[51] Wilhelm Treue, "Carl Duisbergs Denkschrift von 1915 zur Gründung der 'kleinen I.G.'" in *Tradition*, 8, October 1963, pp. 193–227, and Vögler to Duisberg, October 8, 1917, Werksarchiv Bayer-Leverkusen, Autographensammlung Duisberg.

[52] Klass, *Stinnes*, p. 227.

[53] Klass, *Vögler*, pp. 68–71.

the VDMA headquarters from Düsseldorf to Berlin at a more opportune time than October 1914. Economic decision was now truly to be concentrated in Berlin, and the government was finding itself in desperate need of organizations like the VDMA in order to deal with the numerous and widely scattered firms whose assistance was essential to the war effort. A Central Bureau for Export Permits for the Machine Industry was set up under government auspices and placed under the direction of the VDMA Business Manager, Dr. Frölich, on October 21, 1914. In 1916 a Price Bureau (*Preisstelle*) was established under another VDMA official, Dr. H. Seck, with the task of implementing the government's policy of securing maximum export prices for German manufactures. These agencies, as well as a host of new functions connected with procurement and war production, enormously enhanced the prestige and importance of the VDMA.[54]

The result was a spectacular increase in the VDMA membership, which rose from 246 firms employing 189,086 workers on January 1, 1914, to 650 firms employing 408,551 workers on January 1, 1918. On December 31, the VDMA could boast 814 member firms with 522,790 workers. No less important a measure of the organization of the machine building industry, however, was the growth of subsidiary organizations. By 1919 there were 40 trade associations connected with the VDMA. These represented the various branches of the industry, but they were by no means the only organizations. At the end of 1918 there were no less than 94 export conventions and general associations in the industry, and 42 more were in the process of organization. The number of personnel working for the VDMA increased from a modest 30 in 1914 to 115 in 1916, and then leaped to 277 in 1917 and 388 in 1918. Of the last number, 104 worked for the VDMA directly, 76 were employed in the Central Bureau for Export Permits, 42 served in the Price Bureau, and the remainder worked in war-connected agencies attached to the VDMA. Thus, although the majority of the new employees were involved in special tasks arising from the wartime situation, the actual VDMA staff had increased impressively. The machine building industry had a formidable organization at its disposal.[55]

The organization of the electrotechnical industry was slower to develop. The disparity between the two giants of the industry, the Siemens concern and the AEG, and the host of smaller firms, as well as the differences among the latter, had complicated prewar organizational efforts on an industry-wide basis. In 1914, at the instigation of the government but with the willing cooperation of the industrial

[54] Polysius, *Verbandsbestrebungen*, p. 91ff., and Deutscher Maschinenbau," p. 159ff.

[55] For the statistical data, see *ibid.*, pp. 151–152, 187–188, 201–202, 459.

organizations, the Central Association of German Industrialists and the Federation of German Industrialists joined forces for the wartime period in a German Industry War Committee (*Kriegsausschuss der deutschen Industrie*). Branch organizations were established for the various industries, and the electrotechnical industry created its own War Committee for the Electrotechnical Industry in 1916. It was not until March 1918, however, that the various competing organizations finally joined together in the Central Association of the German Electrotechnical Industry (*Zentralverband der deutschen Elektrotechnischen Industrie*—Zendei). The organization developed because of the increasing agreement of all members of the industry on the need for a uniform pricing policy and the success attained in the recently created wartime Price Bureau. As might be expected, the leaders of the industry, particularly C. F. von Siemens and Felix Deutsch, played an important role in its founding. The basic work of the Zendei, however, was directed by its extraordinary Business Manager, Hans von Raumer (1870–1965), a former Treasury official, who was to prove a consummate organizer, lobbyist, and political representative of industry. In 1918, at the beginning of its development, the Zendei was composed of 286 firms employing 145,330 workers.[56] It should not be thought, however, that the work of organization was easy despite the propitious circumstances. In order to bring in the small and medium-sized firms, an effort was made to win over a prominent representative of the latter by inviting him to take a seat on the Zendei board of directors, an invitation he refused because "the large firms will only use the Central Association of the German Electrotechnical Industry to protect their own interests and weaken the small firms. . . ." The chairman of the Zendei, Baron von Uslar, who was also a Siemens director, pointed out that this attitude was typical of "the old mistrust of the small and medium sized firms toward the large firms."[57]

Indeed, the organizational efforts undertaken during the war reflected a wide spectrum of mistrust within industry that seriously complicated the striving to organize all of German industry as well as its various branches. The leaders of the machine building and electrotechnical industries were as anxious as the leaders of heavy industry to heal the rift reflected in the existence of two central organizations of German industry by taking advantage of the War Committee to set up one central association. However, the leaders of the manufac-

---

[56] This account is based on the informative unpublished history of the Zendei in the library of the organization in Frankfurt, hereinafter cited as "Zendei History." There is an insightful biographical sketch of Hans von Raumer by Johannes Fischart in *Die Weltbühne*, 20, October 23, 1924, pp. 622–624.

[57] Baron von Uslar to C. F. von Siemens, April 24, 1918, SAA 4/Lf 724.

73

turing industries were most anxious to increase their power vis-à-vis heavy industry and end their subordination in the existing organizations. To accomplish this, they recognized the need to organize their own industries and to overcome the mistrust of the small and medium-sized firms. Yet the large manufacturing firms and concerns were also anxious not to become the prisoners of their lesser colleagues and thereby be forced into a posture of hostility toward heavy industry. They only wished to be in a better position to bargain with heavy industry and the government. In any case, because of the heterogeneity of the industries and organizations involved, the chief burden of the manufacturing industry's organizing efforts and the initiative necessarily lay with the various trade association business managers, on the one hand, and with the directors of the larger firms, on the other hand.

Although the leadership group involved was relatively narrow, it was difficult to attain unanimity. From December 1915 to January 1916, the question of forming an association "that would give the finishing industries greater influence vis-à-vis heavy industry"[58] was the subject of a discussion between Anton von Rieppel of the MAN and VDMA and the leaders of the electrotechnical industry, Wilhelm and Carl Friedrich von Siemens and the AEG leaders, Walther Rathenau and Felix Deutsch. Rieppel and the two Siemens were most anxious to strengthen their industries within the framework of the Central Association of German Industrialists and effectuate what amounted to a readjustment of relations with heavy industry rather than an open organizational breach. In place of a separate organization encompassing the various industrial organizations engaged in finishing, Rieppel proposed that these organizations form a working partnership (Arbeitsgemeinschaft) to coordinate policy and create a united front within the Central Association.

Rathenau and Deutsch took a different view. They tended toward the Central Association's competitor, the more liberal and regionally oriented Federation of German Industrialists, and they wanted to create a separate organization of finished product manufacturers under the leadership of the electrotechnical industry. This was not out of solicitude for medium-sized and small businesses. On the contrary, Rathenau feared that the working partnership proposed by Rieppel would mean equality between major branches of the manufacturing industries and "music box manufacturers or manufacturers of metal toys." Rieppel, however, felt that Rathenau was being both impractical and unnecessarily fearful. He did not think that the larger asso-

[58] Rieppel to Siemens, December 28, 1915, MAN Werksarchiv Nürnberg, Nr. 02.

ciations like the VDMA and the Association of German Machine Tool Manufacturers (*Verein deutscher Werkzeugmaschinen-Fabrikanten*) were going to subordinate themselves willingly to the electrotechnical industry. As for the small specialty producers, his own experience with the Association of Bavarian Metal Industrialists had convinced him that "with proper handling" such groups could be useful collaborators and that "they never could or would want to play a decisive role."[59]

The Rieppel-Siemens position was supported strongly by the leaders of the VDMA, the chairman, Dr. Kurt Sorge, and the business manager, Dr. Frölich. The Rathenau-Deutsch proposal ran counter to the wartime tendencies toward greater unity within industry as a whole as reflected in the wartime collaboration of the Central Association and the Federation of German Industrialists in the German Industry War Committee and in the constant discussion of continuing this collaboration after the war. The Rathenau-Deutsch idea also went afoul of the VDMA's traditional policy of working within the Central Association. Frölich argued that membership in the Central Association gave the VDMA much greater thrust in achieving legislative objectives in such areas as patents, taxation, and trade policy.[60]

In Frölich's view there would always be conflicts within industry, and the solution to them could not be found in fragmentation, but rather in a systematic effort to secure greater power within the Central Association through a working partnership of the finished product industries, on the one hand, and a reform of the Central Association itself, on the other hand. The reform he advocated, a reform that had the support of heavy industry, was the reorganization of the Central Association on the basis of branch organizations (*Fachgruppen*). The Directorate of the Central Association would then be composed of the representatives of the branch organizations in proportion to their strength instead of being composed of men chosen on the basis of their personal reputations and economic power. Thus, powerful branch organizations composed of numerous subgroups would be in a position to exert strong influence on the Central Association, while their representatives on the Directorate would work for compromise but would also be in a position to pursue an independent policy if compromise was unattainable. Fearful of the Rathenau-Deutsch alternative, heavy industry also accepted this concept, so that by 1916 the

[59] Rieppel to Siemens, January 26, 1916, *ibid.*, and the notes on conversations with the electrotechnical industry leaders on January 13, 1916, in MAN Werksarchiv Nürnberg, Nr. 161.

[60] Frölich to VDMA Board of Directors, August 14, 1916, MAN Werksarchiv Nürnberg, Nr. 171.

Central Association was reformed along the lines advocated by Rieppel, Siemens, and Frölich. These reforms, in both their origin and their character, reflected the interests of big businessmen, who dominated the organizations of both the producers and the manufacturers.[61]

There were solid political and economic motives behind this desire to promote unity on the part of the big manufacturers. They were certain that they were going to have a difficult struggle with the government, where they encountered "boundless mistrust." C. F. von Siemens was convinced that if the finishing industries permitted themselves to be isolated, the government would find it possible to disregard their interests, and the much better organized forces of heavy industry would end up shifting the costs of the war onto their shoulders. At the same time, it was impossible to overlook the trend toward vertical concentration reflected in the expansion of heavy industrialists, such as Thyssen and Stinnes into manufacturing.

In an "age of concentration," Siemens found no advantage whatever in the idea of a sharp organizational division between heavy industry and the manufacturing industries.[62] Also, wartime raw materials shortages, delivery delays, and high prices made the idea of a secure supply of raw materials very attractive, and the manufacturers could hardly overlook the advantages of the substantial capital resources that heavy industry had to offer. Thus, the organizational reforms in the Central Association reflected not only political calculations and anxieties but also real economic tendencies.

In day-to-day economic practice, however, it was difficult to avoid irritating conflicts between heavy industry and the finishing industries. The question of delivery terms constituted the greatest source of contention. Raw materials producers insisted on filling orders at the prices in effect on the day of delivery in order to ride with inflation over long wartime delays in delivery. This made price calculations exceedingly difficult for the manufacturers of finished products, who were finding it increasingly hard to predict materials costs just at a time when these costs were assuming a disproportionately large place in manufacturer cost calculations. During wartime, such difficulties could be fairly easily handled at the expense of the taxpayer, and manufacturers followed the lead of the producers and drew up contracts that not only

[61] *Ibid.*, and Kaelble, *Industrielle Interessenpolitik*, pp. 22–23. Sorge to Rieppel and Sorge to Rötger, August 24, 1916, MAN Werksarchiv Nürnberg, Nr. 116, and remarks of Hugenberg at the February 1917 VdESI Executive Directors meeting, BA, R 13 I/150.

[62] Siemens to O. von Petri, February 19, 1918, SAA 4 Lf/514, Bd. 4, Bl. 128–133.

contained a high provision for risk but that also left the final price to be determined on the date of delivery. The capstone of these inflationary business practices was provided by cost-plus pricing by the military procurement agencies.[63]

Foreign customers, however, took less kindly to the idea that rising prices in Germany might justify either contract cancellation or belated demands for a price higher than that stated in the contracts they had signed. For obvious reasons, they were most reluctant to leave the final price open to significant readjustments. Until the middle of 1917, the machine builders had been able to make a substantial profit on foreign sales to neutrals by purchasing raw materials at domestic prices and then, thanks to government-imposed syndicalization, selling abroad at a high price. This happy situation for the manufacturers changed when the government decided that pig iron and other raw materials used in machine construction could only be delivered when the purchaser presented documentation indicating not only that the material was going to be used for a legitimate purpose but also indicating the specific purpose for which it was going to be used. Raw materials producers now could identify orders for materials that were going to be used in the making of goods for export, and take advantage of a standard contract clause allowing the imposition of a "suitable" (*angemessene*) price increase "from case to case" where some special justification could be found. Deliveries for indirect export (*mittelbare Ausfuhr*) were regarded as justification for such an increase, and initially the raw materials syndicates imposed on German manufacturers the extremely high export price that they charged their foreign customers. In the face of outraged protests from the finishers, they adopted a series of confusing *ad hoc* arrangements, and finally settled down to charging a price between that charged domestically and that charged abroad. The new policy of the raw materials producers, however, had jeopardized the finishing industry's ability to offer foreign customers their goods at high but competitive and stable prices.[64]

This conflict between producers and manufacturers over indirect exports continued a tradition of disagreement, but the changed conditions raised the stakes and emotions. The raw materials shortage significantly increased the dependence of the manufacturers, "which now

[63] On the wartime procurement and business practices, see Feldman, *Army*, esp. p. 385ff.

[64] This description is based largely on the documentary materials. See especially the VDMA petition to the RWA of December 8, 1917, and the Pig Iron Syndicate to the RWA, December 31, 1917, Friedrich-Wilhelms-Hütte Archiv, Nr. 860/14, and the VDMA report on its meeting with the raw materials producers of March 1, 1918, in MAN Werksarchiv, Nürnberg.

in wartime has even reached the point of a refusal to supply on the part of the iron and steel works, and this for the very obvious reason that the finishing of their own raw materials will give them a higher profit than their sale."[65] Although a great concern such as the MAN might contemplate, as it did in 1917, the purchase of its own steel works in order to secure relief from the long delays in delivery, ensure the quality of the raw materials it received, and enjoy the high profits of heavy industry, such thoughts could not be entertained by smaller firms and concerns. Nor were they carried out very often by larger ones. The MAN did not buy a steel plant, possibly because, as C. F. von Siemens noted when he heard about the matter, coal was the raw material in shortest supply, and it was difficult to imagine vertical expansion in manufacturing extending back that far."[66] How, then, were manufacturers to compel producers to compromise?

One possible way to bring producers to heel was to turn to the government, an option that had become all the easier to take by the increased government role in economic affairs. In December 1917 the VDMA did turn to the Reich Economic Office (*Reichswirtschaftsamt* —RWA) to protest the above-discussed pricing policies of the producers, and its petition was followed by an angry counterattack from the Pig Iron Syndicate. Turning to the government to settle interindustrial conflicts was, as Dr. Frölich noted, "ticklish business."[67] A public attack on the pricing policies of heavy industry could only be conducted if the machine construction industry was united in its demands. The producers, however, rapidly compromised with some of their customers and thus sowed disunity among them. Under the circumstances, therefore, it was far more desirable to turn to the VdESI, in which both groups were represented, and settle the issues at hand. This is what Frölich did, and a compromise was worked out in early 1918. The producers agreed to guarantee that the price they asked for material used by manufacturers in goods designated for export would not be subject to retroactive increases at delivery time, but refused to return to the old practice of charging the domestic price without regard for the intended use of their products. They were willing, at the most, to make special concessions in cases where the competitiveness of the manufacturer was clearly at stake because of high raw materials costs. Dr. Reichert, one of whose main tasks in life was to try to keep peace

[65] O. von Petri to Siemens, February 8, 1917, SAA 4 Lf/724.

[66] *Ibid.* The Borsig concern was an important exception, having control over coal mines and steel mills in Upper Silesia since before the war. See Tross, *Aufbau,* p. 113ff.

[67] VDMA Export Committee meeting, May 14, 1918, "Deutscher Maschinenbau," p. 143. See also the sources mentioned in note 67 above.

between the two sides, was much relieved by this settlement. It conformed to his model of the way in which industry should deal with its internal conflicts—that is, not through press campaigns or requests for government intervention but rather through direct negotiation and friendly understanding.[68]

This desire to avoid government intervention and promote industrial self-government cut across the divisions within industry and increasingly bound the various segments of the business community together during the final period of the war. Indeed, by 1918 hatred of the controlled economy had reached fever pitch. A mountain of regulations and bureaucratic irritations coexisted with increasing hoarding, profiteering, and black marketeering, and businessmen yearned for the return of their old liberties and the resumption of normal business conditions. Although the vast majority of businessmen were overtly loyal to the existing regime, they did participate in the general loss of confidence in the regime that was so widespread at the end of the war. Although hardly revolutionary, their sense of commitment and respect had been weakened and the tone of their protests was becoming increasingly sharp.[69]

Much of the business-government conflict centered about the question of who was to control the demobilization and transition to a peacetime economy (*Übergangswirtschaft*). Businessmen feared the bungling military administrators in the War Office, and they worried that the civilian bureaucrats in the Reich Economic Office were concocting schemes to control industry through a network of compulsory syndicates and corporate economic bodies in which the government would play a major role. The influence of anti-Manchesterian academics and the writings of Walther Rathenau and Wichard von Moellendorff (1881–1937), a former AEG employee and one of the most important and influential of the wartime economic advisers and officials, which called for a continuation of some of the methods and institutions of the wartime "state socialism," were found particularly alarming. Moellendorff's conception of the German corporate economy (*Deutsche Gemeinwirtschaft*) was very popular among the younger ministerial officials in Berlin, as were the writings of Rathenau, and businessmen were giving considerable sums of money to fight these

[68] See the June 1918 VdESI Executive Directors meeting, BA, R 13 I/151.

[69] For this and the general discussion that follows, see Feldman, *Army*, pp. 46–61, 170, 277–280; Gerald D. Feldman, "German Business Between War and Revolution: The Origins of the Stinnes-Legien Agreement," in Ritter, ed., *Entstehung und Wandel*, pp. 312–341, esp. pp. 312–321; Schieck, *Wirtschaftspolitik*, p. 14ff.; Jürgen Kocka, *Klassengesellschaft im Krieg 1914–1918* (Kritische Studien zur Geschichtswissenschaft, Vol. 8) (Göttingen, 1973), esp. pp. 57–64.

ideas during the last year of the war.[70] If the desire for industrial self-government and freedom from state control was universal among businessmen, however, there were important nuances in the way in which the specific problems of the transition to a peacetime economy were approached by various individuals and groups within the business community. Merchants engaged in foreign trade were most anxious to have complete freedom to export and import, and they took the most radical position in favor of laissez faire. Small and medium-sized business, which suffered most severely from trade restrictions and raw materials shortages, tended to share the attitude of those engaged in commerce. Big business, in contrast, had suffered far more spiritually than materially from the war economy. They were in a position to temper their desire for freedom with the recognition that complete freedom secured too quickly could produce undesirable results. Although they wished freedom from restrictions as soon as possible, they had the resources to overcome or handle bureaucratic barriers. As might be expected, the most cautious attitude toward the elimination of controls came from the business managers of trade associations and other business organizations. They had a better insight into the advantages of organization and a measure of control for the economy and industry as well as a great stake in maintaining the organizational impetus that the war had given to industry.

Thus, there was a considerable difference of opinion over the tempo of release from government restrictions. When the VDMA board of directors discussed this question at the end of 1917, for example, there was unanimity on the need to terminate government controls as quickly as possible but disagreement as to when this was to occur. A majority favored retaining controls for the transition, but some major industrial leaders wanted immediate and total decontrol. It was typical of the atmosphere surrounding the controlled economy, however, that Sorge showed little concern for this disagreement and stressed instead the basic consensus against control to counteract the "many influential personalities in the government and in the parliaments" who yearned for state socialism and hoped "to retain in the future as much as possible of the state influences shaped by the wartime situation."[71]

The transitional economy came in for more specific scrutiny at the

---

[70] See especially the excellent discussion in Zunkel, *Industrie*, p. 50ff. Also see Arnold Brecht, *The Political Education of Arnold Brecht. An Autobiography 1884–1970* (Princeton, 1970), pp. 162–163. On Rathenau and Moellendorff, see Fritz Redlich, "German Economic Planning for War and Peace," *Review of Politics*, VI, July 1944, pp. 319–326.

[71] Sorge to Rieppel, December 1, 1917, MAN Werksarchiv Nürnberg, Nr. 03/III.

executive committee meeting of the VdESI in June 1918. In this discussion there was general agreement that export controls could not be totally eliminated. Obviously there would have to be restraints on the export of raw materials and military equipment, but there was also a desire to take advantage of the high demand anticipated at the end of the war. Reichert feared that if the export restrictions and the syndicates established in connection with them were dissolved suddenly, the high export prices would collapse immediately, "and this price decrease on the foreign market [would] also make itself felt in a very unpleasant way domestically." Although Reichert regarded it as "self-evident" that German industry would have to bring down its prices, he argued that "this price reduction should not be carried out quicker than necessitated by the pressure of foreign industry. . . ." In response to government inquiries, therefore, Reichert opposed removal of export bans immediately after the war except for items that were not syndicalized or for which demand was minimal.[72]

Reichert's positive attitude toward export restrictions was not universally shared. Director Beukenberg did not think that world prices were destined to drop so quickly in the absence of export controls, and he was greatly alarmed at reports that neutral countries were beginning to build iron and steel plants of their own in order to reduce their dependence on German and other producers. Iron and steel, he felt, should be exported as quickly and as free of restrictions as possible in order to take the "wind out of their sails." Neither Reichert nor Beukenberg seemed particularly concerned about the danger that German firms might export at the expense of domestic consumers, probably because they anticipated no domestic shortages once military demand had ceased and because they presumed that domestic price controls would be terminated. If domestic prices rose to the level of world market prices, then the incentive to favor foreign markets would presumably vanish. Underlying these calculations was the assumption that the value of the German mark would return to its normal level once foreign trade was resumed, and that the restoration of prewar currency relationships would obviate the need of the Reichsbank to insist on payment for German exports in foreign currencies. Only Director Gerwin of the Steel Works Association expressed some concern about the domestic supply, but his considerations revolved around the possibility that domestic price controls might be retained. If price ceilings were abandoned, then export controls would not be necessary to protect the domestic market. If price ceilings were retained, however, then Gerwin thought that there would have to be

[72] VdESI Executive Directors meeting, June 21, 1918, BA, R 13 I/151.

surveillance over exports to make sure that "material destined for domestic use is not misused on foreign markets in order to get higher prices."[73] From the standpoint of the dominant policy makers in the iron and steel producing industry, who discussed these problems both among themselves and with government officials in the early summer of 1918, therefore, the ideal program for the demobilization and transition to a peacetime economy was the termination of domestic price ceilings and the quickest possible abandonment of export controls consistent with maximum profit on the export market. This was to be realized in the context of the most limited government interference and the greatest possible industrial self-regulation.

In Revolution

The failure of the German war effort, the Revolution of November 1918, and the creation of the Weimar Republic did not change these plans for an economic restoration formulated in the closing year of the war. The industrialists held fast to their positions despite these events and with their weapons sharpened by their earlier wartime battles with the imperial bureaucracy and military authorities. Such tears as they had for the old regime—and a surprising number had none—they shed in private, and they proved very imaginative in coming to terms with the trade union leaders, a group they had refused to recognize as representatives of the workers before the war. In a remarkable series of negotiations conducted with almost breathtaking speed and skill in October and November 1918, the leaders of the coal, iron, steel, electrotechnical, and machine construction industries concluded agreements with Carl Legien and other Socialist trade union leaders of a unique character. The industrialists did more than merely recognize the trade unions, agree to collective bargaining, and reluctantly swallow the eight-hour day with the secretly agreed-upon condition that it eventually be implemented internationally. They also joined together with the unions in the so-called Central Working Community (*Zentralarbeitsgemeinschaft*—ZAG), an organization meant to institutionalize collaboration in economic as well as social matters and to compel the government to bow to the will of "the only power left in Germany, the united employers and workers."[74] In this way, the

[73] *Ibid.*

[74] For a full account of these and related events, see Feldman in Ritter, *Entstehung und Wandel*; also, see Gerald D. Feldman, "The Origins of the Stinnes-Legien Agreement: A Documentation," *Internationale wissenschaftliche Korrespondenz zur Geschichte der deutschen Arbeiterbewegung*, 19/20, December 1972, pp. 45–102, and Gerald D. Feldman, "Wirtschafts- und sozialpolitische Probleme der deutschen Demobilmachung 1918/19" in *Industrielles System*, pp. 618–636.

employers sought insurance against socialization and government interference in alliance with the numerically powerful trade unions, and the trade union leaders found an answer to their desire for recognition, fear of chaos, and feeling that they lacked the technical competence to manage the economy without the direction of the businessmen. Both groups shared a complete lack of confidence in the bureaucracy, and they joined together in compelling the Max von Baden government to take the demobilization out of the hands of the RWA and turn it over to a new Demobilization Office under the leadership of Lieutenant-Colonel Koeth. It was anticipated that the newly appointed "dictator" would act in collaboration with the ZAG and follow its wishes, thus providing the state-protected industrial self-government the industrialists had expected two years earlier when the War Office was created. The Demobilization Office began operation on November 7, 1918. Lastly, the industrialists and business managers who made these arrangements—Hugo Stinnes, Jakob Reichert, Anton von Rieppel, Hans von Raumer, Walther Rathenau, Felix Deutsch, Carl Friedrich von Siemens—anticipated using the ZAG to promote a new industrial organization that would encompass all of German industry organized along branch lines and more effectively directed than the Central Association and the Federation of Industrialists.

Little wonder, therefore, that Dr. Reichert could write to a colleague on November 9, 1918:

> The *Arbeitsgemeinschaft* between industry and the unions marches along well. The leadership of the demobilization has come into the best of hands. Serious disturbances are not to be feared. The conclusion of peace, too, can be much better than it now appears as soon as the revolutionary wave has rolled over France and England also.[75]

This precious little bit of commentary on the Revolution of November 9 was undoubtedly produced in the morning before the "wave" had hit Berlin, but it was written in the wake of days of newspaper reports about spreading revolution in Germany. However overly optimistic Reichert's prognostications, they are a good indication of how "economics" was triumphing over "politics" in the Revolution's most crucial hours. Industry had the initiative, and so long as it was able to play upon its expertise and maintain either the reality or the appearance of a united front, it was in a position to preempt, evade, or throw back the most dangerous possibilities inherent in defeat and revolution.

If Reichert was an optimist, Stinnes was a super-optimist, and the

[75] Reichert to O. Petersen, BA, R 13 I/92, Bl. 11.

"merchant from Mülheim" had no intention of letting mistaken past speculations deter him from taking advantage of such promising opportunities as the future might hold in store. For the past two years he had consistently said that Ludendorff would win. Now that Ludendorff had lost, it was time to turn to presumably safer and certainly more familiar forms of speculation. At a meeting in the RWA on October 29, 1918, Stinnes quickly calculated the territorial gains France would make from her victory and then came to the remarkable conclusion that these gains would give Germany definite advantages. He viewed the future supply of minette ore from Lorraine and Luxemburg "not unfavorably" because

> Pure economic considerations will bring the enemy to permit the export of ore to Germany despite the separation of Lorraine from the German Empire and the political annexation of Luxemburg. For one thing Germany has a means of pressure in its possession of the coke needed for the running of the smelting plants, and besides this the Belgian and French iron industrialists have no use for the employment of Luxemburg and Lorraine minette for their industry because they then must find foreign markets for 80% of their production. Thus far the interests of the German and French iron industries are alike. . . .[76]

Although one is tempted to the sarcastic comment that the French should have thought twice about winning the war or at least should have consulted Stinnes before deciding how to benefit from their victory, the fact remains that Stinnes was correct about everything but the immediate psychology of the French. Over the long run, Germany did have the advantages he specified, but it was anything but reasonable to expect "pure economic considerations" to rule French policy after such a long and brutal war. At the same time, some of Stinnes' own economic calculations left something to be desired. He and his supporters appeared completely optimistic about the future of the

[76] RWA meeting, November 7, 1918, KrAMü, Nr. 14 413. Beukenberg agreed with Stinnes on the problems the French would face. See his note to the RWA of November 8, 1918, DZA Potsdam, RWM, Nr. 7291, Bl. 219–221. For a general and informative discussion of these problems, see Georges Soutou, "Der Einfluss der Schwerindustrie auf die Gestaltung der Frankreichpolitik Deutschlands 1919–1921," and Jacques Bariéty, "Das Zustandekommen der Internationalen Rohstahlgemeinschaft (1926) als Alternative zum misslungenen 'Schwerindustriellen Projekt' des Versailler Vertrages," in *Industrielles System*, pp. 543–567; and Jacques Bariéty, "Le Rôle de la Minette dans la Sidérurgie Allemande et la Restructuration de la Sidérurgie Allemande après le Traité de Versailles," in Centre de Recherches Internationales de l'Université de Metz, *Travaux et Recherches* (1972), pp. 233–277.

German mark if only the government abandoned restrictions on raw materials and exports and eliminated wartime regulations that exports be calculated and paid in foreign currency.[77] Sanguine expectations concerning the mark were widely held, and they were shared by the Reichsbank president, Havenstein, a man destined to play one of the sorriest roles in banking history. On the day following this meeting, November 8, the regulation that sales abroad had to be concluded in foreign currency was relaxed, and Reichert took advantage of this to argue that the "inner justification" for an export levy no longer existed.

There can be no question about the fact that Stinnes and the supporters of maximum freedom from government regulations were moving very quickly and with a sense of certainty by no means justified by the events about them. This, however, rather than the truth or falsity of their argumentation, was their great strength. Stinnes' contention about the implications of the coal-minette ore nexus was correct in the long run but hardly a foundation for a tough line in German foreign policy or optimism about raw materials in the short run. His arguments about the future of the mark were to have some slight short-run validity but were to prove completely erroneous in the long run. By force of personality and by the apodictic certainty with which they argued, however, Stinnes and his supporters were able to impose actions upon the government and their colleagues that enabled the iron and steel producers in particular to secure repeatedly the kind of tactical advantage that permitted them to escape the worst consequences of their own long-term and short-term mistakes.

When representatives of the iron and steel producers and the finishing industries met with RWA officials on November 8, the choral singing of the industrialists suddenly assumed a rather contrapuntal quality. Everyone agreed that the military authorities had to be eliminated from economic affairs and that bureaucratic clearances had to be radically simplified. Then, however, differences of opinion began to break through even within the ranks of the producers. Reichert was true to the position he had taken in June. If price ceilings were retained, then export controls were necessary on pig iron and rolled products to protect the domestic supply and to prevent a sudden collapse of export prices. Where there were no syndicates, export controls should be eliminated. Where syndicates existed, the continuation of the syndicates should be left to the determination of the members. Dr. Bruhn of the Pig Iron Syndicate was even more fearful of a complete breakdown of the export syndicates, and he was worried that goods would be exported at "cut-rate prices" (*Schleuderpreise*) if the export bans

[77] RWA meeting, November 7, 1918, KrAMü, Nr. 14413.

were eliminated. The position of these "organization men" (*Verbands-männer*) was criticized by Stinnes and Vögler, both of whom insisted on the termination of export controls and price ceilings. Vögler treated fears of a domestic shortage with contempt on the grounds that the military had been taking 85% of the production and this would now be available for peacetime uses. Stinnes dismissed Bruhn's fears that the syndicates could not survive without the help of government export bans, and he emphasized that "We must be free and deliver to the world."[78]

Because the comments of Reichert, Bruhn, Vögler, and Stinnes were "creating the impression that we are not united"—a dangerous indulgence in the presence of government officials—they retired for private negotiations and came up with a compromise formula under which export controls with simplified clearance procedures would be retained for an interim period. Once the armistice was signed, however, price ceilings were to be lifted as quickly as possible along with the export bans on pig iron and the A and B products. The continuation of export regulation would then lie entirely in the hands of the export syndicates. In short, Vögler and Stinnes accepted the argument made by the cautious trade association managers that export controls be continued until domestic price ceilings were lifted, while the latter gentlemen accepted the substance of the Vögler-Stinnes program, which was the elimination of all government controls and total reliance on industrial self-government. Apparently, Bruhn and Reichert were unwilling to challenge seriously the Stinnes-Vögler assumption that the domestic supply of iron and steel would be satisfactory if price ceilings and export controls were eliminated at the same time.

The representatives of the finishing industries supported this compromise, and it had undoubtedly been designed in part to reassure them, as were promises of moderation in future pricing policies and of an end to the higher charges demanded for raw materials sold for indirect export. At the same time, the leaders of the finishing industries were badly divided over the question of whether or not there should be a continuation of government export controls for their industries. Dr. Sorge, the chairman of the VDMA, warned against an immediate lifting of export bans for the simple reason that it was too early to tell what the consequences would be. Director Emil Guggenheimer of the MAN, one of the most influential men in the machine construction industry, was more interested in getting rid of government controls, and he came up with the novel idea of having the Reichstag pass an enabling act placing the power of issuing export

[78] For this quotation and the discussion in the paragraphs below, see the VdESI report on the meeting, November 8, 1918, BA, R 13 I/189.

bans in the hands of any syndicate if three-fourths of its members voted that they wished to continue export controls. Thus, the government would be eliminated from the picture entirely except as agents of the syndicates in cases where recalcitrant members put up resistance. This solution might have proven attractive if either the businessmen or the ministry trusted the Reichstag, but the 1916 Auxiliary Service Law had demonstrated that the left-wing majority in the Reichstag could do remarkable things to socioeconomic legislation. As a consequence, the future of export controls was left unsettled by the November 8 meeting, and it continued to be debated among the leaders of the finished products industries for the next few weeks.

As in the case of the producers, so the manufacturers tended to split between the industrialists and the business managers, although too rigid division of opinion cannot be made along these lines. Big concerns in the industry such as the MAN and Borsig placed chief emphasis on liberation from state controls and felt strong enough to face the world market without the help of the state and its export bans. Interestingly enough, their attitude was shared by some of the leading officials of the RWA, particularly the liberal Undersecretary Heinrich Göppert and the right-wing Socialist who took over as State Secretary on November 9, August Müller. Müller, who was held in such high esteem by some industrialists that he was to become a serious candidate for the position of Business Manager of the Reich Association of German Industry sometime later, secretly proposed to Guggenheimer that the RWA issue a decree terminating government export controls on all products of the machine construction industry. The decree was to be issued suddenly and without warning, before opponents of the measure had a chance to protest it. Much to the chagrin of Guggenheimer, the business manager of the VDMA, Dr. Frölich, stepped in at the last minute and prevented the action on the grounds that some branches of the industry feared the development of cutthroat competition if the export bans were lifted and manufacturers were thereby permitted to operate outside the trade associations once again.[79]

Guggenheimer understood why Frölich acted to prevent the issuance of Müller's projected decree, and he could not deny the right of self-governing industrial associations to call on the government for the protective mantle of export bans, but Guggenheimer could not resist expressing his contempt for "that part of industry that wants a bailiff and does not feel it has strength enough to bring its own affairs in

[79] Julius Gebauer to Guggenheimer, November 26, 1918, Frölich to Guggenheimer, November 28, 1918, and minute on a telephone call to the MAN from Director Otto Gertung, December 3, 1918, along with other relevant correspondence in MAN Werksarchiv Nürnberg, Nr. 03.

order and places itself under the protective wings of the state."[80] It is important to recognize, however, that while Guggenheimer and Frö- lich seemed to be papering over a misunderstanding, they really did differ on a major question of policy and tactics. Guggenheimer felt that if industry really wanted to be free and self-governing, then it had to accept the implications of its position to the fullest and not protect its pricing policies with export bans. From a tactical point of view, he considered it mistaken to promote syndicalization and there- by give state agencies "the opportunity to extend their syndicalizing ideas still further."[81] Frölich also feared Moellendorff's planning con- cepts, but he felt that maintaining a reasonable amount of economic stability within the context of a revolutionary situation justified a more opportunistic tactic on the issue of controls. Ultimately, industry would benefit: "From the standpoint of domestic politics suspension or establishment of import and export bans is to be viewed from the perspective of creating employment and, above everything else, as a measure against the consumer point of view."[82] Frölich thus succeeded in retaining export bans for all already syndicalized products of the machine construction industry, except where the organizations in- volved requested that they be terminated. Export controls on nonsyn- dicalized products were terminated and, to the satisfaction of all concerned, the entire procedure of granting export permissions was greatly simplified.[83]

Throughout these discussions, the fate of export controls appeared bound up with the maintenance of domestic price ceilings. Here, too, the industrialists had won for themselves a position of decisive influ- ence over government policy, but they were very uncertain and di- vided about how to use their power. The entire issue of price ceilings thus became the subject of a lively debate in the Steel Works Asso- ciation on November 21, 1918. All present agreed that they deserved a price increase because they were selling their products at a loss and could no longer afford to do so now that military production was end- ing. But was it wise to end price ceilings and raise prices substantially in the midst of so inflammatory a political situation where there was so much talk about socialization? As Director Klemme of the GHH argued: "Because of the high war profits the hatred of heavy industry

---

[80] Guggenheimer to Frölich, December 2, 1918, *ibid.* Guggenheimer must have been furious to learn that the Gustavusberg branch of the MAN had been among those requesting a continuation of the export bans.

[81] *Ibid.*

[82] Meeting of the German Industrial Council (*Industrierat*), December 19, 1918, BA, R 13 I/189.

[83] *Stahl und Eisen*, 38:2, November 28, 1918, p. 1121.

has increased immeasurably and what is now planned against industry is a consequence of its false pricing policy." Klemme suggested that they produce at a loss because if they continued to reap profits during so difficult a period, "people will presume that they can place every possible burden upon this industry." Bruhn of Krupp agreed with Klemme and warned that "If we want to continue working with the high dividends, then we are indulging in the same stupidities as the workers."[84]

This view was unpopular, however. Peter Klöckner accused Klemme and Bruhn of asking "that we should go to a living death." He pointed out that perhaps Krupp could afford to lose 200 million marks, "but we have to take care that our plants do not go *kaputt*." August Thyssen also objected to waiting "until we are finally ruined" and to "being bled white" while awaiting the political stabilization that the summoning of a National Assembly might bring. If industry did not at most cover costs, investors would lose all confidence, stocks would fall below par, "and then the Social Democrats will get our well established and well amortized works at a very cheap price," or the Entente would buy them out.[85]

The most resentful industrialists such as Klöckner and Hasslacher threatened refusal to deliver and shutdowns if prices remained fixed or unsatisfactory. Hasslacher urged a united front against the system of price ceilings and an immediate return to the prewar economic order: "We take the view that this government imposed by force (*Zwangsregierung*) does not exist for us when it comes to these questions and that we do what we consider to be right."[86] He was more willing to discuss the matter with the workers themselves and show them the true situation, because "they are not so stupid that they will not understand that." It appears that Hasslacher had a peculiarly extreme interpretation of the meaning of the *Arbeitsgemeinschaft*, and his colleagues were neither prepared to test openly the extent of their independence from the revolutionary regime nor were they particularly sanguine about securing worker sympathy through an exposure of their financial problems. They also knew that they would be asking for nothing but trouble if they pursued Hass-

[84] Steel Works Association meeting, November 21, 1918, HA/GHH, Nr. 3000030/11 for these statements. Klemme's comments are all the more impressive because his boss, Reusch, was uncompromising in his contempt for the new regime in Berlin, with which he initially refused to deal "because he has not completely lost his self-respect." See the report on the Steel Works Association meeting of December 4, 1918, in the ATH Archiv, Stahlwerksverband, 1903–1925.

[85] For the quotations in this paragraph, see the Steel Works Association meeting of November 21, 1918, HA/GHH, Nr. 3000030/11.

[86] *Ibid.*

lacher's intended tactic of shutting down his plants, beginning with the least profitable ones, and refusing to deliver heavy plate to shipyards as contracted on the grounds that the existing price ceilings made the continuation of operations impossible. Bruhn warned Hasslacher that placing the prices in the foreground would guarantee that "the government reds will be at our throats,"[87] while Klemme emphasized the importance of maximizing employment "to maintain peace and order" and condemned the Rheinstahl threats as shortsighted and tactless.

Undoubtedly, Klöckner and Hasslacher to at least some extent found it personally therapeutic to rant in the above manner, and it was certainly a useful way to force their colleagues into a more active posture. In any case, they recognized that heavy industry had a friend in Koeth, who "has always shown himself to be very reasonable; he has a total view of the situation and he undoubtedly will want to and will be able to give good advice."[88] They resolved, therefore, to send a delegation to the Demobilization Office in order to decide whether or not to settle for an increase of the price ceilings or to take the ultimate step of asking for the elimination of price ceilings entirely.

When Koeth met with the industrialist committee in early December he lived up to the faith they had placed in him. He was prepared to drop price ceilings on iron, steel, and rolled products. All he asked in return was that the syndicates set prices that were within "defensible limits," and that the intended measures be delayed until the ban on commercial railroad traffic then in effect be ended. The last request was made to prevent hoarders from buying up iron at cheap prices in order to profiteer when the prices changed. Koeth agreed that unfulfilled government contracts were to be paid according to the new prices fixed by the syndicates, a matter that had worried the industrialists considerably.[89]

The question of what to ask for had thus been answered, and the industrialists could move on to the next problems: how soon and how much? As usual, they were divided. Gradualists such as Beukenberg proposed that price ceilings be raised and maintained until January and then abandoned. The impatient Hasslacher, however, argued that the situation was too uncertain to make reasonable suggestions about any appropriate ceilings. Furthermore, he pointed out that plants in the occupied areas on the left bank of the Rhine were no longer taking

[87] Heavy Plate Syndicate meeting, November 27, 1918, *ibid.*, Nr. 3000033/7.

[88] Steel Works Association meeting, November 21, 1918, *ibid.*, Nr. 3000030/11.

[89] This concern was expressed at the November 21 meeting, *ibid.* For the meeting with Koeth, see Steel Works Association meeting, December 4, 1918, ATH Archiv, Stahlwerksverband, 1903–1925.

orders from Berlin and that the plants on the right bank would be placed at a disadvantage unless they, too, enjoyed freedom in pricing. He felt that Beukenberg's idea of raising price ceilings would lead to a new round of wage demands just at a time when the workers seemed to be quieting down and making fewer claims. Finally, Hasslacher intimated that he was thinking about going much further than simply abandoning official price ceilings in favor of prices set by the syndicates. He pointed in the direction of totally uncontrolled prices by suggesting that the Steel Works Association would have to be dissolved if the works in Lorraine and Luxemburg ceased to be members. Most of Hasslacher's colleagues thought that this was rushing things, but they did not approve of Beukenberg's proposals either. Instead, the Steel Works Association at its December 19 meeting set new prices to be effective January 1, when presumably the price ceilings would be lifted. The impending increases were substantial, jumping from 187.5 to 285 marks per ton for semis and from 235 to 335 marks per ton for bars, although a minority of the producers led by Krupp, the GHH, and the Deutsch-Luxemburg concerns had fought in vain for lesser increases.[90]

This victory for heavy industry was not exacted in opposition to the trade union leaders. On the contrary, the trade union people were consulted regularly and were strongly inclined to identify with producer rather than consumer interests during the period of economic reconstruction. Indeed, the advocates of the elimination of price ceilings urged their colleagues to work through the *Arbeitsgemeinschaften*: "In a group based on parity between the employers and the workers, an . . . industry has an entirely different impact than if the individual works present petitions for the lifting of price ceilings. . . ."[91] Thus, although it would be ludicrous to suggest that industrialists had reason to engage in wild celebration on New Year's Eve 1919, there is very good reason to suggest that the November Revolution brought them as much, if not more, liberation as any other major social group in Germany.

The conditions under which this freedom was won left much to be desired. Translated into economic terms, the sociopolitical unrest of 1918–1919 meant steadily rising costs for raw materials and labor. Of course, the two types of costs cannot be neatly separated. Labor shortages in mining and smelting, low productivity, the introduction of a shorter working day, repeated strikes, and repeated wage demands accompanied by threats of violence and sabotage necessarily had a

[90] *Ibid.*
[91] ZAG to Director Poensgen, December 19, 1918, DZA Potsdam, ZAG, Nr. 5, Bl. 678.

severe impact on the price of coal and iron ore. Nevertheless, the supply and cost of these raw materials were determined by a variety of other factors as well. In the case of coal, the failure to repair or improve mines during the war, Allied demands for deliveries, and shortages of wood and other needed raw materials for coal mining played a major role in the problems. The problems of supply and distribution were compounded by the shortage of rolling stock, the poor state of the transportation system, and the increasing costs of both rail and water transport. It was difficult to move coal to its destination, and the railroads themselves consumed coal at the expense of other industries.[92]

The iron ore question provided a host of serious difficulties. Not only had Germany failed to gain Briey-Longwy, but she had lost control of her most important ore fields, and the industrialists knew that the loss was permanent. France promised to return ore for coke in the Luxemburg Agreement of December 1918 but did not fulfill the promise. At the same time, Germany was cut off from some of her major foreign suppliers by the Allied blockade. In general, however, the German iron producers had adequate stores of ore during 1919. As late as October 1, they had approximately two and a half months supply of phosphorus Swedish ores and five months supply of nonphosphorus Swedish ores. They owed their ample stocks to Koeth's Raw Materials Section in the War Ministry, which had purchased 600,000 tons of Swedish ore in the summer of 1918 and forced the industrialists to accept it despite their unwillingness to do so and complaints about storage problems. By September, they were quite happy to have the reserve, although it should be noted that the ore supplies were not evenly divided and some firms had difficulties. In considering the raw materials situation in 1919, however, it is even more important to recognize that the problems of all the works would have been much greater if they had been permitted consistent and normal use of their raw materials. The constant strikes and work stoppages in the winter and spring of 1919 had the effect of stretching raw materials supplies in the iron and steel industry and mitigating shortages just as the shortages made the actual production losses due to the disturbances less serious than they otherwise might have been.[93]

[92] Schieck, *Wirtschaftspolitik*, pp. 115–122, and the report on the coal situation in 1919 in BA, Nachlass Silverberg, Nr. 145, Bl. 197ff.

[93] See the report of the Reich Commissar for the Ore Supply to the RWM, October 31, 1919, DZA Potsdam, RWM, Nr. 4610, Bl. 156. Extensive material on the negotiations with the Swedes is to be found in HA/GHH, Nr. 30006/11 and 17, and in the ATH Archive, Nr. 450 and 452. On April 14, 1919, the GHH had

Indeed, it is fair to say that the industrialists were far more nervous about their Swedish ore debts and the costs of future ore shipments than they were about immediate problems of supply. In March 1919 the Swedish ore debt payable to Swedish banks amounted to 120 million marks, and it fell due one year after the conclusion of peace or July 1, 1920, at the latest. As noted earlier, the wartime German government had compelled the industrialists to make the debts to Swedish banks payable in kronen in the expectation that the value of the German mark would improve after a victorious war. In their wartime dealings with the Swedish ore monopoly, the Trafikaktiebolaget Grängesberg-Oxelösund, the German industrialists had exerted strong pressure on the concern to intervene with the banks to extend the credits as well as to keep prices low. The Germans threatened that otherwise they would employ more minette in the future. In early 1918, the Swedes, calculating on a German victory, had made important concessions.[94]

Following the German defeat, however, the Swedes began demanding various contract revisions including higher prices to cover the cost increases arising from their own unsettled conditions. The Germans now felt compelled to make concessions even though they recognized that the Swedes were anxious to sell off their excess inventories. Large debtors such as Rheinstahl and Thyssen felt it important to earn Swedish goodwill in view of their long-term dependence on Swedish ores as well as to pay their ore debts as rapidly as possible in order to strengthen Swedish confidence and avoid having the real value of the debt increase because of further deterioration of the mark. Although optimists such as Bruhn of Krupp and the leaders of the Reichsbank urged against paying any of the Swedish ore debt until the exchange value of the mark improved, Thyssen and Hasslacher found little ground to hope for such improvement. They knew that the 400 million in mark assets abroad held by the various steel syndicates had depreciated to half their value during the war and had no reason to entertain the optimism about the mark that seemed to prevail in some industrial circles in No-

---

four months supply of minette and nine months supply of Swedish ores. In November 1918 Krupp had three times as much ore in storage as it had in August 1914 and felt richly supplied. See Krupp WA, VII f 1087 kd 57. On the socioeconomic "checks and balances" operating during the revolutionary period, see Gerald D. Feldman, Eberhard Kolb, and Reinhard Rürup, "Die Massenbewegungen der Arbeiterschaft in Deutschland am Ende des Ersten Weltkrieges (1917–1920)," *Politische Vierteljahresschrift*, 13, 1972, pp. 84–105.

[94] See above, pp. 55–56, and the discussions of January 31, 1918, and March 12, 1919, in HA/GHH, Nr. 30006/17.

vember 1918. Hasslacher insisted that the debts had to be paid rapidly if the Swedes were going to do business with them in the future and that "I want to remain an honest fellow who pays his debts and does not need to claim that I would have paid gladly except for the fact that my government prevented me from doing so."[95] In March 1919 Thyssen was arguing that they should pay a quarter of the debt immediately in order to strengthen Swedish confidence, and apparently he had the cash resources abroad to do so. Both he and Hasslacher, however, wanted the Reichsbank to permit the steel industrialists to retain foreign exchange derived from exports in order to pay the debts. Even if the Reichsbank were willing to release gold itself or to permit the industrialists to use their foreign exchange or other resources to pay the debts, such action would have been a violation of the financial agreements made in connection with the Armistice at Treves on December 13, 1918. For the moment, therefore, the industrialists speculated about the chances of getting an American loan and sought to negotiate further with the Swedes. Naturally, the delay in settling the matter only made it worse, and threatened to undermine the precarious entente between iron producers and manufacturers.[96]

If the greatest problems of the iron and steel industrialists were only beginning in early 1919, however, it must also be recognized that these troubles were developing after the most critical period of the Revolution came to an end. Only days after the lifting of price ceilings the Spartacist uprising in Berlin was put down, Rosa Luxemburg and Karl Liebknecht were murdered, and new elections were held for a National Assembly. The composition of the new National Assembly could hardly be called the fulfillment of heavy industry's dreams, but it did constitute a defeat for radicalism. On February 4 the chief organ of the councils movement, the *Zentralrat*, turned its powers over to the National Assembly, and the latter began its meetings in Weimar two days later. Not far away, in Jena, the men who had founded the ZAG were taking the lead in establishing the most unified and powerful central organization of German business until that time, the Reich Association of German Industry (*Reichsverband der deutschen Industrie*—RdI). Disturbances had by no means ended, but there were brutal free corps units available to end them with the assistance of industrialist financial support. At the same time, the heavy industrialists had enjoyed access to the Demobilization Office and other government agencies to secure contracts and maintain employment in their plants. Broadly speaking,

[95] Meeting of January 16, 1919, *ibid.*, Nr. 3000030/11.

[96] See the correspondence with the German Embassy in Stockholm and related correspondence in BA, R 85/905. Also, see Carl Bergmann, *The History of Reparations* (Boston and New York, 1927), p. 4.

therefore, the iron and steel industrialists had an improved framework within which to deal with the problems arising from the economic policies and decisions adopted in November–December 1918.[97]

Some of the most important of these problems were spelled out by Dr. Frölich of the VDMA in a gloomy report of January 2, 1919. Naturally and justifiably, Frölich emphasized the general political uncertainty, the bad transportation situation, and the coal shortage as major reasons why customers had held back in placing orders and why the conversion from wartime to peacetime production was moving slowly. Many of Frölich's most depressing comments, however, were reserved for the various sanguine predictions made by the iron and steel producers before the turn of the year. The coal shortage and the occupation of the left bank had reduced iron production such that "The fears of an actual iron shortage . . . were only too justified; the projected oversupply of iron has not materialized." Similarly, "The retreat of iron prices hoped for in connection with statements of the iron producing industry has not materialized." Prices had increased in January. New price increases were scheduled for February, and more of the same could be expected in the future. Frölich made it clear that business conditions would never improve if customers continued to await the domestic price reductions and improved exchange rate promised and predicted by the producers.[98] Frölich might also have added that the value of the mark was not rising either, but he suggested that all the talk about dropping export controls had been very premature because the enemy was not going to tolerate the selling of German manufactures at cut-rate prices. Indeed, the Reichsbank had found it necessary to rescind part of its decree of November 1 permitting exporters to calculate in German rather than in foreign currency, but its earlier decision to permit both calculation and payment in either type of currency had produced difficulties and confusion.[99] Following Stinnes' advice had made it more difficult to calculate than ever.

Indeed, the manufacturers were those most directly and immediately affected by the large pig iron price increases of January 1919 and the

[97] On the question of the "timing" of the Revolution, see Feldman et al., in *Politische Vierteljahresschrift*, 13, p. 92ff. On the revolution in general, see Reinhard Rürup, *Probleme der Revolution in Deutschland* (Wiesbaden, 1968). On the RdI, see Fritz Hauenstein et al., *Der Weg zum Industriellen Spitzenverband* (Frankfurt a.M., 1956), p. 118ff., and Friedrich Zunkel, "Die Gewichtung der Industriegruppen bei der Etablierung des Reichsverbandes der deutschen Industrie," *Industrielles System*, pp. 637–646.

[98] Frölich report to VDMA Board of Directors, January 2, 1919, MAN Werksarchiv Nürnberg, Nr. 171.

[99] See the discussion of this problem on March 22, 1919, BA, R 13 I/190, Bl. 1–7.

substantial price increases on most A and B products of January *and* February 1919 (see Table 6). Ironically, the successful collaboration between raw materials producers and the finished product manufacturers in eliminating or reducing government controls at the end of 1918 was being jeopardized by its consequences. Director Hermann Fischmann, a leader in the iron construction and bridge building industry, graphically described these consequences in a lengthy and irate encounter with the producers at the March 1 VdESI Executive Directors meeting. Before the January price increases there had been a flood of customer inquiries in his industry, and although there was little signing of contracts, there did arise the hope "that we could gradually crawl out of the *Schlamassel* in which we found ourselves."[100] Additionally, the government had been giving contracts in order to create employment opportunities. Until January 1, however, it was virtually impossible to get raw materials because producers and merchants were holding back until the price increase went into effect. Then, when it became known that there was going to be another price increase effective February 15, a new and even more "catastrophic" raw materials shortage developed in his industry. Many of Fischmann's colleagues regarded this second price increase "as a first class funeral for the finishing industry." In his own industry, customers either abandoned their plans or decided to employ wood instead of iron in construction. Fischmann did not deny that costs had risen for the producers, but frankly felt that expenses arising from the revolution, such as cost-of-living increases for the workers, should be covered by "certain reserve funds or previously made profits." Also, Fischmann could not understand why the producers continued to charge higher prices for indirect export items now that price ceilings and export taxes had been eliminated. If conditions were so desperate for the producers, then he suggested that they turn to the government and ask for subsidies to cover their costs rather than ruin their customers.

As during the war, however, the thing that most irritated the finished product manufacturers was the way in which heavy industry "exploited its power position" in the implementation of its policy of having customers pay the price in effect on the day of delivery. Quite aside from the fact that this condition made calculation difficult and encouraged the workers to make renewed wage demands because they were constantly witnessing how every wage increase was being passed on in a price increase, there was the enraging fact that producers exploited every transportation delay and conceivable excuse to impose higher

[100] VdESI Executive Directors meeting, March 1, 1919, *ibid.*, 156. Until otherwise noted, the quotations that follow come from this meeting. See also Fischmann to Gerwin, March 6, 1919, *ibid.*, 420, Bl. 16–21.

TABLE 6

The Price of Various Iron and Steel Products, December 1918–June 1919

(Price per ton measured in paper and gold marks)

		December	January	February	March	April	May	June
Foundry pig iron III	PM	156.50	249.00	249.00	339.00	390.00	404.50	438.00
	GM	101.62	127.56	114.54	100.61	112.96	127.45	121.22
Hematite pig iron	PM	223.00	314.50	314.50	314.50	366.50	407.00	418.50
	GM	159.64	161.12	144.66	127.07	122.13	133.01	125.26
Billets	PM	202.50	366.67	366.67	366.67	450.00	450.00	450.00
	GM	145.70	153.69	183.99	161.61	158.28	155.23	142.34
Girders	PM	220.00	320.00	420.00	420.00	420.00	520.00	520.00
	GM	157.49	163.93	193.19	169.70	139.95	169.93	155.83
Merchant bars	PM	235.00	335.00	435.00	435.00	435.00	550.00	550.00
	GM	168.64	171.62	200.09	175.76	144.95	179.73	164.82
Heavy plate	PM	275.00	375.00	500.00	500.00	500.00	615.00	615.00
	GM	196.86	192.11	229.99	202.02	166.61	200.98	184.30

Source: Hans J. Schneider, Zur Analyse des Eisenmarkts (Vierteljahrshefte zur Konjunkturforschung, Sonderheft 1) (Berlin, 1927), p. 103.

prices upon manufacturers for orders already completed and even in transit before a new price increase was to go into effect. This "dictatorial" treatment was calling forth "the most angry and caustic comments," and "already the cry for state intervention is being made here and there with increasing strength."

The idea of the *Arbeitsgemeinschaft*, Fischmann pointedly suggested, "ought above all else to be extended for once to the producer and customer. The two are actually much closer in their economic views and their economic needs than the employer and worker."[101] In making this comment, Fischmann was in no way exaggerating the bitterness felt in small and medium-sized business toward heavy industry for its willingness to make constant concessions to the workers while passing on the costs to its customers, a bitterness that was even creating some sympathy toward socialization of heavy industry in manufacturing circles.

General Director Vögler did not find it easy or comfortable to answer these attacks. He did make a telling point when he argued that a manufacturer purchasing bars in Germany for 400 marks was not being prevented from exporting at a profit because the mark was worth 40–45 pfennig abroad, and this meant that the bars had been purchased, in effect, at a very reasonable world market price of 180–200 gold marks and thus could and should be sold in finished form at a reasonable gold mark price too. Vögler did not explain, however, how long this circle of price increases, currency deterioration, and exchange dumping was supposed to continue or how it was supposed to be stopped. If it were not stopped, then presumably the wartime situation had been perpetuated and with it the justification for price ceilings and export controls. Above all, Vögler feared a restoration of government controls, and he strongly opposed Fischmann's call to use government subsidies as a substitute for price increases. At the same time, the bitterness of heavy industry's customers and the unrest among the workers made it impossible for Vögler to advocate continuing large price increases.

Vögler was keenly aware of the fact that heavy industry's hard-won freedom from government price controls could only be maintained through a measure of moderation and good public relations. At the March 21 meeting of the Pig Iron Syndicate, he fought against proponents of a 90–132 mark price increase on the grounds that it would

101 The influential southwest German manufacturer, Paul Meesmann, made the same point even more harshly, *ibid.* See also the letter of Director Ditges of the Association of German Shipyard Works to the VdESI of April 12, 1919, contrasting the favoritism shown to the workers and the harsh treatment of the manufacturers, *ibid.*, Bl. 51.

produce "socialization in four to six weeks." Instead, he suggested a vigorous program of "enlightenment" to change the public image of heavy industry and explain its economic problems. He suggested that they stop being so secretive about costs because they could make a good case.[102] Lastly, he, Bruhn, and Klöckner urged that the new prices be set in collaboration with the representatives of the manufacturing industries, of the government, and of the workers. This would give all concerned a sense that they were participating or at least well informed, and it would be in the spirit of the *Arbeitsgemeinschaft*. Even Reichstag deputies in the area might be invited to the discussions. In short, Vögler and his colleagues felt confident enough of the justifiability of new price increases to discuss the matter with potential critics and fearful enough of threats to heavy industry to consider such discussion absolutely essential.

The iron and steel producers now began to retreat from the hard policy they had pursued in January and February under the impact of threats from manufacturers and workers and the danger of government intervention. The Pig Iron Syndicate, always the most moderate of the syndicates, took the lead at the beginning of March by refraining from raising its prices and then followed Vögler's advice at the end of the month and discussed its April price increases with representatives of the government, the finished product manufacturers, and the workers. By May, the Pig Iron Syndicate actually cut back its April increase because the government had refused to sanction a price increase for coal and cokes and had thus lowered iron producer costs.[103]

The producers' show of goodwill toward their own industrial customers was even more impressive. In a series of meetings at the beginning and end of April, the finished product manufacturers were persuaded to accept price increases for the most important A and B products effective May 1. At the same time, the iron and steel producers made major concessions in the area of delivery conditions, including a pledge that they would sell their products for one fixed price subject to no retroactive adjustments. They also promised that the new May prices would go unchanged for two months. Second, the producers agreed that delays in delivery, intentional and unintentional, would also no longer be permitted to affect the price. Third, the producer

[102] Meeting of the Pig Iron Syndicate, March 21, 1919, HA/GHH, Nr. 300039/15. Vögler wanted to point out that they were only making a 10 mark profit on pig iron, but Director Bürgers of the GBAG warned against discussing the profit question too much because someone might then "also ask about the profits on the subsidiary plants."

[103] See the various meetings and correspondence of the Pig Iron Syndicate in the Friedrich-Wilhelms-Hütte Archiv, Nr. 860/16.

associations promised to take action against members who sold products at prices higher than those they had set. Finally, the producers agreed to drop extra charges for indirect exports. This April Düsseldorf Agreement between the producers and the manufacturers constituted a systematic attempt to put an end to the wartime business practices that had caused so much friction between the two groups and work toward economic stabilization through a friendly understanding within industry arrived at without the assistance of government intervention or supervision.[104]

The danger of such intervention seemed very great and immediate. Just as the industrialists had tried to escape government regulation at the end of 1918 by privately forming an *Arbeitsgemeinschaft* with the workers, so in the spring of 1919 they were trying to preserve their autonomy by voluntary cooperation and discussion of economic issues with other concerned parties as a substitute for the organizational schemes being hatched in connection with the *Gemeinwirtschaft* and "planned economy" (*Planwirtschaft*) program under development by the RWM. This ministry was now headed by the Socialist Rudolf Wissell, but its program was the work of its technocratic undersecretary, Wichard von Moellendorff. Industry had developed a fondness for Wissell's predecessor until February 1919, August Müller, the Socialist who had distinguished himself by opposing socialization and who had reassured his industrialist friends by telling them that he intended to "free his office from every form of bureaucratism and to make it run along business-like lines." Müller had asked for the confidence of industry and had hoped "to remain in office even if there is a change to the right or the left, because he wants to handle his tasks in a purely objective manner without much politicking,"[105] but his open opposition to socialization had made his retention impossible. Moellendorff had served under Müller, and he was viewed with great suspicion by heavy industry, as he was believed to "have the intention of forcefully syndicalizing the entire iron and steel industry" so that the state could take its profits while dictating its operations.[106] Under Wissell, who like most of the Socialist leaders was remarkably free of original ideas, Moellendorff became the "idea man" of the RWM and thus assured a basic continuity between the prerevolutionary and post-

[104] Undated report by Director Ditges and meeting of April 29, 1919, in BA, R 13 I/420, Bl. 59–61, 67–71.

[105] Guggenheimer to Rieppel, November 25, 1918, MAN Werksarchiv Nürnberg, Nr. 116.1.

[106] Heavy Plate Syndicate meeting, November 26, 1918, HA/GHH, Nr. 3000033/7.

100

revolutionary periods. The notion of a planned economy organized along corporatist lines became the guiding idea of the RWM's activity and thus threatened to bring the fears of heavy industry close to reality. In contrast to Rathenau, who did not always practice what he preached, Moellendorff pursued the idea of a nationalist, corporatist, and technocratic restructuring of the economy with persistence and enthusiasm. It was he who had provided many of the basic ideas for the organization of the war economy, and it was he who continued to provide the most imaginative organizational ideas for the postwar regime.[107]

Moellendorff's essential goal was the reconstruction and rationalization of the German economy on the basis of the most rational organization of production and distribution within the context of the greatest possible national economic autonomy. In his view, the inflationary situation demanded the elimination of wasteful competition, the rigid control of imports to prevent useless expenditure, and the careful control of exports to prevent the loss of vital raw materials and ensure that a maximum profit was made from such exports as were permitted or encouraged. While demanding the subordination of private interests to national interests, Moellendorff insisted that this could never be achieved through bureaucracy but only through the unselfish collaboration of all concerned—producers, manufacturers, merchants, consumers, workers, and the state—in corporate, self-governing organizations (*Gemeinwirtschaftskörper*). Moellendorff thought that defeat gave Germany an opportunity to repeat the accomplishments of Freiherr vom Stein and the Prussian reform movement of the Napoleonic period. Self-government based on broad participation of those concerned was expected to infuse both efficiency and new moral energy into the nation. Because the economy had to be organized if it were to function in an organized way, most of the RWM's efforts in early 1919 were directed toward organizational ends. For Moellendorff, however, these organizational activities were meant to serve as a preliminary to a more substantive change in the operation of the German economy.[108]

Although Moellendorff's theorizing and moralizing propensities worried businessmen, he did enjoy popularity in certain business circles, particularly among some of the leadership of the manufacturing in-

[107] Schieck, *Wirtschaftspolitik*, pp. 23–28, 74–99, and Michael W. Honhart, *The Incomplete Revolution. The Social Democrats' Failure to Transform the German Economy, 1918–1920*, Ph.D. Diss. (Duke, 1972), p. 159ff.

[108] For Moellendorff's ideas, see the collection of his writings in Hermann Curth, ed., *Konservativer Sozialismus* (Hamburg, 1932).

dustries, and he was closely associated with the metal and chemical industries.[109] At the beginning of 1919, this popularity among business-men became more widespread because of the anxiety generated by the extreme left. Big industrialists were suspicious of Moellendorff but by no means completely hostile to him, an attitude that contrasted markedly with the antagonism toward him and his ideas felt by com-mercial and small business interests. Finished product manufacturers had recognized in Moellendorff an ally in their wartime struggle to keep raw materials prices down. He was, it must be remembered, an engineer by profession, and technocratic ideas had some appeal in such circles. At the same time, Moellendorff's emphasis on rationaliza-tion struck a responsive note with such leaders of heavy industry as Albert Vögler. More generally, big industrialists could hardly react in a totally negative way to his schemes for industrial self-government and widespread participation in economic policy formation after they themselves had formed an *Arbeitsgemeinschaft* with the workers. Moellendorff himself seems to have done his best initially to reassure and win over prominent industrialists. Thus, if industrialists sometimes found it difficult to understand exactly what Moellendorff was after, they did not find it too difficult in the context of strikes, unrest, and socialization demands to detect a soothing parallelism of efforts, inten-tions, and sentiments between their own goals and those publicly and privately advocated by Moellendorff.

During 1918–1919, there was a veritable organizational mania in Germany, a phenomenon that probably reflected in part an exaggera-tion of what was supposed to be a peculiarly Germanic talent at a time when the national self-image was in particular need of bolster-ing.[110] In some respects, this organizational activity probably served as a kind of girding of the loins and therapeutic activity in the midst of great uncertainty, above all the uncertainty surrounding the terms the Allies would impose on Germany. Lastly, and no less importantly, organizational changes were required by new, objective circumstances. The restructuring of labor-management relations and the creation of the *Arbeitsgemeinschaft* demanded more effective and inclusive in-dustrial and management organizations. The future reconstruction of Germany's economy and restoration of her position in the world econ-

[109] After his fall from office, he was hired by the Metallgesellschaft and the im-portant chemical firm, the BASF, to serve as an economic adviser. See Richard Mer-ton to H. Schmitz, Historisches Archiv, Metallgesellschaft AG, Privatbriefe Richard Merton, December 11, 1919. He later worked for I. G. Farben.

[110] On the pride in organization, see Jürgen Kocka's stimulating "Industrielles Management. Konzeptionen und Modelle in Deutschland vor 1914," *Vierteljahr-schrift für Sozial- und Wirtschaftsgeschichte*, 56, 1969, pp. 332–372, esp. p. 348.

omy also called forth a desire for more effective and cohesive organization. It was in this context that the iron and steel industrialists discussed the establishment of a self-governing body for their industry to be composed of representatives of industry, labor, consumers, and merchants with Moellendorff's good friend, the head of the Iron Section of the RWM, Baron Paul von Buttlar, in February 1919. Although no one seemed very clear about how these organizations were to function or how permanent they were going to be, organizational planning was a useful way of managing uncertainty and good politics besides, for as Buttlar noted, "it is better to introduce this organization from above before a socialization from below endangers our entire economic existence."[111]

Events were to prove that such mixed self-government bodies were useful even in blunting socialization efforts from below. When serious worker disturbances in the coal mines compelled the Scheidemann government to present a Socialization Law to the Reichstag as well as a specific law applying the more generalized legislation to the coal mining industry, the ultimate result was not socialization in the sense of a change of ownership of the mines, but rather a Reich Coal Council (*Reichskohlenrat*) along the lines advocated by Moellendorff. The very fuzziness of Moellendorff's *Gemeinwirtschaft* doctrines made them acceptable enough to secure a Reichstag majority in this instance, as well as to secure the grudging collaboration of the industrialists.[112]

The fundamental questions, however, were whether the RWM could realize its goals without such extraordinary pressures and how long the industrialists and the RWM could continue to work together despite the fact that their ultimate intentions were quite different. Moellendorff and Buttlar viewed the mixed self-governing bodies as permanent institutions subordinate to national interests and subject to state veto powers. One RWM draft proposal specifically concerned with the iron and steel industry, for example, envisioned a body with five committees: a production committee to undertake the rationalization of the industry, a committee to regulate domestic commerce and prices, a committee to regulate foreign trade and prices, a committee to deal with social questions, and a committee to deal with problems of taxation. In short, the self-governing body was to have extensive powers of regulation in every area of concern to the industry and to be a vehicle for state control of supervision in all these areas.[113] The

[111] Meeting of February 13, 1919, DZA Potsdam, RWM, Nr. 4146, Bl. 87.

[112] Schieck, Wirtschaftspolitik, p. 153ff. Also, see Charles Maier, *Recasting Bourgeois Europe. Stabilization in France, Germany and Italy in the Decade after World War I* (Princeton, 1975), pp. 140–141.

[113] Memorandum of February 24, 1919, DZA Potsdam, RWM, Nr. 4146, Bl. 107ff.

full extent of Moellendorff's intentions were not always made clear in public. In one of his memoranda he outlined a scheme for the creation of supersyndicates that would have a financial basis in the manner of the older private syndicates, but now that state would participate in the investment and in the return. This would have made the trustification and rationalization of German heavy industry a semipublic operation.[114] The aspect of Moellendorff's plans that received greatest emphasis for practical and tactical reasons, however, was the organizational one with its vision of a pyramid-like structure of economic parliaments for industries and regions culminating in a Reich Economic Council (*Reichswirtschaftsrat*).

The industrialists often seemed willing enough to discuss such schemes, but their basic concerns and efforts remained practical and limited and, as Moellendorff's intentions became more apparent, defensive. They were happy to improve upon their already existing organizations, and they were willing to follow the advice Vögler had given to the Pig Iron Syndicate and discuss basic issues with the iron consumers, workers, and merchants. Thus, they pursued the establishment of branch organizations within the framework of the *Reichsverband, Arbeitsgemeinschaft*, and VdESI. On April 10, 1919, they founded, in part at the behest of the RWM, a new German Steel Federation encompassing all iron, steel, and rolled products producers. Within this new Steel Federation the producers discussed pricing and other problems with other interested parties, and it was within its framework that the Düsseldorf Agreement of April 1919 on delivery conditions was concluded. The industrialists presented the Steel Federation as another illustration of the way in which they had learned to "take democratic ideas into account."[115] Although the Steel Federation certainly did lead to an exchange of ideas and points of view as well as to concrete agreements, it was deficient in at least three major respects from the standpoint of the Moellendorff-Buttlar program for the iron and steel industry. First, it was completely voluntary and had no basis whatever in public law. Second, it was purely consultative, and final decision remained with the producers. If the producers sought the approval of iron consumers, trade union representatives, and RWM representatives, they did so for political and public relations reasons. Finally, it provided no mechanisms by which the state could impose its will on all parties in the interests of the general welfare. In essence, the German Steel Federation was a shrewd and sensible effort to preempt government action and evade the implementation of more far-

---

[114] Undated memorandum, *ibid.*, Bl. 301ff.

[115] *Stahl und Eisen*, 39:1, April 17, 1919, pp. 423–424. The protocol of the first meeting of April 10, 1919, is in HA/GHH, Nr. 3000035/3.

reaching organizational ideas. It bridged but did not eliminate the latent conflict between the iron and steel producers and the RWM.

One of the peculiarities of the situation was that it was often impossible for either side to define the conflict because Moellendorff and Buttlar would not allow themselves to be pinned down to a specific statement of their plans. In part, this was due to the political difficulties and uncertainties facing the RWM. It faced strong opposition in the Cabinet and the Reichstag. At the same time, Germany did not have a peace treaty and the definable economic situation that the conclusion of peace was expected to bring with it. Instead of attacking the issue of economic organization head-on, therefore, Moellendorff approached the problem through the side door of export controls. He tried to create the nucleus of his projected self-governing bodies through the establishment of Export Control Bureaus (*Aussenhandelsstellen*) composed of representatives of the producers, consumers, merchants, and workers. At the same time, he concocted complicated schemes and organization charts uniting these bureaus with the various councils, *Arbeitsgemeinschaften*, and branch organizations (*Fachgruppen*) that had been created.[116]

Moellendorff seemed to take particular pleasure in spinning his web of organizations and speaking of their purposes in high-sounding phrases. When he gave such an address to a large number of iron industrialists on May 15, 1919,[117] however, it was quite apparent at the end that he had failed to transmit his ecstasy to his listeners: "A short time went by before anyone asked to speak, for the ideas Herr von Moellendorff had presented were strange to most of those present and the plans unpredictable in their consequences." Vögler finally broke the ice by politely asking if the RWM could not finally present a detailed statement of its intentions on paper so that the industrialists could come to a conclusion based on the answer to such concrete questions as how large concerns were supposed to fit into the proposed self-governing body. Instead of answering, Moellendorff replied by asking for their expert advice on such questions. This may have been a laudable illustration of Moellendorff's desire to prevent bureaucratic regulation and promote true participation, but its chief consequence was to produce true anxiety and increasing mistrust. The industrialists were used to setting up specific organizations for specific purposes and "this kind of grand attempt to organize the *entire* German industry in a unified way in *every* respect has not yet been made." Similarly, the industrialists were used to seeing the draft of a law when the

[116] Schieck, *Wirtschaftspolitik*, p. 194ff.

[117] For the discussion and quotations from this meeting that follow, see BA, R 13 I/191, Bl. 30–47.

government had something in mind, but Moellendorff would only tell them that he wanted a free exchange of ideas and that the RWM's program involved "such a monumental task of legislation that it demands years." The impact of such a statement on men who were convinced that their only ray of hope was an emergence from the past four years of government interference and endless legislation and overorganization can well be imagined. Furthermore, the industrialists now seemed to be facing not only more of the same but the added complication of having to negotiate all their decisions with workers, merchants, and consumers. Because Moellendorff insisted that the self-governing bodies had to have executive as well as consultative powers and that their sphere of activity had to be virtually all-encompassing, the industrialists could only conclude that they were going to lose all their previous autonomy in matters of production and distribution. The entire idea seemed so deplorably impractical as well. Director Bruhn referred to the Moellendorff program as a "house of cards," and warned that "The plans will not accomplish what their proponents promise from them. Much stronger forces will be and will remain at work and will overthrow what we construct here."

It is difficult not to share the industrialists' feeling that the RWM leaders were being monumentally unclear. Moellendorff was also open to the charge of engaging in obfuscation when he suggested an analogy between the self-governing bodies and the *Arbeitsgemeinschaften*. Reichert stated the differences angrily, but cogently and correctly:

> . . . The *Arbeitsgemeinschaft*, above all, is constructed on a free foundation. The Reich Economics Ministry thinks of and needs compulsion. The *Arbeitsgemeinschaft* very wisely limits itself to economic and social *policy*; the Reich Economics Ministry interferes in *business* activity. . . . A further difference between the two structures is that the organs of the *Arbeitsgemeinschaft* are composed on the basis of parity of workers and employers from *industry*. In no case do industrial employers work together with merchants and consumers in the same organs. The solidarity, of whose importance the *Arbeitsgemeinschaft* is convinced, is for us an entirely different one from that presented here by the Reich Economics Ministry.

Reichert also proved himself to be a better historian than either Moellendorff or Buttlar by insisting that it was nonsense to draw an analogy between the RWM's proposals and the principles of self-government advocated by Baron vom Stein a century earlier. To the enthusiastic approval of his colleagues, who now seemed fully recovered from the confusion into which Moellendorff had placed them, Reichert pointed out that

When vom Stein granted the municipalities. . . the right of self-government, it was a matter of actual liberation from close cabinet control in which there was interference in everything. But here we have previously been dealing with a free private economy. But now there shall be compulsory regulation and a lasting controlled economy. (Very true, very true!)

Reichert accused the RWM of being misleading in talking about industrial self-government. It was not purely industrial because it was not limited to industry. Instead, it was a self-government of all those engaged in the economic process (*eine Selbstverwaltung der "Wirtschaftenden"*)—that is, it sought to organize all those engaged in iron *trades* rather than simply those engaged in the iron *industry*. In the end, however, it was not even true self-government because the RWM did explicitly reserve veto powers for itself. Reichert concluded by saying that he would greet "an open and honorable manner of conflict" on the part of the RWM, and he urged the RWM leaders to speak frankly of employing compulsion in the public good rather than of a self-government that served as a mere cover for such compulsion.

This was a peculiar line for Reichert to take, because German heavy industry had not been escaping the perils of the revolution by a policy of excessive clarity and confrontation. Also, Reichert had been quite diplomatic in his dealings with the RWM until this point, and he was to become diplomatic again. There are, however, a number of possible explanations for this hard line. Undoubtedly, Reichert and his colleagues were beginning to find the vagueness of the RWM and the uncertainty about what it was going to do next very nerve racking. Reichert may also have had some personal concern about the continued autonomy of the Export Control Agency for the iron industry that he headed in Düsseldorf. He certainly was influenced by the unrest in business circles, particulary in the Rhenish iron wares industry, where reactions to the RWM proposals concerning Export Bureaus had taken on a truly vitriolic character.[118] Nevertheless, Reichert's attitude and, by implication, his performance received some criticism at the Executive Committee meeting of the VdESI on May 16, the day following the above discussed meeting. Moellendorff's honesty was defended, and one of those present pointed out that Moellendorff had prevented terrible things from happening and that the Undersecretary deserved industry's gratitude. Bruhn and Vögler argued that, for all

[118] Buttlar was subjected to incredible verbal abuse that constituted nothing less than an overt attack on the RWM's authority when he presented the RWM's program to the Rhenish iron wares industrialists at a meeting in Elberfeld on June 14, 1919. There is a detailed account in Oscar Funcke, "Vergangene Zeiten," Buch 2, Deutsches Industrieinstitut, Köln.

their reservations about the RWM plans, industry could only do itself harm by taking an entirely negative position. The industrialists decided, therefore, to apply pressure on the RWM for as concrete as possible a statement of its intentions and to assume a constructive posture on industrial organization while fighting for the principles espoused by Reichert. A joint VdESI and VDMA committee was appointed to pursue these questions with the RWM.[119]

These tactics were followed with considerable success by the leaders of heavy industry throughout June 1919. On June 18, Moellendorff presented his ideas before the Reich Association of German Industry, and Reichert provided another devastating critique. This time, however, there were no imputations of dishonesty, only the usual demands for clarity and the charge of timewasting while Germany's economic fate was being sealed at Versailles.[120] In contrast to the hysterics of the Rhenish iron wares industrialists and the fulminations of the Hamburg merchants, the big industrialists pursued a tactic described with admirable clarity by Vögler in a letter to Director Gerwin of the Steel Works Association of June 24, 1919:

> . . . one can very easily defend the position that, given a choice between socialization on the one hand and planned economy on the other hand, one can go part of the way together with the proponents of the latter. . . . we must always keep in mind that the government, whether it wishes or not, is forced to interfere in the economy. For this reason, it will be better in the total interest of industry to collaborate rather than only to carry on opposition and thereby at least not to make the situation worse.[121]

At the time he wrote this letter, Vögler feared that industry might have to give up what he frankly described as its "dilatory" tactic and go over to a more direct collaboration with the RWM because of what turned out to be a momentary strengthening of Wissell's position. The acceptance of the Treaty of Versailles and the change of government, however, cut the ground out from under the feet of Wissell and Moellendorff, and they resigned on July 12, 1919. The new Bauer government replaced Wissell with a conventional Socialist, Robert Schmidt, and Moellendorff with the academician, Julius Hirsch. Socialization would now have to await the "ripening" of the industries for which it was destined, and liberal economics could now be put into practice.[122]

[119] VdESI Executive Directors meeting, May 16, 1919, BA, R 13 I/156, and report on the VDMA meeting of May 17, 1919 in *ibid.*, 191, Bl. 63–65.

[120] Meeting of June 18, 1919, *ibid.*, 192, Bl. 121–138.

[121] Vögler to Gerwin, June 24, 1919, ATH Archiv, Allgemeiner Schriftwechsel.

[122] Schieck, *Wirtschaftspolitik*, pp. 256–261.

It no longer seemed necessary even to go "part of the way" with a planned economy.

The sustained economic emergency that had begun in war and had been exacerbated by defeat, however, was far from over, and this emergency had served to forge links between and among traditional problems of the iron and steel industry and the novel problems specific to the wartime and postwar crisis. The issues of cartelization, trustification, and the conflicts between producers and manufacturers were not new, but their urgency had been increased by the war and its consequences. Long-term problems of reorganization and restructuring had been quickened with the immediate difficulties arising from territorial and plant losses, while low productivity, social unrest and inflation had qualitatively multiplied problems of supply, prices, and delivery conditions to the point where the cohesion of the business community was threatened in a drastic manner. Insofar as industry stood united, it could entertain the prospect of reversing or at least containing the revolution in industry-state relations that began during the war. If industrial self-government broke down, however, there then existed the real danger that the government would take advantage of immediate economic dislocations to impose permanent organizational changes on the iron and steel industry, subjecting its future development to new forms of external interference and control.

CHAPTER TWO

The Disruption of Industrialist Solidarity, July 1919–April 1920

The signing of the Treaty of Versailles, the resignation of the Scheidemann government, and the fall of Wissell and Moellendorff in June–July 1919 did not trigger but rather accelerated the general drift into chaos on the iron and steel market and the continuing disintegration of the organizations and agreements intended to stabilize the industry. Between July 1919 and April 1920, the gloomy rhetorical question raised by the *Kölnische Zeitung* in an editorial of July 3 was to be a constant theme: "When finally will the unavoidable total collapse come? That is the question that inevitably imposes itself upon everyone who has followed the development of the iron market closely during the last months."[1] The treaty itself set the seal on Germany's enormous losses of plant and equipment in Lorraine and Luxemburg, made likely the loss of other major enterprises after the projected plebiscite in Upper Silesia, and deprived Germany of the Saar for the coming fifteen years. The minette ore fields were lost to German control, and Germany was expected to make huge reparations payments in the form of coal deliveries that were intended for use in the French iron and steel industry. The necessary reconstruction of the German iron and steel industry, therefore, was to be conducted under a series of handicaps designed to favor the French competition, and the enemy advantage was increased by the freezing of the German iron tariff at its pre-1914 level and the imposition of a French right to export iron and steel from the Saar and Lorraine to Germany duty free. Given the shortages of coal in those areas, however, production was very low, and the iron and steel supply of South Germany, normally provided by Lorraine and the Saar, now seemed precarious. In summary, the German economy was thrown back upon a severely reduced productive plant in iron and steel at a time when raw materials supplies and labor productivity were very low within the industrial plant that remained.[2]

The iron and steel market was already in a Hobbesian condition before the signing of the Treaty, and if the departure of Wissell and

[1] *Kölnische Zeitung*, July 3, 1919.

[2] Ferdinand Friedensburg, *Kohle und Eisen im Weltkriege und in den Friedensschlüssen* (Munich and Berlin, 1934), p. 185ff.

Moellendorff caused many industrialists to breathe a sigh of relief, it did nothing whatever to ensure that they could bring their own house into order. The gap between the prices set by the Steel Federation in May and the prices actually paid on the market was growing steadily because the merchants, who were in no way bound by Steel Federation prices, were in a position to take advantage of consumer readiness to pay almost any price for iron and steel products. Although legitimate merchants and their organizations sought to exercise a measure of self-control, the condition of the iron market was such as to invite new and unscrupulous elements into the field, who were more ruthless in their hoarding and speculation than the others. Unfortunately, the producers organized in the Steel Federation were not themselves setting a good example. They proved increasingly unwilling to fulfill their obligations and supply the syndicates in accordance with their quotas, and in June, the Steel Works Association reported that customers were being forced to buy semis from Sweden.[3] In August, the Association reminded its members that their hoarding and discriminatory practices rather than actual shortages were responsible for the failure of the producers to meet their obligations to the railroads, and that it was essential to follow priority lists and supply the railroad system before meeting the demands of less vital industries or exporting.

The producers, however, were more concerned about their solvency than they were about their obligations to either their organizations or society at large. Industrialists suffered from a vertically organized structure of anxiety that began with coal, ore, and scrap and then moved on to the difficulties encountered at every stage and level of production and distribution. The serious coal shortage was likely to be compounded by reparations requirements for delivery of coal to service the French iron and steel industry. The continued depreciation of the currency intensified the problem of the Swedish ore debts and made it appear unwise if not impossible to contract new ones. Because of the ore problems, the scrap supply assumed a greater importance than ever before, and there was an acceleration of the tendency to favor open-hearth production. Although there was plenty of scrap around thanks to the junking of war equipment, the price of scrap was rising anyway, and the collapse of the organizations controlling the scrap supply in July made the situation worse. The iron and steel producers hoarded scrap in anticipation of a future ore shortage, and this was incentive enough to extend the practices of hoarding and speculative selling and buying to the scrap market.[4] It was an environment

---

[3] Steel Works Association meeting, June 18, 1919, HA/GHH, Nr. 3000030/12.

[4] Scrap, which cost 43 marks per ton in July 1914 and 67.50 in January 1919, was 170 marks in July and 675–970 marks by early November, reaching a maxi-

that encouraged everyone to think of themselves first and that undermined the commitment to discipline and organization.

If the restraint that had previously existed, however reluctant it
might have been, now gave way to more unconcealed anger, panic, and
self-seeking, this was in no small measure due to the government's loss
of important sources of legitimacy and authority. The democratic
republic had failed to bring Germany the "Wilsonian" peace that large
numbers of German society had unrealistically anticipated of it, and
the way was open for the political right to reassert itself. The political
background of the events discussed in this chapter was such a right-
wing revival, in which industrialists often played an important role
and in which the fateful legends of the "stab in the back" and the
"November criminals" were being disseminated. At the close of the
period, there were demands for new elections and finally an effort to
force a change of the Socialist Party-Center Party-Democratic Party
Weimar Coalition Government of Gustav Bauer in the Kapp Putsch of
March 1920.[5]

Naturally, this crisis of authority extended to the economic functions
of the regime. The new leaders of the RWM, Schmidt and Hirsch, had
backgrounds in the Food Ministry, were most concerned with the
loosening of import restrictions and, during their early months in office,
operated under the principle that the depreciation of the mark was one
of the best ways to make the Entente realize the necessity of revising
the Treaty of Versailles. As a result, there was an initial tendency to
decontrol exports and imports. Such controls were difficult enough
because of the "hole in the West," that is, the occupation of the left
bank of the Rhine and the deliberate encouragement of smuggling by
the occupation authorities. The loose attitude of the RWM toward
foreign trade controls combined with their willingness to eliminate
controls on foreign exchange purchases and sales were nothing less
than invitations to the further deterioration of the mark already given
such a powerful impulse by the war and the treaty. This, in turn, led
to the other phenomena identified with the inflation: the "buying out"
of Germany by foreigners anxious to secure goods at cheap prices, the
"flight from the mark," and the "flight into real values" (*Sachwerte*).[6]

---

mum for the period of 2200 marks per ton in February 1920. See Schlaghecke,
Bewirtschaftung des Eisens, p. 91. There is an excellent report on the development
of the scrap market and problems related to it by the Raw Materials Bureau of
the Bavarian Ministry of Commerce of November 22, 1921, BayHStA, Abt. I,
MWi 6896.

[5] Erich Eyck, *A History of the Weimar Republic*, 2 vols. (Cambridge, 1962), I,
pp. 129–160.

[6] Schieck, *Wirtschaftspolitik*, pp. 256–260, Honhart, *Incomplete Revolution*,
p. 193ff.

It took some time for Schmidt and Hirsch to reverse these policies, and it required pressure from the forces of industry to compel them to do so in certain cases. As might be expected, the authority of the RWM was not strengthened by its mistakes, and the industrialists found themselves torn between the need for a government strong enough to undertake measures they considered necessary and timid enough to accept their will. The problem was compounded by the fact that industry itself was being badly divided by internal differences between raw materials producers and manufacturers.

The RWM thus found itself in the unenviable position of first abandoning the Wissell-Moellendorff program in July, only to resurrect some of its leading characteristics a few months later. This was because producers who had thought themselves liberated from the threat of government control with the defeat of Wissell and Moellendorff proved unable to maintain disciplined self-regulation and succumbed instead to their anxiety, cupidity, and internal divisions. The inevitable result was a reopening of the rift between producers and their manufacturing customers, and this division at once invited and required a government reaction to industry's incapacity to control the consequences of its freedom in the form of mandatory regulatory agencies designed to restrict industrial self-government.

THE STEEL WORKS ASSOCIATION IN DISINTEGRATION AND THE QUEST FOR ALTERNATIVES

At an earlier period of German industrial history, the iron and steel industrialists had sought security from the trials of economic life in those "children of necessity," the cartels. Now, the opposite was to be the case, and the inflation was to be a "cartel-less period" in which the great concerns tried to reconstruct and to reestablish their strength on their own. After the signing of the Treaty, the Steel Works Association was truly on its last legs, and there appeared to be no further reason for restraint in the burying of the dead. In January 1919, when the Steel Works Association was informed by the Lorraine and Luxemburg works that they no longer considered themselves Association members, a decision had been taken not to recognize their withdrawal for political reasons. The German industrial leaders did not want it said that they had anticipated the peace treaty by their actions.[7] With the signing of the Treaty, the withdrawal of the Saar works in July, and the anticipated resignation of the Upper Silesian works once the plebiscite

[7] Steel Works Association Contract Committee meeting, January 15, 1919, HA/GHH, Nr. 3000030/14.

113

called for by the Treaty had taken place, the facade that had long masked its parlous condition was conclusively eliminated. For all intents and purposes, the Steel Works Association had become a regional organization of Rhenish-Westphalian concerns that sold their products at increasingly unsatisfactory prices and felt like fools every time they actually did so. If some of the members, as mentioned earlier, were withholding their products for direct sale, it was not very hard for them to find justifications for doing so. How long could they stand by and watch the iron merchants profiteer from their virtue? Neither the iron merchants nor the customers could distinguish between Rhenish-Westphalian products and their counterparts from the Saar and Lorraine. Works in the latter territories, however, charged a substantially higher price for their products, and merchants quite naturally based their price on the highest price they paid. Thus, neither the Rhenish-Westphalian producer nor the purchaser of his products were allowed to benefit from the relatively low price of material sold through the Steel Works Association, but the merchant was able to make an extra profit by selling at the prices charged by the outsiders. The situation was made all the more anomalous by the fact that industry in South Germany in particular, but in the Ruhr as well, needed to import from the Saar and Lorraine and was compelled to offer higher and higher prices to prevent the Saar-Lorraine works from turning their backs on the German market altogether.

There were other serious grounds for dissatisfaction with the Steel Works Association. Demand for what had been one of its most important sales items, structural steel, had diminished greatly because so little construction was being undertaken at this time. The Upper Silesian works, like their counterparts in the Saar, could get prices 50–100% higher than those attainable through the Steel Works Association. This fact, combined with the political uncertainty about the future of Upper Silesia and the high production costs in that area, lowered their commitment to the Association. Lastly, some of the concerns heavily dependent on foreign ores, such as Rheinstahl, Thyssen, and the Deutsch-Lux, were dissatisfied with the Steel Works Association's pricing policies and were convinced that they could do a much better job of pricing and marketing if they had "the greatest possible flexibility" and could market independently.[8] Despite all these grounds for opposition to the Steel Works Association, however, some of its

[8] Hasslacher at the June 16, 1920, Rheinstahl Supervisory Board meeting, Rheinstahl Archiv, Nr. 123. On the problems of the Steel Works Association, see also Schlaghecke, *Bewirtschaftung des Eisens*, p. 43ff. There are excellent reports by Florian Klöckner of September 5, 1919, and Baron von Buttlar of January 15, 1920, in DZA Potsdam, RWM, Nr. 4453, Bl. 264–265.

members fought for its survival. On the one hand, they feared that the government would not tolerate the dissolution of the last marketing organizations remaining in the industry. On the other hand, many industrialists felt that an organization created with such difficulty should not be so speedily destroyed and that a day would come when industry would need such organizations again—that is, unless new and more viable forms of organization could be found.

The most systematic approach to the question of an alternative form of organization was taken by General Director Vögler. On July 12, 1919, he provided some of the leading industrialists in the Steel Works Association with a revised and up-to-date version of the memorandum on trustification that he had prepared for Stinnes in October 1918.[9] The territorial and economic changes brought about by the Armistice and the Treaty of Versailles made it possible for Vögler to speak quite definitively about the impossibility of retaining the Steel Works Association in its existing form. The Rhenish-Westphalian, Silesian, and Southwestern works could no longer conduct a common pricing and marketing policy. It was futile, therefore, to attempt the reestablishment of a national organization, and it was necessary to construct an organization on the regional level for Rhineland-Westphalia. Vögler thought such an organization desirable for a variety of political and economic reasons. Politically, he thought it essential because the government would "under no circumstances" permit the individual concerns to operate in total freedom. Although he did not believe that even the more radical Socialists were prepared to have the government take over the large concerns, recent government attempts to socialize the Ilseder Hütte Iron Ore Mining and Smelting Concern[10] demonstrated that the government might indulge in piecemeal socialization. Trustification would discourage such efforts. On the economic side, Vögler considered it doubtful that individual concerns could survive the struggle on world markets in the face of the trustification that had already taken place in the United States and the tendencies in this direction in England, France, and Italy. Vögler was convinced that voluntary industrial organization along the lines he was proposing was necessary for Germany's domestic economic development, and

[9] See above, p. 71. The October 27, 1918, version of the memorandum is reprinted in Klass, Vögler, p. 74ff. The June 1919 version, from which the quotations and discussion below are taken, is to be found in HA/GHH, Nr. 3000030/11.

[10] The Reich had heavily subsidized the expansion of the ore mining operations of this concern during the war with the expectation of partial repayment. This was refused after the war by the concern and led to a nationalization drive that was finally defeated because of divisions within the government, but the government did acquire a one-quarter participation in the concern. There is a good summary in Honhart, *Incomplete Revolution*, pp. 195–204.

115

believed that the development of the chemical industry's IG Farben was a model for the iron and steel industry.

Vögler recognized, however, that the concerns could be brought together only by the prospect of profit through cost reduction in production, administration, and marketing. The main body of his memorandum was a sketch of the way in which an *Interessengemeinschaft* (IG) could promote a greater and more systematic division of labor than that provided by the large individual concerns ruling the industry. A common production program for the rolling mills would make it possible to produce one product or group of products in a plant. Vögler pointed out that it was all the more essential to eliminate the time-consuming switching of profiles because the introduction of the eight-hour day had eliminated the pauses between shifts that had been used to make such changes. Vögler was also convinced that great savings in the realm of production could be made through the exchange of information. He placed particular stress, however, on how much could be saved in the area of capital investment if there was a common policy and division of labor in the construction of docks, mines, and plants for the production of plates, pipes, and other products. Instead of each concern rounding out its own individual production program, it would concentrate on its most efficient operations and expand on the basis of the most rational economic and geographical considerations.

Rationalization would not be limited to the sphere of production, however. Common administration of neighboring production units, common purchasing, common utilization of transportation facilities, common advertising and marketing, and common research and development programs would now become possible. The quality of administrative personnel would be improved through the reward of talent with responsibility on a larger scale. Labor questions would be handled more effectively because "a consolidation of works with hundreds of thousands of workers is an employer organization writ small." It would be easier to recruit labor, and a uniform policy of fringe benefits and profit-sharing might help to relieve social discontent and end that "unholy amalgamation of Socialism with the labor movement," which "in and of itself has in large part produced the present confused political conditions."

American trustification, although it was one factor that spurred Vögler into making his proposals, was treated by Vögler with considerable reservation. He thought it too rigid and believed that it hindered technical progress. Vögler thought it essential that the individual members of the IG maintain an identity of their own and as much independence as possible so that the elimination of harmful external competition would not be accompanied by a stultifying elimination of "internal competition." This was why he advocated the IG. The members, who would join together for fifty years, would maintain their individual identity. They would employ a small amount of capital to create a new corporation to serve as an administrative center for the IG. The business managers of this corporation would be members of the boards of directors of the member corporations, and Vögler anticipated that the IG managers would be taken from the boards of these corporations. The common policies of the IG would be determined by this administrative center, and it would also represent the IG in all economic organizations and syndicates. In conclusion, Vögler hoped that this proposal would bring together six or seven of the major Rhenish-Westphalian concerns, and that a block of these firms would be sufficient to compel the outsiders to join eventually. In the meantime, he was certain that the proposed IG would make it easier to create viable syndicates with outsiders.

The rationalization of the German iron and steel industry and the creation of the *Vereinigte Stahlwerke* (United Steel Works) are heralded by the Vögler memorandum, and it is no accident that Vögler was to play such a major role in these postinflationary phenomena.[11] The main concern here, however, is not the fate of Vögler's ideas after 1924, but rather their reception during the period of inflation. The significance of Vögler's scheme in July 1919 was that it offered, at least in part, an alternative to the unsystematic concern building and plant expansion that was to characterize the inflation. It shows how difficult it is to ask whether or not the inflationary period promoted rationalization. As the Vögler memorandum demonstrated, it certainly did promote the idea of rationalization and, insofar as individual concerns succeeded in realizing various economies within their framework, it promoted the reality of rationalization within such a context as well. As will be shown throughout this study, it did not promote the kind of industry-wide rationalization desired by Vögler. Why, then, did Vögler's basic proposals have to await the stabilization period for a measure of realization?

Vögler's memorandum received its most enthusiastic and uncompromising support from August Thyssen. On July 14 the board of directors of the Thyssen concern voted unanimously to support the formation of an IG. Two days later, on July 16, August Thyssen not only echoed Vögler's proposals at a meeting of the Steel Works Association but also went beyond them.[12] Like Vögler, Thyssen thought

[11] See Klass, *Vögler*, pp. 89–91, and below, pp. 457–459.
[12] Treue, *August Thyssen-Hütte*, p. 235, and Steel Works Association meeting, July 16, 1919, HA/GHH, Nr. 3000030/12.

the chemical industry's IG Farben concern had shown the way for the iron and steel industry both in terms of organizational form and in terms of the gradual process of consolidation. Thyssen felt, however, that the process of fusion should not be limited to the Ruhr and that the works on the left bank of the Rhine and in Upper Silesia would also form regional groups of their own and that the three groups would then reach an understanding. In contrast to Vögler, who treated the potential socialization of the coal industry somewhat fatalistically,[13] Thyssen was convinced that the IG had to have coal as well as iron as a foundation. He argued that such a combination would improve the chances of preventing socialization and give the industrialists involved a virtually impregnable position. Indeed, Thyssen was so enthusiastic about Vögler's idea that he was prepared to lengthen the Steel Works Association temporarily despite his distaste for it on the condition that energetic measures be taken to form an IG.

Ironically, however, Vögler received relatively little support from Beukenberg, Stinnes, and Hasslacher. Beukenberg, whose wartime proposal for a fusion of Phoenix and Deutsch-Lux had inspired Stinnes to elicit the first version of the Vögler memorandum, now was filled with reservations. He noted that there were many more firms in the iron and steel industry than in the chemical industry and that their character varied, some being impersonal corporations and others being family concerns. In contrast to Thyssen, Beukenberg thought that an IG would make socialization easier rather than harder, by consolidating the objects to be socialized. Negotiations for an IG would be long and tedious, and Beukenberg knew that very few of his colleagues were serious about forming an IG at this point but that some of them were very serious about eliminating the Steel Works Association. He warned that Berlin would not tolerate either the dissolution of the cartels or their emasculation and urged that they "also think of the future."[14]

Stinnes and Hasslacher, however, were obsessed with present problems and opportunities. They wanted immediate freedom of syndicate controls and restraints. Stinnes did not reject so much as neglect the ideas he had once solicited from Vögler by praising them without giving any concrete support for their practical implementation. Hasslacher, who was to play a major role in implementing some of Vögler's

[13] See his July 12, 1919, memorandum, where he uses the telling sentence, "whether or not the coal industry will be spared, remains uncertain," *ibid.*, Nr. 3000030/11.

[14] Steel Works Association meeting, July 16, 1919, *ibid.*, Nr. 3000030/12, and Woltmann to Reusch, August 20, 1919, Nr. 3000030/17.

ideas five years later, argued that freedom from syndicate controls was the precondition for the kind of organization advocated by Vögler.[15] Hasslacher rejected Thyssen's proposal, a proposal supported by Reusch also, that the Steel Works Association be temporarily prolonged while an effort was made to create an IG. As for Vögler, he had ended up in his characteristic posture. He was a powerful and convincing advocate of freedom from government restrictions and from the poorly functioning syndicates inherited from the past. At the same time, he urged moderation upon his colleagues and the creation of new and more viable forms of business organization. In practice, however, this meant that just as he ended up serving as one of the most effective servants of Stinnes' business interests even where he had strong doubts about his master's policies, so he ended up marching in step with the more immoderate elements in the industry he sought to stabilize. Vögler was by no means unaware of the problem, because he did as much as he could to prevent a complete descent into anarchy on the iron market, but it did not take him long to doubt the ripeness of industry for the creation of an IG because "For this, things appear at the moment to be going too well for us."[16] It was Hasslacher, not Vögler, who predicted what would actually happen, namely that the formation of an IG would develop out of freedom and disorganization and, he might have added as Vögler was beginning to understand, depression. At the same time, it should be recognized that Hasslacher's stand also constituted a self-fulfilling prophecy, because the existing organizations could not survive, even temporarily, if their members refused to cooperate.

The goal of Stinnes and Hasslacher in July 1919, therefore, was not rationalization of industry as a totality, but rather an opportunity to build up their own concerns and solve their own financial problems through free competition. Rheinstahl had been busy creating its own domestic sales organizations and had formed a very lucrative connection with the iron merchandising firm of Otto Wolff. Wolff, who was becoming a major stockholder in Rheinstahl, was closely connected with Dutch financial and industrial interests, and his firm had numerous foreign outlets operating as foreign rather than German trading organizations. Throughout 1919 the Wolff organization was doing a splendid job of rebuilding Rheinstahl's foreign trade and thereby giving Hasslacher good reason to argue that "every work will do better business abroad individually than through an association. We will do better business under a neutral or enemy trading flag than

---

[15] July 16 meeting, *ibid.*, Nr. 3000030/17.
[16] Vögler to Wiedfeldt, October 25, 1919, Krupp WA III, 225.

119

we would if we came forward with syndicates."[17] When it came to the domestic market, Hasslacher admitted that "out of consideration for Berlin something had to happen," and he was prepared to retain the form of the Steel Works Association to satisfy the government's demand for an organization. He insisted, however, that members be permitted to sell all their products directly. He was prepared to have the Steel Works Association set prices, "provided that a pricing policy precisely the opposite of the old one is pursued, and that means that one makes it possible for the works to profit." Hasslacher's colleague, Director Filius, was no less explicit and argued that prices would have to be determined by costs rather than by "fear of the government."[18]

Stinnes was even more radical than Hasslacher in calling for an end to syndicate controls and higher prices. He rejected the idea of retaining syndicates that bound the firms in the slightest way, even for the sake of appearances, and he argued that the syndicates had done a miserable job of adapting effectively to business conditions. Stinnes openly and bluntly advocated using the advantages provided by the inflation to build up production and promote exports where Germany was in the best position to compete, namely in finishing:

> If we have the coal we need, our country will be the natural land of quality production, on the one hand, because of our exchange situation, and, on the other hand, because of our wages, which, in view of our exchange situation, are the lowest in the world. The pricing policy that we have been pursuing has proven totally false. If we continue to follow it, then we will make things such that individual works will go under. The first work that goes under will be bought out and that will be the signal for a general nationalization. We must operate as has been done in the coal

[17] July 16, 1919, meeting, HA/GHH, Nr. 3000030/12. On Wolff's operations, see Chapter 4 below. They were discussed by Hasslacher before the Rheinstahl Supervisory Board on January 16, 1920, Rheinstahl Archiv, Nr. 123. A good illustration of how Wolff (and Rheinstahl) operated under neutral flags was the Dutch firm of Dikema and Chabot, an old and well-reputed Dutch merchant house which, after its owner's death, came under Wolff's control and was, in effect, "the Otto Wolff firm in Holland operating under the clever retention of an old and well-established name." Woltmann to Reusch, HA/GHH, Nr. 3000033/12.

[18] For these various quotes, see the July 16 meeting, *ibid.* Hasslacher's view was shared by Joseph Schumpeter, who argued at the time that "every merchant who smuggles a carload of coal into a factory through all the artificial barriers does more for his people than all the learned writers who—in a completely pre-Marxist manner—act as if human beings have a free choice among all the possible forms of organization." See Joseph Schumpeter, "Sozialistische Möglichkeiten von Heute," *Archiv für Sozialwissenschaft*, 48, 1920–1921, pp. 305–360, p. 360.

industry. We must get together with the workers and give them what they deserve; then we will get the prices we need.[19]

Stinnes rejected the argument of some of his colleagues that the proper thing to do was to try to bring down both prices and wages, and he asked them, in effect, to turn their backs on the attempts at stabilization made during the previous months. He was convinced that high paper wages would keep the workers on the job, just as he knew that high paper profits made it possible to liquidate debts and permit expansion. In short, Stinnes' disagreement with Hasslacher was purely tactical. Hasslacher hoped to keep the government at bay with fake syndicates, whereas Stinnes hoped to keep the workers at bay with inflated currency and not have to pacify the government in any way.

Many of the other industrialists participating in this discussion of July 16 were not as optimistic or as daring as Hasslacher and Stinnes. Director Woltmann of the GHH and Klöckner were certain that the government would not accept a syndicate that controlled neither sales nor prices, and they privately believed that the entire discussion was "a maneuver with the object of blackmailing us into higher prices."[20] This certainly seemed true in part, but it underestimated the very real antagonism felt by Hasslacher and Stinnes toward the Steel Works Association. Director Bruhn, not entirely reflecting the attitude of some of his colleagues on the Krupp Board of Directors, took his usual position of warning that it was easier to tear down syndicates than to build them anew. Nevertheless, it was difficult to find answers to the complaints raised by Hasslacher and Stinnes. As a large producer of merchant bars and structural steel, Hasslacher's Rheinstahl was being hurt by the fact that the syndicate offered it such a low price in comparison to the price that merchants would eventually receive. These were items that were ultimately almost always handled by merchants, and it was understandable that Hasslacher wished to have the advantage of working through his own organizations. Producers of semis were being less badly affected by the Steel Works Association policies because most semis were used for self-consumption, and there was considerable agreement that some form of syndicate was necessary for dealing with the state railways. Attitudes toward the syndicates, however, not only varied according to the relative importance of various types of production and the specific financial difficulties of individual firms, but also according to the economic philosophies and prognostications of individual industrialists. Bruhn, for example,

[19] July 16, 1919, meeting for this and the discussion in the paragraph, HA/GHH, Nr. 3000033/12.
[20] Woltmann to Reusch, July 17, 1919, *ibid.*

believed in syndicates with the kind of conviction that enabled him to brush aside all objections of the moment; Vögler was ever on the lookout for opportunities to promote rationalization; Stinnes was constantly attuned to speculative possibilities. At the same time, all were making the best guesses they could as to where the most promising immediate business prospects lay.[21] Under the existing circumstances, this disorderly state of affairs was hardly very surprising, but the confusion contrasted rather sharply with the claims industrialists had made about the potential effectiveness of industrial self-government. At the same time, this confusion began to serve as an invitation to state intervention.

The need for government props to shore up the tottering industrial organizations was clear in the case of the Steel Works Association. In October 1918 its members agreed to continue the policy of short-term prolongations and extend the Association until June 30, 1919. On April 10, 1919, the Association again voted an extension until September 30, 1919. The real test came in July. On July 24 a majority of the remaining members of the Steel Works Association voted for the prolongation of the Association until December 31, 1919, in opposition to a minority led by Rheinstahl. Under the contract provisions, all members would be released from their contract provisions effective August 1 if this minority did not change its position. When the latter did not occur, the government employed its special powers under the demobilization ordinances to prolong the Steel Works Association until November 30, 1919, but this was communicated privately to the members in the hope that it would induce them to come to terms on their own. If there was to be a private agreement, however, it had to be made before September 1 or the members would again be released from their contract obligations. In August the majority again voted to renew the contract until December 31, largely because they wished to avoid RWM intervention, but Rheinstahl and Deutsch-Lux opposed renewal. They ostentatiously absented themselves from further discussion and indicated that they no longer felt bound by the contract. As a consequence, the RWM acted on August 28, 1919, and openly extended the Steel Works Association until March 1, 1920. As can be imagined, those who had fought to prevent government intervention were irritated at Hasslacher and Stinnes and worried about renewed government intervention. Reusch disgustedly noted: "The position of the Rheinische Stahlwerke that has incited this intervention by the government is very regrettable. 'The spirits that I have summoned, of them will I never be free.' I fear that in the future we will have a government commissar sitting regularly in the syndicate."[22]

The prolongation of the Steel Works Association is illustrative of the manner in which the RWM under Schmidt and Hirsch was being pushed and pulled into a more interventionist posture by the economic situation and by the inability or the unwillingness of the industrialists to control the consequences of their liberty. Although Schmidt and Hirsch had abandoned the long-range organizational schemes of their predecessor and were generally lacking in a real program, they could hardly overlook all long-range considerations in their efforts to cope with immediate problems. Hirsch believed that trustification was essential to the future of the iron and steel industry and, employing tactics not very different from those of Moellendorff, hoped that government encouragement would lead the industrialists to take an initiative. The coal problem gave Hirsch the handle he needed to promote this goal. It was clear to all that the entire complex of production, supply, and pricing of iron and steel products hinged on the coal supply, and it was no less clear there was going to be a coal shortage in the fall and winter coupled with transportation difficulties. The Reich Coal Commissar had already reduced the self-consumption and coal purchasing allotments of the iron and steel plants in June. He was planning further restrictions designed to favor those plants in a position to take maximum advantage of transportation facilities. A curtailment of iron and steel production and the actual shutting down of some plants were anticipated. Clearly, this was a situation conducive to rationalization and consolidation in the industry. Dr. Kind, the Reich Commissar for the Iron Trades in the RWM, thought that the situation was ideally suited for the government to promote the much discussed trustification of the industry. In a memorandum of August 21, 1919, he urged the RWM to use the coal supply problem to encourage fusion. Kind's emphasis, however, was on encouragement rather than action. He warned that industrialists and bankers were nervous about the government's taxation plans and the recurrent threats of socialization. They needed to be reassured that the government was not planning to play a far-reaching role if they were to engage in serious discussions and follow them up with action.[23]

---

[22] Reusch to Karl Haniel, August 4, 1919, *ibid.*, 30019300/5. The details of these various prolongations and conflicts between the government and Rheinstahl and Deutsch-Lux may be found in DZA Potsdam, RWM, Nr. 5602, and Rheinstahl Archiv, Nr. 650.

[23] Kind's memorandum is to be found in DZA Potsdam, RWM, Nr. 4616, Bl. 299ff. Although a government commissar, Kind was paid most of his income by

The truth of Dr. Kind's remarks was amply demonstrated when Undersecretary Hirsch held a meeting with the leading producers on September 11 to discuss "the impending coal emergency and its effect upon the iron industry and pending cartel questions."[24] He advertised the meeting as a strictly confidential and purely exploratory discussion in which he hoped that everyone would speak frankly. Hirsch told the industrialists that the government preferred self-help to state intervention. As might be expected, the industrialists agreed with this principle and then launched an attack on the Reich Coal Commissar. They warned against allowing him to expand his prerogative of allocating coal among the concerns by permitting him to allocate coal among the various plants within concerns. While urging that the government permit them to shut down plants as they deemed economically desirable, they warned against the government itself trying to undertake such measures with "expert" assistance. Although it was usual for the industrialists to argue that the government summon "experts" from industry before making decisions, Peter Klöckner now argued that it was impossible to find true experts because "every expert is at the same time an interested party."

The industrialists showed remarkably little enthusiasm for the rationalization proposals of the RWM and expressed an almost boundless distrust of the government. They did not deny that some cutbacks in their coal supply might be necessary, but they insisted that such coal problems could best be handled by a friendly understanding among neighboring plants on an *ad hoc* basis. When Hirsch gingerly suggested that such last-minute agreements could prove economically wasteful and tactfully inquired if it might not make more sense "to speed up somewhat the unavoidable process of fusion at the outset," he received a bit more frankness than he had probably bargained for when he began the discussion. Klöckner informed him that "We do not need to play hide-and-seek here. Industry as well as the banking world has no confidence in the present government. The situation is

---

the Steel Federation. Economics Minister Schmidt did not seem to know this and was shocked when he learned about it from Peter Klöckner, who was angry at Kind for persuading the RWM to eliminate the compulsory scrap marketing organizations in July 1919. Klöckner had an interest in them and suffered by the change. Although Kind was friendly to industry, he did not seem to please Vögler and Stinnes very much either, because he supported syndicalization. Vögler accused him of being "completely in the line of Bruhn," and Stinnes agreed with Vögler in hoping that Kind could be thrown out of office soon. See Vögler to Stinnes, October 30, 1919, Nachlass Stinnes, in private possession. The document was generously placed at my disposal by Prof. Henry Turner.

[24] For the discussion and quotations from the meeting of September 11, 1919, that follow, see DZA Potsdam, RWM, Nr. 4616, Bl. 264–272.

still too incalculable. . . ." Hirsch was informed that until uncertainty about the government's tax plans was reduced, no one was going to supply the large amounts of capital necessary for trustification. Director Kurt Wiedfeldt of Krupp added that businessmen and bankers were worried about state bankruptcy and also worried about talk of socialization. He concluded that "The general uncertainty and concern about the future causes every firm to keep its financial situation as liquid as possible above all so that, if it is necessary, it can at least have as respectable a bankruptcy as possible."

The underlying tone of unpleasantness in these remarks showed that many of the industrialists had lost their taste for a statesman-like posture in the face of the general economic difficulties and such irritations as the taxation program of Finance Minister Erzberger, which was designed to tax war profits heavily and corporate as well as individual wealth.[25] They were now prepared to pursue their own interests even at the expense of alienating the government. The change is ironic when one considers the more diplomatic handling of the much more dangerous Wissell-Moellendorff administration of the RWM by the big producers. Politically, however, the right was beginning to recover while the seemingly desperate economic situation created a "now or never" attitude among some of the producers. Iron industrialists now felt either strong enough or desperate enough to declare that they were "primarily responsible to their stockholders and could not take responsibility for giving out their stockholders' money solely in the interest of the rest of the German economy,"[26] and actually to threaten noncompliance with the orders of Coal Commissar Köngeter. The latter could only respond by warning of the "serious consequences" that resistance would bring, and it was rapidly to become clear that industrialist aggressiveness was forcing the weak Schmidt-Hirsch administration into increasing aggressiveness itself.

This breakdown of the armistice between the producers and the government was to have more lasting consequences in the area of pricing than in the altercations over the coal supply or the theoretical discussions about fusion. In the late spring and early summer the Steel Federation had tried to pursue a moderate course despite the growing disparity between its prices and the prices actually paid on the market. The prices set in April were allowed to stand for May, June, and July. On July 10, to the joy of the manufacturers and the extreme irritation of the minority of producers led by Hasslacher and

[25] On the Erzberger program, see Klaus Epstein, *Matthias Erzberger and the Dilemma of German Democracy* (Princeton, 1959), p. 369ff.

[26] Meeting with Coal Commissar Köngeter on September 16, 1919, see DZA Potsdam, RWM, Nr. 4616, Bl. 221–222.

Stinnes, the producers decided not to raise prices for July despite an increase in costs. (See Table 7.) They wished to await the effects of a government effort to reduce food prices and thereby stabilize wages. It was this decision of July 10 that had pushed the opponents of the Steel Works Association into taking such an extreme stand at the meeting of July 16 discussed earlier, where they argued that it was better to raise wages if this was the only way to raise prices. The majority of the producers, however, were unwilling to sabotage the government's efforts at this point, and they also noted that the trade union leaders strongly opposed a price increase and demanded stabilization. There was a price increase in August, but it was moderate and justifiable by any standard. Furthermore, just as the majority of producers demonstrated moderation in the pricing decisions in the Steel Federation, so too did they maintain their agreement with the finishing industries on delivery conditions of April.[27]

By September, however, it was patently clear that the chaos on the market and the increasing dissatisfaction of the producers would lead to demands for a significant price increase in October. The RWM Commissar at the Steel Federation, Florian Klöckner, the brother of Peter Klöckner and a leading industrialist himself, was no friend of government controls, but he had to admit that the differences among the various prices charged for the same iron and steel products had produced a "situation of complete anarchy" on the iron market from which merchants rather than producers or consumers had the greatest advantage. As might be expected, Klöckner opposed the reintroduction of price ceilings, but he argued that the RWM "had in the future to secure itself a much greater influence over future pricing decisions by the producers as well as by the merchants." He proposed that the government's wartime influence on pricing through the auditing of cost calculations be reintroduced "so that, as far as possible, exaggerated demands could be rejected with official sanction."[28] Klöckner was urging that the RWM depart from its policy of relative inaction and no longer limit itself to exerting tacit pressure by attending pricing discussions at the Steel Federation and expressing its views after decisions had been made. Instead, the RWM was to conduct its own investigations prior to Steel Federation meetings and decide on what it would allow. This procedure, however, had certain ambi-

---

[27] See the July 10, 1919, meeting and the memorandum of the Association of German Shipyard Works, July 2, 1919, in BA, R 13 I/420, Bl. 63–65, 75–78, 92; also, Woltmann to Reusch, July 17, 1919, HA/GHH, Nr. 3000030/12, and Schlaghecke, *Bewirtschaftung des Eisens*, p. 62.

[28] Florian Klöckner to RWM, September 5, 1919, DZA Potsdam, RWM, Nr. 4453, Bl. 264–265.

TABLE 7

The Price of Various Iron and Steel Products, July 1919–April 1920
(price per ton measured in paper and gold marks)

		July	August	September	October	November	December	January	February	March	April
Foundry pig iron III	PM	438.00	516.50	516.50	651.50	651.50	913.50	1323.50	1625.00	1665.00	1775.00
	GM	121.97	115.19	90.19	101.97	71.42	82.03	85.78	68.86	83.36	125.00
Hematite pig iron	PM	460.50	573.50	573.50	735.50	735.50	1718.50	2120.00	2125.50	2338.50	2350.50
	GM	128.24	127.90	100.14	115.12	80.63	111.38	93.65	110.92	164.68	212.39
Billets	PM	450.00	575.67	575.67	575.67	1050.00	1050.00	2072.00	2072.00	2072.00	2776.00
	GM	132.28	139.38	109.13	129.13	90.44	134.70	97.22	95.77	116.40	163.73
Girders	PM	520.00	715.00	715.00	965.00	965.00	1715.00	1715.00	2620.00	2685.00	2772.00
	GM	144.81	159.46	124.85	151.04	105.79	154.01	111.15	111.03	134.42	195.21
Merchant bars	PM	550.00	745.00	745.00	995.00	995.00	1745.00	1745.00	2650.00	2715.00	2802.00
	GM	153.16	166.15	130.09	155.74	109.08	156.70	133.09	110.17	132.70	186.62
Heavy plate	PM	615.00	835.00	835.00	1185.00	1185.00	2235.00	2235.00	3415.00	3435.00	3435.00
	GM	171.26	186.22	145.80	185.48	129.91	200.70	144.86	144.72	171.97	241.90

Source: Hans J. Schneider, *Zur Analyse des Eisenmarkts* (*Vierteljahrshefte zur Konjunkturforschung*, Sonderheft 1) (Berlin, 1927), p. 103.

guities, because it meant a preemption of the self-governing prerogatives of the Steel Federation. The industrialists knew that the government was interested in the decisions of the Steel Federation, and they
had exercised some care about securing government approval despite
the absence of official price ceilings. All along, however, they had
assumed that prices agreed upon by all parties in the Steel Federation—producers, consumers, and workers—would be accepted by
the RWM. Klöckner's procedure, which was adopted by the RWM,
thus opened the way to a potential conflict.

Although it might sound surprising that an industrialist like Florian
Klöckner was proposing greater RWM involvement in pricing decisions, it is important to remember the lack of unanimity among producers on the question of pricing. At the meeting in the RWM on
September 11, for example, Sandmann of the Thyssen firm and Wiedfeldt of Krupp argued that domestic prices should be permitted to
reach the level of world market prices, while Peter Klöckner warned
against letting this happen too quickly. Hirsch and his colleagues in
the RWM, however, had no intention of permitting domestic prices
to soar because this would have raised the cost-of-living and the wage
demands of the workers while ruining the export advantages of German manufacturers. These conflicting points of view were reiterated
at a meeting between the RWM and representatives of the industrialists on September 30, at which time the RWM officials insisted that
the firms calling for a price increase present cost calculations justifying their demands. Thus, the procedure advocated by Florian Klöckner
was being followed.[29]

At the Steel Federation meeting of October 8, however, this procedure led to conflict when the Steel Federation defied Dr. Susat of the
RWM and voted for a compromise increase of 250 marks proposed by
Klöckner, which was above the 200 marks Susat would allow but below the 300 marks the producers, manufacturers, and workers in the
RWM were prepared to accept. Economics Minister Schmidt and
Undersecretary Hirsch were distressed by this action, which they
viewed as "an infringement of the authority of the state,"[30] but the
matter was not so simple. There were no price ceilings, and there was
no law that required the Steel Federation, which was a purely private
organization, to accept a RWM veto, particularly where all interested
parties in the Federation had come to an agreement. Although the
Federation members had made a practice of securing RWM approval
for their decisions, the RWM had not been insisting on an investigation to justify increases above some fixed amount on which it had

[29] See *Stahl und Eisen*, 39:2, October 16, 1919, p. 1263.
[30] Meeting of October 8, 1919, HA/GHH, Nr. 3000035/3.

settled. Ernst Poensgen of the Phoenix concern, who had replaced Beukenberg as chairman of the Steel Federation, tried to mollify the ruffled feelings of the RWM officials by securing a few concessions from his colleagues. The tension between the RWM and the producers was exacerbated during the coming months, however, when the scenario of the October Steel Federation meeting was more or less repeated with different numbers and the industrialists paid increasingly less heed to the "small souls" running the RWM.[31]

This contempt for the RWM felt by the producers was accompanied by a growing aggressiveness and ruthlessness in the fall and winter of 1919–1920. The most important measure of this aggressiveness was not to be found in the realm of price increases in the Steel Federation, but rather in the sphere of delivery conditions. On October 9, Poensgen announced the end of the Düsseldorf Agreement of the previous April:

> Reliable calculation has become an impossibility because of the leaps taken by the exchange rate. The works committed an act of stupidity with their agreement about stable prices at the end of April that cost much money. Therefore, we cannot maintain the previous practice of selling at stable prices, and we must go over to sliding prices again.[32]

As might be expected, the iron consumers were more than a little alarmed at what one of them characterized as "a declaration of bankruptcy for our entire iron trade." Dr. Fabian of the state railways pointed out that the government was already having to purchase through the black market and warned that "sliding prices mean sliding business morals."[33] The trouble was, as Dr. Susat pointed out, that morals were deteriorating anyway because the prices fixed by the Steel Federation were not being honored. Both Fabian and Susat were correct, but the decision to abandon stable prices was only the beginning of a series of extremely ruthless practices with regard to delivery conditions. In December the Pig Iron Syndicate began demanding payment in foreign currency calculated at an artificially low rate, and the firms in the Steel Works Association soon joined with demands not only for payment in foreign exchange but also for partial payment in scrap calculated below the market price.[34] By the end of 1919 it had become clear that the producers were fleeing from the mark and seeking their salvation by attempting to charge so-called world market

[31] Reusch to Wieland, February 25, 1920, *ibid.*, Nr. 300193901/29.
[32] October 9, 1919, meeting, *ibid.*, Nr. 3000035/3.
[33] *Ibid.*
[34] Schlaghecke, *Bewirtschaftung des Eisens*, pp. 91–92.

prices. This was a policy, however, that not only defied the RWM but also cut across the interests of the finished product manufacturers.

Under these conditions, organizational questions were necessarily more political than economic in character. Few producers were willing to consider seriously Vögler's trustification proposals and RWM encouragement of rationalization because neither the political situation nor the inflation made them attractive. The producers who were most ruthlessly exploiting the inflation were those most opposed to the retention of the Steel Works Association for the obvious reason that organizations of any kind meant greater possibilities for control, whereas producers trying to save the existing organizations were moved by political considerations and the calculation that industrial self-government was the surest means of warding off government intervention. The inability of the producers to maintain unity in their own house and their business practices, however, made them increasingly vulnerable to state intervention, particularly because of the accompanying breakdown of their relations with their manufacturing customers.

"ONWARD TO WORLD MARKET PRICES!"

The period between November 1919 and April 1920 was one of exacerbated materials shortage and moral deterioration in the German business community, and the iron and steel industry exhibited both features at their worst. Transportation difficulties compounded the problems created by the coal shortage. There was frost, flooding, equipment deterioration, blockades in the Baltic, railroad strikes, and a shipping shortage. The depreciation of the mark had made it difficult to purchase Swedish ores in any case, but in January it proved impossible to move even 150,000 tons of German ores because of the transportation problems. Hoarding, black marketeering, and smuggling were the order of the day. The "hole in the West" made it possible to smuggle out an estimated 150,000 tons of iron and steel a month and thereby deprive the domestic economy of vitally needed material. The unwillingness of the German government to set up a firm customs boundary at the eastern border of the unoccupied zone for political reasons, and the rapacity of the occupying powers in refusing to permit Germany an effective border control in the West, were of great importance in turning the country into a gigantic bargain basement for foreign purchasers. Germany was being "bought out," and it took the German government and German manufacturers some time to develop the export controls necessary to sell at appropriate prices. While the iron and steel producers abandoned all restraint in their pricing policies, the finishing industries began to run out of capital necessary for the purchase of raw materials and the continued operation of their plants. Their wartime reserves were being used up and domestic demand was declining despite the continued hunger for materials. The producers had decided to pay their Swedish ore debts and maintain their financial solvency at all costs, and the manufacturers felt that these costs were being transferred to them. The result was a bitter debate and conflict between the iron and steel producers, on the one hand, and the finished product manufacturers, on the other hand.[35]

This conflict over the producer slogan of "onward to world market prices" (*Heran an die Weltmarktpreise*) was conducted on both a theoretical and a practical level. Although the latter is crucial for an understanding of the political and institutional decisions taken in connection with the organization of the iron and steel industry, the former is important for a comprehension of the total environment in which decisions were being made. It is easy enough to relate interests and theoretical positions, and considerable evidence will be provided later as to the extent to which monetary, fiscal, credit, and business policies were defended and pursued by political and industrial leaders with an interest in promoting inflation for political and economic reasons.[36] Contemporary understanding of the inflation, however, was extremely inadequate. Indeed, the term "inflation" was scarcely used in the literature on monetary theory, let alone understood. The leading officials of the Reichsbank were particularly ignorant in matters of monetary theory, and although they had sought to prevent and discourage critical discussion of their note coverage policies and generous credit policies, the evidence suggests that they sincerely believed in their highly formalistic notions concerning what actually constituted money as well as in their obligation to provide the economy with the means necessary to keep operating.[37] Similarly, many businessmen persisted in believing that "a mark equals a mark" and failed to comprehend or did not wish to comprehend that they were cheating themselves when they exported at prices calculated in German currency. Furthermore, it is essential to have a dynamic appreciation of the manner in which positions and attitudes changed or became modified by constantly

[35] Valuable information on the economic situation is provided by the monthly reports of the RWM sent to the President of the Republic. For the reports of January–April 1920, see BA, R 43 I/1147, Bl. 32ff.

[36] See especially Chapters 5–6.

[37] See Czada in *Finanz- und wirtschaftspolitsche Fragen*, pp. 10–17, for a good discussion of the problem and the literature. An important work on the status of monetary theory at the time is Howard S. Ellis, *German Monetary Theory 1905–1933* (Cambridge, 1937), p. 203ff.

changing, unfamiliar, and unpredictable situations. Clearly, for example, the producers never would have concluded the April Düsseldorf agreement with the manufacturers if they had the conviction that they were going to regret it as an "act of stupidity" in October. As shall be shown, even among industrialists who knowingly and skillfully employed the inflation to their advantage, there was a considerable sense of unease while doing so as well as a desire to return to normal conditions. Under these mercurial circumstances, there was bound to be a very close relationship between theory, or what passed for theory, and practice.

Fittingly enough, the focus of much of the theoretical debate among businessmen was provided by the speeches and writings of the business manager of the VdESI, Dr. Jacob Reichert, who presented his views to a variety of business audiences throughout the fall of 1919 and then gave them final and comprehensive form in a highly influential pamphlet written in November 1919 and published in December 1919 under the title "The Way Out of the Exchange Emergency" (*Rettung aus der Valutanot*).[38] In his argument, Reichert proved true to the most fundamental characteristics of his career as business manager of the VdESI. He sought to reconcile producer and manufacturer interests by proving that what was good for the former would benefit the latter if only the manufacturers followed the lead of the producers and adjusted to their wishes. At the same time, he defended the notion of state protection of industrial interests under maximum industrial self-regulation. The outcome was a neatly packaged argument that sounded remarkably convincing to those wishing to believe it and that did considerable credit to Reichert's talents as an "organization man" if not to his abilities as a theorist.

Reichert's explanation of the fall of the German mark was more descriptive than analytical and was not lacking in tendentious qualities of a political nature. After reminding his readers of those happy prewar years when small exchange difficulties were easily remedied by the export of gold, he pointed out that all countries involved in the war suffered from a diminution in the value of their currencies. Although Germany suffered the most in this respect, it was not until the "November revolution condemned Germany to powerlessness"[39] that the collapse of the mark assumed the character of a long-term and

[38] Jacob Reichert, *Rettung aus der Valutanot* (Berlin, 1919). There is a strong relationship between the economic and political views of Reichert and those of his more famous DNVP party colleague, Karl Helfferich. See John G. Williamson, *Karl Helfferich 1872–1924. Economist, Financier, Politician.* (Princeton, 1971), pp. 342n, 387.

[39] *Ibid.*, p. 8.

dangerous phenomenon. It might be pointed out that this suggestion that the November 1918 Revolution was an economic stab-in-the-back fitted in very nicely with the analogous political and military legends being fomented by Field Marshal von Hindenburg before the Reichstag subcommittee investigating the German collapse during the very month Reichert was writing his pamphlet. The latter was not the place for Reichert to give full expression to his political inclinations, however, and he did not blame everything on the Revolution.[40] Appropriately, his major concern was with the immediate economic situation, and he sought to convince his readers that it was a mistake to base economic policy on the expectation that the mark would rise in value if one waited long enough. Reichert confessed that he had entertained such delusions himself. Initially, he thought that the termination of price ceilings would lead to a brief series of price increases and then stabilization. Then, at the beginning of 1919, he thought that domestic and world prices would fall into line as German prices gradually ceased to rise and world prices began to sink. It had now become clear to him, however, that the wartime price controls, however justified, were taking their revenge, that Germany was finding it impossible to get a favorable balance of trade, and that Germany was being bought out because of her insufficient export controls and a deteriorating currency. In his view, the time had come for a more active policy that would "unconditionally base itself upon the facts"[41] rather than upon hopes. Otherwise, Germany would face collapse and new revolutionary upheavals.

There were two keys to the solution of the exchange problem in Reichert's view. The first of these was the rigorous control of imports and exports. Reichert could and did boast of a very early and active role in this area. In the fall of 1915 he had been one of those to bring the exchange question to the attention of the government, and he had been important in promoting the creation of export syndicates as well as directly involved in the entire question in his capacity as head of the Central Agency for Export Permits for Iron and Steel Products. In the fall of 1918 he had been reserved about the elimination of government export controls, although he did tend to accept the argument that the elimination of domestic price ceilings would eliminate the need for most export controls.[42] He quickly reverted to his earlier position of support for export controls, however, in early

[40] He was more explicit at private meetings, as for example at the VdESI Executive Directors meeting on February 27, 1920, where he argued that the "revolution alone cut the ground from under our feet," BA, R 131/157. See also Eyck, *History*, p. 137ff.

[41] Reichert, *Rettung*, p. 9.   [42] See above, p. 85.

1919, and although he was highly critical of the Wissell-Moellendorff organizational schemes, he felt that they were absolutely correct in their demand for the control of imports and exports. By contrast, Reichert could not abide the relaxed policies of the Schmidt-Hirsch regime. In Reichert's view, it was essential to prevent unnecessary imports and just as essential to control exports to prevent continued exportation at cut-rate prices either out of ignorance or out of a desire to keep up relations with foreign customers. He pointed out that Germany was being bought out and cheated of a proper return on her materials and labor. At the same time, he remarked that foreign employers, trade unions, and governments were complaining bitterly about German dumping and beginning to take countermeasures.

In making this case for export controls, Reichert could exploit the authority of some of the leaders of the manufacturing industries, and he stressed an article by Felix Deutsch of the AEG that demonstrated the extent to which manufacturers of cranes, machines, locomotives, and other manufactured products were selling at prices far below those of non-German competitors.[43] Indeed, Reichert's view of Schmidt and Hirsch was widely shared in industrial circles. Hans von Raumer, the business manager of the Central Association of German Electro-Technical Manufacturers, to provide yet another significant example, was particularly distressed by the foreign trade policy of Schmidt, who seemed to feel that German dumping would compel the other powers to recognize Germany's economic problems and give Germany an international loan to help the defeated nation back on her feet.[44]

Reichert, however, did not stop with the employment of his criticism of the absence of sufficient export controls as a weapon against the RWM. He also very shrewdly criticized the manufacturing industries in order to drive home his argument for what he considered to be the second key to solving the exchange problem, namely, an unrestricted and unhampered development of domestic prices. It was here that Reichert departed from the views of Wissell and Moellendorff as well as from the majority of the manufacturers.[45] He noted that although the quantity of iron and steel exported had diminished substantially between 1914 and 1919, the value of these exports had increased considerably, whereas the value of manufactured products exported, despite their greater intrinsic value, had increased far less.

[43] Reichert, *Rettung*, p. 13ff., for his discussion of the import-export question. The Deutsch article appeared in the *Vossische Zeitung* on November 9, 1919.

[44] Raumer to Saemisch, November 24, 1919, BA, Nachlass Saemisch, Nr. 8, Bl. 40.

[45] Reichert to Moellendorff, November 24, 1919, and Moellendorff draft of his reply in which this was expressed, BA, Nachlass Moellendorff Nr. 4.

How was the difference between the export profits of the iron and steel producers and those of the manufacturers of finished products to be explained? In part, Reichert attributed it to ignorance of the currency situation, overestimation of foreign competition, and insufficient organization. These aspects of the problem could be handled through strict export controls. Yet this was not the whole answer. No less important in explaining the low export profits of the manufacturers was the low domestic prices they paid for their raw materials! The iron and steel producers understood what world market prices were really all about because they were compelled to purchase foreign ores. They knew the difference between the mark and the krone; they knew the prices that should be charged for German exports. Manufacturers, in contrast, were unable to learn this lesson because they paid such low prices for German iron and steel, and they would not learn this lesson until the domestic price of German iron and steel was permitted to rise freely to world market levels.[46]

This clever twist Reichert gave to his argument for export controls was hardly very convincing by itself, because rigorous export controls might have proven "education" enough for the manufacturers. The chief force of Reichert's argument for a free pricing policy was directed against government efforts to prevent the producers from following the policy he was advocating. Reichert attacked the "evil dilettantism" of Minister Matthias Erzberger, whose tax programs and plans to reduce currency circulation and to consolidate the debt were viewed with great suspicion by the business community. The only point on which Reichert agreed with the hated Finance Minister was on the need to increase production. Similarly, Reichert was utterly contemptuous of recent declarations by Schmidt and Hirsch in favor of consumer protection and action against profiteers. Reichert could not accept Hirsch's argument that "consumer socialism" was necessary so long as there was a scarcity and that effective action could be taken against profiteering. Business immorality, according to Reichert, was the product of controls in the first place, and the way to protect consumers was to increase production and to eliminate the incentives for hoarding. This could only be done if one obeyed the "law of world market prices," for "The exchange rate is so all-powerful that all producers must bow before it whether they want to or not. It is the exchange rate that rules and guides prices. How can one speak of the superior power of the producers over the consumers?"[47] The only solution, therefore, was to free prices of all restraints and permit them to rise to their natural levels. Reichert recognized that this would

[46] Reichert, *Rettung*, pp. 23–25.
[47] *Ibid.*, pp. 56–57.

135

increase the domestic cost of living, and he argued that salaries and pensions would have to be increased and that everything possible should be done to raise wages. Like Stinnes, Reichert was no supporter of wage stabilization, and he expected the union leaders and the employers to work together in keeping wages high.[48] Thus, strict import-export controls at Germany's borders and the elimination of informal and formal controls within Germany constituted Dr. Reichert's prescription for Germany's dire economic situation. He sang a veritable paean to the glories that the elimination of domestic price restraints would bring:

> It alone helps to increase the national production of goods, to a complete satisfaction of domestic demand, to an increase of the quantity and value of exports, to a better regulation of imports and exports, to a strengthening of our foreign credit, to a way out of the exchange emergency, to the prevention of our being drained of goods, to the payment of our debts, to an increase of our tax receipts, to an increase of our national wealth. All this will be created for us by the enlivening and refreshing power of free price determination and individual entrepreneurship.[49]

As might be expected, Reichert's program received its strongest support in producer circles, because it encouraged them to continue the pricing policy they either were pursuing already or were inclined to pursue. Nevertheless, even here there were critics of both key aspects of his program. Although everyone agreed that German firms had been selling too cheaply abroad, not everyone felt that effective preventive action could be taken through export controls. Reusch, for example, fatalistically argued that the channels of trade were too complex to be controlled effectively.[50] Reusch, however, unlike Director Bruhn of Krupp and General Director Becker of the Stahlwerke Becker, came to the conclusion that domestic pricing had to be freed of restraints despite his own support of a relatively moderate pricing policy. Bruhn and Becker, in contrast, were convinced that allowing domestic prices to rise very rapidly was a very dangerous experiment. They wondered if it even made sense of talking about "world market prices" when so many currencies had diminished in value and where conditions fluctuated in such a confusing manner. At the same time, they feared that

[48] "There must be no talk of a reduction of wages," *ibid.*, p. 58.

[49] *Ibid.*, pp. 69–71. Reichert seems to have been very fond of this enthusiastic paragraph, which he repeated with the same elation at the VdESI meeting of February 27, 1920, BA, R 13 I/157, and in an article summarizing his views in *Stahl und Eisen*, 39:2, November 20, 1919, p. 1435.

[50] For Reusch's views, see *ibid.*, p. 1436.

the experiment of a rapid *de facto* devaluation of the mark involved serious social risks. If the attempt to bring domestic prices into line with world market prices in the context of a wage-price spiral failed because of speculation on the money market or other untoward economic developments, then Germany could find itself in the position of having suddenly to reduce excessively high wages and prices. They did not think that wage reduction could be accomplished without serious labor conflicts and domestic disturbances.[51]

Predictably, the strongest opposition to Reichert's program came from the finished product manufacturers. With the exception of mavericks such as the Altona machine builder, Director Johannes Menck, who argued passionately for the elimination of every type of control on exports, imports, and domestic prices,[52] most manufacturers recognized the need for foreign trade controls. What they objected to was Reichert's advocacy of attempting to reach world market prices and his casual approach to a price-wage spiral. They contested the theoretical as well as the practical foundations of this position. The influential General Director Otto Schrey, the Chairman of the Association of German Railroad Car Manufacturers, pointed out that the liquidity needed to meet the domestic price increases advocated by Reichert could be met only by "putting the printing presses into motion" and pointedly asked "is that a measure likely to improve our exchange rate?"[53] Schrey also wondered who would have the courage or the money to raise wages as speedily or as substantially as might be necessary if Reichert's proposals were followed. Lastly, Schrey did not fully comprehend Reichert's passion to reduce the difference between Germany's domestic and foreign prices in view of the advantages that this difference had brought in the struggle to restore Germany's position on world markets.

Reichert remained remarkably cheerful and confident in the face of these attacks. He was firmly convinced that they would have to "obey the all-powerful law of the world market," but he reassured his critics that world market prices would continue to go up for a long time and that Germany would retain her export advantages if the policy of export controls he advocated were followed. Reichert and his chief ally among the finished product manufacturers, Director Menck,

[51] For Becker's views, see *ibid.*, pp. 1431–1433; Bruhn's arguments appear in an article in *ibid.*, November 6, 1919, pp. 1356–1359.

[52] *Ibid.*, November 27, 1919, pp. 1492–1493. Menck may have been reflecting the general view of the Hamburg merchants, who opposed all foreign trade controls.

[53] For this quotation and the discussion below, see the February 27, 1920, VdESI Executive Directors meeting, BA, R 13 I/157.

sought to persuade the finishers that much of the hoarding and cheating on the iron market would be eliminated if there was freedom in domestic pricing. Few manufacturers, however, were willing to join Menck and declare that they were ready to pay any price for raw material, and their experience did not lead them to share Menck's certainty that they could get material for any price. Director Moritz Klönne, a Dortmund machine manufacturer, saw only one way out of the situation confronting the manufacturers, and that was the reintroduction of government controls, "naturally on a reasonable basis but in such a way that the iron consuming industry in Germany is supplied first and that then the surplus can be exported."

As Klönne's comment demonstrates, the debate over Reichert's program and the producers' practices was something more than an enriching intellectual exercise designed to enliven the pages of *Stahl und Eisen*[54] and to provide stimulating discussion at VdESI meetings. Much of the decorum was on the surface, and it covered an accelerating tendency on the part of the manufacturers to take their complaints and demands to the government. Indeed, the government received a mountain of manufacturer protests during this period. The tone and emphasis of these petitions varied, however. Klönne, for example, who was the head of a newly organized Association of Employers of Medium-Sized and Small Factories of the Iron Industry, placed more emphasis on supply than on prices in his letters to the RWM. He and his colleagues were prepared to surrender exchange they received from exports to help the producers pay their ore debts if only the producers would supply needed raw materials. For other manufacturers, however, prices assumed an equally important or even higher place in their petitions for relief when the producers began demanding partial payment in foreign exchange or scrap. A Dortmund railroad equipment manufacturer, Both & Tilmann, thought that although the operation proposed by Reichert of raising domestic to foreign price levels might cure the practice of exporting at cut-rate prices, the increased prices combined with the constant wage increases granted in the course of "endless negotiations in the *Arbeitsgemeinschaften*" would ruin small corporations lacking the capital and credit needed to sustain such policies.[55]

[54] *Stahl und Eisen*, 39:2, 1919, ran a lengthy series of commentaries and articles by prominent industrialists on all sides of the question in its October and November issues.

[55] Both & Tilmann to the RWM, November 29, 1919, DZA Potsdam, RWM, Nr. 5679, Bl. 45–48; Klönne to RWM, November 19, 1919, *ibid.*, Nr. 4610, Bl. 81ff,, and December 5, 1919, *ibid.*, Bl. 119–121; Henrich to Siemens, February 27, 1920, SAA 4/Lf 669.

The bitterest complaints about prices, however, were made concerning those hidden in the form of special payment conditions in foreign exchange and scrap. The Motorenfabrik Berusse reported in March 1920 that the rolling mills were demanding a quantity of scrap double in weight to that of every delivery and that they were offering only 80 marks for 100 kilos when the going market price was 180–200 marks. Perhaps the most fulsome expression of the difficulties and anger of the manufacturers was provided by the United Association of Textile Machine Builders in a gravamina to the RWM of March 26, 1920. This association pointed out that it was well supplied with contracts, but that a large proportion of these had been made before the catastrophic decline of the mark and had been drawn up for payment in marks. These contracts required nine to twelve months for completion because of the kind of work required and because of the raw materials shortage. The decline of the mark, however, had required that many of these contracts be cancelled or renegotiated to prevent serious financial losses. In the midst of this situation, the Pig Iron Syndicate and other raw materials suppliers suddenly began demanding partial payment in foreign exchange at an exchange rate calculated at 30% below what the same foreign currency was rated on the money market. The textile machine builders denied that they possessed such quantities of foreign exchange, and they wanted to know where heavy industry received the right to insist on a rate of exchange less favorable than that offered by the banks.[56]

It should not be thought that all the complaints came from one side or that all the justice was to be found on the side of the manufacturers. One of the latter, for example, expressed criticism of its fellows and outrage "that a part of today's manufacturing industry purchases iron and steel in marks at domestic prices and then sells the finished goods at export prices in foreign exchange. . . ."[57] Furthermore, it should be noted that the miscalculations made by manufacturers in their export pricing policies reflected an ignorance and misinformation that could hardly be blamed on the producers. The VDMA seems to have done a miserable job of supplying up-to-date intelligence to its members.[58] What must also be recognized, however, is that the entire economic situation was one that gave the producers immense advantages and power over the manufacturers. It was natural for some of these manu-

[56] United Association of Textile Machine Builders to RWM, March 26, 1920, DZA Potsdam, RWM, Nr. 4540, Bl. 220–227, and Motorenfabrik-Berusse to RWM, March 4, 1920, *ibid.*, Nr. 5683, Bl. 149–150.

[57] Otto Mansfeld and Co. to RWM, March 4, 1920, *ibid.*, Nr. 4540, Bl. 22–23.

[58] Oscar Funcke, "Wirtschaftspolitik," Industrieinstitut for the transcript of the special membership meeting of the VDMA on February 19, 1920.

facturers to turn to the state for help. This was done with little enthusiasm and much desperation. C. F. von Siemens, for example, although certainly a supporter of the free market, felt that the "catastrophic period" in which they were operating required "special measures" backed by "the power of the state" so as to prevent "individual excesses."[59] Such insight and moderation was not to be found so easily among the iron and steel producers, and this prevented the kind of unanimity or at least goodwill among businessmen that usually succeeded in minimizing government intervention. It was the serious division within the business community that made it possible and even necessary for the RWM to take the initiative.

GOVERNMENT REGULATION OF THE IRON TRADES

It would probably be more accurate to say that the RWM was driven into action by the inability of the producers to come to terms with the manufacturers, because it hardly demonstrated much initiative with regard to the problems of the iron trades before the late fall of 1919. In fact, as shown earlier, the Schmidt-Hirsch regime had begun by taking a friendly attitude toward the producers and by limiting itself to defensive actions where there were difficulties. In the field of organization, the RWM had prolonged the Steel Works Association because the industrialists failed to offer any real alternative after they had been invited to do so. The RWM had encouraged trustification and had been rewarded with the insulting suggestion that a better atmosphere for such action could be created by a change of government. Also, the RWM had been both sympathetic and helpful in the matter of Swedish ore debts and had enthusiastically supported the producers' claim that they needed to export in order to get the exchange required to pay the debts. In October 1919 Hirsch told the industrialists that the RWM believed that the producers should be allowed to export at least as much as was necessary to cover the costs of its raw materials imports.[60]

One of the peculiarities of the situation was that the RWM never seems to have discovered the actual extent of the Swedish ore debts or how much the concerns owed individually. When it tried to get this information in late April 1920, it was told by the industrialists that the Reich Finance Ministry had received all the information it needed

[59] Siemens to L. Hirschberg, February 4, 1920, SAA 4 Lf/514, Bd. 7, Bl. 243–244.

[60] Meeting of the Merchant Bar Association, October 9, 1919, HA/GHH, Nr. 3000031/6. See also Bruhn to Buttlar, November 15, 1919, DZA Potsdam, RWM, Nr. 4453.

concerning the origin of the debts, the amounts involved, and the dates on which the various payments fell due. The steel industrialists refused to provide any new information on the grounds that such new information would give "a completely different and inaccurate picture of the actual situation." This was because "some of the works had covered the debts in another manner at great sacrifice in order to ensure further deliveries."[61] In fact, the evidence shows that most of the debts were paid between November 1919 and April 1920, and that the last debts of the total of about 200 million gold marks that were owed were paid in October 1920.[62] The information given to the Finance Ministry was nothing more than a claim for government compensation on the grounds that the wartime debts had been contracted at the government's insistence. In general, the government refused such claims for "indirect war costs," a practice all the more justified in this case because the industrialists seem to have undertaken the risk during the war with the expectation of a major exchange profit.[63]

Their claim for compensation becomes all the more dubious, however, because it is hard to discover wherein lay the alleged "great sacrifice" made by the concerns to pay off their debts. Sacrifice had been urged upon them by the Hamburg banker, Max Warburg, who used his excellent Swedish connections to attempt the mediation of an arrangement with the Swedes under which the debts would be extended in return for various securities from the industrialists. Others had proposed that a credit be taken from the Reichsbank, and Finance Minister Erzberger seems to have proposed that an extension of the Swedish loans be backed by the Reich in the form of a lease to the Swedes of the government-owned Hibernia mines. In this way, the Swedes would have received security and the mines would have been protected from possible Allied seizure for reparations purposes. At a meeting of October 30, however, the majority of the concerns involved, particularly Rheinstahl, Hoesch, the GBAG, the GHH, and Thyssen, refused to consider taking any further risks or putting up any securities in connection with the debts. They were resolved to pay them no matter what the consequences. In early November, Warburg complained bitterly that ". . . it is wrong not to take advantage of the good disposition of the Swedes, who want to be accommodating. We really drive ourselves into the abyss if now each businessman, insofar as he does not produce for export, secretly sells marks in order to meet his obligations. If that continues, then the mark notes will soon be

[61] See the notes of the discussion between the industrialists and the RWM officials on April 24, 1920, HA/GHH, Nr. 3000035/6.
[62] Schlaghecke, *Bewirtschaftung des Eisens*, p. 32, and the discussion below.
[63] Discussion in the RWM of April 24, 1920, HA/GHH, Nr. 3000035/6.

141

unmarketable."[64] It is impossible to tell how much steel industry mark sales abroad to secure foreign exchange to pay Swedish ore debts were responsible for the severe drop in the exchange value of the mark in November, but it is difficult to imagine that such surreptitious sales did not play a role.[65]

There is clearer evidence for the other methods employed by the industrialists in eliminating their Swedish ore debts. It shows that the combination of relaxed exchange controls after July 1919, the policy of securing partial payment in exchange from the manufacturers in the winter of 1919–1920, and increased liquidity arising from the sale of property lost under the Peace Treaty helped to relieve the situation of the producers considerably. Between July 1, 1919, and January 1920, Krupp paid 12 million of the 16.8 million Swedish kronen it owed. Nevertheless, Krupp was still hard pressed at the beginning of 1920, and Director Wiedfeldt urged that Krupp keep up with the other concerns in demanding partial payment in foreign exchange for its domestic sales. The methods by which the debts were completely eliminated are clearly stated in an internal report, which points out that because of the unfavorable exchange rate and the anxieties about the debts, "we had to push consideration of our domestic customers somewhat into the background and turn more strongly to export. . . . As a consequence of the depreciation of the mark, the profits were splendid at times."[66] Rheinstahl's relentless policies also seem to have proven advantageous, because Hasslacher was able to report that the concern's 100 million mark debt would be paid by the end of January 1920.[67] Similarly, Vögler was able to report in April 1920 that the sale of Deutsch-Lux holdings in Lorraine, for which it was also to receive compensation from the German government, would bring enough to pay, among other things, the entire Swedish ore debt.[68]

If the steel producers did make a sacrifice in order to pay their ore debts, it was a political one arising from the inability of their customers and the RWM to tolerate the methods by which the debts were being paid and the degree to which the producers exploited the debt to maximize their profits. As noted above, the RWM could never get satisfac-

[64] Warburg to Wiedfeldt, November 10, 1919, Krupp WA III, 225. On the Erzberger plan, see Wiedfeldt to Hugenberg, December 9, 1919, *ibid.*, 224.

[65] See Table 5, above, p. 56, and Appendix I. It will be remembered that in March 1919 Thyssen had indicated his desire to employ his liquid resources abroad to pay off the debts. See above, p. 94.

[66] See the memorandum on "The Krupp Firm in the World War," Krupp WA VII f 1088, and Wiedfeldt to Bruhn, January 8, 1920, *ibid.*, 224.

[67] Supervisory Board meeting, January 16, 1920, Rheinstahl Archiv, Nr. 123.

[68] Supervisory Board meeting, April 12, 1920, Friedrich-Wilhelms-Hütte Archiv, Nr. 123/19.

tory information about the debts and was constantly told that the best way of handling the matter was to permit the firms to export as much as possible and to have direct disposal over foreign exchange proceeds rather than indirect control through the Steel Works Association. To these demands, voiced particularly by Thyssen and Rheinstahl,[69] were added the arguments of some of the producers that domestic prices should be allowed to reach the level of world market prices. The RWM could not accept the Reichert program, and it was insistent that something be done to establish uniform prices throughout Germany for the various iron and steel products that were low enough to permit manufacturers to survive and sufficiently high for producers to pay their costs.

As a mechanism to accomplish these ends, the RWM suggested an equalization fund (*Ausgleichskasse*), such as already existed in the coal industry, through which firms with higher costs and firms in the occupied areas would receive an extra share of the price paid for iron and steel sales. Naturally, the entire scheme presupposed effectively functioning syndicates capable of arriving at a uniform price and administering the funds received from sales. Although there seemed to be some inclination in certain producer circles to consider this solution during September and October, the continued opposition of the Rheinstahl and the Deutsch-Lux concerns to the Steel Works Association and the actions of the major producers following the further deterioration of the mark in November broke down the efforts to reach a compromise on this basis.[70]

The RWM responded to this situation on December 8 with the draft of a decree establishing price ceilings and an equalization fund for the iron and steel industry. The decree prohibited private arrangements involving premium payments for rolled products, the delivery of scrap at lower than market prices, or the payment in foreign exchange at rates lower than those in force on the day of payment. The RWM commissar at the Steel Federation was empowered to oversee the administration of the decree, and penalties involving sequestration, fines, and even imprisonment were provided for its willful violation.[71]

The proposed decree was justified in a lengthy memorandum signed by Dr. Hirsch that explained why the RWM viewed it as "the only possibility of relieving the insupportable conditions existing on the iron market and effectively acting against the often proclaimed intention

[69] Steel Works Association meeting, June 18, 1919, HA/GHH, Nr. 3000030/12; Merchant Bars Export Association, October 9, 1919, *ibid.*, Nr. 3000031/6; and meetings of March 25 and April 24, 1920, *ibid.*, Nr. 3000035/6.

[70] Meeting of various syndicates on October 4, 1919, BA, R 13 I/415.

[71] Copies are to be found in O. Funcke, "Vergangene Zeiten," Book 2, Industrie-institut, and in HA/GHH, Nr. 3000035/5.

143

of heavy industry of speedily adjusting our price to the world market price."[72] The memorandum painted a dismal but rather accurate record of the iron market following the termination of price controls in January 1919. The RWM stressed the inaccuracy of industrialist predictions that Germany would "soon be swimming in iron," and pointed to the continuous price increases, the encouragement of black marketeering and profiteering by the varying prices, the favoritism showed by some suppliers, the unfair payment conditions, and the complete disintegration of efforts to maintain the prices set by the Steel Federation. In the view of the RWM, something had to be done to ensure the iron supply needed by the manufacturers for the proposed reconstruction of northern France and Belgium, for the railroads, and for the housing construction program planned by the government for the coming year. The government could no longer put its faith in the promises given by the industrialists. The RWM was in no way mollified by the fact that the producers claimed that they were satisfied with the prices going into effect on December 1. The RWM thought these prices unjustifiably high and argued that they were based on the costs of the least efficient firms or those most indebted because of dependence on foreign ores. The RWM had accepted these price increases only because of its intention to introduce price ceilings and an equalization fund. A single domestic price was necessary if merchants were to be controlled. The RWM refused to accept the argument that the state did not have enough authority to control prices and countered with the somewhat uninspiring argument that even a small improvement over existing conditions would mean significant progress.

The memorandum sought to counter industrialist arguments that an equalization fund would provide a premium for incompetence, would be technically impossible to administer, and could become the basis for creating an iron tax. According to the RWM's investigations, a fair average price for bars in December 1919 was 1,400 marks per ton, not the 1,750 marks decided upon in the Steel Federation. What the RWM suggested was that the 350-mark difference between the two prices be taken and put into the equalization fund in order to pay the extra costs involved in pig iron imports—about one-tenth of the total being used— to reimburse importers of foreign ores and the Upper Silesian works for their extra costs, and to reward firms making financial sacrifices in order to satisfy pressing domestic requirements. Thus, no special premium was being given for high production costs but only for specific external expenses. The RWM could not find any serious technical barriers to implementing their scheme because this method had worked

[72] *Ibid.*, for this and the other quotations and discussion of this memorandum.

144

in other industries. Finally, the government denied that it had any intention of introducing an iron tax.

Instead of issuing the decree on price ceilings and the equalization fund immediately, however, the RWM felt that it was necessary to secure the approval of the Economic Policy Committee of the Reichstag at its meetings on December 15–16, 1919. This procedure gave the producers a further opportunity to delay RWM action. VdESI representatives were able to contact some of the deputies as well as the press and express strong opposition to the RWM's plans. Undoubtedly, this helped to sway the most influential members of the committee, if not against the RWM's contention that action had to be taken to correct the situation on the iron market, then at least in the direction of encouraging the RWM to make yet another stab at agreement with industry. Deputy Philipp Wieland, a member of the Democratic Party and a Württemberg metal industrialist, opposed the scheme for an equalization fund and pushed through a resolution calling on the RWM and industry to resume negotiations with the object of creating a self-governing body for the iron trades composed of representatives of industry, commerce, the crafts, the consumers, and the workers. If these negotiations failed, "the committee would take appropriate measures in common with the government."[73] Wieland, who was favorably impressed with the way an analogous self-governing body had been working in his own industry, was convinced that his proposal was the best way to steer a middle course between the undesirable controls of the wartime period and the chaos being created by the total freedom of the present period. Through his resolution, which was accepted unanimously, he hoped "to build a bridge for the iron industry" from which to escape from the plan of the RWM. In a personal letter to his fellow Swabian, General Director Reusch, Wieland urged that "You and your colleagues in the iron and steel industry ought to take a conciliatory attitude in the negotiations and offer to cooperate in a self-governing body." Reusch, in his reply, promised to try his utmost but caustically remarked that "The government makes it difficult to take a conciliatory attitude toward it in the negotiations. It sends forth into the world the most unbelievable charges."[74]

Although Reusch himself certainly played a more reasonable and responsible role than some of his colleagues, it is difficult to see how he could justify his animosity and impatience with the RWM in the

[73] Report by Reichert, December 19, 1919, BA R 13 I/193, Bl. 59. See also the comment by Buttlar at the Steel Federation meeting of December 20, 1919, HA/GHH, Nr. 3000035/5, and the report on the Reichstag Economic Policy Committee hearings in DZA Potsdam, RWM, Nr. 4453, Bl. 160–162.

[74] Wieland to Reusch, December 20, 1919, and Reusch to Wieland, December 27, 1919, HA/GHH, Nr. 30019390/29.

145

light of his own experiences in trying to maintain the Steel Works Association and his own knowledge about the way some of his colleagues had resisted any and all measures to regulate the iron market. This resistance continued. Although the producers had been compelled by the Reichstag committee's decision to discuss the *form* of organization to be created among themselves and with the government, the basic point to many of them was opposition to *any* organization at all on the grounds that the future could not be foreseen and they had to be in a position to defend their own security. Fritz Thyssen made the point clearly to the RWM representatives at the Steel Federation meeting on December 20 by arguing that "In the end it is *we* who are responsible for the economic organizations we lead, and we cannot calmly cooperate if no guarantee is offered that business will be run in an economically sound manner."[75] Thyssen insisted that pricing policy had to be based on the presumption of further cost increases by emphasizing the Swedish ore debts and insisting that the only way to guarantee that Germany would have ore in the future was to guarantee that the ore could be paid for in the future. The producer concerns, he claimed, had now used up their silent reserves and their stores of raw materials, and they were compelled to operate on the basis of present income and present raw materials requirements. Thyssen's argument did not contain an explanation of what the rest of the German economy was to do about its present and future security while the iron and steel producers devoted exclusive attention to their own problems. It also did not state the basic reason for the producers' opposition to an equalization fund. This was provided by Vögler, who accepted the arguments of the government representatives and some of his colleagues that only strong syndicates could administer such a fund and then insisted that "we cannot now create strong associations because the conditions are unpredictable."[76] Once again the fundamental contradiction in industry's position came to the surface. The industrialists insisted on industrial self-government and then argued that conditions were too unclear and uncertain to make effective industrial self-government possible.

Vögler was too shrewd and effective a businessman not to recognize the problematic nature of his own position. He was convinced that industry would have to come up with definite proposals for a self-governing body if it were to escape an equalization fund, price ceilings, and partial sequestration of production. Following the December 20 Steel Federation meeting, he sent Reusch a series of suggestions that combined the loosest form of syndicate organization with a formaliza-

[75] Steel Federation meeting, December 20, 1919, *ibid.*, Nr. 3000035/5.
[76] *Ibid.*

tion of the Steel Federation's existence as a mantle organization for the industry. Thus, although individual associations would be created for the various products of the industry to determine prices and general sales conditions, actual sales both at home and abroad would remain in the hands of the individual firms. Every firm would be allowed a certain percentage for export based on its previous month's production, but the types of production exported would be left to the discretion of the individual firms. Those firms having Swedish ore debts would be given an increment to their export quotas. The Steel Federation would oversee the entire industry, and it was to be composed of representatives of the producers, the manufacturers, the merchants, and the government and to be organized on the principle of parity between industry and labor. Vögler believed that this constituted the maximum program on which the leading producers could be brought to agree.[77]

If anything, however, Vögler's program only served to highlight the continued difficulties of the producers in developing an effective answer to the demands for government controls. Reusch spotted immediately the unsatisfactory aspects of Vögler's proposals. Indeed, Reusch did not place much more confidence in the moral commitments of his colleagues under the existing circumstances than did the government. He argued that the maintenance of domestic and foreign prices could be achieved only by posting financial bonds and imposing strict penalties, and he doubted that the weak arrangements proposed by Vögler would be sufficient.[78]

In the meantime, positions actually hardened rather than softened. In order to maintain some semblance of external order and organization in the industry and possibly to reassert its authority as well, the RWM decreed a further extension of the Steel Works Association until May 1, 1920. When Deutsch-Lux and Rheinstahl again refused to follow the decree on legal and economic grounds and began to sell A products independently, the government took Director Klinkenberg of the former concern and Directors Hasslacher and Filius of the latter concern to court. The cases dragged on at various appeal stages until 1924. The significance of the situation in 1920 was that these firms had openly attacked the authority of the government and had increased the tensions between the producers and the RWM. Having continuously argued that the government lacked the authority to impose its will on the economy, some of the industrialists seemed to be anxious to prove the point in no uncertain terms as well.[79]

[77] Vögler to Reusch, December 23, 1919, *ibid.*
[78] Reusch to Vögler, December 30, 1919, *ibid.*
[79] See pp. 124–125 and note 27 above.

147

The producers had created a committee to set up guidelines for negotiations with the RWM, and its labors were concluded on January 6, 1920. These guidelines again revealed the testy nature of the relationship between the two sides and the reluctance, not to say resentment, felt by the producers. The guidelines began with three "preconditions": unlimited freedom with regard to the setting of prices, restoration of the coal quotas allowed the smelting plants in October 1919, and a promise by the RWM that the "mistaken measure" of prolonging the Steel Works Association would not be implemented. Assuming that these preconditions were met, the industrialists were prepared to create a self-governing body for the iron trades—representing the producers, merchants, manufacturers, and workers—which they proposed calling the *Arbeitsgemeinschaft* of the Steel Federation. From the standpoint of the producers, the most important issue in the negotiations over the creation of such a self-governing body, as in the days of Moellendorff, was the issue of "independence in decision making." If absolutely necessary, the producers were prepared to concede a veto power to the government when unanimity was lacking in the self-governing body. In matters of pricing, however, this veto would be allowable only if the prices asked went beyond costs plus a "reasonable profit that would guarantee the economic security of the works" and if the value of exports exceeded the old and new debts for ore.[80]

On January 9–10, preliminary discussions were held between the RWM and the producers. Discussions then continued throughout the month and, in addition, the RWM met with representatives of other interest groups. Indeed, haggling continued until the beginning of April over various provisions of the drafts drawn up by the RWM, but there would be little point in following these in detail. Essentially, the problem for the producers was that they were able to win individual battles but not their war with the RWM. They had managed to defeat two of the possible three suggested ways of organizing the industry. The Reichstag committee had killed the equalization fund idea. The maintenance and creation of effective syndicates, always warmly supported by Director Bruhn of the Pig Iron Association, was rejected by a large number of producers. Thus, the only solution that remained was the self-governing body along the lines once advocated by Moellendorff and Baron von Buttlar and successfully evaded by the producers until its resurrection. As always, the central issues were the questions of how "self-governing" the new body would be and the nature of its composition. The battle over these issues, however, was

[80] Meeting of January 6, 1920, BA, R 13 I/415, Bl. 60–63.

not decided in the aforementioned meetings as much as by the day-to-day conflicts over prices and delivery conditions that undermined the position of the producers by dividing them from other segments of the business community and making it possible for the RWM to draw upon the schemes previously developed by Moellendorff and Buttlar and create what was to be called the Iron Trades Federation (*Eisenwirtschaftsbund*—EWB).[81]

What accompanied the formal discussions over the organization and character of the EWB, therefore, was a constant testing of the extent to which the producers and consumers could adjust their differences independently of the government. The RWM, in its turn, sought to play upon these divisions for its own purposes. When the Pig Iron Syndicate raised prices on January 8 despite strong consumer objections, the RWM approved the increase in part but reserved its approval of that portion of the increase meant to cover the Swedish ore debts until such time as its application could be regulated by the proposed self-governing body. Two weeks before, the RWM had followed up consumer complaints about the Pig Iron Syndicate's intention of asking for partial payment in foreign exchange by making official inquiries with the latter association. The Pig Iron Syndicate replied by informing the RWM that it was aware of the complaints and that a committee of producers and manufacturers had been formed to work out the problem.[82]

These negotiations, conducted between the Pig Iron Syndicate and the VDMA on February 2 and February 14, were extremely difficult and complicated because it was virtually impossible to find an equitable arrangement satisfactory to both sides. Pig iron producers were willing to supply domestic manufacturers only if the latter effectively guaranteed the former a substantial portion of the export profits on machines by paying a substantial amount of foreign exchange for the pig iron at an artificially low rate of exchange. Manufacturers were irked at the notion that their foreign exchange payments to the producers should be undervalued and were concerned that machine builders producing for the domestic market not be required to buy pig iron with foreign exchange and that old contracts not be affected by the new arrangements. Under the circumstances, confusion and misunderstanding were inevitable. After oscillating between an arrangement to have manufacturers pay for their pig iron in proportion to their exports and an agreement to have exporting manufacturers pay one-third of

[81] For the negotiations, see DZA Potsdam, RWM, Nr. 4453.

[82] *Stahl und Eisen*, 40:1, January 15, 1920, p. 99, and the correspondence between the Pig Iron Syndicate and the RWM in DZA Potsdam, RWM Nr. 4540, Bl. 31ff.

their pig iron purchases in foreign exchange pegged at a fixed rate of exchange lower than that prevailing on the money market, the latter solution was accepted by the VDMA leaders on February 14 and was then paraded as an illustration of the "values of objective collaboration" between heavy industry and the manufacturers.[83] It had proven impossible to make special arrangements for manufacturers who had already signed contracts with foreign customers, however. In the end, the VDMA could only advise its members to calculate this higher price in their contracts containing so-called pig iron clauses. That is, they were encouraged to employ the clauses permitting retroactive price increases based on increases in the costs of pig iron during the period when the contract was being fulfilled. If Reichert had been right about anything in his pamphlet it was about the way in which the producers could compel the manufacturers to follow their lead in raising export prices. An entire extraordinary membership meeting of the VDMA on February 19 was devoted to such questions as the employment of sliding-scale prices for both domestic and foreign contracts and the annulment of contracts concluded at fixed prices or in marks. Although there was loud applause for speakers attacking the exporting of raw materials and even suggesting that there should be a discriminatory tax on the export of unfinished products, Dr. Reichert thought that the meeting had gone "not unfavorably for the iron producing industry."[84] Undoubtedly, he was impressed by the official line of the VDMA leadership as well as by the speech of Dr. Guggenheimer calling on industry to solve its own problems without government help.

Guggenheimer's correspondence at this very time, however, does not speak very well for industry's ability to solve its own problems. If anything, it demonstrates the incredible confusion and disorder existing in business circles, a condition already demonstrated by the negotiations between producers and iron consumers on February 2 and February 14. Guggenheimer had been infuriated by these negotiations because he thought that the VDMA had done a miserable job of conducting them, a view held not only by the MAN but also by two other great manufacturing firms, Borsig and Siemens. Instead of turning back to the VDMA, however, Guggenheimer turned to the Reich Association of German Industry (RdI) and, on February 16, asked its business manager, Dr. Simons, to open new negotiations between producers and manufacturers. A meeting of leading members of the RdI on February 20 muddled the situation still further, when

[83] See VDMA to C. F. von Siemens, January 30, 1920, SAA 4/Lf 715, and the VDMA circular in the special membership meeting of February 19, 1920, O. Funcke, "Wirtschaftspolitik," Industrieinstitut.

[84] *Ibid.*, and the undated report by Reichert in BA, R 13 I/194, Bl. 191–195.

Reichert presented a letter from the Pig Iron Syndicate repudiating its agreement with the VDMA and asking that customers pay foreign exchange for the pig iron in proportion to their exports. Naturally, the chief VDMA negotiators with the Pig Iron Syndicate, Frölich and General Director Reuter of DEMAG, were offended by the unilateral abrogation of the agreement. At the same time the industrialists representing the large manufacturing firms raised differing objections to all the proposals that had been under consideration.[85]

The situation was indeed peculiar and reflected the immense variety of firms and interests within the manufacturing industry and the difficult problem of coordinating the interests of large concerns like the MAN, which did not feel bound by the VDMA's decisions and looked to the RdI, with those of the mass of members who did look to the VDMA for leadership. Business managers such as Dr. Frölich of the VDMA and Director Schrey of the Association of German Railroad Car Manufacturers were often at loggerheads with the directors of large firms. Frölich appears to have viewed his constituency in broader terms than simply serving the interests of the major concerns like the MAN with its large capital resources and its directors, like Guggenheimer, who were willing and able to fight for their position without calling on the government. It is interesting to note that although Guggenheimer was not given a copy of the record of negotiations between the VDMA and the Pig Iron Association, Frölich sent his friend in the RWM, von Buttlar, a draft of his report for the latter's "confidential information."[86] It is difficult not to conclude that Frölich in no way shared Guggenheimer's urgent sentiment that there only be "no intervention of the government." Indeed, the search for a solution through the RdI as desired by Guggenheimer had failed to work also because the RdI had decided as a result of the above-discussed meeting of February 20 "to refrain on its part and instead to leave the matter to the iron producing and manufacturing industries."[87] That was where it had been before the RdI ever discussed the issue, and the Pig Iron Association's repudiation of its agreement with the VDMA had demol-

[85] The Guggenheimer Correspondence is in the MAN Werksarchiv Nürnberg, Nr. 031/IV. See especially Guggenheimer to Simons, February 16, 1920, and Guggenheimer's notes on the February 20 meeting in the RdI and his letter of February 23 to the MAN directors along with the Pig Iron Syndicate note to Reichert of February 18, which was appended. Further see VdESI Executive Directors meeting of February 27, 1920 in BA, R 13 I/157. Guggenheimer's views were shared by Director Henrich of Siemens, see Henrich to C. F. von Siemens, February 27, 1920, SAA 4/Lf 669.

[86] Frölich to Buttlar, DZA Potsdam, RWM, Nr. 4540, Bl. 46–52.

[87] RdI meeting of February 20, 1920, in MAN Werksarchiv Nürnberg, Nr. 031/IV.

151

ished such remnants of goodwill as had survived between the two groups after their meetings of February 2 and February 14.

All this encouraged the RWM to take a hard line, and the ministry's inclination to take action was being fed by the continued chaos of the industry, the flow of petitions and complaints from the iron consuming industries, and its own tug-of-war with the producers. To the usual battle over prices was now added a new and even more acrimonious conflict over the government draft of the projected Iron Trades Federation, and the government assumed the initiative and increased pressure in both areas. It resisted the price demands of the producers—not that the official prices had much to do with reality in any case—and some producers responded by refusing to supply the RWM with information on costs to justify their price demands. Then there was a nasty quarrel over the naming of producer representatives to the newly formed Export Control Board (*Aussenhandelsstelle*) in Düsseldorf. The RWM insisted that the delegates be appointed by February 25 in a letter dated February 14 that reached the hands of the producer organizations on February 23. The producers objected that this did not give them enough time and suggested that the matter be handled in connection with the formation of the Iron Trades Federation, but Buttlar replied that the producers had been aware of the RWM's plans since December and that the RWM would name the producer representatives if the associations failed to do so. Director Gerwin suspected that this was the RWM's deceitful way of creating an Export Control Board without the participation of industry so that it could organize the industry's export business in such a manner as to create an equalization fund through the back door. That is, exporters of finished products would pay an export tax that would be used to compensate producers having Swedish ore debts. The government did in fact proceed just as Gerwin intimated, and the new bureau was set up on March 1 in Düsseldorf and was told to operate along the aforementioned lines. The situation had deteriorated to the point where both sides were living up to each other's worst expectations.[88]

The quarrel over the projected EWB, however, came to the forefront in the late winter of 1920. The case against the government proposal was stated most forcefully by Dr. Reichert at the VdESI Executive Directors meeting of February 27. Reichert noted that the RWM had steadily modified its drafts to the point where the EWB, as now planned, could be considered a self-governing body in name only. In reality, it gave the government such prerogatives that "the power of the government in the regulation of the iron trades will thereby be

[88] Gerwin at the VdESI meeting of February 27, 1920, BA, R 13 I/157 and *Stahl und Eisen*, 40:1, March 11, 1920, p. 375.

stabilized like a *rocher de bronze* or *de fer*."[89] He noted that the producers had been singled out for controls and that the manufacturers were not being "blessed" with a similar organization—not that he wished one on them. Where the producers had demanded at least 50% of the seats in the EWB, the government draft had given the majority to the manufacturers and merchants by providing for 34 producers, 12 merchants, and 24 manufacturers with an equivalent number of labor representatives for each respective group. Reichert's greatest complaint, of course, concerned the veto power provided the RWM. The producers had sought to persuade the government to accept the finality of all EWB decisions taken with a two-thirds or larger majority, whereas the government demanded unanimity before relinquishing its right to veto EWB decisions and its right to take independent action if a disagreement between the RWM and the EWB could not be resolved by negotiation.[90]

The chief impression that emerges from Reichert's remarks, however, is that he found the aggregate character of the government's draft rather than its individual provisions to be the most infuriating thing about it. In giving EWB pricing decisions the force of government-ordained price ceilings, in providing for compulsory inventories, sequestrations, confiscations, fines, and prison sentences, the government draft suggested not a transition from wartime to peacetime economy but rather a restoration of wartime controls without the justification of a wartime emergency and with a very punitive intent.[91]

It must be said that Reichert did have a point in viewing the draft as a one-sided effort to control the producers. Not only did they not have 50% of the votes or appear to have any effective means of escaping the RWM veto powers, but they also had to face the hostility and ideological tensions that would arise between employers and workers. The German Metal Workers Union had left the *Arbeitsgemeinschaft*, and it was difficult for the producers to imagine that they would be reliable voting partners in the EWB. Furthermore, many of the trade union leaders had been talking about running the iron trades in conformity with the idea of an "economic community," a concept that Reichert thought eliminated with Wissell and Moellendorff. Finally, Reichert thought that the entire RWM program was impractical. He did not think it possible to maintain a single domestic price in Germany, and he was equally sceptical about the RWM's notions of controlling the industry's foreign exchange supply, regulating the com-

[89] BA, R 13 I/57.
[90] The draft is to be found in *ibid.*, 416, Bl. 302ff.
[91] Reichert at the February 27, 1920 meeting, *ibid.*, 157.

pensation of the Swedish ore debtors through a special export tax, and, more generally, managing the iron trades through such a body. Once again, he questioned the authority of the government: "One fails to recognize that the state authority in its present form has been diminished enormously through the revolution. In order to carry through such a restrictive law one needs above all a state authority and a respect for individual officials that neither we in our circles have and that those outside the iron trades certainly do not have."[92] Thus, Reichert continued to plead and to hope that industry would pull together at the last minute and organize things on a voluntary basis.

Reichert's power of persuasion, however, was inadequate to overcome manufacturer mistrust. When Schrey pointed out that the manufacturers could not be expected to "commit harakiri" and that they could no longer live on producer promises, Reichert asked Schrey not to blame persons or groups—a peculiar statement for a supporter of the stab-in-the-back legend—but rather circumstances: the lost war, lost territories, "hole in the West," loss of state authority, bad currency, and "six years of economic revolution" and government controls. This cold comfort was followed up with the no less chilling proposition that the manufacturers adjust precisely to those conditions they found intolerable and stop "exaggerating" the difficulties involved.[93]

The contradiction in Reichert's argument was that he asked the manufacturers to yield to the force of circumstances and implied that they were exaggerating their plight while he assumed it perfectly natural for the producers to manipulate circumstances to their own advantage and did not think that there was anything exaggerated about the producers' cries of financial anguish. Yet, as Reichert himself noted with some distress—and as RWM officials had noted with amused interest—the producers were quite prepared to support price ceilings for one of their vital raw materials, scrap, while objecting to price ceilings on their own products.[94] Indeed, what Schrey, Frölich, and others were making clear to Reichert and the producers was that the manufacturers could learn how to deal with "circumstances" and cease playing the role of passive victims. Just as the producers had decided that the situation warranted the dissolution of their Steel Works Association and a policy of every concern for itself, so the manufacturers had come to the conclusion that they had to band together in a demand for state intervention but also in the defense of their own interests. They, too, now took the path of self-help and, on February 27, they founded the Federation of Iron Consumers (*Bund*

[92] *Ibid.* [93] *Ibid.*

[94] *Ibid.*, and Guggenheimer's notes on the February 20, 1919, RdI meeting in MAN Werksarchiv, Nürnberg, Nr. 03/IV.

der Eisenverbraucher), a federation of the various manufacturing organizations formed so that they would "have a united representation of consumer interests over against the producers and the government in order to prevent the possibility of one consumer group being played off against another in the self-governing body."[95] Directors Reuter and Schrey seem to have played a leading role in forming the group, which reflected an increasing solidarity among the iron consumers.

This solidarity among the iron consumers, as usual, was anything but perfect, and although there was a general resentment against the producers that bound the consumers together, there were considerable differences among them with regard to the compromises they were prepared to make and the techniques they wished to use in making their interests felt. The electrotechnical industrialists were much less generous when it came to the payment of the iron and steel producers in foreign exchange because they had to purchase and import a larger variety of raw materials than the machine builders, but relations within the electrotechnical industry appear to have been somewhat less tense than in the machine construction industry because of the domination of the AEG and Siemens and the fact that Hans von Raumer worked in close collaboration with these concerns. In the VDMA, relations between the large concerns and the business management of the association were not always of the best. Thanks largely to the development of Export Control Boards, the number of trade associations connected with the VDMA grew from 40 in 1919 to 124 in 1920.[96] This meant that the smaller and medium-sized firms in the industry were now organized and that their business managers could play a very active role in VDMA affairs, a situation that was encouraged by the enthusiastic business management of the VDMA in Berlin. Frölich and his colleagues thus felt that they had a broader constituency than the prominent industrialists from the large concerns. Furthermore, they appear to have been supported in this attitude by prominent representatives of certain of the larger machine construction firms such as Reuter of DEMAG, the Cologne-Kalk factory owner, Becker, and the Berliner, Waldschmidt, all of whom were quite antagonistic to heavy industry. However, other large firm representatives, particularly Guggenheimer of the MAN, were not very happy with the way Frölich operated. Just as Guggenheimer had objected to Frölich's enthusiasm for export controls in 1918,[97] so now he objected to the way the VDMA business management seemed to approve of government intentions with regard to the EWB. Guggenheimer of the MAN and

[95] For the founding meeting, see MAN Werksarchiv Nürnberg, Nr. 03/IV.

[96] "Deutscher Maschinenbau," p. 458.

[97] See above, pp. 87–88.

Deutsch of the AEG were both surprised and angered when VDMA leadership sanctioned the RWM draft, a draft they had not even read at the time of its approval by Frölich and Reuter. Guggenheimer took the position, and with some obvious justification, that "it is certainly necessary that the directors of great firms, which are represented in the Association and particularly when they sit on the Board of Directors [of the VDMA], be informed about such important matters."[98] Unlike the VDMA leaders, who had lost faith in direct negotiations between producers and manufacturers outside the mechanism of the projected EWB, Guggenheimer and other leaders of major concerns as well as the highly influential Hans von Raumer continued to believe in direct producer-manufacturer negotiations. The big problem, from their perspective, was whether or not they could bring the two sides together before the government took final action.

On March 3, Guggenheimer, Raumer, and another MAN Director, Otto Gertung, drew up the terms for a possible agreement. They suggested that the policy of paying in foreign exchange in proportion to exports be continued, but that demands for payment in scrap and insistence on the calculation of exchange at a low rate be discontinued. In addition, Gertung introduced the idea of creating a referee empowered to make sure that both sides maintained the agreement and to levy penalties against violators. On the following day, March 4, Guggenheimer, Raumer, and Director Henrich of Siemens presented these proposals to Stinnes and Vögler, who found them acceptable. This little group of major industrial leaders, who had also been so instrumental in creating the ZAG and RdI, and who, as shall be shown, were deeply involved in the process of vertical concentration then taking place,[99] agreed to pursue a common line at the discussion of the projected self-governing body planned for the following day at the RWM's Economic Advisory Council. They would try to have the entire matter delayed until the outcome of the proposed direct negotiations were known. Their goal was to bury the EWB by means of a friendly agreement within the business community through the well-tried tactic of delay.[100]

Both sides kept to their bargain at the March 5 meeting of the Economic Advisory Council. Vögler, Bruhn, Guggenheimer, and Deutsch all put in a plea for delay in the hope that private negotiations would prove successful, and their united front forced Frölich to

[98] Guggenheimer to MAN directors, March 8, 1920, MAN Werksarchiv Nürnberg, Nr. 03/IV.

[99] See above, pp. 82–83 and Chapter 4.

[100] Guggenheimer to MAN, March 8, 1920, MAN Werksarchiv Nürnberg, Nr. 03/IV.

weaken his support for the EWB by declaring that he would have to delay taking a final position. The Prussian and Bavarian state representatives strengthened the pressure for delay by taking very seriously producer claims that the proposed organization might actually endanger the iron supply. Thus, Hirsch, Buttlar, and the trade union representatives had a difficult time arguing for immediate action, but much of the discussion about a four-week delay was academic. The RWM had no intention of holding back its draft and intended to send it to the Reichsrat and Reichstag committee for approval, but this process was certain to take a few weeks. Whatever the case, the RWM was not going to stand by idly while awaiting the conclusion of a "friendly agreement" between producers and consumers.[101]

The chances for such an agreement are difficult to estimate. Guggenheimer felt certain that "the threatening danger of a decree concerning the Iron Trades Federation will . . . elicit a certain flexibility from both sides and make an agreement easier."[102] Similarly, Vögler thought that the manufacturers had lost some of their taste for the EWB after learning that a high export tax was going to be imposed on finished products. Objectively, the most hopeful sign was a recognition on the part of some of the producers that the manufacturers had legitimate complaints and that something had to be done about them. At a meeting of the producers on March 9, Bruhn went furthest in this direction and noted that there was "much that is right" in the criticisms of the producers because "Under the influence of Reichert's pamphlet prices have been sent soaring and then not kept to." Klöckner warned that "the excitement in consumer circles is much greater than one suspects, and there is a certain justification for it."[103] Even more impressively, some producers were prepared to make actual concessions. Klöckner and even the very relentless Director Filius of Rheinstahl argued that no more than 25% in foreign exchange should be demanded of any manufacturer no matter how great the latter's exports, while Director Klotzbach of Krupp went so far as to argue that offers of more than 25% payment in foreign exchange should be refused in order to bring order to the market and prevent favoritism in the area of supply.

Over against such promising tendencies, one must set the powerful resistance to effective organization in producer circles. As usual, only Bruhn supported the creation of new and effective syndicates "all along

---

[101] VDMA circular of March 8, 1920, *ibid.*, Nr. 03. See also the report of the Bavarian delegate to the Reichsrat, Dr. Rohmer, March 5, 1920, BayHStA, Abt. I, MH 15 610.

[102] Guggenheimer to RdI, March 8, 1920, MAN Werksarchiv Nürnberg, Nr. 03/IV.

[103] Meeting of March 9, 1920, BA, R 13 I/416, Bl. 278–287.

the line" as the best way of preventing the EWB from becoming a reality. Bruhn received no support from his colleagues. Even such friends of syndicates as Director Klemme of the GHH and Peter Klöckner had simply given up their support of Bruhn in face of the implacable opposition of Stinnes and Hasslacher. Justifiably, Bruhn was pessimistic and thought that "the decree will become law in some form, and it seems doubtful . . . that it will be possible to pull its teeth at the last minute."[104]

Unfortunately for the proponents of a friendy agreement between producers and manufacturers, the Kapp Putsch and the strikes and disturbances that followed it during the last half of March made a continuation of negotiations impossible. By the end of the month, such advantages as might have been gained by speedy private negotiations were lost because the RWM draft had already been approved by the Reich Cabinet on March 9, at which time complaints about iron shortages, high prices, and outrageous payment conditions had actually increased.[105] The general political situation increased the sense of uncertainty and tension. Guggenheimer and his friends had thus lost the race against time and circumstances. On March 26 he still hoped that the RdI would take the initiative and seemed to think that the rumored resignation of Undersecretary Hirsch would delay government action.[106] While Guggenheimer grasped at such straws, Bruhn seems to have simply given up all hope. Thus, on March 29 he wrote to Buttlar, with whom he was on friendly terms, that because some leading producers had resisted the creation of the syndicates Bruhn had consistently advocated, effective action among the producers was impossible.[107] Because Bruhn, who along with Vögler was the chief negotiator on the producer side in the negotiations with the manufacturers, believed that a private understanding between producers and manufacturers was also out of the question, the creation of the EWB appeared unavoidable.[108]

Vögler seems to have recognized this point. At the Reichstag Economic Committee meeting on March 31 called to consider the final draft for the EWB, Vögler proposed that the EWB be formed but that "it be made possible for it in its first meeting to once again take a

[104] *Ibid.*

[105] See the discussion, March 9, 1920, DZA Potsdam, RWM, Nr. 4455, Bl. 142.

[106] Guggenheimer to RWM, March 26, 1920, MAN Werksarchiv Nürnberg, Nr. 03/IV.

[107] Bruhn to Buttlar, March 29, 1920, DZA Potsdam, RWM, Nr. 4455, Bl. 153–155.

[108] Guggenheimer to RdI, April 1, 1920, MAN Werksarchiv, Nürnberg, Nr. 031.

stand on the value of creating a self-governing body."[109] That is, its first action after being formed would be to consider its justification for existence. Directors Schrey and Frölich spoke for the manufacturers in support of the government. Although recognizing that the method proposed by the government as embodied in the decree remained to be tested, they insisted that some regulation was unavoidable after efforts at a private understanding had come to naught. Their real feeling was perhaps better expressed in the concluding lines of a report sent by Schrey to his colleagues in the railroad car construction industry. He reported that the Reichstag committee and the Reichsrat had approved the government draft with minor modifications and went on to point out that "Thereby a regulation of the iron trades has been attained in which the consumers can have a significant say about the distribution of the available quantities of iron."[110] The organization advocated by Moellendorff and so successfully resisted by the producers had now been called into existence, albeit without his program and only because of the breakdown of cohesion within the business community. Nevertheless, it was a significant event because the producers seemed to have been placed on the defensive for the first time, and it appeared as if it might be possible to develop economic policies in the iron trades that would give priority to consumer interests. Also, it demonstrated that the government could play on the divisions in industry to reassert its authority in matters of economic policy. The question now, however, was the extent to which the new EWB constituted a real opportunity for the non-producer forces that could be made to work or whether it was an instrument erected by the exigencies of the moment that was at once too little and too late.

[109] VDMA report of April 9, 1920, *ibid.*, Nr. 03 and the Report of the Economic Policy Committee in *Verhandlungen der Verfassungsgebenden Nationalversammlung. Stenographische Berichte und Drucksachen* (Berlin, 1919 ff.), Vol. 343, No. 2887, p. 3254 ff.

[110] Circular of April 1, 1920, signed by Schrey in MAN Werksarchiv Nürnberg, Nr. 03/II.

CHAPTER THREE

Unity Restored: The Struggle for Decontrol, 1920–1921

The development of Germany's wartime and postwar inflation was not a smooth and continuous one, and it was anything but simple for state officials and industrialists to adjust to its imperatives. Institutions and policies designed to meet specific situations were condemned to rapid obsolescence, and lessons learned from one set of circumstances had rapidly to be unlearned or modified to meet suddenly changed conditions. All this had important psychological and political effects. It placed a premium on self-preservation and rapid adaptability and put on the defensive all those who strove to create programmatic or institutional frameworks designed to promote a collective response to the confused situation. Not only governmental but also industrial leaders easily found themselves identified with arguments and mechanisms suddenly inappropriate to existing conditions. In the iron trades, this was to be well illustrated after March 1920 by the dilemmas of persons as diverse in their interests and intentions as Jakob Reichert and Baron von Buttlar. They had played major roles in the respective responses of industry and government to the crisis on the iron and steel market in the fall and winter of 1919–1920. In the spring of 1920, however, the situation seemed to change radically and provided these men and all those involved in the iron trades with what appeared to be a new set of conditions and problems that rendered much of what had been said and done earlier obsolete.

Throughout the fall and winter of 1919–1920 Dr. Reichert had been advocating his dual policy of state export controls and unrestricted domestic pricing on the assumption that the value of the mark would continue to decline for some time to come. Although it is certain that some producers, such as Hasslacher and Stinnes, did not need Reichert's writings and speeches to inspire their pricing policies, Reichert's influence does seem to have been very important because his critics attributed many of the actions taken by the producers directly to his pronouncements.[1] It will be remembered that the chief criticism of

[1] The influence of Reichert's *Rettung aus der Valutanot* is specifically mentioned by O. Funcke in the chapter on the EWB in his "Vergangene Zeiten," Industrie-institut.

Reichert's program had been directed against his advocacy of rapid increase of domestic prices and wages because it was feared, among other things, that German industry might find itself in serious trouble if Reichert's assumption that the mark would continue to depreciate but that the decline of its domestic purchasing power would lag behind its depreciation on foreign markets proved false. His critics were worried that world market prices might drop while the external value of the mark stabilized at existing values or even improved. Such a combination of circumstances would ruin the export advantages enjoyed under depreciation, whereas the increase of prices and wages advocated by Reichert would intensify the competitive disadvantages that Germany would suffer under more stable conditions. Reichert's opponents were fearful of embracing the inflation too fully because they recognized that the inflation was only to Germany's advantage so long as German domestic prices and wages lagged behind those of her competitors. Similarly, they did not think it wise to lose sight of the dangers of stabilization even when pursuing inflationary price and wage policies and were wary of too rapid an increase of prices, and particularly of wages, at which they might suddenly have to stabilize.

Economic developments between March 1920 and May 1921 demonstrated the validity of these criticisms of the Reichert program and made a mockery of his prophecies. The value of the mark increased substantially in the spring of 1920 and, except for a comparatively mild renewed depreciation in August–November 1920, remained relatively stable for the entire year.[2] To be sure, Germany continued and would for some time continue to enjoy an export advantage because of the relative low value of her currency compared to those of her chief competitors, but it had now become clearer that the pursuit of "world market prices" and the casual attitude toward wages espoused by Reichert were hardly appropriate to the delicate condition of the world economy.

When Reichert, in a report to the VdESI on June 20, 1920, somewhat sheepishly expressed concern over the deteriorating export market and the fact that foreign customers were now cancelling orders placed when the value of the mark was lower, Reichert's critics sorely tried to embarrass him.[3] Director Bruhn, who never had been convinced by Reichert's arguments and who had fought to keep the Pig Iron syndicate from making a total surrender to the "law of world market prices," had to be dissuaded from using the syndicate's business report to make comments of self-congratulation and remarks

[2] See Appendix I.
[3] VdESI Executive Directors meeting, June 22, 1920, BA, R 13 I/158.

161

about how "fateful" it would have been if domestic prices had been as high as advocated.[4] At the same time, the sudden change in market conditions resulted in some amusing and embarrassing episodes for both producers and consumers, which cast an interesting light on the problems of the preceding months. A railroad car manufacturer that had placed the same order with three rolling mills—whether the firm was trying to hoard or simply casting about wildly for material is unclear—suffered the considerable shock of having all three orders filled. Similarly, the railroad system suddenly found itself oversupplied for the first time in years, and merchants who only a short time before had behaved as if they deserved beatification for supplying their customers at astronomical prices were prepared to sell at a sacrifice.[5] Of course, it would be impossible to estimate how much had been hoarded, and it must be remembered that the superfluity of iron and steel in 1920–1921, insofar as it existed, was a consequence of market conditions rather than of a significant increase in production. Nevertheless, the glut on the iron market in the spring of 1920 provided unmistakable proof of the abuses that had led to the foundation of the Iron Trades Federation (*Eisenwirtschaftsbund*—EWB).

Although it remained possible to debate the wisdom and appropriateness of Dr. Reichert's program in the context of the time and conditions under which it was devised, after April 1920 the industrialists were confronted with both the unintended and the intended legacy of the Reichert program. The EWB belonged distinctly to the former category. It was the response of the RWM and the manufacturers to the iron shortage and the pricing policies pursued by the producers, and it was a humiliating symbol of the failure of the producers to settle their differences with the iron consumers before government intervention. Although the producers who followed Reichert's advice on domestic pricing certainly made money, they had to pay for these financial advantages with the loss of autonomy and the other difficulties presented by the new EWB. Ironically, however, the EWB was founded at just the moment when the conditions that had led to its creation were disintegrating. The fundamental question, therefore, was whether the producers could take advantage of the changed economic situation, that is, the increased supply and tendency toward

---

[4] Apparently Bruhn was dissuaded by Director Wirtz of the Friedrich-Wilhelms-Hütte, who in a letter of September 13, 1920, warned the former against sowing discord within industry because "a not-to-be-underestimated number of the members of the iron industry and even of other industrial branches held and still hold, whether rightly or wrongly, another point of view." Friedrich-Wilhelms-Hütte Archiv, Nr. 860/17.

[5] For these incidents, see the June 22, 1920, VdESI Executive Directors meeting, BA, R 13 I/158.

lower prices, to conciliate the iron consumers and prevent Baron von Buttlar and other enemies of heavy industry from realizing their goal of limiting producer autonomy through the EWB.

Where Reichert had opposed the EWB with all his might, he had been a warm advocate of self-governing export control boards. Furthermore, there can be no question that export controls were essential if German manufacturers were to be prevented from selling at cut-throat prices. The increased value of the mark and the worldwide depression in 1920–1921, however, raised serious questions about the continued utility and desirability of a thoroughgoing system of export controls. At a time when successful competition on world markets demanded speed and flexibility, businessmen were bound to complain about bureaucratic procedures and minimum prices imposed by the Export Control Boards. Thus, even this pillar of Reichert's program was now open to challenge. Furthermore, the changed economic situation also meant that businessmen were going to take a much less lighthearted attitude toward labor demands than that advocated by Reichert. They would no longer be as willing to grant wage increases, and they would no longer be prepared to follow Reichert's unresisting policy with regard to the so-called export levy (*Ausfuhragabe*). In a successful effort to foil Erzberger's plans to tax the export profit arising from the exchange rate, the business representatives on the ZAG concluded a compromise with their trade union counterparts under which a special levy, calculated at an average of 5%, would be levied on export profits for social purposes.[6] The government accepted this proposal, and it would have represented a successful arrangement for the businessmen if the economic situation had not changed so drastically just when the government began to implement it. By the spring of 1920, however, this export levy, like the Export Control Boards and the EWB, came under attack as noxious hindrances to business recovery in depressed market conditions.

Nevertheless, even during this period of relatively poor business conditions, Pangloss rather than Cassandra had more to offer the iron and steel producers. The reaction to their policies in the fall and winter of 1919–1920 had come too late to correct the situation from which the producers had profited, while the depressed conditions of 1920–1921 drove the segments of the business community back together and undermined the institutions set up to guarantee public control. At the same time, as will be shown in the following chapter, the producers were able to employ old and new profits to engage in that program

[6] See Heinrich Kaun, *Die Geschichte der Zentralarbeitsgemeinschaft der industriellen und gewerblichen Arbeitgeber und Arbeitnehmer Deutschlands* (Jena, 1938), pp. 76–80.

163

of vertical concentration for which the inflation was so famous. Thus, 1920–1921 was a time when private power enjoyed and consolidated new victories over public power and when the producers gained new tactical advantages in their relations with the manufacturers and the workers.

THE FAILURE OF THE EWB

On April 23, 1920, the newly created "parliament of the iron trades," the EWB, held its first plenary session in the large meeting hall of the *Stahlhof* in Düsseldorf. It was an impressive assemblage, because not only the 70 regular delegates but also most of the deputy delegates, who had an advisory vote in the deliberations, and a host of RWM and other government representatives appeared. The regular delegates were divided into three groups, 34 producers, 12 merchants, and 24 primary consumers, and each of these groups was equally divided between employers and workers from the groups represented. The seating arrangements were curiously at odds with much of the theory underlying the *Gemeinwirtschaftskörper*. The government representatives sat in an elevated position looking down on the "self-government" taking place below them, and although employers and workers were supposed to be partners within their respective groups, the producer-employers and the merchant-employers sat together on the right, whereas the consumer-employers sat together on the left. The worker representatives occupied the middle table and the ends of the side tables. Undoubtedly without intention, these seating arrangements reflected the peculiarities of a corporatist organization partially founded on class organizations. Most of the work of the EWB was not to be done in plenary session but rather in the working committees established under the decree: the Pig Iron Committee, the Inland Iron Trades Committee, the Foreign Trade Committee, and the Committee for the Regulation of Imports from the Saar and Lorraine. Even these, however, were to be committees of 60 or 70, and the size of the EWB and its committees caused one critical newspaper to remark that it almost appeared as if the EWB was "the creation of the Düsseldorf innkeepers."[7]

Such a creation would undoubtedly have been more palatable to the producers, the merchants, and even some of the manufacturers than the institution created by the RWM. The Decree of April 1, 1920, that created the EWB had been hastily promulgated, and the opposition to its provisions were known to both the Reichstag Com-

[7] *Kölnische Zeitung*, May 9, 1920.

mittee that had approved it and the RWM, both of which had declared their willingness to consider proposals for revision. In his opening remarks at the plenary meeting of April 23, therefore, Buttlar assured those present that he did not regard the EWB as an "ideal solution" to the problems faced by the iron trades but only as an "expedient" (*Notbehelf*) to alleviate the difficulties that had arisen. He asked for cooperation and assured the assembled that convincingly argued proposals for changes in the decree would receive consideration and action.[8]

As called for by the decree, the Chairman (*Vertrauensmann*, literally Trustee) of the EWB was to be chosen from the producer-employer group, and Director Ernst Poensgen of the Phoenix concern was unanimously elected upon that group's recommendation. Poensgen assured Buttlar and the EWB that he would try to fulfill his tasks with objectivity and impartiality. Speaking for his producer colleagues, however, he declared that the producers could not regard the decree as a "happy solution," and he made it clear that they "must even now refuse responsibility for its successful implementation." However, they intended to show goodwill now that the decree had the force of law and would try to bring about "a viable regulation of the German iron trades." Thus, it was clear to all that the producers and their allies had very definite changes in mind.[9]

The second plenary meeting of the EWB on April 24 began at ten o'clock in the morning and ended at two the following morning. Such marathon meetings were to repeat themselves fairly frequently, and in later years Poensgen looked back on these meetings, which he counted among his "unhappiest memories," and paid tribute to a "rear end hardened on the rowing bench"[10] for his capacity to hold out through these battles when his colleagues were often ready to give in. By all accounts, however, Poensgen owed his success as chairman of these meetings to more than *Sitzfleisch*: "Ernst Poensgen understood how to combine the nonpartisanship of the chairmanship with his role as the representative of the interests of his party in such a way that

[8] The printed record of these meetings of April 23–24, 1920, may be found in numerous archives. I have found the fullest report in the Friedrich-Wilhelms-Hütte Archiv, Nr. 866/08. See also DZA, Potsdam, RWM, Nr. 4455, Bl. 164–165, and BA, R 13 I/416, Bl. 265ff.

[9] *Ibid.*

[10] Remarks of General Director Dr. Ernst Poensgen at a celebration in his honor on October 17, 1941, printed as "Ernst Poensgen–Die Ehrung im Stahlhof am 17. Oktober 1941" in *Verbindungsstelle Eisen für Schrifttum und Presse, Düsseldorf, Stahlhof* (1941), p. 38. Apparently Poensgen was happier in 1941 when such "Marxist" institutions as the EWB were a thing of the past, although let it be said that he added the Nazi years to his many unhappy memories after 1945.

his dual role aroused no objection. The calm and authoritative way in which he handled the material assured him of success. There were enough highly combative men among the iron producers available to present a more radical and even the most radical point of view and who thereby, perhaps unconsciously, made possible the effectiveness of Poensgen's position. . . ."[11] As might be expected, the basic work was done neither in the plenary nor in the committee meetings, which were usually filled with lengthy statements of conflicting opinions, but rather in the caucuses of the various groups and in the private negotiations between them that punctuated the movement from one deadlock to another in the formal meetings. Although the length of the April 24 session testified to the difficulty involved in resolving differences in the body, therefore, it was not to be atypical. It must also be said, however, that it produced more results than later meetings, namely, a lengthy series of proposals for changes in the Decree of April 1 that testified to the continued power of the iron and steel producers.

The basic objection of the producers to the EWB was, of course, the very fact that it existed, but its most infuriating feature was the concept of "self-government" that it reflected. In their view, the RWM had not created a constitution under which the iron trades would take responsibility for their own regulation but had instead arrogated the regulation of the iron trades to RWM commissars while creating an EWB that was little more than "an organ for the execution of instructions given by the Reich Economics Ministry."[12] Thus, the RWM had reserved the right to determine the composition of the EWB, the products to be regulated by it, the allocation of iron and steel for domestic use and exports, and the allocation of exchange, imports, and scrap after "consultation" (*nach Anhörung*) with the EWB or with its "understanding." It also reserved the right to examine the books and records of private firms. The formula, "after consultation," was familiar to the businessmen from the day of the Empire. They had found it demeaning then, and they regarded it as even more unacceptable at the hands of the new regime.[13] Nor were they mollified by the formula, "after understanding," for however much this might have been a concession in the eyes of the RWM officials who drafted the decree, the businessmen could not consider the EWB a true instrument of self-government so long as the RWM retained either general

[11] O. Funcke, "Vergangene Zeiten, Buch 2," Industrieinstitut.

[12] EWB resolution addressed to the Reichstag Economic Policy Committee requesting changes in the EWB Decree of April 1, 1920, in BA, R 13 I/416, Bl. 261ff.

[13] See Reichert's interesting remarks at the VdESI Executive Directors meeting of November 18, 1920, BA, R 13 I/159.

veto powers or the specific powers it had reserved to itself. Under §19 the RWM commissars could impose a suspensive veto on any decision of the EWB. If agreement could not be reached after ten days, then the RWM would decide the issue "after consultation" with the Reich Economic Council or one of the Council's committees. Also, the above procedure could be employed in any case where at least six members of an EWB committee appealed a committee decision to the RWM.

At the meeting of April 24, the producers, with relatively little difficulty, secured overwhelming or strong majority support for changing nearly all these provisions in such a manner that the EWB would have sole discretion. With similar intent, the producers carried an amendment limiting the suspensive veto of the RWM to decisions and elections with less than a three-quarter majority and to elections and decisions viewed as "dangerous to the public interest." Should the RWM and the EWB prove unable to reach an agreement on these matters within ten days, then the decision was to be made by the Reich Economic Council and the Reichsrat, not the RWM. These resolutions were not the only victories won by the producers. Upon their motion, the number of producer representatives was to be raised from 34 to 36, thus giving them 50% of the votes (§34). Finally, it was recommended that the provision allowing for imprisonment as well as fines for violation of EWB decisions be eliminated.[14]

In most of the above-mentioned issues, as well as in a good many minor ones, the producer-employers had the support of the merchants and the consumer-employers, but they also had the support of the workers. The worker representatives, most of whom had been named by the *Zentralarbeitsgemeinschaft*, were won over to a radical reduction of the RWM powers and to numerical equality for the producers with the combined merchants and consumers by a guarantee of worker parity on the EWB committees. Under §8 of the EWB Decree, the number of worker representatives on the committees could be reduced by a maximum of three with the approval of the labor delegates in the plenum. This provision reflected the belief that the trade unions might not have enough delegates with the desired expertise to staff the committees and that they would be willing to yield some of their seats to more competent employer colleagues. Because the trade union delegates were very jealous of their rights in economic matters, however, they were most anxious to have their parity guaranteed and gladly traded a variety of concessions to the producer-employers in return for elimination of the offensive provision. Undoubtedly many of the labor delegates were convinced as well that the EWB should

[14] EWB meeting of April 24, 1920, in Friedrich-Wilhelms-Hütte Archiv, Nr. 866/08.

167

be truly self-governing and objected to the patriarchal character of the RWM's powers.[15]

A similar combination of practical and ideological considerations moved the consumer-employer group to support the amendments. Although some of them had played an important role in bringing the EWB into existence, the vast majority had always opposed the Wissell-Moellendorff schemes, and they had accepted the EWB "with a heavy heart" as a necessary evil. The EWB might restore some of the balance in the relationship between producers and iron consumers, but it could not eliminate the continued dependence of the latter upon the former or obliterate the mutual interests of producers and manufacturers as employers. Having shown their teeth by calling on the government and having organized into a Federation of Iron Consumers in early March to present a united front on the Export Control Board and in the EWB, they were now prepared to be more conciliatory where they deemed it safe. They, too, believed in industrial self-government and easily joined with the producers in demanding true power for the EWB. At the same time, they were prepared to give the producers formal equality just as they were willing to eliminate some of the more humiliating provisions of the decree with regard to penalties.[16]

Thus, the consumers and producers were careful to limit their battles to those issues where confrontation was unavoidable. The longest and most difficult debate, therefore, revolved around §11, which obligated the producers to give priority to the demands of their domestic customers not only over their foreign customers but also over their own needs.[17] From the standpoint of the producers, this provision could not be fulfilled, and they considered it a prime illustration of the antiproducer animus and amateurishness that characterized the entire decree in their eyes. On the one hand, it appeared to presume that the productive capacity of the works was completely within their control. No provision was made for nondelivery due to strikes, coal shortages, foreign occupation, etc., and no consideration was given to the fact that delivery within a month might prove impossible. On the other hand, the provision that the works had always to make their

[15] *Ibid.* It should be noted, however, that the Socialist German Metal Workers Union (DMV) had only two instead of its allotted fifteen delegates at the meeting because it had resigned from the ZAG in October 1919 and refused to have its delegates named by the ZAG. Thus, the most radical and important of the unions was underrepresented.

[16] See O. Funcke's interesting discussion in the *Bergische-Märkische Zeitung* of June 14, 1920, in the section on "Rohstoffe" of his memoirs in the Industrieinstitut.

[17] Decree on the Regulation of the Iron Trades of April 1, 1920, *Reichsgesetzblatt* (Berlin, 1920), p. 435ff.

self-consumption secondary to the satisfaction of EWB demands ignored the extent to which manufacturing plants producing for essential domestic purposes were attached to many of the producer works and were threatened with shut-down if the provision were carried out literally in time of severe shortage. In short, to what extent were vertically organized concerns obligated to supply raw materials to producers of essentially needed manufactured products that they were producing themselves? In the virtual unanswerability of this question lay the strength of the producer argument that problems of short supply could be answered only by increased production, not bureaucratic regulation. In the abuses to which the provision addressed itself lay much of the consumer desperation that had led to their acceptance of the EWB. As might be expected, the new version finally agreed upon by the two groups lessened but did not resolve the dilemma by specifying that the obligation to supply domestic customers first was to be fulfilled "insofar as this is not made impossible by conditions not under the influence of the works" and insofar as the materials used by the works for their own needs was not "primarily essential." Although guaranteeing that the producers would not be called upon to do the impossible, the new version left hanging the obligations of the producer concerns engaged in manufacturing to the "pure" manufacturers. Finally the producers were successful in gaining support for the change of two other economic provisions of the decree that they considered particularly dangerous. They objected strongly to the favoring of producer export rights to works using foreign ores alone and won the inclusion of a passage permitting exports for the purpose of maintaining foreign customers (§13). They also won a majority for the elimination of a provision allowing the establishment of an equalization fund taken from export profits to cover the extra cost of imports of raw materials from the Saar, Lorraine, and Luxemburg into South Germany.[18]

The lengthy and serious catalogue of revisions of the EWB Decree discussed above constituted a challenge to the RWM and particularly to Baron von Buttlar, who had framed the Decree. Buttlar appears to have exercised considerable restraint at the meeting, reserving comments to small matters of detail and openly questioning an EWB resolution on an important matter only in the case of the EWB demand that it determine the quantities allowed for export. In the latter instance, he noted that under law the RWM was the only authority that could give export permits and that this right could not be transferred

[18] See the juxtaposed original and EWB version in BA, R 13 I/416, Bl. 252–253, and Reichert's discussion of the various proposed changes in the VdESI Executive Directors meeting of November 18, 1920, in *ibid.*, 159.

to another body. In general, however, Buttlar withheld comment on the proposed changes, which were formally presented for submission to the Economic Policy Committee of the Reichstag on May 31, 1920. In reality, however, Buttlar could afford to be silent, for he would have the last word. All changes would have to have the approval of the RWM and the Reich Cabinet, as well as the Reichstag Economic Policy Committee and the Reichsrat. In submitting the proposed changes, Poensgen made no effort to match Buttlar's restraint. As a parting shot on behalf of the producers, he pointed out that the proposed changes would eliminate "certain hardships and impossible conditions," but that the government ought to consider the fact that the preconditions under which the decree had been issued had changed and that this made the EWB a "superfluous and production-hindering restraint upon our economic life."[19]

The conditions that had led to the creation of the EWB *had* changed. Demand had been reduced by a worldwide depression and the exchange rate had improved and stabilized. In the spring and summer of 1920 domestic requirements were easily satisfied and market conditions forced producers to reduce their prices. Although anxieties concerning the domestic supply increased in the fall and winter because of the usual coal supply problems and the additional coal delivery burdens imposed by the Spa Agreement between Germany and the Allies of August 1920, some relief was found through coal imports from abroad and increased use of lignite. Most important, market conditions kept demand low in comparison to the previous year, and these conditions persisted through the spring.[20]

These changed market and supply conditions did not eliminate conflicts between producers and consumers, but they did reduce their intensity and made agreement easier. Ironically, the first act of the EWB was to raise the official price ceilings. On the one hand, the producers claimed that the last official prices set by the Steel Federation on February 1 did not cover increased costs. On the other hand, everyone recognized that those prices bore little relation to what was actually being paid on the market. Thus, at its first meeting on April 25, the Inland Committee, with five dissenting labor votes, accepted producer claims that prices for May should be raised 800–1,000 marks. However, the past practices connected with payment in foreign exchange or scrap were outlawed, and a three-man commission composed of a producer, a worker, and a RWM representative was set

[19] Included in the EWB resolution calling for changes, *ibid.*, 416, Bl. 261.
[20] See the reports of the RWM to the President of the Republic, April 1920– September 1921, in BA, R 43 I/1147, Bl. 127ff.

up to examine the cost calculations of a number of the works.[21] At the end of May, new prices were set for June and July which were 215–760 marks lower than those set at the end of April. Thus, for the first time in six years, prices were lowered on iron and steel products. This trend toward lower prices for prolonged periods was repeated at EWB meetings in July and October (see Table 8).[22]

Although the early months of 1921 were filled with rumors of yet another price ceiling reduction, this was strongly resisted by the producers on the grounds that their costs in no way justified such action. The desire to avoid serious altercations before the London Conference on reparations and the general uncertainty surrounding the reparations question, an uncertainty heightened by the Allied occupation of Düsseldorf, Duisburg, and Ruhrort on March 8, further delayed pricing decisions in the EWB. Although there was a general reluctance to set lower price ceilings, the play of the market was turning this into a rather academic question. Producers felt compelled to sell below the price ceilings, and sentiment was growing for the elimination of price ceilings altogether on the grounds of superfluity. On April 23, 1921, a year to the day after the EWB had held its first meeting, it abolished its price ceilings with the proviso that the RWM could reinstitute price ceilings subject to the approval of the Inland Committee within eight days of RWM action. Thus, the first year of the EWB's operation ended with the nullification of its most basic functions, and the *Kölnische Zeitung* voiced the sentiments of its many critics and opponents by suggesting that the EWB "Die at the right time!"[23]

Throughout this first year the hostility of the producers toward the EWB continued and even intensified. Nevertheless, the existence of the EWB had a sobering effect. In an unguarded moment, the Upper Silesian steel industrialist, Ewald Hilger, frankly stated that the unwillingness of certain producers to renew the Steel Works Association had "compelled the government to take the path of the Iron Trades Federation."[24] The creation of the EWB had permitted the liquidation of the Steel Works Association, but its demise was treated with nostalgia and the hope that a return of normal circumstances would bring the day when the EWB would be replaced with a Steel Works Asso-

[21] Reports on the meetings in Friedrich-Wilhelms-Hütte Archiv, Nr. 866/08.

[22] See O. Funcke's excellent discussion of the first year of the EWB in analysis of May 1921 in the chapter entitled "Rohstoffe," Industrieinstitut. Also, see the editorial, "Ein Jahr Eisenwirtschaftsbund," *Kölnische Zeitung*, April 24, 1921.

[23] *Ibid.*

[24] VdESI Executive Directors meeting, June 22, 1920, BA, R 13 I/158.

TABLE 8

The Price of Various Iron and Steel Products, April 1920–December 1921
(price per ton measured in paper and gold marks)

1920		April	May	June	July	August	September	October	November	December
Foundry pig iron III	PM	1775.00	1789.50	1739.50	1739.50	1659.50	1659.50	1659.50	1659.50	1659.50
	GM	125.00	161.70	186.70	185.05	145.95	120.17	102.21	90.21	95.45
Hematite pig iron	PM	2338.50	2350.50	2150.50	2150.50	1910.00	1910.00	1910.00	1910.00	1910.00
	GM	164.68	212.39	230.81	228.78	168.03	138.36	117.68	103.86	109.89
Billets	PM	2776.00	2776.00	2776.00	2485.00	2485.00	2485.00	2118.00	2118.00	2118.00
	GM	163.73	282.37	292.48	289.89	208.06	171.31	145.71	108.48	114.78
Girders	PM	2772.00	3620.00	3105.00	3105.00	2740.00	2740.00	2740.00	2340.00	2340.00
	GM	195.21	327.10	333.26	330.32	241.05	198.48	168.81	127.24	134.63
Merchant bars	PM	2802.00	3650.00	3200.00	3200.00	2840.00	2840.00	2840.00	2840.00	2840.00
	GM	186.82	329.72	343.35	340.43	289.78	205.65	174.98	132.68	140.39
Heavy plate	PM	3435.00	3435.00	4700.00	4040.00	3595.00	3595.00	3595.00	3090.00	3090.00
	GM	241.90	424.69	433.62	429.79	316.27	260.41	221.49	168.03	177.78

1921		January	February	March	April	May	June	July	August	September	October	November	December
Foundry pig iron III	PM	1659.00	1659.00	1659.00	1509.00	1484.00	1484.00	1484.00	1484.00	1484.00	1484.00	2124.00	3250.00
	GM	107.34	113.65	111.57	99.76	100.45	89.86	81.26	73.93	59.41	41.50	33.91	71.08
Hematite pig iron	PM	1910.00	1910.00	1910.00	1910.00	1810.00	1810.00	1810.00	1810.00	1810.00	1810.00	2700.00	3891.00
	GM	123.58	130.84	128.46	126.27	122.03	109.60	99.11	90.17	72.46	50.61	43.10	85.11
Billets	PM	1995.00	1995.00	1995.00	1682.00	1682.00	1682.00	1832.00	1832.00	1832.00	3552.00	3552.00	3552.00
	GM	129.08	136.66	134.17	131.89	113.40	101.85	92.10	91.26	73.34	51.23	56.71	77.69
Girders	PM	2340.00	2340.00	2340.00	2340.00	1737.50	1800.00	2100.00	2340.00	2340.00	3150.00	3775.00	4390.00
	GM	151.41	160.30	157.37	154.70	117.17	109.00	114.99	116.57	93.68	88.08	60.27	107.83
Merchant bars	PM	2440.00	2440.00	2440.00	2440.00	1775.00	1800.00	1900.00	2150.00	2440.00	2850.00	2850.00	4765.00
	GM	157.88	167.15	164.10	161.31	119.67	109.00	104.04	107.10	97.68	76.45	65.61	110.02
Heavy plate	PM	3090.00	3090.00	3090.00	3090.00	1850.00	1725.00	1775.00	1930.00	2350.00	3050.00	4300.00	5365.00
	GM	199.94	211.67	207.81	204.28	124.72	104.46	97.19	96.14	94.08	85.29	68.65	117.35

Source: Hans J. Schneider, Zur Analyse des Eisenmarktes (Vierteljahrshefte Zur Konjunkturforschung, Sonderheft 1) (Berlin, 1927), p. 103.

ciation once again.[25] The implication that voluntary association could have prevented and still might ameliorate compulsory organization was important in inspiring the Pig Iron Syndicate to extend its existence for three years.[26]

Although the producers sought to use the poor market conditions, the falling prices, and the ungainliness of the EWB to argue for its elimination, they had only mixed success in convincing their manufacturing colleagues. The strongest manufacturer case against the EWB was made by Hans von Raumer, who had opposed it from the start, but his arguments in part refute some of those used by the producers in precisely the same cause. Raumer argued, and here much in tune with the producers, that economic decisions could not be made by majority vote, that it was impossible to find a correct way of dividing votes among the many interests involved, and that just as it was wrong for producers to give consumers a voice in their pricing policies while retaining full responsibility for the financial survival of their enterprises, so was it wrong for consumers to be identified with decisions that ran against their own interests. In contrast to the general line taken by the producers, however, Raumer thought the voting arrangements in the EWB unfavorable to consumer interests. He pointed out that the merchants had similar interests to the producers and "the workers are easily inclined to agree to price increases because they hope to have an easier time thereby in presenting increased wage demands."[27] Raumer felt that the customers were inhibited in the defense of their interests by fear of reprisals and other considerations and that they were "without influence" as a result. Thus, on the one hand, passivity on the part of the consumers meant a surrender to the producer effort to use the EWB "as an instrument to justify their policy." On the other hand, resistance and appeals to the veto power of the RWM made the consumers appear as supporters of the controlled economy. Under these circumstances, Raumer claimed, the EWB was useless and, because of the greater stabilization of the mark and decline in prices, unnecessary as well. As an alternative, Raumer pleaded for a return to negotiations within a limited circle on the basis of goodwill and, above all, for strong primary consumer organizations that would fight for their interests. Raumer was particularly concerned with the avoidance of conflict at a time when

[25] See the editorial, "Vom Stahlwerks-Verband zum Eisenwirtschaftsbund," *Stahl und Eisen*, 40:1, May 20, 1920, pp. 673–677.

[26] See Wirtz to Wenzel, June 11, 1920. Friedrich-Wilhelms-Hütte, Nr. 866/08, and Klotzbach, *Roheisen-Verband*, p. 232ff.

[27] Raumer to the VdESI, June 21, 1920, BA, R 13 I/416, Bl. 199ff., for this and the remaining quotations from and discussion of his position.

"all disunity within industry leads to attacks promoting Socialist tendencies." Raumer and the Zendei, of which he was business manager, therefore, constituted a strong anti-EWB force in the Federation of Iron Consumers. Indeed, Director Henrich of the Siemens-Schuckert concern privately suggested to Reichert that the EWB prices "be strongly undersold by a number of smelting works because that would be the quickest way to show that the Iron Trades Federation is unnecessary and has to be eliminated."[28]

Political, therefore, as well as economic incentives forced the producers to sell below EWB prices in the winter of 1920–1921, and the decision to eliminate price ceilings in April 1921 was undoubtedly encouraged by this. Nevertheless, the evidence suggests that economic considerations were more important than political ones in the April 1921 decision. The producers had taken a hard line for as long as they could with regard to the price ceilings despite their actual underselling of EWB prices. They fought for higher official prices than they actually charged for two reasons. First, as a leading manufacturer put it, "The great sense of power developed over the long boom which had lasted many years worked against the prospect of their appearing as the economically weaker party in times of recession."[29] More than a psychological disposition was involved, however. The producers were not amused by consumer attacks on their pricing policies and also felt that many manufacturers were not doing their share to lower prices. A particularly nasty altercation took place in the VDMA Board of Directors meeting of September 16, 1920, when Justizrat Waldschmidt of Loewe & Co. and General Director Becker of the Kalker Maschinenfabrik placed the entire blame for the economic crisis upon the "profiteering pricing policy" of the raw materials syndicates during the first quarter of 1920. Director Wedemeyer of the GHH took the offensive for the producers. He argued that "the perennial accusations against the raw materials industry . . . ought to stop," especially because the machine building industry had also demanded very high prices.[30] Clearly, the producers were very sensitive

[28] Reichert to Poensgen, July 15, 1920, *ibid.*, Bl. 177–179.

[29] Funcke in his article of May 1921 in "Rohstoffe," Industrieinstitut.

[30] Wedemeyer to Reusch, September 23, 1920, HA/GHH, Nr. 300193000/5. In a friendlier exchange, C. F. von Siemens, whose concern was in the process of forming an IG with Deutsch-Lux to be discussed in the next chapter, responded to Vögler's accusations that the electrotechnical industry was not following the lead of the producers by pointing out that it had begun its efforts to hold down prices in March 1920 and thus had no reason to respond to the EWB May price decreases. See Siemens to Vögler, December 21, 1920, SAA 4/Lf, Bd. 10, Bl. 119–120. On June 15, 1920, an article appeared in the *Rheinisch-Westfälische Zeitung* suggesting that the electrotechnical industry needed to be blessed with an institu-

that it was they, not their customers, who were being called upon to control their prices. Hence the producers sought to make their point in each debate over price ceilings, while the majority of the consumers in the Federation of Iron Consumers, ably led by Director Schrey of the Association of German Railroad Car Manufacturers, insisted on the maintenance of the EWB, not because they were satisfied with it, but because it gave them a measure of control over the producers and some guarantee against a return of 1919–1920 conditions.[31]

Yet another major reason for producer opposition to a sharp reduction of official prices commensurate with the prices actually being charged was that the producers considered it of fundamental importance that they demonstrate the ill effects of continued wage increases and the eight-hour day and thereby show that their costs had not declined with their declining prices. Director Wirtz of the Friedrich-Wilhelms-Hütte, for example, opposed Bruhn-Klotzbach proposals to lower pig iron prices in February 1921 because "it is absolutely essential that worker and consumer circles really experience directly the consequences of the steady wage increases. . . ."[32] The manufacturers in the EWB were not insensitive to such reasoning, and they felt strongly that price ceilings should not be allowed to drop below costs. Thus, in April 1921, when the leading manufacturers saw that it would be impossible to create a viable price ceiling that at once took into account costs and a reasonable profit while at the same time corresponding to the realities of the market, it was they, not the producers, who proposed that the price ceilings be suspended. They recognized that this would please the producers while at the same time benefiting the manufacturers who were naively using the EWB price ceilings as a guide in the purchase of raw materials. Consequently, a "friendly agreement" to suspend the chief functions of the EWB could be made among the employers even if they did not find it possible to join together with the object of eliminating the EWB itself.[33]

In any case, the actual elimination of the EWB by means of an employer agreement was impossible because the workers would not allow it. At the same time, the posture gradually assumed by the worker representatives in the EWB increased the dissatisfaction of

tion like the EWB. The heavy industrialists subsequently denied charges that they had inspired the article. See Sorge's comments at the June 22, 1920, VdESI meeting, BA, R 13 I/158.

[31] See Funcke's May 1921 article in "Rohstoffe," Industrieinstitut.

[32] Wirtz to Vögler, February 12, 1921, Friedrich-Wilhelms-Hütte Archiv, Nr. 120.

[33] See Funcke's May 1921 article in "Rohstoffe," Industrieinstitut.

all the employers with the EWB. The ideology underlying corporatist organizations of this type was at least in one major respect similar to that of the *Arbeitsgemeinschaft*, i.e., the notion that workers and employers had common interests as producers that were at once anterior and and superior to differences arising from their class situations. This notion assisted employers in coming to terms with the necessity of collective bargaining without surrendering their prewar ideological baggage about the identity of employer-worker interests or the notion that the "true" representatives of the workers were those who worked in the plants and were in direct contact with its problems rather than the union secretaries. Also, the employers were reinforced in these beliefs by the attitudes of at least some of the non-Socialist labor representatives and by the difficulties workers had in dealing with the technicalities of setting prices for iron and steel products.

It would appear that some of the workers did look to the employers for the expert technical information needed to make pricing decisions and were easily won over by arguments based on expertise or what appeared to be expertise. At the same time, they could easily be influenced against producer demands by a show of employer ill-temper and, more importantly, by the attitude of the RWM representatives. The producer-employers, however, were not always willing to do all that was necessary to take advantage of the potential support of the workers although they were well aware of the need to make some efforts in this direction. Thus, for example, they might refuse to supply friendly worker representatives with cost calculations because "the determination of individual figures is very difficult and easily leads to misunderstandings which could give rise to completely confused ideas."[34]

Such employer-producer blandishments and efforts at persuasion as there were, however, were of little avail in the case of the representatives of the Socialist Metal Workers Union (DMV), the most powerful and important of the industrial trade unions and the most radical. The DMV had withdrawn from the ZAG and the branch *Arbeitsgemeinschaften* in October 1919, when its membership replaced its conservative Majority Socialist leader, Alexander Schlicke, with the Independent Socialist, Robert Dissmann. It sent less than its allotted representatives to the first meetings of the EWB in April 1920, and they ostentatiously demanded that the EWB Decree be changed to have the DMV representatives named directly by the union itself or through the General Confederation of German Trade

[34] Wirtz to Wenzel, June 11, 1920, Friedrich-Wilhelms-Hütte Archiv, Nr. 866/08.

Unions (ADGB) rather than through the ZAG. When it appeared that the employers were going to try to use the situation to force the DMV back into the ZAG, the DMV refused to participate in the EWB and compelled the Deputy Chairman of the EWB, Hans Böckler, to withdraw until the DMV won its point. Finally, after lengthy and confused negotiations, the DMV representatives were seated in July 1920 independently of all ZAG influence and with the promise that an appropriate change in the decree would be made in connection with the general revision being planned.[35]

As can be imagined, the relative absence of the DMV at the first meetings and its complete absence during the first months of the EWB's existence were not bemoaned by the employers. Not only was it easier for the employer-producers to win out in the voting, but they were also spared large amounts of Socialist agitation. The DMV constantly sought to expose what it viewed as the profiteering of heavy industry and, while viewing the EWB with suspicion and dissatisfaction, pointedly warned that "The heavy industrialists have every reason to fear *any* judge unbribed by its money."[36] After entering the EWB in full force in July 1920, the DMV representatives sharply attacked the manufacturers and non-Socialist trade union representatives for making compromises with the producers and rejected the charge that the DMV was disturbing the economic peace: "What peace? Between the classes there is no peace, there can be no peace."[37] The producers were quick to take up such statements as further ammunition against the EWB.

The combined performance of the workers and the RWM representatives at the late October 1920 EWB meetings, however, had the effect of further intensifying producer opposition to the EWB as well as driving all the employers together. First, worker solidarity in the Inland Commission forced the producers to reduce prices by 400 marks instead of the 250 marks originally intended. Then, to the much greater distress of the producers, a producer effort to encourage exports and improve their international competitiveness by lifting the 25% export quota and the maximum price restrictions was blocked by the worker representatives on the Export Commission in collaboration with the RWM. The RWM, while quite cognizant of the need to in-

[35] These negotiations can be followed in detail in DZA Potsdam, RWM, Nr. 4455, esp. Bl. 216–223.

[36] *Deutsche Metallarbeiter-Zeitung*, June 20, 1920.

[37] Article by "Hasche" entitled "Eisenwirtschaft," in *ibid.*, August 21, 1920. "Hasche" was the pseudonym of the leading DMV representative in the EWB, the Remscheid trade union secretary Schliestedt. See Reichert's caustic remarks at the VdESI Executive Directors meeting, November 18, 1920, BA, R 13 I/159.

crease exports, was anxious to employ the export profits to reduce domestic prices and tried to use the situation to implement the old idea of an equalization fund. The RWM urged the workers to present a resolution providing for a special tax on export profits toward this end. The proposal incensed the producers, who felt burdened by the social export levy and viewed a further tax along with the hated equalization fund as an unwarranted assault at a time when the economic situation was particularly difficult. Although Director Bruhn wished to have the worker resolution discussed in a caucus with his colleagues, presumably in order to attain a compromise that would save the intended relaxation of export restrictions, Peter Klöckner angrily insisted on an immediate vote on the worker resolution. The latter was defeated in a tie vote along class lines. The workers responded to this brusque rejection of their proposal by rejecting the employer resolutions. Needless to say, the workers celebrated the strength they had demonstrated in the EWB, and the DMV began to find unanticipated virtues in the EWB. It now seemed to be "a factor, which to be sure cannot bring the socialization of the iron industry but which can bring a decisive reduction of the exploitative appetites of heavy industry."[38]

As might be expected, the producers complained bitterly of the sabotage of their efforts to retain German competitiveness in the world-wide economic depression by the Socialist labor leaders. They were even more irritated, however, by the actions of the RWM, which had served to instigate and encourage the worker resolution. Almost immediately following the October 1920 meetings, the industrialists sent a sharp protest to the Economics Minister, Ernst Scholz, a People's Party (DVP) politician who had taken over the ministry in June 1920. Clearly, they had much to complain about. The various articles dealing with the EWB in the DMV's *Metallarbeiter-Zeitung* and in other labor newspapers were highly inflammatory and openly urged the use of the EWB in the class struggle. Industrialists argued that the non-Socialist labor leaders in the EWB were being "terrorized" by the DMV representatives, and that the latter continually threatened to make the former "morally dead" if they dared to vote with the employers. Yet the producers had good reason to suspect that such intimidation might not have been successful if Baron von Buttlar, who

---

[38] *Deutsche Metallarbeiter-Zeitung*, November 6, 1920, and article by A. Leonhardt, "Aus dem Eisenwirtschaftsbund," *Deutsche Werkmeister-Zeitung*, October 29, 1920. It is interesting to note that the trade unionists complained about the failure of other government agencies with voting power in the EWB, the Reconstruction Ministry and the Railroad Authority, to support the RWM.

was now viewed increasingly as a sinister enemy, had not instigated the workers. Producers had overheard Buttlar ask the DMV leader Schliestedt if he had gotten the workers together yet and had seen Buttlar caucus with the labor leaders during meals and before crucial votes.[39]

By the late fall of 1920, however, the employers not only had cause to complain about what the EWB had become, but also about what it threatened to become in the future. There were disturbing reports that Economics Minister Scholz, despite the presumed friendliness of his party to industry, wanted to increase the number of *Gemeinwirtschaftskörper* and use them for purposes of corporate tax levies and equalization of burdens. The idea was most unappealing to producers, who remembered the difficult struggles over quotas in prewar cartels and who could well imagine the conflicts that would erupt in matters of taxation.[40] More concretely and immediately, however, the producers found themselves in a state of war with the RWM bureaucracy, especially with Hirsch and Buttlar. A major cause of their hostility was the manner in which the RWM officials had responded to the proposed changes in the EWB decree.

There *was* something provocative about the manner in which the RWM officials had drafted their response to the changes in the EWB decree proposed by the EWB in April–May 1920, because the new draft turned many of the most important EWB proposals upside down. Both the attitude and the concrete proposals of the RWM officials were impolitic because it was highly unlikely that the Reich Cabinet itself, the Reichstag Economic Policy Committee, or the EWB as a body were prepared to deal serious new blows to the producers under the depressed economic conditions and the difficult international problems of late 1920 and early 1921. Furthermore, the experiences with the EWB had hardly been satisfactory enough to suggest that it could easily be strengthened against the will of the producers.

For all intents and purposes, the only serious concession the RWM made to producer wishes was the elimination of prison sentences for the violation of EWB regulations. Otherwise, the RWM opposed the EWB proposals both in general and in detail. The RWM bluntly challenged the conception of a "self-governing body" implicit in the EWB resolution. In its view, a self-governing body does not imply "complete freedom of decision making and immunity from the action of administrative bodies of the state but rather self-determina-

---

[39] Poensgen to Scholz, October 28, 1920, BA, R 13 I/416, Bl. 70ff., and VdESI meeting of November 18, 1920, *ibid.*, 159.

[40] *Ibid.*

tion within the framework of tasks assigned by law and under the general supervision (*Oberaufsicht*) of the state."[41] This interpretation of "self-government" did not permit very far-reaching concessions to the EWB. The RWM claimed that it was making great concessions to the EWB by substituting "in agreement with the Reich Economics Minister" in place of "after consultation" with the EWB or "after understanding" with the EWB. When it came to the fundamental question of its suspensive veto and its power to make final decisions where an agreement with the EWB could not be reached, however, the RWM argued that it could not surrender its ultimate responsibility.

The RWM, however, demanded something very substantial in return for these very modest concessions to the EWB's wishes, and as usual the demand was being made on the producers. The EWB resolutions had called for giving the producers half the votes in the EWB, and providing the other two groups, consumers and merchants, with the other half. The RWM insisted that the minority status of the producers not only be maintained but actually intensified through the introduction of an entirely new group of "final consumers" (*Endverbraucher*) into the EWB.[42] To begin with, the RWM argued, cogently, that the so-called producer minority was a fiction because the merchants almost invariably voted with the producers. Many of the iron merchants were partially or fully owned by the producers. Also, because the merchant commissions were based on a percentage of price, the merchants had a natural interest in higher prices. The RWM, however, also applied similar arguments to the manufacturers. Many of them, too, it was argued, were financially dependent on the producers, thanks to the process of vertical concentration that was taking place. Furthermore, there was a conflict of interest between those who built machines and those who used them in that the former had an interest in high prices and therefore were willing to support high producer prices in order to impose high prices for manufactured producers on the final consumers. In short, the RWM was now making a real distinction between primary and final consumers and was trying to respond to the pressure of consumer organizations, state and local authorities, and local train and streetcar companies by granting their organizations representation in the new consumer category.[43] Thus, in

[41] The RWM draft and commentaries is to be found in *ibid.*, 416, Bl. 238ff.; see Bl. 243 for this quote. To contrast the RWM position with the EWB resolutions, see *ibid.* and above pp. 167–169.

[42] *Ibid.*, Bl. 243. Under the new draft, 12 final consumers would be added to the ranks of the EWB, and the producers would have 34 of the 80 votes.

[43] For the correspondence with these various interests, see DZA Potsdam, RWM, Nr. 4456–4457.

place of the relatively simple change requested by the EWB, the RWM had seen fit to launch an attack on "producers" in general. In return, it was to be speedily attacked for "consumer Socialism."[44] At the same time, the entire debate opened up a dreary and insoluble discussion of who should be represented in a body like the EWB.

As indicated earlier, the tactical situation of the RWM was poor. The producers could point with justification to the DMV's introduction of class conflict into the EWB, could use the October 1920 meetings to demonstrate their powerlessness, could argue that the primary consumers had been voting with them and were critical of the EWB and, above all, could point to an economic situation in which they were compelled to undersell official prices and were facing stiff foreign competition in exports. All this they did in a series of letters to Minister Scholz in November and December 1920 as soon as a small group of producers were confidentially informed of the new RWM draft.[45] It must be said that it was a bit late and a rather unpropitious time for the RWM to have discovered the "final consumers," and the German admiralty had a point in arguing to the RWM that "If you want to reach any kind of goal in the economic area, then it can only be done through a dictator, that is, through a state agency with sufficient powers."[46] Within the government itself, the RWM also met opposition from the Foreign Office and the Treasury. The former pointed out that the strength of final consumers was impressive enough already because the DMV delegates regarded themselves as representatives of the final consumers.[47] The Treasury, under Hans von Raumer's leadership since June 1920, also constituted a useful producer ally against "consumer socialism" if not against the primary consumers.[48] The difficulties of the RWM officials were further compounded by the leakage of the new draft in mid-December and its publication in the newspapers. This made it hard for the RWM to present the draft to the Cabinet for approval before its contents had become widely known among interested circles.[49]

The greatest obstacle faced by the RWM officials seeking to

[44] Director Nothmann to Reichert, November 10, 1920, BA, R 13 I/416, Bl. 108ff.

[45] See VdESI notes to the RWM of November 19, December 3, and December 16, 1920, in *ibid.*, Bl. 51ff. It learned of the RWM draft on November 11.

[46] Admiralty Councilor Friedrichs to Buttlar, November 24, 1920, DZA Potsdam, RWM, Nr. 4457, Bl. 132.

[47] Foreign Office to RWM, December 10, 1920, *ibid.*, Bl. 140–141.

[48] Raumer asked to address the cabinet in opposition to the RWM draft. See the minute of Schäfer of the Reich Treasury Ministry, February 4, 1921, *ibid.*, Bl. 77. Raumer was a DVP deputy.

[49] Reich Commissar for the Iron Trades to RWM, January 18, 1921, *ibid.*, Bl. 40.

strengthen their position against the producers, however, was that the political situation increasingly interfered with their intended actions while the economic situation militated against controls. Just as the fall of the mark at the turn of 1919–1920 and the Kapp Putsch had played into the hands of the RWM, so now the bourgeois composition of the Fehrenbach Cabinet ruling Germany between June 1920 and May 1921 and the continual foreign policy crises of 1921 combined with poor business conditions further undermined the government's capacity to take a strong hand internally, weakened the case for the EWB, and strengthened the producers. As mentioned earlier, the economic situation had led to the elimination of price ceilings and thus the practical emasculation of the EWB in April 1921. The economic interests of the producers and manufacturers now seemed to run along virtually parallel lines, because price ceilings were clearly dysfunctional in a depressed market. At the same time, the manufacturers had been irritated by both the workers and the RWM and were more inclined than ever to concentrate on their common interests with their fellow employers in the producer camp. The tactical advantage lay with the employers because a majority vote was necessary for the reintroduction of price ceilings under the EWB voting regulations. If the employers stood together, they could defeat any worker resolution to restore price ceilings.[50]

Here, indeed, was the worker dilemma. The DMV delegates and other labor delegates fought for price ceilings in order to preserve the "principle of co-determination . . . the participation of the workers in economic and pricing questions."[51] However, the co-determination right of the labor organizations was a function of the inflationary emergency rather than of any permanent structure of economic decision making, and its survival depended on the peculiar arrangements necessary to meet the inflationary emergency. The moment these arrangements lost their rationale, the workers were placed in the strange situation of having to defend institutions threatened with obsolescence in order to maintain their rights of participation. The fragility of labor's rights was thus manifest.

Economic conditions in the spring and summer of 1921 worked in favor of the employer position, as did the political difficulties in connection with reparations and Upper Silesia. Businessmen were troubled by the depressed market conditions and political problems, but some found encouraging the vision of stabilization induced by the improvement of the German currency since the spring of 1920. As one

[50] Funcke, "Rückschau," of August 19, 1922, in "Rohstoffe," Industrieinstitut.
[51] See Reichert's report on the Inland Committee meeting of April 22, 1921, BA, R 13 I/418, Bl. 207–208.

businessman reported: ". . . Industry returned to stable prices, and there was a belief in wide circles in an impending recovery so that it was held in the most important iron industrialist circles that the process of recovery demanded a return to full responsibility among all business circles. The improvement of the mark in the summer of 1921 had even led otherwise very cautious industrialists (Vögler, etc.) to give preference in exports to business that could be done in marks over business that had to be done in strong currencies."[52] By mid-summer 1921, prices reached their lowest level, and the producers were hungry for domestic orders.

In August 1921, however, the situation began to change as the value of the mark began to fall. Consumers of raw materials, however, had failed to take advantage of the period of low prices and were reluctant initially to believe that the impending boom was real. Producers had become increasingly dependent on exports, and the fall of the mark naturally encouraged them to export as much as possible to cover their rising costs. By September there was heavy demand both at home and abroad, prices began to increase rapidly, and the fear developed that the situation of fall and winter of 1919–1920 was going to be repeated all over again. The trade union leaders were quick to note the change and began to call for the reintroduction of price ceilings. The RWM responded to complaints from some consumers and workers and its own growing concern by sending officials on surprise visits to producers to examine their books and report on the question on reintroducing price ceilings.[53]

The experiences of the EWB, however, had sobered both the producers and their customers, and the lessons of the previous twelve months had not been lost. The two sides and the non-Socialist trade unions were talking things out in the Steel Federation, and the producers were being very cautious in their pricing policies. The RWM found it difficult to challenge the cost calculations that lay at the base of the producer pricing policies, although it argued that the export profits justified a lowering of domestic prices. Similarly, although the RWM had received cabinet approval for its proposed changes in the EWB decree, the forces united in the Steel Federation increasingly argued that they were prepared to drop their own demands for changes in return for the RWM's abandonment of its proposals. In short, producers and consumers were demanding the status quo in the iron trades, insisting that their private collaboration in the Steel Federation was truly effective and that price ceilings would only de-

[52] Retrospective survey by Klemme for Woltmann, December 27, 1923, HA/GHH, Nr. 300000/5.
[53] Funcke, "Rückschau" of August 19, 1922, in "Rohstoffe," Industrieinstitut.

stabilize the market further and lead to renewed black marketeering. In August, the Steel Federation urged its members not to exceed the last official price ceilings and to sell at stable prices. When evidence mounted in September that this request was being violated, the RWM decided to summon a meeting of the Inland Pricing Commission of the EWB to consider the reintroduction of price ceilings.[54]

It was natural for iron consumers suddenly confronted with claims that their orders could not be met or inordinately high prices to conjure up bitter memories of the winter and spring of 1919–1920 and to argue that a repetition of the latter situation could only lead to sharper export controls and the reintroduction of price ceilings. Indeed, when Director Lippart of the MAN complained to Reusch at the end of September, Reusch himself suspected that the export market was being unduly favored, especially by Rheinstahl, where the influence of the Cologne iron merchant, Otto Wolff, was dominant. Reusch's well-informed subordinate, Director Klemme, however, made a much more differentiated comparison between the situations in 1920 and 1921. He too feared a repetition of some of the experiences of early 1920 if the mark continued its deterioration. Although some major consumers had been shrewd enough to buy up huge amounts of iron at cheap prices during the summer, others were now caught short. Some producers, such as the GHH, were sold out until the beginning of the year, and no one was willing to sell their production at the last EWB prices. Klemme doubted, however, that the shortages and high prices were the consequence of excessive exports because the export market had been bad for weeks. It was known, to be sure, that Hoesch was favoring its foreign customers and claiming that it was going to have to curtail its domestic production program, but the real difficulty appeared to be that firms such as Hoesch, Rheinstahl, and Thyssen were refusing to fulfill old contracts without special premiums or price increases and were often reneging on old contracts or delaying their fulfillment in order to meet more recent orders made at more favorable conditions. Klemme urged, therefore, that a front be formed within the industry against excessive exports and other undesirable practices, but that no support be given to increased export restrictions because the exports were essential for their survival.[55]

The RWM, for its part, was reluctant to decree price ceilings. On the one hand, court decisions had called into question its legal right to do so. On the other hand, it seemed impossible to alienate both the producers and the manufacturers by decreeing price ceilings against

[54] See the relevant documents in DZA Potsdam, RWM, Nr. 4458, Bl. 61ff.

[55] Lippart to Reusch, September 27, 1921, and Reusch to Lippart, October 2, 1921, and Klemme report of October 5, 1921, in HA/GHH, Nr. 300193010/13.

their will and then having the RWM decision thrown out by a negative vote of the EWB. At a meeting of the manufacturer representatives with the RWM on September 26, it became clear that the former had decided that the powers of the EWB were more useful as a threat than as a reality. Thus, Oscar Funcke admitted that some of the abuses of early 1920 were being repeated, but he minimized their importance. In general, he felt that costs justified the prices being demanded and that "moderation" was being practiced by the producers. At the same time, it was only just that consumers pay a certain penalty for their mistaken decision to hold back on their purchase of raw materials when prices were low. Funcke urged that they "strengthen the backs of those works charging moderate prices while threatening price ceilings if moderation is not pursued."[56]

Baron von Buttlar placed very little faith in friendly understanding between the producers and the consumers, an attitude that reflected both his own prejudices and his reading of the past history, but he found himself in a very weak position at the EWB meetings of October 18–20, 1921, where both the reform of the EWB Decree and price ceilings came up for discussion. He could not prevent the burying of his efforts to change the EWB Decree in favor of consumer interests. Even the DMV representatives recognized the pointlessness of trying to change the EWB in any serious way. After securing an agreement that they could name their representatives independently, they helped make unanimous the withdrawal of the changes the EWB had proposed in late April 1920. Shortly thereafter, the RWM withdrew its draft of the changes in the Decree to avoid the "bitter economic and political conflicts" they would generate.[57]

The proposal to reintroduce price ceilings at the October 19 meeting was rejected thanks to employer unanimity. When Buttlar argued that price ceilings had to be reintroduced to ensure that domestic prices remained below world market prices, Schrey, speaking for the iron consumers, sang a paean to producer-consumer collaboration. He argued that the good result of the EWB was that it had increased the "confidence between the individual groups of delegates," and that "the best experience had been had with the private agreements between consumers and producers."[58] In view of the difficult political situation

[56] Meeting of September 26, 1921, DZA Potsdam, RWM, Nr. 4458, Bl. 157–160, and "Rückschau" by Funcke of August 19, 1922, in "Rohstoffe," Industrie-institut.

[57] Jotten to Schmitt, November 9, 1921, DZA Potsdam, RWM, Nr. 4459, Bl. 10–12.

[58] The official record of the meeting is to be found in the Friedrich-Wilhelms-Hütte Archiv, Nr. 866/08. There are useful details added by Reichert in BA, R 13 I/418, Bl. 112–114.

in Upper Silesia and in view of the uncertainty about changes in the price of coal, the consumers had decided to reject the reintroduction of price ceilings.

Employer harmony was further in evidence when the producers reported that the group of producers, manufacturers, and merchants that had been meeting privately to set guiding prices (*Richtpreise*) would continue to meet and that workers were invited to join. The DMV refused to accept this invitation, but clearly this was not much regretted by the employers. Fundamentally, the situation existing before the EWB and, more specifically, before the breakdown of producer-manufacturer relations in the summer of 1919, had been restored. Prices were being set privately on the basis of discussion among the interested parties. A friendly understanding had been reached that these price guidelines would be held to by producers, and the producers also promised to fulfill all domestic contracts and orders to the greatest extent and with as much speed as was possible. Manufacturer leaders friendly to this agreement, such as Hans von Raumer of the electrotechnical industry, viewed these negotiations favorably and praised the "skillful approach" of the producers that had led to the RWM's defeat. At the same time, however, he worried about the long-term commitment of the producers to this agreement once the danger of price ceilings had passed and argued that the producers could be held to their part of the bargain more easily if a coal clause were built into the arrangement that automatically increased prices a certain percentage if coal prices increased. In any case, he and his colleagues wanted to know of every violation of the agreement.[59] Allied to Hans von Raumer were the more moderate leaders among the producers, such as Vögler, who explained recent retroactive price increases, not unconvincingly, by the depreciation of the mark, the high cost of ores, and the waves of strikes. Vögler fought hard against efforts to introduce sliding-scale prices, promised that he would always fight against them, but feared "not to be able to win out over the long run." This would lead, in his opinion, to a return of controls and "a new era of profiteering."[60]

For the moment, however, the producer efforts to undermine the EWB had met with success. The changed business conditions in 1920–1921 certainly had much to do with this, as had the poor experience with the EWB and the dysfunctional class warfare conducted by the DMV. The process of vertical concentration was not without its influence in smoothing producer-consumer relations either. Another RWM effort to introduce price ceilings went down to defeat in the Domestic

[59] Zendei directors meeting, October 20, 1921, SAA 4/Lf 730.
[60] Vögler to Köttgen, *ibid.*, Nachlass Köttgen, 11/Lf 265.

Pricing Commission on December 15, 1921, this time by a vote of 24–12.[61] The DMV leaders had lost control of their worker colleagues. Whether or not the producers could maintain control in their own camp remained to be seen. The *Kölnische Zeitung*, always hostile to the EWB, rejoiced, but warned the producers "to agree in good faith with their customers and avoid all force. . . ."[62]

EXPORT CONTROLS UNDER ATTACK

The benighted history of the EWB was only one example of how Germany's unpredictable economic and political situation gave birth to peculiar and problematic institutions whose existence and evolution reflected shifting alignments within the business community as well as among business, labor, and government. The convoluted development of the EWB, however, was as nothing compared to that of the institutions and controversies surrounding the control and taxation of exports. In order to render intelligible the debates over these issues in 1920–1921, therefore, it would be well to summarize their chronological development as well as the fundamental functions of export controls and export levies.

Both export controls and export levies, of course, had their origins in the war. The initial function of the controls had been to prevent the export of strategic materials needed for the national defense and to make sure that such exports as were permitted did not fall into enemy hands. Subsequently, the controls became a means of ensuring high export profits in the government's efforts to combat the depreciation of the mark and secure foreign exchange. Throughout the war, the ultimate responsibility for the granting of export permits and the determination of prices rested with civilian and military agencies, initially the Reich Office of the Interior and the Prussian War Ministry, later the Reich Economic Office and the War Office. Despite universal and often justified complaints about slow and bureaucratic procedures, the basic need and value of the controls were clearly recognized. Given the shortages in neutral states, delays were not likely to mean the loss of orders, and the minimum price regulations in wartime guaranteed not merely that exporters would not overlook the exchange value of the mark or drive down prices by needless competition, but that they would actually charge and receive all that the traffic would bear. At the same time, the much-hated but indispensa-

---

[61] See the memorandum by Schmidt, November 28, 1921, BA, R 13 I/418, Bl. 99–102, and Friedrich-Wilhelms-Hütte Archiv, Nr. 866/08, for the official protocol of the meeting.

[62] *Kölnische Zeitung*, January 24, 1922.

The industrialist who ruined the exchange rate of the mark to improve exports. From *Vorwarts*, June 24, 1923.

ble "Delivery Work Certificate" (*Lieferwerksbescheinigung*) ensured that material presented for export or the raw materials used in a product presented for export had not been sold to the exporter for domestic use at low domestic prices.

As noted earlier,[63] the wartime government made every effort to employ the organizations, personnel, and expertise of industry in its management of the economy, and this was the case in foreign trade controls as well. On November 3, 1914, a Central Bureau for the Export Certification of Iron and Steel Products was set up under Reichert at the Berlin headquarters of the VdESI, and Central Bureaus were then set up in Essen and Düsseldorf as export control work expanded. Similar Central Bureaus were set up for the machine construction and electrotechnical industries during the war. At the end of the war, many of the bureaucratic regulations surrounding exports eased, but the government retained its basic power to control imports and exports and the Central Bureaus continued to function for those areas where controls were maintained. Furthermore, until October 1919 the Central Bureaus had no formal powers of decision making and were mere advisory bodies. The right to grant export permits (*Stempelbefugnis*) ultimately rested with the Reich Commissar for Exports and Imports.

Nevertheless, many of the trade association leaders, particularly Reichert, Frölich, and Raumer, favored export controls as a means of organizing their industries, controlling the merchants, and maintaining high profits. During 1919, therefore, they found themselves fighting a two-front war. On the one hand, they opposed business elements, especially in the Hanse cities, desiring to free trade of all restrictions. On the other hand, they fought for greater industrial self-administration of export controls and against the Wissell-Moellendorff plans to use the export controls as a means of launching the planned economy program. The RWM leaders were successful in bringing together producers, consumers, merchants, and workers in a self-governing organization for the metal industry, but they failed in the case of the iron trades and machine construction industry, where the industrialists succeeded in warding off co-determination in the crucial areas of basic policy making and price examination.[64]

Having battled to save industrial self-government against Wissell and Moellendorff, the industrialists next had to battle against Schmidt

[63] See above, pp. 59–61, for the more detailed discussion and sources. Also, see the useful narrative discussion by Franz Weber of the VDMA in *Stahl und Eisen*, 40:1, April 8, 1920, pp. 473–476.

[64] For the skillful manner in which they negotiated with the object of keeping worker co-determination limited and keeping export controls separated from the RWM *Planwirtschaft* schemes, see the RWM meeting of July 9, 1919, in BA, R 13 I/192, Bl. 77–86.

189

and Hirsch in the summer and fall of 1919 in order to save export controls. Reichert, Raumer, and other trade association officials and industrialists were compelled to mobilize not only their colleagues in industry but also the labor leaders in the ZAG to fight against the RWM's free trade policies and its concessions to South German and North German particularism, which took the form of decentralizing export controls through the granting of decision-making powers to newly created "Delegates" of the Reich Commissar. Ultimately, however, the RWM was forced to reverse its policy when it became apparent that Germany was being "bought out" in the fall and winter of 1919–1920. Faced with enormous raw materials shortages, the hoarding of foreign exchange by exporters, increasing foreign threats of retaliation against German exchange dumping, and mounting criticism of German businessmen for failing to keep contracts, the RWM was compelled to change its policy. At the same time, a startling article entitled "The Buying Out of Germany" by Felix Deutsch of the AEG in the *Vossische Zeitung* of November 9, 1919, helped make businessmen aware of the need for export controls, as did Reichert's "Way Out of the Exchange Problem."[65]

Yielding, therefore, to both pressure and necessity, the RWM, with the approval of the Reichstag Economic Policy Committee and the Reichsrat, issued a decree on December 20, 1919, empowering the Reich Commissar for Exports and Imports to ban the export of goods and then to permit their export subject to conditions laid down by himself or by those to whom he delegated his authority. The Commissar could delegate his authority to Export Control Boards or other agencies, and the old Central Agencies were to be replaced by such boards.[66] The result of this decree was the creation of many new export control boards, the revamping or renaming of old ones, and the delegation of commissarial authority to the heads of these boards, the so-called *Reichsbevollmächtigte*. In the case of the iron and steel industry, Reichert continued to function as before, although the Export Control Board for Iron and Steel formally established on May 1, 1920, was completely independent of the VdESI in a formal sense. Reichert and the steel industrialists were now compelled to discuss export policy within the context of an organization composed of producers, consumers, and merchants organized along lines of parity between management and labor, but he had succeeded in keeping this participation by others purely advisory in function. In essence, Reichert and

---

[65] See above, pp. 133–135, and the ZAG meetings in the summer of 1919 in DZA Potsdam, ZAG, Nr. 28, Bl. 153ff., and Graham, *Exchange and Prices*, pp. 80–82.

[66] *Reichs-Gesetzblatt 1919*, pp. 2128–2129.

his fellow *Reichsbevollmächtigte* were empowered to grant or deny export permits within the guidelines established by the Reich Commissar, and the major and difficult work of price examination was done by a large staff of price examiners selected, by and large, by the trade association managers who headed the export control boards. For all intents and purposes, therefore, the actual control of exports was in the hands of the trade associations and their staffs.[67]

The boards and their powerful chairman were authorized to charge fees to cover the costs of the boards, and they were also responsible for the collection of the so-called social export levy (*soziale Ausfuhrabgabe*) provided for in the Decree of December 20, 1919. The concept of an export levy designed to appropriate some portion of the export profit for the treasury was practically coincident with the development of export controls for the purpose of improving foreign exchange during the war. The wartime export levy was very modest and was dropped during the revolution. As might be expected, the Finance Ministry under Erzberger was particularly interested in employing a large export tax as a major instrument of fiscal and economic policy. It contemplated nothing less than a 25–30% export tariff (*Ausfuhrzoll*) with the goal, not only of helping the fiscus, but also of influencing the domestic economy. Specifically, by virtually confiscatory taxation of export profits, Erzberger hoped to discourage exports at the expense of the domestic market and to discourage the granting of inflationary wage increases. Thus, the Finance Ministry was more than happy to have a well-organized network of Export Control boards at hand to administer and collect such a tariff.[68]

This was not what the industrialists had in mind when they threw their weight behind export controls. They did, however, face a dilemma, for it was impossible to argue that industry was entitled to maintain its entire export profit when this profit owed so much to government controls as well as to the backing industry received for its position from the labor leaders in the ZAG. The dilemma was resolved when Raumer and the trade union leader Legien were able to come to an agreement. Both men opposed the creation of an export tariff. Raumer warned that such a tariff, "when it is once introduced and its effect upon the Reich's finances is recognized, would only be eliminated again with great difficulty. It would apply to the individual industries equally in the way it is calculated and thus under certain

[67] There are good discussions in the retrospective histories of the relevant trade associations: BA, R 13 I/13, Bl. 43ff., "Deutscher Maschinenbau," p. 228ff., and "Zendei History," p. 53ff.

[68] See the discussion by Dr. Dalberg of the Finance Ministry in *Stahl und Eisen*, 39:2, December 18, 1919, pp. 1594–1596.

circumstances could act as a total barrier to exports. We should also not overlook the fact that the industries are, without exception, greatly in need of capital and therefore that a part of the export profit has to be left to them. Excessive profits will be covered by taxation, and the financial interests of the Reich, therefore, will not be neglected."[69] Legien added to these arguments by noting that there was a danger that the Entente might seek to seize the proceeds of such a tariff. Raumer and Legien, therefore, felt that it would be much safer and less noticeable if a minimum levy of 5% were imposed on export invoices for the restricted purpose of supplementing pensions to mitigate some of the untoward effects of the inflation. It was understood that this levy was to be applied elastically and could even be reduced below 5% in the case of industries unable to bear the cost. Thanks in large measure to the ZAG's pressure, the Finance Ministry's tariff proposal was eliminated from the Decree of December 20, whose provisions now foresaw the creation of an "exchange levy" to be paid into the Reich Treasury and to be used for social purposes.[70]

The ZAG victory was ambiguous, however, and the social export levy created some extraordinarily delicate problems when the RWM finally announced the export levies it intended to charge in a decree of April 22, 1920, that is, four months after it had provided for the levy when creating the export control system. Effective May 1, 1920 (subsequently changed to May 10, 1920), levies of 3–6% were to be imposed on iron and steel products and levies of 6–8% on the products of the machine building and electrotechnical industries. Back orders already approved by the export control boards were to be free of the levy insofar as they were filled before July 1, 1920.[71] Had the levy been imposed in the winter, when the value of the German mark was particularly low and the exchange profits of the businessmen were high, it would have provoked little controversy because it had been accepted by the businessmen in principle. When the value of the mark improved while export business declined, however, the imposition of the levy was certain to provoke opposition. Industrialists could and did accuse the RWM of having missed the chance to impose the levy when it would have served its purposes without seriously hurting business. The RWM explained its delay by the difficult negotiations Germany had been conducting with the Allies concerning the closing of the "hole in the West," negotiations that had at long last been

[69] ZAG directors meeting, November 18, 1919, DZA Potsdam, ZAG, Nr. 29, Bl. 5.

[70] See the remarks of Undersecretary Hirsch at a meeting of the RWM Section Heads on December 11, 1919, in DZA Potsdam, RWM, Nr. 4184, Bl. 12.

[71] *Stahl und Eisen*, 40:1, April 22, 1920, p. 560.

brought to a fruitful conclusion with an Allied promise that Germany would be able to control the entry and exit of goods in the occupied areas. The RWM claimed that an effective control of exports and a successful application of the export levy would be possible only if the "hole in the West" was closed.

This explanation does not appear completely satisfactory, however, because even the RWM recognized that the moderate levies it intended to impose initially were likely to be evaded. It would seem that, as usual, effective government action had been hampered by conflicts within the government and timidity on the part of the RWM. The Finance Ministry and the RWM had been quarreling throughout March, the former insisting that the decree of December 10 in no way precluded the imposition of a tax confiscating the entire exchange profit of exporters, the latter warning that the export control boards did not have the manpower needed to determine individual profits and insisting that the export levy not be used as a means of controlling the domestic supply of raw materials or keeping the domestic price levels low. In the case of iron and steel, for example, the RWM intended to look to the EWB to set policy rather than employ the export levy to force a policy with regard to export quotas and domestic prices. In any case, the failure to settle such basic issues as late as March suggests that the confused condition of Germany's government was more important than the confused condition of her customs boundaries in delaying the "moderate" schedule imposed at a time when the German control of her own customs borders still was incomplete.[72]

The ranks of business were no less confused than those of the government. Although both producers and manufacturers agreed that the changed business conditions and intensifying world economic crisis would require the easing of export controls and export levies, they were quite divided as to whether these controls and levies should be eased or eliminated. Furthermore, the lines of division changed and shifted in 1920–1921 with changes in the international and economic situation. Nevertheless, there is a basic story of growing hostility toward export levies and export controls throughout the business community. As might be expected, the brunt of the initial attack was borne by the export levy.

The announcement of the levies in the spring of 1920 provoked outrage and particularly sharp reaction in the machine building industry, and this despite the fact that the industry's leaders had promoted export controls and appeared to work well with the labor representatives

[72] RWM to Reichsbank Direction, April 10, 1920, BA, R 43 I/1172, Bl. 288ff.; RFM to RWM, March 19, 1920, *ibid.*, Bl. 281–282.

in the industry's export control boards. Thus, when von Buttlar announced at a March 12 meeting with the industry's leaders that there would be a 6–8% levy on machines as well as a ½% charge for the costs of export controls, the government was attacked for its "unsteady export and price policy."[73] The machine building industry stood to be most adversely affected by the levies. The government had reasoned that the export profit would be greatest in the case of finished products employing German labor and German raw materials purchased at relatively cheap or controlled domestic German prices. Acting on this proposition, the highest rates were imposed on machines. Unhappily, the application of so sensible a theory did not always prove fair in practice because many manufacturers had paid a price for their raw materials that was disproportionately high in relation to what they could ask for the finished product. They now faced being overtaxed on what they had already been overcharged. Special problems also arose because of the lengthy periods involved in filling contracts in the machine building industry. According to the RWM regulations, the levy had to be calculated in foreign currency at the time that an export permit was requested and then paid in the mark equivalent at the time of export. Manufacturers now feared that they could lose money if the mark continued to increase in value and they had to pay the levy in marks calculated at an old rate of exchange. Also, many manufacturers had reached agreement with their customers before the schedule went into effect, but they had not reported the contract to the export control boards. They considered it unfair that such orders would be subjected to the levy, just as they regarded it as unfair to be required to pay the levy on long-standing orders that had not been entirely filled on July 1, 1920. The RWM's regulations connected with the imposition of the levy had increased the speculative nature of the machine building industry's export business, a condition that had caused anxiety enough before the levy. Underlying all the above objections, however, was concern over the increasing feebleness of the export market, a matter of no small moment to an industry that had the repeated experience of being the first to suffer and the last to recover in times of depression.[74]

This combination of factors explains the very spontaneous and angry response of the machine construction industry to the government's announcement of the levies. Acting under the pressure of its member organizations, the VDMA held a protest meeting at the Herrenhaus

[73] Meeting of the Export Committee of the VDMA, March 12, 1920, "Deutscher Maschinenbau," Heft 10/1920, p. 120.
[74] *Ibid.*, and Polysius, *Verbandsbestrebungen*, p. 38.

in Berlin on May 19, 1920, to which government representatives were invited. In the keynote speech delivered by General Director Becker of the Humboldt firm in Cologne-Kalk, the government was castigated for the delay in imposing the levies and warned that these levies, under existing conditions, would lead to the shutting down of plants and the laying off of workers. Becker pointed out that foreign customers were not in the business of serving as a "welfare institute for the German people" and would not be so kind as to revise contracted prices upward to cover the levy in the same manner in which many had revised contracted prices upward to take account of currency fluctuations. A resolution was passed calling on the ZAG to take the changed economic situation into account and support "the complete elimination of the levy as quickly as possible."[75]

In a curious commentary on the meeting, the Socialist newspaper *Vorwärts* criticized the industrialists for not using the available time to prepare for the levies and pointed out that the brusque manner with which trade unionist comments at the meeting had been received would harm the *Arbeitsgemeinschaft*. It then commented, however, that much of the problem lay with the excessively high raw materials prices the manufacturers were paying, and that the latter could count on the trade unions in their struggle with heavy industry. The VDMA was thus shrewdly reminded that it possibly had greater enemies than the trade unions and greater problems than the export levy and that the sledgehammer approach typified by the meeting was unwarranted.[76]

The VDMA meeting and its resolution also was viewed as impolitic in important industrial circles. It was considered an unnecessary provocation before the Reichstag elections scheduled for June 6 and, in Vögler's words, "a catastrophe" from the standpoint of industry-labor relations in the ZAG as well as from the standpoint of securing relief from the export levy. Particular criticism was leveled against Dr. Sorge, who as chairman of the VDMA had signed the invitation to a meeting organized to protest implementing an agreement he, as chairman of the Reich Association of German Industry and as chief industrial negotiator in the ZAG, had made with labor. Industry was thus open to the charge of violating its agreements. Sorge sought to defend himself at the RdI's board of directors meeting on June 9, 1920, by arguing in agreement with his VDMA colleague Reuter, the general director of DEMAG, that such serious criticisms notwithstanding, "the meeting must not have been so unwanted by the authorities and perhaps even

[75] Reported in the *Frankfurter Zeitung*, May 20, 1920.
[76] *Vorwärts*, May 20, 1920.

195

by the worker representatives because through this protest an excuse has been created for the adjustment of the social levy . . . to the changed situation."[77]

Sorge's argument received a measure of confirmation from Jakob Reichert at the Executive Directors meeting of the VdESI on June 22. While criticizing the VDMA protest meeting from a political viewpoint, Reichert admitted that it had made easier the securing of worker support for export levy reductions. Reichert persuaded the VdESI leaders that the best tactic at the moment was to avoid an all-out attack on the levy that would alienate the trade unions. Instead, he urged that efforts be made to persuade the government to delay implementation of the levy and to permit downward revision of the schedules. He hoped that this method of "extracting its fangs" would make it possible eventually to eliminate the levy entirely.[78] This tactic was pursued by no less a personage than Hugo Stinnes at the meeting of the Economic Policy Committee of the Reich Economic Council on July 6, 1920. Stinnes declared that he had always been an "unconditional opponent" of the export levy because it was based on too optimistic an assessment of long-term world market conditions, but he insisted that "the first obligation of those in the *Arbeitsgemeinschaft* must be to keep their word." Stinnes dismissed the inconveniences and injustices of the export levy as minor matters, but he stressed that "the question of employment or unemployment is of such great importance that nothing should be allowed to exist which in any way hinders the gaining of orders,"[79] and he urged that the levy be eliminated for every product where this was the case.

The tactics advocated by Reichert and Stinnes were precisely those pursued by industry in the initial struggle against the export levy. On July 13 the heads of the various export control boards met and developed a series of recommendations to the government. The most basic of these was the temporary elimination of export levies, presumably as long as business conditions remained poor, but the basic thrust of the recommendations was much less extreme. The most important practical recommendations were that the export control boards be called upon to reduce or eliminate the levies on items for which market conditions were poor, that the date on which shipment of old orders

[77] RdI directors meeting, June 9, 1920, in MAN Werksarchiv, Augsburg, Nr. K 75, Bl. 86ff.

[78] VdESI Executive Directors meeting, June 22, 1920, BA, R 13 I/158.

[79] Reich Economic Council, Economic Policy Committee, July 6, 1920, DZA Potsdam, RWR, Nr. 1, Bl. 120. Relationships in the ZAG did need smoothing over after the VDMA performance. At the May 20, 1920, meeting of the ZAG directors, RdI representatives apologized to the trade union leaders, *ibid.*, ZAG, Nr. 30, Bl. 187.

free from the levy be moved up from July 1 to October 1, and that special arrangements be made for the payment of the levy on large orders over an extended period. During the ensuing months, these and other demands were met. Rates on numerous items were significantly reduced and even eliminated, the government responding more or less rapidly to the plaints of various industries, many of these often being supported by factory councils fearful of shut-downs and lay-offs. As business conditions worsened, industry was able to move more actively against the export levy. In August, without prior consultation with the ZAG, the RdI voted to support the elimination of export levies for all goods, and in September, Reichert, a DNVP Reichstag Deputy, secured the unanimous vote of the Reichstag Economic Policy Committee for the elimination of levies on all industries that had done 50% less export business in August than they had on the average during the previous months. While the government and the trade union leaders persisted in maintaining the export levy in principle and in maintaining token export levies wherever possible, concessions were made until the renewed depreciation of the mark in the fall of 1921. The government's initial position had been weak because it had acted so tardily and because it had published its rate schedule without any consultation with the industries involved. It was compelled to remain on the defensive so long as the less favorable business conditions and the relative stability of the exchange rate continued.[80]

The struggle against export controls built up much more slowly and much less uniformly than the battle against the export levy. To some extent, hostility against the latter spilled over into hostility against the former. It could be and was indeed argued that the idea of the export levy and the means of its administration derived directly from the idea of export controls administered by export control boards.[81] Needless to say, the chief charges against export controls were other than those connected with the export levy. Fundamentally, it was argued that export controls imposed bureaucratic delays on the conduct of business that cost businessmen important orders, that price examiners often did not know what they were doing, and that the morality of German businessmen was being ruined by the constant evasion of the regulations by profiteers (*Schieber*) employing bribery,

[80] The work of revising the rates began in the spring, see Steinbrinck to the VdESI members, May 15, 1920, and Reichert to the various groups, June 14, 1920, in BA, R 13 I/194, Bl. 89–90 and 55–56, and Reichert's report at the VdESI Executive Directors meeting, September 21, 1920, BA, R 13 I/158. Changes may be followed in the regular reports in *Stahl und Eisen*, 40–41, for 1920–1921.

[81] It should be noted that goods unregulated by export control boards were also free of export levies.

rebates, forgery, smuggling, and every conceivable form of chicanery to undersell the minimum prices. Nevertheless, so long as German industry enjoyed the export advantages of a low exchange rate on the mark and continued to operate in the glow of the exchange dumping that characterized the fall and winter of 1919–1920, there was not only minimal opposition to export controls but, as noted earlier, warm support and enthusiasm.

Probably the most enthused of the enthusiastic was Jakob Reichert, who, as Reich Trustee for the oldest and most successful of the export control agencies, defended export controls with verve and vigor at meeting after meeting, particularly in his reports to the Executive Directors of the VdESI. Reichert was not alone in his support of the export control system, which was backed strongly by the leaders of the manufacturer trade associations. In examining the record of Reichert's defense of export controls, however, it is difficult not to escape the impression that Reichert had an emotional attachment to the control of exports, an activity in which he had been engaged since 1914, which gave him important powers in the state as well as in the business community, and enabled him to organize an entire staff that included many ex-officers, the most notable of which was the U-Boat hero, Captain Steinbrinck. The export control system was very congenial to an "organization man" like Reichert, and his increasingly futile efforts to keep the VdESI directors behind him at the successive executive director meetings in 1920–1921 are not only revealing of changing conditions during the period but also provide a piquant illustration of what could happen if a trade association manager in the iron and steel industry forgot who was the boss.

At the VdESI meeting on June 22, Reichert was able to present a strong and uncontested case for export controls. The contrast between the millions made in the iron and steel industry thanks to the export controls and the millions lost in the machine building industry because of its failure to have adequate controls in 1919 was accurate and convincing. Furthermore, business conditions still were not bad, although he had to admit that "the good old days of splendid export profits are undoubtedly over and that profitability would depend more upon cost reduction and increased emphasis upon trade with the weak-currency nations (*Unterpariländer*) in eastern Europe."[82] While in basic agreement with a recent statement by Reich Commissar for Exports and Imports, Ernst Trendelenburg, that it was undesirable to react to changed market conditions by switching from "exchange dumping," that is, the exploitation of the depreciated exchange rate, to the tradi-

[82] Meeting of June 22, 1920, BA, R 13 I/158, for the quotations and discussion in this paragraph.

tional mode of dumping by selling abroad more cheaply than at home, he would not rule out any method, for "the chief thing is that we keep our industrial plants operating." Although prepared to give full employment primacy over other considerations, an argument that was going to give Reichert much trouble in the future, Reichert expressed alarm at suggestions that the narrowing gap between domestic and foreign prices justified the elimination of export controls. He warned that there was no reason to believe "that our exchange will remain stable at its present height," and he was successful in winning his listeners over to a policy of continued support of export controls coupled with a strong effort to reduce export levies.

Things were not so simple when the Executive Directors met again on September 21, that is, after three months of worsening business conditions. Under the impact of an exchange situation less favorable to exports, poor market conditions, and rising domestic production costs, the RdI had already weakened its stand on export controls by declaring that the decision to maintain or abandon controls was to be left to the individual branches of industry in consultation with the RdI. The VdESI's support for export controls, therefore, had to be treated as a question rather than as a presumption, and Reichert's position was all the more difficult because he was asking the directors for approval of a series of guidelines for export control boards recently developed by the Reich Economic Council at Trendelenburg's request. It was difficult to present these guidelines at the very moment when commitment to the system was diminishing.

The sentiment of Reichert's critics was most clearly and ably expressed by a wire manufacturer, Director Eduard Hobrecker, who sarcastically remarked that Reichert had sung such praises of the export control boards in his opening remarks as to leave the impression that if industry did not already have these agencies, then it should create them. Although conceding that Reichert's export control board had served the iron industry well, Hobrecker emphasized that it was still bound by RWM decisions and was not flexible enough to respond rapidly to changing economic conditions. Hobrecker would not deny the importance of getting good prices abroad, but he insisted that the maintenance of production and employment was more important. In his view, and here Hobrecker was supported by representatives of the sheet and high-grade steel producers, export controls were costing the steel industry vitally needed business. He was not prepared to exempt the export control system from the more general effort to dismantle the controlled economy, and while not pleading that the export controls be eliminated overnight, he urgently requested taking the posture that "as soon as possible German industry be given back again that freedom of movement which it unconditionally needs and which it will not misuse."[83]

Reichert came to the defense of export controls, as always, by stressing that the boards were superior to private syndicates and cartels because merchants were forced to participate and no one could remain an outsider and still export. At the same time, the setting of most policies and the crucial examination of prices were done by people from the trade associations, and this meant a high degree of industrial self-government. Did they prefer to have these tasks done by an organization like the EWB? Furthermore, so long as Germany was barred from imposing tariffs under the Peace Treaty, import controls were necessary, and import controls made export controls necessary to protect domestic supplies of vital materials. He reminded his listeners of foreign protests against German dumping, the constant danger of retaliation, and the need to make sure that German businessmen kept to their contracts and did not invite further complaints ruinous to their reputation. Whatever the evils of export controls in Reichert's view, they were the lesser evil when compared to the chaos of complete decontrol and its alternative, the total control that was socialization. Finally, Reichert reminded them of the political realities. Even if the control boards were abolished and everything was left to trade associations, cartels, and syndicates, it had become quite clear that these no longer had their old autonomy. They were being used by the state to serve consumer interests and often in subservience to the labor organizations. It was a point that Reichert, an experienced Reichstag deputy, could drive home with force and shrewdness:

> Gentlemen, undo the Revolution, push the workers back into their previous position, make them somewhat more powerless in economic policy than they now are, then you can regulate foreign trade completely as you will. Today you will find no Reichstag and no Reich Economic Council and above all no government for this. . . .[84]

The weakness of Reichert's position, however, was that his colleagues were in no way rejecting his reminder that "politics is the art of the attainable." All that they were saying is that their aims might be attained at some future date and that the way should be paved for the dismantling of export controls by an appropriate position on the question. In the end, this purpose was served by a resolution declaring that the directors, while wishing for the "speediest possible dismantling of export controls," considered their temporary retention in

[83] Meeting of September 21, 1920, *ibid.*
[84] *Ibid.*

the iron and steel industry necessary. Within the VdESI at least, Reichert and the supporters of the export control system had now been placed on the defensive.

During the last months of 1920, a renewed depreciation of the mark that had set in at the end of the summer of 1920 and some improvement in the export market reduced the clamor for an end to export controls, but at the turn of the year the value of the mark began to increase again while depressed business conditions returned. What meaning did these events have for export controls and the export levy? In an important speech in January 1921, "The World Economic Crisis and Foreign Trade," Reich Commissar Trendelenburg argued that these oscillations demonstrated the importance of maintaining export controls and the export levy. He anticipated that a pattern was developing in which mark depreciation and export booms would be followed by mark appreciation and export depressions with each set of circumstances promoting the other, modified or interrupted only by developments such as the setting of Germany's final reparations bill and monetary speculation. The fundamental problem, in his view, was maintaining stable prices at home and in foreign trade under such conditions, and he found the answer in export controls. Given the instability of the mark, export prices had to be made as independent of the fluctuation of the mark as possible, and this could only be done if these prices were calculated at world market prices in the better foreign currencies. At the same time, it was essential that the domestic prices be calculated in marks if the German economy was not to be deprived of the indigenous currency that was the basis of its finances, and it was also essential that the domestic price structure be kept relatively insulated from the fluctuations of the mark abroad so as to maintain price stability at home. Furthermore, just as export controls were necessary to protect Germany from wasting her substance and provoking foreign reprisals, so the export levy was necessary to ensure a fair distribution of export profits. Trendelenburg was fully aware of the difficulties involved with the measures he was defending. The handling of 20–30,000 export permits a day could not be accomplished without the expertise and cooperation of the business community itself, and the decision concerning the export duty, although relatively easy in the case of mass-produced articles and uniform products, was extraordinarily difficult in the case of specialized goods because it was hard to tell at what point the price of such goods was no longer competitive. In the last analysis, however, what concerned Trendelenburg was not the organizational problem. He recognized that his countrymen were "unusually inventive when it comes to organizational forms."

In his view, what they lacked was "the will to organization, the cheerful submission of the individual to the whole."[85] Reichert, who was a subordinate of Trendelenburg in his capacity of Trustee for the Export Control Board for Iron and Steel Products, was impressed with the Trendelenburg speech and seems to have thought that it would make good and persuasive reading for the members of the VdESI executive board prior to their meeting of February 22, 1921. He sent it to the board members with warm words of recommendation, and as the meeting was to show, to Reichert's unanticipated discomfort, some of them had done their homework.

If Reichert had any goal at this meeting, it was to maintain the VdESI's commitment to the resolution of the previous September in the face of strong hostility to the export control boards on the part of the producers. The context of the discussion had changed in two important ways, however. First, there was a distinct shift in the tone and character of the VdESI's leadership. Although the organization had always been dominated by the Northwest Group and by the leaders of heavy industry in the Ruhr, the territorial losses under the Treaty strengthened this regional domination of VdESI. To be sure, the VdESI meetings were chaired by Justizrat Meyer of the Ilseder Hütte, and the Upper Silesian, Ewald Hilger, and Reichert and his staff devoted great amounts of time and energy trying to keep the peace between primary producers and manufacturers. Since June 1920, however, the executive directors of the VdESI had been meeting jointly with the executive committee of the Iron Producing Industry's Branch Group (*Fachgruppe*) of the Reich Association of German Industry, and the latter's chairman, Paul Reusch, alternated chairmanship of the VdESI executive directors' meetings with Meyer and Hilger. Although this formal arrangement had the obvious advantages of preventing duplication of discussions and contradictory decisions by two executive committees of significantly overlapping composition, it necessarily increased the direct influence of heavy industry within the Berlin VdESI meetings, an influence made all the more potent by Reusch's powerful and domineering personality. This phenomenon paralleled the direct intensification of heavy industry's influence over manufacturing through vertical concentration.[86]

The second major change in the context of the discussions was that the reparations issue and foreign policy increasingly dominated the concerns of the industrialists after January 1921. The inevitable con-

[85] Ernst Trendelenburg, *Weltwirtschaftskrise und Aussenhandel. Vortrag gehalten am 26. Januar 1921 in der deutschen Hochschule für Politik in Berlin* (Berlin, 1921), p. 32. A copy is to be found in BA, R 13 I/196.
[86] For material on these organizational changes, see BA, R 13 I/4.

flict over the final reparations figure at the impending London Conference and the threat of sanctions introduced important new considerations into the discussion of export policy. These considerations, however, further enhanced the position and voice of the Ruhr leaders, who would be the first to feel the brunt of sanctions as well as the economic group whose cooperation would be most essential in any reparations settlement.[87]

At the February 1921 meeting, the great iron and steel producers were in a fighting mood, and the tocsin was sounded at the very start by Reusch, who took the view "that we should let the negotiations [in London] break down without regard for the consequences if the Entente does not significantly reduce its demands. . . ."[88] Reichert, of course, was no less incensed by the Allied demands than Reusch, but the international situation further undermined his efforts to save export controls. It was known, for example, that the Allies were proposing to collect part of the reparations in export taxes, and Reichert tried very hard to persuade his colleagues to blame Erzberger's old plans to confiscate export profits and not the export control boards. General Director Beukenberg, however, was not prepared to be deflected from his understanding of the situation by inflammatory references to the right's favorite scapegoat. He pointed out that the Germans, in pursuing a policy of keeping export prices often as high as 50% above domestic prices and at a minimum of 12½% above domestic prices, had actually been showing the Entente exactly where they could collect money from the Germans with impunity.

Similarly, Reichert did not fare very well with his few cautious, tentative indications of approval to a suggestion by Foreign Secretary Simons that many of the Allied complaints about German dumping as well as many of Europe's economic problems could be solved by international cartels and economic agreements. Although Reichert did not feel that an international cartel system was possible so long as Germany needed to maximize her exports to pay reparations, he did think that this approach might work for some products. Such proposals for international economic cooperation, however, ran directly counter to the thinking of the leading producers. Hasslacher saw no reason whatever to negotiate an international cartel agreement with the French iron and steel industry so long as the inequality reflected in the Versailles *Diktat* provided the background and the terms would be such as to force Germany to limit her production while France picked up a quota that included the production of Lorraine and Luxemburg. The

[87] Bergmann, *History of Reparations*, p. 53ff., and Chapter 5, below.
[88] VdESI Executive Directors meeting, February 22, 1921, BA, R 13 I/159, for the discussion of and quotations from the meeting that follow.

simple fact was that whereas France needed German coal, Germany had much less need for French ores thanks to the increased use of Swedish ores as well as of the Siemens-Martin process.[89] Hasslacher spelled out the strategy of the German steel producers with great clarity:

> We can only come to the top again if we are able to exploit on world markets the advantages which we believe we have achieved in costs and productivity as a result of the exertions we have made during the last two years. We think we have the advantage with regard to costs as well as because of the technical methods made possible by the use of other types of ores. Today we do not need minette, at least not to the old degree, and the French should first choke on their minette and crude steel, and then they can come to us and ask to make cartels.

Reusch, too, opposed an international understanding so long as Germany's productivity had not reached its maximum and the French were having major difficulties that made cartelization more advantageous for them than for the Germans. In Reusch's view, Germany's underselling of the Entente on world markets was a political weapon of no small importance: "Let our enemies have to sell at a loss for just a while, and then they will collapse and come to us with conditions that are favorable for us and that we can accept." Thus, Reusch was not prepared to treat international complaints about German dumping with the same concern as Trendelenburg and Reichert. Although Hasslacher and Reusch had differed and continued to differ very strongly in their domestic pricing policies, economic and international political developments had brought them much closer together on matters of industrial organization. One of Reichert's strongest points in favor of export control boards over the traditional cartels and syndicates was the fragility of the voluntary organizations in the recent past. Hasslacher, who had played no mean role in breaking up the Steel Works Association, could now use the international situation to transform his opposition to such organizations into a patriotic virtue. He warned against any "fixed forms," be they cartels, be they export control boards, which stood forth in the open as instruments that might be used to bend Germany and German industry to an enemy's will.

Indeed, just as the opponents of the Steel Works Association in 1919–1920 had attacked that organization because strict adherence to its pricing policies had turned honest businessmen into fools, so now Reusch was pointing out that the great works could not go on obeying

[89] See below, pp. 348–349 for a fuller discussion of the German iron and steel industry's development during this period.

the export regulations when "thousands upon thousands of contracts are reported to the export control boards and put on the books at the prescribed prices for which then rebates are given abroad in one form or another." Reusch, with considerable support from many of his colleagues, warned that business morality was going down the drain and that dishonesty would soon "reach dimensions that will make our hair stand on end" if export controls were retained. He suggested that Reichert was either naive or not telling all he knew about violations of the export price regulations. In any case, he did not think it wise "to eternalize in the protocol all the details that have come to our ears in the course of time." More basically, Reusch argued that German industry could best flourish under conditions where it was free to produce and sell according to its own necessities. Industry did not need a "nursemaid" to tell it what to do.

Reusch had sweetened his attack on Reichert with a measure of recognition for the relative success of Reichert's export control board and recognition for Reichert's valiant efforts to make the system work. Hasslacher, however, seemed to feel that Reichert had stepped completely out of line when he undertook to distribute Trendelenburg's speech with favorable comment, and he intended to put Reichert in his place. As far as Hasslacher was concerned, the central point of the Trendelenburg speech was that everything had to be regulated from Berlin, and this idea was "false." Hasslacher attributed the loss of the war to economic direction by professional bureaucrats who lacked expert knowledge, and he thought that this lack or expertise had only increased after the war and that its ill effects had been only somewhat mitigated by corruption. He expressed particular loathing for the notion that the price examiners were capable of evaluating 30,000 pieces of business a day and reminded his listeners that the very concept of an examiner implied a person who knew more than those he was investigating and that neither Trendelenburg, nor Reichert, nor most of the other officials involved had ever "really sold or handled iron."

What was obvious from Hasslacher's ill-tempered remarks, which insultingly lumped Reichert and his men with government officials and exuded all the suspicion of "organization men" felt by "men of practice," was that Reichert's traditional claim that his export control board represented industrial self-government no longer found acceptance. Similarly, the tactic of concentrating industry's attack on the export levy was not working either. Beukenberg bluntly told Reichert that he viewed the export levy as a minor matter in comparison to the business that was being lost and the danger of unemployment being created by export controls. Reichert did receive some support at the meeting, but it did not do him much good. One Cologne businessman complained that the large firms in his trade association had forced the leadership to abandon price examination with the proviso that they would not sell much under the world market price, but they had then gone on to dump their products on the world market at prices below even the German domestic price. Reichert had already made this point by remarking that the elimination of export controls would deprive the small and middle-sized firms of protection "while the great concerns are in themselves strong enough to weather the competition." The fact was that for both political and economic reasons the big industrialists were arguing that their survival and the employment of their thousands of workers were more important. They recognized that export controls still served some useful function for specialized products and small orders in the manufacturing industry, where world market prices were not easily established and negotiations lengthy, but they considered them unsuitable for the sale of mass articles where often "the deal is concluded within five minutes or not at all."

Indeed, Reusch and his colleagues were intent on eliminating every pocket of resistance at Reichert's disposal, and they were severely critical of his ideological pretensions. To Reichert's statement that "strict discipline in industry is better than unbridled competition," Reusch and Hasslacher replied that they were in no way advocates of anarchy. They were prepared to accept export and import bans imposed by the government for sound political or economic reasons, and they were prepared to accept self-limitations insofar as they were willing to organize voluntarily: "All we want in general," Reusch declared, "is the elimination of every control when we are allowed to export." Reichert had sought to prevent what he called the "merchant spirit" from prevailing, and he seems to have forgotten that the men he was serving were in the business of selling as well as producing. It was made clear to him that he could maintain his position on export controls only if he had the backing of those who employed him, and that backing had disappeared. It would have been suicidal to have played off the manufacturing supporters of controls against the heavy industrialists, and the former were in a cooperative mood in any case. Also, the day's experience was not conducive to faith in the steadiness of anyone's convictions in economic matters. Indeed, there were powerful forces now in manufacturing who opposed controls, for as Reusch, to an interjection of "unfortunately!" and laughter, reminded his colleagues, "I, too, am a bit engaged in manufacturing." Thus, it was a much chastened Reichert who himself framed the resolution that conveyed the sense of the meeting. The resolution was careful to maintain a distinction between imports and exports and between the products of the manufacturing industries and those of heavy industry such as bars, wire, and sheets. The VdESI continued to support import controls and said nothing about export controls for manufactured products, but it called for the "speediest possible dismantling" of export controls in heavy industry.

Life was much easier for Reichert when the VdESI Executive Directors met again on May 6, 1921, for his formal conversion into an opponent of export controls was at once smoothed by events and of little practical consequence. The breakdown of the reparations discussions in London, the Allied occupation of Düsseldorf, Duisburg, and Ruhrort on March 8, and the revival of the "hole in the West" through the creation of a Rhine customs boundary made the continuation of even import controls appear futile. Reichert was also able to report that he had met with a large number of the groups producing iron and steel products and that most of them wished to end export controls. Under these circumstances, Reichert was able to announce that export controls no longer had their old significance and to take the view that those wishing to maintain export controls should do so on a voluntary basis. At the same time, it also became fairly clear from Reichert's report that neither export controls nor export levies were going to disappear simply because of VdESI resolutions. The worker representatives on the ZAG and the EWB were not prepared to see the export control boards eliminated because they wanted to retain a voice in these matters. Although they had made numerous concessions on the export levies, they were not prepared to abandon them either. The RWM had actually planned to conduct a speedy dismantling of export controls, Reichert reported, but labor pressure had prevented this. Clearly Reichert was correct when he had argued that the Revolution was not so easily undone.[90]

VdESI resolutions, however, like those of the October 21, 1921, meeting, which reiterated the demand for the elimination of export controls and the export levy, were futile for the time being. The London Ultimatum, which fixed the German reparations bill at 132 billion gold marks, was accepted by the new Wirth government in May. The government refrained from further efforts to eliminate export controls because of trade union pressure and also because the drop in the value of the mark in the fall of 1921 gave export controls renewed importance. At the same time, the Wirth government began to employ the export levy for fiscal, rather than purely "social" purposes, and the levies were substantially increased in November.

At the turn of 1921-1922, therefore, it was clear that the opposition to the controlled economy had consolidated and become strengthened

[90] See above, p. 200. For the meeting of May 6, 1921, see *ibid.*, 160.

over the course of the previous year and a half, but it was no less clear that a stalemate had been reached. The EWB had been neutralized but not eliminated, and the export control system and export levies seemed to be reviving from the relative monetary stabilization that had nearly destroyed them. This stalemate reflected the general incoherence of the period between the spring of 1920 and the fall of 1921. The inflation was anything but over, but the relative stability of the mark created the prospect that stabilization was not far off. At the same time, industry continued to enjoy advantages on a depressed world market, and its leaders wished to continue doing so for economic and political reasons. The German export boom continued, but not in the manner of late 1919 and early 1920. As one industrialist put it in February 1921, "In the meantime conditions on the world market have changed in such a manner, that certain countries are actually heading for a catastrophic collapse, and unemployment, especially according to reports I have received from England, increases daily. . . . Our prices, therefore, cannot be set as crudely as they were about a year ago, and one needs to calculate carefully in order to be able to compete at all abroad."[91] The German advantage, in short, had become precarious, particularly when the mark failed to depreciate while other countries lowered their prices because of depression, and this pushed German businessmen to demand maximum flexibility. For example, sometimes it made sense to conclude contracts in foreign exchange, sometimes not, but in any case, "It certainly cannot be of use to the German economy if through a stubborn insistence upon payment in foreign exchange no orders come in, but rather it is precisely in the interests of the German economy that we maintain employment for our workers for so long as there is still any profit in it at all."[92]

This was the general mentality behind the attack on controls in 1920–1921, and it assisted the reconstitution of cooperation between heavy industry and manufacturing. At the same time, this cooperation also reflected the substantial penetration of manufacturing by heavy industry during the same period. It seemed as if German industry was restructuring itself along lines determined by its own inner tendencies and that these would override all other forms of control and direction. Alongside the elaborate organizational network through government agencies and trade associations, there developed a vertical concentration process of significant proportions. The ultimate relationship of these tendencies, however, remained uncertain. As Trendelenburg noted in his January 1921 speech, it was by no means clear if German

[91] Wirtz to Krieger, February 22, 1921, Friedrich-Wilhelms-Hütte Archiv, Nr. 861/07.

[92] *Ibid.*

industry would reconstitute itself along cooperative lines or if "strong-er forces building within the private sector by means of trustification, of vertical organization, will give our planless economy support and direction. . . ."[93] The post-1918 aggressiveness of German heavy industry received its most extreme expression in the vertical concentration process of the inflationary period, and the time has come to direct attention to this phenomenon.

[93] Trendelenburg, *Weltwirtschaftskrise*, p. 31.

CHAPTER FOUR

Vertical Concentration

The organization and regulation of the iron trades and the relations between raw materials producers and their primary consumers cannot be examined solely from the perspective of intraindustrial relations and the problem of government intervention. Both contemporaries and retrospective observers considered the massive efforts at vertical concentration undertaken by industry itself as the most fundamental and effective attempt to organize and regulate the production, allocation, and marketing of iron and steel and the products manufactured from them. An exclusive emphasis on the "superstructure" of economic activity represented by interest groups and ministries would mean neglect of the "substructure," where important forces were at work. The dangers of such neglect were noted by a contemporary critic, who pointed out that the RWM had restricted itself to influencing only the market situation through the EWB, but had stood by inactive in all matters concerning the problems of production and actual industrial organization. Undersecretary Hirsch and his colleagues encouraged rationalization and fusions in general, but they made no effort to determine the form and character they took.[1] There was a large and decisive sphere of industrial concentration that took place in complete independence of governmental or even industrial trade association influence and that ultimately determined many of the economic realities with which German society had to reckon. Some of these instances of vertical concentration during the inflation proved to have long-term viability and have lasted to this day. Others did not. All, however, were profoundly influenced by the specific economic and sociopolitical conditions of the period and took on forms decisively influenced by these conditions. In some crucial instances, in fact, mergers and communities of interest must be understood politically as well as economically.

The political context of vertical concentration is of such tremendous moment because, as Joseph Schumpeter noted, it was a period of "deadlock . . . in which neither "capitalist" nor "socialist" policy prevailed. As a sort of compromise, the capitalist engine was allowed to work, but was put under a pressure that prevented it from working

[1] See the interesting memorandum by Dr. Stellwaag in DZA Potsdam, RWM, Nr. 4457, Bl. 55ff.

"One has the best overview of the situation from here."

"No, from here."

From *Simplicissimus*, Vol. 26, No. 49 (March 1, 1922), p. 664. By Th. Th. Heine. Courtesy of Professor Dr. Erich Seeman.

according to design." Schumpeter was highly critical of the attempt made "to handle the essentially intracapitalistic problems of this period by anticapitalistic methods,"[2] and the development of the EWB certainly gives substance to this criticism. As shall be shown, vertical concentration was frequently viewed as an alternative to the meddling and muddling represented by the EWB as well as to the syndicates, which had proven as unable to hold together under private auspices as they had proven obnoxious to industrialists when held together under government tutelage.

Yet is is also somewhat difficult to determine the "design" according to which the capitalist "engine" was supposed to have worked, for as Schumpeter himself noted in his brief mention of the concentration movement during this period, "The losses of territory, often cutting through the domains of concerns and upsetting established relations between materials or steps of production, also necessitated reorientation. Many unshapely and unmanageable monsters resulted, which were unable to live as soon as the contours of reality emerged from the fog."[3] Thus, insofar as vertical concentration represented, as it did, the effort of private industry to reorganize and rationalize autonomously, some effort must be made to comprehend the immediate problems and conceptions of reality motivating the industrial leaders as against the realities that finally emerged.

Needless to say, this is more easily said than done. Although there are satisfactory discussions of the general motives for the concentration movement during this period, descriptions of the forms it took, and outlines of the great concerns, their holdings, and their connections, there is very little historical work that demonstrates how and why the actors performed as they did.[4] This is not surprising given the paucity of sources available, and the task is fairly hopeless for many of the major concerns of the period. However, it is possible to approach the problems dealt with in this chapter empirically.

[2] Schumpeter, *Business Cycles*, II, p. 702.

[3] *Ibid.*, p. 763.

[4] The most important work is Tross, *Aufbau*. The useful publication of the Deutscher Metallarbeiter-Verband, *Konzerne der Metallindustrie. Eine Darstellung der Entwicklung und des gegenwärtigen Standes der grossen Konzerne der deutschen Metallindustrie* (Stuttgart, 1923) seems to be largely a plagiarism of Tross but does contain some interesting additional information. Maschke's *Konzern* is exceptional as a concrete case study of concern building based on examination of the primary sources. There is also a fine unpublished work by W. Freund, "Die Siemens-Rheinelbe-Schuckert Union (1920–1926)" (1960) in the SAA 54/ Lm 123 based on the sources. I have employed both these works, but have relied mainly on the documents because my purposes are somewhat different than those of the two authors.

We have excellent records for two of the most important vertical communities of interest (*Interessengemeinschaften*—IG's) formed during the inflation. The first of these is the most famous of all the vertical combinations created during the inflation, the Siemens-Rhein-Elbe-Schuckert Union (SRSU), usually identified with the person and program of Hugo Stinnes, but often erroneously called the "Stinnes concern." The other is the expansion of the Gutehoffnungshütte, owned by the Haniel family and managed by Paul Reusch. In both cases, the center of interest will be on the way in which two great manufacturing concerns, the Siemens concern and the MAN, came into combination with raw materials producers, respectively, the Rhein-Elbe Union and the GHH. Although the expansion of heavy industry into manufacturing was not entirely novel, it had never previously attained this scale and significance. The availability of material for these two case studies is particularly fortuitous because they developed in a peculiar mixture of competition and collaboration with one another and can thus be integrally related to one another. At the same time, the complexity of their development, the scope of their operations, the centrality of their positions in German economic life, but also their differing fates permit extrapolation from their history in order to reach here and in the remainder of this study some generalizations and conclusions about the character, function, and viability of the vertical concentration process during the inflation.

THE TALE OF TWO CONCERNS

The birth of the SRSU as well as the complex of circumstances surrounding the GHH's acquisition of the MAN began with a series of conversations among Director Otto Henrich of Siemens, General Director Albert Vögler of Deutsch-Lux, and Hugo Stinnes in the winter of 1919–1920. These discussions took place at a very crucial period in the development of Deutsch-Lux and at a time of great stress for Siemens, conditions reflecting the general reorganization and reconstruction of heavy industry then beginning, on the one hand, and dire shortages of raw materials and capital in the manufacturing industries, on the other hand.

Deutsch-Luxemburg, a concern in whose strength and vigor its founder and chief stockholder, Hugo Stinnes, took particular pride, had been torn apart by the loss of the war and the Versailles Treaty. At the end of October 1918, the Supervisory board had empowered Stinnes and Vögler to take whatever measures they deemed necessary in connection with the concern's holdings in the Saar, Luxemburg, and Lorraine. Since that time, the two men had been successfully liquidating these cherished possessions under highly favorable terms. Substantial amounts of cash were expected from the German government, which had obligated itself to compensate all such losses provided that these funds were used for the reconstruction of the industrial enterprises involved within Germany. These amounts, however, were not yet determined. Much more important at this time were the direct sales of the threatened holdings to foreign firms anxious to secure the plants involved before their own governments interfered in the matter and willing to pay a high price in their own currencies. Here, Stinnes and Vögler made substantial gains. The French company that had bought up the prized plants at Differdingen agreed, among other things, to supply Deutsch-Lux with 500,000 tons of ore and 200,000 tons of metal at favorable prices for the coming thirty years. With the monies received from the liquidations, Stinnes was able to eliminate his Swedish ore debts and other obligations and begin systematically to replace his losses through the acquisition of new plants in the Ruhr and elsewhere.[5]

This process of reconstruction moved in two directions. First, Stinnes intended to strengthen Deutsch-Lux's relatively weak coal base, and he had long dreamed of penetrating into the coal empire of the Gelsenkirchener Bergwerke AG (GBAG), headed by Emil Kirdorf. The GBAG had been forced to divest itself of almost all its iron and steel plants by the treaty, and Kirdorf was showing interest in Stinnes' proposals for the formation of an IG between the two concerns. Second, he and Vögler were anxious not only to replace their losses but also to continue their highly profitable traditional policy of fabricating the bulk of their production and to accelerate their expansion into finishing and manufacturing. Because the high costs seemed to prohibit the construction of new plants, they wished to combine with existing firms, either through fusion or community of interest. The idea of an IG with Phoenix, first broached during the war, continued to interest them apparently, although they were to abandon it, probably because such a combination would have created the impression that they were trying to gain monopoly power in the steel industry and have provoked antagonism. In any case, it was viewed mainly as a means of expanding Deutsch-Lux's steel base and not as an active attempt to realize Vögler's idea of rationalizing the industry through

[5] See the Deutsch-Lux Supervisory Board meeting, April 12, 1920, Friedrich-Wilhelms-Hütte Archiv, Nr. 123/19; Vögler to Siemens, September 14, 1920, SAA 4/Lf/635; Paul Ufermann und Carl Hüglin, *Stinnes und Seine Konzerne* (Berlin, 1924), p. 28, Klass, *Stinnes*, p. 222ff.

[6] See above, pp. 115–117, and the remarks in the exposé by Henrich of December 1919/January 1920 in SAA 54/Ld 273.

horizontal organization.[6] For Stinnes, vertical concentration was a matter of principle, because "I do not share the view of the creators of the great American trusts, that every branch of industry must be separate from the others and take care of itself with the single purpose of the greatest possible return."[7] He believed that the return would be much greater if they worked in solidarity with one another. Such expansion into fabrication and other industries interested Stinnes far more than the rationalization of the steel industry advocated by Vögler, but Vögler certainly believed in the need for vertical expansion. Thus, for example, Vögler participated directly in the work involving Deutsch-Lux acquisitions of Philipp Weber GmbH in Brandenburg, and shipbuilding facilities in Emden.

Deutsch-Lux's assumption of complete control of the Philipp Weber Company in 1919 was very much on Director Henrich's mind in his discussions with Vögler in December 1919. Unlike Vögler, who was deeply concerned about the reconstruction and rationalization of the steel industry, Henrich was active in a newer industry and had reason to be fairly well satisfied with its organization and with the progress that had been made in cutting costs and keeping it competitive. Henrich's chief worry was raw materials, and his recognition that Germany was so short of coal and iron caused him to work consistently "to avoid differences between heavy industry and the finished products industries."[8] Siemens' most pressing raw materials problem at the time was securing sufficient supplies of steel plate for dynamos (*Dynomoblech*). Most of the supply came from Upper Silesia, and Henrich feared that if the area came under Polish control, the Poles might prove unwilling to sell their production for "bad German currency." When Henrich mentioned the problem to Stinnes during a conversation, the latter suggested that his recently acquired Brandenburg facilities could produce dynamo plate. Henrich found the suggestion quite attractive. The company already had three Siemens-Martin furnaces, and a necessary fourth furnace could be easily added. It was near Berlin, where there were large quantities of scrap and which was the center of the electrotechnical industry. Because both the scrap and the steel could be transported by water, it had transport advantages over every other part of Germany. The company also had "a labor force which is not infected by Berlin conditions,"[9] a matter of no small concern to a strike-plagued Berliner. In short, Henrich had good reason to follow up Stinnes' suggestion in further discussions with Vögler, and they developed a proposal under which the two concerns would evenly

[7] Quoted in Klass, *Stinnes*, p. 225.
[8] Henrich exposé, December 1919/January 1920, SAA 54/Ld 273.
[9] *Ibid.*

215

divide the costs of expanding the Brandenburg facilities to produce the necessary steel plate for dynamos. Siemens would be a silent partner with limited liability, while the management would remain in Deutsch-Lux's hands.[10] This arrangement was necessary, Vögler explained, because the plant could not continue to benefit from the coal self-consumption rights enjoyed by Deutsch-Lux unless the latter was at least 80% in possession. Siemens, however, would have equal share of all profits made on the new facilities as well as first call on its production with guaranteed German market prices. Vögler anticipated that delivery might start as early as October 1920.

Vögler did not think that Stinnes would raise any objections to the above proposal, but he was wrong. Stinnes did not like the idea of keeping a separate account for one portion of the Brandenburg production, and he urged that Siemens simply lend half the money required for the new construction with the guarantee of first call on production. Henrich was irritated by what he considered Stinnes' "somewhat petty standpoint." He did not want to play the "banker" in a matter of such vital concern, and he reminded Stinnes in a conversation on January 5, 1920, "that Berlin industry has a great mistrust of heavy industry, and Herr Stinnes here has an opportunity to allay this mistrust by setting up this plant in common with us on an absolutely straightforward basis."[11] The most curious and even extraordinary aspect of this conversation among Henrich, Stinnes, and Vögler, however, was the way in which the somewhat soured flirtation concerning the Brandenburg works gradually mushroomed into a project aimed at tying together Deutsch-Lux, the MAN, and Siemens in a community of interest until at least to the year 2000, "and this in a form that allows each of the concerns its financial and economic independence, but pools the profits of the concerns."[12]

When Henrich and Vögler resumed their negotiations on January 16, the expansion of Philipp Weber had become a sideshow. The IG project now stood in the forefront of consideration. Vögler pointed out that the GBAG would have to be included "in order to secure for ourselves the broadest coal basis that exists in Germany," and then began to sketch the form he thought the IG might take. Although uncertain as to what would be most favorable from a tax standpoint, Vögler operated with the model of a limited liability corporation as the most suitable institutional embodiment for the IG. It would have the traditional boards of supervisors and directors, who would be

[10] On this form of organization, the Kommandit Gesellschaft, see Beckerath, *Modern Industrial Organization*, p. 56.
[11] Henrich Exposé, December 1919/January 1920, SAA 54/Ld 273.
[12] *Ibid.*

taken from the member concerns, each of which would of course remain juridically and administratively independent. The IG supervisory board would include the chairmen of the boards of the member concerns: Arthur Salomonsohn of the Deutsche Bank (GBAG), Stinnes (Deutsch-Lux), Baron von Cramer-Klett (MAN), and C. F. von Siemens, whereas the IG board of directors would include the leading directors of these concerns, respectively, Kirdorf, Vögler, Rieppel, and Henrich, as well as engineering, financial, and marketing specialists. A special director would be assigned to represent the IG in the various trade associations, and Vögler was hopeful that some of the supervisory board members would also be Reichstag deputies.[13]

Naturally, the future of this hastily sketched scheme depended on the reactions of the GBAG and the MAN. Vögler was optimistic about Kirdorf's response and was planning to meet with the MAN Nürnberg director Gottlieb Lippart as well. Emil Kirdorf and his brother, Adolf, were indeed quite receptive to most of what Stinnes and Vögler proposed, and were prepared to go so far as to have the GBAG fused with Deutsch-Lux because they were so impressed by the "progressive character" of Stinnes' concern and were worried about their age and the short supply of able managers in the GBAG to replace themselves. It thus took some effort for Stinnes and Vögler to persuade them "that a fusion of such great companies would carry with it many disadvantages; the administration would be bureaucratic, and flexibility and technical advance would be significantly set back by a fusion. The two companies should under all circumstances be allowed to remain, as such, free and independent of one another, and should only be bound by the head corporation with regard to the major guidelines."[14] In the end, however, the Kirdorfs agreed to an IG. Insofar as the expansion of the IG to include finishing organizations was concerned, they were enthused about Siemens' membership but were less happy about bringing in the MAN because they thought it too small in comparison to the other concerns to be involved. Apparently, however, they were prepared to give way to Stinnes' arguments that they "could not do without the MAN in the future because of technical development. He [Stinnes] referred to the oil motor for shipping . . . the diesel motor, the gas machine, the developmental capacities of tractors

[13] *Ibid.* Henrich pointed out to Vögler that Siemens & Halske would also have to be added to the IG. Three days after this discussion Stinnes, Vögler, and Siemens were elected to the Reichstag in the January 19, 1919 elections. Later, a decision was made to place Emil Kirdorf on the IG board of supervisors and to recognize his age and distinction by giving him the first two-year term of the intended rotating chairmanship.

[14] Reported by Henrich in an undated exposé, SAA 54/Ld 273.

and similar technical perspectives, which we (i.e., Vögler and Henrich) had also always placed in the foreground of our discussions, in accordance with the principle followed from the very beginning that the concern must be in the technological forefront. . . ."[15]

Despite their interest in an alliance with Siemens and the MAN, however, Stinnes and Vögler tended to give priority to the IG with the GBAG. When Vögler proposed that this formidable heavy industrial block be erected before the adhesion of Siemens and the MAN, Henrich raised strong objections. This was no small matter. Vögler indicated that he wanted as much parity among the member concerns of the IG as possible and hoped that they would arrange to give equal dividends, but he confessed that he had not made much progress in devising a method for dividing the profits. The problem was most easily soluble between concerns like Deutsch-Lux and the GBAG because they produced similar products and had similar structures. The Siemens concern, however, had a very complex financial structure, and it could not be easily brought into an equitable relationship with its projected heavy industrial partners. The proposed procedure, therefore, created the real danger that a structure would be created and a series of arrangements made into which Siemens would not agreeably fit. Henrich preferred to have all the problems worked on at one and the same time, and undoubtedly preferred to deal with the two heavy industrial giants before they had formally cemented their relationship.[16]

Nevertheless, not only Henrich but also his employer C. F. von Siemens, abandoned this demand at a decisive breakfast meeting with Vögler and Stinnes at Berlin's famous Hotel Adlon on February 10. Stinnes announced that Dr. Salomonsohn, the chairman of the GBAG supervisory board, enthusiastically supported the IG project and went unchallenged when he urged that, "in order not to complicate things," the GBAG-Deutsch-Lux IG be formed before the IG's with Siemens and the MAN.[17]

[15] *Ibid.* The financial weakness of the MAN relative to the other proposed members is clear from a comparison of their capital stock and obligations:

	Capital Stock	Obligations
	(in millions of marks)	
GBAG	185	54
Deutsch-Lux	130	78.8
SSW	200	73.5
MAN	36	25 (loans and mortgages)

[16] *Ibid.*   [17] *Ibid.*

What is all the more striking about this crucial meeting is that most of the basic and difficult problems remained unsettled. The pressing problem of gaining a secure supply of steel plate, which had triggered the discussions, was now enveloped by a much larger and as yet unrealized project, and the critical profit-pooling arrangements were completely fuzzy. Here, as on other occasions, Stinnes seems to have silenced objections through his extraordinary capacity to "sell" his project by a peculiar mixture of hard calculation and fantasy.

Stinnes suggested all sorts of ways in which a connection with himself as well as the projected IG would place Siemens in a position to benefit from every conceivable technological advance and industrial wave of the past, present, and future. Stinnes knew, for example, that Siemens was trying to become a major supplier of the Italian automobile firm of Fiat, and he suggested that Siemens' position with Fiat would improve immensely because Stinnes, along with Fiat, had interests in Austria's largest iron and steel producer, the Alpine Montangesellschaft. This seemed reasonable enough, as did Stinnes' interest in the oil motor for ships, new sources of oil, and the supplying of Siemens with lignite from the Riebeck'schen Bergwerksgesellschaft in which Stinnes had an interest and on whose supervisory board he sat. Stinnes' industrial spectrum hardly stopped here, however, for beyond oil loomed wood and the substitution of cellulose for cotton. The discussion took a very strange turn as Stinnes announced a plan to use his Dutch connections to buy for 15 million paper marks a huge forest complex in the vicinity of Minsk from a Russian countess whose husband he had once assisted and Vögler informed Henrich that he had already begun to wear a suit made out of long cellulose fibers, "although he had not dared to go out with it in the rain." Undoubtedly, so experimental an attitude from so relatively cautious and sober a man as Vögler was reassuring, and fiber suits certainly had much more of a future and were in much less danger of disintegration than Stinnes' prospects in Minsk. In any case, the general directorship of Deutsch-Lux was well worth an experiment with unconventional clothes. It is less easy to understand why Henrich should have been so enthralled by Stinnes' plan "to forge together a community of interest that begins with wood and ends with the completed machine,"[18] and one wonders if the Siemens director was not suffering from an excessive will to believe if not from excessive ambition or cupidity.

Although Stinnes evidently did have the ability to cast a spell on many of his fellow businessmen through his single-minded pursuit of a boundless entrepreneurial vision, it is doubtful that C. F. von Siemens himself was ever as impressed with it as was Henrich. Siemens

[18] *Ibid.*

had never shown much enthusiasm for vertical concentration. He had contemplated the question in 1917, for example, when he was informed that the MAN was considering the purchase of a steel plant because they were chaffing under their dependence on raw materials producers, the long delays in deliveries, and the difficulties of assuring the proper quality of what was finally delivered. Siemens faced the same problems, and the idea of profiting from the fabrication and finishing of one's own raw materials was tempting. Yet Siemens came to the conclusion that it would not make sense in the electrotechnical business because "we use too many kinds of raw materials and semifinished goods and most of them in very different forms."[19] He had shown much more interest in horizontal organization, particularly in marketing, and he had made some effort to work through such possibilities during the war before coming to the conclusion that they could not be realized.[20] Apparently the AEG had often proposed collaboration, not only in marketing but also in production, but the Siemens concern had finally rejected proposals for formal ties for a variety of reasons. As Henrich explained, aside from the fact that the leaders of the two concerns differed sharply in their views on many economic and business issues, there was the very real danger that "the world would view such a connection simply as trustification for the purposes of creating a monopoly and dictating prices through this monopoly and, given the sick attitudes dominant today, this would lead to state intervention."[21] Furthermore, the high demand for electrotechnical products and the pricing arrangements made through the Zendei, whose founding Siemens had done so much to inspire, diminished the incentives for horizontal concentration. Most important, it could be argued that this form of concentration in no way solved the most pressing problems they were facing. It would double their worries about getting raw materials as well as intensify the impact of any bad business conditions that might arise for the industry, and it did not promise Siemens a really significant source of new capital. In short, at a time of great political and economic uncertainty as well as increased economic burdens, an arrangement with the AEG seemed to offer little security when compared to what the IG with Stinnes and Vögler appeared to promise. Although Siemens himself was probably disinclined to make an overly dramatic response to the aforementioned problems, he apparently felt obliged to take into account the above arguments as well as what he later called the "artificially increased anxiety of many members of the

---

[19] Siemens to O. von Petri, February 23, 1917, and Petri to Siemens, February 8, 1917, *ibid.*, 4 Lf/671. See also above, p. 78.

[20] Siemens to Vögler, December 27, 1925, *ibid.*, 635.

[21] Undated memorandum by Henrich, *ibid.*, 54/Ld 273.

family,"[22] who feared to have their fortunes completely tied up in the concern if it had to stand and bear all the burdens of the present and future without substantial assistance.

Both Director Henrich and his colleague Director Jastrow were much more enthusiastic about the IG than Siemens, and they played on the concrete problems of raw materials and capital shortages in pressing for an affirmative decision in various internal memoranda written during the spring of 1920. Henrich predicted that iron and steel production would remain at low levels for years to come, and argued that "works which organically belong together will join in communities of interest."[23] Because the entire economy depended on the maximum export of manufactured products containing as much German labor and material as possible, the issue of quality control of raw materials, always a headache for his industry, and the problem of making heavy industry feel that it had a greater stake in supplying the domestic market than in exporting, a source of so much recent conflict, could both be dealt with by means of vertical concentration. Furthermore, because heavy industry disposed of far greater capital resources and had much easier access to short-term capital than the manufacturing industries, vertical concentration would also mean some relief of his firm's capital shortages.

The Siemens' leaders were constantly preoccupied with the short-term and long-term problems of raising capital throughout this period of negotiation with Stinnes and Vögler. In February 1920, Siemens issued 47 million marks worth of new stock along with a 60 million mark bond issue, but this capital increase was viewed as little more than a "drop in the bucket," useful "to cover our copper needs for about two weeks."[24] They wanted to encourage foreign investment but feared that foreign interests would use the inflation to gain control of Siemens and sought to ward off this danger by pursuing the strategy increasingly employed at this time of transforming stock, in this case the stock held by the Siemens family, into preferred stock with thirty times the voting rights of regular stock. German (and family) control could be maintained by such means. Henrich and Jastrow, in their argu-

22 Siemens to Vögler, December 27, 1925, ibid., 4/Lf 635. As a member of the Siemens concern, Heintzenberg, noted retrospectively on July 23, 1947: "If Carl Friedrich decided despite all this [i.e., his reservations] to agree to the proposals for concluding the IG, he was compelled to do so by the consideration that given the uncertainty of the economic future in 1920, it was appropriate for reasons of caution to distribute the economic risk upon a broader basis," ibid., 54/Ld 273.

23 Undated Henrich memorandum, ibid.

24 Ibid., and Siemens concern to the Prussian Minister of Commerce and Industry, February 16, 1920, in volume on Siemens & Halske in the Deutsche Bank Archiv, Frankfurt/Main.

ments for the IG with Stinnes, emphasized that "such normal methods of creating capital" were inadequate during a period of raw materials shortages and fluctuating exchange rates and that it was necessary to "employ the capital liquidity of other enterprises"[25] in dealing with these acute short-term credit problems as well as the longer-term needs. In their view no single concern could handle its credit and capital needs alone, and they needed a "broader basis" if they were going to attract foreign money and if they were going to manage what had apparently become a long-term task of allocating and appropriately manipulating foreign exchange. An IG could perform these functions, because "It is necessary to have the bank kept, a central institute which, without interfering in the settlement of individual transactions and without disturbing individual enterprises in the disposition of their internal affairs, will take over the role of the financier, the clearing house."[26]

It would be misleading to suggest, however, that the IG proponents at Siemens were moved solely by serious but mundane considerations of raw materials and capital. An IG with Deutsch-Lux and the GBAG required considerably broader justification because it only required common sense to see that such a combination in no way fulfilled many of the traditional functions of industrial concentration. The relatively sober Jastrow noted that however gigantic the proposed IG, it would not be in a position to monopolize production, an aim more easily attained by horizontal than by vertical organizations. Nor could there be any serious cost reduction through rationalization of production and marketing in so far-flung and heterogeneous an empire based on such variegated production. Nevertheless, Jastrow's sense of such a conglomerate's potentialities was little less than Henrich's, but the latter's rhapsodic and fulsome description of what it could and would accomplish is the most revealing:

... The first thing to do is to set up an economic program for the new economic body (*Wirtschaftskörper*), to regulate imports and exports and the exchange question; to reduce the costs of new acquisitions; to consolidate foreign enterprises and representatives; to appropriately deal with business cycles, preparing ahead for future better periods in times of slack, limiting sharp recessions through the production for stockpiling (*Lagerfabrikation*) of appropriate items. We need to take advantage of technical improvements ... and to create an economic body which ought not to go unnoted and unasked for any project that comes up in this world. ...[27]

[25] Undated Henrich memorandum, SAA 54/Ld 273.
[26] Jastrow memorandum of April 7, 1920, *ibid.*
[27] Undated Henrich memorandum, *ibid.*

222

In contemplating these lines, it seems clear that the driving force behind the IG was not simply raw materials and capital problems or even the advantages that Stinnes and Siemens could gain from one another's far-flung sales organizations at home and abroad. Certainly there is the vision of economic enterprise under conditions of vastly reduced risk. The IG would always have something to sell because it would have a membership that produced practically everything, and it could afford to produce even in hard times because its members could always serve as customers for one another and because its capital base would be large enough to withstand the strains. The IG would always be able to sit in the eye of economic hurricanes.

It should be no less clear that there was a profoundly political conception underlying the proposed plan for economic collaboration, and that in referring to an "economic body" with an "economic program," Henrich was elevating this IG beyond the normal industrial combination. Just as Stinnes, Vögler, and Henrich had played a decisive role in creating the *Arbeitsgemeinschaft* with labor during the revolution in defiance or disregard of the government and the traditional industrial organizations, so now they were collaborating in the formation of a gigantic *Interessengemeinschaft* designed to function in the sphere of intraindustrial relations in the manner that the *Arbeitsgemeinschaft* was meant to function in labor-management relations. The style of thought about the relations among industrialists, labor leaders, and bureaucrats that inspired the ZAG ran parallel to that fueling the IG project. Indeed, for Stinnes, the similarity was quite explicit, and he hoped that the security provided by "large economic structures" would promote "a better relationship with employees and workers."[28] When Vögler and Henrich emphasized the need to have strong IG representation in the Reichstag—and Vögler, Stinnes, and Siemens were members of the Reichstag—they had more than lobbying in mind. The IG represented to them an economic program, the economic program that a weak government had been unable to formulate and that the leading industrial organizations could not formulate because of their inability to cut through intraindustrial conflicts.

These political considerations were fully explicated by Henrich's collaborator, Jastrow. The IG, Jastrow pointed out, was being created "out of the emergency of our time." Economic ruin and government incompetence had forced each enterprise to go its own way, "to set up its own economic plan untroubled about the others beside itself." Moellendorff's *Planwirtschaft*, with its "healthy basic idea" of a strong consolidation of industrial groups, failed because of the form in which

[28] Oscar von Petri at the MAN Supervisory Board on November 13, 1920, Guggenheimer notes, MAN Werksarchiv Augsburg, Nr. K56.

it was presented by the RWM. Little could be expected of Moellen-dorff's successors, and industry would have to help itself. Collaboration was in the air, and it had led to a proliferation of branch organizations for the various industries, but these were proving inadequate to the tasks confronting industry. The prewar cartels and syndicates had, in the meantime, collapsed. An economic program satisfying all industrial interests required, in Jastrow's view, vertical organization. Experience had shown that neither the "sick" state nor the existing industrial organizations could create such organization and that it could only be done "through the self-help of individual enterprises."[29] The projected IG, in short, was to be an economic state within the state. It is difficult to imagine an economic enterprise founded on more extraordinary and grandiose political pretensions, and the style of formulation reflects the extent to which the crisis of authority in the Weimar state encouraged an untamed pluralism and permitted the already heightened self-assertiveness of businessmen like Henrich and Stinnes to move well beyond the bounds of what was desirable not only from a broad political standpoint but also from a business point of view.

In reality, the formation of combinations among firms and concerns was not some kind of lofty arrangement made according to high-flown principles by men elevated beyond the toss and tumble of daily affairs. Rather, it involved risky decisions inspired by motives containing various mixtures of fear and ambition in the context of disorderly if not downright anarchic conditions, and the final results were as much the product of shady dealing and happenstance as they were of cool calculation. Relations of power, the advantages of the strong over the weak, and similar mundane factors were determinant in these events, particularly when they involved lesser giants like the MAN. The latter was in no position to state its terms in the manner of Siemens, and it could not deal with Deutsch-Lux or the GBAG on equal terms. Joining the projected IG or in any formal arrangement with a great raw materials producer would mean loss of cherished independence as well as intensification of the much resented subservience of southern Germany to the Ruhr and Berlin. If the MAN directors and supervisors were seriously contemplating the formation of an IG with a raw materials producer, as they were, then it was for very concrete and unpleasant reasons in which *grosse Politik* in the manner of Stinnes and Henrich played very little role.

This leading South German concern had always suffered from its distance from the sources of raw materials and chief customers in the North, and in happier prewar days its leading director, Anton von Rieppel, had actually contemplated expansion in the Ruhr and the

[29] Jastrow memorandum of April 7, 1920, SAA/54 Ld 273.

securing of a position in the Steel Works Association so as to give the MAN the advantages of a self-consumer. He found, however, and this somewhat ironically in the light of subsequent developments after the war, that the only steel producing company strongly involved in fabrication was the GHH, a concern well beyond the MAN's powers of acquisition. In 1910 the MAN did build a plant in Duisburg that manufactured large gas machines and cranes, and this was meant to serve as a first installment on further penetration into the North. The war interrupted this effort, and the discussion of expansion into steel production in 1917 did not lead to concrete action. In 1919, the MAN found itself deprived of its previous easy access to the Saar coal and Lorraine iron, more dependent on Ruhr supplies than ever before, and overwhelmingly burdened by the increased costs of materials and labor. The Duisburg plant, despite its favorable location, had never been properly integrated into the MAN's production program and had become a serious financial burden.[30]

In December 1919 a decision was made to raise the capital stock from 36 to 54 million marks and to issue bonds as well. In the second half of 1920, the firm found it necessary to repeat this with a 46 million mark stock issue and another bond issue. Although these capital increases were all the more justified by the fact that the capital base of the MAN had been far too low, the MAN's 80 million mark bank debt and its increasing dependence on the banks were viewed with anxiety by its leadership.[31] Most of the directors were convinced that they would have to enter an IG with a raw materials producer, and Rieppel seems to have been much taken with the IG project Henrich unfolded to him in a conversation in Berlin early in 1920. Henrich reported that "... Reichsrat von Rieppel told me that such ideas had been waltzing about in his brain for years, and he would be happy to help in the creation of such a structure before he retires."[32] Needless to say, there was a measure of self-consolation in Rieppel's remarks because he had always contemplated an IG in which the MAN would play the dominant role, a situation obviously precluded by the general circumstances as well as by the specific project Henrich advocated. Yet the project could be considered appealing in many respects to Rieppel. There had long been close relations and collaboration between the MAN and the

[30] Fritz Buchner, *Hundert Jahre Geschichte der Maschinenfabrik Augsburg-Nürnberg* (n.p., 1940), pp. 138–150.

[31] Maschke, *Konzern*, pp. 144–145.

[32] Undated early 1920 memorandum by Henrich, SAA 54/Ld 273. Henrich gave his exposé of December 1919/January 1920 to Rieppel and later sent it to Dr. Lippart, a MAN Nürnberg director, where it is to be found in the MAN Werksarchiv Nürnberg, Nr. 121 and 171.

Schuckert works in Nürnberg. Indeed, because of its production program in motors and turbines, the MAN needed close contact with the electrotechnical manufacturers, and Rieppel had also discussed various forms of potential collaboration and combination with Geheimrat Deutsch of the AEG in 1919. The possible arrangement with Siemens was particularly attractive to Rieppel, however, because of the Nürnberg connection and for political reasons. Rieppel had also been involved in the founding of the ZAG with Henrich, and he appears to have worked closely with Henrich in the Association of German Engineers during the war.[33]

Within the MAN, however, there was strong hostility to the entire IG idea from at least one director, Otto Gertung, who urged that the MAN try to hold out financially.[34] He implied that this could be done through the MAN's "friends" in Switzerland, particularly the Bern businessman Carl Winkler, with whom the MAN participated in a Swiss holding company and who had assisted the MAN financially by lending it large sums of money and buying a substantial portion of the new stock issue well above par in April 1920. Furthermore, Winkler had good contacts in the United States, who expressed interest in the MAN and seemed willing to invest in the MAN.[35] At the same time, Director Guggenheimer of the MAN and Director Deutsch of the AEG, who were both prominent members of the German industry's peak association, the RdI, were also involved in discussions with Americans, apparently with the object of securing a large loan for a group of prominent German firms in need of money. In late May 1920, however, Rathenau and Deutsch reported to Guggenheimer that the Americans were losing interest because the increased value of the mark made investment in Germany more expensive at a time when money was becoming scarcer in the United States due to recession. The AEG executives also reported that the Americans were not in the least interested in long-term financial commitments and insisted in dealing exclusively in commercial paper that could be sold on the market at will. The Americans would not give money to a group of German firms that might be formed with the object of attracting foreign investors but rather wished "to choose the individual flowers for the bouquet themselves."[36] By the late spring of 1920, therefore, the prospects of signifi-

[33] For the negotiations with the AEG, see *ibid.*, Nr. 151. On the role of Rieppel in the founding of the ZAG, see Feldman in Ritter, *Entstehung und Wandel*, p. 329, and in *IWK*, 19/20, p. 64ff.

[34] Memorandum of April 14, 1920, MAN Werksarchiv Nürnberg, Nr. 171.

[35] Maschke, *Konzern*, pp. 155–158, and the informative letter from Director Endres to Reusch, July 6, 1921, HA/GHH, Nr. 300193010/4.

[36] Memorandum by Guggenheimer on his discussions of June 4, 1920, with Rathenau and Deutsch, June 5, 1920, MAN Werksarchiv Nürnberg, Nr. 03/V.

cant American capital investment in the MAN were far from promising.

Gertung had not based his arguments against an IG with Stinnes
solely on such prospects, however, and he had also warned that so
mammoth an IG would make the MAN completely dependent on the
raw materials producers and particularly on the "energetic, determined
and strong personality" of Stinnes "who will dominate the entire alliance."[37] Gertung felt that it was safer to depend on a combination of
state protection through the EWB and *ad hoc* private agreements with
suppliers to secure raw materials, and he warned that an IG with
Stinnes would alarm the Entente, deprive the MAN of sympathy it
enjoyed because of its South German character, and make a negative
impression on the trade unions.

Rieppel conveyed these and other objections to Stinnes and, in late
June, Stinnes turned to the problem of selling the IG project to the
MAN leaders in his characteristically fulsome and frank style.[38] As
might be expected, Stinnes pointed out that the IG offered finishing
concerns like the MAN what they would supposedly need most in the
future, "the securest possible means of procuring money and independence in raw materials and semifinished goods so that they can
make plans and commitments for a longer period without too great a
risk."[39] The political situation provided additional reasons for entering
an IG, however. It was a way of getting around the Factory Councils
Law passed that year, because the fundamental policies of the member concerns could be decided without involving the individual factory councils. There were important tax advantages because the inventory tax would not apply to goods sold within the IG as part of
an overall production program, and the sum total of taxes on profits
would be lower if those profits were pooled. Stinnes was particularly
anxious to contest the notion that the IG would constitute some sort
of ungainly bureaucratic organization in which independence and initiative would disappear, and he hammered at the point that the IG
form had been deliberately chosen to, among other things, maintain
the independence and initiative of its members. They would be free
to purchase and sell outside the IG if it were to their interest, and they
would be free to seek participation in other enterprises. Stinnes could

---

Also, see Guggenheimer's "travel notes" of May 14, 1920, in MAN Werksarchiv
Augsburg, Nr. K56, Bl. 38.

[37] Memorandum of April 14, 1920, MAN Werksarchiv Nürnberg, Nr. 171.

[38] Discussion in Berlin among Stinnes, Rieppel, Endres, and Gertung on June 23,
1920, MAN Werksarchiv Nürnberg, Nr. 171; Rieppel to Siemens, July 1, 1920, and
Stinnes to Rieppel, July 2, 1920, in SAA 4/Lf 635/1.

[39] Stinnes to Rieppel, July 2, 1920, *ibid.*

not deny, of course, that in the case "of such great undertakings the last word would have to lie with the business management of the community of interest,"[40] but he pointed out that the MAN's freedom of action was being much less purposefully restricted by its current raw materials and financial problems. Implicit in Stinnes' arguments was that the IG represented a more desirable form of dependency than the MAN's dependency on the banks because the IG constituted a form of industrial self-financing based on informed decision making. The company embodying the IG at the summit was likened by Stinnes to a "leading bank." It would decide general policy, financial policies, distribution of production on the basis of maximum advantages, guidelines for purchasing and sales, and it would have the final word on new construction and expansion recommended by member concerns. Stinnes envisioned that these decisions would require a two-thirds majority. Stinnes hoped, therefore, that the MAN would not feel that it was losing its independence or that it would not have an important voice in the affairs of the proposed IG.

Similarly, Stinnes was most anxious to allay anxieties connected with his own person from both a business and a sociopolitical perspective. He dismissed fears that his enormous outside interests would dominate the IG or that the entire structure would depend on himself. On the one hand, he emphasized that his private interests outside Deutsch-Lux would be kept strictly separate from his interests in the IG. On the other hand, he stressed that the IG and its members would have everything to gain from his outside interests because he would obviously favor the IG and, wherever possible, give it the benefits of his international organization and connections. Stinnes deprecated the sociopolitical reservations Rieppel had conveyed on behalf of his colleagues. Although the Entente would certainly treat the gigantic IG with "a certain caution," the IG would be respected for its size and power and would be considered first in all important matters. Here, Stinnes undoubtedly had in mind the reconstruction contracts for the war-devastated regions in connection with the reparations settlement. As for his reputation abroad, Stinnes pointed to his role in negotiations with the Allies which, in his view, confirmed that it "can in no way be called bad."[41] Labor's reaction to the IG was not to be feared because, as Stinnes noted, the labor leaders understood the necessity of "com-

[40] *Ibid.*

[41] *Ibid.* Stinnes was also gaining popularity in South Germany, thanks to his tough nationalist utterances at the Conference with the Allies in Spa. As Oscar von Petri of Siemens-Schuckert reported, "The person of Herr Stinnes has also become very popular in South Germany because of his excellent speech at Spa. It was a real joy that finally a German found the right words to say," Petri to Siemens, July 15, 1920, *ibid.*, 4/Lf 671.

binations from raw materials to the last stage of fabrication." Stinnes was no less confident in dismissing the notion that the MAN had anything to gain from remaining known throughout the world as a purely South German firm.

Most important, however, Stinnes wanted to have the MAN leaders understand that the IG was good business. It had been suggested that Deutsch-Lux would find supplying the MAN a burden at times of great demands for iron and steel, and Stinnes responded that the greatest profits would always be made in manufacturing be the times good or bad. It was necessary to maintain steady employment and maximize gains through a coordinated policy between raw materials producers and manufacturers. Characteristically, Stinnes then moved from this effort to convince those with whom he negotiated of the economic correctness of his program to the harsh insistence that they embrace the grand design on his terms or not at all. He had little patience with timid suggestions emanating from Rieppel and others in the MAN for weaker forms of relationship binding for less lengthy periods than the thirty years initially proposed. Stinnes "categorically declared that he could not deviate from the basic principles of his program. The economic goal can only be reached if we go the whole way at once."[42] The MAN would have to make a full commitment to the IG, therefore, or solve its problems by some other means.

Rieppel came to the conclusion that Stinnes did, indeed, offer the best solution to the MAN's difficulties. Although Rieppel certainly was impressed with Stinnes' "unbounded energy and activity," he did not approach the project with anything comparable to Henrich's almost ecstatic enthusiasm. For Rieppel, Stinnes, although remarkable as an individual, was in no way unique in what he was doing. The Ruhr steel producers were all expanding into finishing, and Rieppel feared that, as these firms increasingly consumed a larger and larger portion of their own production in their own finishing operations, great consumers like the MAN would be left "hanging in the air." He regarded the Iron Trades Federation and the Reich Coal Bureaus as "unusable means" of securing South Germany's raw materials needs, and it is not difficult to see how the continuous reports of heavy industrial expansion would undermine such confidence as Rieppel might have had in government-supported agencies. He cited the Gutehoffnungshütte as an illustration of what was going on. It had taken over Haniel & Lueg in Düsseldorf with its foundries, steel plant, hammer and press work, machine plant, and mine shaft building facilities; it had bought up the important Eisenwerk Nürnberg, vorm. Tafel & Co., which had always been an important MAN supplier; it had gained control of the ship-

[42] Stinnes to Rieppel, July 2, 1920, *ibid.*, 4 Lf/635/1.

building facilities of the Deutsche Werft in Hamburg, acquired the steel wire works of Boecker & Co. in Gelsenkirchen, and taken over the Osnabrück Copper and Cable Works. Rieppel undoubtedly could have added more detail about how Paul Reusch, a Swabian by birth, was moving into South Germany, not only by taking over the Nürnberg iron works but also the Esslinger Machinenfabrik, which had recently tied up with the GHH for the usual reasons of raw materials and capital need. In any case, neither Reusch nor Stinnes had left much to the imagination, and from Rieppel's perspective, which was that of an aging South German businessman facing an unpleasant present and a potentially even more unpromising future, the differences between Reusch and Stinnes were largely matters of style and personality: Rieppel found Reusch, who openly stated his intention of placing the "entire finishing of his own iron and steel production in his control as effectively as possible" to be "ruthless and crude" whereas Stinnes "is more skillful, clearer in his goals and counts less upon the power at his disposal than upon a conviction of the necessity of his proposals and intentions."[43] This comparison demonstrates the anxiety and reluctance with which Rieppel argued for the IG with Siemens and Stinnes. Indeed, if he found any consolation in his conclusion, it was that the IG would strengthen the MAN's already close relations with the Schuckert works in Nürnberg.

Rieppel and C. F. von Siemens were counting on the support of one another in dealing with Stinnes and Vögler, as their correspondence after July 9, when the MAN formally decided to pursue further the possibilities of joining an IG with a raw materials producer, demonstrates.[44] Despite the MAN's interest in negotiations with Stinnes and Siemens, however, the summer months came and went without further negotiations with the MAN. For that matter, there was no further progress in the negotiations between Siemens and his projected heavy industrial partners either. There was one major event that should have moved matters along. On August 18, 1920, the GBAG and Deutsch-Lux signed the agreement creating the Rhein-Elbe-Union, which was to begin its formal existence on October 1, and the supposed basis for bringing in the manufacturing firms had thus been created. Apparently, the delay was caused by the summer vacation schedule of the key men at Siemens, but the delay irritated Rieppel and left MAN leaders with the impression that interest in the project had somehow evaporated.[45]

[43] Rieppel memorandum of July 5, 1920, MAN Werksarchiv Nürnberg, Nr. 171.

[44] Rieppel to Siemens, July 10, 1920, SAA 4/Lf 635/1, and Guggenheimer travel notes, November 3, 1920, MAN Werksarchiv Augsburg, Nr. K56.

[45] On developments during the summer and the correspondence of September 1920 discussed above and below, see the comments by Petri at the MAN Super-

The delay was also creating difficulties for both Vögler and Siemens, who had renounced the right to pursue other possible connections for their respective concerns until a decision about the IG had been made. Finally, the negotiations were reopened with an outburst of correspondence in mid-September, which followed shortly upon a visit by Siemens to Vögler. Siemens had been finding it difficult to think through the question of devising a basis for the quota according to which the IG profits were to be pooled. The small capital base of the MAN in comparison with its intended partners was a source of particular difficulty. Because the MAN had been steadily raising its capital base to 100 million marks, however, the possibility of an adjustment of the relations among the concerns now presented itself. Siemens contemplated setting up two fairly balanced finishing groups within the IG, one composed of Schuckert and the MAN, the other being Siemens & Halske. As Siemens privately suggested to the Schuckert General Director, Oscar von Petri, who was also a MAN supervisory board member, the two firms would constitute a "South German group," and this would create a measure of regional balance in the IG as well as a practical solution to the quota question. Unhappily for Siemens, however, Rieppel was in no condition to respond to the initiatives of Siemens and Vögler because he had become seriously ill. The effort to remobilize the negotiators and revitalize the negotiations with the MAN had come too late, and matters were taking an entirely new turn.

The comparison Rieppel had made between Stinnes and Reusch in his memorandum of July 5 had been no casual one, and the distaste for Reusch expressed in the comparison was deeply felt. The takeover of the Eisenwerk Nürnberg in 1919 by the Haniel interests, whom Reusch served, had distressed the MAN leaders. The Eisenwerk Nürnberg had been an important MAN supplier, and the MAN was represented on its supervisory board. Its takeover by a concern so heavily engaged in finishing as the GHH raised the spectre of new competition for the MAN on its home territory as well as a significant incursion by Ruhr industry into South Germany.[46] Reusch was as anxious to reduce such fears as he was to make incursions into the South German market now opened up for exploitation because the Peace Treaty had cut off the Saar and Lorraine from Germany. Thus, he made a special point of trying to soothe ruffled feelings by giving official guarantees that he did not intend to compete with the MAN in South Germany and by keeping MAN members on the Eisenwerk Nürnberg supervisory board.

---

visory Board meeting of November 3, 1920 in *ibid.*; Siemens to Rieppel, September 13, 1920, and Vögler to Siemens, September 14, 1920, in SAA 4/Lf 635; Petri to Siemens, September 16, 1920, in *ibid.*, 635/1 and Vögler to Stinnes, September 10, 1920, Nachlass Stinnes. The Rhein-Elbe contract is in SAA 54/Ld 273.

[46] Cramer-Klett to Reusch, June 30, 1919, HA/GHH, Nr. 300193010/10.

These efforts seem to have won him some goodwill within the MAN, although Rieppel refused to forgive what he evidently considered an illegitimate invasion. Contacts between the GHH and the MAN were increased thanks to Eisenwerk Nürnberg supervisory board meetings and the continuation of the traditional cooperation between the man who now became Reusch's chief agent in South Germany, the director of the Eisenwerk Nürnberg, Lambert Jessen, and MAN Nürnberg directors Otto Gertung and Ludwig Endres. It appears that the last-named directors tried desperately and vainly to get Rieppel to assent to discussions with Reusch about possible GHH-MAN collaboration during the summer of 1920. Reusch himself approached the subject directly on July 9 at an Eisenwerk Nürnberg supervisors meeting, where he and Karl Haniel expressed regret to Baron von Cramer-Klett, the chairman of the MAN supervisory board, about the MAN's negotiations with Stinnes and pointed out that the GHH would have been interested in an IG with the MAN also. The Baron said nothing at this time because he did not want to be disavowed by Rieppel, but he corresponded with Rieppel about the matter subsequently without making any headway.[47]

By mid-September, however, Rieppel was so sick that he could be expected to be away from business affairs for months to come. Yet this was only one, albeit a major, barrier to negotiations with Reusch that had been eliminated. Not only had the negotiations with Stinnes and Siemens progressed quite far, but the MAN was also now being actively courted by yet another major Ruhr concern, Rheinstahl. The latter had approached Rieppel with an offer to purchase the MAN's Duisburg plant, which had proven a financial lodestone for the MAN of the worst sort, and was also prepared to guarantee the MAN raw materials as part of the arrangement. There was to be no financial participation by either of the firms in the other, but their connection was to be fortified by having one or more supervisory board members in common. If Reusch were now to become an active wooer of the MAN, therefore, he would have to face the competition of the two suitors already at the door.[48]

Reusch was not the romantic type. He approached his prize with threats and won it by entering through the back door. In all fairness, however, it must be said that he did so only after he became certain that the latter would be unlatched. Through Jessen, he intimated to Baron von Cramer-Klett that the Eisenwerk Nürnberg would have to

[47] Jessen to Reusch, September 14, 1920, *ibid.*, and Guggenheimer travel notes, November 3, 1920, MAN Werksarchiv Augsburg, Nr. K56.

[48] Guggenheimer travel notes of October 26, 1920, and report to the MAN board of supervisors by the directors, November 2, 1920, in *ibid.*

find new customers if the MAN were to become obligated to another raw materials producer, and when Jessen reported that the Baron and other MAN directors were favorable to an alliance with the GHH, Reusch proceeded to play on the unadventuresome, conservative, and South German provincial tendencies of the Baron.[49] The Baron distrusted the "powerful personality" of Stinnes and thought the bigness of the proposed IG more suitable to America than South Germany. Reusch was straightforward and businesslike. He bluntly stated that any connection between a raw materials producer and a manufacturer in the existing circumstances was bound to favor the former but argued that a profit-pooling arrangement such as that proposed by Stinnes would prove disadvantageous when conditions favored manufacturers once again. In place of such an agreement Reusch offered a "kind of community of interest" that "requires no contracts or arrangements," namely, "participation by taking over a large portion of stock."[50] At the same time, the MAN could rest assured that once the GHH assumed "a more or less dominant" role in the affairs of a manufacturing enterprise, the latter could expect the financial support and raw materials it needed without having to surrender its independence as an enterprise and its Bavarian character. Cramer-Klett was impressed by the style, leadership, and tradition of the GHH, which he thought "would also be secure in the next generation,"[51] and although he was in no position to terminate the negotiations with Stinnes and Rheinstahl, he was able to persuade the MAN directors to consider an alliance with the GHH seriously.

Thus, when the MAN board of directors met on October 15, 1920, they had three projects to mull over and pursue before presentation of the various options to the supervisory board. Because the three options seemed to offer a solution to the MAN's financial and raw materials problems, they were variously judged as to which left the concern "the greatest legal and economic independence."[52] An arrangement with Rheinstahl unquestionably ranked first in this regard because all that was involved was the sale of the Duisburg plant and an agreement on raw materials. The collaboration with the GHH would leave the

[49] Jessen to Reusch, September 14, 1920, and Reusch to Jessen, September 21, 1920, in HA/GHH, Nr. 300193010/10.

[50] Reusch to Cramer-Klett, September 21, 1920, *ibid.*, and Maschke, *Konzern*, p. 149. Certain portions of the original letter are not quoted in Maschke. It is important to bear in mind that the term *Interessengemeinschaft* covered every form of contractual relationship short of fusion, see above, p. 38.

[51] Guggenheimer notes on the MAN supervisory board meeting, November 3, 1920, MAN Werksarchiv Augsburg, Nr. 56.

[52] Report by Buz to the supervisory board on November 2, 1920, in *ibid.* for the discussion below.

MAN with "a certain dependence through the (stock) participation, but generous treatment with far-reaching freedom of action and an arrangement that would involve no diminution of the MAN's external status." Furthermore, the arrangement with the GHH would not preclude sale of the Duisburg plant to Rheinstahl, and it might eliminate burdensome competition in production between the MAN and GHH. The IG with Stinnes appeared to offer the least agreeable arrangement, a feeling much heightened by the dissatisfaction of the MAN directors with the quota offered in negotiations that same day.[53] Although the IG purported to offer equality among the members, it really meant, in the MAN directors' view, "substantial dependence because of financial influence, disproportionate strength of the raw materials works, the slenderness of our quota, and the personal influence of Herr Stinnes. Disturbing also is the size and vastness of the concern as well as the potential conflicting private interests of Herr Stinnes." At this meeting of October 15, however, no attempt was made to make a final choice among the alternatives. Instead, Endres and Lippart were instructed to negotiate with Rheinstahl, and Adolf Eberbach, a mysterious go-between serving Carl Winkler and other MAN officials, was told to join with Cramer-Klett in discussions with Reusch. A meeting with Stinnes on the quota question was also to be arranged. Complete information on the three projects was then to be presented to the supervisory board for purposes of comparison and final decision.

Unhappily for the MAN directors, Cramer-Klett made a shambles of this perfectly sensible procedure. There is no evidence that he acted in bad faith, but there is every reason to believe that the Baron's hostility to the IG with Stinnes, a hostility shared by Eberbach and by Winkler, who feared Stinnes' domination and argued that his "American friends" were unwilling to invest if Stinnes were involved, predisposed the Baron to act precipitously when he feared a Stinnes victory. According to plan, the Baron contacted Reusch to arrange a meeting in Frankfurt, and Reusch proposed October 25 or November 12. Suddenly, however, the Baron became alarmed by reports of large-scale purchases of MAN stock, and he telegraphed Reusch asking for an immediate meeting. On October 24, Cramer-Klett and Eberbach met Reusch in Frankfurt, and the Baron offered to mediate the purchase of a large amount of MAN stock by the Haniel group, to support the GHH's acquisition of a substantial portion of a new stock issue, and

[53] I have found no record of these negotiations, but in addition to the reference at the meeting of the MAN supervisory board of November 3 and in the Buz report of November 2, they are referred to as forthcoming in a letter from Siemens to Stinnes of October 10, 1920, and are noted retrospectively in a letter from Buz to Siemens of November 9, 1920, SAA 4/Lf 635/1.

to combine his voting strength with that of the GHH to secure the Haniel group two seats on the MAN supervisory board. In taking this drastic step, Cramer-Klett was acting under the understandable but false presumption that Stinnes or persons acting for Stinnes had been buying up the MAN stock. The presumption was understandable because Stinnes, in one of the notable coups of his career, had just that month secured majority control of the Bochumer Verein, one of the greatest and most venerable Ruhr steel companies, from the banker and noted inflation speculator, Hugo Herzfeld. Although it was widely presumed that Herzfeld had been buying up the Bochumer Verein for Stinnes, this was not in fact the case. Herzfeld had been prepared to sell the Bochumer Verein to Dutch interests, and Stinnes was quite honest in claiming that he had saved this important firm from foreign control. The entire affair, however, created a public sensation. It occurred in the midst of wild speculation with industrial shares, and the MAN was a natural object of speculation throughout this period because of the continuous rumors about its forthcoming connection with some great raw materials producer. Cramer-Klett, therefore, was misinformed, but his fears were understandable, particularly because there had been large MAN stock purchases in September.[54]

If the Baron had acted in good faith and within his rights, however, he had also gone far beyond the letter and spirit of his mission as defined by the board of directors on October 15. The situation was all the more aggravating to the MAN directors because Rheinstahl had come up with a very attractive offer in its negotiations with Endres and Lippart. It offered the MAN a total of 68 million marks for the Duisburg plant and its stocks, along with an agreement to supply the MAN with coal and iron at reduced prices and favorable payment terms to help the MAN compete for foreign bridge building contracts. There were to be some common supervisory board members, and Rheinstahl held out the prospect of joint participation in a marketing enterprise. In summary, Rheinstahl offered money, raw materials, and competitive

---

[54] In Maschke, *Konzern*, p. 160, it is argued that Cramer-Klett's action on October 24 was in consonance with the decisions taken at the MAN directors' meeting on October 15. As demonstrated above and argued below, this was not the case. On the Bochumer Verein stock sale, see the supervisory board meeting of Deutsch-Lux, October 28, 1920, in Friedrich-Wilhelms-Hütte Archiv, Nr. 123/19, and on Herzfeld, see Paul Ufermann, *Könige der Inflation* (Berlin, 1924), pp. 91–96. The interpretation of the Bochumer Verein purchase given here is based on comments at the MAN supervisory board meeting on November 3, 1920, where Oscar Schlitter of the Deutsche Bank and Franz Urbig of the Disconto-Gesellschaft, both of whom were in the banking consortium supporting Stinnes, reported on the matter. See MAN Werksarchiv Augsburg, Nr. K56. On the MAN stock speculation, see Jessen to Reusch, September 13, 1920, HA/GHH, Nr. 300193010/10.

advantages while in no way reducing the MAN's autonomy in the manner demanded by either Stinnes or Reusch. Endres and Lippart had made a point of keeping Cramer-Klett and Eberbach informed about the excellent progress of the Rheinstahl negotiations, but had themselves been kept in the dark about what was transpiring in Frankfurt. They only discovered what Cramer-Klett had done after the conclusion of his agreement with Reusch.[55]

The Baron explained his actions to the board of directors on October 26 and tried to demonstrate all the advantages of an alliance with the GHH. He pointed out that the arrangement with Reusch would bring in 85 million in cash as well as a promised large loan and assistance with the MAN's foreign exchange needs. The MAN would remain unrestricted as to where it secured its raw materials but would become a favored customer for the GHH. Indeed, the GHH was willing to invest a total of 120 million marks in the MAN on the basis of a "gentlemen's agreement" alone. Furthermore, the Baron insisted that the alliance with Reusch would not preclude the sale of the Duisburg plant to Rheinstahl, but that it would be more advantageous than the loose arrangement proposed by Rheinstahl because the MAN would gain a "first-class stockholder" with much greater financial strength than that possessed by Rheinstahl. At the same time, the Baron left no doubt in the minds of his listeners that they were facing a *fait accompli*. If they disavowed him, he intended to resign as chairman of the supervisory board. He would then be free to use his 25% of the MAN stock to block every other project and force through the arrangement with the GHH.[56]

Fundamentally, there was little principled objection to an alliance with the GHH among the MAN directors present, but much general irritation at the loss of freedom of choice. A disavowal of the Baron would have meant an open battle for control that would be damaging to the firm, because it was inconceivable that the GHH would not fight to retain what it had won. The directors did decide to write an honest report for the supervisors, however, in which they compared the various projects and made it perfectly clear that the Baron had presented them with a *fait accompli*. Yet they insisted that there were great advantages to an alliance with the GHH, which was known for "its cautious and sound financial policy and its honorable business practices." They concluded that "The entire structure of the GHH and its previous record of calm and steady development and its limitation to a definite

[55] MAN supervisory board, November 2, 1920, MAN Werksarchiv Augsburg, Nr. K56.

[56] Board of Directors meeting, October 26, 1920, *ibid.*

production program leads us to expect that we will not be drawn into far-flung and overly vast involvements."[57]

When the MAN board of supervisors met to consider the matter on November 3, the entire affair came in for renewed criticism, particularly from the bankers on the board, Oscar Schlitter of the Deutsche Bank and Franz Urbig of the Disconto-Gesellschaft. They did not question either the Baron's motives or his right to act as he had, but they regretted the precipitousness with which he had acted. Schlitter insisted that the Baron could have found out from them if it had been Stinnes who was buying up MAN stock because they were in a position to know, just as they were in a position to know that Stinnes had "saved [the] Bochum[er] Verein for Germany."[58] Urbig thought that Stinnes had been shabbily treated by the MAN, which had written to him asking for negotiations in September and had never given him a chance to offer a more generous quota after the October negotiations with Siemens. It thus appeared that the MAN had negotiated in bad faith. On a more practical level, there was considerable worry about what the alliance with the GHH might do to the MAN's relationship with Siemens-Schuckert. This delicate matter was stressed by both Schlitter, who had discussed the matter with Siemens, and the Siemens-Schuckert general director, Oscar von Petri, who was a MAN supervisory board member and, quite naturally, a strong advocate of the IG with Stinnes and Siemens. They knew that the turn of events was a serious blow to Siemens. This becomes all the more apparent when one notes that as short a time before as October 10, Siemens had told Stinnes that he would make his own adhesion to the IG dependent on the MAN's participation. This attitude had changed by November 3, and Petri reported that Siemens would join the IG with Stinnes in any event because it had more "far-reaching" reasons to do so than the MAN. In expressing the hope that the "relationship to SSW would not suffer," however, Petri was making it clear that the MAN could lose one of its best customers because of its new relationship to the GHH.[59]

Because the MAN supervisors knew that they could not reverse the Baron's actions, however, most of their discussion on November 3 was devoted to improving the terms of the agreement with Reusch. Quite aside from the sense that Reusch had not made a sufficient commitment to long-term MAN interests and sensibilities, there was considerable dissatisfaction with the actual cash terms on which the new MAN stock issue was being offered to Reusch by Cramer-Klett. The actual

[57] Report by Buz of November 2, 1920, *ibid.*
[58] MAN supervisory board meeting, November 3, 1920, *ibid.*
[59] *Ibid.*, and Siemens to Vögler, November 2, 1920, SAA 4/Lf 635/1.

details are of minor significance,[60] but the discussion concerning them and the debate over the amount of pressure they were to place on Reusch for more favorable terms are interesting in that they are most revealing of the complex and tense relations among raw materials producers, manufacturers, and bankers at this time.

One of the most unpleasant ironies of the situation was that there was some doubt that the conditions that had led the MAN to seek a closer relationship with a raw materials producer were as valid as they had been earlier that year. Some felt, for example, that the raw materials shortage was not serious and that there would be a surplus in 1921 as demand and prices fell. The bankers and MAN directors blamed much of their financial problem on the "profiteering policy" (*Wucherpolitik*) of heavy industry, for as Endres angrily pointed out, producers had made as much as 2,500 marks on a price of 4,000 marks a ton. Although Schlitter and the others recognized that "Reusch has always fought the profiteering policy of heavy industry," the bankers felt that it was dangerous to depend on the goodwill of persons instead of formal arrangements. Reusch had been allowed to gain the upper hand, and there was an underlying sense at the meeting that this was in no way justified by the economic and financial situation. The Rheinstahl solution seemed much less drastic, and it was argued that because of the expected depression and reduction of demand, the sums gained from Rheinstahl combined with cutting back and rationalization within the MAN would have sufficed to meet the MAN's needs. Endres pointed out that the manufacturing industry would have to cut back in line with the cutback taking place throughout the world, and Urbig gloomily stated that "for Germany there can only be the dismantling of the eight-hour day."[61] Turning from the larger problem to the more immediate one, Urbig argued that Reusch would be in a position to gain at the MAN's expense and the expense of the stockholders in recession as well as boom. If conditions turned bad, then the GHH would use its position in the MAN to depress dividends, and the MAN would have to engage in "endless write-offs" on its unused stores of

[60] The Baron had offered Reusch 18 million in MAN shares, of which 6 million were still held by the MAN, at 400%, i.e., 72 million marks. There was then to be a new 50 million mark stock issue of which the GHH was to get 32 million at 150%. Schlitter was outraged by the latter part of the arrangement because he was certain that the new stock would sell at 300% on the market and could find no justification for the bargain offered Reusch. *Ibid.*, and Maschke, *Konzern*, pp. 150–151.

[61] MAN supervisory board meeting, November 3, 1920, in MAN Werksarchiv Augsburg, Nr. K56.

materials, thereby lowering share prices and permitting a full takeover by the GHH.

It was in this hapless mood that the MAN supervisory board voted to pursue further negotiations with the GHH and try to secure more satisfactory terms. On November 7, Cramer-Klett, Eberbach, and two MAN directors met with Reusch at the latter's Württemberg estate, Kathrinenhof, and made the so-called "Pact of Katharinenhof." Reusch agreed to pay a higher price for the stock he was to buy from the new stock issue, and the MAN leaders promised to support the alliance with the GHH and the election of Reusch and Haniel to the MAN supervisory board. This arrangement was confirmed by the supervisory board a few days later, at which point Urbig and Schlitter urged that the GHH participate in the MAN by at least a third.[62] On November 9, the MAN formally broke off negotiations with Siemens, but expressed the hope that the good business relations between the two concerns would persist.[63] By mid-November 1920, therefore, almost a year of negotiations among these various concerns with the purpose of forming stronger bonds between raw materials producers and finished products manufacturers were coming to a conclusion.

From a purely formal standpoint, the arrangements between the GHH and the MAN were far simpler than those involved in the formation of the SRSU because all that was involved in the former was a large stock participation, not the formation of a new company or complicated profit-pooling arrangements. As it turned out, the MAN-GHH combination led to a full year of conflict, and much of it attracted newspaper and public attention. To be sure, the various parties initially adhered to the "Pact of Kathrinenhof." The MAN sold its Duisburg plant to Rheinstahl, and the latter announced the purchase at the beginning of December. At the general stockholders meeting of the MAN on December 15, the supervisors and directors of the MAN supported the election of Reusch and Haniel to the supervisory board, and Reusch kept a promise he had made to support the election of Carl Winkler as a third new member of the board. Winkler had backed the GHH against Stinnes and had solemnly promised Reusch to stand behind GHH policies. Cramer-Klett used the occasion of the meeting to emphasize the benefits to be expected of the new relationship as well as the high degree of independence left to the MAN in its internal organization and policies. The meeting, however, was not the peaceful affair it was intended to be. A stockholder who was a prominent member

[62] Reusch agreed to pay 215% instead of 150% for the new stock, Maschke, *Konzern*, p. 151.

[63] MAN to Siemens, November 9, 1920, SAA 4/Lf 635/1.

239

of one of Stinnes' companies sought unsuccessfully to suspend the meeting on the grounds that Rieppel was not present to speak against the decisions that had been taken.[64]

These were not to be the last difficulties Reusch encountered with Rieppel, who resigned from the MAN with much fanfare, and thereby compelled Reusch to defend the GHH against repeated accusations of exemplifying the North German effort to dominate South Germany by force. Reusch fought back by means of direct contact with political leaders such as the Bavarian Minister of Commerce and later Reich Economics Minister Eduard Hamm, as well as through Haniel-controlled newspapers in the region.[65] Such influence became all the more necessary as Reusch became convinced that he needed majority control of the MAN rather than the qualified minority with which he had originally contented himself. He secured this absolute majority of 52% in the course of 1921 by having Jessen and various firms in the Haniel group buy up the necessary stock.[66] This decision, however, led to a conflict with Winkler, which was dragged through German and Swiss courts with all the attendant bad publicity but with no consequences whatever for the GHH's control.[67] These conflicts proved terribly distressing to Cramer-Klett, who had entertained rather benign visions of what the connection with the GHH would be like and who does not seem to have anticipated Reusch's eventual assumption of majority control. Feeling unable to settle the conflicts in the supervisory board, the Baron resigned, and Reusch took advantage of the opportunity to ask Oscar von Petri to become chairman of the MAN supervisory board. This recementing of the relations between the MAN and

[64] *Kölnische Zeitung*, December 16, 1920.

[65] See Reusch to Cramer-Klett, December 20, 1920, and Cramer-Klett to Reusch, December 30, 1920, HA/GHH, Nr. 300193010/10, on the Rieppel problem. On Hamm, see Hamm's minute on his meeting with Jessen, December 27, 1921, BayHStA, MWi, Nr. 6879. There is considerable correspondence between Hamm and Reusch in the latter's papers. Hamm served as a State Secretary for Cuno from November 1922 to August 1923 and as Reich Economics Minister in the first Marx government from December 1923 to January 1925. In the spring of 1920, Karl Haniel, at the request of "nationally minded Bavarian economic circles," participated in the reconstruction of the influential *Münchener Neuesten Nachrichten*. Reusch handled these matters for Haniel, and the former has an interesting correspondence with numerous right-wing newspapers and journals with which Haniel became associated. See the unsigned and undated memorandum in HA/GHH, Nr. 40010120000/1.

[66] Although Reusch made a practice of using dummy shareholders, this was essential in the MAN case because under the MAN by-laws no shareholder was allowed more than 500 votes.

[67] On Winkler's machinations and motives, see Endres to Reusch, July 6, 1921, HA/GHH, Nr. 300193010/14.

240

Schuckert at the end of 1921 was only one indication that the stormy first year of the GHH-MAN connection was ending with a clear victory for the GHH and, as will be shown later, with increasing attention to the substantive production and marketing problems of the Haniel concern.[68]

The formation of the Siemens-Rheinelbe-Schuckert Union, which officially came into existence on December 30, 1920, following up the stockholder meetings of the member concerns a few days previous, was an infinitely less quarrelsome affair than the GHH-MAN alliance despite the IG's complicated structure and character. To be sure, questions of status and prestige and problems of geographical rivalry were by no means absent. Siemens, for example, would not hear of having the IG named the "Rhein-Elbe-Siemens Union" because "I consider it self-evident that the manufacturing industries can in no case appear under the names of heavy industry."[69]

However, neither trivial nor even very substantive issues were allowed to stand in the way of the IG's creation, a remarkable situation in a contract meant to remain in effect until September 30, 2000. This is particularly apparent with regard to the profit-pooling arrangements, which were never actually implemented throughout the IG's slightly more than five-year history. These arrangements seemed simple enough. The three dominant partners, Deutsch-Lux, GBAG, and Siemens & Halske, raised their capital to equal levels and stood as equal partners in the IG, whereas Siemens-Schuckert assumed a lesser claim on profits in proportion to its lower capital stock. The ratio was to be 1:1:1:0.45. Each year, the partners were to present preliminary balances setting forth gross profits before write-offs and the setting aside of reserves. The total sum would then be divided according to the aforementioned ratio; specific portions would be allocated for write-offs and reserves, and the rest distributed as pure profit. Although this arrangement made some sense in the case of the GBAG and Deutsch-Lux, it made little sense when the two Siemens partners were brought in—Schuckert had nothing to write off because it was scarcely involved in fabrication. Under this scheme, therefore, Schuckert would receive more than it deserved, whereas any effort to correct this would, for complicated reasons, leave some other partner feeling cheated. As long

---

[68] See Maschke, *Konzern*, p. 158ff. Reusch made Cramer-Klett chairman of the Eisenwerk Nürnberg supervisory board as part of an effort to smooth things over. See also Petri to Siemens, December 24, 1921, SAA 4/Lf 671. The affairs of the MAN were extensively reported in the *Münchener Neueste Nachrichten*, esp. September 17, 1921, December 21, 1921, December 22, 1921, October 31, 1922, and December 25, 1922, to be found in BayHStA, MWi, Nr. 6879.

[69] Siemens to Berthold, November 15, 1920, SAA 4/Lf 635.

as the inflation lasted, it proved impossible to calculate the profits and no effort was made to implement these arrangements. When stabilization came, neither Siemens nor Vögler were able to figure out how to do so. As Siemens confessed with admirable candor five years after signing the agreement, ". . . one would have to search a long time before one can find an example of greater inconsequence in the formulation of an agreement of such an important and long-lasting nature. If these conditions were to come out into the open, then it would be a disgrace of the first order for all who bear responsibility for it."[70] How then, one must ask, did businessmen of such stature sign an agreement without clearly thinking through or even understanding one of its most fundamental provisions?

Siemens thought that the fundamental mistake had been the mode of procedure imposed by Stinnes and Vögler, namely, the conclusion of the Rhein-Elbe Union and the attempt to fit the manufacturing industries into its mold. Although it is true that the SRSU was regarded as "the continuation of the Rhein-Elbe Union,"[71] and that the latter contract was the model for the former, this is only a partial explanation for the willingness of those involved to overlook the peculiarities of the profit-pooling arrangements. In reality, there had been just as much of a will to overlook these questions in the creation of the Rhein-Elbe Union, as is evident from Vögler's own description to Siemens in September 1920:

> . . . the most important [question] naturally, is the proportioning of the profits of the individual concerns. As you know, Gelsenkirchen and Deutsch-Lux, after lengthy consideration, have agreed to treat one another on a completely equal basis. A purely material evaluation of the assets is almost impossible in so economically chaotic a period as today's and does not lead to the goal in any case. But the chief thing will be whether the collaboration is economically correct, whether the grade of effectiveness of each enterprise will be improved thereby. The two existing works in the IG had come to this conclusion at the time they made the consolidation. . . .[72]

Clearly the "most important" question was not really the most important question, at least not at the time. Under conditions of inflation, all calculations of assets and profits were somewhat arbitrary and unpredictable. The real goal was security, security for the concerns in financial and raw materials matters and security for the stockholders,

[70] Siemens to Vögler, December 27, 1925, *ibid.*

[71] Gemeinschaftsrat meeting, December 29, 1920, *ibid.*, Nachlass Haller, 11/Lb 108.

[72] Vögler to Siemens, September 14, 1920, *ibid.*, 4/Lf 635.

"especially the permanent stockholders," who would receive a "steady [and], as far as possible, secure return."[73]

Siemens' decision to join the IG was, in this sense, quite in harmony with the spirit and psychology that had moved Rhein-Elbe into existence. In presenting the contract to the stockholders, Siemens frankly spoke of it as an "insurance contract" (*Versicherungsvertrag*) from both a "branch" and a "territorial" point of view.[74] It guaranteed protection against materials and capital shortages and against the ill effects of business fluctuations, but it also ensured that if "political difficulties" in one part of the Reich hampered or stopped production, then some part of the IG would continue working. It was, after all, a national organization encompassing the Ruhr, Berlin, and Bavaria. He could also argue that the IG would increase financial security. There would be more capital available for expansion, and large sums would be saved now that the necessity of maintaining vast stores of raw materials for emergency purposes was obviated. The IG was viewed as an important step in the direction of industrial self-financing, and outside money would no longer carry the same threats of foreign or bank control. Although the new IG did get help from a banking consortium, Stinnes was able to dictate the terms and insist that the banks play a role no greater than Stinnes or Siemens and that their "position not be given a significance which they should not have from an industrial standpoint."[75]

If the quest for security constitutes the fundamental reason why the SRSU ultimately came into being, particularly from the perspective of Siemens' decision, it must also be remembered that the SRSU itself was an extraordinary conglomeration of concerns with vast potential. Its coal base was two and a half times larger than that of its nearest competitor, Krupp, and although it was second to Krupp in steel production, the addition of the Bochumer Verein to Deutsch-Lux had given the SRSU enormously increased production as well as opportunities for significant rationalization. Once established, it enjoyed the largest self-consumption rights of any concern in the Rhenisch-Westphalian Coal Syndicate. Furthermore, its fabricating facilities and manufacturing plants and its worldwide marketing organizations, when added to the aforementioned heavy industrial production base, made it the most formidable industrial organization in German history until that time. Although the SRSU rested on the principle of the independence of the member concerns in their internal organization and day-to-

[73] *Ibid.*

[74] His interesting speech is quoted in Ufermann and Hüglin, *Stinnes-Konzerne*, p. 50.

[75] Stinnes to Salomonsohn, November 9, 1920, SAA 4/Lf 635.

day operations, it also rested on the proposition that all parts of this mammoth IG had the interest and obligation to serve their common good and to accept general policies designed to bend their activities in this direction. Thus, if the SRSU was designed to provide security, it also was framed with more exciting visions in mind. Furthermore, instrumentalities were created for the realization of these broader goals. One of these was the provisions for the exchange of supervisors and directors among the member concerns. Another was for the establishment of concern bureaus within each concern. The most important, however, was the umbrella corporation (*Dachgesellschaft*) embodying the IG, which was housed in Düsseldorf and headed by a supervisory board and a board of directors composed of personnel from the member concerns. This umbrella corporation was expected to play a decisive role in all large financial questions and general policies concerning production, marketing, and public relations. In short, it was meant to act as an "economic body" with an "economic program" in the sense envisioned by Stinnes, Henrich, and Jastrow.[76]

THE BALANCE SHEET OF VERTICAL CONCENTRATION

The case studies under discussion are only two simplified illustrations of vertical concentration in the iron and steel industry during the inflation, and even they have emphasized and will continue to emphasize certain key combinations within more complex business structures. It is necessary to leave largely unexplored the virtually impenetrable relationships between these concerns and the holdings of their principal stockholders. Stinnes' own concern, a confusing network of coal merchandising, shipping, and other enterprises, had few formal connections with the SRSU, but this ostensible independence of the two blocks of enterprises veiled a good deal of practical interconnection and collaboration. Similarly, it is difficult to measure the benefits derived by the GHH from the independent operations of the Haniel concern which, for example, in 1920 created an IG between its important Zollverein mines and the Phoenix concern. If nothing else, the GHH's financial strength certainly was buttressed by the great profitability of the Haniel enterprises.[77] Furthermore, the SRSU and GHH are illustrative of another fundamental fact, namely that there were important differences in style, character, and organization among the concerns that took the lead in the concentration movement as well

[76] See Tross, *Aufbau*, pp. 122–125, and Jastrow memorandum on the SRSU organization of December 21, 1920, in SAA 54/Ld 273.

[77] See Ufermann and Hüglin, *Stinnes-Konzerne*, p. 57ff., and Tross, *Aufbau*, p. 98.

as in the manner in which these combinations were formed and organized. Deutsch-Lux and the GBAG were much more heavily engaged in primary production than the GHH, the latter having a long tradition of emphasis on fabrication and manufacture as its most important activities. Also, the problems and goals moving Stinnes and Reusch were quite different. The former's were vaguer and more grandiose because his empire was so large and complex and because he sought maximum maneuverability rather than the rounding out of a specific production program and the penetration of particular markets that characterized the GHH expansion. Finally, the organizational modes of combination were different, and these differences reflected not only the size and stature of the concerns involved but also distinct preferences on the part of the participating industrial leaders. If there was any general characteristic, it was a preference for some form of community interest rather than fusion, a choice dictated after March 1920 by the severe tax disadvantages of fusion under the new tax laws but also by a firm belief in the superior efficiency of decentralized management.[78]

When one turns to the other great industrial groups under consideration here, there then emerges a variegated collection of concerns all more or less vertically organized but each according to its own way for its own particular reasons and with individual raw materials bases and production programs (see Tables 9 and 10). Krupp did not participate much in the general expansion of holdings characteristic of the period. To be sure, Krupp shared in the general tendency of the steel firms to increase their coal base through combinations with coal companies, but Krupp's iron and steel base was intact thanks to its own massive facilities and its consortial connections with Rheinmetall and Mannesmann. Krupp's fundamental postwar problem was making up for its lost advantages as the major military producer of the Reich by converting to peacetime production and entering the fields of locomotive and truck production and other new areas on a large scale. It was toward these ends and to solve patent problems that it entered into a few IG's, as it did with the Baden agricultural firm of Fahr and the Dresden photographic equipment firm, the Ernemannwerke AG. Krupp's greatest stress, however, was on the reorganization and conversion of its existing plant facilities.[79] A similar policy, albeit with a much more intense emphasis on rationalization and modernization,

[78] *Ibid.*, pp. 193–195. Tross, however, overestimates the importance of tax considerations when he argues that it was the decisive reason in the decision of Deutsch-Lux and the GBAG to form an IG rather than a completer merger. See above, p. 217.

[79] Tross, *Aufbau*, pp. 34–43.

TABLE 9

A Comparative Overview of the Concerns (I)

Concern (without consortial participants)	Capital Stock on January 1, 1922 (in 1,000 marks)	Obligations on January 1, 1922 (in 1,000 marks)	Capital Stock and Obligations on January 1, 1922 (in 1,000 marks)	Capital Stock on January 1, 1918 (in 1,000 marks)	Increase of Capital Stock from 1918 to 1922 (in percent)
	1	2	3	4	5
Siemens-Rheinelbe-Schuckert Union	1,189,236	564,330	1,753,566	616,436	93
Krupp	506,000	295,650	801,650	273,600	85
Phönix	324,600	44,902	379,502	151,600	114
Haniel	296,000	62,073	358,073	99,000	197
Stumm	228,530	125,917	354,447	117,110	95
Henschel-Lothringen-Essener Steinkohle	333,900	15,450	348,350	235,800	42
Klöckner	259,500	71,907	331,407	136,400	91
Thyssen	47,690[a]	278,348	326,038	44,500[a]	7
Rheinstahl	199,600	32,810	232,410	78,700	154
Hösch-Köln-Neuessen	189,800	19,123	208,923	52,800	259
A.E.G.	1,640,750	349,408	1,990,158	319,410	413
Borsig	65,000	—	65,000	65,000	—

Participation (in thousands of tons)

Concern (without consortial participants)	Rhenish-Westphalian Coal Syndicate					Pig Iron Syndicate	Steel Works Association[b]			
	Coal	Coke	Briquettes	Self-consumption	Total		Semis	Railroad Material	Structural Steel	Total
	6	7	8	9	10	11	12	13	14	15
Siemens-Rheinelbe-Schuckert Union	16,714	3,192	1,082	4,898	21,612	575	224	482	414	1,120
Krupp	5,553	2,118	295	3,093	8,646	150	160	253	74	487
Phönix	5,140	1,282	71	2,473	7,613	20	134	215	111	460
Haniel	3,117	220	216	1,635	4,752	140	14	184	67	265
Stumm	2,088	563	100	900	3,338	555	39	94	130	263
Henschel-Lothringen-Essener Steinkohle	6,061	1,407	1,180	—	6,061	95	—	—	—	—
Klöckner	3,630	946	72	1,511	5,141	145	112	145	137	394
Thyssen	3,650	35	—	2,723	6,373	212	52	214	192	458
Rheinstahl	5,510	1,179	324	1,100	6,610	37	77	142	52	271
Hösch-Köln-Neuessen	6,172	1,084	—	905	7,077	10	—	85	86	171
A.E.G.	—	—	—	—	—	—	—	—	—	—
Borsig	—	—	—	—	—	—	—	—	—	—
Total participation of the concerns	57,985	12,106	3,340	19,238	77,223	1,939	812	1,814	1,263	3,889
Inclusive of consortial participation	—	—	—	—	—	2,089	767	1,626	1,097	3,470
Total participation in syndicates	119,547	26,221	5,626	21,743	141,290	3,210	1,225	2,441	2,254	5,920
Percent participation in total syndicate quota	48.8	46	59.5	88.5	54.5	65.0	62.5	66.5	48.7	58.7

[a] Exclusive of the mining shares (Kuxe) of the August-Thyssen Hütte.
[b] Dissolved since July 1, 1920.

Source: A. Tross, Der Aufbau der Eisen- und eisenverarbeitenden Konzerne Deutschlands (Berlin, 1923), p. 122.

TABLE 10

A Comparative Overview of the Concerns (II)

(a) without, (b) with consortial participations and looser connections	Blast Furnaces		Converters				Siemens-Martin Furnaces				Electric Furnaces		Capacity Puddling Ovens	Total Capacity of the Steel Works in Tons
			Acid		Basic		Acid		Basic					
	No.	Capacity in Cbm.	No.	Capacity in Tons	No.	Capacity in Tons	No.	Capacity in Tons	No.	Capacity in Tons	No.	Capacity in Tons		
	1	*2*	*3*	*4*	*5*	*6*	*7*	*8*	*9*	*10*	*11*	*12*	*13*	*14*
Siemens-Rheinelbe-Schuckert-Union	27	13,130	8	24	5	120	7	141	33	1,650	2	18	21	1,953
Krupp (a)	17	7,295	6	33	6	150	1	25	57	1,986	3	32	—	2,226
Krupp (b)							3	49	62	2,101				2,365
Phönix	18	8,175	—	—	8	160	—	—	21	875	1	10	5	1,045
Hamiel	12	5,305	—	—	6	150	—	—	15	563	1	3	—	716
Thyssen (a)	14	6,635	—	—	6	180	1	5	30	915	5	78	—	1,178
Thyssen (b)	20	8,735					2	35	54	1,584	9	112		1,911
Stumm	19	8,180	—	—	4	100	—	—	38	1,306	2	16	12	1,422

Henschel-Lothringen-Essener Steinkohle	4	1,790	—	—	—	—	—	—	—	—	2	16	8	340	—	—	—	356
Klöckner (a)	10	5,690	—	—	4	—	—	40	{1	—	—	19	795	{42	—	—	7	{835
Klöckner (b)	16	7,790	—	—	—	—	—	—	—	—	—	—	—	—	—	—	—	{1,576
Rheinstahl	6	3,330	—	—	—	—	4	70	—	—	13	—	43	1,464	—	—	6	513
Hoesch-Köln-Neuessen	7	3,630	—	—	—	—	4	59	—	—	9	—	9	576	—	—	—	635
A.E.G. (a)	—	—	—	—	—	—	—	—	—	—	—	15	385	{4	26	—	411
A.E.G. (b)	—	—	—	—	—	—	—	—	—	—	—	—	—	{7	39	—	424
Borsig	4	1,350	—	—	—	—	—	—	2	20	10	—	10	205	—	—	12	225
Totals (a)	138	64,510	—	14	—	57	—	47	—	1,029	13	207	268	10,039	18	183	63	11,515
Totals (b)	144	66,610	—	—	—	—	—	—	—	—	16	261	297	10,823	27	238	—	12,408
Totals for Germany (inclusive of Silesia and the Saar)	272	109,870	16	—	62	83		1,682	28	360	512	17,329	61	474			132	19,908
Percentage in concerns	53	60.7	87.5	92	56.7	61.2		57.2	72.5	58	62.5	44	50.2	47.8				62.4
In Rhineland-Westphalia exclusive of the Siegerland, the District of Wetzlar and the Saar																		
Totals (a)	125	57,925	14	—	57	48		1,029	20	297	331	11,530	36	299			70	13,212
Totals (b)	111	54,425	14	—	57	43		929	14	241	247	9,468	23	211			24	10,906
Percentage in concerns	89	94	100	—	100	89.5		90.2	70	81.3	74.7	82	64	70.6			34.3	82.5

Source: A. Tross, *Der Aufbau der Eisen- und eisenverarbeitenden Konzerne Deutschlands* (Berlin, 1923), p. 125.

was pursued by Thyssen. Although Thyssen had lost most heavily of all the steel concerns from the standpoint of the value of the works it was compelled to alienate under the peace treaty, it had the great advantage of retaining "a completely intact and self-contained complex of works"[80] within Germany. Thyssen chose to concentrate on the strengthening of this base and to pursue a very moderate policy of expansion through various joint participations with his fellow Catholic industrialist, Peter Klöckner, with whom he joined in 1920 in control of large works in the Siegerland, especially the Geisweider Eisenhüttenwerke.

The Klöckner concern, like the Stumm concern, had suffered heavy losses under the peace treaty, and both groups lacked Thyssen's advantage of a solid industrial base in Germany on which to fall back. Consequently, both concerns employed the substantial liquid resources acquired from the sale of their old holdings to enter into a series of IG's and participations. The most important of Klöckner's IG's were with two large iron and steel producers, the Hasper Eisen- und Stahlwerk in Haspe and the Georgs-Marien-Bergwerks- und Hüttenverein in Osnabrück. In addition to the joint participations with Thyssen noted above, Klöckner also shared with Otto Wolff participation in another important iron and steel producing company, Van der Zypen in Wissen, a company in which Thyssen also had an interest. The reconstitution of the Stumm concern was accomplished rather differently, because the concern used its money to purchase and participate in a number of important works, such as the Gelsenkirchener-Gussstahl-und Eisenwerk in Gelsenkirchen, which became the center of the concern, but also in a number of works, many of them quite small, spread throughout Germany.[81]

In contrast to the concerns at least ostensibly organized with a view toward the solution of raw materials and production problems, the Otto Wolff concern remained rooted in its Cologne iron marketing house and was never meant to form a coherent vertical structure in the sense of the vertically organized concerns with which it was most closely associated, Rheinstahl and Phoenix. Wolff remained satisfied with a significant minority participation in those and other large works, such as Van der Zypen, and made utilization of his marketing organization his only major requirement. Rheinstahl and Phoenix found this arrangement extremely advantageous, and it helped these concerns to expand and improve their own operations.[82]

[80] Treue, *A-T-H*, p. 197, and Tross, *Aufbau*, pp. 57–66.
[81] *Ibid.*, pp. 84–93, 66–76.
[82] *Ibid.*, pp. 118–119.

Given this variegation in the concentration process during the inflation, what general conclusions about vertical concentration during the inflation may be drawn from the two case studies that have received the major emphasis as well as from the other illustrations mentioned? One must begin any analysis with the very fact of concentration itself. The postwar situation and the inflation increased concentration in the iron and steel industry and strengthened the position of the mixed works in the Coal Syndicate. The coal shortage pushed forward a process that had been going on for some time. Thus, Hoesch's major act of expansion in 1920 was its IG with the Köln-Neuessener Bergwerksverein.[83] However interested in expansion into manufacturing, the first object of most of the concerns in 1919–1920 was the acquisition of a secure coal base. This was done despite threats of socialization and government controls. The Rheinstahl board of directors, who succeeded in gaining control of the Arenberg mining group, urged the board of supervisors to move in this direction in June 1919 because "without denying the fact that the danger of socialization is still not over, and that in addition the still existing and probable intensification of controls over coal will not permit a full exploitation of all the advantages of one's own mines, nevertheless we believe that the possession of yet another source of one's own coal to be such a valuable security that we urgently request permission to acquire possession."[84] Vertical concentration in the inflation meant that fewer great concerns controlled more coal production and possessed a larger portion of the Coal Syndicate's self-consumption rights than ever before.

Similarly, postwar development promoted the massive concentration of productive capacity in iron and steel within a smaller group of great concerns now more centered than before in the Rhenish-Westphalian industrial region. A true measure of this concentration is only partially garnered from the quotas of these concerns in the defunct Steel Works Association (Table 8). Such figures fail to take into account the production of works taken over by the concerns that had never belonged to the Steel Works Association. Far more revealing is the fact that by 1921 a dozen concerns controlled 62.4% of Germany's steel production capacity and 82.5% of the capacity of Rhineland-Westphalia. (See

[83] *Ibid.*, pp. 98–108.

[84] Rheinstahl supervisory board meeting, June 24, 1919, Rheinstahl Archiv, Nr. 123. Indeed, on May 7, 1919, Bergassessor Otto Krawehl wrote to Hasslacher saying that the relatively poor returns of the mines at the time made it a good moment to enter into combinations with them before "socialization" measures would make such combinations more difficult in the future, *ibid.*, Nr. 166. See also Peter Wulf, "Regierung, Parteien, Wirtschaftsverbände und die Sozialisierung des Kohlenbergbaues 1920–1921," in *Industrielles System*, pp. 647–657.

Table 9.) The latter region, which had been responsible for 59% of Germany's crude steel production in 1913, was responsible for 76.6% of such production in 1921.[85]

Where before the war some concerns had held back from expanding into manufacturing, now all the great concerns took this path. Rheinstahl, for example, acquired the machine building plant of the MAN in Duisburg and Phoenix acquired the Reiherstieg dockyards and machine plants in Hamburg. As has been shown, finishing and manufacturing works needed secure supplies of raw materials and were short of capital because of constantly increasing materials and labor costs. The raw materials producers had both to offer. The sale of works lost under the peace treaty combined with government compensation for these losses and the large profits made from the sale of raw materials gave them disposal over large amounts of capital. Where a manufacturing concern like the AEG had to increase its capital stock 413% between 1918 and 1922, the iron and steel producers at the very worst were able to keep below half this percentage during the same period. Whatever the damage done to the iron and steel producers by the war, it should be clear that the war did strengthen their relative position within the German economy enormously.[86]

What is less clear is what the war and the inflation did to their absolute position, and the problem of answering this question existed for contemporaries well before it came into existence for the historian. In January 1921 an arbitration board was assigned the task of deciding if the industrialists of greater Duisburg should be compelled to pay the wage increases demanded by the unions. It decided in favor of the workers and against heavy industrialist claims that "the assembled reserves, write-offs and other forms of security contained in the balances are necessary for the coming period of bad business conditions." (See Table 11.) The arbitration board pointed out that heavy industry had "an extraordinarily good business year" behind it, that the "capital invested in heavy industry had been trustified in a manner harmful to the general interest" and that heavy industry had "prepared itself very well for the coming period of bad business conditions by the conclusion of communities of interest and other transactions."[87]

This evaluation became the subject of debate in the RWM between

[85] Wiel, *Wirtschaftsgeschichte*, p. 238.

[86] In 1920, of the corporations increasing their capital stock, those that were engaged solely in mining and smelting increased their capital stock on an average of 13.4%; those engaged in both raw materials and manufacturing production increased their capital stock an average of 2.9%; those engaged in manufacturing alone increased their capital stock by 18.9%. Tross, *Aufbau*, p. 154.

[87] DZA Potsdam, RWM, Nr. 2267/1, Bl. 45–47.

TABLE 11

Profits of the Most Important Iron and Steel Concerns for the Business Years 1919–1920 and 1918–1919 (in millions of paper marks)

Work	Gross Profit Without Carryover		Write-offs and Reserves		Net Profit Including Carryover		Percent		Dividends		New Carryover	
	19–20	18–19	19–20	18–19	19–20	18–19	19–20	18–19	19–20	18–19	19–20	18–19
Phönix	68.94	24.56	21.25	21.93	50.48	11.73	20	8	21.20	8.48	4.62	2.75
Rheinstahl	50.08	8.02	36.00	8.00	14.13	2.72	10	6	13.00	3.60	0.51	0.05
Bochumer Verein	26.62	8.21	9.13	8.49	17.50	3.37	15	5	10.50	2.85	2.49	—
Deutsch-Lux	55.56	44.17	29.00	29.00	27.45	16.11	12	11	15.60	14.30	0.74	0.84
Krupp	90.11	—	10.55	31.93	89.56	—	—	—	—	—	4.22	—
Gutehoffnungshütte	55.98	9.59	29.53	9.19	35.83	2.68	20	6	2.40	2.40	1.58	0.28
Mannesmann	54.12	9.64	7.52	4.61	51.15	9.78	20	6	5.16	5.16	7.08	4.53
Hoesch	81.68	8.08	11.42	25.98	31.78	—	24	0	—	—	0.97	—
Bismarckhütte	26.66	8.19	13.28	8.08	13.57	1.31	28	5	1.10	1.10	0.40	0.18
Hasper Eisen	11.02	3.14	5.18	2.01	5.87	2.11	20	10	1.30	1.30	0.97	0.03
Laurahütte	59.99	—	10.10	4.33	49.98	—	20	0	—	—	0.23	—
Georgsmarienhütte	8.97	4.52	6.81	4.90	2.29	0.16	8	0	—	—	0.23	0.16
Van der Zypen	20.62	4.75	5.39	3.51	16.15	2.92	30	10	1.70	1.60	1.60	0.93
Gelsenkirchener Guss-stahlverein	8.10	—	3.14	1.31	5.05	—	10	10	0.45	0.45	0.48	0.12

Source: Alfons Schlaghecke, *Die Preissteigerung, Absatzorganisation und Bewirtschaftung des Eisens 1914–1920*, diss. Phil. (Giessen, 1920), p. 68.

Ministerial Director Imhoff and Baron von Buttlar. The former contested the notion that the previous year had been a good one for the concerns because, from an economic standpoint, the assembled reserves would have to be sufficiently high to permit plant renewal within an appropriate period of time. Imhoff argued that this was not the case, that the necessary reserves were not available, and that the misleadingly high dividends were really nothing more than payments from capital rather than distributions of net profits. Such payments were possible, in Imhoff's view, only because the steel industry was producing half as much as it had before the war and had not yet felt the incentive to undertake the necessary renewals of its plants. Lastly, while recognizing that "trustification" could be harmful to the public interest if it entailed monopolization, Imhoff insisted that the concentration then going on was beneficial in that it promoted industrial efficiency through exchanges of information and better fuel economy and that it would aid in the battle against unemployment under worsening business conditions.[88]

Baron von Buttlar was less taken with the alleged woes of the steel men, and he responded to Imhoff's presentation of the industry's economic problems with an emphatic *"wrong."* Buttlar's fundamental point was that the steel men had gained enormously from the inflation because they were paying the interest on their obligations along with many of their domestic debts in paper currency that was worth a fraction of its prewar value. To be sure, the dividends were also being paid in paper money, but he did not see why stockholders should not "suffer from the monetary devaluation just as others must."[89] He disagreed completely with Imhoff's notion, which conformed to that of some industrialists,[90] that the reserves needed to equal renewal costs for the entirety of the plants involved and argued that only those portions of the plants that had deteriorated were to be written off, and then only at the going purchase price. Buttlar felt that the rest of the needed monies should be raised through capital stock increases.

Arguments could be made for both points of view. Buttlar was correct, of course, in noting that the steel companies were paying interest and debts in devalued currency. He might also have added that the flight into "real values" (*Sachwerte*) accompanying the inflation constituted a great boon for the industrialists as well. When Stinnes paid a reported 230 million marks for his Bochumer Verein shares, he paid the equivalent of 15 million gold marks for what was worth 70 million

[88] *Ibid.*   [89] *Ibid.*

[90] See the revealing articles by General Director Zörner, "Bilanz and Steuerrecht," in *Technik und Wirtschaft*, 15 (September 1922), pp. 449–461 and 488–500, esp. 488–489, and Maier, *Recasting Bourgeois Europe*, pp. 214–215.

gold marks.[91] More generally, Buttlar's insistence that capitalistic enterprises should finance their expansion in a capitalistic manner instead of expecting employees and consumers to bear the costs had more than a little merit even if it was becoming a bit quaint in the context of actual practice. Imhoff, however, was also calling attention to some important realities. Inflation, naturally, meant high nominal profits, dividends, and wages. In reality, the profits were a meager percentage of prewar gains, and the dividends, although impressive on paper and useful to trade union leaders pressing for higher wages, were also significantly lower in actual value and, indeed, proportionately lower with respect to profits than before the war. To be sure, major stockholders received all kinds of hidden benefits and were given stock options, but it must also be said that the great concerns intensified their traditional policy of granting steady but moderate dividends while trying to retain as much capital as possible for the purpose of securing independence from banks and other outside sources of capital.[92]

Throughout this period one detects a relatively severe attitude toward stockholders, a condition reflecting their dependency on the goodwill of the industrial leaders. As Reusch noted in February 1920, he was doing the stockholders, not the GHH, a favor by increasing capital stock at that time. It was they who thought that additional shares would provide them with greater financial security than their depreciated marks.[93] Although prepared to help out his major stockholders when they needed money by repurchasing stock, he refused to coddle them by paying an excessively high rate when share prices were inflated on the market. He flatly rejected arrangements proposed by stockholders designed to give them higher dividends at the expense of the GHH's control over its stock and dividend policy.[94] In short, Reusch was willing to guarantee the interests of the stockholders as far as possible, but he intended to prevent their control of company policies.

Stinnes and Siemens took a similar posture toward their banking allies. On December 29, 1920, Dr. Salomonsohn of the Disconto-

---

[91] Klass, *Stinnes*, p. 231.

[92] Here I follow what seems to me the judicious evaluation of Bresciani-Turroni, *Economics of Inflation*, pp. 261–262, rather than that of Schlaghecke, *Bewirtschaftung des Eisens*, pp. 69–71, who, like Imhoff, tends to neglect the fact that real profits were being made. See also Tross, *Aufbau*, p. 156.

[93] Reusch to Wiskott, February 9, 1920, HA/GHH, Nr. 300193002/3. The general belief that stocks were a hedge against inflation, an error not unfamiliar to Americans of the 1970s, was held until 1922 when experience demonstrated otherwise. See Bresciani-Turroni, *Economics of Inflation*, p. 262ff.

[94] Reusch to his supervisory board, February 26, 1921, and Reusch to Wiskott, July 21, 1921, HA/GHH, Nr. 3001900/0–1.

Gesellschaft sought to increase the power of the banks in the IG by proposing that a quarter of newly issued preferred stock be thrown on the market, but this was vetoed by the industrialists, as was a second effort on May 20, 1921. Stinnes opposed any increases in the capital stock and warned that preferential stock constituted no guarantee against efforts by foreigners to gain control.[95] Self-financing was clearly preferred over capital stock increases, and the banks were not going to be given an opportunity to buy more stock than it was absolutely necessary for them to have. When a leading banker declared that "the great industrial corporations generally dominate the banks and not the reverse,"[96] he was telling the truth.

To say that the inflation encouraged a shift of wealth and economic power to industrial leaders and away from banks and other holders of securities, however, is not to demonstrate that the actual financial and productive condition of industry was satisfactory. The great leaders of German industry did not feel overly secure despite their supposedly strengthened condition. In part, this was due to the confused and uncertain times, and Reusch could therefore declare in February 1920 that "it cannot even be foretold if we will close out the coming months with many millions in profit or many millions in losses,"[97] even though the GHH was doing very well at the time. More important than such generalized anxiety, however, was that the normal objective indicators of the condition of their companies had been undermined, to a great extent by themselves. The inflation placed enormous discretionary power into the hands of industrial leaders when setting up their balance sheets, a situation hardly conducive to business morality and destructive of efforts to relate planning to a clearly defined economic situation. As Siemens confessed to Vögler in 1925: "Because of the inflation we have, in part through force of circumstances, in part through our own fault, allowed ourselves to be driven into unclear circumstances, into engaging in obscure manipulations, which can no longer be allowed to remain under orderly conditions. . . ."[98]

The practice of drawing up so-called mixed balances, that is, balances calculated in paper marks for some items and in gold marks for others, provided glorious opportunities to bend and twist the balances

[95] See the protocol of the December 29, 1920, meeting in SAA, Nachlass Haller, 11/LB 108, and Sempell to Haller, April 6, 1922, *ibid.*, 11/Lb 391.

[96] Director Klaproth of the Hannoverische Bank to Director Wassermann of the Deutsche Bank, May 10, 1920, Hannoverische Bank Akten, Deutsche Bank Archiv, Frankfurt/Main.

[97] Reusch to Wiskott, February 9, 1920, HA/GHH, Nr. 300193002/3.

[98] Siemens to Vögler, December 27, 1925, SAA 4/Lf 635. On this problem, see Bresciani-Turroni, *Economics of Inflation*, p. 262, and Zölner in *Technik und Wirtschaft*, 15, p. 449.

to serve specific purposes. When the question of the legitimacy of such balances was discussed in 1921, heavy industry fought to maintain the method "because it believed that through significant undervaluation of inventories, through the writing off of the abnormal increases in the fixed costs, and through the formation of other open and hidden reserves, it could prevent the disappearance of capital."[99] Such practices, however, posed both long-run and short-run problems. What would happen when the day of stabilization came and assets had to be valuated in terms intelligible to one's successors and appropriate to existing economic circumstances? During the inflation the valuation of assets was so arbitrary that there was little linkage between stated assets and actual and potential productivity.[100]

Nor was it very clear how much capital would be needed and where it would come from. In April 1921, a cautious man like Vögler could express concern that the total capital of the IG was hardly a billion marks whereas sales constituted ten to twelve billion. This disproportion disturbed Vögler, who thought at the time that the mark was stabilizing and was worried about having the working capital necessary for expansion and modernization. When the Finance Committee of the SRSU met in May, however, the sense of having a sufficient capital supply dominated over the recognition that the supply would begin to diminish as new projects were undertaken, while the anticipation of stabilization of the mark at its existing level rendered the SRSU willing to grant long-term loans. By the end of 1921, the high point of liquidity seemed to have passed, while the SRSU's large construction programs, renewed depreciation of the mark, and galloping costs were beginning to undermine the financial resources of the SRSU. Although in January 1922 the SRSU hoped to finance itself through gains from an increase in coke prices, it was compelled to turn to the banks, the Reichsbank, and other outside means of support after June 1922. Increasingly, the strength of the SRSU and other concerns became a function of public and private lending policies rather than of simple capital and reserve resources. Needless to say, the capacity of these concerns to marshal such assistance bespoke their strength and capacity to secure such support for their existence and their policies.[101]

The decision of the Duisburg arbitration board and the debate between Imhoff and Buttlar mentioned above, therefore, dealt only with

[99] From the very revealing report by Director Baur of Krupp, October 20, 1923, Krupp WA IV 1405.

[100] This foreshadows the problem that arose in the stabilization, when it was debated as to whether gold balances should be established on the basis of "intrinsic value" or "earning capacity." See Bresciani-Turroni, *Economics of Inflation*, p. 274ff.

[101] For this discussion, see Freund's study of the SRSU in SAA 54/Lm 123.

certain aspects of a much broader problem. The evaluation of the activities of the iron and steel industrialists in 1920–1921 was much less a question of the highly ambiguous results that appeared on paper, both those available to the public and those hidden from the public view, than the question of their relative advantage and whether or not their activities were conducive to a healthy reconstruction of the German economy. The government never seriously analyzed this question, that is, whether or not the vertical concentration movement as conducted by the heavy industrialists was the most rational way to organize the industrial sectors involved. This is not surprising because the section of the RWM dealing with iron consisted of three persons, none of whom was an expert in the field. Although not very well informed as to what was going on—the analyses made were taken from newspaper reports—and in no way active in guiding what was happening, however, the government did in effect promote the vertical concentration movement in both word and deed. It supported fusion and rationalization as principles, permitted tax and lending policies favorable to concentration, and, in paying compensation to the various concerns compelled to alienate old holdings, as required by the peace treaty, it specified that the monies so acquired had to be spent on reconstruction without in any way attempting to determine what the best mode of reconstruction was. In effect, the government left the reconstruction of the economy to the industrialists and accepted passively a program designed to eliminate government interference.[102]

It is important to note that Stinnes and Vögler had made an ideology of vertical concentration during those hectic months in the summer and fall of 1920 when they were forging the SRSU. They did this in the course of their efforts to present a counterprogram to the various schemes for the socialization of the mining industry being considered by the Commission on the Socialization of the Coal Industry that had been set up after the Kapp Putsch. The two industrial leaders argued in memoranda to their colleagues in industry as well as in various public pronouncements that coal should under no circumstances be separated from other industrial branches because this would run counter to the entire effort by industry to maximize energy utilization through establishing organic relationships between production and consumption. Naturally, this argument was extended to the relations between steel producers and their primary consumers as well. Vögler, who had

---

[102] See the revealing memorandum by Dr. Stellwaag in DZA Potsdam, RWM, Nr. 4457, Bl. 55ff. When RWM officials tried to draw up a report on vertical concentration in 1921, their primary source was the newspapers. See *ibid.*, Nr. 2267/1, Bl. 28ff. Naturally, it was hard for the RWM to get suitable experts because, as Stellwaag pointed out, such persons could make more money in private industry.

abandoned his fatalistic attitude toward coal socialization of 1919, insisted that respect had to be shown for the "technical-economic motives" responsible for the manner in which concerns were being created, and he took the lead in helping his colleagues to consider ways of utilizing energy to maximum advantage. As chairman of the Association of German Foundry Engineers' Committee on Fuel Economy (*Wärmewirtschaft*), he argued effectively that "in order to prevent the intervention of the state," some type of "economic community" was necessary, and he urged "a consolidation of the power networks in certain industrial districts with the inclusion of the mines and the city electrical works."[103]

Stinnes preached the same message in the Socialization Committee, where he insisted that increased productivity could only come through a system that "brings consumers and producers into close, indeed, the closest connection."[104] He cited two combinations in which he was a direct participant, that of Deutsch-Lux and the GBAG and that of the lignite-producing Roddergrube and the Rheinisch-Westfälische Elektrizitätswerke, as practical examples of what he meant. These cases were also used as illustrations of a much broader reorganization of the German economy being advocated by Stinnes and Vögler under which the Reich would be divided into economic districts based on close collaboration between industrial producers and industrial consumers governing their own affairs. RWM officials were fully aware of the implications of these proposals, which were designed, among other things, to push the Berlin bureaucracy into the background and place the Rhenish-Westphalian industrial area in the foreground.[105]

These ideas met with alarm in industrial as well as in government circles. Otto Wiedfeldt, the leading Krupp director, found the Stinnes-Vögler program "interesting," to be sure, but also anxiety-producing. He was aware of Vögler's July 1919 memorandum recommending the trustification of the Ruhr steel industry, and he thought that Vögler was preparing the ground for the "future iron trust . . . which we are moving towards for general reasons. . . ."[106] In August 1920, when he wrote these lines, Wiedfeldt thought it perfectly understandable that Vögler

[103] See the meeting of August 20, 1920, HA/GHH, Nr. 30104/3, and Vögler's memorandum, "Die Sozialisierung des Bergbaues," September 20, 1920, in BA, Nachlass Silverberg, Nr. 135, Bl. 58–62. Also, see Wulf in *Industrielles System*, pp. 653–657, and Maier, *Recasting Bourgeois Europe*, p. 215ff.

[104] Stinnes before the Sub-Committee on Socialization, October 25, 1920, in BA, Nachlass Silverberg, Nr. 141, Bl. 95–96.

[105] See Alexander Rüstow, who was in the RWM during the early 1920s, to Paul Legers, December 3, 1927, BA, Nachlass Rüstow, Nr. 18. There is interesting material on the RWE in the unpublished history in its Essen library.

[106] Wiedfeldt to Bohlen, August 5, 1920, Krupp WA IV 1999.

should design programs in consonance with Deutsch-Lux's interests and in which Stinnes was bound to play a leading role. In the summer of 1921, however, when the danger of coal socialization had passed and the economic future seemed dark for the steel industry, Wiedfeldt was much more resentful, fearing that the Rhein-Elbe Union was "only a step along the path to the complete trustification of the Rhenish-Westphalian iron industry that Stinnes is contemplating. He will try to group as many works as possible about himself and then present the question: 'Do you want to go along under the conditions I lay down or do you want to go against us in isolation?' "[107]

Wiedfeldt was overestimating Stinnes and Vögler's interest in an iron trust at this point and, as has been shown, the connection with Siemens involved an attempt to create a relatively self-contained organization based on vertical rather than horizontal principles. It would have been difficult for the SRSU to accommodate an iron trust within its framework, as was to be demonstrated in 1926, and Wiedfeldt was himself anticipating a situation that was only to arise after the stabilization. Nevertheless, he was able to anticipate this situation because the fundamental problem that Vögler's initial trustification program was meant to answer, namely the rationalization of the steel industry, was to become increasingly pressing as the initial postwar conditions and shortages began to abate. The alliance Stinnes and Vögler had forged between heavy industry and the particularly advanced electrotechnical sector could only serve, in a sense, to place the relative retardation of the heavy industrial sector in a more glaring light.

This is strikingly evident in a report written by Director Jastrow of Siemens, who undertook a personal survey of the heavy industrial plants of the SRSU in April 1921.[108] Jastrow emphasized that the initial impression of great complexity created by the huge conglomerations of power plants, cokeries, smelting plants, rolling mills, foundries, and machine plants was really very misleading. Although truly impressive from the standpoint of its dimensions, the entire mass of operations were "in reality astoundingly simple." Jastrow had nothing against simplicity, but he was disturbed by the confusion everywhere in evidence because of overlapping and uncoordinated production programs in the foundries and rolling mills and by the way in which major fabrication and finishing operations had been lodged in inade-

---

[107] Wiedfeldt to Bohlen, July 8, 1921, *ibid.*, III 226.

[108] Jastrow took his tour on April 3–13, 1921, and signed his report on April 20, 1921. The discussion and quotations from the report that follow are based on the document in SAA 54/Ld 274.

quate old repair workshops converted to new uses. He was surprised at the absence of plants that gave one the "impression of modern mass fabrication."

Jastrow had undertaken his journey filled with "high expectations" because of the steel industry's reputation for technological progressiveness, but he returned "greatly disappointed." It appeared to him that the technological accomplishments of the industry were purely dimensional in nature and that such real technological advances as were in evidence had come in from the machine construction and electrotechnical industries. Indeed, Jastrow was often deprecatory in his description, as when he described the electrical steering of a bloom roll train (*Blockwalzenstrasse*) as a "technological pearl in the otherwise far extended field, forest, and meadow technology" of a steel works. He found the fabrication plants for large products primitive and incomplete because they were based on the simplistic notion that large plants were nothing more than big versions of smaller ones. Similarly, Jastrow found the gas works a "technical disappointment" and thought it "completely astonishing" that Thyssen was the only firm in the Ruhr to employ the gas turbine.

It is obvious that Jastrow was viewing the Rhein-Elbe Union from the perspective of his own industry and his special engineering interests. The evidence does suggest, however, that Jastrow was basically correct. His criticisms were not very different from those of Vögler in his July 1919 memorandum, and both the rationalization efforts then being undertaken by Thyssen and the more massive efforts at rationalization undertaken after the inflation were designed to deal with precisely the sort of conditions outlined by Jastrow.[109] Furthermore, Jastrow was fair enough to recognize that the nature of heavy industry necessarily gave the iron and steel men a very different orientation from their colleagues in manufacturing. Where the latter dealt with highly individualized and complex products or with intricate mass production problems, the former operated on a more primitive level in which grosser questions of maximizing plant operation and solving transportation difficulties took precedence over more refined technical considerations. Similarly, the heavy industrialists dealt in fungible wares and needed few sophisticated marketing techniques because they had little concern about how the products of their foundries, rolling mills, and fabricating plants were employed in the manufac-

---

[109] See above, pp. 115–117, and Robert Brady, *The Rationalization of German Industry. A Study in the Evolution of Economic Planning* (Berkeley, 1933), p. 103ff., and D. Warriner, *Combines and Rationalization in Germany, 1924–1928* (London, 1931), pp. 31–32.

ture of more complex products. Their major concern, in short, was to produce, and the market was only a problem if a crisis caused a reduction of demand and plant utilization.

Jastrow's description of the mentality of the steel producers provides important clues as to why the reconstruction of heavy industry took the form that it did. Theoretically, the losses under the peace treaty, labor problems, reduced productivity, and the expanded capacities of foreign competitors all militated for rationalization of heavy industry as well as greater emphasis on fabrication. In practice, the trend toward rationalization was limited by a variety of very immediate considerations. To begin with, low productivity and shortages placed a premium on production rather than efficiency, while the entire postwar economic and political situation undermined the syndicates and promoted individual reconstruction rather than planned or collective action on either the public or private levels. The government was too weak to impose its will, and most of the time it was lacking in the ideas that were necessary to deal with such problems. As mentioned earlier, the government compensation for losses under the treaty were spent on reconstruction, but much of this was employed in the coal sector. Indeed, much of the postinflationary rationalization would be concerned with repairing the damage of short-term investments made to meet immediate shortages by the shoring up and expanding of mines and works that needed to be shut down. Rationalization on an individual firm level often meant the duplication of work done in other firms. Thus, if Thyssen was wisely modernizing his operations, he was not alone in this effort. It is known that Thyssen was partial to Vögler's trustification proposal and, like Vögler, he had come to the conclusion that the time was not yet ripe. His rationalization efforts were designed to strengthen his own position for the expected time when stabilization and overproduction in heavy industry would require rationalization. When that time came, Thyssen would be prepared to enter on the most favorable terms possible. This position was understandable under the circumstances, and the plant expansions of the inflation, whether of long-term value or not, could be viewed as "productive unemployment support" at a time of social unrest, but it may also be questioned whether this was the best way to reconstruct the German iron and steel industry.[110]

The long-term need for modernization and rationalization in heavy industry, whether conducted immediately or put off until necessary,

---

[110] *Ibid.* The relationship between the reconstruction of the iron and steel industry and foreign policy problems will be dealt with more extensively in the last two chapters of this study.

does suggest that the capital strength that heavy industry had employed to woo or coerce the finishing industries was often a transitory phenomenon. In this sense, Krupp, which suffered severe capital difficulties because of its enormous reconversion problems and hence pursued the cautious expansion policy mentioned earlier, was more symptomatic of the problems in heavy industry than its neighboring concerns, many of which were employing their temporary liquidity to expand in any and every direction. This was why Wiedfeldt seemed to be continuously anticipating conditions that were only to arise after the stabilization. Similarly, he was an early advocate of ruthless rationalization policies.

In a memorandum of October 1919, Wiedfeldt pointed out that the constantly mounting costs of labor and materials threatened to bring Krupp to financial ruin. He urged Gustav Krupp von Bohlen und Halbach to decentralize the various sections of the firm and compel the various member works to demonstrate their capacity to survive by proving their profitability. He warned that "one can almost draw a mathematical curve showing when monetary resources will in all probability be used up. Then we can do business on credit for some time, but after that we will be at the end."[111] Bohlen would not accept these proposals, however. In a lengthy rebuttal in January 1920 he urged caution in reorganization until conditions had become more stable, doubted that decentralization would have the good effect on Krupp's image that Wiedfeldt expected it to have, and emphatically rejected a ruthless rationalization policy conceivable if an American bought the firm and "could throw everything into the scrap heap . . . without any consideration for the past and without moral obligations," but out of the question "so long as the firm is associated with the name of Krupp."[112]

Actually, the much less traditionalistic Wiedfeldt was not adverse to giving Americans a voice in Krupp's affairs, and he returned to the charge in the summer of 1921, when he thought that the worldwide depression presaged what he considered to be the inevitable overproduction of iron and steel. Krupp would need large sums of money to rationalize, he argued, if the firm were not to go bankrupt or fall prey to Stinnes' imperialism, and he did not think that the Dutch financial help Krupp had been receiving would suffice. He urged that Bohlen turn to Rockefeller or U.S. Steel even if this meant an American voice in company affairs. Wiedfeldt was fully aware that Krupp would be

---

[111] "Finanzlage der Firma und Änderungen im Gesellschaftsbau," October 1919, Krupp WA IV 1263.

[112] Bohlen to the Krupp directors, January 5, 1920, *ibid.*, 1432.

criticized and somewhat isolated if it took this step, but argued that it would help the firm's foreign trade and liberate its pricing policies.[113] As it turned out, Krupp continued to manage during the inflation thanks to bank loans, Dutch assistance, its stock holdings in various enterprises such as Mannesmann, and sufficiently satisfactory business conditions to enable it to sell its production. The evil day was yet to come.

Precisely the situation created by the inflation, however, made rationalization less significant than the building up of marketing possibilities for the great concerns. As Jastrow had noted, the iron and steel men were more concerned about moving their production than about rationalization. Given the demand for German production in the world, even during the worldwide depression of 1920–1921, there was a real opportunity to restore Germany's position on world markets by taking advantage of the depreciated mark. Under these conditions, great importance was attached to the development of marketing organizations or the association with such organizations. Otto Wolff immediately comes to mind in this connection. Wolff had earned a somewhat bad reputation in many circles as a notorious war profiteer, and a man who manipulated the stock market "less in the sense of bringing about a rationalization of the plants than for the purpose of the greatest possible profitable manipulation of the securities market."[114] It certainly was true that Wolff had made his fortune selling iron for Krupp and others during the war. Furthermore, he had nothing against speculation, and he was an admirer of the Great French speculator of the revolutionary era, Gabriel Julien Ouvrard. In his interesting biography of Ouvrard of 1932, however, Wolff was anxious to stress Ouvrard's patriotic services to France, and he was critical of Ouvrard's boundless speculative drive and impecunious end. He compared Ouvrard to Napoleon, and he viewed the downfall of both as deriving from the same lack of moderation.[115] If Wolff did not share the fate of Stinnes after the inflation, it was no accident, and the evidence suggests that Wolff was misjudged by his critics. Indeed, although plenty of speculation accompanied the concentration movement, it is generally a mistake to think that speculation was the dominant motive for the concern builders.[116]

In Wolff's case, the object of his concern was neither simply to make

[113] Wiedfeldt to Bohlen, July 8, 1921, *ibid.*, 226.

[114] See the Stellwaag memorandum, DZA Potsdam, RWM, Nr. 4457, Bl. 69.

[115] Otto Wolff, *Die Geschäfte des Herrn Ouvrard. Aus dem Leben eines Genialen Spekulanten* (Frankfurt a/M, 1932), p. 271ff. Wolff was a man of broad interests and talents, as this intriguing work suggests.

[116] Tross, *Aufbau*, p. 157.

speculative gains nor to act, as was often charged, as a front man for the turning of German concerns over to Dutch control. His basic concern was not rationalization either. That was the task of the directors of Phoenix, Rheinstahl, de Fries, and van der Zypen, the major steel companies in which he participated and in whose basic production policies he seldom interfered. As noted earlier, Wolff was a great merchant, and his object was to serve himself, the concerns with which he was associated, and at times even the German economy with his impressive organization both at home and abroad. Wolff's Dutch operations were not viewed with suspicion but rather with approval by the government, and Wolff was heavily involved in the close economic cooperation between Holland and Germany during the inflation. Thus, shortly after his first substantial purchase of Phoenix stock in the fall of 1919, which was discreetly handled by the Deutsche Bank and the private bank of Delbrück, Schickler & Co., Wolff mortgaged 12 million marks worth of Phoenix, Rheinstahl, and de Fries stock in return for a 40 million mark loan from the Finance Ministry repayable at 4% yearly interest with the principal to fall due beginning in November 1922. Wolff retained the voting rights of this stock, which the Reich in turn mortgaged as security against payment of a mineral oil delivery agreement with the Dutch Bataafsche Petroleum Maatschappij. This arrangement enabled the Reich to provide securities required by the Dutch for vital imports valued in gulden while it enabled Wolff to secure a mark loan that he was subsequently fortunate enough to be able to repay in devalued currency. Wolff controlled important trading companies in Holland, at times under assumed names, and he participated in various consortia with Dutch industrialists and bankers, but Holland was the logical place for both the Reich and private entrepreneurs to turn in an unfriendly post-World War I Europe. Although Wolff exercised his stock options to increase his control over Phoenix in 1921 and gave his colleagues in a Dutch consortium a large voice in Phoenix affairs, the arrangements with the Dutch could be viewed and were viewed by the government as particularly useful from the German standpoint. Under arrangements between Phoenix and the Royal Dutch Smelting and Steel Factories, the latter supplied the former with pig iron to be turned into steel and then reexported to Holland. This enabled Phoenix to employ its facilities and workers while saving on ore and coke costs as well as on the use of foreign exchange for raw materials purchases. Of course it would be ludicrous to view Wolff's operations as a patriotic endeavor, and it is reasonable to suppose that he did quite well thanks to his connections with Erzberger and other politicians. Furthermore, the Wolff group was notorious for favoring the foreign over the domestic market in 1919–1920.

Yet Wolff had plenty of company in this regard, and his example was followed by others in the effort to restore Germany's world market position as well as to rationalize somewhat the marketing operations of Germany's leading companies.[117]

Participation in foreign marketing organizations and the building up of such organizations, therefore, constituted an exceptionally important and positive element in the concentration movement during the inflation. The GHH was particularly active in this respect. In February 1920 it gained 100% control of a Dutch trading firm, the N. V. Goederentransport Maatschappij Rollo, which it used to penetrate into the Dutch market and the colonial markets of Holland and England. This was followed by 50% participation in the J. G. Goudriaan Industrie— en Export Maatschappij, which marketed railroad tracks. The GHH also established a foothold in Sweden with an eye toward the future development of its Baltic and Russian trade.[118] Ultimately, however, the most important marketing organization serving the GHH was the N. V. Algemeene Ijzer- en Staal- Maatschappij "Ferrostaal." Originally created by a consortium of German and Dutch businessmen and bankers for the purpose of selling off German war materials and field railroad equipment after the war, the firm rapidly developed into a worldwide trading organization for light rails and rolled steel products. It began servicing the GHH in 1921, and the latter soon took over 40% of its stock.[119]

The Ferrostaal services were of immense importance. The GHH was given a preference over all other Ferrostaal customers in the sale of its production by the organization's worldwide network of outlets and was thus spared the costs and risks of setting up its own trading organization. It did not have to engage in the difficult negotiations necessary to compete with competing trade organizations like those of Stinnes or of foreign firms. Through the Ferrostaal and organizations like it, the GHH and other concerns were able to dispose of inventories even during the world crisis of 1921, when, as Ferrostaal reported, the relatively low value of the mark meant that "insofar as orders being given, they are going first to Germany."[120] Reusch placed great hopes in Fer-

[117] The operations connected with the Phoenix stock dealings of Wolff may be followed in the volume entitled "Phoenix AG f. Bergbau u. Hüttenbetrieb. Okt. 1919–Okt. 1922," in the Deutsche Bank Archiv, Frankfurt/Main. See also the relevant articles in the *Kölnische Zeitung* on April 30, October 11, and October 21, 1920, and Deutelmoser of the Foreign Office to Chancellor Wirth, September 26, 1921, BA, 43 I/1173.

[118] Maschke, *Konzern*, pp. 163–165.

[119] *Ibid.*, pp. 183–184.

[120] Report of February 24, 1921, and Director Nathan to Reusch, November 4, 1921, HA/GHH, Nr. 300193022/0–1.

rostaal, anticipating that it would become "one of the greatest trading organizations that exist," so that "we can be assured of work in bad times because business conditions in the world do not normally proceed in a uniform way. . . ."[121]

One of the most important expectations of the founders of the SRSU was that the marketing organizations of Siemens and Stinnes would combine their forces as much as possible. Siemens at this time had the largest foreign organization of any company in the world. The Rhein-Elbe group controlled a string of important trading firms at home and abroad, e.g., the widespread German house of Heinrich August Schulte and the Swedish Aktieselskabet Sydvaranger in Christiana. Additionally, however, there was the expectation that the trading organizations of Stinnes' private concern with its huge network of organizations throughout the world and the important A. G. Hugo Stinnes für Seeschiffahrt und Überseehandel, Hamburg, in which much of this trading activity was centered, would be of service as well. In July 1921 important steps were taken in this direction at a meeting in which agreements were reached to eliminate or settle in a friendly manner points of competition between the Siemens and Stinnes organizations abroad. In the area of marketing, therefore, the SRSU, like the other concerns under discussion, offered expanded and more effective marketing organizations to its member firms, organizations that gathered invaluable intelligence and that aggressively operated to restore Germany's trade.[122]

There is thus no neat and simple way to evaluate the vertical concentration movement during this period. There was much expansion of holdings and reconstruction of plants which were of short-term benefit to the concerns involved and to the economy as a whole because they increased productivity and maintained high employment. Some of the expansion was inorganic in nature, wasted resources through duplication of effort, and expanded capacities beyond long-term need. The inflation, along with the weakening of political authority, encouraged the creation of what Walther Rathenau rightly called "economic duchies,"[123] and as was the case with the political duchies of old, some already demonstrated the capacity to maintain themselves and develop further from a viable base while others were too far-flung and incoherent in their character to enjoy more than an interesting but limited glory. Here again, the GHH and the Siemens-Rheinelbe-Union emerge as useful prototypes in helping the historian to draw some conclusions.

[121] Concern meeting, Oberhausen, October 24, 1921, ibid., Nr. 3001900/1.
[122] Discussion among SRSU leaders in Hamburg, July 14, 1921, SAA Ld 273.
[123] Bresciani-Turroni, Economics of Inflation, p. 215.

There is a peculiar contradiction between the harshness of Reusch's personality and the delicacy and skill with which he developed his concern, just as there is a contradiction between the speculation and uproar surrounding the acquisition of the MAN and the purposeful and impressive manner with which it and the GHH's other acquisitions were brought into relatively harmonious association with one another. When the Ferrostaal directors suggested that the member firms of the GHH might raise objections to the GHH connections with Ferrostaal because they had their own outlets, Reusch responded that "my people are not in the habit of acting in violation of my instructions, and I am not in the habit of putting up with violations of my instructions."[124] Yet Reusch was careful to make clear that he did not intend to force the member firms to use Ferrostaal. He did not try to eliminate the various outlets of the concern members but rather to coordinate them, a process that went on until 1938. More generally, he was careful to at once take a lively direct interest in the affairs of each member firm and, at the same time, to pay heed to need for autonomy and a sense of self-importance. He undertook a grueling schedule of personal visits to these firms, which stretched from Hamburg to Munich, and he made a point of having the concern meetings located at the headquarters of the various firms to emphasize his commitment to decentralization. These meetings, at which common problems and policies were reviewed and coordinated, were organized through a Concern Bureau (*Konzernstelle*) set up under Director Paul Schmerse. The protocols of these meetings show that Reusch and Schmerse were careful not to press for common policies where differences among the members seemed too great. The object seemed to be voluntary coordination of interests because it was advantageous to all concerned. It was expected that the member firms would purchase from one another when price and quality equalled what was being offered by outsiders, but it was a general rule that firms were to purchase where they were best served.[125]

Reusch made it clear in word and deed that he planned to do everything possible to ensure that member firms received the raw materials they required. He asked the concern works to make quarterly inventories of their raw materials requirements and ordered that in times of shortage the GHH rolling program be organized "according to the needs of the finishers in the concern and not the concern merchants."[126] Concern works were permitted to emphasize their connection with the GHH when trying to assure customers that they would have the raw

[124] Reusch to Müller-Nico, October 2, 1921, HA/GHH, Nr. 300193022/1.
[125] Maschke, *Konzern*, p. 219ff.
[126] *Ibid.*, p. 222.

materials needed to deliver finished goods on time. At the same time Reusch emphasized that this policy of supplying the concern members had to find its limits in the need of the GHH to secure foreign exchange to purchase ores because he would not purchase foreign exchange on the market. The GHH had an understandable desire to export, particularly when, as in 1921, the export profit was 50% higher than the domestic price. For reasons of principle and interest, Reusch had always supported a moderate pricing policy within the steel industry, and he approved of special terms for raw materials sold for use in export products. Similarly, he was a strong supporter of stable prices. The manufacturing firms in the concern were appreciative of Reusch's desire to improve their export position and were in full agreement with his policy that "Germany must export as much as possible so that the enemy states find themselves in worse and worse circumstances and are thereby finally brought to reason."[127] It is notable, however, that Reusch did not try to compel other concern members to follow his lead in all matters of economic policy. Thus, in June 1921, while Reusch was calling for the termination of export controls, the MAN, with Reusch's knowledge, was asking the government to retain those controls.[128] In general, the evidence suggests that Reusch's working relationship with the leading directors of the concern firms was based on mutual respect and considerable friendly feeling as well.

Reusch was appropriately generous with money where he felt such help was justified, and the GHH acted as a "credit bank" for the concern members as part of a deliberate policy to prevent the firms from building up bank debts. Not only did the GHH thus provide an easier and more agreeable source of credit, but it also charged a much lower interest rate than the banks while sharing with the banks the rather unpleasant experience of frequently being paid back in depreciated currency. This is not to say that Reusch was always willing to support the daughter companies every time they asked for help or sought to expand, and he argued that firms should earn their capital and that "too tempestuous an expansion is unhealthy and will revenge itself someday."[129] This cautious attitude reflected Reusch's entire approach to the construction of his concern. He sought to maximize the stability of the concern by the elimination of competition in the production programs of the member firms and by encouraging exchanges of information and collaboration, e.g., between the MAN and the Esslinger Maschinenfabrik in the manufacture of Diesel motors. In his modest

---

[127] Concern meeting, October 21, 1921, HA/GHH, Nr. 3001900/1.

[128] MAN to Foreign Trade Section of the Foreign Office, June 23, 1921, *ibid.*, Nr. 3001930/0.

[129] Maschke, *Konzern*, pp. 215–216.

acquisition policy after 1920, Reusch kept these conservative aims in mind. He gained control of the Munich firm, Fritz Neumeyer AG, in order to eliminate it as a potential competitor of the MAN, but he turned down an excellent opportunity to acquire the Magirus AG, a fine Württemberg firm manufacturing busses and trucks, on the grounds that "the need for material that could be supplied by us is so small that the matter has no interest for us."[130] If Reusch was one of the great concern builders of the inflation, it was because he employed the advantages provided by the inflation to expand a long-established concern in a manner that at once increased its security and permitted it to pursue an aggressive policy in the domestic and world market.

In contrast to the Haniel concern, the SRSU was a more complex and a more problematic form of vertical concentration from the very outset, and the historian faces the problem, noted before, of properly appreciating a failure for the functions it did serve during the period of its existence. The problem is complicated by the need to understand the policies and motives of Hugo Stinnes, who was the dominating personality in the SRSU, and although it would be false to argue that Stinnes ultimately determined the policies of the SRSU, it would be fair to say that it was he who defined the parameters within which it operated and gave it decisive impulses. Although Stinnes often stated that a day would come when the demand for raw materials would abate and the finished products manufacturers would have the upper hand, the evidence suggests that he "believed to his very end in a continuation of the lively demand for coal and iron."[131] Important expansion was undertaken in the heavy industrial domain. This was reflected in the acquisition of majority control of the Oesterreichische Alpine Montangesellschaft in the spring of 1921, the most important Styrian ore, iron, and steel concern. This acquisition gave the SRSU an important base from which to penetrate into the markets of south-eastern and eastern Europe as well as a strong position in Upper Silesian heavy industry. The SRSU also expanded into the lignite industry following its founding. Another important acquisition was the Gebrüder Bohler & Co., AG Berlin and Vienna, an important high-grade steel producer with major works in Germany and Austria. At the same time, work was begun on the development and expansion of

[130] Reusch to Haniel, February 20, 1922, and other correspondence on Magirus in HA/GHH, Nr. 3001900/1. On his rationalization efforts, see the memorandum on "Vereinheitlichung der Fabrikationsgebiete der GHH," *ibid.*, Nr. 300193010/17. On the Fritz Neumeyer problem, see Maschke, *Konzern*, p. 169.

[131] Emil Kirdorf, in his unpublished "Erinnerungen" in the GBAG Archiv, Nr. 200/01/3.

the works in the Ruhr. In September 1921 Stinnes and Vögler placed great stress on the "necessity of complementing the good foundations of the concern in ore, coal, and furnace capacity by increasing our capacity to transform iron and steel into rolled products,"[132] and a large program for new construction was planned for 1921–1922 that included, among other things, a new plant for pipes. All this, however, was very traditional, and the problem remained as to how the production programs of the two groups in the SRSU might be brought into greater contact.

From the point of view of production alone, it was hard to understand what was to be gained from an IG between the Rhine-Elbe Union and Siemens, particularly after the MAN dropped out of the picture. Jastrow already pointed to the key sources of difficulty in his memorandum of April 1921 following his inspection of the heavy industrial side of the SRSU. Jastrow found Stinnes' desire for an association with Siemens difficult to explain. As Jastrow pointed out, the logical expansion of heavy industry had to be "first in seeking combination with such works as employ iron most extensively, that is, shipbuilding, steam boiler works, locomotive construction, bridge building, iron construction, iron merchandising, and only secondarily . . . automobile construction, the entire area of building small and large machines and, finally, electrotechnology."[133] The IG had been created with the vision of an "economic body" producing practically everything in the industrial spectrum, but Jastrow evidently had an extremely difficult time defining exactly how this spectrum was going to be formed between its extreme ends. Apparently, Jastrow rapidly lost his early enthusiasm and came to the conclusion that Stinnes was less moved by any conception of vertical concentration than by a desire to benefit from Siemens' foreign outlets and by the advantages to be derived from the magic of the Siemens name itself.[134] Such an explanation, however, is probably too simple and neglects both the historical conditions under which the SRSU was founded and the fact that Stinnes was very much given to the contemplation of new schemes of industrial development.

There is every reason to believe that Stinnes, like Siemens, initially expected mutual advantage from a close connection between raw materials production and manufacturing, the latter being secure in its raw materials requirements, the former having a guaranteed customer in hard times. There is no evidence that Stinnes thought much of the

[132] Meeting of September 26, 1921, SAA, Nachlass Haller, 11 Lb 108, and Ufermann and Hüglin, *Stinnes-Konzerne*, p. 34ff.

[133] Jastrow memorandum of April 20, 1921, SAA 54/Ld 274.

[134] Freund study of the SRSU in *ibid.*, Lm/123.

warnings of skeptics such as Director Deutsch of the AEG, a strong critic of vertical concentration, who did not think that such arrangements would really work.[135] Furthermore, the SRSU did provide some advantages to Siemens in the management of its raw materials problems. In 1920–1921, Vögler was able to provide considerable assistance to his counterpart at Siemens, Director Köttgen, in the reduction of raw materials inventories and the selling off of excess supplies that had been stocked in anticipation of shortage. Less tangibly, the SRSU certainly gave Siemens and its customers a much greater sense of security about the raw materials supply.[136]

Nevertheless, the overall evaluation made by Siemens of its dealings with its heavy industrial partners in this area for 1920–1922 was justifiably reserved. Siemens did receive important high-quality coal deliveries for its porcelain factories from within the SRSU, but most of the coal needs of Siemens continued to come from Upper Silesia. It was not until the spring of 1922 that Siemens gave way to pressure from the GBAG and began to take more of its coal. Purchases of iron and steel from SRSU members by Siemens increased from 10% to 25% of all such purchases between 1920–1921 and 1921–1922. However, Siemens had always been most concerned about the quality of what it received and the promptness with which it was delivered rather than with mere amounts, and in both those respects the results were very mixed. There had been some improvement in quality, but all the suggestions for such improvements came from Siemens. The Siemens people were most distressed throughout 1921–1922 by late deliveries. As a consequence, Siemens had found it necessary to purchase outside the SRSU to cover its needs until the SRSU steel arrived, and this resurrected the problem of overstocking that seemed to have been solved during the previous year. As Director Deutsch had correctly warned Stinnes, Deutsch-Lux's enthusiasm for meeting Siemens' demands at times when it could sell elsewhere would be limited by the advantages to be gained from supplying less demanding and often more lucrative customers. Furthermore, it is reasonable to believe that Stinnes was also more aware of the truth of Deutsch's prediction that Siemens

[135] See Deutsch's testimony to investigators in 1927, discussed below. See Ausschuss zur Untersuchung der Erzeugungs- und Absatzbedingungen der deutschen Wirtschaft. *Verhandlungen und Berichte des Unterausschusses für allgemeine Wirtschaftsstruktur (I. Unterausschuss). 3. Arbeitsgruppe. Wandlungen in den wirtschaftlichen Organisationsformen. Erster Teil. Wandlungen in den Rechtsformen der Einzelunternehmungen und Konzerne* (Berlin, 1928), pp. 407–408.

[136] Köttgen to Vögler, November 16, 1920, Deutsch-Lux to SSW, November 18, 1920, Köttgen minute, January 6, 1921, in SAA, Nachlass Köttgen, 11/Lf 129, and Vögler, to Köttgen, November 21, 1921, and Köttgen to Vögler, December 28, 1921, *ibid.*, 255.

would not prove a really reliable customer for his steel in hard times. Although this thesis could not be tested much during the first two years of the SRSU's existence, it was obvious that Siemens could be supplied from competing sources. Furthermore, at the maximum, Siemens could employ only 10% of Deutsch-Lux's production, and much of this only in the form of special orders. Although it is difficult to tell how sincere Stinnes was when he remarked to Deutsch a year after the founding of the IG that it was wrong to think of himself as a man of vertical constructions alone and that he had become a man of horizontal constructions, there is every reason to believe that Stinnes understood that the linkages in the SRSU from the standpoint of production were far from ideal.[137]

Ultimately, such linkages were necessary if the SRSU was to fulfill the high expectations on which it was founded and become something more than a conglomerate. It must be remembered that the MAN leadership began to question the absolute necessity of a close alliance with a raw materials producer just before it surrendered to the GHH. The Siemens leaders had good reason, indeed better reason, to raise the same issue. However, the GHH-MAN combination evolved in a way that was highly promising from the standpoint of coordination of production programs and marketing arrangements. Stinnes and Siemens were anxious to build up areas of production coordination as well, but this was extremely difficult because of the reasons Jastrow had analyzed so well. Heavy industry and the electrotechnical industry serviced one another, but at a great distance, and there was a strongly felt need to develop mediating areas of industrial endeavor. Expansion seemed necessary.

One potential area of expansion was the automobile industry, a prospect raised at one of the earliest meetings of the SRSU Council (*Gemeinschaftsrat*) on December 29, 1920, when Vögler reported that Deutsch-Lux had been approached by three automobile works, two of which were Benz and Adler, seeking a connection. Both Deutsch-Lux and Siemens had made a beginning in this industry, the former controlling the Dinos Automobilwerke in Berlin, the latter running the Protos-Automobile GmbH in Berlin-Siemensstadt. While the Council agreed that "a consolidation of automobile fabrication in order to avoid uneconomic competition and to make possible the mass production of specific types of automobiles"[138] was necessary, they decided to put off further action until they could determine whether or

---

[137] See the undated report on deliveries within the SRSU in *ibid.*, 54/Ld 13, and Deutsch's comments cited in note 135 above. Also, see Siemens to Vögler, December 27, 1925, SAA 4/Lf 635.

[138] Meeting of December 29, 1920, *ibid.*, Nachlass Haller, 11/Lb 108.

not a major automobile manufacturer could be integrated into the SRSU's various production operations. The matter appears not to have been taken up again, and the reasons are not hard to find. During the war, the various automobile companies had been encouraged to over-expand their plants by the government, but nothing had been done to reduce the number of firms in this new and highly individualistic industry. As a consequence, the end of the war left the industry vastly overexpanded and in a continued state of individualistic competition for a shrunken market. There was bad mismanagement, as in the case of Daimler, fruitless competition in the production of luxury cars of various types, heavy government taxation discouraging the purchase of such cars, and severe foreign competition. Although both industrial leaders and bankers recognized the need to consolidate the industry and bring it into closer connection with its raw materials suppliers, conditions of production and the market were not conducive to effective action, and the industry was allowed to drift through the inflation. In any case, the problems involved were quite beyond the material and psychological resources of the SRSU leaders at this time.[139]

There were, however, other projects of a major nature that attracted the attention of the SRSU leaders, particularly in the field of locomotive construction. The locomotive plants were large consumers of raw materials and had large government contracts. Thus they attracted the strong interest of the heavy industrial side of the SRSU, whereas the Siemens group also wished to expand its construction of electric locomotives. Also, locomotive works, with their capacity to build large boilers, could be of assistance to Siemens' construction of electric power works. When the famous Cassel firm of Henschel approached Siemens with the idea of entering the SRSU, therefore, the matter was pursued energetically, especially at the end of 1921 when Henschel formed an IG with Hanomag, the large Hannoverian producer of locomotives, trucks, and machinery. Henschel-Hanomag's combination had been created in defiance of a major Hanomag stockholder, the Breslau locomotive manufacturer, Linke-Hofmann. Linke-Hofmann stood in an IG relationship to the heavy industrial producer Lauchhammer AG in Riesa, on the one hand, and to Siemens' great competitor, the AEG, on the other hand.[140] Thus, the Henschel-Hanomag combination was a defeat for AEG interests, which caused no end of glee at Sie-

---

[139] Excellent material on the state of the automobile industry is to be found on the volumes on Daimler-Benz in the Deutsche Bank Archiv, Frankfurt/Main. See especially the memoranda of Dr. Jahr of the Rheinische Creditbank of 1919 and 1924.

[140] Vögler to Salomonsohn, June 21, 1921, SAA 4/Lf 635/1. This volume also contains important correspondence with Henschel. Also, see Tross, *Aufbau*, pp. 77ff. and 103ff.

mens, and it was only natural for the Siemens concern to send Director Albert Werner of Schuckert to pay a call on his uncle, Director ter Meer of Hanomag.

In discussions on January 24, 1922, Werner sought to seduce Henschel-Hanomag into the SRSU with a catalogue of all the advantages that could be offered by its extent and size: connection with a concern whose capital base and productivity gave it a very different position in the world from that of any individual work; the possibility of participation in the rebuilding of eastern Europe through the gaining of concessions and the accessibility of large credits for such purposes; a vast marketing organization; security and contracts in times of poor business conditions. Yet the SRSU-Henschel-Hanomag connection failed to materialize. The major reason was that Henschel-Hanomag already stood in an IG relationship with the coal and steel producers joined in the so-called Lothringen group that had been forged together after 1918 by Otto Gehres, a Hanoverian industrialist and banker, and the SRSU was in no position to accommodate this complex of concerns.[141]

Indeed, throughout the discussions with Henschel there was concern about the danger of creating an organizational monster. Vögler was particularly worried that the SRSU would become unbearably clumsy if it had a new administrative center in Cassel. He was also concerned about the fact that Henschel seemed very short of skilled technical personnel. This meant that all the new designing and technical planning would have to be done by Siemens people, and if this were to be the case, then Vögler wondered if it did not make sense for Siemens gradually to expand its facilities at Siemensstadt and move into locomotive construction as well as into the construction of Diesel machines, steam turbines, and perhaps expand its automobile construction. In making this suggestion, Vögler's thoughts, probably not accidentally, were running along lines parallel to those of Stinnes, who was coming to the conclusion that the electrotechnical group in the SRSU had to take up turbine, locomotive, and Diesel motor construction. Siemens initially reacted to these ideas somewhat critically because of the shortage of skilled workers and their low productivity, but he had also come to feel that it was a mistake for Siemens to limit itself to electrotechnical production. In any case, Stinnes pursued the idea with his usual intensity.[142]

These questions of turbine and motor construction once again

---

[141] See the minute of ter Meer of January 24, 1922, and a report to Siemens of January 30, 1922, in SAA 4/Lf 635, as well as the correspondence in *ibid.*, 4/Lf 635/1. On Gehres, see Wenzel, *Wirtschaftsführer*, p. 704.

[142] Vögler to Siemens, August 16, 1922, SAA 4/Lf 635/1, and SRSU Council meeting, September 26, 1921, *ibid.*, Nachlass Haller, 11/Lb 108.

brought the SRSU into contact with the MAN and reopened the question of collaboration. Of course, it was necessary to bring Reusch into all agreements now, but the relationship between Reusch and Vögler was a good one, and Reusch understood the importance of maintaining the MAN's collaboration with Siemens. Such cooperation was particularly important to the MAN Nürnberg, which received 70% of its turbine orders from Siemens and was running into difficulty because of inadequate coordination between its turbine production and Siemens' generator production. This was of great importance for the development of Diesel motors. Reusch wanted to solve this problem by consolidating the MAN-Siemens construction bureaus in Berlin, but Vögler felt that more was needed from Reusch by way of financial investment, expansion, and coordination of production.[143]

When Stinnes entered into the discussions in March 1922, he did so with his characteristic opposition to half-measures. He was worried about increasing AEG competition and was impressed by the way in which the AEG and Linke-Hofmann had successfully coordinated their generator and turbine production. Furthermore, the great engineer of the Rheinish-Westfälische Elektrizitätswerke, Goldenberg, had once told him that the combination of these two objects of production in the same place could be rich in technical consequences. Consequently, Stinnes came to the conclusion that the SRSU had to control its own turbine production and that Reusch would have to bring this part of the MAN's activity within the framework of the SRSU if the happy relationship between Siemens and the MAN were to continue. Reusch suggested milder forms of association, particularly through joint participation in the expansion of locomotive and turbine construction at the Neumeyer works in Munich, but Stinnes was insistent that this would not solve his problem, and Köttgen tried to sell the SRSU to Reusch by arguing that the size of the SRSU and its huge sales operation required that it be in a "position to deliver complete plants from the foundations to the last piece of equipment."[144]

In private conversation among the SRSU leaders, however, only Stinnes seemed prepared to stick to his extreme position. He stubbornly insisted, against the views of Köttgen and Vögler, that the two types of production had to be conducted on the same site and, to their horror, went so far as to suggest that the Siemensstadt production could be moved to Nürnberg or vice versa. Vögler and Köttgen were not taken with the idea of uprooting enormous amounts of equipment and

[143] Vögler to Siemens, July 9, 1921, *ibid.*, 4/Lf 635/1.
[144] Report on a discussion in Nürnberg, March 7, 1922, HA/GHH, Nr. 300193010/17.

abandoning large groups of skilled workers, and they were unprepared to duplicate the MAN's work in the turbine field as threatened by Stinnes because "this will demand monumental amounts of money and labor and will take a very long time."[145]

The conflict between Stinnes and Vögler was an old one. Vögler had continuously warned against excessive acquisitions and overexpansion at Deutsch-Lux, often in vain. In collaboration with Köttgen after the founding of the SRSU, he took a critical attitude toward the almost daily inquiries by firms seeking to join the SRSU. Köttgen felt that they had to distinguish between requests made for association because of what he called a "vertical point of view"[146] and those made simply to solve liquidity problems. Vögler was prepared to consider combinations with other firms only if they did not cost much capital and seemed to hold a certain promise of advantage in the disposal of inventories. Both Köttgen and Vögler shared a common anxiety that they would run short of operating capital, and this became a major problem in 1922. As will be shown in the next chapter, the SRSU certainly helped the member concerns to raise working capital from the private banks and the Reichsbank and to organize the distribution of this money more efficiently than would have been the case otherwise, but the funds were not available for Stinnes to carry out his threats against Reusch. By the second half of 1922 more conservative policies took hold, and Stinnes was telling Siemens "to get into contact with all its customers who have ordered large equipment and see to it that no more machines are begun than can actually be received and paid for."[147] From the standpoint of the further development of the SRSU production program, such as it was, this situation could only mean stagnation in the attempt to chart a coherent course of development.

It is doubtful, however, that such coherence was possible for the SRSU. What, after all, was the "vertical point of view" Köttgen talked about? For Stinnes it seemed to be some vague notion that all forms of production were ultimately connected, and because he was interested in producing and marketing practically everything, the possibilities of vertical combination were almost boundless. This is not to say that Stinnes did not have visions of the future potentialities in many areas of production, but the times were not propitious for their realization, and he did not have the knowledge to master the questions of detail. For Vögler and Reusch, and probably for Köttgen, the "ver-

[145] *Ibid.*

[146] Köttgen to Vögler, March 29, 1921, and Vögler to Köttgen, April 1, 1921, SAA, Nachlass Köttgen, 11/Lf 104.

[147] SRSU Finance Committee, June 27, 1922, *ibid.*, Lb 82.

tical point of view," involved expansion within a defined domain, and the problem with the SRSU was that the domain had been defined so broadly as to lack coherence.

Ultimately, the SRSU must be presented to history as men like Werner and Köttgen tried to present it to potential new members. They were correct in emphasizing that it offered a larger capital base with greater opportunities for gaining credit than that possessed by other concerns and that it offered an enormous network of marketing outlets both at home and abroad. Furthermore, to argue that the SRSU was unable to create a coherent production program and that its promise in the area of raw materials supply was overblown is not to say that the SRSU did not serve its members in very important areas during the period under discussion. In addition to the major areas described above, there were also a wide variety of forms of collaboration of mutual advantage, particularly where personal relationships were as excellent as those between Vögler and Köttgen. For example, Vögler would volunteer his services to Siemens by offering to cause difficulties at a Rheinmetall stockholders meeting where the AEG was planning to bid for control. Stinnes would heed a request by Köttgen to use his influence as a major stockholder in a mining company to get a contract for Siemens that would otherwise have gone to the AEG. Köttgen and Vögler would collaborate in trying to keep great machine industry concerns such as the MAN and DEMAG from feeling deprived of orders by carefully coordinating their business policies.[148]

Lastly, the political character of the SRSU must not be forgotten. Köttgen fought against criticisms of the pricing policies of the steel industrialists in his own trade association and in meetings at the RWM, and he did so with statistical material and arguments supplied by Vögler. Similarly, he battled against the free trade policies prevalent in his industry's trade association. In October 1921, the IG members met to agree on a common policy toward the various tax measures being considered by the Reichstag and government, and thanks to its connection with Siemens, heavy industry now had entré to deputies from the left-wing bourgeoisie parties as well as to its friends in the DNVP and DVP.[149] Vertical concentration was a major means of ensuring that "friendly cooperation" between heavy industry and the manufacturing industries that had been so hard to achieve during the previous years. The undermining of the EWB and the gradual mobili-

[148] For these examples, see Vögler to Siemens, July 12, 1921, *ibid.*, 4/Lf 635/1; Köttgen to Stinnes, March 24, 1921, *ibid.*, Nachlass Köttgen, 11/Lf 265; and the correspondence between Köttgen and Vögler of May–June 1921 in *ibid.*

[149] See the Vögler-Köttgen correspondence of November 1921 in *ibid.* and discussion in the SRSU of the new tax bills on October 11, 1921, in *ibid.*, 11/Lf 104.

zation against all aspects of the regulated economy that had emerged from the war must be understood against this background of vertical concentration, which helped to disintegrate such brief identification between the primary and the final consumer as there had been. Vertical concentration during the inflation, whatever its successes and failures from the standpoint of business and productive operations, was therefore extremely important in strengthening the economic and political power of heavy industry and of promoting collaboration between rival sectors of big business. It was a fundamental factor in the way in which the industries involved dealt with hyperinflation in 1922–1923.

CHAPTER FIVE

1922: From Low Interest to High Principle

In 1922–1923 rapidly increasing inflation gave way to hyperinflation and culminated in the collapse of the mark and the subsequent stabilization. It is unpolitical and unhistorical to interpret the German inflation as the consequence of "passivity" and "lack of policy" dictated by prevailing economic theories and fear of the political consequences of mass unemployment.[1] Leaving aside the question of how passivity in the face of inflation for political reasons can be described as "lack of policy," one must note that so benign a presentation is extremely misleading because it veils the continuity of policy as Germany moved from inflation to hyperinflation and even to stabilization.

Certainly it is true that by means of her protracted inflation, Germany and certain groups within German society bought time and advantage in dealing with a host of internal and external problems that appeared insoluble by more conventional economic methods. Informed contemporaries both without and within German society well understood that Germany's low mark "enabled her to return to her former overseas market and to open up new ones" and "saved Germany from the crushing burden of unemployment under which the remainder of the world has laboured so heavily." They could only conclude "that there must be a large section—or perhaps it would be better to say a powerful section—of the German nation which considers a low rate of exchange its most effective commercial weapon, and is in no hurry to lay it aside. . . ."[2] Prevailing economic theory may have indirectly buttressed the deliberate policy of using inflation to reconstruct the German industrial plant, regain world markets through an export drive, and support relative social stability at home through the maintenance of high employment levels. Ernst Troeltsch nevertheless came very close to analyzing the real source of German policy when, in 1922, he wrote of *Der Staat der Grossindustrie*, and expressed fear that the authority of the state would be buried by big business's effort to dominate it.[3]

[1] Laursen and Pedersen, *German Inflation*, p. 123.

[2] J. W. F. Thelwall and C. J. Kavanagh, *Report on the Economic and Financial Conditions in Germany to March, 1922* (Board of Overseas Trade) (London, 1922), pp. 8–9.

[3] Ernst Troeltsch, *Spektator-Briefe. Aufsätze über die deutsche Revolution und die Weltpolitik 1918/1922* (Tübingen, 1924), p. 241ff.

"What do you think of the condition of German Industry?"

"Catastrophically, favorable."

From *Simplicissimus*, Vol. 26, No. 40 (January 1, 1922), p. 543. By E. Thöny. Courtesy of Michael Thöny.

"Passivity" in the face of mounting inflation may have been encouraged by the dogma that stabilization could not be attempted until reparations demands were reduced to an "acceptable" level and Germany received a foreign loan, although there certainly were those both inside and outside the government who understood that the prerequisite for a foreign loan was that Germany put her economic house in order. In any case, the most dogmatic expressions of the aforementioned dogma often came from heavy industrialists, who blocked government efforts at fulfillment of the treaty through a conciliatory policy abroad and a rigorous taxation policy at home.[4]

Such considerations serve as a warning against a historicist acceptance of events as they transpired, against a myopic appreciation of the German inflation for real and exaggerated benefits that overlooks the actual interests that were being served. Germany was doomed to a particular type of stabilization in large measure because of the socio-political conditions of the Weimar Republic. In examining the concluding period of accelerated inflation, hyperinflation, and stabilization, therefore, it is necessary to concentrate on the terms on which the inflation was to be ended and the stabilization effected and on the question of which industrial groups would emerge with the tactical advantages so fundamental for the determination of subsequent socio-economic policy. As has been shown, the great industrialists, especially the leaders of heavy industry, had managed to seize the tactical advantage during the demobilization, the inflationary upsurge at the turn of 1919–1920, and the relative stability of 1921 to either evade government controls or diminish their effectiveness, while at the same time they had managed to create bastions of economic power through vertical concentration. How would they fare in 1922–1923 under the impact of intensifying inflation and political disorder?

The answer to this question was very much a function of industrial politics as pursued by the leaders of heavy industry during these years, but its development did not run along the smooth path that might make either its description or its comprehension easy. The years 1922–1923 will be treated in separate chapters despite a certain overlapping of economic conditions from 1921 to 1922 and from 1922 to

---

[4] For new perspectives on the reparations question, see Peter Krüger, "Die Rolle der Banken und der Industrie in den deutschen reparationspolitischen Entscheidungen nach dem Ersten Weltkreig," in *Industrielles System*, pp. 568–582, and Hermann J. Rupieper, "Industrie und Reparationen: Einige Aspekte des Reparationsproblems 1922–1924," in *ibid.*, pp. 582–592. Also, Peter Krüger, *Deutschland und die Reparationen 1918/1919. Die Genesis des Reparationsproblems in Deutschland zwischen Waffenstillstand und Versailler Friedensschluss* (Stuttgart, 1973), and Ernst Laubach, *Die Politik der Kabinette Wirth 1921/22* (Lübeck and Hamburg, 1968).

1923 because the Ruhr occupation in January 1923 marks an interruption in the kind of dénouement to the story presaged by developments in 1922. The Ruhr occupation suddenly revives many of the accommodations and conceptions that had developed during the war and demobilization and that were breaking down at the end of 1922. In 1923, it almost seemed as if history were providing a précis of itself through a relatively rapid and traumatic recapitulation of some of the most basic tendencies of the previous few years.

These stormy concluding two years of the inflation, however, are also ones in which there was an increasing effort by the leaders of heavy industry to realign what might be called the "lower" and "higher" levels of business policy. It must be remembered that the industrialists performed a variety of roles necessarily productive of inner conflict. Understandably, their primary concern was the fate of the enterprises for which they were responsible, but even here there were difficulties of distinguishing between the interests of the stockholders and the interests of the enterprise. Furthermore, what seemed good for one aspect of a concern's operations was not necessarily good for another, and conflicts among coal, iron, and finishing interests were often conflicts within concerns themselves as well as conflicts among different branches of industry. Thus, even within concerns there were different interests that divided leaders from one another and within themselves. In times of crisis and high risk demanding unusual behavior because the margin at which one was operating was anything but clear, a great many of the decisions taken seem unintelligible because they were in fact confusing and confused. And how much more was this the case when the economic policies of the concern, of the industries of which it was a member, and of the state had to be brought into consonance? The presumption that public interest and private interest should be in harmony may be viewed as the cant of businessmen in the twentieth century, but it is extraordinarily difficult for great industrialists, in their capacity as "economic leaders," to sustain themselves comfortably for a long period under conditions where they are convinced that general economic policies are mistaken, and that they themselves are pursuing policies that, however necessary at one level, will ultimately revenge themselves. The capitalist ethic and the managerial ethic are heavily laden with notions of sin and retribution which operate at all levels of functional behavior. Business opportunities must be grasped, or the concern will lose to its competitors; immediate dangers must be dealt with at all costs, or the concern will become their victim. Yet contraction must follow expansion, bust must follow boom, and great violations of "economic laws" must be followed by great penalties. Economies must be "cleansed," and the *Sanierung*,

283

however painful to all participants in the economic order, must ultimately strengthen the strong while eliminating the weak. As "economic leaders" and representatives of *Die Wirtschaft*, the industrialists believed these things and felt a responsibility to bring socioeconomic policy into line with the "realities" as they saw them.

In sum, the various functional roles of the industrialists provided a large range of rationalizations covering a multitude of sinful and virtuous actions, from the most selfish pursuit of self-interest as an expression of their primary obligation to their enterprises, "low policy," to lofty demands connected with state policy on both the domestic and foreign fronts, "high policy." But most of the industrialists would have been less than human if they could have been basically satisfied with a condition in which they felt that their own policies were not consonant with the general welfare of the economy, and if they did not presume a harmony between their prescriptions and what was required by the nation as a whole. The pursuit of a "lower policy" had to be rationalized by the inability to pursue a "higher policy," and opportunities to break through to the harmonization of the two were continuously being sought. It was this uncomfortable engagement in dangerous "low policies" and the effort to develop and implement a "higher" policy, as well as the oscillation between the two, that characterize heavy industrialist behavior in 1922–1923, that render its confused character somewhat intelligible, and that bring this study itself now into more direct contact with the broader and more familiar sociopolitical problems of the history of the Weimar Republic.

THE LAST FLING

Commencing in the spring of 1921, when Germany accepted the London Ultimatum, the external value of the mark was seriously and regularly influenced by the reparations problem and other exogenous influences arising from the peace treaty. Domestic and foreign speculators as well as all those who had cause to deal in international currency transactions were continuously responding to the various crises surrounding the implementation of the peace treaty. Such responses not only occurred on the occasion of real losses, such as the Upper Silesian settlement in the fall of 1921, and the actual German payments in foreign currency under the London Ultimatum, which did not begin until August 1921 and which terminated in July 1922, but also took place to the tune of international politics as played out in the various successes and failures in the negotiations pertaining to reparations moratoria, foreign loans to Germany, and government changes and domestic crises in Germany and France. Furthermore, the value of the mark had been rendered all the more parlous by Reichstag legislation of May 8, 1921 which, for the coming three years, relieved the Reichsbank of the requirement that it maintain a one-third reserve for its outstanding bank notes and thereby eliminated all remaining restrictions on its issuance of notes.[5]

The great German heavy industrialists were not passive spectators or outsiders to these events. Rather, they directly influenced them, and more frequently than not in a negative direction. The classic instance of the latter was the so-called credit action of the Reich Association of German Industry between September and November 1921, an "action" that degenerated into inaction because the plan was sabotaged by Hugenberg, Stinnes, Hasslacher, and other leaders of heavy industry. The plan would use industry's credit abroad as a means of guaranteeing a foreign loan to help German economic recovery while compensating industry for its assistance and acceptance of various compulsory measures toward this end by means of significant tax benefits. Both important industrialists in the Wirth Cabinet, particularly Walther Rathenau, and its leading industrialist supporters, Directors Wiedfeldt and Sorge of Krupp, Hans von Raumer, and Carl Duisberg, intended it to become a way both to ward off growing sentiment for compulsory seizure of "real values" in the hands of the industrialists and to make a positive contribution toward the policy of "fulfillment" while simultaneously securing foreign assistance and a greater foreign commitment to Germany's economic future. Hugenberg's opposition was frankly political; he opposed the stabilization of the democratic state. Paul Silverberg of the mining industry, as well as Hasslacher and Stinnes, however, opposed the policy of fulfillment on the grounds that it would not work and objected to the compulsory aspects of the plan. Although it was impossible to make a really effective response to Wiedfeldt's charge that compulsion was necessary because it was evident that those who had not volunteered their exchange to the government for the August reparations payment had made fools of those who had because that foreign exchange had doubled and tripled its value in marks by November, it was no less evident that Hasslacher and Stinnes had no intention of giving up their foreign exchange if they could avoid doing so. Stinnes intimated that industry might give up more exchange voluntarily, but made the denationalization of the railroad system a precondition for the credit action. More broadly, he demanded the freeing of industry from its bonds—a none-too-subtle reference to the eight-hour day as well as all other aspects of the "controlled economy"—and a conservative budgetary policy. Although the Wirth government was by no means unsympathetic to some of the

[5] See Appendix I and Bresciani-Turroni, *Economics of Inflation*, p. 55ff.

policies Stinnes advocated, it was not prepared to turn the state-run enterprises over to private hands and have them serve as a guarantee to industry that it would be repaid its financial sacrifices on behalf of the Reich. Stinnes, and with him an important segment of German industry, had made it clear that they would not lend their weight to stabilization except on their own terms. Because the Wirth government was politically too weak to impose its terms on industry and unable to implement the effective taxation policy and control of the printing press that were the keys to terminating the inflation, the result was a stalemate in which "high policy" was surrendered to "low policy."[6]

All of German heavy industry was not prepared to join Stinnes in consciously and unhesitatingly promoting the disastrous drift into hyperinflation in 1922. There was a general belief and hope until the second half of 1921 that the relative stabilization of the mark since the late winter of 1920 would have permanent results. In the last months of 1921, however, this attitude gave way to a greater fatalism about the continuation of inflation and an increasing proclivity to adapt to it in a "semi-automatic" manner.[7] In short, the tendency to resist the further development of inflation deteriorated, but in contrast to 1919–1920, this surrender to inflation was not accompanied by quite the same tension between producers and primary consumers that had characterized the wild pricing and hoarding of raw materials at the earlier time. Rather, it was characterized by an increasing and relatively successful effort of mutual accommodation within the framework of galloping inflation.

These proclivities were already on the march at the end of 1921 when, it will be recalled, coal shortages, reduced iron and steel production, increased domestic demand, and rapid mark depreciation seemed to presage a return to the unhappy conditions at the turn of 1919–1920. Responses to the situation were rather different, however. A very major step toward the automatic adjustment of steel prices to increasing costs was taken on November 9, when the EWB Inland Commission voted that 3.50 M per ton for iron and steel was to be added for every one mark increase per ton in the price of coal. This rather schematic approach was revised in January, when a scale of automatic increases was set up based on the amount of coke and coal

---

[6] On the credit action, see the important and stimulating article by Lothar Albertin, "Die Verantwortung der liberalen Parteien für das Scheitern der Grossen Koalition im Herbst 1921. Ökonomische und ideologische Einflüsse auf die Funktionsfähigkeit der parteienstaatlichen Demokratie," *Historische Zeitschrift*, 205 (1967), pp. 566–627, and Laubach, *Kabinette Wirth*, p. 84ff.

[7] Czada in *Schriften des Vereins für Sozialpolitik*, 73, p. 28.

employed in the production of various types of iron and steel products, but the November action set the basic precedent of automatically pegging iron and steel price increases to basic cost increases.[8]

The introduction of a "coal clause" did not eliminate debate concerning steel pricing, but there was an unquestionable tendency for all sides to be "reasonable." Thus, when the RWM sent a memorandum to the EWB at the beginning of December urging a reduction of the guiding prices for steel sold domestically on the grounds that the works were making a large export profit, the Inland Commission did the reverse of what the RWM requested when it met in the middle of the month. It responded to the deterioration of the mark during the previous weeks and to increased production costs by supporting a substantial increase in the guiding prices—that is, it followed the recommendations of the producers. In contrast to 1919–1920, the latter maintained discipline and renewed the Pig Iron Syndicate.[9] This renewed interest in organization did not reflect a concern with consumer interests, however. As was to become quite apparent throughout 1922, those industries that were organized and syndicalized were in a much better position to respond effectively to galloping inflation than those that were not. At the same time, heavy industry had learned that if it did not maintain its organizations, the government and consumers would dictate policy, and that a more conciliatory policy had to be adopted whenever possible. When the RWM called for the reintroduction of price ceilings, only the metalworker (DMV) representatives on the EWB backed the idea, whereas the other labor representatives along with the consumers joined with the producers in opposing ceilings. In return, the producers relinquished some of the independence to set prices that the Steel Federation had regained when an EWB committee of twelve representatives of producers, consumers, and merchants based on parity between labor and management was set up to review Steel Federation decisions.[10]

Undoubtedly, the bad experiences with the EWB and price ceilings contributed to this compromise, as did the increased interlocking of producer and consumer interests through vertical concentration. There was also a sense, however, that the turn of 1921–1922 was more like the turn of 1920–1921 than like the turn of 1919–1920. In all three cases, fuel problems and reduced productivity and mark depreciation had caused anxiety about future supplies and led to a spurt in demand, but only the first case had been fairly protracted. At the turn of 1921–1922 the tempo of inflation and demand seemed to be slowing down, just

[8] *Kölnische Zeitung*, December 16, 1921, and January 7, 1922.
[9] *Ibid.*, December 23–24, 1921, and Klotzbach, *Roheisen-Verband*, p. 240ff.
[10] See the RWM report of January 24, 1922, in BA, R 43 I/1147, Bl. 284ff.

as it had in 1920–1921. Raw materials producers and manufacturers were quite busy, but they were largely engaged in filling back orders, and there was a holding back on new orders. Some speculated that the slowing of inflation and increased foreign competition would lead to a reduction of demand and of domestic prices. Under these circumstances, producers and consumers had little economic motivation for a repetition of the 1919–1920 performance. By March 1922, however, anticipations of reduced prices had evaporated as the decline of the mark resumed, and domestic prices began to keep pace with the dollar rate for the first time. Fear of renewed price increases on a more massive scale than ever before now drove up domestic demand, and the economy entered a renewed period of feverish activity in which the massive steel shortages of 1919–1920 were not to be repeated thanks to greatly increased production but in which many of the other sources of tension between consumers and producers could be revived.[11]

What had happened? The failure of the Cannes conference in January to produce the desired alleviation of the reparations burden and the appointment of Poincaré as French Prime Minister undermined the psychological expectations on which continued slowing down of inflation might have been based and encouraged renewed flights of capital and speculation against the mark. From December through February there were major railroad strikes which had severe economic and political effects, and major strikes occurred in the Düsseldorf and Dortmund iron and steel industry. The results of this severe labor unrest were short-term reductions in production and an acceleration of the constantly rising freight and labor costs. Reparation payments in kind, particularly in coking coal, created further hardships because there was a shortage of coke and pig iron, and Germany was compelled to import both these products, in which she had been self-sufficient before the war and in which she was potentially self-sufficient, in order to satisfy her immediate needs. These needs, however, were not the "natural" ones of her economy in 1922, but rather those created by a great flurry of demand on the domestic market, which reflected a renewed hoarding of goods and heavy expenditures on plant construction.

The rising costs and uncertainty in early 1922 were particularly alarming to many iron and steel producers because they could argue with some justification that they were incurring substantial losses on the orders they had accepted in September, October, and November

[11] See the RWM reports of January–June 1922 in *ibid.*, 1147–1148, for the discussion of economic conditions in the text as well as the monthly reports on economic conditions in *Stahl und Eisen*, 42:1–2. See also Bresciani-Turroni, *Economics of Inflation*, p. 23.

1921, orders they were filling and for which they were being paid in early 1922. The steel producers conformed to the stable price policy of the EWB and continued their own efforts in 1921 to sell at fixed prices, but the contracts they negotiated made no provision for the currency depreciation and increased costs. The steel producers thus faced a nasty dilemma. Any new major increases in costs would only make the losses on the old contracts even greater, whereas the effort to revise the old contracts, a procedure allowable under court decisions, was bound to make for unpleasantness in customer relations. Calculability seemed to be vanishing once again under the wave of higher costs, which also threatened exports because of the tendency of domestic prices to keep up with the dollar rate. Both steel producers and their primary consumers had outstanding contracts on which they might suffer large losses, and both groups faced rising domestic costs which jeopardized their export ability. When Stinnes, Silverberg, and other leaders of the coal industry began to fight for a massive increase in coal prices in January and February 1922, therefore, most steel producers and primary consumers joined in opposition to this policy.

The battle between Stinnes and his allies in the coal industry, on the one hand, and the coal consumers, on the other, was fought out not only in the Reich Coal Council at the end of January but also in the highest councils of the Reich Association of German Industry, to which it was brought by angry consumers on February 22, 1922. In this conflict, Stinnes found himself ranged not only against traditional moderates in pricing matters such as Reusch and Wiedfeldt, but also against Hasslacher and even his trusted General Director, Vögler, as well as against leaders of the manufacturing industries such as Funcke, Guggenheimer, and Reuter.[12] Stinnes insisted that the time had come to bring coal prices up to world market levels because this was the only way Germany could become self-sufficient in coal again with respect to both quality and quantity. He pointed out that Germany was already importing large amounts of English coal, and that it was dysfunctional to pay world market prices for this coal while continuing to sell German coal at 60% of the world market price. Furthermore, the British, upset at the manner in which German reparations coal was going to the French at the domestic German price, were also demanding that the Germans raise their prices. Reiterating the views he had been expressing since 1920, Stinnes argued that the German coal industry had neglected its obligation to expand its production by open-

[12] See Woltmann to Reusch, February 16, 1922, HA/GHH, Nr. 30019323/8; RdI meeting of February 22, 1922, in *ibid.*, Nr. 30019320/2; Steel Federation meeting of February 28/March 1, 1922, in *ibid.*, Nr. 3000035/3; Rheinstahl supervisory board meeting, April 3, 1922, Rheinstahl Archiv, Nr. 123.

ing new shafts and especially to improve the quality of its production by building new cokeries since the war. Such expansion was necessary now if Germany were to achieve the self-sufficiency she needed. If there was sufficient production, then it would also be possible to end the regulation of coal distribution and related controls. Above all, however, Stinnes presented the coal price increase he supported as a part of his general policy of employing the inflation to build up German industry to maximum strength and advantage for the eventual stabilization. He noted the iron industry had every reason to support the coal industry because its future depended on Germany's coking capacity. With the birth rate decreasing, Germany would someday lack the body of miners and shafts needed if she did not use the opportunity now presented to create a basis for the industry's future: "For now is the last moment in which to build the shafts and the coking ovens from the needed price increase of coal. Once the stabilization of the currency has taken place, then we will have the same struggles the other countries are going through. In order to endure them, we must undertake the necessary preparations now."[13] Hence, Stinnes and Silverberg objected to the idea that the coal tax might be increased as a means of satisfying the British demand for a diminution of the difference between the German and world market price of coal. This danger that the government might tax away the price difference was precisely what had triggered the extreme level of the coal industry's demands. The industry wanted the whole difference to finance its own expansion and did not want the money to flow into the state's coffers any more than it was willing to raise money by the normal means of going to the capital market.

Funcke of the iron wares industry objected along with his colleagues to viewing everything from the perspective of the coal industry and was unmoved by Stinnes' long-range considerations because the immediate consequences would be so devastating. Funcke warned that steel prices would be driven beyond world market prices, and Germany would cease to be competitive abroad. Hence, he could only support a limited coal price increase and pointed out "that naturally this increase cannot be the means for new plant construction, and one must turn much more to the capital market for this purpose."[14] These objections were quite to the point. Many businessmen were more than slightly suspicious that Stinnes was looking after his own interests at the expense

[13] RdI meeting of February 22, 1922, HA/GHH, Nr. 30019320/2, and Stinnes at the Reich Coal Council meeting, January 24, 1922, BA, Nachlass Silverberg, Nr. 148, Bl. 20ff. For the 1920 arguments, see Maier, *Recasting Bourgeois Europe*, pp. 213–215.

[14] RdI meeting, February 22, 1922, HA/GHH, Nr. 30019320/2.

of everyone else. In this they were correct, for Stinnes did indeed hope, among other things, that the coal price increase would enable the heavy industrial group in the SRSU to finance its construction projects without turning to outside sources of capital. These projects were by no means solely in the coal mining field, and many of Stinnes' critics in the Reich Association meeting on February 22 noted that there would be no way to control the actual use of funds gained from the coal price increase without setting up new onerous controls.[15]

Leading steel men, however, were no less critical than the manufacturers. Reusch opposed an immediate effort to attain world market prices and thought the time chosen particularly unfortunate because of its great uncertainties. He believed in a gradual adjustment to world market prices, hopefully through an improvement of Germany's currency, that would finally put an end to the wage-price spiral. He accused the mining industry of failing to do enough to improve its plant in the past and argued that it was wrong to expect everyone to pay the price of its failures. Some of the sharpest criticism came from Vögler, however, who questioned the value of the coal price increase for plant expansion in the coal industry and thus, by implication, for its intended use in the self-financing of the IG, and argued that such an increase would simply further destabilize the economy by increasing all other costs and promoting sliding-scale prices. He considered the latter undesirable in both the iron producing and manufacturing industries, and Vögler also warned that wage increases without productivity increases would only perpetuate the crisis.[16]

The conflict here was between a conventional wisdom, as reflected in the remarks of Reusch, Vögler, and their concurring colleague Wiedfeldt, and the unconventional wisdom of Stinnes. Whereas the former wished to benefit from the export advantages of the inflation, they feared that promotion of the inflation would undo these advantages by intensifying its pace to the point of its yielding no further returns. Hence one had to benefit where one could but work for stabilization by the conventional means of fighting increased labor and materials costs and trying to improve productivity. At this time, however, Stinnes was arguing that "with our workers we can never attain higher production,"[17] and chose to emphasize quality improvements instead. Improved coking would reduce transport costs because less coal would

---

[15] *Ibid.* For an illustration of the suspicions concerning Stinnes' motives, see Wieland to Reusch, February 8, 1922, in *ibid.*, Nr. 30019390/29. On the SRSU plans to use the coal price increase profits for expansion, see the SRSU Finance Committee meeting of January 12, 1922, SAA 54/Lm 123.

[16] RdI meeting of February 22, 1922, HA/GHH, Nr. 30019320/2.

[17] *Ibid.*

have to be transported and wasted. At the same time, he and his supporters played down the role of wages in coal costs by pointing out that the German miner was making three shillings a day whereas the British miner was making between eight and ten shillings per day, and he implied that whatever the coal mining firms did not take from the increase in coal prices the miners were going to demand in higher wages anyway. As usual, Stinnes was prepared to give the workers "their due," just so long as he was able to take what he felt due him as well, and he seemed convinced that it was to industry's advantage not only to bear more inflation but even to promote it at this point. The Reich Association of German Industry, which was never very effective when different points of view clashed head on, was in no position to truly reconcile these differences of opinion. The Business Manager, Dr. Bücher, sagely concluded the meeting of February 22 by declaring that both sides had a point and urged the coal mining industry leaders to keep in mind the recent wave of increased costs and prices when determining its price increase. On March 1, 1922, coal prices went up 133 marks per ton.

For the moment, the coal price increase did some of the things Stinnes said it would do, for as Reusch anticipated, the "profit from coal is now completely satisfactory; the mines can now make the necessary new outlays out of their profits."[18] As he, Vögler, and others had feared, however, the battle over the tempo of adjustment to inflation now simply shifted to other quarters, namely their own. The old 1921 contracts appeared even more financially disastrous after the coal price increase, and the calculation of domestic prices was more difficult than ever. At the same time, there was much talk of a "latent inventory crisis," and a general recognition that the export market could not be taken for granted now that there was increasing competition in iron and steel from France and England and not, as previously, from Belgium alone. To be sure, not all optimism had evaporated with regard to exports, and the steel industry launched a big advertising campaign abroad in May 1922.[19] Yet Germany's competition was stronger and German exporters, confronted with decreasing foreign production costs, tariff barriers, and, frequently, the need to offer a "hate rebate" (Hassrabatt) as an inducement to former enemies to buy German goods, faced an uncertain future. Anxieties over the foreign market only served to intensify the problem of making the overheated domestic market pay as much as it could bear for as long as the "flight into

[18] Concern meeting, February 27, 1922, MAN Werksarchiv Augsburg, Nr. K 56.

[19] The decision was taken at a meeting of April 27, 1922. See Steel Works Association to Reusch, May 3, 1922, HA/GHH, Nr. 3000030/20.

goods" lasted. The coal price increase of March 1 simply gave the coup de grâce to the already much regretted stable pricing policy of 1921, and the fateful turn toward sliding-scale prices had become unavoidable.

In the iron and steel industry, the formal change from stable to sliding-scale prices took place at the Steel Federation meetings of February 28–March 1, 1922, meetings interesting not only because of this change but also because they became typical of the continuing battle that was to be fought for the rest of the year over the character of pricing policy.[20] As usual, Ernst Poensgen chaired the meeting, and he skillfully based the discussion on the assumption that a major change of policy was inevitable. He explained at great length that this was necessitated by the "complete incalculability of present and especially future circumstances," made a point of mentioning the "coal pricing policy being pursued against the resistance of the iron industry," and emphasized that the member works had been losing money under the stable guiding prices of the past, which often failed to cover soaring costs even at the moment they were being set. Many of the concerns wanted to eliminate every constraint and have complete freedom in setting their prices, and Poensgen warned that "at the very least we must introduce sliding prices from here on despite all the serious reservations that can be made against them." The proposal for complete freedom in the setting of prices was not a ploy, because it won by a narrow margin of 169 to 166, and it is a measure of the uncertainty concerning the advisability of taking this drastic step that the Thyssen and Stumm concerns divided their votes on the question. The very moderate Director Klemme of the GHH voted against the motion only "because the proponents of freeing prices largely stood in the camp that lacked any sense of moderation in setting prices and would have . . . hastened the collapse of the price structure."

Given the narrowness of the margin, the producers did not feel that they could seriously seek to impose their will in this respect on the manufacturers and merchants and settled instead for sliding-scale prices—that is, prices that left open adjustment for changes in costs between the date on which an order was placed and the date on which delivery was made. As the meeting with the consumers on the afternoon of February 28 demonstrated, however, this was a wise tactic because the latter came to terms with sliding prices "relatively easily." They, too, were saddled with contracts from 1921 that were making things difficult, and they could hardly deny the producers that which

[20] The discussion and quotations that follow are taken from the reports by Director Klemme of the GHH in HA/GHH, Nr. 3000035/3.

293

they wanted for themselves. Thus, producers and manufacturers were united in their willingness to abandon fixed prices.[21] They also agreed that foreign exchange could be demanded for raw materials to be used in manufactured products for export. In contrast to 1919–1920, this practice was now viewed as advantageous because it permitted both producer and manufacturer to calculate on a more solid basis. What it meant, however, was that a substantial amount of domestic business in Germany would now be calculated and paid in foreign currency.

There was considerably more disagreement over the extent of the increase to be made in the guiding prices, particularly among the producers, where the moderates representing Klöckner, Krupp, and the GHH argued for a 1,000-mark increase whereas Filius of Rheinstahl and Trowe of Hoesch characteristically led the extremists with a demand for a 2,000-mark increase before compromising on the 1,500-mark increase that had been calculated to be the actual increase in costs since February 1. This compromise was then presented as a non-negotiable demand to the manufacturers and merchants, who were offended by the *Diktat* but were divided over its justifiability. Whereas some thought 1,500 marks excessive, others argued that "under the present business conditions an increase of 1,500 marks could still be bearable and wanted willingly to give the works something in view of the great losses which the works had suffered in the past." As usual, Baron von Buttlar was not sympathetic to the producers, but it is interesting that the 1,100-mark increase he proposed actually exceeded the 1,000-mark increase advocated by the moderate producers. The final decision was to accept the 1,500-mark increase with 100-mark reductions for certain rolled products (see Table 12).

This sort of haggling was to continue throughout the year and, as will be shown, was to take on a particularly bizarre quality as the figures discussed became more and more astronomical. The difficult problem is to explain what can be learned about industrial problems and attitudes during this chaotic period from these rather peculiar pricing debates, a problem that would be difficult even were one dealing with "normal" pricing discussions under "normal" conditions. The differences among the producers with regard to pricing policy must be explained in terms of differences in the situations of the various firms and concerns involved as well as in terms of the differing styles of the various industrial leaders. Although information on such matters is difficult to come by, there is fortunately some information available on two concerns that stood as antipodes in the pricing discussions, the GHH and Rheinstahl and their respective general directors, Reusch

[21] *Ibid.*, and *Kölnische Zeitung*, March 27, 1922.

TABLE 12

The Price of Various Iron and Steel Products in 1922
(price per ton measured in paper and gold marks)

		January	February	March	April	May	June	July	August	September	October	November	December
Foundry pig iron III	PM	3,250	3,371	4,136	5,473	5,800	6,136	7,845	11,951	26,044	34,591	92,800	157,475
	GM	71.13	68.09	61.10	78.95	83.93	81.15	67.61	47.68	75.01	48.05	54.93	88.20
Hematite pig iron	PM	3,891	3,979	4,744	6,264	6,435	6,724	8,265	13,802	30,004	40,334	113,754	175,858
	GM	85.16	80.38	70.08	90.36	93.12	88.92	70.35	51.07	85.93	53.23	66.48	97.28
Billets	PM	4,230	4,680	5,945	8,270	8,270	8,525	9,660	18,518	38,750	62,558	156,397	236,994
	GM	92.58	94.54	87.82	119.30	119.67	112.74	82.23	68.52	110.97	82.56	91.40	131.09
Girders	PM	4,930	5,440	6,920	9,635	9,635	9,937	11,290	21,642	45,463	73,415	180,950	273,329
	GM	107.90	109.89	102.22	139.00	139.42	131.42	96.10	80.08	130.20	96.89	105.75	151.19
Merchant bars	PM	5,030	5,550	7,050	9,810	9,810	10,640	11,470	21,958	46,003	74,279	183,100	276,171
	GM	110.09	112.11	104.14	141.52	141.95	133.75	98.85	88.06	132.51	100.92	108.00	154.77
Heavy plate	PM	5,630	6,220	7,805	11,000	11,000	11,930	12,860	24,654	51,507	83,488	206,253	311,413
	GM	123.22	125.64	115.29	158.69	159.17	157.77	109.46	91.22	147.51	110.18	120.54	172.26

Source: Hans J. Schneider, Zur Analyse des Eisenmarktes (Vierteljahrshefte zur Konjunkturforschung, Sonderheft 1) (Berlin, 1927), p. 103.

and Hasslacher. The illustration is all the more interesting because these two men appear to have been quite friendly and to have been in general agreement on most political questions.

The moderate pricing policies of the GHH and Reusch can hardly be explained by the notion that they were having an easy time of it economically in early 1922. On February 10 Reusch instructed his subordinates not to make any new foreign ore purchases because the GHH did not have enough foreign exchange on hand. At the concern meeting on February 27, he told the finishing firms in the concern that they and other customers would have to supply more foreign currency from their exports to pay for supplies.[22] Throughout the preceding months, the GHH had sought to keep up with the demand of the concern works, a demand that had increased 80% while production necessary to meet it had increased only 25%. Reusch made it clear that this heavy supplying within the concern would have to be cut back as general domestic demand was increasing sharply. Obviously, however, the GHH had been supplying its concern members to such a high degree that it had suffered less than those iron and steel producers who had supplied outside customers to a greater extent during the period of rapid mark deterioration. Yet, as noted earlier, Klemme was tempted to support uncontrolled pricing at the February 28 meeting of the Steel Federation, and he did support sliding-scale pricing. Reusch could hardly afford to face increasing demand outside the concern during the coming months without such protection. Furthermore, for all its support of stable pricing, the GHH had contacted its customers who had placed orders in late 1921 and arrangements were made for retroactive additional payments for orders already delivered and for price revision in the case of orders still to be completed. In short, the GHH seems to have been somewhat less affected by the changed conditions between 1921 and 1922 than some other concerns, but it did have outside customers, and it was revising old contracts. The revision of old contracts seems to have been accomplished very smoothly, often at the initiative of customers themselves, and apparently this was due to the concern's excellent reputation as a supporter of stable prices and its relative reasonableness when requesting price changes.[23]

In substance, there was not much difference between the policies pursued by Hasslacher and Rheinstahl and those pursued by Reusch and the GHH, but it would seem that both the pressures on the former and the intensity of their response was much greater than in the case

[22] Concern meeting, February 27, 1922, MAN Werksarchiv Augsburg, Nr. K 56, and Reusch circular of February 10, 1922, HA/GHH, Nr. 30006/11.
[23] Klemme to Woltmann, December 27, 1923, *ibid.*, Nr. 300000/5.

of the latter. Hasslacher, like Reusch, seems to have supported stable prices in the fall of 1921, and they both opposed Stinnes' coal pricing policy. Once the major coal price increase had taken place, however, Hasslacher and his directors Filius and Esser became the leaders of an extreme response as evidenced by their posture at the Steel Federation meetings as well as by the rigor with which they pursued the revision of old contracts. One inspiration for Hasslacher's actions certainly becomes apparent if one looks ahead to Rheinstahl's general stockholders meeting of November 1922, where he was accused of losing millions in 1921–1922 by selling at stable prices. Hasslacher defended himself by arguing that the policy had been pursued for the benefit of the entire economy as well as to keep the rolling mills fully employed through the acceptance of small orders. He praised the Rheinstahl direction for being the first to recognize that the stable pricing policy would "have led to the ruin of German industry because of the continuing inflation,"[24] and he assured the stockholders that the concern had made up for the losses and had received additional payments on unprofitable contracts through "friendly agreement" with its customers. Clearly, the general directors of family-owned concerns like the GHH and Krupp were less subject to such open and sharp attacks on the way they conducted their business operations, particularly where the relationship between the chief stockholder and the general director was as close and supportive as that between Karl Haniel and Reusch. Hasslacher seemed to enjoy less maneuverability despite Otto Wolff's practice of leaving the practical running of affairs to general directors of companies in which he had a strong interest, and Hasslacher's approach to contract revision was not quite as "friendly" as he pretended.

Throughout March 1922, Rheinstahl's organizations sent letters to their customers reminding them that the courts had ruled that contracts could be annulled or revised where the terms had changed to the disfavor of either party as a consequence of circumstances arising from the war and revolution. Consequently, Rheinstahl was going to terminate contracts made in 1921 unless new prices could be agreed upon. In cases where the customer offered a price that Rheinstahl did not deem adequate, it was prepared to make delivery at the going price on the day of delivery so as not to do damage to the customer's operations and then have the ultimate price settled "in a friendly manner in court." When the GHH's Maschinenfabrik Esslingen received such a letter and failed to reach an agreement on price with Rheinstahl, Reusch decided to call in his lawyers and in so informing Hasslacher,

[24] *Kölnische Zeitung*, November 9, 1922.

concluded his letter with the remark that "I hope you do not take it ill if I here openly state that I think that the Rheinische Stahlwerke by its attitude on the pricing question is rendering a disservice to the entire German iron industry."[25] Soon thereafter, Rheinstahl's contract revision letters received even greater notoriety when one was sent by an angry customer to the *Kölnische Zeitung* for publication. This customer pointed out that Rheinstahl, which was not mentioned by name, and the other producers were begging for domestic orders between September and December 1921, and that it was difficult to understand why the steel producers should not share some of the difficulties faced by the rest of German industry. Hasslacher, however, was not very moved by either the private or the public criticisms.[26] He told his supervisory board in April that "It is indicative that it is not the customers, but rather the competition, to whom the expansion of our marketing organization is in any case a thorn in the flesh, that seeks to oppose us in the Iron Trades Federation as well as here and there with regard to prices. There can be no doubt, however, that with few exceptions there will be all along the line understandings with our customers on our terms or on the basis of a compromise, so that we can count with complete certainty on showing profits from the beginning of the second half of the business year."[27] As for Reusch's complaints, Hasslacher irritatedly informed Reusch that Rheinstahl's practices were no different than Thyssen's, and that the big complaints had not come from "consumers" but rather from "producers." Hasslacher obviously had the GHH in mind, and he reminded Reusch that "Your firm is in the fortunate position of supplying the largest portion of the products falling within the province of the Steel Federation to its own concern works and is not therefore as hard hit by developments as the other works."[28] Although Reusch denied that this was true at the time, April 1922, Hasslacher obviously had scored a point.

Yet the conflict between the GHH and Rheinstahl over pricing policy was to continue, and they remained at opposite ends of a spectrum whose variations reflected peculiar combinations of special interest, differing evaluation of the immediate and future situation, and differing and uncertain estimates of their own margins as well as of what the market would bear. The situation was not one that lent itself to

[25] Rheinische Handelsgesellschaft Stuttgart to Maschinenfabrik Esslingen, March 17, 1922, and Reusch to Hasslacher, April 1, 1922, in HA/GHH, Nr. 300193011/0.

[26] The concern involved was Rheinstahl, because the letter was exactly the same as that cited in the last note. See *Kölnische Zeitung*, May 30–31, 1922.

[27] Supervisory board meeting, April 3, 1922, Rheinstahl Archiv, Nr. 123.

[28] Hasslacher to Reusch, April 5, 1922, and Reusch to Hasslacher, April 10, 1922, HA/GHH, Nr. 30019390/4.

precise evaluation either on the part of the actors or on the part of the historian.

The leaders of the manufacturing industries participated in this helplessness and second guessing. As mentioned earlier, they had accepted sliding-scale pricing because they needed it themselves, and they could hardly deny the producers the rights they wished to and had appropriated for themselves. When it came to the actual pricing of raw materials, their participation in pricing discussions had limited utility because they did not feel capable of challenging producer cost calculations very effectively. Funcke, for example, thought little of the value of average calculations presented by the producers because conditions varied from work to work, and he suspected that the averages reflected an adding together of the least favorable components of the various works.[29] Of course, this corresponded to the long-standing criticism of cartel pricing policies. Since the war, however, there had been a greater insistence on public accountability and various degrees of official control and inspection of cost calculations. The RWM, assisted by EWB representatives, made a regular practice of visiting leading steel works and auditing the cost calculations and often came to the conclusion that the demanded prices were too high. There were also occasions on which it came to the opposite conclusion. What one fails to find, however, is a systematic critique or questioning of the basic principles on which the cost calculations were made. The producers, after all, were also often critical of one another. What should have been the price increase on March 1? The 1,000 marks advocated by the moderates, who evidently felt that the failure to cover all increased costs would nevertheless find compensation in continued ability to maintain production and sell more at home and abroad for a longer time? The 2,000 marks advocated by the extremists, who evidently felt that both security and greatest profit lay in covering all costs and then taking all that one could at the moment? The 1,100 marks advocated by von Buttlar because it was based on a "fair and accurate" evaluation of costs? Or the 1,500 marks finally accepted precisely because it was a figure on which the majority could agree and conformed most accurately to the estimated cost increase by the producers?[30]

[29] O. Funcke, article of February 9, 1923, on "Eisenfragen" in the volume of his memoirs entitled "Rohstoffe," Industrieinstitut.

[30] The records of the price audits by the RWM for the years 1920–1922 may be found in DZA Potsdam, RWM, Nr. 4564–4565. They demonstrate the variety of calculation methods and special production problems of the industrial concerns and in no way go beyond the cost calculations on individual products to deal with the relationship between losses or gains within one part of a concern as over

One fundamental and all-important fact in the situation, however, was that the locus of decision making was by and large the producer group, and it was argued by those friendly to industry and opposed to the controlled economy of the recent past that this was where the decision making belonged, namely, in the hands of those with the immediate responsibility for German industry's survival. The *Kölnische Zeitung* granted that the RWM was careful in its estimates of costs and was trying to be fair, but the paper insisted that it could not adequately take into account all the considerations of the industrial leaders themselves, who bore "the entire responsibility for their decisions."[31] Although it recognized that one could debate about how much was necessary for maintenance and what was a fair profit, the paper warned against the development of "strict rules for price calculation, since the effects of such a practice are not forseeable." The editorial concluded that everyone wanted stable conditions but that "until now the government—this is not meant as a reproach—has not been able to bring these about."[32] Therefore, it is the duty of the government to permit the businessman to fulfill his responsibilities toward his firm.

All this sounded very reasonable, but it did not answer the question of how one was to make a decision among the various pricing policies advocated by the producers. The end effect of the posture advocated by the *Kölnische Zeitung*, which was the effective policy pursued with minor variations throughout 1922, was to increase the tendency to leave matters to "circumstances." The variations, insofar as they did not arise from the conflict among the producers themselves, were induced by outside pressures in the form of RWM challenges to producer cost calculations and renewed labor agitation in the EWB. Motions for the reintroduction of price ceilings had been defeated twice, in October and December 1921, and they were defeated for a third time in April 1922. The last vote was along strict class lines, however, and this was an employer setback when compared to the December 1921 vote in which labor had been divided.[33]

---

against those in another. If any conclusion may be drawn from these audits, it is that the major works took no losses on their production and made greater profits on their more advanced fabrication. At the same time, they consistently anticipated renewal costs and other less clear cost factors by renegotiating the bases on which they were calculated.

[31] "Zur Preispolitik des Stahlbundes," *Kölnische Zeitung*, April 7, 1922.

[32] *Ibid.*

[33] *Stahl und Eisen*, 42:1, April 6, 1922, pp. 563–564; April 27, 1922, p. 684. See also, *Kölnische Zeitung*, April 20–21, 1922; *Deutsche Bergwerks-Zeitung*, April 27, 1922, and *Rheinische-Westfälische Zeitung*, April 24, 1922. The last two articles are to be found in Funcke, "Rohstoffe," in the Industrieinstitut.

The employers were cooperating with one another, as evidenced in the EWB votes and the collaboration between the heavy industrialists and the VDMA at this time in the revision of 1921 contracts. Indeed, the VDMA had moved in the direction of sliding-scale prices as early as November 1921, and had actually had to answer producer complaints on this score before the producers themselves went over to sliding-scale pricing.[34] There is also evidence that heavy industry was now in a stronger position to influence and pressure the VDMA and was doing so. Much of this pressure came from Reusch and the member firms in the GHH, particularly the prominent VDMA members associated with the GHH, Directors Lueg, Mayer-Etscheit, and Wedemeyer, as well as from the MAN, Directors Guggenheimer and Lippart. In their judgment, the VDMA had become a "hydrocephalus" since it had moved from Düsseldorf to Berlin in 1914.[35] It pursued a policy dictated by the business managers of the VDMA and its various member associations, and this *Geschäftsführerpolitik* was backed, according to the GHH leaders, by an overgrown and expensive staff of employees. They took the position that "The VDMA today is at best meaningless if not harmful for us since in its stand against the economic interests of the large works and in its effort to win over the small and tiny machine producers, of whom it has taken hundreds as members, it no longer fulfills its purpose."[36]

The GHH directors had a particular distaste for two of the three VDMA chairmen, Reuter and Becker, but they had greater respect for the third chairman, Ernst von Borsig, who, like Reusch, straddled heavy industry and manufacturing in his own business operations. Appropriately enough, it was Borsig who responded to their threat of resignation from the VDMA at the end of February 1922 by holding a meeting with the leading Haniel group directors a few months later to answer complaints about the VDMA's role in the EWB and with regard to export controls. Although Borsig reminded the GHH leaders that industry had to stand together and that this required some consideration for small and medium-sized firms, he recognized that the EWB and the export control boards had provided points of abrasion between the two industrial groups. He was hopeful that export controls could be eliminated and that, in any case, the VDMA could be organizationally separated from the export control boards by the beginning of 1923. He also prom-

[34] "Deutscher Maschinenbau," p. 374, and appended VDMA directors meeting of February 17, 1922, Heft 6/1922.

[35] Guggenheimer travel notes, February 27, 1922, MAN Werksarchiv Augsburg, Nr. K 56.

[36] Mayer-Etscheit to Guggenheimer, February 2, 1922, in *ibid.*, unabgesetzte Korrespondenz 1922, Bl. 112.

ised organizational reforms that would reduce the large variety of influences playing a role in VDMA policy determination. Clearly, Reusch and his friends were in no position to eliminate Becker and Reuter or immediately eliminate Frölich, who had begun his career with the GHH, and it would be difficult to provide an exact measure of their success at this time. Given the strength and importance of the GHH and MAN, however, one may be certain that this pressure counted for something, and it is noteworthy that even Becker assumed a relatively conciliatory attitude toward heavy industry at the VDMA membership meetings in May 1922. He emphasized that prices were being set in collaboration with the producers, that many conflicts were being settled amicably, and that the manufacturers had a responsibility to prove their claims against producers before making loud complaints.[37]

Nevertheless, it is also possible to overestimate producer discretion in pricing. Throughout April, May, and June an effort was made to keep prices relatively stable, an effort assisted and encouraged by the relative slowdown in the depreciation of the mark and the desire to do everything possible to maintain German competitiveness on world markets. Only the Pig Iron Syndicate increased its prices in April and May, and here employers and workers joined together in arguing that the insufficient coke supply and the need to import pig iron required the increases.[38] At the May 31 Steel Federation meeting, however, there was dispute over pricing once again after two months of unchanged guiding prices. All the producers were aware of the fact that a price increase would meet with manufacturer and merchant opposition, and the producers themselves were divided despite increased coal, labor, and freight costs since the end of March. The relative improvement in the mark and the desire to encourage business at home and abroad moved one group to oppose increases, whereas the group supporting increases argued that one had to charge what the market would bear. After deciding on a compromise increase of 535 marks, the producers confronted the manufacturers only to find that the latter categorically refused to accept the price increase. It became clear that a price increase based on a vote of a majority of the producers without any support from the manufacturers would only have been "grist on the mill of Herr von Buttlar," and Poensgen, speaking for the Phoenix concern, which had divided its vote on the compromise, as well as with his immense authority among the producers, "brought the Trowe-Filius group to its senses" by declaring that he "would not go along

[37] Borsig to Reusch, March 25, 1922, and Reusch to Borsig, March 26, 1922, in *ibid.*, Bl. 114, 119, and *Stahl und Eisen*, 42:1, May 25, 1922, pp. 825–826.

[38] *Ibid.*, April 6, 1922, p. 563, and May 4, 1922, pp. 719–720.

with a price increase without the collaboration of the consumers and merchants."[39] In the end, it was decided to implement a 535-mark increase only if coal prices were increased again in June, and on June 20 this increase along with some other slight increases were imposed. On July 1 the automatic operation of the coal clause led to a further increase.[40] Until the end of July, however, neither the resistance of the moderates in the producer camp nor that of the consumers as potentially backed up by the RWM had been broken.

In June, the iron and steel industrialists seemed almost to be catching their breath on the inflationary treadmill before the next six months of even greater exertion. It was becoming increasingly apparent that they would be spinning at a faster pace than ever before. The economy was running full speed. Developments on the labor market, where coal miners and other workers were deserting their jobs for work in neighboring countries or work in the highly paid construction industry, were causing severe production difficulties in the coal industry as well as labor shortages in important areas. The most significant and illustrative measure of the situation is perhaps provided by the SRSU. Since the beginning of the year, it had been engaged in a massive construction program which Stinnes hoped to keep completely self-financed despite the fact that it involved, among other things, the construction of a pipe rolling mill at the Bochumer Verein, a new central cokery between Bochum and Gelsenkirchen designed to establish direct contact between the mines and the smelting plants, and the expansion of the Weber work in Brandenburg.[41] Although rumors were flying about in April 1922 that the IG was going to join the trend toward large new capital stock increases, Stinnes let it be known that he was opposed to such a measure. A capital increase was in fact under active discussion within the concern at the time, but the view that a capital stock issue in marks would involve an "extraordinary watering of the stock" without really solving the long-range problem was one that Stinnes' colleagues found persuasive.[42] Although Stinnes' view that so large an IG could and should make it through without such a measure and even without significant outside help continued to conform to the realities of the situation in the spring, the prognosis for the future was bleak. Siemens was unwilling even temporarily to place financial resources at Deutsch-Lux's disposal because he anticipated that these would be needed for his own concern's use in the

[39] Klemme report of June 1, 1922, HA/GHH, Nr. 3000035/3.
[40] *Stahl und Eisen*, 42:2, June 29, 1922, p. 1034.
[41] *Kölnische Zeitung*, May 10, 1922.
[42] See the correspondence of April 19–20 in SAA, Nachlass Haller, 11/Lb 387.

very near future and that, in any case, "one can well assume that the money shortage on the heavy industrial side will be no passing one. . . ."[43]

The credit crisis, which had developed throughout the German economy since the beginning of the year, hit the SRSU in June, when it was compelled to ask its bank consortium for a 2 billion mark loan. Salomonsohn and Schlitter, however, were only willing to grant 800 million because "the great banks have already granted credits to a degree which practically oversteps what is allowed under a healthy banking policy."[44] This situation put Stinnes and his colleagues in a very sober mood, and they ordered the cessation of all construction that was not absolutely necessary, a command that reverberated throughout the mammoth organization. Thus, even in the crucial mining sector, the GBAG decided to cut all new construction by 60%, whereas Deutsch-Lux terminated all new construction, and Siemens cut back on all that was not deemed absolutely necessary. In part, this represented a systematic effort on the part of heavy industry to fight the "uncontrolled wage policy of the construction industry" and exert the "desired influence on the development of wages" in general, but the dominant consideration was the financial one.[45]

Somewhat to the irritation of his colleagues at Siemens, Stinnes told them to inquire whether customers who had ordered large machines still wanted them before actually undertaking new construction. Köttgen was less concerned than Stinnes about such orders, which constituted only 10% of Siemens sales, but he promised to go over every major order, "one by one." Even more annoying was Stinnes' insistence that the electrotechnical industry was "earning too little" because of its "mistaken pricing policy." He thought it a mistake to employ the "arithmetic method" of charging a stable price and then adding surcharges to cover increased costs and insisted that the only proper contract under the existing conditions was one that charged total cost on the day of delivery. Although admitting that the surcharges (*Teuerungszuschläge*) added at the end of 1921 had been too small, the Siemens people thought that Stinnes had overstated his criticisms and were reluctant to overthrow all the complicated formulas developed by the industry's trade association.[46]

On the heavy industrial side of the SRSU, however, there was a

[43] Letter by Haller, April 20, 1922, in *ibid*.

[44] Finance Committee meeting, June 27, 1922, in *ibid*. Lb/82.

[45] GBAG directors meeting, June 17, 1922, GBAG Archiv, Nr. 121/15 and Deutsch-Lux directors meeting on June 17, 1922, in SAA 11/Lf 129/131.

[46] Siemens Secretariat to C. F. von Siemens, June 29, 1922, in *ibid*., 4/Lf, Bd. 15, Bl. 80–82.

strong tendency to close the gates of the fortress and man the towers against the customer. On July 1, instructions went out designed to ensure further savings now that all unnecessary construction and expansion had been terminated. Insofar as there were new orders placed by the concern works, they were to be placed within the concern even if delivery were to be slower than with the competition. Similarly, higher prices charged by concern works were not to be rejected immediately in favor of lower bids from the competition but rather negotiated within the SRSU. Finally, billing procedures were to be speeded up, payment deadlines strictly enforced, customers with late payments warned, and interest and penalties charged whenever possible.[47]

These trends were reflected on an industry-wide level in the pricing discussions in the Steel Federation and the EWB at the end of July. Their background was the final and most calamitous period of mark depreciation before the Ruhr occupation, which had been triggered by the failure of Germany to secure a foreign loan at the beginning of June, the murder of Rathenau on June 24, and France's threatening attitude in July. Efforts by the Reichsbank to shore up the mark had only limited successes, whereas the flight from the mark into goods increasingly became a flight into foreign exchange. While the boom continued, the rapidity of mark depreciation and the tendency of domestic prices to increase and keep pace with the dollar rate assumed unheard-of proportions. When the Steel Federation met on July 31, therefore, "The negotiations were generally characterized by the domination of the view that the development could no longer be stopped, so that even the works which had previously promoted moderation now stood opposed to intervention."[48]

The sense of desperation was particularly heightened by the intensification of the government's efforts to force exporters to surrender their foreign exchange on July 29, but few were so desperate as to accept the remedy proposed by Trowe and Filius. These gentlemen were trying to find a way "under which an automatic regulation of iron prices could be established whereby the constant need for negotiations could then be eliminated."[49] They proposed that the entire price schedule be tied to the development of pig iron prices, a proposition that undoubtedly seemed very promising from their point of view because the coal situation and the shortage of pig iron had increased pig iron prices even when the steel prices had been kept relatively stable. Furthermore, pig iron prices were already pegged to a series of "clauses,"

[47] Sempell to Wirtz, July 1, 1922, Friedrich-Wilhelms-Hütte Archiv, Nr. 120.
[48] Steel Federation meeting, July 31, 1922, HA/GHH, Nr. 3000035/3.
[49] Ibid.

such as coal, freight, and the foreign exchange rate, so that price increases were virtually automatic. Little enthusiasm was shown for this formula, however, because it would have done little more than shift the center of debate from the Steel Federation to the Pig Iron Syndicate and EWB Pig Iron Committee in a dubious attempt to base the price of 1 million tons of steel on 100–150,000 tons of pig iron. One cannot help wondering if this was the sort of "unschematic" approach to pricing the *Kölnische Zeitung* had in mind in its April editorial advocating the producer determination of pricing.[50]

It was a measure of producer radicalization since the end of May, however, that where the producers at that time had decided not to ask for a price increase without the cooperation of the merchants and consumers, there were now producers who were prepared to battle for complete freedom in pricing if the merchants and consumers would not accept an 8,000 mark per ton increase. Although the GHH and Klöckner were opposed to the 8,000 mark demand, the majority of producers refused to consider the 7,000 marks offered by the consumers and would not even give the 250–350 mark reduction that the latter transparently would have been happy to accept. More important, however, was that the consumers and merchants were informed that this 70% price increase could not be expected to last for more than a week before a new price would have to be negotiated! Although ideas as to the exact mode of adjustment varied among the producers, there was general agreement that minimally it would be necessary to have weekly meetings to consider the development of the exchange rate. Thus, eight days later there was another 1,600 mark increase in the steel prices, and the merchants joined in with a demand for a 25% increase in their commissions.[51]

The development of the foreign exchange rate, which made Sisyphus labor of the effort to make prices keep pace with it because decisions were rendered obsolete on the very day they were taken, necessarily also made a mockery of all efforts to take a longer perspective on any problem. "High policy" seemed impossible except for a principled objection to actions that inhibited flexibility. This was evident on August 2, when a group of major coal and iron industrialists met in Essen to discuss the possibilities of putting pressure on the French to reduce their demands for German coking coal by boycotting French pig iron and importing the more expensive English material. The additional costs were to be divided among the works according to an assessment schedule (*Umlage*) so that individual concerns would not suffer dis-

[50] See above, p. 300.
[51] Steel Federation meeting, July 31, 1922, HA/GHH, Nr. 3000035/3, and *Stahl und Eisen*, 42:2, September 7, 1922, p. 1407.

proportionately. Many concerns were willing to bear the financial sacrifices involved, whereas others doubted that it really would reduce French coal demands because the French could always make money selling the German coal they did not use abroad. True to form, Hasslacher, although sharing the reservations of those who felt that the action would not bring the desired results, also warned that they were going to create a "new compulsory economy in the form of the notorious equalization funds."[52] What really decided the day in favor of those who opposed the action was the news arriving in the middle of the meeting that the exchange rate of the mark had undergone a further serious deterioration. The purchase of English pig iron now represented such a financial burden that further discussion of the proposed boycott had to be suspended until the currency situation improved. It should also be noted that the steady need to import pig iron and the efforts to favor English pig iron tended to dampen the impact of the iron industry's efforts at this time to persuade both the iron consumers and the public of the need to raise the old iron tariff significantly once Germany was allowed to raise iron tariffs again at the beginning of 1925. Although it was possible to argue that Germany had rebuilt her pig iron production capacity and would be flooded with foreign pig iron once stabilization occurred, it was difficult to give a sense of the reality of the problem when the Pig Iron Association was privately negotiating with the government for momentary relief from the pig iron tariff in order to import more from England! On no level, in short, was the situation conducive to "high policy."

Such "high policy" as there was consisted of doing battle against government efforts to make effective such vestiges of the controlled economy as had survived the ravages of the intensified inflation. When the government sought to increase the social export levy in August, the iron industry launched a strong campaign against it and employed the VdESI's Steinbrinck to lobby in the ministries and in the Reich Economic Council against Hirsch and others who argued that it was only proper to raise the tax when the mark was depreciating in order to ensure that the Reich did benefit from foreign exchange profits that were made and that exporters did not secure all the benefit from the export advantages derived from the lower German wage rates, freight rates, and coal costs. The iron and steel industry was in a particularly advantageous position to lead such a campaign because even Hirsch had to admit that iron costs had exceeded the monetary depreciation benefits fairly regularly, although Hirsch also emphasized the enor-

[52] For the quotation and the discussion in this paragraph, see the report on the industrialist discussion in Essen of August 2, 1922, and Köngeter to Reichert, July 13, 1922, in BA, R 13 I/394, Bl. 68–70, 82–83.

mous gains all the industrialists were making from the low interest rates they were paying as well as from the monetary speculation.[53]

The battle over the social export levy was a protracted one that dragged on between the inconclusive debates held in the Reich Economics Council in August and the drastic reductions of the levies that were to take place in the late fall. A much more pressing and immediate danger for the producers in the fall was the RWM's efforts to reintroduce price ceilings on iron and steel. At a time of high labor unrest and public alarm over the inflation, there was bound to be a public reaction to the pricing policies of the Steel Federation that would attract the attention of the government. The RWM responded to the public outcry by asking for and receiving the Reich Cabinet's permission to demand a reintroduction of price ceilings in the EWB. Within the government, the greatest oppositon to price ceilings came from the ministry most heavily dependent on steel deliveries, the Reich Transport Ministry, which pointed out that "when price ceilings are set up, the goods are not delivered."[54]

There were good reasons to have reservations about the RWM's price ceiling proposals at this point, and it would seem that the real object of that ministry was not so much to reestablish price ceilings as to reassert some measure of control over pricing policy if only for reasons of public relations. In his presentation to the EWB on August 15, Imhoff of the RWM stated frankly that conditions had changed since 1920 and that the ceilings would have to be changed every week and would have to be equipped with coal, freight, and exchange clauses. Furthermore, there would have to be many price ceilings to cover material from the Saar, Lorraine, Luxemburg, Upper Silesia, material made with the use of English coal, and material imported from other countries. Predictably, the producers responded to this fantastic presentation, which makes one wonder if Imhoff was really sincere, with unanimous rejection.[55]

Although the discussion in the Inland Commission over the price ceiling question was long and tedious, it was obvious that there was very little support for price ceilings except within the ranks of labor, and even here only from the DMV representatives. The major interest

[53] See Blank to Reusch, August 12, 1922, in HA/GHH, Nr. 300193024/1, the RWR Economic Policy Committee meetings of August 17, 1922, in DZA Potsdam, RWR, Nr. 9, Bl. 46–51, and *Stahl und Eisen*, 42:2, September 7, 1922, p. 1411.

[54] Cabinet meeting of August 15, 1922, in Ingrid Schulze-Bidlingmaier, ed., *Die Kabinette Wirth I und II. Akten der Reichskanzlei. Weimarer Republik*, 2 vols. (Boppard am Rhein, 1973), II, p. 1011.

[55] Report by Klemme on the August 15, 1922, EWB meeting, in HA/GHH, Nr. 3000035/3.

of the leading DMV representative, Schliestädt, in fact, appears to have been regaining some voice for the trade unions in pricing decisions rather than the reintroduction of price ceilings per se. In any case, Peter Klöckner skillfully deepened the rift in the labor camp and won goodwill among the manufacturers and merchants by successfully pushing through a proposal that they revive the EWB committee that had participated in the Steel Federation pricing decisions between December and March. Although not a formal organ of the EWB, the committee was instructed to report to the Inland Commission about its work. It was anticipated that pricing discussions would be held at least every ten days. This was not the first experiment with such an arrangement, but even labor had divided over price ceilings. Schliestädt seemed tamed by this fact and now seemed anxious to collaborate in the Pricing Committee in the same manner in which he had already been collaborating for some time in the Pig Iron Committee. Also, the Vice President of the EWB, Weimann, a Christian Union representative, was assigned to the committee as an expert and was given the task of evaluating the cost calculations of the works, participating in the inspection of books with the RWM, and explaining the cost calculations to the labor representatives on the EWB. It cannot be said that these arrangements made a very substantive difference at the next pricing discussion of August 31, however, where a compromise increase of 37,020 marks was reluctantly accepted by the manufacturers.[56]

In September, as steel pricing degenerated into almost meaningless haggling every ten days at which producers increasingly sought to get all they could regardless of the consequences, the moderate Klemme reported in utter disgust: "Nothing resembling a higher point of view is given consideration in the negotiations anymore; it seems as if everyone sees the collapse coming closer and closer and wants to still grab for himself beforehand whatever can be snatched up. Sobriety will only return when the orders are stopped or annuled, and that is not yet the case . . . one speaks so much and so urgently of losses that one finally believes in them oneself."[57] By the end of the month, however, the tide seemed to be turning against Trowe and other radicals among the producers, whose imaginative schemes to tighten up delivery conditions and insistence on the most ruthless implementation of every clause and every formula devised and employed in pricing during the previous months, only demonstrated their capacity to remain "stiff necked and uninstructable" in the face of warnings about the

[56] *Ibid.*, and report by Klemme on the August 31, 1922, meetings in *ibid.*
[57] Report by Klemme on the September 11, 1922, meeting in *ibid.*

"threatening change in the situation, the continuously increasing competitive possibilities of the outside world."[58] On September 29, Klemme actually persuaded his colleagues to wait ten or twelve days before demanding another price increase.

By October 10, the desperateness of the situation was even more in evidence. The value of the mark had suffered new shocks, but there was "the greatest uncertainty as to what the market could still take in price increases" because of the greatly reduced demand at home and abroad. When it was proposed that they go over in whole or in part to prices calculated in gold marks, Klemme warned that other industries would then follow suit. Once Germany went over to gold mark wages and gold mark prices, "our competitive possibilities on the world market will be finished and the collapse all along the line will be sealed."[59] That is, Germany would no longer benefit from the relatively low domestic wages and prices at home, for with the change to calculation in gold marks the process by which German domestic wages and prices were catching up with those in the rest of the world and even exceeding them would have been completed. At the same time, Klemme warned that calculation in gold would threaten industry's control over its foreign exchange because "the government would regard such an action as a friendly invitation to take the procurement of exchange out of industry's hands, to demand the surrender of exchange from exports, and to undertake the distribution of exchange to industry in accordance with demonstrated needs."[60] Open conversion to gold mark calculation, in short, would introduce transparency into the situation and eliminate the maneuverability provided by the paper marks.

August Thyssen found Klemme's position most convincing and came to the view that "we must unquestionably remain with the old paper marks until a new strong government finds a way out."[61] For the moment, however, there was no "new strong government," and the game with paper mark increases continued. The consumers were playing it too, and ironically, Klemme's effort to keep the lid on was ruined by Schrey, who claimed that his railroad car manufacturers could no longer operate on the basis of ten-day periods and had to have prices set every three days! Trowe and Filius took advantage of this unexpected turn of events to secure a 67.7% price increase and an agreement to have prices regulated every Tuesday. Every other Tuesday would be "exchange Tuesday," when steel prices would be regulated

[58] Report by Klemme on the September 29, 1922, meeting in *ibid.*
[59] Report by Klemme on the October 10, 1922, meeting in *ibid.*
[60] *Ibid.*   [61] *Ibid.*

anew with attention to the exchange rate, whereas on other Tuesdays the parties involved would meet to negotiate concerning the other aspects of the price question.

As became obvious during October and November, however, it was becoming increasingly difficult to raise prices because of the collapsing market and the increasing labor unrest in the Ruhr and among the metal workers throughout Germany. Also, the consumers were extremely restive, and bitterness against heavy industry was increasing. When Carl Duisberg of the chemical industry complained to Vögler about iron prices in late November, Vögler was quick to supply him with information trying to demonstrate how the inflation had eaten up his industry's capital and given it enormous debts at a time when prices on the world market were dropping. He went on to point out that "If we change the payment conditions, which is naturally something that is repeatedly being considered among us, then the need for credit in the manufacturing industry will become so extraordinarily great, that I fear that we will ruin our own business."[62] Similar warnings were voiced by Poensgen at the November 21 Steel Federation meeting, where he argued out that the market could no longer take the price increases, that a reduction in prices was necessary and all the more necessary if the workers were to be kept from voting for price ceilings at the December 5 EWB meetings. Prices were in fact reduced 25,000 marks on December 5, but then payment conditions were made much harsher on December 12, and this produced great bitterness among the primary consumers.[63] As 1923 approached, however, the dilemma was obvious. The game seemed to be up, but the players continued to play it in the old way for lack of anything better to do. The entire situation was well summarized by Hasslacher in a report to his supervisory board on December 8, 1922, in which he pointed out that the monetary depreciation was making the financial situation "ever more tense" and forcing the concern to procure its working capital either in exchange bills or in foreign exchange. Although prices were sufficiently high for there to be surpluses on the books, he feared that these would be insufficient to maintain operations over the long run if the currency continued to depreciate. Yet, he concluded, "so long as there is no change in our foreign and domestic policy, there is nothing left to do but operate in the way we have until now."[64]

[62] Vögler to Duisberg, November 27, 1922, Werksarchiv Bayer-Leverkusen, Autographensammlung Duisberg.

[63] See the relevant Klemme reports in HA/GHH, Nr. 3000035/3.

[64] Rheinstahl supervisory board meeting, December 8, 1922, Rheinstahl Archiv, Nr. 123.

311

Hasslacher's statement reveals the underlying foundations of the iron and steel pricing policies of 1922, namely, a relentless hunt for foreign exchange combined with a tendency on the part of big business to drown itself and the economy in every conceivable form of paper currency in order to secure the liquid means necessary to keep going. Stinnes was simply the most famous and explicit representative of these practices, serving as their spokesman and consummate practitioner. In one of his many speeches against export controls and the export levy in the Reich Economics Council, Stinnes pointed out in February 1922 that because of the instability of the exchange, ". . . all business today has by and large become an exchange insurance business and otherwise a speculative business. In every great firm today the securing of exchange, the buying up of exchange at certain times, is actually the chief matter of concern, and trade in goods has stepped completely into second place. I tell you quite openly, when one today undertakes payment obligations in connection with the receipt of raw materials, then I would consider him very irresponsible under the circumstances, particularly when it comes to exports from Germany where we are accepting orders three or four months ahead, if he did not secure the foreign exchange by purchase in advance at a fixed price (*auf Termin*) for the time when he had to pay for the wares and if he did not make sure that when this time came he was in a position to assure that he could get the foreign exchange through export. . . ."[65]

In order to understand what all this meant in practice, one need only turn to the SRSU, where exchange policy was actively discussed and debated in the fall of 1922. As usual, Stinnes did not think that the Siemens group was doing quite enough to protect itself against the inflation. Stinnes claimed that the heavy industrial groups in the SRSU had long pursued a policy of turning half of all mark payments they received into secure liquid capital by purchasing foreign exchange at fixed terms immediately. Stinnes viewed this as a particularly sure way of operating because whatever one might lose by purchasing this foreign exchange if the value of the mark went up, one gained by the corresponding improvement of the purchasing power of the other half of the monetary resources. It seems that the Siemens Financial Director, Haller, was somewhat surprised by this "policy" because he had understood that the SRSU's basic policy since July 1921 had been to retain one-third of its liquid resources in foreign exchange, a decision based on arrangements made with the Reichsbank and only sub-

[65] RWR Economic Policy Committee, February 17, 1922, DZA Potsdam, RWR, Nr. 7, Bl. 238.

stantially violated in agreement with the latter at times when the value of the mark underwent serious deterioration.[66]

According to Haller, the Siemens policy was only somewhat different from the Stinnes policy in that Siemens had not fixed its foreign exchange-mark ratio in any way but rather operated on the principle that the Siemens group would seek to cover its "needs" (*Bedarf*) in part through foreign exchange stores maintained in long-term supply and in part through the immediate purchases of exchange from proceeds received in marks. This policy was conducted after negotiation with the Reichsbank and Finance Ministry in order to avoid suspicion of hoarding, but Haller pointed out that the "concept of 'need' was as broadly construed as possible in that long-term need was included."[67] In reality, therefore, the differences between the two groups in the IG were not so great. As Haller noted, "In general, internally we have followed the principle of having as much exchange and as little marks as possible when the mark is falling and whenever possible to have debts in marks, and to follow the reverse principle when the mark is rising."[68] What this meant in practice was that between January 1 and September 1, 1922, the percentage of Siemens & Halske's liquid assets in foreign exchange had increased from 18 to 97% and that of Siemens-Schuckert from 25 to 88%.[69] Deutsch-Luxemburg was simply more extreme in this connection and, as Vögler told Siemens in September 1922, had not maintained any of its liquid resources in marks since the beginning of the year and had avoided any exchange losses between July and September by taking its 400 million mark proceeds from domestic sales of July and selling them in a forward transaction on August 31 and then selling this foreign exchange for marks, presumably in payment of operating expenses, at the end of August. Such speculation demonstrates how the great concerns could manage to weather the immediate storms of hyperinflation by dealing in both foreign exchange and marks. Insofar as there was a difference between Deutsch-Lux and Siemens, it was in the way the two concerns evaluated their stocks of goods. Haller emphasized that whereas the liquid resources of Siemens had dropped 5.5 million dollars since the beginning of the business year, its stocks of material had risen 7 million dollars in worth. Vögler was less impressed with the "flight into real values" in the form of goods and argued "that stores of material which exceed operating requirements are uneconomic at present. In general, the world market shows a falling tendency. A continuous depreciation

[66] Haller to Siemens, September 11, 1922, SAA 4/Lf 635.
[67] *Ibid.*   [68] *Ibid.*
[69] See the Freund study of the SRSU in *ibid.*, 54/Lm 123.

of stocks is thus occurring. A correspondingly larger store of exchange is more correct, therefore, and has the advantage of bringing in interest and not lying fallow."[70]

These practices were not what the government had in mind in desperate but basically futile efforts to gain effective control of foreign exchange holdings for purposes of paying reparations and vital import costs. Since October 1921 the Reichsbank had been given partial control over foreign exchange received from exports, and regulations were tightened in February 1922 when, under Allied pressure, the government ordered that permission to export be made contingent on the agreement to surrender foreign currency proceeds for German marks. The Reich Commissar for Exports and Imports was allowed to make exceptions, however, and he normally did so for all firms capable of demonstrating that they did any form of business abroad involving foreign exchange. Needless to say, this made the ban on conducting business in foreign exchange and holding on to it ineffective for the most significant cases of those engaged in such business. The actual control of foreign exchange transactions for industry was given to the Export Control Boards, which determined the amounts to be surrendered from foreign sales and the amounts that might be kept by firms to meet their obligations. In April 1922, the Export Control Board for iron and steel products set a minimum requirement that 25% of the foreign exchange received from abroad be surrendered to the Reichsbank. In October, this was raised to 33⅓%, but given the extent of transactions involving foreign exchange, it should come as no surprise that officials frankly stated that "it is well known that one of the chief reasons for the deterioration of the mark is to be found in the fact that industrial circles are keeping more exchange than they need."[71] As Klemme, Thyssen, and others had recognized, the basic industrialist retention of control over proceeds in foreign exchange was largely contingent on the continued calculation in marks as well as foreign exchange in the course of normal business, and this explains the reluctance of industrialists to calculate entirely in gold marks to which must of course be added the export advantages accrued from the continued use of depreciating marks to pay domestic costs. Calculation in fixed values would have enabled the government to determine precisely how much foreign exchange the industrialists needed at any given time, just as the calculation of wages and certain other costs in a stable currency or value would have eliminated certain export advantages.

[70] Vögler to Siemens, September 6, 1922, *ibid.*, 4/Lf 635.

[71] Dalberg at the Exchange Advisory Council meeting, October 1, 1922, BA R 38/505. See also Graham, *Exchange and Prices*, pp. 83–87, and *Stahl und Eisen*, 42:1, April 20, 1922, p. 64; 42:2, October 26, 1922, p. 1638.

When the government made a desperate effort to tighten up the regulations with a new Emergency Exchange Decree in October, which was meant to prohibit the employment of foreign exchange in domestic transactions, it ran into a storm of protest from industry which, to be sure, loudly proclaimed the need to provide the government with as much foreign exchange as possible but insisted that the new regulations were intolerable. In contrast to 1919–1920, objections now came from manufacturers as well as producers, the former arguing, as did the MAN, that it had to pay suppliers like Thyssen in foreign exchange for rolled steel to be used in the completion of export orders because otherwise "a very undesirable uncertainty in the calculations will be the consequence."[72] In short, large firms like these had already given up both on calculating and dealing in marks in vital areas of business transactions pertaining to exports. The conflict with the Wirth government over this issue, which had broader political implications to be discussed later, was settled in favor of industry in a manner that let the public be fooled while permitting the government to save face. As Guggenheimer confidentially reported from Berlin to his colleagues in the MAN, the bourgeois parties under business influence had formed a nine-man committee under the chairmanship of Hans von Raumer which had devised for the chancellor implementing regulations (*Ausführungsbestimmungen*) for the Exchange Decree.[73] Thanks to such assiduous labor and lobbying, the ban on the employment of foreign exchange in domestic commerce for the purpose of indirect export was eliminated, and the industrialists continued to retain basic control over their foreign exchange supplies.

In the government's efforts to impose and implement stricter exchange controls, it received relatively little assistance and support from the Reichsbank which, under the leadership of General Director Dr. Havenstein, pursued credit and monetary policies that will forever excite wonder and that mark him as one of the great incompetents of banking history. A firm believer in the balance of payments theory, Havenstein came to the view that his primary responsibility was that of a helpless producer of money and credit in order to satisfy the insatiable demand for the paper that was considered necessary to keep the economy going. Thanks to his discount and credit policies, which were unbelievably generous in both their scope and their low rates, he aided, abetted, and promoted those great industrialists who were using the inflation, whether out of design or felt need or both, to serve

[72] MAN Gustavsburg to Guggenheimer, October 24, 1922, MAN Werksarchiv Augsburg, Unabgesetzte Korrespondenz 1922, Bl. 122.

[73] Guggenheimer to MAN Gustavsburg, October 26, 1922, *ibid.* and Laubach, *Kabinette Wirth*, p. 290ff.

their interests. It was, after all, the employment of the printing press and the credit policies of the Reichsbank that made possible the speculation against the mark and the various foreign exchange manipulations discussed above, as evidenced by the fact that the cessation of these banking policies would one day terminate the speculation. Nevertheless, Havenstein, with his misplaced pride in the printing capacity of the Reich Printing Office and his panic every time the printers went out on strike, has too long stood alone as an object of derision.[74] His policies were warmly supported by many of the leading lights of German banking and industry, and the initiative for the policies pursued in the fall and winter of 1922–1923 came from them.

To begin with, there was a growing tendency in the second half of 1922 to employ and accept commercial bills in place of normal currency. Thus, at a meeting of the leading Ruhr industrialists on August 2, "all those present were in agreement that in view of the intensifying need for credit, customer's commercial bills will play an increasing role, and that the works and particularly the trade associations cannot do anything against this tendency. A special promotion of payment with commercial bills by the trade associations was not deemed desirable. It was deemed preferable to let the natural development take its course."[75] Actually, there was nothing new about the discounting of commercial bills by the Reichsbank. Before the war, the noncash cover of the Reichsbank notes had largely consisted of commercial bills. Since the war, however, commercial bills had fallen into disuse because of the employment of payment by checks, and until the summer of 1922 treasury bills (*Reichsschatzwechsel*) dominated among the forms of noncash cover and commercial bills remained of negligible significance in this connection. Thus, the inflationary source of the Reichsbank's noncash cover had largely been "governmental." Thanks to the large-scale resurrection and employment of commercial bills in the summer of 1922, the Reichsbank now added a "private" inflation to the "governmental" one. Understandably, bankers and industrialists had long felt that the reintroduction of commercial bills and their discounting by the banks were highly desirable, but the high liquidity and periodic uncertainty about ability to deliver goods had acted as a barrier to this development.[76] With the intensification of inflation since the beginning of 1922, the withdrawal of short term foreign funds German money market, and the growing shortage of cash on hand, however, commercial bills appeared

[74] Czada in *Schriften des Vereins für Sozialpolitik*, 73, p. 15ff.
[75] Meeting of August 2, 1922, Friedrich-Wilhelms-Hütte Archiv, Nr. 860/19.
[76] Czada in *Schriften des Vereins für Sozialpolitik*, 73, p. 28ff.; Bresciani-Turroni, *Economics of Inflation*, p. 75ff., and Whale, *Joint Stock Banking*, p. 210ff.

both attractive and vital for the continued operation of business. The Reichsbank leaders viewed the potential dangers of the easy credit policy to the private sector implied by the massive increase in the discounting of commercial bills with surprising equanimity. On the one hand, although it was understood that the employment of such paper would increase the amount of paper in circulation and intensify the inflation, it was felt that "production policy" had to be put before "currency policy" (*währungspolitische Gesichtspunkte*) and that the benefits of maintaining production and trade would outweigh such negative monetary consequences as might arise.[77] On the other hand, the Reichsbank leaders argued that a continuation of its low discount rate, which had remained at 5% until July and then gradually rose to a ludicrously low 12% in January 1923, was desirable because it kept production costs and prices low. Instead, the Reichsbank felt that such ill effects as might arise from its low discount rate could be remedied by a selective credit extension policy that would favor only those worthy of credit.[78] Translated into practical terms, this meant that the giants of industry would be given easy access to credit and, under conditions of rising prices, would be encouraged to borrow still further because they were continuously being allowed to repay their debts at interest rates so low as to permit them to underpay even the principal. Thus, the Ruhr industrialists, who had agreed to let this "natural development" of using commercial paper take its course in early August, were quite prepared to give nature something of a push as their credit problems increased by early September.

In this effort, they had much support and assistance from other industries, and thus the promotion of the Reichsbank policy of discounting commercial paper at low discount rates became the policy of the Reich Association of German Industry at its meeting of September 6, 1922. Indeed, there was not a policy of the Reichsbank subsequently condemned by monetary theorists that did not receive the encouragement of the leaders of German industry. Havenstein's fondness for the printing press and disregard of its consequences was widely shared. Because there was a constant shortage of currency due to the incapacity of firms to pay their bills and wages under steadily rising prices, money production was a pressing problem. The RdI Business Manager, Geheimrat Bücher, praised Havenstein for his efforts, thought it splendid that the Reich Printing Office could produce about 1.9 billion marks a day, spoke warmly of Havenstein's plans to produce even more, and urged that the industrialists do their share in

[77] RWM report, January 14, 1923, R 43 I/1148, Bl. 282.
[78] Reported at the RdI directors meeting, September 6, 1922, HA/GHH, Nr. 3001240/4.

317

helping Havenstein's production problems. Paying wages had been a problem, and Bücher had discussed it with Reichsbank officials who, like he, felt that it could temporarily be solved if the large works would print their own coupons (*Gutscheine*) that would serve as money in local stores until the Reichsbank could catch up with demand by printing the money necessary for its redemption. One of Bücher's colleagues from the textile industry sagely noted that "I do not believe that the value of the German mark will be all that much influenced by the fact that we are printing more currency,"[79] and Stinnes made optimistic remarks to the effect that the Reichsbank would be able to produce 3.8 billion per day by October 1. Stinnes' greatest concern, like that of his colleagues, however, was with the creation of credit, and he declared that "The credit and currency shortage can only be eliminated if the Reichsbank can be brought about to perform the great deed that it did at the outbreak of the war when it accepted every type of bill that was presented to it."[80] Stinnes thought it a great mistake that the Reichsbank and commercial banks had sought to cover their needs and the credit needs of industry by accepting so many treasury bills and had neglected to employ the enormous credit resources that might be created through the discounting of commercial bills at low rates. His views were widely shared, and little attention was paid to the complaints of one textile industrialist, who argued that "Through commercial bills the credit problem is only put off a bit, but then we will stand before the same catastrophe afterwards."[81] A decision was made to go to Havenstein to urge him to revise his credit lists and to expand his generous policies toward reliable firms.

This Reichsbank policy became the basis for substantial lending to the SRSU and other concerns in the fall of 1922. The heavy industrial group's old policy of covering its losses by forward transactions in foreign exchange was no longer possible in the fall because of the rapidity of the mark's deterioration, a fact that explains Stinnes' desire to promote Havenstein's "great deed" of massively reintroducing the discounting of commercial bills at the time, and Stinnes found a "new way" of raising capital by this means. The SRSU members were asked to calculate the sum total of invoices in September for deliveries within the concern. Stinnes then arranged with Havenstein to have commercial bills discounted in the Reichsbank in the amount of these invoices. In October, this method of credit creation through the discounting of commercial bills was expanded to encompass the discounting of bills based on presumed inventory dispacement for a three-

---

[79] Müller-Oerlinghausen at *ibid.*

[80] *Ibid.*   [81] *Ibid.*

month period. The Reichsbank did set limits to the amounts that could thus be discounted, however, and these amounts did not cover the enormous needs of the SRSU, which had to be raised from other quarters. The scramble for credit did in fact cause some tensions within the SRSU, where the enormous needs of the heavy industrial group led it to lay claim to the lion's share of the Reichsbank credits whereas the Siemens group was urged to get its money from more expensive private banks. Although this policy made some sense in terms of the former's huge needs, C. F. von Siemens was more than mildly irritated to receive telegrams requesting that he supply the Alpine Montagesellschaft with money when he was starving his own works and depriving them of the development "which we desperately need if we are not to be overshadowed by our competition."[82]

By December 1922, however, the entire range of practices connected with the hyperinflation of the last half of that year were becoming counterproductive in that what is today known as a "stagflation" had developed—that is, continuing inflation in the context of reduced demand both at home and abroad. "Low policy" had reached its limits, and a way had to be found to pursue "high policy" once again.

TOWARD AN ECONOMIC PROGRAM

Throughout late 1921 and 1922, and particularly as conditions became more critical in the late spring and early summer, the leaders of German industry were keenly aware of the fact that they had been living from hand to mouth intellectually and politically as well as in their day-to-day business practices. The abortive credit action in late 1921 had been anything but helpful to the domestic and foreign image of German industry. First, the industrial leaders had offered to assist the government by backing its fulfillment policy with their credit, and then they effectively withdrew the offer by making demands of a socioeconomic and political nature that appeared all the more selfish because of the suddenness and brutality of their presentation. The image of German industry abroad was in something of a parlous state in any case. Whatever the benefits of the inflation, German producers for export had done little to enhance their reputations by their repeated breaking of contracts, changing of prices, and delivery delays. On a more general political level they were accused of promoting the inflation, failing to support internal stabilization, and sabotaging the

[82] Siemens to Kirdorf, December 23, 1920, SAA 4/Lf 635, and SRSU Finance Committee meeting, September 21, 1922, *ibid.*, 11/Lb 82, and Köttgen to Sempell, October 2, 1922, Sempell to Köttgen, October 4, 1922, and Köttgen to Sempell, October 5, 1922, in *ibid.*, Nachlass Köttgen, 11/Lf 129.

policy of fulfillment. German industry thus found itself being tarnished with the same brush employed by the French in their accusations that the German government was using reparations as an excuse not to bring its economic and financial house in order.[83]

Privately, leading German industrialists were prepared to agree with some of the French charges. Reusch noted in mid-August that reparations alone could not be blamed for the currency depreciations and that Poincaré was correct in insisting that the "German government bears significant responsibility for the depreciation of the mark."[84] Paul Silverberg, who was often acting as the mouthpiece for his friend Stinnes at this time, also felt that "there is a kernel of truth" in France's charges against Germany.[85] Needless to say, the industrial leaders were not talking about their own responsibility but rather of the responsibility of the government and the left-wing organizations and parties. Reusch was particularly brutal in his criticism, declaring that "We do not have a government in Berlin but rather many bureaus with, aside from a very few exceptions, more or less poor bureau supervisors," and that "The chief activity of the government has limited itself to following after public opinion and satisfying the wishes of the masses." From this he could only draw the conclusion that "The outside world will only again have confidence in us when we have a government that maintains order domestically and regulates our finances through a policy of strict economy."[86] At the same time, the industrial leaders were also convinced that they would have to move beyond criticism and take the initiative to remedy the failure of Germany to come up with a positive program at home and abroad. As Sorge pointed out to his colleagues in the Reich Association of German Industry, "We must admit that we ourselves don't really know what we want. In this there lies a great danger, for our enemies can use this to put us in the wrong before the world by saying that the Germans are showing bad faith because they do not make any positive proposals. . . ."[87]

To remedy this programmatic deficit as well as to be prepared for an anticipated new series of economic and political shocks, the directors of the RdI established a Special Committee for an Economic Program at their meeting on June 18, 1922. The Special Committee, which included such important leaders of heavy industry as Vögler and Sil-

[83] See, for example, Thewall and Kavanagh, *Report . . . March 1922*, p. 15; Laubach, *Kabinette Wirth*, p. 69ff.

[84] Reusch to Batocki, August 14, 1922, HA/GHH, Nr. 400101790/0.

[85] Silverberg at a RdI Special Committee meeting, August 9, 1922, BA Nachlass Silverberg, Nr. 312, Bl. 73.

[86] Reusch to Batocki, August 14, 1922, HA/GHH, Nr. 400101790/0.

[87] Sorge at a RdI Special Committee meeting, August 9, 1922, BA, Nachlass Silverberg, Nr. 312, Bl. 79–80.

verberg, the committee chairman, and of the manufacturing industries as Funcke, von Raumer, and Guggenheimer, was strongly assisted by the business manager of the RdI, Hermann Bücher, and his staff. In short, it was an elite committee whose work received high priority. Although not a member of the committee in regular attendance, Hugo Stinnes took a very direct interest in its work, which he influenced strongly through Silverberg and Vögler. The Special Committee began meeting in late July 1922 and continued through the fall and winter, gradually developing a series of guidelines on a host of subjects by the end of the year before its work was permanently interrupted by the Ruhr occupation. This interruption, however, did not rob the committee's work of importance. The ideas developed by the committee served as the foundation for the RdI program accepted at the Cologne membership meeting of 1925. More important for the purposes of this discussion, the Special Committee became the mechanism by which the great industrialists could concretize and consolidate the program they considered essential for ending the inflation and stabilizing the economy. As such, it constituted a seizure of the initiative and a basis for mobilizing the business community comparable to that of the 1917–1918 preparation for the transition from a wartime to a peacetime economy as well as a consolidation and coherent articulation of the basic socioeconomic beliefs of Germany's dominant industrial leaders. The object of the enterprise, as Oscar Funcke pointed out in a revealing retrospective account, was not simply to take a stand on immediate questions of the day. Rather, "there was a persistent effort . . . to form a general understanding of the problems of political economy, not as a science, but rather as a collection of those vantage points from which a political orientation could proceed. An entire ideology was created, which was held to in economic circles for many years."[88] This ideology stressed freedom from state interference and the maintenance of profitability through low taxes, wages, and social expenditures. Great attention also was paid to monetary and trade questions, but at the beginning, "an extraordinarily important role was played by . . . the struggle against the eight-hour day."

What is interesting about the formulation of the RdI program in

[88] Funcke in "Vergangene Zeiten, Buch 4," Industrieinstitut. The records of the Special Committee are to be found in Funcke's memoirs and in the Silverberg Nachlass in the BA, Nr. 312–313. For the 1925 RdI program, see *Tagung des Reichsverbandes am 23., 24., 25. Juni 1925 in Köln. Juli 1925* and *Deutsche Wirtschafts und Finanzpolitik. Dezember 1925* (Veröffentlichungen des Reichsverbandes der Deutschen Industrie, Nr. 28–29) (Berlin, 1925). For an analysis of the Special Committee's work from the perspective of foreign affairs, see the unpublished Ph.D. dissertation of Hermann-Josef Rupieper, "Politics and Economics: The Cuno Government and Reparations, 1922–1923" (Stanford, 1974), p. 122ff.

1922, with its basically unsurprising and traditionally oriented stress on freedom from state controls and conventional modes of cost reduction and inducements to trade, is the order of priorities and the emphases that informed the committee's work within this framework. Although ostensibly concerned with foreign as well as domestic policy, the former was treated by some of the industrial leaders with an indifference that arose from a sense of futility. Bücher, who placed greater stress on foreign policy initiatives than the Special Committee chairman, Silverberg, provided the committee with some general guidelines that involved the usual attacks on Versailles for ruining the world economic balance, a call for equal treatment for Germany, a demand for a definitive settlement of the reparations question that would not involve an assault on Germany's economic substance, and a long-term international loan. Silverberg and Stinnes were unwilling to give top priority to the foreign policy question, however, because there seemed to be no way to bring France to reason so long as the British were so preoccupied with their Indian, Irish, and domestic difficulties that they were unable to conduct a strong foreign policy and so long as the United States refused to play a responsible role in world affairs. More fundamentally, however, Stinnes argued that "A basis must be created for our negotiations in foreign affairs so that we are not told at every negotiation that the German economy is managed in such a way that it always operates with a passive balance of trade. . . ."[89] Whatever the reservations felt about Stinnes' and Silverberg's insistence on a somewhat rigid order of priorities that would place domestic before foreign affairs in the work of the Special Committee, therefore, this procedure seems to have been endorsed by the RdI directors at their meeting of September 6, 1922.[90]

At this same meeting, which appropriately enough was the one at which it was decided to urge Havenstein to discount commercial bills on a large scale, support was also given to the Special Committee's decision not to give stabilization of the currency top priority in its domestic program. Initially, the textile industrialist, Dr. Abraham Frowein, urged giving priority to monetary stabilization, but he was overruled on two counts by his colleagues on the committee. First, Frowein was reminded that stabilization depended on a definitive reparations question, and he soon himself asserted with due conviction that "So long as our enemies are insisting upon squeezing money out of us that we cannot pay because of our balance of payments, we can-

[89] RdI directors meeting, September 6, 1922, HA/GHH, Nr. 3001240/4.

[90] The opponents of this procedure were to take the initiative again at the end of the year, see Rupieper in *Industrielles System*, pp. 586–587.

not in my view do anything."[91] The second reason for the opposition to making domestic currency stabilization the major item of the RdI domestic program was that stabilization would have to be coordinated with wage policy. As Silverberg pointed out, it would "at least temporarily" be necessary to keep two types of currency in operation to make sure that wages would not be stabilized at too high a level when one finally stopped paying them in depreciating currency. Frowein was quick to get this message too: "If we stabilize in such a way that the wages are not too high, then we will be able to say to the workers: You should earn more, but only when you also work more."[92] This was precisely what Silverberg had in mind in making the currency question secondary to the creation of "domestic economic order." Stinnes could not have agreed more, and he warmly supported the Special Committee's order of priorities at the RdI directors meeting of September 6, when he declared that *First increased labor productivity must come, then the stabilization of the currency on the day when we are certain that the reparations question has been solved.*"[93]

Although the Special Committee took up a host of domestic economic problems, its primary emphasis was on the productivity question, and this emphasis reflected the dominance of Stinnes and heavy industry in the RdI councils. As Funcke noted, no matter how many other issues were discussed, "Stinnes with his incredible concentration (or one-sidedness) always came back to the productivity question. . . ."[94] Stinnes was more than ably seconded by Vögler, however, and above all by Silverberg, who volunteered to write the domestic program and whose own one-sided emphasis on the productivity question caused a certain measure of discomfiture among his colleagues from other industries. Clemens Lammers of the cellulose and paper industry pointed out that a distinction had to be made between the heavy industries and the manufacturing industries because worker productivity had improved substantially in the latter, and this point was seconed by Dr. Frank of the chemical industry, who considered worker productivity in his industry to be satisfactory. They had little incentive, therefore, to attack the eight-hour day, although they undoubtedly shared in the general disapproval of the "schematic" eight-hour day enforced by the government since the Revolution. Silverberg and Vögler remained unmoved by their remarks because they regarded increased hours of work as the key to Germany's economic salvation.

[91] Meeting of September 6, 1922, HA/GHH, Nr. 3001240/4.
[92] *Ibid.*
[93] *Ibid.* The italics appear in the original.
[94] Funcke in "Vergangene Zeiten, Buch 4," Industrieinstitut.

They argued that an improved balance of payments required a capacity to export manufactured goods at reasonable prices, and the latter required the cheapest possible domestic production of coal and raw materials.[95] Silverberg reminded his colleagues that worker productivity in manufacturing industries was closely tied to work at machines and depended much less on individual will to work than in the primary industries. He and Vögler were furious at the government and the trade unions for allegedly undermining the initiative of the workers, and particularly the coal miners. On the one hand, the industrialists objected to the policy of fulfillment which gave the workers the sense that the gains from increased labor would simply flow into the pockets of the Entente. On the other hand, they objected to the labor policies pursued since the war. Although the major object of their effort was the elimination of the eight-hour day, that issue does not appear openly in the protocols of the initial Special Committee meetings. Instead, the stress was placed on the need to restore piece work, to reestablish wage differentials between old and younger and skilled and unskilled workers, and to terminate the endless stream of wage increases granted by government-supported arbitration boards. Vögler was adamant on the necessity of tying higher wages to higher productivity and argued that only in this way could they attain the desired increase in productivity. The hours of work question, therefore, was being attacked through the wage question, and the burden of Germany's economic well-being, indeed her survival, was being laid squarely on the backs of the workers.

This very one-sided approach to the distribution of the social costs of a lost war and of the burdens of maintaining German competitiveness on world markets was criticized by some committee members. The textile industrialists Frowein and Hans Jordan reminded Vögler that the purchasing power of wages paid in marks was something less than satisfactory and that there was much that industry itself could do to lower costs by improved techniques. The most telling and penetrating commentary came from Dr. Lammers, however, who strongly suggested to his colleagues that waste rather than rationalization had characterized some of the recent developments in German entrepreneurship and that worker productivity was not the only problem to be solved. He criticized the tendency toward "unproductive" and "uneconomic" plant expansion and concentration, much of which failed to take the "substantially changed economic conditions" into account. He

[95] August 9, 1922, Special Committee meeting, BA, Nachlass Silverberg, Nr. 312, Bl. 103–104. The discussion here is based on the lengthy protocol of this revealing meeting in *ibid.*, Bl. 73–106.

warned against artificially creating "supposed values which are fated from the outset to go down to destruction."[96] Although Lammers was more concerned with the preservation of small and medium-sized business than he was with rationalization, his critical remarks served to point up the very narrow conception of cost reduction and increased productivity emphasized by Silverberg and Vögler. Although not openly confessed, it appeared that the costs of rationalization were also to be laid on the backs of the workers. Rationalization, however, was not discussed. Instead, the issue was shunted aside by Bücher, who declared that superfluous productive capacities were "unavoidable" under the circumstances, would have to be corrected by the operation of the world market, and therefore constituted a problem best solved after the productivity question had been tackled.[97]

The decision to attack the economic problem by stressing increased worker productivity and to build the RdI program about this point was as simple as it was politically explosive. Underlying it was a deep-seated resentment against the Weimar regimes that had ruled Germany as well as against the gains made by the workers as a consequence of the Revolution. At the same time, there was a most peculiar tension between the desire to put the workers in their place and the desire to see if one could not come to terms with the more "reasonable" elements in the Social Democratic Party and increase productivity with their support and assistance. Silverberg was convinced that "one day it will come to a miners strike,"[98] but he agreed with Stinnes that they had neither the power nor could they take the responsibility for such a strike under existing circumstances. English experience had taught that such a strike could only be risked by the employers if it were prepared in cooperation with the government in such a way as to ensure security, sufficient quantities of coal, and sufficient quantities of food. Otherwise, public support would be lost, and without that and government backing, more would be lost than gained from a labor conflict. The time for an open economic battle with the workers, therefore had not come, but the time did seem ripe for a political and propaganda battle. Silverberg argued that the RdI, backed by the program they were developing, could and should openly reveal the "sins of the Socialist government" and trade union leaders.[99] He believed that this would win support for the German cause abroad, where it was felt that foreigners, particularly the Americans to whom they were looking for a loan, would appreciate a hard line toward the Socialists, who

[96] *Ibid.*, Bl. 101–102.   [97] *Ibid.*, Bl. 104–105.
[98] *Ibid.*, Bl. 88–90 for his remarks on this subject.
[99] *Ibid.*, Bl. 90.

according to the new German ambassador to Washington, Dr. Wiedfeldt of Krupp, the Americans regarded as a species of Bolshevik.[100]

The members of the Special Committee themselves did not identify the Social Democrats with the Bolsheviks, of course, and they recognized that Bolshevism had made some contributions to the disciplining of the workers. Although they rejected it for obvious reasons, they also opposed counterrevolution as "little suited to our purposes."[101] Thus, whereas attacking the Socialists and driving them from the government seemed to be reasonable political goals, they also wished to woo them, and both von Raumer and Silverberg, advocates of Stinnes' *Zentralarbeitsgemeinschaft*, urged that the RdI seek to win the support of Socialist and even Independent Socialist theoreticians who had demonstrated some command of economics and who had shown an understanding for the productivity question. Such persons were viewed as open to "scientific" argumentation and less susceptible to mass pressures than the Socialist politicians and trade union leaders. The anticipated fusion of the SPD and USPD in September was viewed as a favorable opportunity. Similarly, they hoped to win over influential writers in the left liberal press. Within heavy industry, however, there was some difference of opinion concerning this approach of trying to win over worker leaders through persuasion. Vögler, who seemed to be distancing himself from the *Arbeitsgemeinschaft* idea, thought Silverberg's and Raumer's tactical proposals "extraordinarily dangerous,"[102] whereas the ever cantankerous Reusch, who had never supported the ZAG, bluntly wrote to Silverberg that "The unwillingness to work cannot be fought through the joint collaboration of workers and employers, but only through a strong government which had the courage to proceed energetically and ruthlessly."[103]

Although the tactical differences between Reusch and Silverberg were important both in 1922 and subsequently, they by no means represented a substantive difference of opinion on basic principles, and both men could certainly agree that the Wirth government lacked the necessary authority to force the workers to increase productivity. It must hastily be added, however, that it also lacked the authority to bring the great industrialists to heel, and that the industrialists had been permitted to play the role of rebellious subjects whenever they did not have their way. Their performance as taxpayers during the inflation had made a mockery of Erzberger's efforts in 1919–1920 to reform the tax structure in such a way as to tax great wealth. Instead, actual tax collection had become more inequitable than ever.

[100] Reported by Lammers, *ibid.*, Bl. 100.
[101] *Ibid.*, Bl. 80.   [102] *Ibid.*, Bl. 98.
[103] Reusch to Silverberg, August 30, 1920, HA/GHH, Nr. 30019320/2.

The industrialists had warmly supported the introduction of a withholding tax on wages in 1920, and by 1922 about 75% of the state's receipts from taxes on income came from this source. This produced bitterness among the workers, who were compelled to pay their taxes at full value at the moment of income receipt whereas those paying taxes on income that was not subject to withholding were allowed to do so with the depreciated marks of 1922 on income received in 1920! The turnover taxes and consumption taxes naturally hit the consumers much harder than they hit the producers, but the situation was exacerbated because business turned these taxes over to the government every quarter. This meant that businesses received a continuous *de facto* interest-free public credit that was paid off in devalued currency. As has been shown, the entire tax structure favored concentration and conglomeration by reducing corporate taxes and eliminating inventory taxes on internal deliveries within concerns.[104] All this did not stop the RdI leaders from complaining about the tax burdens in the most bitter terms and calling for "a fundamental reform of the entire German tax system." They frankly noted that "the taxes in effect at the present time and their technical implementation are only bearable thanks to the inflation." Because, by implication, stabilization carried with it the danger that the tax system might actually function as it was intended to—that is, to appropriately tax individual wealth and corporate profit —it was argued that "It is necessary to push the production promoting point of view into the foreground in preparing for a modern tax program."[105]

The role heavy industry was permitted to play in the foreign affairs of the Reich was a further illustration of the lack of authority possessed by the Wirth government and its predecessors. The question at issue was not so much that industrialists were both encouraged and used by the government to undertake negotiations with industrial and political leaders of foreign powers, but rather that the industrial leaders were permitted to circumscribe the range of agreements and the types of accommodations that Germany could make with her former enemies, particularly France, and that they were allowed to exceed their prerogatives by setting political as well as economic conditions in domestic and foreign affairs. Thus, in negotiations with the French between 1919 and 1921, the heavy industrialists had refused to give serious consideration to French proposals for collaboration between French and German heavy industry because they insisted on rebuilding their capacities to the point where they could negotiate from a

[104] Witt in *Industrielles System*, p. 411ff.

[105] Draft of an economic program for the Special Committee in BA, Nachlass Silverberg, Nr. 312, Bl. 71.

position of strength. The government had been powerless to prevent the implementation of this policy, although concessions permitting the more rapid growth of French production might have alleviated international tensions and created economic conditions of longer-term benefit to the economic development of Europe and even Germany. By 1922, German heavy industry's iron and steel production capacity had reached the point where its leaders could begin to contemplate negotiating from strength and employing the soon-to-be tariff weapon to bring the French to terms. As noted earlier, however, this increased capacity was veiled by the reparations deliveries of coal. Yet when Frölich of the VDMA expressed concern in April 1922 that German industry would not be able to supply domestic demand if tariffs were raised above prewar levels as demanded by heavy industry, he was provided with a list of twelve major concerns engaged in major expansion of their basic productive capacities and was told that the list was far from complete. He was warned that Germany would be flooded with French iron and steel products the moment the coal supply was sufficient and that the tariff was necessary if the iron and steel industry was not to be ruined.[106]

It was from this sense of potential strength and capacity as well as from his usual splendidly developed sense of self-importance and self-interest that Stinnes conducted various private negotiations with Allied industrialists and statesmen in the summer and fall of 1922. Stinnes and his colleagues had been merciless in their criticism of Rathenau for concluding the so-called Wiesbaden Agreement with the French Minister Louis Loucheur in October 1921, an agreement on the payment of reparations in kind for the purpose of reconstructing the devastated regions of France. The agreement foresaw the creation of self-governing bodies composed of government officials, industrialists, and trade union leaders as well as of those Frenchmen who were to be recompensed for their losses. The political goals were to depoliticize the reparations issue, show German good faith, and promote commercial relations. The organizational structure was designed to ensure that contracts were equitably distributed among German firms and that the social interests of labor were not disregarded. Stinnes attacked the agreement because, in his view, it made too many concessions to

[106] See Soutou and Bariéty in *Industrielles System*, pp. 543–567, and Maier, *Recasting Bourgeois Europe*, chap. 4, for the general discussion here and below. Also, Frölich to Reichert, April 12, 1922; Pig Iron Syndicate to VdESI, April 24, 1922; Steel Works Association report, April 27, 1922, in BA, R 13 I/349., Bl. 135–145. The list of expanding works included the Bochumer Verein, Thyssen, Mannesmann (which was building smelting plants for the first time), Phoenix, Georgsmarienhütte, Van der Zypen, Röchling, Maximilianshütte, Siegen-Solinger Gussstahlverein, Klöckner, Krupp, Gewerkschaft Luthertaufe in Gotha, and Stahlwerk Becker.

France, and he regarded the entire organization as a piece of Rathen-auian planned economics that would add to the malfunctioning of the already "controlled" economy.

In September 1922, however, he shocked all of Germany by sud-denly appearing as a convert to "fulfillment" and outdoing the mur-dered Rathenau with his own Stinnes-Lubersac Agreement, an agree-ment privately negotiated between himself and the President of the General Confederation of Enterprises for the Reconstruction of the Devastated Regions, the Marquis de Lubersac. Like the Wiesbaden Agreement, the Stinnes-Lubersac Agreement was designed to provide reparations in kind to aid French reconstruction, but unlike the earlier agreement, no provision was made for the participation of either the government or the trade unions. Instead, the tasks of acting as an agent between the French and the German firms as well as the actual distribution of contracts was to be done by Stinnes' Aktiengesellschaft für Hoch und Tiefbau in Essen, a large construction firm Stinnes had set up within the framework of the SRSU to realize one of the initial intentions he had mentioned when first creating the SRSU, namely, giving it a major role in the reconstruction of the devastated regions. In return for its services, the firm was to get a 6% commission on the price of what was delivered, prices, it must be added, that would be based on what was being paid on the French market and that could therefore bring in a substantial exchange profit. Furthermore, the agreement provided that the French would relinquish a percentage of German coal deliveries in return for an increased supply of construc-tion materials with the understanding that the coal would be used to produce material for reparations in kind. Needless to say, the distribu-tion of this coal would be handled by Stinnes' coal firm, albeit in collaboration with the Coal Syndicate, and this would further enhance his already enormous power in the coal industry.[107]

The entire arrangement was a stunning illustration of how Stinnes combined the relentless pursuit of his special interests with political pretensions of the most unrealistic kind. The self-interest involved was so transparent as to invite enormous public criticism. His sudden conversion to collaboration with the French in the proposed manner could easily be explained by the downturn in business opportunities and a looming depression, and it illustrated the imagination as well as the desperation with which Stinnes was searching for new sources of liquidity for his giant and tenuously founded operations. Nevertheless,

---

[107] See Eyck, *History*, I, pp. 186–187; Ufermann, *Stinnes-Konzerne*, pp. 68–71; Laubach, *Kabinette Wirth*, pp. 73–78, 286ff; David Felix, *Walther Rathenau and the Weimar Republic. The Politics of Reparations* (Baltimore and London, 1971), p. 105ff.

Stinnes sought to save the nation for himself as well as himself for the nation, and his arrangement with de Lubersac was part of a "great plan" confidentially imparted to Ebert, de Lubersac, Poincaré, and the American Ambassador Alanson B. Houghton in late October 1922.[108] Stinnes entertained the notion that he could use the agreement and the promise of future assistance from German industry to induce the French to forget about guarantees and sanctions and to terminate the Rhineland and Saar occupations by April 1, 1923. In return for this, the German workers would work an extra two hours per day overtime for the coming ten or fifteen years in order to maintain an active balance of trade and pay interest on a gold loan for the reconstruction of France and Belgium. In return for the gold loan, Germany would stabilize the mark, terminate all domestic controls designed to protect German consumers, ban strikes for five years, reform her tax laws "to stimulate thrift," and sharply reduce government personnel and expenditure. Social justice for those members of the middle class and pensioners hurt by the inflation would be provided by state-granted temporary minimum annuities. Finally, the European nations, inclusive of Germany, would then "approach the U.S. of America in order to try to arrange the indebtedness between the nations and thus make possible a final liquidation of the consequences of the war of 1914–18."[109] Unhappily for Stinnes, whose capacity to mix fantasy and reality was second only to that of the militarist he had once so heartily supported, Ludendorff, it was much easier to do business with an ambitious dueler like de Lubersac than it was to deal with Poincaré or the Americans. Foreign experts were hardly fooled by what one American State Department official called a "gigantic German trust with a French tail,"[110] and the Americans were not prepared to offer the political and economic assurances that might have made Poincaré seriously consider the program. Although the Wirth government, desperate for help in the "depoliticization" of reparations and the financial relief it would bring, encouraged Stinnes' efforts, it did so with few illusions.

The reality was that even Germany's strongest friends abroad, such as John Maynard Keynes, neither expected France to surrender such security as she had gained under Versailles nor agreed with Stinnes' argument that Germany could do nothing to stabilize her economy by herself so long as she did not receive the definitive reparations set-

[108] The relevant documents are reprinted and discussed in G. W. F. Hallgarten, *Hitler, Reichswehr und Industrie* (Frankfurt am Main, 1955), pp. 11–19, 47–61.

[109] *Ibid.*, p. 54.

[110] Comment by W. R. Castle, Head of the West European Section of the U.S. State Department, *ibid.*, p. 59.

tlement and long-term loan accompanied by a moratorium on reparations payments. Specifically, they were convinced that the Reichsbank could use its gold reserves to support an action undertaken on behalf of the mark and that the government was in a position to exercise greater control on foreign exchange transactions as well as on its own expenditures. In short, they rejected the official German view that all stabilization was impossible so long as the balance of trade remained unfavorable and the reparations question remained unsettled. This critical posture toward the Reichsbank's policies was fully shared by the leaders of the RWM under Wirth, Schmidt, and Hirsch, who severely criticized the Reichsbank and whose strict Exchange Decree of October 12 had provided such sharp attacks and criticisms from German industry.[111]

Indeed, throughout October and early November, Wirth found himself in an increasingly impossible position. On the one hand, he felt that he needed the support of Stinnes and industry to gain credibility abroad and he wanted to widen the base of his government to the right to include industrial leaders and the industrialist-supported DVP. On the other hand, not only the Social Democrats in the RWM, but also German experts such as Moritz Bonn and Rudolf Hilferding and, most painfully for Wirth, the foreign experts whose expert opinion he had solicited, came down on the side of policies supporting immediate measures of stabilization that provoked strong opposition from the industrialists. Back in September, Bücher had declared in the RdI that *"The gold in the Reichsbank is the last reserve that we have in order to meet a more severe economic crisis.* Under no circumstances should it come into question in dealing with the Reparations Commission."[112] This view was fully supported by Havenstein, who responded to attacks from Schmidt and Hirsch by placing himself behind heavy industry's priorities of increasing productivity, settling reparations, and only then undertaking stabilization. The attack on the October Exchange Decree from heavy industry, therefore, was highly political in character because it was employed not only to undermine the unwelcome provisions of the decree itself, but also to push for the set of priorities being developed in the RdI program.[113]

If literally implemented, this was a program that could only lead to open conflict, and as August Thyssen revealed in a personal letter to Wirth of October 14, some industrialists were prepared to push the

[111] Laubach, *Kabinette Wirth*, p. 286ff., for this and the general discussion below.
[112] RdI meeting of September 6, 1922, HA/GHH, Nr. 3001240/4. Italics in the original.
[113] See Laubach, *Kabinette Wirth*, p. 292, and above, p. 315.

government in that direction. Thyssen considered the "undifferenti-ated eight-hour day" to be "the greatest misfortune that the Revo-lution could bring to Germany" because it had lowered productivity at a time when higher productivity was more important than ever before. He was bewildered as to how Germans who had worked ten hours a day during the prosperous years before the war could expect to live even better than then by working eight hours a day under the Versailles *Diktat*. He pleaded with Wirth to place himself "at the head of a movement for an increased working day" and not to shy away from the battle it would inevitably bring.[114]

The high point of the industrialist campaign, however, came on November 9, 1922, the fourth anniversary of the German Revolution, when Stinnes, with the official sanction of the RdI, delivered a major address before the Reich Economics Council which was widely re-ported and then circulated in brochure form for the "enlightenment" of the public. In it, he declared quite bluntly that he had "always fought the stabilization of the mark at any price," that the time had not come for stabilization, and that "the precondition for any success-ful stabilization in my view is that all wage conflict and strikes are banned." As was to be expected, the extra two hours per day of work Stinnes felt essential was presented as a matter of "life and death:"

> For this reason I believe that we in Germany must have the cour-age to say . . . to the people: You can keep the eight-hour day, but for the forseeable future you must work the additional hours with-out overtime pay (*Überbezahlung*) until you have an active balance of payments and additionally so much surplus as is necessary to live and to pay the interest and amortization on the loan that is absolutely necessary for the stabilization of the mark and for the payment of reparations. . . .[115]

Stinnes' speech undermined Wirth's efforts to persuade the Socialists to enter a Great Coalition cabinet running from the SPD to the DVP. Wirth sought to bridge the gap between the contending positions in his Reparations Note of November 13 in which he committed his gov-ernment to a stabilization effort for the first time and promised to do everything possible to straighten out Germany's finances and to raise

[114] Thyssen to Wirth, October 14, 1922, BA R 13 I/1132, Bl. 359–362.

[115] Hugo Stinnes, *Mark-Stabilisierung und Arbeitsleistung. Rede von Hugo Stinnes gehalten am 9. November 1922 in Reichswirtschaftsrat* (Berlin, 1922), pp. 9–10. This effort to dispense Stinnes' wisdom to a wide audience through a cheap brochure was further embellished by an apparatus of footnotes designed to explain basic economic concepts and difficult words (e.g., "doctrinaire" and "nu-ances") for the man on the street. Needless to say, the "enlightenment" thereby given compounded the tendentiousness of the speech itself.

productivity. Nevertheless, it was one thing to put intentions on paper, another to realize them tangibly in the form of a Great Coalition cabinet, and although the DVP demanded the introduction of industrial leaders into the cabinet and SPD support for a program that would allow exceptions to the eight-hour day, the SPD refused to surrender to such terms. On November 14, 1922, Wirth and his cabinet resigned and were succeeded by a bourgeois minority government under the chancellorship of the politically unaffiliated head of the Hamburg-America Line, Heinrich Cuno. Not only did Germany have a leading businessman to head its government for the first time, but it also had a new Economics Minister from heavy industry in the person of the former Hessian Minister of Finance, Johannes Becker, who had been made a director of Rheinstahl at the beginning of 1920 to deal with various sociopolitical and financial tasks involving lobbying in Berlin. It appeared as if big business was in the saddle at last.[116]

Industry had, of course, been longing for a strong business-oriented regime, and the absence of such a government had served as a rationalization and justification for letting things drift and engaging in the "low policy" of day-to-day adjustment to the inflation. This was explicitly stated by Thyssen in early October when he came down on the side of maintaining paper mark pricing "until a new strong government finds a way out," just as it was demonstrated in mid-December when Hasslacher fatalistically told his supervisory board that "So long as there is no change in our foreign and domestic policy, there is nothing left to do but operate in the way we have until now." Hasslacher's fatalism in December, however, illustrates that there was some ambivalence in heavy industrial circles as to whether the Cuno regime, already in power a month when Hasslacher made his remark, was the type of "new, strong regime" for which Thyssen had been waiting.[117]

Cuno owed his appointment, in fact, to the confidence felt in him by Reich President Ebert, and although Cuno had good connections in heavy industrial circles, particularly with Reusch, he was by no means a man of heavy industry. A leading executive of the Hamburg shipping industry, Cuno tended to the cosmopolitan, internationalist, free-trading views of the Hanseatic businessmen as exemplified by the attitudes of his close associate, the banker, Max Warburg. Cuno was suspicious of Stinnes, with whom the Hamburg-America Line had had some unpleasant business dealings, and he did not share many of Stinnes' political views.[118] In general, he was less rigid than the heavy

[116] Laubach, *Kabinette Wirth*, pp. 306–314, and Rupieper, "Politics and Economics," p. 62ff.

[117] See above, p. 311.

[118] See Karl-Heinz Harbeck, ed., *Das Kabinett Cuno. 22. November 1922 bis 12.*

industrialists. This was already in evidence before he became Chancellor when, in September, as a member of the RdI board of directors, he challenged the rigid priorities set forth by Silverberg's Special Committee and insisted that domestic and foreign affairs could not be separated and that "the healing of our internal circumstances depends on the healing of the external ones."[119] This is not to say that Cuno disagreed with the substance of the domestic economic program or the basic attitudes toward the relationship between state and economy underlying it. He advocated *the separation of economics from politics* so that "our economic freedom of movement should not be hemmed in by politics," and he opposed false compromises and called on industry to stand up to the workers.[120]

Two months later, as Chancellor of a minority government, with a Labor Ministry in the hands of a Centrist close to the Christian trade unions, Heinrich Brauns, an Economics Ministry in the hands of a politician associated with heavy industry, Johannes Becker, and a powerful political opposition on the left and right watching the government's actions from the Reichstag, Cuno was finding it somewhat more difficult to separate economics from politics and avoid compromises. True to his own convictions, he continued the foreign policy of Wirth outlined in the latter's Reparations Note of November 13—that is, a policy of promising to undertake measures of internal stabilization before securing a definitive reparations settlement and a foreign loan. Like Wirth, Cuno ran into the opposition of Hugo Stinnes and other heavy industrial leaders, and Cuno took the occasion of a major speech before the Reich Economics Council in Hamburg on December 12 to point out that "the relationship between economic circles and the government should also be one in which the government takes the lead and the business community (*die Wirtschaft*) supports the government."[121] In his efforts to tone down the demands of the heavy industrialists, Cuno was supported by Economics Minister Becker, whose political experience and responsibility compelled him to be reasonable, as well as leading businessmen such as Duisberg, the banker Louis Hagen, and Warburg. On most occasions, Reusch also proved loyal and helpful, but it was extraordinarily difficult to persuade Reusch and

---

August 1923. Akten der Reichskanzlei. Weimarer Republik (Boppard am Rhein, 1968), p. xixff. (Hereinafter cited as *Kabinett Cuno*). Much can be learned about Cuno from his papers in the Hapag Archiv in Hamburg as well as from the Warburg papers in Brinckmann, Wirtz u. Co. in Hamburg and the correspondence between Cuno and Reusch.

[119] RdI directors meeting, September 6, 1922, HA/GHH, Nr. 3001240/4.
[120] *Ibid.*
[121] *Kabinett Cuno*, p. 64n4.

Klöckner that demands for a premature Allied evacuation of the Rhineland could not be made the precondition of a reparations settlement.[122]

Cuno did have the weight and support within business circles to
gain the necessary backing for a reparations plan for which he vainly
tried to gain Allied acceptance in his feverish efforts to ward off a
French invasion of the Ruhr, but it is also clear that his abortive efforts were made more difficult by heavy industry. Insofar as he did
have heavy industrial assistance in foreign relations, as he did in the
private negotiations between Stinnes, Klöckner, and Silverberg, on
the one side, and French industrialists, on the other, these were conducted on terms defined by the former. Stinnes believed that long-term
collaboration with the French was possible and necessary because a
natural division of labor existed if Germany could supply the coal and
finished iron and steel products, whereas France supplied the ore, pig
iron, and semifinished products, but he rejected the notion of an interpenetration of French-German interests that did not involve German
participation in French enterprises as well as the reverse. More important, as Silverberg informed Finance Minister Hermes, the success of
all such agreements with France or any other Allied power depended
on "domestic economic and political order."[123]

Indeed, during the last weeks before the Ruhr invasion, heavy industry was as uncompromising and as frank in its demands as Cuno
had advised the business leaders to be at the September RdI directors
meeting. Certainly the domestic political policies of the Cuno regime
were looked on with greater favor than those of its predecessors by
big business. Aside from such welcome personnel changes as the replacement of Schmidt and Hirsch by Becker and Trendelenburg, the
Cuno regime was strongly committed to the reduction of government
expenditures and raising productivity as well as to the elimination of
economic controls as rapidly as possible. The appointment of a Reich
Austerity Commissar (*Reichssparkommissar*) on November 23 with the
task of trimming all the fat from the administration was greeted as a
major step toward these goals. Nevertheless, the intentions and capa-
bilities of the Cuno regime in domestic affairs were as nothing compared to what Silverberg wanted it to do in a program he distributed
with great liberality to his industrialist colleagues and the government
under the title "Reconstruction of the German Economy."[124]

The program was meant to be the working draft of the Special Com-

[122] Meeting of December 16, 1922, in *ibid.*, pp. 73–74.

[123] Silverberg to Hermes, December 26, 1922, BA R 43 I/i133, Bl. 148–150, and
Kabinett Cuno, pp. 91–92n4 and 136–137n3.

[124] For the program, as discussed below, see BA, Nachlass Silverberg, Nr. 313,
Bl. 3–8.

mittee, and Silverberg hoped that it would shortly be discussed within the RdI executive. He began by laying down the basic principles underpinning his concrete proposals: the primacy of "work and production," the need to maintain Germany's industrial base and to promote its technical development, the need to maintain "respect for property" by preserving and expanding the capital on which it rested, and the need for a "fundamental renunciation of interference by all public authorities and administrations in the production and distribution of goods." Turning then to concrete measures, he called for the "elimination of *all* demobilization decrees and the agencies and institutions arising from them," as the first and most important item on the agenda. As he noted in an appendix dealing with "immediate necessities," with this measure "the eight-hour day falls." Thereupon followed a lengthy and remarkably inclusive catalogue of proposals for the elimination of all regulations against profiteering through price controls and regulations, the termination of all export controls and export levies, the banning of labor contracts negotiated on a national level or for any area larger than those defined in a series of economic regions to be carefully drawn up, and the banning of trade union interference in the affairs of individual plants. He demanded that the workers and the employer in a plant be allowed to conclude private agreements on wages and hours even when these violated existing labor contracts between the organizations, and he insisted that the courts be allowed temporarily to increase the normal working day whenever an agreement toward this end could not be reached by the parties involved. He went on to propose that all matters pertaining to the coal industry be effectively turned over to the Coal Syndicate for decision, that all publicly owned enterprises be privatized, that strikes in the public sector be banned, that rents be unfrozen, that exchange controls be eliminated, and that the Economics and Labor Ministries be combined because "social policy cannot be a purpose unto itself." Fundamentally, the program was nothing less than a socioeconomic counterrevolution, because the call for "a cleansing of the entire postrevolutionary legislation"[125] was explicitly designed to eliminate what labor considered to be its greatest gain from the Revolution, the eight-hour day, and to weaken severely the collective bargaining arrangements that had developed out of the war and the Revolution. At the same time, Silverberg was also intent on banning government interference to preserve the social peace in the form of arbitration boards whose decisions might be declared binding by the Labor Ministry. In short, there was much in the Silverberg

---

[125] Silverberg to Hermes, December 26, 1922, BA R 43 I/1133, Bl. 148. The dismantling of the demobilization decrees would also pave the way for large-scale unemployment by removing restrictions on the shutting down of plants.

336

program that looked back to 1914, and if there was a willingness to deal with the unions, it was only on the most general level and basically on employer terms.

Silverberg was careful to point out that his programmatic outline, which he modestly suggested made no pretension of being a complete survey of the monumental problems involved, represented his own views because he had not had a chance to gain prior approval from his colleagues. Yet he was "convinced that the views set down therein, aside from individual details, are shared in the main by all my professional colleagues."[126] Undoubtedly, the basic principles and desires expressed in the program were widely shared among leading German businessmen, particularly the heavy industrialists, but a distinction must be made between the fantasy life of businessmen and their realistic desires and expectations. If it had ever been discussed in the RdI, the Silverberg draft certainly would have encountered strong resistance from representatives of the more advanced sectors, such as Carl Duisberg, who told Silverberg that "In your demands . . . you are returning to Manchesterianism without retaining and appropriating for your program that which is good in what the last decades have brought us."[127] On the tactical side, Duisberg rejected presenting the workers with a *Diktat*, urged compromise, and warned against fighting "historical development." Even Reusch, who seldom shied away from conflict and who was most sympathetic to the idea of using Silverberg's draft as a basis for discussion, found it rather unrealistic. He thought that Silverberg exaggerated Germany's internal freedom of action and felt that the importance of the Versailles Treaty and the restrictions it imposed had been neglected. However hateful to Reusch was most of what had happened since 1918, he felt compelled to point out "that you treat certain domestic political changes that have taken place in many areas because of postwar conditions as if they did not exist," and Reusch did not anticipate that these could be changed in the "forseeable future." Lastly, Reusch disliked the number of things that Silverberg wanted to "forbid" and "ban," and he urged that such words be used sparingly and that a more positive tone be taken with as few demands for legislation as possible: "We want as few laws as possible and as much freedom as possible."[128]

The government leaders who received Silverberg's reconstruction program found its implementation most difficult to imagine. Finance Minister Hermes, who had solicited a copy from Silverberg because

[126] *Ibid.*

[127] Duisberg to Silverberg, January 12, 1923, BA, Nachlass Silverberg, Nr. 298, Bl. 87–88.

[128] Reusch to Silverberg, January 13, 1923, HA/GHH, Nr. 400101290/35.

he wanted information on industrialist thinking in connection with the reparations question, simply buried the document in his files. A similar course was recommended by officials of the Reich Chancellery, where Cuno had sent the document for consideration.[129] To be sure, Silverberg's views, particularly on the eight-hour-day question, were shared in some political circles, but both in the Reich Economics Council, where the problem of a new hours of work law to replace the Decree of November 23, 1918, had been debated for some time, and in the programmatic guidelines developed by the DVP, DDP, and Center in November 1922, a frontal assault on the eight-hour day had been carefully avoided. Instead, the latter recommended "speedy passage of an hours of work law with the fixing of the eight-hour day as the normal work day while permitting legally defined exceptions by contractual or governmental means to relieve the distress of our economy."[130]

However "grotesque" Silverberg's program, it was no more so than many of the demands made by Stinnes and Thyssen, particularly with respect to the crucial eight-hour-day question. That issue was a matter of particular significance to the iron and steel industrialists because the twelve-hour day with its two-hour pause had long been considered essential to the functioning of their continuously operating plants, where an actual increase in labor productivity per hour by other than technical improvements was impossible. The eight-hour day had been condemned as inefficient from the standpoint of permitting adequate repair and maintenance and of allowing for the necessary readjustments for the changing of profiles and the production of certain products. It was argued that the eight-hour day was bad for the workers too because it gave them inadequate opportunity to rest during their working day. The steel men claimed that the lower costs and higher efficiency of the ten-hour working day and twelve-hour shift had enabled them to maintain employment in hard times and that this policy was now placed in jeopardy. It was quite clear that the eight-hour day was a reform that the unions had only been able to win because of the Revolution and even then only with the proviso that it depend on the conclusion of an international agreement establishing the eight-hour day everywhere. Although the international agreement was never ratified, the "schematic" eight-hour day became anchored in law by the Decrees of the Council of Peoples' Commissars in November 1918. Thus, to

[129] Ministerial Councilor Kempner to State Secretary Hamm, January 6, 1923, BA R 43 I/1133, Bl. 170. Some of Silverberg's demands were characterized as "grotesque."

[130] For these guidelines see BA, Nachlass Silverberg, Nr. 298, Bl. 82. On the general problem see Ludwig Preller, *Sozialpolitik in der Weimarer Republik* (Stuttgart, 1949), p. 267ff.

both the workers and employers, it became a symbol. To the former, it represented *the* achievement of the otherwise aborted Revolution. To the latter, it was a concession granted under duress in an agreement that had not been lived up to, and its maintenance was the product of the decree of a regime of dubious legitimacy that conflicted with basic economic necessities.[131]

When it came to attacking the eight-hour day overtly, however, the steel men had had a difficult time. They had contemplated a frontal assault on the eight-hour day in early 1920, a time when they were being obstreperous about a host of matters, and the VdESI had been prepared to formally request the RdI to demand openly "that the ten-hour day again be made the normal working day in industry."[132] The Kapp Putsch, however, had made the continuation of this effort most inadvisable. Also, it was difficult to launch a major campaign for a longer working day when raw materials shortages, transport difficulties, and the desire to employ as many people as possible hampered efforts to work at full capacity and maximum efficiency. Consequently, they concentrated their attacks on the "schematic" eight-hour day, where they shared grievances, some of which were quite legitimate, with other industries. At the same time, they joined in the demand for increased productivity and overtime work on the railroads and in the coal mines. In both cases, it was possible to score economic points because the railroads had been bloated with personnel and their operation was quite open to criticism for much of the period, whereas the need for increased coal production was apparent to all. Furthermore, the increased productivity of the mines under a series of overtime agreements in effect at various times since 1920 was useful in making the case for increased hours throughout industry. As far as the iron and steel industry was concerned, the question as to whether or not the eight-hour day actually increased costs and reduced productivity significantly was hotly debated, not only in Germany but in the other steel-producing nations. The official position of the German steel-producing organizations was that the introduction of the eight-hour day had been a mistake from both points of view, although the actual results of surveys undertaken were far from unambiguous.[133] When

131 For the various technical arguments against the eight-hour day in the iron and steel industry, see the material sent by Steinbrinck of the VdESI to Walcher of the RWM on October 24, 1922, DZA Potsdam, RWM, Nr. 4619, Bl. 22ff.

132 See the report by Bülow at the VdESI Executive Directors meeting of June 22, 1920, BA R 13 I/158.

133 On the railroad situation, see, for example, the VdESI Northwest Group meeting on December 21, 1920, and related materials in HA/GHH, Nr. 30019321/1. For the ambiguity of the reports, see the material sent by Steinbrinck to the

Judge Gary, the American steel leader, made inquiries among his German colleagues, he was given positive as well as negative evaluations of the eight-hour day, but the former were deliberately provided "in order to sidetrack them and raise their costs."[134] The major consideration for the steel leaders, however, had little to do with the actual functioning of the eight-hour day. From the outset, they viewed the elimination of the eight-hour day as a mechanism by which to lower wages. This was quite explicitly stated by a VdESI official in 1920, who pointed out that wages could not be reduced directly because of the high cost of living. Workers, therefore, had to be persuaded to work more hours for the same pay. In this way, industry could achieve "at least an indirect reduction of wages."[135]

What was a shrewd calculation in 1920 became a shrill demand by the end of 1922. The combined pressure of reparations demands and the closing of the gap between domestic and world market prices as well as the growing prospect of stabilization and depression made the industrialists insistent on cost reduction through increased work and reduced wages. Behind this insistence lurked anxiety over the potential irreversibility of labor's gains and an anger expressed by Reusch when he remarked that "What is to blame for the collapse of the mark and the difficult circumstances created among us is in large measure the laziness to which the German people have succumbed since the war. . . . "[136] There was all the more reason to place the burden on the workers because matters were progressing to the point where the raw materials producers and manufacturers were at one another's throats once again and relations even within heavy industry left something to be desired. The emphasis on productivity was something that could unite businessmen at a time when most of the other things they were doing seemed to be dividing them.

Tensions between raw materials producers and finishers had been mounting because the former were able to use their pricing organizations such as the Coal Syndicate, the Pig Iron Syndicate, and the Steel Federation to keep pace with the inflation at the expense of their customers. Furthermore, the principles on which heavy industrial pricing were based were recognized by many to be at once exploitative and self-defeating because they only intensified inflationary tendencies. Stinnes, supported by many industrial leaders, had fought against laws

RWM, October 24, 1922, DZA Potsdam, RWM, Nr. 4619, Bl. 22ff. Also, see the survey in the VdESI history, BA R 13 I/13, Bl. 77–78.

[134] Reichert to Deputy Pinkerneil, November 16, 1922, Bergbau Archiv. Bestand 15, Bd. 67.

[135] Bülow at the VdESI Executive Directors meeting, June 22, 1920, BA R 13 I/158.

[136] Reusch at a meeting on December 16, 1922, HA/GHH, Nr. 300193008/12.

prohibiting profiteering (*Wuchergesetze*), often under the claim that this was the only way to protect small businessmen and shopkeepers from being ruined by regulations limiting the bases of price calculation to costs. He argued that the only just basis for pricing was reproduction costs (*Wiederbeschaffungskosten*)—that is, the price needed to permit the seller to reproduce the product.[137] Although it certainly was true that the laws against profiteering had largely been inequitably applied against small businessmen and shopkeepers, Stinnes was really serving himself in supposedly serving them because sophisticated anticipatory pricing was most easily accomplished by those organized to sell goods most susceptible to such pricing, i.e., raw materials producers like himself. Knowledgeable persons in the manufacturing industries were not fooled by Stinnes' arguments, which were otherwise widely accepted in certain governmental and industrial circles. A well-known engineer and economic expert from the electrotechnical industry, Emil Schiff, for example, tried to enlighten Cuno on the subject. He pointed out that "price increases to make up for the depreciation of money mean only the cultivation of artificial purchasing power" with an "endless price and wage spiral" as the result. He considered the industrial pricing policies not only "monopolistic in the worst sense" but also "fundamentally false" because it was a "mathematical impossibility" to "maintain the substance" of the producing concerns by implementing the "theory of renewal costs" and the "theory of reproduction costs" expounded by the heavy industrialists and apparently accepted by the RWM. Instead of giving the "monstrously overburdened economy" the relief it needed by pricing according to actual immediate costs, the situation was being made worse not only for the present but also for the future in a most unjust manner:

> The attempt of the businessmen to liberate themselves from the effects of the inflation must therefore fail, as is already clearly demonstrated; only a few raw material monopolists can succeed in the end. But in the meantime, the most fateful redistribution of capital is taking place, and left in the lurch are the state and the communes along with all those who are not participants in the economic process primarily as producers, among them our most valuable intellectual workers. . . .[138]

The more sensitive and politically alert of the heavy industrialists could not but be aware of the dangers of the situation. The effectiveness of the business community as a coherent and united pressure

[137] See his remarks at the RdI directors meeting on September 6, 1922, *ibid.*, Nr. 3001240/4.

[138] Emil Schiff to Cuno, December 24, 1922, BA R 43 I/1133, Bl. 171–172.

group was in danger because of increasing criticism of heavy industry's blatant domination of the RdI.[139] The criticisms were all the more alarming because they came from powerful industrial leaders such as Carl Duisberg, whose complaints about steel prices led Vögler to send him detailed cost analyses with a plea that he counter criticisms of his industry's pricing policies.[140] Whatever his success with Duisberg, Vögler had no success with the many hostile members of the electrotechnical industry despite the valiant efforts of the Siemens' director Köttgen to employ material supplied by Vögler to gain a hearing for the steel men. The Zendei directors accepted the pricing policies of the coal syndicate because the soaring prices of wood in 1922 and the 40% coal tax made that industry's cost calculations sound convincing, but the steel prices were viewed as excessive. Not only was Köttgen told to warn the steel industrialists to stop their excessive pricing, but hostility was further demonstrated when the Zendei directors voted against an increase in iron tariffs called for by the iron industry because "the iron prices are soaring and once the protective tariff is there, then the electrotechnical industry will suffer even more."[141] Köttgen's appeal to the "higher point of view" represented by the principle of industrial solidarity made little impression. His argument that an individual attack on the proposed iron tariff by the Zendei would have little effect and that collaboration with the VDMA was needed but that this would be difficult to get because of "the close connection between machine construction and the iron industry"[142] was considered a more telling point. Raumer was sent by the Zendei to negotiate with the VDMA, and Köttgen hoped that Borsig and Reusch would offset the enthusiasm that other VDMA leaders might show for the formation of a common front against the iron producers. All this was most unpleasant, in any case, and to it was being added growing bitterness over the stricter payment conditions being imposed by the steel industrialists. *Die Wirtschaft* seemed to be falling apart.

At the same time, however, the steel industrialists had increasing economic inducement to show moderation at the turn of 1922–1923 because, as noted in the last section, the loss of export business and the danger of a market collapse on the domestic front militated for lower prices, and they began to reduce prices in December. If necessity made them willing to take the lead in price reduction, however, it also caused them to take the initiative in pushing for the stabilization

[139] Bücher to Reusch, January 2, 1923, HA/GHH, Nr. 30019320/7.

[140] Vögler to Duisberg, November 27, 1922, Werksarchiv Bayer-Leverkusen, Autographensammlung Duisberg.

[141] Köttgen to Vögler, December 28, 1922, SAA, Nachlass Köttgen, 11/Lf 265.

[142] *Ibid.*

of wages. In short, an effort was being made to bring "low policy" and "high policy" into line, and to make some of the principles being expounded in the developing RdI program a living reality. Unlike Silverberg, however, the steel men understood that tactical skill was necessary. On December 19, the Steel Federation lowered the price on bars by 23,000 marks per ton, but noted that the policy of price reductions could work only if costs could be kept stable. They pointed to the possibility of increased coal prices in January as the chief threat because the miners were demanding a wage increase on January 1. Hence, it was deemed essential that such a wage increase not take place. In accordance with this conclusion, the Northwest Group of the VdESI and its employer organization (Arbeno) resolved to petition the RAM and RWM to refuse the worker demands and, at the suggestion of Vögler, to send a delegation to the Mine Owners Association (*Zechenverband*) to participate in the negotiations with the unions. The delegation would be composed of leading directors from the mixed concerns of Rheinstahl, Phoenix, Hoesch, and the GHH—that is, those firms engaged in coal as well as iron and steel production. The concerted character of the heavy industrialist action became all the more obvious on December 22—that is, only three days after the Steel Federation meeting and one day after Arbeno had officially notified the coal leaders of its wishes, when the Mine Owners Association informed all the German employer associations that the government opposed a wage increase on January 1 and that a wage increase on January 15, when bread prices were scheduled to go up, might also be prevented if all industries followed the lead of the mining industry and refused all wage increases.[143]

From the perspective of the heavy industrialists, it was a hopeful way to begin the new year, but the first days of 1923 brought new frustrations even before they brought the dramatic occupation of the Ruhr. An arbitration board had decided to grant the miners a wage increase effective January 1, but the actual effect of this action remained unclear because the Coal Syndicate resolved on January 2 not to grant any increases before January 15. The real blow to the steel industrialists' policy came from within industrialist ranks itself, where the Pig Iron Syndicate increased prices on January 4. Klemme and the other moderates in the Steel Federation were furious at its meeting on the 9th:

I [Klemme] characterized the action of the Pig Iron Syndicate as undisciplined. After the Northwest Group along with the *Langnam-*

[143] Arbeno to Mine Owners Association, December 21, 1922; undated memorandum to RAM; Mine Owners Association to VdA, December 22, 1922, Bergbau Archiv, Bestand 13, Bd. 307.

verein had decided upon the petition to the Reich Labor Ministry, and the Steel Federation had supported this "high policy" by holding back the price on January 2, the solo performance of the Pig Iron Syndicate cannot be defended. Once "high policy" is decided upon, then it must be held to by every group.[144]

Poensgen agreed with Klemme, but the dike had been breached again, and the majority voted for the maximum price increase demand made at the meeting, a 43,000 mark per ton increase. As Klemme noted, the vote was carried by works that tended to pay no attention to Steel Federation prices anyway, while the Hoesch representative repeated his already familiar threat that "if he did not succeed in his demand, then he will not be bound by the decisions."[145] Obviously, it was hard to rise above "low policy," and questions of discipline and authority were not limited to those employed in the workshops.

Nevertheless, it would be a mistake to think that the year 1922 had not brought important gains for the iron and steel industrialists in their efforts to maintain their economic position and stock their political arsenal. However grim the future seemed, foundations for the future had been laid. Their productive capacity was higher than ever since the war, and they had found ways to manage in the midst of worsening inflation. As one trade union leader who, like his colleagues, was no longer taken in by *die Wirtschaft's* pretensions to wisdom and honor, bluntly told the industrial representatives in the ZAG, "If it cannot be said that German industry does not have any interest in the stabilization of the mark, still it cannot be belied that it has found a means of getting out of the worst distress through self-help. Industry and commerce employ this means in the form of reproduction prices. . . ."[146] Labor was demanding that the constant reduction of real wages come to an end, and that it too be permitted to calculate its wages in the manner used by employers to calculate their prices. If the inflationary boom was collapsing, however, the industrialists had also demonstrated an ability to harden their ideological stand in preparation for the forthcoming and inevitable stabilization and *Sanierung*. The slogans of increased productivity and reduced labor and social costs provided the magic formulas on which their cooperation in any future settlement of reparations and stabilization were to be based, and they had demonstrated an increasing capacity and willingness to fight against labor and consumer protection. To be sure, at the turn of 1922–

[144] Meeting of December 9, 1923, in HA/GHH, Nr. 3000035/3.
[145] *Ibid.*
[146] Fritz Tarnow at the ZAG discussions on November 10–11, 1922, in DZA Potsdam, RWM, Nr. 12, Bl. 349.

1923 the outcome of these efforts remained uncertain, and the path to stabilization was far from clear. The terms on which they expected it to take place, however, were now quite explicit and were being driven into the consciousness of the nation. The question was whether they could be held to in the face of the French invasion of the Ruhr on January 11, 1923, when "high policy" was elevated beyond questions of hours and wages and was redirected to the exalted heights of national unity, self-sacrifice, and social peace in the name of patriotism.

CHAPTER SIX

1923: From Ruhr Occupation to Twelve-Hour Shift

The Franco-Belgian occupation of the Ruhr, which began on January 11, 1923, ushered in a year of such turmoil and complication in every aspect of German political, economic, and social life that efforts at a full-scale treatment or, as in this chapter, attempts to focus on certain limited but crucial aspects of the story, necessarily compel the historian to do even more violence to the fullness of reality than usual. Nevertheless, a focus on the German iron and steel industry is by no means inappropriate. The condition of that industry at the end of 1922 was symptomatic of the extent to which France was losing the "economic war after the war" and of the conditions that pushed her to drastic action.

This is not to say that the French invaded the Ruhr primarily because the German iron and steel industry was making good its losses in productive capacity under the Versailles Treaty while its French counterpart, thanks to its dependence on Ruhr coke, languished despite the vastly expanded capacity created by the acquisition of Lorraine and seemed condemned to competitive inferiority even if it should one day produce to capacity. Insofar as it is possible to penetrate the "governmental anarchy of France"[1] and pinpoint the chief motives and goals of the French invasion, it would seem that its basic and minimal objective was to force a comprehensive financial settlement to relieve French fiscal difficulties through the procurement of "productive guarantees" for the payment of reparations. Primarily, the pressure of the French occupation was to be the main instrument for bringing Germany to terms, although the creation of a separate Rhenish state was a supplementary outcome for Poincaré and a major goal of certain other French policy makers.[2]

---

[1] Jacques Bariéty, "Les Réparations Allemandes Aprés la Premiére Guerre Mondiale: Objet ou Prétexte à une Politique Rhénane de la France (1919–1924)" in *Bulletin de la Société d'histoire Moderne*, 5th series, No. 6 (1973), pp. 20–33, esp. p. 33.

[2] *Ibid.*, pp. 26–27; Rupieper in *Industrielles System*, pp. 589–590; Greer, *Ruhr-Lorraine Problem*, p. 81; Karl Dietrich Erdmann, *Adenauer in der Rheinlandpolitik nach dem Ersten Weltkrieg* (Stuttgart, 1966), pp. 71–78. The most judicious and informed discussion of French policy is Walter A. McDougall, "French Rhineland Policy and the Struggle for European Stabilization: Reparations, Security, and Rhenish Separatism, 1918–1924," unpublished dissertation (Chicago, 1974), p. 216ff.

Unrestricted work day; 9 hour work day. From *Vorwarts*, February 17, 1924.

If coke deliveries and German recovery in iron and steel played a secondary role in actually bringing on the Ruhr occupation, however, it is still likely that Poincaré hoped that the military action would strengthen the economic condition of the French iron and steel industry, and significantly improve its negotiating position when the limitations on German tariff sovereignty under the Versailles Treaty terminated on January 10, 1925. In a more fundamental way, however, the recovery of the German iron and steel industry had a great deal to do with the German policies that drove the French into the Ruhr. Potentially, the Treaty of Versailles might have shifted the balance of heavy industrial power in Europe from Germany to France by depriving Germany of minette and the important plants of Lorraine, Luxemburg, the Saar, and Upper Silesia and by slowing down her reconstruction through forced coke deliveries to her competitors. In reality, however, there was what might be considered a negative collaboration between French and German heavy industry to make sure that this very hypothetical potentiality was never realized. A substantial portion of French heavy industry did not believe in its own promise, was convinced that the Germans would only supply coke by agreement rather than by force, and was fearful of being saddled with an overproduction of minette, iron, and steel. Although some French industrialists had hoped that the French government would force the Germans to accept French participation in German enterprises as a means of solving French difficulties and ensuring French success, French heavy industry in general sought compromise with its German counterpart and was particularly active in this respect in 1922.[3]

French businessmen never enjoyed the influence in Paris that German steel men enjoyed in Berlin, however, and the French government gave primacy to political and fiscal considerations in the formulation of its policies. German steel men, by contrast, resisted cooperation with their French colleagues until they could face the latter from a position of strength and equality. In 1920–1921 they sabotaged German governmental proposals to use interindustrial collaboration and French participation in German enterprises as a means of mitigating the terms of the Versailles Treaty. The German steel men simply ignored the risk of future overproduction and virtually courted French action in the Ruhr by insisting on the primacy of their own reconstruction and opposing any German governmental efforts to fulfill the treaty in a manner that touched on their capital base or limited the rebuilding of their productive capacities. In short, their posture toward reparations

---

[3] Bariéty in *Industrielle System*, pp. 559–560. He argues that a French "heavy industrial project" was at least implicit in the Treaty of Versailles provisions, and that the first revision of the treaty lay in the frustration of this "project."

was a direct function of their reconstruction policies, and it may be reasonably hypothesized that the latter policies undermined such chances as there were for Franco-German industrial collaboration of a type that might have made compromises between the governments easier and relaxed the reparations stalemate that had become so irreconcilable by 1923.[4]

If Stinnes and certain other heavy industrialists displayed a more conciliatory attitude toward French industry in 1922, it was in part because Stinnes' predictions of November 1918 were coming true as well as in anticipation of the problems arising from an increasingly foreseeable stabilization. As Stinnes had foretold and Hasslacher had wished, the French were "choking" on their minette and hungry for coke, whereas German steel production was well on the road to recovery and certainly was superior to that of its European competitors.[5] The Germans had accelerated their tendency to employ higher-quality Swedish ores rather than French minette because of their greater emphasis on fuel economy after 1918, and in 1922 consumption of minette in Rhineland-Westphalia had been reduced to 13% of all ores consumed as against 22.5% of ores consumed in 1913, whereas the Scandinavian share of ores consumed had risen from 22% in 1913 to 28% in 1922. The import of these ores was by 1922 based on long-term arrangements with the Swedes. At the same time, the dependence on ores of all kinds was being reduced by an acceleration of the trend toward Siemens-Martin process production, so that by 1924 the prewar relationship between the latter and Thomas process production had been reversed in favor of Siemens-Martin steel. To be sure, pig iron production in 1922 was only 48% of what it had been in 1913, but German crude steel production was 67% of 1913. In the Ruhr proper, production of crude steel in 1922 was 91% of what it had been in 1913.[6]

All things being left equal, therefore, it was clear by 1923 that Germany had regained her competitive advantage as a producer of iron and steel products and that in any attempt to regulate the conse-

[4] This is well argued by Soutou in *Industrielles System*, pp. 543–552. See also Charles Maier, "Coal and Economic Power in the Weimar Republic: The Effects of the Coal Crisis of 1920," in *ibid.*, pp. 530–542. For an important and stimulating interpretation of French policy in the years immediately after the signing of the treaty, see the unpublished dissertation of Marc Trachtenberg, "French Reparation Policy, 1918–1921" (Berkeley, 1974).

[5] See above, p. 84 and p. 204.

[6] See the important reports, "L'industrie du Fer dans la Ruhr," produced by the Mission Interalliée de Contrôle des Usines et des Mines, *1914–1924. Dix Ans du Développement Industriel Allemand*, 10 vols. (Brussels, November 1924), esp. III, pp. 67–68, 25ff., IV, p. 21ff. Also, Warriner, *Combines*, pp. 161–168, and Wiel, *Wirtschaftsgeschichte*, pp. 226–227, 238.

quences of overproduction after stabilization, the Germans would have a negotiating advantage. Even in the attempt to prevent things from "being left equal," however, the French were fated to have a difficult time reversing the balance. Economically, the realization of the French government's reparations demands seemed to require the further development of German productive capacity and its rationalization in order to enable Germany to procure the necessary surplus through exports. As one contemporary argued, "preposterous as the idea may seem, the problem of markets for the French iron and steel industry could be much more readily solved if France were paying reparation to Germany."[7] Politically, the reparations demands, with their requirements of deliveries in kind and of financial backing of the government by German industry, strengthened the hand of German industry and, as Moritz Bonn noted, thereby "prepared the ground upon which the kings of the Republic placed in power by them [i.e., the reparations claimants] would try to realize the rule of business (*die Wirtschaft*) over the state."[8]

The year 1923 was one in which both the extent and the limits of heavy industry's power in the Weimar Republic were to be revealed and defined. In 1922, the leaders of German heavy industry had launched an overt counteroffensive against the governmental incursions into their affairs that had developed since the war, as well as against the gains made by labor in war and revolution, and continued to fight French efforts to reap the economic advantages anticipated from Germany's defeat. The industrialist stabilization program, with its call for the dismantling of all controls, reduction of wages and increase of hours, and settlement of the reparations issue on terms that were tantamount to the reestablishment of Germany's economic superiority on the European continent, constituted an unabashed and single-minded strategy to consolidate and protect the gains of inflation by virtually restoring pre-1914 techniques and conditions. In 1923, the industrial leaders were compelled to fight the battles so well prepared in 1922 under conditions that were not of their own choosing and that were to be very costly to themselves in many respects. The results, more often than not, were tactical victories bought at unanticipated cost rather than strategic breakthroughs. Nevertheless, the balance was to fall largely in their favor, and they were to succeed in making the costs and disadvantages for others greater than for themselves. Therein would lie the major area of continuity between inflation and stabilization.

For the purposes of this discussion, the concluding year of the inflation will be divided between the period of passive resistance—that is,

[7] Greer, *Ruhr-Lorraine Problem,* p. 225.

[8] Moritz Bonn, *Das Schicksal des Deutschen Kapitalismus* (Berlin, 1926), p. 57.

from January to late September 1923—and the subsequent period when passive resistance was terminated, the new currency was introduced, and a variety of new arrangements in domestic and foreign policy were made that laid the foundation for the middle years of the Weimar Republic. During the first period, Germany was ruled by the Cuno government until August 13 and then by the first Stresemann Great Coalition cabinet. The second period encompasses the latter cabinet, until October 6, then Stresemann's reorganized Great Coalition cabinet, which left office on November 30, and finally the first months of the bourgeois cabinet of the Centrist Wilhelm Marx.

SURVIVING PASSIVE RESISTANCE

An initial consequence of the Ruhr occupation was to create a situation in which, as Cuno expressed it, "politics must take precedence over economics."[9] As in 1914, the primacy of political considerations was identified with a suspension of political and social conflict, and both government and industry were agreed on the need to avoid conflict with the workers in order to carry out the policy of passive resistance. Coal, as usual, led the way. On the evening of January 9, the Coal Syndicate, in anticipation of French action, voted to move its operations from Essen to Hamburg and thereby deprive the French of the organizational and informational resources necessary to control coal supply and distribution. The employers thus began by making a "first sacrifice" aimed at inspiring "respect and courage" among the workers.[10] Naturally, the coal industrialists also recognized that the basis for their effort to hold the line on wages had evaporated, and they accepted the arbitrated wage increase effective January 1 that they had previously been so resolved to reject. Similarly, the impending conflict over the draft of an hours-of-work bill designed to permit exceptions to the eight-hour day was suspended by the government, which decided to extend the demobilization decrees on the eight-hour day scheduled to expire on March 31.[11]

The iron and steel industry was not slow to give evidence of its own willingness to make important sacrifices to support passive resistance. The firms cancelled all minette ore deliveries called for in their contracts with their French and Luxemburg suppliers.[12] On January 18 an effort was made to stiffen the backs of the Reich railroad administration. When the latter asked if the iron industry was prepared to

[9] *Kabinett Cuno*, p. 218.   [10] *Ibid.*, p. 126.

[11] *Ibid.*, pp. 127, 218–219n6.

[12] Paul Wentzcke, *Ruhrkampf. Einbruch und Abwehr im rheinisch-westfälischen Industriegebiet*, 2 vols. (Berlin, 1930–1932), I, p. 401.

support the refusal of the railroad authorities to transport coal confiscated by the French even if this meant French interference with the railroads harmful to the iron industry's operations, the industrialists replied affirmatively. They intended to set a "good example" for the workers and strengthen the hand of the Cuno government.[13] A sensationally "good example" was provided by Fritz Thyssen and a number of his colleagues, who were arrested by the French on January 23 for their refusal to violate the orders of the Reich Coal Commissar and deliver coal to the French.[14] Among the heavy industrialist leaders, Paul Reusch was certainly one of the most supportive of passive resistance, and he played an important role in encouraging Cuno to hold firm and intensify propaganda on the home front. He was "of the firm conviction that the struggle in the Ruhr will last months" and that the French would only be brought to terms after their smelting plants had been closed three or four months and the franc fell sharply.[15] Underlying such seemingly sober calculations in the case of Reusch and some of his like-minded colleagues, however, there was also a burning nationalism and commitment to a policy of "holding out" that reflected a real sense of pride and anger. Thus, he told a group of French industrialists who happened to have the misfortune of visiting him on the day of the occupation that "you can probably destroy our economy and rob us of our wealth, but we will not let you break our national pride."[16] In an interview with the *Nation*, he made the rather remarkable comment that "we will go to the extreme and transform ourselves into Communists and deliver our goods to the workers before we surrender ourselves in the face of French machine guns. . . ."[17]

What was demanded of the industrialists in the first months of 1923, however, was not a metamorphosis of so extraordinary and improbable a nature, but rather the confidence necessary to hold out and a willingness to exercise restraint and make sacrifices. Public postures did not always conform to private anxieties and concerns. For example, it was quite splendid of the VdESI to vote enthusiastically at its membership meeting on January 1919 to boycott French, Belgian, and Luxemburg goods and to terminate business relations with enemy firms for the duration of the occupation.[18] The discussion in the Northwest Group ten days later, however, was less inspirational, because the debate as

---

[13] Woltmann to Reusch, January 18, 1923, HA/GHH, Nr. 300193008/7.

[14] Wentzcke, *Ruhrkampf*, I, pp. 184–185.

[15] Reusch to Haniel, February 8, 1923, HA/GHH, Nr. 300193000/6.

[16] Quoted by Reichert in the draft of a report to Meyer, undated but certainly of January 1923 in BA R 13 I/98, Bl. 89.

[17] January 26, 1923 interview, HA/GHH, Nr. 300193008/21.

[18] VdESI history, BA R 13 I/13, Bl. 99–100.

to whether or not to supply the French with the export and import data the latter were demanding as a precondition for permitting Germans to engage in foreign trade demonstrated that many industrialists were not very happy with the January 19 decision. Director Vielhaber of Krupp, who certainly shared Reusch's nationalist sentiments, was depressed and simply felt "that the strength of the French is much greater than our own, and that they will be able to hold out much longer than we. Despite everything, we will still come to a bad end. He gave up everything, so to speak, for lost."[19] It was hard for Ruhr industrialists to forget that competitors in the unoccupied areas had stolen their customers during the last French incursion in 1921, and some felt discomfort over the idea of severing all business connections with enemy suppliers and customers because this could mean that they would have neither the work nor the money to run their plants. Thus, although the industrialists had been turning down French requests for statistics, particularly after Thyssen's arrest, some doubted that so rigid a policy was well advised. If such a policy was finally adopted at the end of January despite the reservations, it was in part because the industrialists were well aware that the French could use such information in their efforts to tax German industry or to harm it in other ways and in part because it was politically difficult to argue against Reichert when he pointed out, "now that we finally have a government which stands very firm, it also has to have the support of industry. . . ."[20]

As Reichert and other enthusiasts for passive resistance were subsequently to complain, however, the government was not completely firm itself. Although banning payment of duties, fees, and taxes to occupation authorities and prohibiting official intercourse and collaboration with the occupation authorities, it refused to go on record in favor of breach of contracts and issue decrees giving legal force to the boycott voluntarily voted by the VdESI on January 19 and subsequently supported by the RdI in March. Thus, whereas firms such as Thyssen refused to trade with the enemy and broke contracts with foreign firms on the grounds of intervention by a "higher power"—that is, their inability to violate German law and deal with the "illegal" French customs authorities at the borders of the occupied zones—firms in the unoccupied areas frequently traded with the enemy with the excuse that they would otherwise be subject to suit for breach of contract or on the less sophisticated grounds that their "existence" depended on continued trade with the French and Belgians. In early March, Reusch not only

[19] Ernst Lueg to Reusch, January 30, 1923, reporting on a Northwest Group meeting, January 29, 1923, HA/GHH, Nr. 300193008/7.
[20] *Ibid.*

noted with displeasure that firms in the unoccupied areas were using "every opportunity" to "out-compete" Ruhr firms, but was even compelled to chide the MAN for taking a contract that it could well have left to Haniel and Lueg in Düsseldorf. If Reusch could not keep order in his own well-managed house in this respect, one can well imagine what was going on under less watchful eyes.[21]

As during the war, so during the Ruhr occupation, decisions taken to meet immediate problems arising from the emergency were strongly influenced by considerations of short-term and long-term interest and often served to heighten rather than to disrupt the continuity of development. The special problems of the occupation were easily integrated into longer-term issues and areas of controversy. When Economics Minister Becker called for an easing of tariffs and freight rates in order to meet some of the problems created by the occupation, for example, he was dealing with problems that had long-range implications. The question of the future pig iron tariff had already become a matter of serious controversy between heavy industry and its customers before the occupation, and the iron producers were understandably nervous over the implications of even the most temporary of iron tariff reductions. They had to support a temporary relaxation of tariffs in the early months of the occupation because 75% of the nation's productive capacity lay within the occupied zone, but Reichert made it clear that this renunciation was to be temporary and could "only be tolerated for a fixed period."[22]

In the meantime, the two sides remained extremely sensitive to both dangers and opportunities. The tug-of-war between them became acute in the spring, when the producers could argue with considerable justification that the unoccupied area had been richly supplied with foreign iron and steel, there were domestic producers lacking work because of this, and tariff-free imports therefore should be restricted only to those products where there was demonstrable shortage and then only on a case-by-case basis. There was plenty of evidence that firms were "fleeing into goods" in order to evade exchange controls and enjoy a later advantage, and the producers probably also had a point in arguing that the English were deliberately keeping prices low in order to get the Germans used to employing English materials. However, the arguments of German manufacturers that the price of German pig iron was too high was not without merit either. By summer, the

[21] See the Steel Federation meeting of February 27, 1923, HA/GHH, Nr. 3000035/3b; Reusch to Lippart, March 5, 1923, *ibid.*, Nr. 300193010/13, and VdESI history, BA R 13 I/13, Bl. 99–100.

[22] Meeting of February 9, 1923, DZA Potsdam, RWM, Nr. 4530, Bl. 14, and *Kabinett Cuno*, pp. 238–239.

immediate issue had been decided largely in favor of the producers, and rebates were limited to a very few products where there was a demonstrable shortage. Poor business conditions and ample supplies of raw material, albeit at high prices, led at the end of May to the termination of what the producers considered a dangerous precedent, but these very conditions also made the consumers more hostile to the tariff.[23]

Producers and consumers were in much greater harmony when it came to asking the Transport Ministry to reduce freight rates and reintroduce certain prewar preferential rates that had been dropped in 1914 and had not been reintroduced when the railroads were taken over by the Reich in 1919. Thus, when the industrial groups from the producer and manufacturer camps appeared at a meeting with the government representatives on February 10, Baron von Buttlar, now an official of the VDMA rather than of the RWM, and Reichert found themselves in the unfamiliar situation of joining in the same cause, albeit with different arguments. Buttlar pointed out that the engineering industry could not carry out its voluntary boycott of enemy firms and products if it continued to suffer from inordinate transportation costs, whereas Reichert emphasized that heavy industry had to receive some reward for agreeing to the rebates on pig iron tariffs and suggested that freight rate reductions were a good way to lower raw materials costs for manufacturers as well. Needless to say, this effort to reduce freight rates fit in well with the steady stream of complaints against the Reich Railroad Authority and demand for such reductions and preferential treatment since 1919. Not untypically, producers and manufacturers were most in harmony when they could unite at the public expense. Despite pressure from the Steel Federation and efforts by Reich Economics Minister Becker to get the Transportation Ministry to make concessions, however, the latter refused for fiscal reasons.[24]

The tension between patriotism and self-interest that existed so strongly even during the early and supposedly most ebullient phase of the Ruhr occupation was particularly in evidence in the pricing discussions in the Steel Federation. The events of January not only set back the effort that was being made at the time to stabilize the value of the mark through restraint on prices and wages, but it also sent the mark into a sharp tailspin. Consequently, insofar as there were restraints on prices, they were largely political. At the January 23 meeting of the Steel Federation,[25] Poensgen pointed out in the preliminary

[23] For the various meetings and discussions of this problem see BA R 13 I/201, Bl. 49, 55–56, 81, 85–87.

[24] On this issue, see DZA Potsdam, RWM, Nr. 4530, Bl. 13ff.

[25] For the discussion and quotations see HA/GHH, Nr. 3000035/3b.

discussion among the producers that although it would be possible to argue "that the moment has come to free prices completely," such an action would "endanger the united front." To control the workers, it was necessary to continue allowing their participation in pricing discussions. Having paid this tribute to the principle of solidarity with the workers, however, it rapidly became apparent that Poensgen was not really giving away much because "in his view, it is today less a question of the price itself than of demanding a further diminution of the time allowed for payment in order to protect the works from a catastrophic depreciation of the currency." Poensgen argued that they faced a choice between a sliding paper mark price with reduced payment periods or a stable gold mark price with the existing payment conditions remaining in force. Poensgen seemed to favor the latter approach, and he reported that, in negotiations conducted in Berlin between his colleague, Director Gerwin, and the iron consumer leaders Schrey and Becker, the latter showed "understanding" for the producer need to protect themselves, and, although opposing changes in the payment conditions, were prepared to accept pricing in gold marks or gulden.

In the ensuing discussion among the producers, Klemme stood more alone than usual in arguing for moderation, an isolation all the more remarkable and painful because of the political context in which the discussion was being held. He warned that pricing in gold marks or gulden "would be a political misfortune and would bring us under serious suspicion," and urged that the appropriate thing to do under the circumstances was to extend payment deadlines in order to maintain employment and economic activity. Klemme concluded his futile sermon by pointing out that "during the next weeks, when everything is at stake, the works ought not to think about material advantages."[26] Recent reductions in time allowed for payment, however, had only served to stir the imaginations of Klemme's colleagues, and this, combined with the alleged willingness of the manufacturers to have prices stated in gold marks or gulden, did nothing to raise the patriotic level of the occasion. If Klemme had any success at all, it was in persuading his colleagues to dissemble by continuing to state prices in paper marks while privately setting gulden prices with customers "in suitable cases." Because their South German customers had already become accustomed to paying their bills in this manner for some months, the true novelty of such price arrangements would only lie in their further extension. At the same time, the producers also decided to propose a change in payment terms to the manufacturers and merchants designed to reduce the period in which customers were allowed to pay their

[26] *Ibid.*

bills to one week unless they were prepared to pay the cost of additional mark depreciation for being granted the privilege of payment by the 15th of the month following delivery.

Unhappily for Poensgen and Gerwin, the discussion with the merchants and manufacturers on January 23 turned out not to be quite as harmonious as they had been led to expect by the latter's "understanding" attitude in Berlin. In Düsseldorf, the manufacturers would consider neither the stating of prices in a stable value nor a change in payment conditions, and although it was easy enough to reach agreement on the latest paper mark price, the businessmen found themselves quibbling over various proposals to change the payment terms and finally decided to set up a committee to discuss the subject. All in all, Klemme did not think that "the negotiations had taken a course worthy of the present situation."[27] Furthermore, things were not much better on the following week, when an agreement on harsher payment conditions was reached after much debate.[28] Only at the end of February did these battles come to an end and give way to a new cycle of moderation. A decision was made to support the government's efforts to hold prices stable as well as to prevent efforts by some firms to employ stricter payment conditions than those set forth by the Steel Federation. The consumers, merchants, and workers responded with warm expressions of gratitude to the producers for these actions, and a spirit of harmony replaced the strife that had prevailed within the Steel Federation during the first six weeks of the Ruhr occupation.[29]

The sources of this change are not difficult to discover. It was only in late February that the cutting off of the Ruhr became economically effective. To be sure, the French had issued various ordinances controlling imports and exports by requiring the mediation of their authority, but, as Reusch reported on February 16, "there are ways and means of getting around these regulations. For the time being, we do not take these regulations tragically."[30] Both the government and the industrialists recognized, however, that the occupation would become increasingly onerous with time and that the real problems were yet to come. Economics Minister Becker warned that the government would have to provide massive assistance to prevent economic collapse in the occupied area, and in this warning he echoed the views of the Ruhr industrialists themselves.[31] The changing situation was mirrored

[27] Ibid.
[28] Meeting of January 30, 1923, ibid.
[29] Meeting of February 27, 1923, HA/GHH, Nr. 3000035/3b.
[30] Reusch to Haniel, February 16, 1923, HA/GHH, Nr. 300193000/6.
[31] Kabinett Cuno, pp. 238–239.

in Reusch's correspondence. On February 25, he reported to Karl Haniel that "I made a one-time purchase of 100,000 gulden and then sold them again at an advantage. The shortage of money forbids another speculation. During the next months we will have to live off our foreign exchange. Vögler told me ten days ago that he was already compelled to sell 20,000 English pounds."[32] The day before, Reusch had, in fact, written to Vögler pointing out that their money was running out and urging a discussion within a small circle of steps to be initiated with the Reich government so that the Ruhr works could continue to hold out.[33]

As during the war, the burden of the national effort was being shifted to the government, and harmony within industry and between industry and labor was to be maintained at the expense of the public purse. Unlike the wartime situation, however, government support of industry during the passive resistance was based almost solely on large-scale credits rather than on purchases. The risking of the nation's currency in the national cause was more blatant and overt. As Reusch expressed it in early February, "not much more is to be saved of the German mark. The question at the moment is not how the monetary situation will further develop. First the battle in the Ruhr must be victoriously carried through."[34] As during the war, there was also an assumption in governmental and in some industrial circles at the beginning that the battle would be of relatively short duration, and it was this that seemed to make the economic risks tolerable.

Nevertheless, there were also important differences between the war and the passive resistance situations from the standpoint of financing and likely outcome. First, the fact of inflation could not be ignored in 1923 as it had been by and large throughout the war. Second, no one could have the illusion that the costs of passive resistance would be paid by the enemy in the same way that so many Germans had believed that the costs of the war would be paid by the enemy. In contrast to the war, what was being sought through passive resistance was a negotiated settlement on terms bearable to Germany. The goal was a reduction of French demands and an international loan, but there was a general consensus that both reparations and international financial assistance would have to be paid off through increased German productivity. Paradoxically, therefore, the Ruhr conflict had to be fought with greater consciousness of the economic dangers and the future implications of what was being done than the war precisely because the actual stakes were so tangible and real instead of speculative

[32] Reusch to Haniel, HA/GHH, Nr. 300193000/6.

[33] Reusch to Vögler, February 24, 1923, ibid., Nr. 30019390/25.

[34] Paul Reusch to Hermann Reusch, February 2, 1923, ibid., Nr. 400101298/3a.

and imaginary. In concrete terms, this meant that success depended not only on providing the credits needed to keep the Ruhr action going but also on supporting the mark for as long as possible so as to prevent immediate and complete collapse. At the same time, the entire question of how the social and economic burdens of a settlement would be distributed within German society hung like a black cloud over the entire passive resistance effort.

During the period February–April 1923, much of the negotiation between and among representatives of industry, the Reichsbank, and the government was concerned with the twin problems of supporting the mark at some steady level and arranging the credits needed by industry to keep passive resistance going. The necessity of supporting the mark was obvious even to Reichsbank President Havenstein, who, for a change, collaborated with government stabilization efforts, and willingly backed the mark support action with the gold and exchange resources of the Reichsbank. Indeed, to some extent Havenstein even restricted certain industrial credits as a means of forcing industry to give up foreign exchange to a government exchange fund set up to back a fifty million dollar gold loan. Thanks to these efforts, introduced on January 31, the depreciation of the mark, manifested in an exchange rate that had moved from 7,525 marks to the dollar on January 2 to 41,500 marks to the dollar on February 1, was arrested, and the exchange rate was maintained at a level of about 21,000 marks to the dollar until the support effort collapsed on April 18. From the very outset, however, Havenstein, Finance Minister Hermes, and the cabinet regarded the action as a temporary one doomed to ultimate failure because it was "an absurdity in the context of the economic situation."[35] Initially, they seemed to think that it would hold up for four weeks, although Havenstein and Hermes told Reusch around February 15 that the Reichsbank had enough exchange to shore the mark up for as long as six weeks. In fact, the action lasted twelve weeks, but this hardly demonstrates more than that the participants underestimated the extent to which they could prolong an action of whose ultimate collapse they were justifiably convinced.

Havenstein would only legitimate the mark support action in political terms on the grounds "that a further increase in prices would have made the continuation of the united front impossible."[36] Throughout

[35] Ministerial discussion, April 19, 1923, *Kabinett Cuno*, pp. 399–400. See also Jean Claude Favez, *Le Reich devant l'occupation franco-belge de la Ruhr en 1923* (Geneva, 1969), p. 211ff., and Reusch to Haniel, February 25, 1923, HA/GHH, Nr. 300193000/6.

[36] For the quote and information that follows see Woltmann's report to Reusch on a meeting of February 26, 1923 in *ibid.*, Nr. 300193003/8.

he was distressed that the effort had, in a sense, been too successful in that he wanted to keep the exchange rate at 23,000 to the dollar instead of 21,000 marks to the dollar. This distress was shared by Becker and by exporters who felt that the exchange rate stabilization had taken place at a level harmful to exports. Yet Havenstein also recognized that the situation had been beneficial in reducing the costs of English coal imports, which, along with food imports, placed an enormous burden on the economy during the Ruhr occupation. In line with this attempt to maintain a stable exchange rate, Havenstein, the industrialists, and the trade union leaders supported government attempts to maintain prices and wages at stable levels.

As noted earlier, however, the self-restraint in pricing at the Steel Federation meetings at the end of February had as its background the fact that the concerns were no longer seeking their survival in higher prices but rather in government credits. When Havenstein subsequently complained that industry had not fulfilled his expectations in subscribing to the gold loan that was a part of the mark support action, he did note that heavy industry put on the best performance in this regard. This, however, was anything but surprising. They had every reason to make some contribution to the effort. To begin with, heavy industry was spared the brunt of Havenstein's efforts to restrict credit as a means of preventing industry from using Reichsbank credits to purchase foreign exchange and forcing it to surrender exchange. Havenstein fully accepted the arguments of the Ruhr concern leaders that their credit and foreign exchange demands were valid.[37] Second, and far more important, Havenstein's discussions with the leaders of heavy industry about their contribution to the gold loan took place in the context of the Ruhr industrialists' appeals to Havenstein and the government for large-scale credits to assist them in finding the money necessary to continue their support of passive resistance. Indeed, when one reads the sources concerning Havenstein's discussions with the heavy industrialists at the end of February, it is difficult to tell exactly which credits are being discussed, those of industry to the government or those of the government to industry.[38]

The two forms of credit were inseparable because Havenstein was asking the industrialists to support the mark with a gold loan so that

[37] *Kabinett Cuno*, pp. 320–321n5–6 and p. 400 and RdI circular of February 21, 1923, in HA/GHH, Nr. 30019320/2. At a meeting of February 26, 1923, Director Klönne of Krupp pointed out "that the foreign exchange will have to be provided chiefly by the works outside the occupied area. H[avenstein] recognized this and wants to extract the foreign exchange from the unoccupied area by restricting credit," *ibid.*, Nr. 300193003/8.

[38] *Ibid.*

360

the government could support the industrialists with the credits needed to keep up the resistance in the Ruhr. Thus, Vögler proposed that the great concerns sign up for 5% of the total 200 million mark gold loan in such a way that each concern would provide one gold mark for every ton of crude steel produced in 1922 by its plants, the amount repayable within three years in marks or dollars depending on the desire of the lender. Havenstein then announced that he was thinking of giving 100 billion marks in credit to the Ruhr concerns completely unencumbered by demands for the surrender of foreign exchange. Beyond this, however, he was willing to reward industry's contribution to the gold loan by lending 80–90% of what was being contributed. It should be noted that this loan to industry would be in paper marks and would be repayable in paper marks as opposed to the gold loan to the government, which was repayable in the currency of industry's choice. When Director Woltmann of the GHH reported on this meeting to Reusch, the latter responded in a manner that at once captured its logic and carried it to its ultimate conclusion:

> I agree to the proposals of Herr Vögler provided that all the rest of the works accept them too. If the Reichsbank strongly supports us with credits on the one hand, then we must, on the other hand, also support the government in the bringing in of its gold loan. It would be advisable if, in connection with the signing of the gold loan, we would negotiate with Havenstein over a further credit beyond the 100 billion already placed at our disposal with the object of giving the individual works further credits in relation to their participation in the gold loan.—We should not therefore remain satisfied to have 90% of the gold loan signed up for by us lent out, but must present further credit demands beyond this.[39]

What is significant about these credit arrangements and the various arrangements to be discussed below is not that there was anything improper or deliberately abusive about the credit demands of the iron and steel industrialists, and it would be misleading to argue that the industrialists were trying to make money out of the national crisis, let alone engaging in "treason" against the nation.[40] Formally, it was the government, after all, that had summoned the Ruhr to passive resistance, and the conditions that developed were conducive neither to normal financial nor to normal business practices. The question of how much of the substance and of the future of their concerns the industrialists should have been prepared to risk for the success of passive resis-

[39] Reusch to Woltmann, February 28, 1923, *ibid.*

[40] As is argued by Günter Hortzschansky, *Der nationale Verrat der deutschen Monopolherren während des Ruhrkampfes 1923* (Berlin, 1961), p. 178ff.

tance, assuming that such success really was possible, was no simple one. The scale of problems faced by the heavy industrialists was far greater than it was for most other businessmen. To be sure, their resources were also far greater, but it must be recognized that they did make an initial effort to employ their own resources as much as possible. During the first months of the occupation they did not take advantage of the government's willingness to implement its wage guarantee (*Lohnsicherung*) and provide funds to pay the costs of unproductive labor or prevent layoffs. Basically, they used their own money and the credits they received to pay their workers until the end of June. Their policy, however, was strongly influenced by the government's pressure and demand that the steel men first use up their credit resources, and it lasted only so long as they were able to maintain and dispose of their production in one form or another.[41] As will be shown, they took full advantage—indeed, special advantage—of the government wage guarantee when they concluded that it was needed. Similarly, they made full and skillful use of the credit facilities open to them by the Reichsbank and the government, and perhaps what is most significant about the large credits demanded and received by the great iron and steel concerns at the time is precisely their availability. They, far more than any group in German society, were in a position to make claims about the economic resources of the country, to bargain hard to minimize their risks, and to gain such security and advantage as could be gained in the unfortunate circumstances of the time. Consequently, it was they who also faced the strongest suspicion and opposition, a situation that made them feel peculiarly justified in complaining about their plight and that strengthened their proclivity to protect themselves as best they could.

The difficulties involved in evaluating the credit arrangements made during the Ruhr occupation are further complicated by the fact that decisions were taken by all concerned on the basis of imperfect information and false expectations. This was particularly the case during the stage of development that followed Havenstein's grant of 100 billion marks in credits to the iron and steel industry in February. As Reusch had indicated, more credits would be needed, and negotiations were held among Havenstein, the industrialists, among whom Peter Klöckner played a prominent role, and Finance Ministry representatives in early March. The scheme developed during these negotiations, which was modeled on similar arrangements being made with the coal industry, reflected the confusion that existed on all sides. The Berlin authorities, faced with the enormous task of supporting passive resistance, were anxious to give as little credit as possible and espe-

[41] See Poensgen's remarks at a meeting of May 9, 1923, HA/GHH, Nr. 300193008/19, and VdESI history, BA R 13 I/13, Bl. 97.

cially to avoid bearing the full brunt of supporting heavy industry. The industrialists were aware of this and wanted to keep their own obligations under control. They were desirous of finding ways and means of securing their immediate needs at little risk to themselves and with minimum complication in their relations with the government. Because all concerned believed in a "relatively short duration of the Ruhr action,"[42] a decision was made to support the industry through a credit issued on its unsold production. Thus was born the Steel Finance Corporation (Stahl-Finanz-Gesellschaft mbH), a limited liability company composed of the eleven leading Ruhr steel concerns, whose task it was to "purchase" the unsold production of the member concerns with bills discountable at the Reichsbank.[43] The transactions were guaranteed by the Finance Ministry. Following the restoration of normal conditions, the concerns would be obligated to buy back their iron and steel. Any profit or loss resulting from a change in the price between the date of purchase and the date of resale would be divided between the Reich and the concern involved on the basis of 90% of the gain or loss going to the Reich and 10% to the concern involved. To keep administrative and other arrangements as simple as possible, no account would be taken of special qualities of steel or differences in profiles, and the price of certain basic types of pig iron would be used for all products. In the initial discussions among the concerns regarding the plan, the need of the concerns was assessed at 270 billion marks divided in the following proportions, proportions that remained representative throughout the history of the Steel Finance Corporation:[44]

Deutsch-Luxemburg (including Gelsenkirchen and the Bochumer Verein)	52
August Thyssen Hütte	33
Phoenix	33
Rheinstahl and van der Zypen	31
Krupp	25
Gutehoffnungshütte	24½
Stumm	21
Mannesmann	20
Hoesch	17
Klöckner	7
Rombach	6½

[42] Remarks by Klemme at meeting of May 9, 1923, HA/GHH, Nr. 300193008/19.

[43] The most important sources on the Steel Finance Corporation I have found are in *ibid.* and DZA Potsdam, RWM, Nr. 4531–4534.

[44] March 16, 1923, meeting in HA/GHH, Nr. 300193008/19. At this meeting, the works also agreed to participate in the same proportions to the tune of 2,500,-000 gold marks in the government's gold loan.

The launching of the Steel Finance Corporation was no simple matter, however, and it took four weeks of haggling before the contracts were finally signed on April 14, 1923. On the industrialist side, there was the usual quest for 100% protection against the risk that changed market conditions or changed exchange rates would lead to losses when the time came to buy back their production from the corporation. On the government side, there was anxiety about accepting all the risks that might arise from the arrangement, particularly because there was a Reichstag committee overseeing such contracts, but also because of the obviously precarious financial situation of the country. In the early phase of the negotiations in mid-March, the industrialists seem to have taken the initiative and made far-reaching demands of the Finance Ministry for a guarantee against bearing any of the costs of changed market or currency conditions when the time came to buy back their steel and even went so far as to threaten that if "the necessary guarantee is not given, then the works can do nothing but undertake reductions in their plants and in this manner reduce the danger of losses as much as possible."[45] This most unpatriotic threat was combined with a suspicious effort to interpret the Finance Ministry's readiness to accept the full risk of a depreciation of the mark as a readiness to accept the full risk of an appreciation of the mark or the establishment of a new currency.[46] The Reich, in other words, was to bear all the losses and to enjoy none of the gains that might eventuate from future currency developments. After much negotiation, Finance Minister Hermes proposed at the end of March that both sides share in the risks of a currency change and that the industrialists take half their credits calculated in paper marks and the other half calculated in pounds sterling.[47]

The industrialists were quite unhappy about this offer, but many of them were no longer in an aggressive and blackmailing mood. Some of the concerns were now desperate to get credits because it was becoming apparent that their needs would only increase in the foreseeable future, and they were worried that the ailing Hermes, already in a "very defeatist" mood, might decide against granting them more than a 300 billion mark credit.[48] Vögler, whose Deutsch-Luxemburg firm already had 96,000 tons of production in storage and whose directors had decided only shortly before to "make the most far-reaching use of

[45] Meeting of March 27, 1923, and Becker to Hermes, March 19, 1923, in *ibid.*

[46] Klöckner and Stinnes to Hermes, March 19, 1923, and comment by RFM official, DZA Potsdam, RWM, Nr. 4331, Bl. 31–33.

[47] Discussion of March 29, 1923, HA/GHH, Nr. 300193008/19.

[48] Meeting of April 10, 1923, and report of April 17, 1923, in *ibid.*

364

the possibilities offered"[49] by the impending Steel Finance agreement, and Poensgen, whose Phoenix concern had 135,000 tons in storage, were nervously urging the granting of a 600 billion mark credit as well as the inclusion of the Reichsbank's previous 100 billion mark credit to the steel industry. If the last credit were included in the Steel Finance arrangement, then it could be prolonged for two additional three-month periods and not have to be repaid in the very near future. In the face of nervous Finance Ministry officials, who were compelled to run back and forth between the impatient industrialists and a recalcitrant Hermes, "everyone in general took the view that it was necessary to pull back to what was absolutely necessary and not to overdo things. The important thing now above all is to get the agreement signed and sealed without delay. As far as the extent of further credits is concerned, one could, in Vögler's view, best come to an understanding with Havenstein in private first."[50] If Havenstein could be counted on, however, the Finance Ministry officials still had to be taught that the wrath of heavy industry was a more serious matter than their efforts to represent the views of Hermes. At the crucial stage of the negotiations, "Klöckner and Vögler let loose and were like a lightning storm, and one could see how the privy councilors were shaking in their boots."[51] The lesson was well learned, and Hermes' officials decided that it was easier to spend an hour and a half at his bedside persuading him to sign the agreement than it was to continue to discuss the fine points of the agreement with the industrialists.

On April 18, four days after the signing of the Steel Finance Agreement, the mark support action collapsed, and a new period of rapid depreciation set in. It was rumored and reported in the newspapers that the effort to support the mark had been sabotaged by the industrialists, and particularly by Stinnes, who had purchased a large quantity of foreign exchange just before the event. There can be no question about the fact that Stinnes did not support the government policy. On the one hand, he felt that it was ruining the export opportunities of industry in the unoccupied area, a view that was shared to some extent by Becker and Havenstein.[52] On the other hand, as a leading importer of English coal for the Reich Railroad Authority and industry, he directly benefited from the resale of high-priced coal imports and had an interest in mark depreciation. The evidence suggests, however, that not Stinnes alone but also the railroads were culpable in the

[49] Deutsch-Lux directors meeting, April 11, 1923, SAA 11/Lf 130.

[50] April 17, 1923, report, HA/GHH, Nr. 300193008/19.

[51] *Ibid.*

[52] See Stinnes' remarks at a discussion of March 29, 1923, in Nachlass Stresemann, Reel 3098, Serial 7114H, Frame H145343.

situation and that Stinnes could claim that he had no choice but to carry out the foreign currency purchases in order to get the coal that had been ordered a considerable time before. Ultimately, however, the collapse of the mark support effort was inevitable given industry's unsatisfactory support of the gold loan and the Reichsbank's inability to continue supporting the mark without exhausting its resources.[53]

The collapse of the mark support action on April 18 made it seem as if the industrialists had acted most precipitously in rushing ahead with the signing of the Steel Finance arrangement only four days earlier. The requirement that they take half their credit calculated in pounds sterling now seemed truly onerous, but subsequent developments demonstrated that Vögler was correct in arguing that the important thing was to establish the basic credit mechanisms while leaving the solution of other difficulties to subsequent negotiation. Now that the mark was depreciating again, the industrialists had the inestimable advantage of really having something to complain about. They were outraged at the demands made on them and annoyed even at Havenstein for making public criticisms of industry's failure to stand behind the gold loan. Their entire case against the government's failure to give them what they considered to be proper support was fully spelled out by one of Poensgen's colleagues in a letter of April 28 which sought to explain why some concerns had been reluctant to take advantage of the Steel Finance credit and which called on Poensgen to renegotiate the agreements. The industrialist pointed out that although his concern needed the credit, he had not yet taken advantage of it because of the risks involved. Prices were below costs, and costs were rising due to reduced production and the increased ore costs caused by the mark depreciation. Thus, the works were showing losses to begin with, and yet they were being asked to take credits calculated in pounds sterling at a time when the mark was depreciating much faster than their prices were rising. If the mark could depreciate as much as 40% in a matter of days, what would happen over months and how could the industrialists procure the astronomical number of marks necessary to pay back mark credits taken out months before calculated in pounds sterling? He indignantly pointed out that "It is impossible to speak of a credit in the actual sense of the term when the credit includes such dangers that the works are compelled to seek security against the particular risks of the credit in order not to be wiped out by having accepted it." In his view, the question as to the type of credit taken, be it a credit calculated in goods (*Sachwerte*),

[53] See *Kabinett Cuno*, pp. 399–404, 421ff., 458ff., and Foreign Exchange Advisory Committee meetings of March 6, April 10, and April 21, 1923, in BA R 11/505. Also, see Maier, *Recasting Bourgeois Europe*, p. 367.

foreign exchange, or paper marks, had to be left to the individual concerns involved. With remarkable disingenuousness and self-righteousness, the industrialist concluded his argument by pointing out:

It is incomprehensible that the ministry has fought against giving paper mark credit until now when one considers that only the paper mark is valid everywhere in Germany, that the Reichsbank only discounts paper mark bills of exchange, that it deducts the exact amount of paper marks stated on the bills when they fall due, and that furthermore all the banks have only one type of account, that they give paper marks and later demand back the same number of paper marks along with interest and charges, and that finally, in our entire economic life no distinction is made between paper marks which are given and are then received back, and that even in the case of Reichsbank notes only the number of paper marks are given which appear on their face irregardless of the note's date of issue.[54]

Assuming that the author of these lines had not recently arrived from another planet, he certainly must have been aware of the extent to which currency depreciation had disadvantaged creditors and of the multitude of ways in which his own industry had, since the war, sought to protect its own interests vis à vis its customers while taking maximum advantage of its creditors. Surely the accountants on this man's staff were as competent as those in the Banking Division of Krupp, which provided the following exquisitely graphic description of the wonders of paper mark credits on June 4, 1923:

Our paper mark debts have remained the same (as last Saturday), namely about 80 billion. But the result in gold marks under a depreciation factor of 17,800 is only 4,445,000 over against the 6,046,000 of the previous week, thus giving an improvement of our status by 1,601,000 gold marks.

Our supply of foreign exchange has also remained about the same, that is

in total	7,489,000
less the Dutch debt	1,733,000
	5,756,000
after subtracting the abovementioned	4,445,000
There is a plus of	1,311,000 gold marks

[54] Unsigned letter to Poensgen, DZA Potsdam, RWM, Nr. 4531, Bl. 110-113.

You can see herein a substantial improvement of our status which has simply developed through the depreciation of the paper mark.[55]

The pean to the continued sanctity of the paper mark, therefore, must be taken as another illustration of the manner in which the steel industrialists were seeking to protect themselves from all risk while in no way acknowledging the right of the state to demand that some reasonable measure of the risk be shared by the economically powerful leaders of heavy industry.

All this is not to say that the terms of the Steel Finance Agreement did not present problems for the member concerns because of the rapid depreciation, but only to say that they did not have quite as much cause to feel as sorry for themselves as they evidently did. In early May, they decided against seeking a dissolution of the Steel Finance Corporation, despite its disadvantages, "since it could perhaps be made serviceable for other purposes."[56] Instead, they went to the Finance Ministry and asked to have the credit calculated in paper marks and to have the right to discount their bills at the Reichsbank at 6% instead of 18%.

As it turned out, the steel concerns made great use of the Steel Finance credits in the spring and summer of 1923. Not only did certain concerns, particularly Deutsch-Lux, Phoenix, and Krupp, find them essential for their continued operation, but the arrangement was also viewed as advantageous because it was a means of assuring that the Reich would fulfill its obligations to compensate the concerns for damages and losses incurred through the sequestration of production by the occupying powers, because such losses were deductible from the amount owable on the credits. From the standpoint of the Reich, the Steel Finance Corporation had the advantage of providing a means by which the productive maintenance of the industry could be continued for as long as possible. The result was a compromise on both sides in which the Steel Finance Corporation was continued and new credits periodically granted. Although refusing to drop its insistence that some part of the credit be calculated in foreign exchange, the Finance Ministry agreed to reduce the amount of the first credit so taken from 50% to 33⅓%. Subsequently, on the occasion of further increases in the amount of the credit in June and July, a new arrangement was created under which the amount of the credit calculated in English pounds would decrease as a work took advantage of the credits from a maximum of 25% on the initial credit to a minimum of 5%

[55] Banking Section of Krupp to Ministerial Director Schäffer, June 4, 1923, WA Krupp IV, 2560.

[56] Meeting of May 9, 1923, HA/GHH, Nr. 300193008/19.

on subsequent credits.[57] Of course, the industrialists complained about even this 5% on the grounds that they were unable to export. Despite the iron industry's claim that it was "an exchange-needy rather than an exchange-producing industry,"[58] however, the government was convinced that the large works had sufficient foreign exchange at their disposal to be able to take at least 5% of their credit calculated in a foreign currency. As will be shown, there was good reason for the government to hold this conviction. Furthermore, in May and June the steel industrialists gave up their restraint in pricing and no longer suffered from the disadvantages arising from their effort to keep prices stable, disadvantages they certainly were experiencing in April. (See Table 13.) Finally, the industrialists had the great advantage of being allowed to discount their bills of exchange connected with the Steel Finance credit at the ludicrously low rate of 6%. Of course, they protested this rate in the usual manner.[59]

Although constantly complaining about the terms of the credit, it was quite clear that a number of the concerns were more than anxious to expand them and were constantly pressing for new credits. Krupp took the lead and asked that the Steel Finance Corporation be expanded to include credits on manufactured goods such as locomotives, railroad cars, bridges, agricultural machinery, etc. As one of the most active users of the credits and as one of the concerns most heavily engaged in finishing, it was particularly anxious to have the Steel Finance expanded so as to cover its needs more adequately. This seemed all the more necessary because, by summer, 96% of its steel plant was inactive, but its finishing works were operating at 70% of capacity. During July and August an arrangement was made to cover finished production as a means of expanding the credit for those in need of it, and the government agreed to keep this expansion in mind when granting new credits through the Steel Finance Corporation.[60] Thus, during the summer of 1923, the Steel Finance Corporation came to include in its purchasing activities not only all forms of crude, semi-finished, and rolled products but also finished products produced by the works. Additionally, at the request of the Zendei and the VDMA, it undertook temporarily to pay the steel firms for goods they were unable to deliver to electrotechnical and engineering works in the unoccupied areas. More important, at the initial request of Deutsch-Lux and Thyssen, the Steel Finance Corporation became the trustee for a

---

[57] See the report on the credits and Steel Finance Corporation to the RFM, June 15, 1923, in DZA Potsdam, RWM, Nr. 4531, Bl. 262–264, 118–120.

[58] Meeting, May 28, 1923, in HA/GHH, Nr. 300193008/19.

[59] Meeting, July 26, 1923, *ibid.*, Nr. 30070/11.

[60] Meetings, July 26 and August 24, 1923, in *ibid.*

TABLE 13

The Price of Various Iron and Steel Products, January–December 1923
(Price per ton measured in paper and gold marks: paper marks stated in thousands)

		January	February	March	April	May	June	July	August	September	October	November	December
Foundry pig iron III	PM	263.6	716.5	645.3	623.6	1,245.0	2,634.7	8,924.8	127,063.4	—	—	—	—
	GM	73.41	115.47	128.11	109.33	113.06	102.26	109.10	114.45	113.94	109.65	107.52	106.37
Hematite pig iron	PM	265.8	749.5	678.3	656.6	1,280.8	2,667.7	8,957.8	—	—	—	—	—
	GM	62.07	112.70	134.38	112.71	112.79	101.81	106.41	115.46	112.74	108.44	106.78	106.37
Billets	PM	347.0	937.5	872.7	1,132.6	2,685.0	9,084.8	—	—	—	—	—	—
	GM	81.05	140.97	172.89	194.41	236.54	346.72	—	—	—	—	—	137.00
Girders	PM	401.6	1,088.7	1,034.0	1,013.3	1,316.8	3,141.0	10,707.3	—	—	—	—	—
	GM	93.80	163.71	102.85	173.94	115.96	119.88	127.19	—	—	—	—	160.50
Merchant bars	PM	405.3	1,098.2	1,043.3	1,327.9	3,161.5	11,075.9	—	—	—	—	—	—
	GM	108.84	178.83	207.07	179.63	118.42	123.30	143.09	175.80	200.43	204.73	195.21	160.50
Heavy plate	PM	457.2	1,238.5	1,176.0	1,152.7	1,496.8	3,563.1	12,119.5	—	—	—	—	—
	GM	106.78	186.23	232.98	177.86	131.81	135.98	143.96	143.96	143.96	143.96	143.96	177.50

Source: Hans J. Schneider, Zur Analyse des Eisenmarktes (Vierteljahrshefte zur Konjunkturforschung, Sonderheft 1) (Berlin, 1927), p. 103.

20 trillion mark credit to finance their construction and expansion programs. The idea of such a credit was very appealing to the RWM because it constituted a form of "productive" work.[61]

By June 1923, however, the payment of unproductive labor costs had become inescapable and, if passive resistance were to be continued, it became necessary for the government and the steel industrialists to come to an agreement designed to ensure that the workers continued to be paid and the plants kept open despite the fact that the employers had every economic reason to shut down operations. On June 5 an agreement was signed between the government and the Employer Association of the Northwest Group of the VdESI (Arbeno) arranging the government wage guarantee for the industry. Under this agreement, the works were divided into five local groups, each of which was to have a commission composed of an equal number of employers and workers, which would be assigned the task of evaluating industrial requests for government wage payments. The Reich was to pay two-thirds of unproductive wage costs and the employers the remaining one-third, and the extent of "unproductive labor" was to be determined on the basis of a comparison between the production for each hour of labor during the month in question as compared with the average hourly production for the three last months of 1922. This formula, which was developed by the industrialists, met with some objection from the RWM and RFM, which pointed out that the difference between hours worked before and after the Ruhr occupation was not necessarily attributable to the occupation itself because bad business conditions could have produced similar effects. Nevertheless, the formula was accepted, and the determination of the amounts involved as well as their distribution was placed in the hands of the aforementioned commissions—that is, the parties most interested. On July 13, a supplementary agreement was signed providing that the government would pay more than two-thirds of the unproductive wages if production fell below 50% of the last months of 1922 and would pay full unproductive wages if production dropped to below 10% insofar as the concerns were unable to cover costs. Furthermore, two-thirds of the payments involved were to be provided in advance as calculated on the basis of the government's contribution during the previous month.[62] These arrangements were designed not only to meet rising wages and prices, but also to meet the tremendous increase in the number of plants shut down or working at very low levels of pro-

[61] Vögler to Hermes, July 26, 1923, and Thyssen to RFM, July 26, 1923, DZA Potsdam, RWM, Nr. 4531, Bl. 197–211.

[62] Reichert to Imhoff, August 28, 1923, and related reports and documents in *ibid.*, Nr. 4620, Bl. 2–3, 69ff., 262–263.

duction. By early summer, the blast furnaces and steel mills of the Ruhr were grinding to a halt, although finishing operations were continuing, and the iron and steel industrialists certainly had cause for concern.[63]

Under such alarming and progressively deteriorating conditions, it was quite natural for the industrialists to extend the logic of the government's credit and support payments and argue that unproductive operating costs (*Regiekosten*) as well as unproductive labor costs should be covered by the government. These were general administrative expenses, the salaries of plant officials uncovered by wage contracts, social expenditures for pensioners, medical facilities, canteens, etc., light and power for the works, general maintenance costs, and local taxes. The demand that the government compensate industry for these costs was first raised by the Phoenix concern, and the RWM undertook to investigate the matter by sending its assessors to the Hörder Verein in late June at a time when it was working at two-thirds of capacity. The RWM officials concluded that the unproductive operating costs were 300% greater than the unproductive wage costs. The coverage of these expenses, therefore, was no small matter, and some of the steel men initially were unenthused about the pressure Phoenix had applied for such payment for at least two reasons. First, they were fearful that if one asked for too much, one would get nothing. Second, some of the industrial leaders were chary of Phoenix's decision to invite the RWM officials to audit the costs of finished products. As General Director Springorum of Hoesch noted, "Previously the Reich Economics Ministry has only troubled itself about the costs of pig iron and crude steel. It is dangerous to bringing it around to concerning itself with the costs of finishing also."[64] Apparently, however, the other concerns ended up following Phoenix's lead because of the increasing unproductivity of their works and the attendant financial problems. In the late summer, the VdESI was demanding the restitution of unproductive operating expenses on behalf of the entire industry. Although the ratio of unproductive operating expenses to unproductive wage costs necessarily diminished as a plant became more unproductive, the VdESI claimed that unproductive operating costs constituted at least 150% more than unproductive wage costs, and that the government should therefore add this amount to its wage support payments. This the government refused to do, primarily for fiscal reasons, although it had made such a concession to the coal industry.

[63] See the detailed report by the Düsseldorf Metal Workers Union leader. Karl Wolff, July 16, 1923, August-Bebel-Institut, NB 158b.

[64] At the Northwest Group meeting, June 19, 1923, Krupp WA IV, 1404. See also the RWM minute of June 20, 1923, in DZA Potsdam, RWM, Nr. 4620, Bl. 9.

To compensate the steel industrialists, however, they were given more favorable treatment than other industries in the wage guarantee and credit arrangements.[65]

The huge sums of credits and outright contributions to costs as well as the later compensation for damages suffered raised all kinds of questions among contemporaries as to how these sums were paid, how they were used, the actual extent to which they were necessary, and the degree, if any, to which the iron and steel industrialists were taking unfair advantage of the situation or receiving more than they deserved. The same questions arise for the historian, and there is no easy and simple way to answer them because of the abnormality of the conditions under which they arose. Passive resistance meant collusion between government and industry in a whole series of secretive, surreptitious, and shady activities, and it undoubtedly helped further to break down inhibitions already weakened by years of instability. For example, every effort was made to keep the Steel Finance agreements secret because it was feared that the French would feel freer to confiscate material if they believed that it was the property of the German state rather than that of private persons.[66] Conditions in the occupied areas were not conducive to effective government auditing of the claims made by the concerns. Because payments from the Reich for the support of passive resistance were confiscated at every available opportunity by the French, proper control of the payments was made even more difficult by the fact that they had to be handled surreptitiously. The Reichstag committee that reviewed the various grants of credit and outright payments raised a host of questions and issues even when approving most of what was done. The committee recognized that "a distinction between the unproductive and productive portions of expenditure is practically impossible,"[67] and thus called into question the basic distinction on which much of the aid to the industrialists was based while in no way providing anything more viable as an alternative. Many members of the committee believed that the concerns were not doing all they could to improve their financial status by new stock issues and employing private credit resources. There was some suspicion that firms in the occupied area were gaining an unfair advantage from the credits received for expansion because such credits were not provided to concerns in the unoccupied area. The most common charge against the concerns, however, was that they were using the monies received to buy foreign exchange, and these charges

[65] Reichert to Imhoff, August 28, 1923, *ibid.*, Bl. 80–84.

[66] Reich Commissar for the Iron Trades to RWM, May 27, 1923, *ibid.*, Nr. 4531, Bl. 124.

[67] Report on its meeting of August 10, 1923, in *ibid.*, Bl. 220–221.

continued despite the fact that the government required a declaration of foreign exchange holdings from the concerns as a precondition for receiving Steel Finance credits.

The iron and steel industrialists, of course, were extremely anxious to convince the government, Reichstag, and public that they were not receiving unfair advantages and were not misusing funds. In July, when they campaigned at the Labor Ministry and the other ministries to have the full cost of their unproductive wages paid by the Reich, they arranged a special meeting with Stresemann and other party leaders to forestall charges "that the iron industry was trying to get special advantages for itself through direct pressure on the government."[68] The situation became worse in August and September as social tension and criticism of heavy industry mounted and as the inability of the government to support the progressively rising costs of passive resistance was more openly indicated by the new Stresemann government and its Socialist Finance Minister, Rudolf Hilferding, who was threatening to reduce expenditures on the Ruhr.[69] Reichert insisted that it was impossible to save money on the Ruhr because of the increasing adjustment of wages and salaries to gold values and the progressive unproductivity of the works, and persuaded Hilferding not to mention saving on the Ruhr in a speech before the full Reichstag, but he was unable to prevent Hilferding from taking action to control and reduce expenditure on the Ruhr in early September. Hilferding demanded that the industrialists fill out detailed questionnaires supporting their claims for wage supports and credits, while the industrialists complained that the agency in Hamm charged with supplying wage and other funds was not doing so quickly enough to keep up with the inflation.[70] The industrialists were angry, but they were also anxious, and they oscillated between threats that they would shut down entirely and throw the workers on the streets with all the ensuing consequences and pleas that the government give them the money they needed so that they and the Reich could be spared the domestic and foreign policy consequences of massive unemployment in the Ruhr. They were particularly fearful of the consequences for their own domestic image. They did not want to be the first and only industry to shut the workers out and thereby invite the press to cry that "the iron industry gave a stab-in-the-back to the Ruhr struggle."[71] Reichert, who

[68] Blank to Reusch, July 7, 1923, HA/GHH, Nr. 300193024.

[69] Report on August 24, 1923, Reichstag Committee meeting in *ibid.*, Nr. 300070/11.

[70] There were grounds for these complaints. See the memorandum by Imhoff of September 15, 1923, in DZA Potsdam, RWM, Nr. 4620, Bl. 67–68.

[71] Reichert at meeting of September 12, 1923, in the RAM, HA/GHH, Nr. 3001100/18.

as a member of the Nationalist Party certainly must have had a very keen sense of how devastating and effective such accusations had been when leveled by himself and his colleagues against the Social Democrats with regard to the Revolution, was very alarmed. As he told the steel men, "We must understand that a scapegoat will be sought in the event of a collapse of the resistance on the Ruhr, and everything is at work to make the iron industry responsible."[72]

As part of the campaign to exonerate the iron and steel industry from the charges made against it, Vögler sought to counter the notion that the industry had received undue support from the Reich, or indeed very much support, in connection with the Ruhr struggle. On September 11, he sent a letter to Becker's successor as Economics Minister, Hans von Raumer, pointing out that the thirteen great iron and steel concerns of the Ruhr had only taken 0.08% of the "contributions employed for the Rhein and Ruhr."[73] Reichert followed this up on September 17 with a letter claiming that the industry had only received 25.3 billion in paper marks to pay for unproductive labor costs. The picture presented by Vögler and Reichert, however, was misleading. It did not include any mention of the 21.6 trillion paper mark credits (86 million gold marks) provided through the Steel Finance Corporation between April 14 and September 15, and it only included certain categories of the so-called *Rhein-Ruhr Hilfe* and not the wage guarantee funds paid out under the special agreements between the Labor Ministry and Arbeno made in June and July. In reality, a total of approximately 189 trillion paper marks had been paid to the industry in wage supports by September 9, which is in no way to deny that the industrialists often received this money in depreciated form because they could not wait and had to pay their workers with their own resources.[74]

As always, the question of the extent to which the industrialists were using the credits they received to make unwarranted purchases of foreign exchange or to use the funds to purchase unnecessary raw materials was as widely asked as it was difficult to answer. To have information to deal with such allegations, Reichert made inquiries among the various concerns and received the uniform response that the concerns were in no position to speculate with the credits they received, that they did not have enough exchange for their own needs, and that they had been using their limited supplies to keep the Ruhr

---

[72] Reichert at meeting on September 11, 1923, *ibid.*

[73] Vögler to Raumer, September 11, 1923, *ibid.*, Nr. 30019390/25.

[74] Reichert to various ministers, September 17, 1923, DZA Potsdam, RWM, Nr. 4541, Bl. 129ff., and RFM report, *ibid.*, Nr. 4620, Bl. 104, and RWM report, *ibid.*, Nr. 4532, Bl. 98a–100.

struggle going. Reusch characterized as "evil libels" suggestions that the credits were being used improperly, and pointed out that between July 1 and September 13 he had used no less than 460,411 of the GHH's reserve of Dutch gulden to buy food for his workers.[75] Armed with such replies from the concerns, Reichert furiously accused their accusers of harming the national effort and ruining industry-labor relations in the Ruhr by spreading false rumors. The steel men now threatened to fight back if the government did not exonerate them. On September 24, the Nationalist deputy Quaatz and Vögler's secretary and lobbiest in Berlin, Dr. Freund, warned the Reich Chancellery that they would have to answer newspaper charges against the steel industry, and the government responded by begging them not to stir up the polemics still further. In return for restraint on the part of the industrialists, the government agreed to hold a press conference indicating that it had asked the industrialists not to reply to the charges being made for the moment. In fact, the government went even further in its effort at accommodation by allowing the RWM to reiterate the industrialists' claim that they had received only 0.08% of the help given to the Ruhr while making suitably vague references to the fact that the industry had "mortgaged its entire substance" in return for undisclosed amounts of credit.[76]

Such statements hardly eliminated suspicions that the steel concerns had used portions of their credits to purchase foreign currency or to accumulate unnecessarily large stores of raw materials. Not surprisingly, the evidence is complicated and ambiguous. Although there is evidence, for example, that Reusch had engaged in the common practice of currency speculation early in the year,[77] there is no reason to doubt that he was telling the truth in his above-mentioned response to Reichert. Furthermore, as will be shown, he could afford his virtue. Nevertheless, there is reason to question the apparent generalization of his self-righteousness to include all his colleagues. Hans von Raumer, surely no enemy of industry, knew better. As he explained to the cabinet shortly after taking over his ministry and around the very time Reusch was protesting his own innocence and that of his colleagues, "It is necessary to gain more strict control over the exchange received from exports. The abuse has always been that industry, every time we come too close to its stores of exchange, flees into goods. It has pro-

[75] Reusch to Reichert, September 13, 1923, and his letter to Reichert of August 30, 1923, in HA/GHH, Nr. 400101222/7.

[76] Reichert to Stresemann, September 17, 1923, and various ministers in DZA Potsdam, RWM, Nr. 4541, Bl. 129–133; RWM minute of September 28, 1923, and information release in *ibid.*, Nr. 4541, Bl. 115–116.

[77] See above, p. 358.

cured and stored large stocks of foreign raw materials instead of foreign exchange. . . ."[78]

There is some evidence that not only exchange procured from exports but also monies received from Ruhr credits were used in such a manner. For example, the Finance Ministry was most disturbed to learn in August that Rheinstahl had used Steel Finance credits to buy 10,000 British pounds and 600,000 Czech kronen in order to pay for lumber purchases. Because it was impossible to import such material into the occupied zone in August 1923, the ministry could only conclude that the purchases constituted "a collecting of factory materials for future use,"[79] and sought to terminate the practice by requiring stricter accounting from the Steel Finance Corporation. Although the Rheinstahl General Director, Hasslacher, conceded slight impropriety in the end by arguing that he should have used coal finance rather than steel finance credits for the purchase,[80] the issue of whether or not he should have made such purchases and payments at all does not appear to have been clarified. Indirectly, Hasslacher demonstrated why such clarification was so difficult and why the funds given by the Reich were so difficult to control when he commented in response to the Finance Ministry's inquiries that "in a corporation such as his own it is self-understood that financial dispositions are handled in a unitary manner and therefore that the means must be taken from where they can most efficiently and easily be gathered without considering whether the needed money is earmarked for an iron, a coal or some other type of plant."[81] Even under normal conditions, let alone under the peculiar ones of 1923, it was difficult to follow the internal financing of great concerns or to evaluate their justifiability in general economic or immediate economic perspective. Although the government began gathering reports on all flights of capital over one billion marks during the summer of 1923, this could only assist in the investigation of blatantly suspicious cases. It did not resolve the question of whether or not the large payments of Mannesmann in Hannover to Mannesmann in Komoton, Czechoslovakia, or of Stinnes in Berlin to the Bismarckhütte in Poland, which were not deviations from normal business practices within and among concerns, were justifiable under the circumstances.[82]

[78] Cabinet meeting of August 23, 1923, 1748/D765417.

[79] Minute of August 30, 1923, DZA Potsdam, RWM, Nr. 4532, Bl. 9, and discussion of September 7, *ibid.*, Bl. 36.

[80] Minute of September 26, 1923, in *ibid.*, Bl. 43.

[81] Quoted in RFM letter to Steel Finance Corporation, September 19, 1923, HA/ GHH, Nr. 300193008/19.

[82] See the long lists for the summer of 1923 in DZA Potsdam, RWM, Nr. 7695.

The issue of justifiability is one that can be viewed from a variety of perspectives. The Ruhr occupation simply drove to the extreme the entire dilemma of how the special interests of privately owned corporate enterprises were to be reconciled with those of a society in the throes of a continuous domestic and international crisis. As the Ruhr began to shut down in the summer and fall and the industrialists responded with the demand for wage payments and more Steel Finance credits, government leaders and some Reichstag deputies wondered if the industrialists were doing all they could by way of employing their own resources, raising money, and taking advantage of credit facilities available to them outside the government and the Reichsbank. The steel men stoutly resisted the repeated suggestions in August and September that they issue new stock in order to raise capital. They argued that the old stockholders, especially those in the family-based concerns, did not have sufficient money to satisfy the needs involved, that it was difficult to interest foreign investors under the existing circumstances, and that a watering of the capital stock of the concerns would create the danger of foreign control. Furthermore, they pointed out that the issuing of new stock required time and involved technical difficulties. These arguments were not without substance, but the real issues lay elsewhere. The fact was that this would not be the first time the concerns had watered their stock. There had been a good deal of stock watering throughout 1922 when they wanted available capital for their own purposes. Furthermore, they were aware of techniques whereby stock could be issued without running the risk of foreign control and had restricted the voting rights on new stock issues in the past. The basic question was how much information and security they were going to give up for the cause, and the answer was that they operated from a very definite if not neatly defined conception of retaining that which was necessary by way of information and resources to avoid risking their survival. Thus, when the government began asking for all types of detailed information concerning their needs as a precondition for further credits and wage payments, Klöckner took the view that all the Reich needed to know was that they were not using Reich funds to hoard foreign exchange or securities of various kinds and warned that "The remaining statistical material could be used against us sometime."[83] When hard pressed, they frequently reminded the government that it was the Reich, not private property owners, that was responsible for reparations just as it was responsible for the passive resistance and the economic problems arising from it. The final answer to the government urging that industry sacrifice more of its own resources was that "the works opposed these demands in

[83] Meeting of August 24, 1923, HA/GHH, Nr. 300070/11.

378

the strongest way and emphatically emphasized that what was involved here simply was the paying of the costs of the Ruhr war (*Ruhr-kriegskosten*) for which the Reich has the responsibility."[84]

As at the turn of 1919–1920, when the steel industrialists solved their Swedish ore debt problems in a manner most consonant with their own security, so in 1923 they did not fail to make basic decisions in their own favor. This is particularly evident when one recognizes that the year 1923 was not without its increases of capital stock and other major capital transactions in the iron and steel industry. The two leading concerns in the Otto Wolff group achieved particular notoriety in this respect, albeit in different ways. In June Rheinstahl raised its capital by 160 million marks and laid the groundwork for an additional 40 million mark issue. The 160 million mark issue was signed over to a bank consortium which, however, was not given the right to place it on the market. Rheinstahl let it be known that the entire stock emission was really intended as "a hedge against the liquidation of the Ruhr action." In order to cover unpaid credits, the concern was prepared to "employ its most yearned for currency, namely its stock, advantageously in some way," such as, for example, sale for foreign exchange.[85]

The path chosen by Phoenix in June–July 1923 was different and caused considerable sensation because it was widely viewed as the "Hollandization" of one of the greatest of the concerns. The affair was really more complicated than the misleading slogan suggested, and its actual impact on the policies of Phoenix in the later phase of the Ruhr occupation is difficult to measure. The Phoenix directors, led by Poensgen and Fahrenhorst, alarmed by the enormous increase of the concern's debt to 20 billion marks, anticipating financial needs of a high order and the dangers involved in having only its stored production to back up its credit requirements and desirous of having some security at the ending of the Ruhr conflict, resolved to invite the further participation of Dutch capital in the concern and to permit Dutch interests a greater voice in Phoenix affairs in return for a substantial loan repayable on very favorable terms. Specifically, Phoenix raised its capital stock from 300 to 600 million marks and, in return for a loan of 10 million Dutch gulden, the repayment of which was not to begin until after the Ruhr conflict was over and whose use was to be restricted to productive purposes designed to enhance the concern's well-being, Phoenix turned over the 300 million in new stock to the Dutch banking group as a security for the loan. If Phoenix paid its debt, then it would retain an option on the stock and could regain full disposition of it in five years—that is, in 1928. However, it could con-

[84] Reichert to RWM, August 28, 1923, DZA Potsdam, RWM, Nr. 4620, Bl. 80ff.
[85] *Vossische Zeitung*, June 14, 1923, in *ibid.*, Nr. 4531, Bl. 129.

trol the disposition of the stock in the intervening period so long as it fulfilled its obligations.[86]

The Reichstag committee overseeing the Steel Finance credits was so alarmed about the reported plans of Phoenix that on June 22 it instructed the government to issue no further credits to Phoenix until the concern demonstrated to the government's satisfaction that the arrangement discussed above precluded a Dutch takeover of the concern and did not involve tax evasion or flight of capital from Germany. The fear of foreign control over the concern had a very tangible basis because, in contrast to previous participation by Dutch interests, the holding company formed to control the new stock issue was given voting rights. The evidence suggests, however, that the Phoenix directors were careful from the outset to protect themselves against the charge and the reality of foreign control. The preferred stock involved was divided equally among the three German Phoenix stockholders and the two Dutch bankers placed at the head of the holding company, and this ensured a German majority. Naturally, the problem was not entirely resolved by formal arrangements of this type. On the one hand, the "Dutch" interest in Phoenix was a very complicated one because it had always been linked with Otto Wolff's involvements there. On the other hand, the Dutch interest and influence could be very real because it was a source of credit that Phoenix wanted and needed, and many Phoenix stockholders were frustrated by the lack of clear information they received from the directors and by what they considered to be poor treatment.[87]

The RWM cleared the Phoenix arrangement and publicly expressed its conviction that it did not involve either tax evasion or flight of capital. Understandably, the formal arrangements involved were designed to take as much advantage of tax loopholes as possible, but those involved could hardly be blamed for doing what had become the accepted. However, the Phoenix directors could certainly be charged with extreme generosity toward their Dutch creditors and a willingness to give exceptional immediate advantages to the latter in order to secure a long-term credit that would be independent of the fate of the mark. Thus, at a time when Phoenix stock was selling at 700,000% more than its nominal value on the German exchanges, the Dutch consortium was receiving the new stock at its par value and thereby making a 1.5 billion paper mark profit. This seemed particularly inappropriate

[86] For this discussion of the Phoenix transactions see DMV, *Konzerne der Metallindustrie*, pp. 225–227, and the correspondence and reports in DZA Potsdam, RWM, Nr. 4534, especially the report of the Reich Commissar for the Iron Trades of July 1, 1923, in Bl. 21ff.

[87] See especially the *Handelsblatt* report of July 8, 1932, in *ibid.*, Bl. 41.

at a time when the concern was chasing after Steel Finance credits and government funds for unproductive wage and operating costs. It appears that Phoenix was prepared to be even more generous in giving the holding company full dividend rights to the stock and was only dissuaded from doing so by Oscar Schlitter of the Deutsche Bank, to whom Fahrenhorst turned for technical advice. Schlitter did not think that the services of the Dutch creditors were proportional to Phoenix's generosity in providing its stock at par value and offering full dividend rights to boot. In his view, like that of the left-wing critics with whom he normally was not associated, the low price of the stock "could hardly be justified," and the offer of dividend rights simply left the arrangement open to "doubly sharp criticism from all sides."[88] In the end, the Dutch consortium was given a right to interest on the dividends but agreed to surrender its right to the dividends themselves. The entire arrangement, however, was an interesting and notable illustration of the lengths to which a concern could go in protecting itself from the insecurities of the situation whatever the problems from the standpoint of the national economic and political interest.

The Ruhr occupation was not conducive to major capital transactions in the West, but this did not prevent a good deal of "business as usual" in other parts of Germany and Europe. Indeed, new stars were rising higher on the horizon, and 1923 was a very active year for Friedrich Flick, who was to gain considerable notoriety during the coming decades and who had already distinguished himself during the war and afterward by his operations on the scrap market and his mysterious but patently profitable speculations. The base for this career of empire building was the fairly modest one of the Charlottenhütte in the Siegerland, where Flick was the chief stockholder and general director. After an abortive and almost disastrous effort to penetrate the Ruhr through coal mine and steel company stock purchases in 1920, Flick retreated before the combined resistance of Thyssen and Klöckner and turned eastward. The major expansion of his interests in 1921 took place on both sides of the Polish border, where he gained a controlling interest in the Bismarckhütte, the Kattowitzer Bergbau AG, and the Oberschlesische Montanwerke.[89]

With the Ruhr cut off from the rest of Germany in 1923, control of works in the Siegerland and other unoccupied areas was particularly advantageous, and the situation encouraged Flick to look for new op-

[88] Schlitter to Fahrenhorst, June 19, 1923, and related correspondence in the volume on the Phoenix AG für Bergbau und Hüttenbetrieb in Deutsche Bank Archiv, Frankfurt/Main.
[89] For Flick's early career see the colorful and well-informed biography of Günther Ogger, *Friedrich Flick der Grosse* (Bern, Munich, Vienna, 1971), p. 46ff.

portunities. One of the most interesting of these was an abortive one. When he learned that Krupp was prepared to sell its stock in Mannesmann in the spring of 1923, Flick expressed interest in the matter through Dr. Bruhn, and because Flick was prepared to let Krupp continue to have its representatives on the Mannesmann supervisory board, it was thought that Flick's interest was not a speculative one but rather an effort to promote collaboration between his Upper Silesian enterprises and the Mannesmann works in Czechoslovakia. The Flick offer seemed all the more appealing to the Krupp directors because they were convinced that "Flick can pay in foreign exchange,"[90] and because he seemed to want a close relationship with Krupp and would be acceptable to the Mannesmann direction. The latter had vetoed a sale of stock to Otto Wolff because it was feared that Wolff would try to ruin the Mannesmann marketing organization as evidenced by his efforts to penetrate Mannesmann's Balkan marketing outlets. Krupp was reluctant to sell its stock in Mannesmann to its neighboring concerns, particularly Rheinstahl and Phoenix, because they might seek to disturb Krupp's good business relations with Mannesmann. Flick, therefore, seemed to have much to offer. Unfortunately for him, however, the Krupp directors decided to drop the matter after it was intimated that their chief would veto it because "the person of Herr Flick was discussed already at an earlier time and . . . Herr von Bohlen expressed himself to the effect that he found his personality unsympathetic."[91] Subsequently, the bank involved found a purchaser who, it reported, was capable of paying in pound sterling and was "not a merchant, but a good industrial firm."[92] Whatever its distress and need to raise foreign exchange in 1923, it is remarkable that no need was so pressing as to bring Krupp to sell stock to parties socially unacceptable to its master!

Stinnes and Vögler did not share Krupp's social prejudices, and they did splendid business with Flick in 1923, which brought the latter into the ranks of the Ruhr industrialists. Stinnes was anxious to decentralize his heavy industrial holdings at a time when conditions in the Ruhr were so uncertain, and Flick could offer help in this regard. Consequently, in April 1923, Stinnes, acting for the SRSU, bought half of Flick's 80% interest in the Bismarckhütte, for which he gave Flick 250,000 pounds sterling and 12 million in IG stock, 10 million marks of which were Bochumer Verein shares. Through this arrangement,

[90] Wendt to Schäffer, May 2, 1923, and Schäffer to Bussmann, April 28, 1923, for the details of the proposed transaction, in Krupp WA IV, 1396.

[91] Schäffer to Wendt, May 3, 1923, *ibid*.

[92] Discussion of May 19, 1923, *ibid*.

Stinnes also developed an interest in the Kattowitzer Bergbau AG. Arrangements were made for Flick's Charlottenhütte to supply ore and pig iron to the works in the East, and the IG was to give steel and coke in return. The connection was also of great importance for the IG's operations in central and eastern Europe, where the Alpine Montangesellschaft was the linchpin. In fact, Stinnes hastened to sell his interest in the Bismarckhütte to the Alpine. On the one hand, the Alpine was thereby assured a coal basis, if not directly because the Upper Silesian works produced little coke, then indirectly because those works were in a position to trade their coal for Czech cokes.[93] On the other hand, it was necessary that the industrial works across the Polish border be in the hands of an Austrian concern such as the Alpine, because the Poles would thereby be unable to use their right to liquidate German property in their new territories. Further protection was provided by the heavy Italian and British interest in the Alpine. Thus, at a time when the western holdings of Stinnes and others were in such difficulty, concern expansion and large financial transactions were still possible in other areas. Indeed, through these transactions and others, such as Flick's creation of an IG between Linke-Hofmann-Lauchhammer and the Oberschlesische Eisenindustrie A.G., the foundation was being laid for important subsequent trends in the iron, steel, and finishing industries.

It is important not to exaggerate the expansionist operations of the great concerns in 1923, but it is necessary to recognize that they did not only suffer in 1923 and that many demonstrated a remarkable capacity to tap and monetize resources. A full survey of such resources is impossible, but there is important evidence demonstrating their existence. The SRSU, as has already been noted, made substantial use of its access to Reichsbank loans and, on the heavy industrial side, was one of the leading employers of the Steel Finance and Coal Finance credits. At the same time, it apparently had important credit possibilities abroad, a matter of great importance because, as in the case of Phoenix, an increasing need was felt to secure credits in foreign currency and thereby acquire resources that would be free of the fate of the mark. This was more difficult for the heavy industrial side of the IG than the electrotechnical side, but Deutsch-Lux and the GBAG were known to have sources of credit in Holland and Switzerland. The

---

[93] DMV, *Konzerne der Metallindustrie*, p. 212, is misleading on this point because the authors erroneously argue that the Kattowitzer coal was suitable for coking. See the detailed memorandum on the negotiations with Flick and the Alpine of April 19, 1923, in SAA, Nachlass Haller, 11/Lb 389. Also, see Ogger, *Flick*, pp. 68–79, and Ufermann and Hüglin, *Stinnes-Konzerne*, p. 52ff.

situation for the electrotechnical group was much simpler because of its enormous foreign organization, which enabled it to secure foreign currencies of every type.[94]

In the quest for domestic credits, Krupp seems to have been in a particularly favorable position as a traditionally protected concern of the Reich for military and perhaps sentimental reasons. Consequently, it "always stood," as its very active banking division director in Berlin, Schäffer, put it, "in a special relationship to the Reichsbank."[95] It had a special 60 billion mark credit from the Reichsbank until July, when it requested that the amount be increased to 100 billion. The Reichsbank directors resisted this initially and urged Krupp to use Steel Finance credits, and it was they who promoted the idea that the Steel Finance credits be expanded to include credits on finished products. When this effort ran into momentary difficulties, however, the Reichsbank leaders confidentially assured Krupp that it would receive the credits it needed through a direct paper mark credit should such credit not be forthcoming from elsewhere. It was well known that Krupp had raised credits in Holland and continued to have substantial credit there, and it is interesting to note that in a survey of the firm's financial status in October 1923—that is, after the termination of passive resistance and at a time when the condition of the industry was presumably more parlous than ever—Director Nathan of the Dresdener Bank concluded that if unproductive work were terminated, then "he viewed the condition of the firm as in no way unfavorable since sufficient resources were available." He urged against seeking a new foreign credit because the Dutch credit had not even been used yet, and he advised getting the needed money by "drawing upon our exchange and credit resources" as well as through the sale of Krupp's stock holdings in various concerns such as Mannesmann, Rheinstahl and, possibly, the Grusonwerke, or by taking a mortgage on the last-named enterprise.[96]

One of the most detailed and impressive descriptions of how strong a concern could remain and how confident its leaders could feel in the midst of the events of 1923 was provided by Reusch in a report to August Haniel on September 5, 1923. Turning first to the Gutehoffnungshütte itself, Reusch noted that its mobile worth lay in its stock of production in storage, which amounted to 150,000 tons of iron of all sorts. This did not include 20,000 tons of rolled material the GHH had managed to get to England, presumably through a combination of

[94] See the Freund study of the SRSU, SAA 54/Lm 123.

[95] Minute by Schäffer, July 6, 1923, Krupp WA, 1405. The volume contains a full record of Schäffer's negotiations in Berlin.

[96] Meeting of October 25, 1923, in *ibid.*, IV 2560.

English influence, bribing French railroad authorities, or both. Of the 150,000 tons, only 4,132 tons were owed in exchange for credits taken or emergency money (*Notgeld*) issued in the name of the GHH to make up for the currency shortage in Oberhausen. Domestic customers had bought 34,000 tons, and they had consigned the money for the material months before and were awaiting delivery as soon as conditions permitted. Thus, Reusch was in a position to discount yet another 111,868 tons of material and had even received some foreign exchange thanks to the sale to England mentioned above. Then, there were "still other liquid resources, which I don't want to go into here." Insofar as the GHH was concerned, therefore, he concluded that "for the moment the affairs of the Gutehoffnungshütte are not in a bad way," despite the fact that they had used up part of their silent reserves. He was confident that he could "steer the ship Gutehoffnungshütte through the coming storms without suffering serious damage."[97]

In considering the concern works as a whole, Reusch came to a similar conclusion of measured confidence. Most of the firms in the concern had managed to make it through without debts, and those compelled to go into debt because of the "insanely increased wages and salaries" remained fundamentally solid and secure. To reduce costs in these firms, he had ordered a reduction of working hours despite the large number of orders to be filled. Furthermore, "There are resources everywhere which we can draw upon and which will hopefully help us through the coming hard times. If the authority of the state can be halfway maintained, then I do not have any fears for the survival of these enterprises."[98] Reusch was a patriot, an enthusiast for passive resistance, and a man who wanted the authority of the state maintained—but not at the expense of the economic interests for which he felt ultimately responsible.

Through such careful husbanding and attention to one's resources, it was possible to look to the future with a greater sense of security than was possible for many other groups in German society. The workers at the MAN Augsburg plants, for example, did not take so kindly to the reduction of hours Reusch was imposing, and in a meeting on September 5, 1923, they declared that they were not ready to "sacrifice their existences" as the finale to their previous years of unbearable sacrifice and insisted "that the government and industry do everything so as to make it through the present circumstances as rapidly as possible since in the final analysis industry has made monstrous profits through the misguided financial and credit policy and thereby

[97] Reusch to A. Haniel, September 5, 1923, HA/GHH, Nr. 300193000/5.
[98] *Ibid.*

contributed to the present inflation."[99] The trade union leaders and the workers in the Ruhr as well as in the unoccupied areas of Germany had demonstrated remarkable loyalty and steadfastness in the face of the French occupation, but the spring of 1923 brought with it a growing demoralization and a despairing sense that no matter how the tragedy ended, they were going to bear the greatest sacrifices. A moving statement of the bitterness and intensifying class conflict in the Ruhr was provided by the Metal Worker Union secretary, Karl Wolff, in a report of July to the union leadership in Stuttgart, when, after cataloguing the large number of plants shut down, he went on to discuss the "demoralization of the workers" while " the entire bourgeoisie of the Ruhr blusters." He went on:

> Certainly you also know—the newspapers don't hide it anymore—that heavy industry negotiates with the other side, and we stand here, rifle at rest and wait to see what Stinnes plots with his comrades. . . . One can just feel in one's bones that negotiations are going on between French industry and them, that perhaps an understanding has already been reached in part. At whose cost would it be made? Only at the cost of the working class.[100]

Rumors of secret dealings among the industrialists and of treasonous relations between German industrialists and the French in connection with various separatist schemes were not new. They dated back to the Revolution. As with most rumors, they had some basis in fact. There were industrialists, of whom Hugo Stinnes was the most prominent, who hoped to settle the political conflict between the French and the Germans by means of an arrangement between the industrialists of the two countries. However, there were differences among the industrialists concerning this, as concerning many things, and Stinnes' plans were rather imperialistic for a defeated power and certainly did not involve a "sell-out" to the French. Furthermore, at a certain stage of the Ruhr crisis, Stinnes' plans became connected with schemes for a Rhenish state, albeit not with the ideas of the true separatists.[101] The rumors, however, were also misleading because they were based on crude Marxist notions that the capitalists of the world could unite and determine the policies of states. Although Stinnes also entertained such fantasies, as did many industrialists, French heavy industry never enjoyed the power or influence of its German counterparts. Even though the rumors were misleading, the anxious sense that developed among the workers that it was they who were going to pay the bill for whatever

[99] Report of September 10, 1923, *ibid.*, Nr. 300193010/11.

[100] Report by Wolff of July 16, 1923, August-Bebel-Institut, NB 158b.

[101] See below, p. 445ff.

arrangement was made was fully justified. The common denominator of all the plans and efforts by the industrialists to settle the Ruhr issue was precisely the effort to make the workers pay for the settlement with the gains of the Revolution.

The basic view of the trade union leadership was that the object of passive resistance was to demonstrate to the French the necessity of negotiation, but that Germany's position was weaker than that of France and that passive resistance had to be accompanied by timely and acceptable German offers given in good faith and having behind them the backing of German industry. To some extent, Stinnes agreed with the trade union people on the limitations of passive resistance. On March 29, Stinnes asked his party colleague Stresemann to discuss the political and economic situation and frankly told the DVP leader that "with regard to the Ruhr, he did not see how we could hold out against France, which can unquestionably hold out longer."[102] This was precisely the message that Leipart, the Socialist trade union leader, had expressed to State Secretary Eduard Hamm the day before.[103] Stresemann was somewhat surprised to find Stinnes so pessimistic because Vögler had been adamant in his opposition to negotiation in his discussions with Stresemann only a few days earlier. Stinnes assured Stresemann that he agreed with Vögler's assessment of the effectiveness of passive resistance and argued that "it would always remain a great achievement for Germany that through this resistance it was made clear that one cannot do anything one wants to Germany." However, Stinnes chose to emphasize that the resistance could not be viewed as "an end in itself" but only as "a means to the goal" of freeing the Ruhr and getting a reparations settlement. Stinnes agreed "with certain reservations" to a recent speech by Stresemann calling for the taxation of "real values" as part of any definitive reparations settlement and that the Reich would one day have to mortgage the "real values" of the country. However, in return, industry would demand the end of the controlled economy and the eight-hour day. Stinnes was convinced that the Socialists would accept the latter "necessity."[104]

There is evidence that Stinnes was partially correct and that there was, if not "complete accord," at least a good measure of Socialist agreement that a settlement would require some temporary concessions on the eight-hour day.[105] The problem was that the industrial leaders were insistent that the chief burdens be placed everywhere but on their shoulders and that they made their demands, which were

[102] Minute of March 29, 1923, Nachlass Stresemann, 3098/7114H/H145343–345.
[103] *Kabinett Cuno*, pp. 348–349.
[104] Minute of March 29, 1923, Nachlass Stresemann, 3098/7114H/H145343–345.
[105] See below, p. 409.

often simply outrageous in the context of their resources, with incredible arrogance and insensitivity. This was demonstrated at its worst in the second half of May, when the RdI was called upon by Cuno to give substance to a German reparations offer sent to the Allied governments on May 2. It proved a disappointment and unacceptable to both the powers involved in the occupation and those who were not, but it did hold forth the prospect that the German government would enact laws enlisting the entire economy—that is, industry included—as security for the loans that would be made to Germany in connection with any settlement.[106]

The government's difficulties in securing industrial support, even for an inadequate offer, was made evident when Cuno and Becker met secretly with the RdI presidium on May 15 to discuss the question. The government leaders were berated by Stinnes and Bücher for failing to consult properly with industry prior to making the offer of May 2 and were urged to avoid such behavior in the future and to take advantage of industry's excellent foreign connections by using industrialists in the conduct of negotiations. Klöckner made it clear that industry would not consider foreign participation in German enterprises and that it would turn down any mortgage on the German private industrial plant whose size or conditions were deemed ruinous and which were not coupled with major "domestic reforms" that ensured that "the workers, through more intensive work, increased the profitability of the works." Under no circumstances would industry tolerate the mortgaging of customs receipts, the direct turning over of stocks and bonds to foreign creditors, or the use of capital. The "solution" would have to be found first and foremost through a mortgaging of the works and resources of the federal and state governments, an industrial guarantee, and an intensification of productivity. Cuno basically accepted the notion that the property and works of the Reich had to be put up as first security, and the only resistance put up by the government appears to have come in rather sheepish form from Becker, who pointed out that the coupling of worker productivity with the industrial guarantee at this time seemed inappropriate "since then the defensive front on the Ruhr will collapse immediately." This view was not shared by Stinnes and others, who felt that the workers would understand the necessity. In fact, the basic notion that industry had to place its cards on the table won out in a meeting of the RdI leaders on the following day in the face of arguments by Sorge that some attention should be paid to choosing the right psychological moment because "The mood

[106] Bergmann, *History of Reparations*, p. 191ff.; Maier, *Recasting Bourgeois Europe*, pp. 368–369.

in the political parties, from the left far into the People's Party, is in no way friendly to industry."[107]

This mood was in no way improved when, on May 25, the RdI officially responded to Cuno with a note drawn up by the same individuals who had been constructing the RdI economic program. Although some of the harshness of Silverberg's initial draft of the note was eliminated, the final version concocted by Lammers and Bücher was sufficiently provocative to cause a wave of anger throughout the country. They began by complaining that industry had not been consulted in the making of the German offer of May 2, apparently under the assumption that the foreign policy of the Reich had to be made with the advice and consent of the RdI, and then went on to declare that the chief burden of any guarantee must fall on the Reich, which would have to mortgage its railroads and other economic operations. Consequently, the state works had to be run according to "principles of private enterprise" if their value was to be maintained for such purposes. Industry itself was prepared to assume 40% of a 500 million gold mark guarantee, but only under three basic conditions beyond the obvious one of stabilizing the economy and the political situation. First, the state was to cease interference in the economy through the elimination of export controls and other vestiges of the controlled economy as well as through the elimination of the demobilization agencies and the termination of state arbitration in labor-industry conflicts. Second, the creation of a tax system that would encourage capital accumulation necessary to the maintenance and development of industry was essential. Third, productivity had to be raised through the creation of an hours-of-work law permitting contractually agreed upon exceptions to the eight-hour day and by permitting industry to relieve itself of paying unproductive wages, i.e., restoring its right to fire workers at will.[108]

Even highly placed industrialists found cause to criticize the RdI document. Thus, v. Thyssen-Bornemisza considered it a "great mistake internally and externally" and, as the "co-owner of a great enterprise," warned against making a reparations offer on the basis of it because "the outside world will never understand that the economically weaker element namely the Reich with its railroads, etc., should do more than industry, agriculture, shipping, and commerce, etc. If one wants to commit oneself to figures, then I would reverse the relationship to one-third by the Reich and two-thirds by industry, agriculture, etc."[109] The trade unions, of course, took the same view and went beyond it

[107] For the RdI meetings of May 15–16, 1923, see HA/GHH, Nr. 30019320/7.
[108] *Kabinett Cuno*, pp. 508–513.   [109] *Ibid.*, p. 539n3.

by accusing industry of an unwillingness to pay taxes and declaring their own unwillingness to surrender the eight-hour day and the limitations on the employer right to dismiss workers. They objected to the industrialist demand that all social considerations be eliminated and that the economy be based on a pure profit motive. They were most penetrating, however, in their attack on the political implications of the RdI "offer." They accused the RdI of turning the relationship between industry and the state "upside down" and of negotiating with the state as an "independent power." The trade unions found it "unbearable that industry is trying to use its economic power to set conditions for the fulfillment of state necessities," and pointed out that "the authority of the state must be unbearably weakened if the government of the Reich gives way to the conditions set up by the Reich Association."[110]

By July 1923 the authority of the state was severely weakened indeed, and the Cuno government was on its deathbed because of the divisions within it and its incapacity either to formulate a clear policy or to implement one. As Raumer told Stresemann: "In my view the Socialists cannot be considered wrong in saying that the Cuno cabinet is conducting a very unskillful domestic policy and above all that its handling of economic problems is completely planless and free of ideas. It is unfortunate that the disappointment in this regard unites capitalists as well as Socialists in making the same criticisms."[111] It was utterly incredible, for example, that Finance Minister Hermes continuously failed to respond to Cuno's requests for a tax program on the grounds that a program could not be developed until the reparations issue was settled and that no special tax to cover the Ruhr costs was levied until August 1923. By and large, the old system of taxes payable in paper marks was continued while the government and the Reichsbank provided one credit after the other that were also repayable or largely repayable in paper marks. Within the government there was a recognition of the need for a new policy, but a complete inability to deal forcefully and forthrightly with the problem.[112]

A similar uncertainty, confusion, and lack of direction prevailed in the handling of the crucial problem of exchange controls. On June 22, 1923, exchange controls were finally stiffened by a decree forbidding the sale of marks directly or indirectly to persons abroad and requiring that all transactions in foreign exchange be done at an officially estab-

[110] *Ibid.*, pp. 537–539.

[111] Raumer to Stresemann, July 23, 1923, Nachlass Stresemann, 3098/7117H/H14749ff.

[112] *Kabinett Cuno*, p. 640n6, and Bresciani-Turroni, *Economics of Inflation*, p. 62.

lished rate. This effort to put a stop to the flight of capital and to reduce speculation was opposed by Economics Minister Becker and various business circles on the not entirely invalid ground that it would make foreign trade very difficult by creating an artificial exchange rate in Berlin that could not be respected abroad. Becker did not sign the decree himself, which made his opposition publicly visible, and he had the dubious satisfaction, one month later, of sending Cuno a memorandum dated July 23 in which he was able to point out that the entire situation had led to an increase of illegal activities, a withholding of exchange, and a dampening of business activity. On August 8 the exchange rate was freed, and the result was an enormous demand for exchange and a renewed plummetting of the mark.[113]

Cuno's dilemmas were, in fact, enormous because, like Wirth at the end of the latter's tenure of office, his desire to gain the support of industry placed him in conflict with the political requirements of representing the interests of the entire nation. Of all the important industrialists, Reusch seemed to stand most solidly behind him. Reusch was an ardent believer in holding out on the Ruhr even at the cost of sacrificing Germany's economic ability to pay reparations afterwards and he, like Cuno, believed that this posture would serve as an effective inducement in bringing the French to the negotiating table.[114] The failure of this policy, a failure really created by the unsatisfactory nature of what the Germans were offering which made it difficult for Allied critics of the French occupation to have an effective voice in Paris, only served to make the domestic situation more difficult as well and to leave Cuno open to the charge of having failed to take advantage of the diplomatic opportunities available at the time when passive resistance seemed strongest. At the same time, Cuno could not help but be disappointed in the May 25 RdI offer, and this led to severe tension with some industrial leaders, particularly Stinnes, with whom the Chancellor was reported to have had a furious altercation at the end of June. Stinnes was supposed to have stormed out of the room after Cuno told him to change his tone because "I am not an employee of yours, and if I were, I would still forbid you to speak to me in such a tone."[115]

Apparently, this kind of problem did not arise with Reusch, who skillfully and persistently sought to push Cuno in the direction desired by most of the leading industrialists. Noting the failure of the June exchange decree, for example, Reusch discussed the matter with Cuno and then wrote to him about his pet project of banning the import of

[113] *Kabinett Cuno*, pp. 650n2, 652ff., 716–717n2.
[114] *Ibid.*, pp. 412–415.
[115] *Ibid.*, p. 650n3.

all luxury articles such as tobacco, coffee, tea, and "everything not absolutely necessary for human life" because it is "much better for the Reich to provide temporary unemployment payments and to compensate the industries involved in one form or another, then to continue the present uncontrolled import policy."[116] Reusch thought that all the exchange decrees were "ripe for the trash can" and that industries such as the tobacco and chocolate industries could well bear suffering a shut-down caused by an import ban until the end of the year because "We are in the midst of a war and must consequently take war measures."[117] Reusch's proposal was not entirely unjustified because there had been large imports of nonessential goods due to the government's unwillingness to harm domestic industries or to hurt trade relations with friendly nations, but as State Secretary Hamm noted in a memorandum considering these problems, such an import ban was not enough. Greater control of the foreign exchange of firms engaged in international commerce was also required. By implication, this meant that Reusch and his colleagues would have to accept restraint and controls. However, as Hamm also realized, such measures would "contradict the recently developed government program of restoring the free movement of the economy."[118]

The fundamental effort of the Cuno regime at its termination was to regain the support of industry and to secure a large loan in foreign exchange from industry in return for an economic program in keeping with industry's desires. The elimination of export controls played a central role in this program, which was developed by State Secretary Albert and the former Siemens director, who exercised great influence on the chancellery, Otto Henrich.[119] Cuno had approved of this program, and industry had agreed to support the new loan program. The entire character of this arrangement and the degree to which Cuno was sinking into captivity to industry was well illustrated by a meeting of August 1 attended by Cuno, Albert, Stinnes, Vögler, Warburg, and Hamm to discuss the loan and various tax schemes. As Warburg reports:

> Vögler then offered 50 million gold marks in foreign exchange if one disbands the export control boards; or, if this cannot be done, then if one relieves those firms that deliver exchange of the export controls for a series of months. Jokingly, I [Warburg] character-

[116] Reusch to Cuno, July 11, 1923, HA/GHH, Nr. 400101290/119.
[117] Reusch to Cuno, July 19, 1923, in *ibid.*
[118] *Kabinett Cuno*, pp. 716–719.
[119] *Ibid.*, p. 682ff. See also the memorandum on the policies of the government at the transition from Cuno to Stresemann in BA R 43 I/1493, Bl. 287–293, and Rupieper, "Politics and Economics," p. 374ff.

ized this last proposal as immoral, and it rapidly disappeared from the discussion.[120]

It was indeed little more than a bribe, but it demonstrates how far things had gone by way of industrialist self-assertion in Germany that Vögler could make such a proposal in the face of the highest officials of the land with impunity. It was a good illustration of why the Cuno regime had become untenable.

ENDING PASSIVE RESISTANCE AND THE EIGHT-HOUR DAY

Understandably, Cuno's departure on August 13 was viewed with regret by some industrialists, and Stresemann's Great Coalition cabinet was considered an unfortunate turning point in the Ruhr conflict as well as in domestic policy making. Reusch was particularly upset because he believed that Cuno was "at the high point of his foreign policy success" thanks to England's recent open criticism of the French policy, and he felt that Cuno had made a great mistake in stepping down under Socialist pressure. Although not very well acquainted with Stresemann, Reusch had no doubt that "a day would come when all the industrial interests would have to take a stand against him."[121] Within less than three weeks of the change of government, Reusch was complaining that "Stresemann is the chancellor of capitulation. The chancellor speaks and his Social Democratic ministers act and will force him in a very short time to negotiate directly with France. . . ." Reusch feared that the Finance Ministry, under the Socialist Rudolf Hilferding, would cease supporting the resistance and that "the one productive activity of the government, namely the printing of notes, will reach its end."[122] When Stresemann finally declared an end to passive resistance on September 26, Reusch took the occasion to resign his membership in the DVP.[123]

As one of the most conservative and nationalistic of the heavy industrialists, Reusch was at once ahead of many of his colleagues in sensing that Stresemann's broadly based and truly political conception of the national interest was incompatible with the narrow and interest-bound ideas of the heavy industrialists, but at the same time he was falling behind many of his colleagues in coming to the realization that the passive resistance policy was hopeless and ultimately a lost cause. On

---

[120] Warburg, unpublished memoirs, 1923, p. 55, in Warburg Papers.

[121] Reusch to W. Tafel, August 15, 1923, HA/GHH, Nr. 4001012017/11.

[122] Reusch to A. Haniel, September 5, 1923, *ibid.*, Nr. 300193000/5.

[123] Reusch to Friedrich Blumberg, September 26, 1923, *ibid.*, Nr. 30019393/0.

the domestic political front, Stresemann and his first Economics Minister, Hans von Raumer, were convinced that attention had to be paid to the means by which certain of the ends desired by industry were to be achieved, and they felt that a purely one-sided solution to the major economic and social issues facing the country could only lead to an intensification of domestic conflict. Stresemann was fully aware, as was noted in the cabinet on August 23, that the "passive resistance of the workers is also directed of late against the German employers."[124] If possible, he wanted to achieve the major goals of industry, particularly decontrol of the economy and extension of the hours of work, with rather than against labor. The logic of this position was sketched by Raumer weeks before the new government was formed when he pointed out that a new, Great Coalition government would have to undertake tax reform and demand sacrifices on the part of the propertied classes for the payment of reparations. Only with a willingness to make such sacrifices on their part would it be possible to demand of the workers "a major concession in the area of working conditions. The business can only be handled step by step (*Zug im Zug*)."[125] Just as Raumer wished to extend the working day, so did he wish to get rid of export controls, but Raumer understood that the Socialists were tenaciously holding on to the controls because the Export Control Boards were a means by which they could exercise some direct influence, however tenuous, in matters of economic policy. Consequently, he felt it necessary to offer new "imponderables" in place of those being sacrificed and suggested that *Arbeitsgemeinschaften* be set up for the various branches of industry in which worker representatives could continue to have a voice in the general discussion of the economic problems of the various industries. Obviously, this was a much less crude approach to the elimination of export controls than the one taken by Vögler. Implicit in that difference, however, was the conflict between the aggressive, politically insensitive, and narrowly interest-oriented policy favored by many of the heavy industrial leaders as against the more moderate, realistic, and flexible posture advocated by Stresemann, Raumer, and other moderate bourgeois politicians and businessmen.

In the initial weeks of the new cabinet, however, Stresemann, Raumer, and Hilferding did seem to secure a measure of cooperation from heavy industry. At a meeting with the RdI leaders on August 22, the latter went so far as to tell Hilferding that some compulsion would have to be used to get businessmen to give up foreign exchange in

[124] Cabinet meeting, August 23, 1923, 1748/D756439.

[125] Raumer to Stresemann, July 23, 1923, Nachlass Stresemann, 3098/7117H/Hi45749ff.

support of a new gold loan, although they took the occasion to ask for an amnesty for previous foreign exchange decree violators. Stresemann seemed to agree that "the financial emergency of the Reich was so great that possible moral reservations against an amnesty have to be set aside." As it turned out, the political reservations were less easily disposed of, and the matter was dropped. More generally, Bücher demanded that "if the propertied now again have to make a special sacrifice, then a sense of sacrifice must be shown by the workers." Here, too, Stresemann was forthcoming. He agreed that "an increase of productivity is an unconditional necessity" and promised that his cabinet would work toward this end. However, he insisted that primacy had to be given to ending the foreign and domestic crisis and asked that industry stand behind him. Sorge promised this collaboration in the name of the RdI, and thus the formal relations between the new government and industry began auspiciously.[126]

Some of this moderately helpful and cooperative behavior must be attributed to the growing panic over the future of passive resistance and a fear on the part of the industrialists for their own fortunes.[127] Most industrialists were not as bull-headed, impervious, and secure as Reusch. To be sure, they could and did take a tough line in foreign affairs on the surface. Thus, on August 20, 1923, Otto Wolff met with Stresemann in Berlin to discuss his recent meeting with General Denvignes, who was the economic adviser to the French commander in the Ruhr, General Degoutte.[128] Denvignes had invited Wolff to a private discussion of ways and means by which the existing stalemate might be ended, and Wolff reported that he had told the Frenchman that the first steps must come from France, that German workers would not serve the French if the latter tried to run German industry themselves and that, however true it might be that collaboration between the industries of the two countries was a necessity, the first thing that was needed was for "France to place money at Germany's disposal so that she might build up the economy once again." Denvignes found this demand "astonishing" because he apparently did not feel that the financial support of Germany was the intended outcome of the Ruhr occupation. He also did not feel that Wolff's suggestion that Germany try to pay reparations to France but cease payment to other reparations claimants would prove consonant with French sensibilities. De-

---

[126] For this meeting of August 22, 1923, see Krupp WA VII, f. 1076.

[127] See the references to this panic at the Cabinet meeting of August 20, 1923, 1748/D756418ff. Also, see Maier, *Recasting Bourgeois Europe*, pp. 390–391.

[128] For this discussion from Stresemann's report see Gustav Stresemann, *Vermächtnis. Der Nachlass in drei Bänden*, edited by Henry Bernhard, 3 vols. (Berlin, 1932), I, pp. 94–95. However, the date there is erroneously given as August 21. For the original see Nachlass Stresemann, 3099/7188/H145858–859.

spite Wolff's alleged bravura in dealing with Denvignes, however, the industrialist expressed his fundamental pessimism quite plainly to Stresemann. He reported that the mood in the Rhineland was "very bad," that separatist feelings were growing, and that the government might even be well advised to consider setting up a separate Rhenish state that would include a part of the Ruhr as a means of stiffening the backs of the Rhinelanders. Wolff was not the only industrialist urging negotiations with the French. Stinnes and Vögler were saying the same thing to Stresemann at the end of August, and Stinnes was arguing that something had to be done within a fortnight.[129] If Reusch thought Stresemann the "chancellor of capitulation," therefore, he could only do so in the knowledge that Stresemann was keeping company with some of Reusch's most illustrious colleagues. Reusch was informed, for example, of a secret Düsseldorf Chamber of Commerce meeting on August 29, in which there was unanimity on the need for a speedy understanding with France and a feeling that "if we don't get a solution soon, no plane would be quick enough to fly to Paris in order to sign everything that is demanded."[130] It was well known that there were many firms engaged in the purchase and resale of goods confiscated by the French, and in mid-September Reichert was informing Reusch that two of the most outstanding victims of these confiscations, Klöckner and Wolff, were conducting secret negotiations with the French.[131]

In August and September, however, these *pourparlers* were very tentative and very much in the background, whereas the economic and social conditions promoting an end to passive resistance and major efforts toward stabilization in both industrial and governmental circles were clear and obvious. In the summer of 1923, the tendency of German domestic market prices not only to reach but also to exceed world market prices crested and then moved toward a seemingly unassailable peak. The advantages of the inflation—low real wages, low coal and transport prices, low real interest on mortgages, unvalorized taxes— were simply evaporating, and German industrialists were left with the raw and brutal reality of having to sell overpriced goods produced at excessive cost.[132] In August 1923, the price of industrial raw materials in Germany was 1.2% above England and 4.4% above France, although

[129] Cabinet meeting, August 30, 1923, 1748/D756499. Indeed, Wolff and Stinnes had been impatient with Cuno and had sent out feelers to the French as early as April 1923, but Poincaré would not negotiate. See Rupieper, "Politics and Economics," p. 273.

[130] Report of meeting, August 29, 1923, HA/GHH, Nr. 300193020/1.

[131] Blank to Reusch, September 15, 1923, *ibid.*, Nr. 300193024/3.

[132] Bresciani-Turroni, *Economics of Inflation*, pp. 140–141.

still 15.8% below the United States. By October, German prices were almost 20% above France and England and 6.4% above those of the United States. Businessmen had, by this time, learned altogether too well the art of calculating in gold marks according to the exchange rate and setting prices that included replacement costs. Wages were also being set according to an index number of the cost of living provided by the Reich Statistical Bureau. In short, prices and wages increased rapidly, but producers no longer enjoyed the cost-price benefits of the previous period of inflation. The government was no longer willing to suffer a constant loss on the real value of its receipts either, and freight rates and utility rates were being calculated in gold marks on the basis of the exchange rate. Furthermore, the government was collecting the new taxes finally passed in late August in connection with the Ruhr conflict on a gold basis and was moving in the direction of valorizing all its tax receipts.[133]

The inflation was now unbearable for most industrialists because they could no longer profit from it on world markets and were compelled to struggle with all its disadvantages. The government could not even supply enough paper currency to pay wages, and the local governments and major concerns were issuing emergency money while impatiently awaiting new supplies from the Berlin printing presses. Even so tightly run a concern as the GHH felt itself compelled to issue 750 trillion marks in uncovered emergency money by mid-August before Reusch ordered that no more such money be issued unless covered by the discounting of Steel Finance credits.[134] The sense of chaos was heightened by the fact that the concerns could not tell what their real costs were and were employing formulas based on prewar prices to which they then added supplementary amounts designed to account for world market price increases. The almost hysterical incantation of the need to cut costs and increase productivity reflected this situation of real ignorance about present and future conditions and intensified the desire for a firm basis of calculation in real values. This combination of circumstances put an end once and for all to the ambivalence and uncertainty among the industrialists as to the desirability of going over to pricing in gold or other stable values.

The uncertainty had been a very real one because of the hermaphroditic accounting and pricing practices, now in gold marks or foreign currencies, now in paper marks, which had been crucial to industry's capacity to enjoy the best of all possible worlds during the bulk of the inflation. So long as the paper mark remained in existence as the basic

[133] *Ibid.*, pp. 70–72, and Gerhard Bry, *Wages in Germany, 1871–1945* (Princeton, 1960), p. 232.

[134] See the correspondence of August 17–18, 1923, in HA/GHH, Nr. 300070/7.

currency, it had been possible to get enormous amounts of credit in paper at low interest rates and to employ credit instruments, such as bills of exchange, to secure operating capital. In the final phase of the inflation, however, no amount of such credit could prove sufficient, and the clear intention of the Stresemann government to reduce the flow of credits signaled the fact that the game was up. The need for new sources of credit based on real values that would be both paid in stable currency and repayable in a like manner was becoming apparent, although this need was handled in different ways by the different concerns involved. Clearly, however, such credits could not be poured down the bottomless pit of passive resistance.

Yet, there had been one major barrier that had served to inhibit the conversion to an open policy of pricing in gold marks, and that was wages. It seemed obvious that once prices were stated in terms of gold marks, wages would have to follow very soon thereafter. There is evidence, however, that the policy of the industrialists, and even the policy within industrial concerns, was far from coordinated in this matter. It all depended on the perspective one took. Insofar as the industrialists, and particularly heavy industrialists whose wage bill was less significant than those of the manufacturers, concentrated their attention on securing a maximum return for the sale of their products, they pushed for stricter delivery conditions and the greatest possible degree of calculation in stable values. Insofar as they reflected on the implications of their pricing policy for labor costs, they were reluctant to be too obvious or stringent in their drive to calculate in stable values. Within the Pig Iron Syndicate and the Steel Federation, the first perspective tended to be dominant, and by early July there was strong pressure for pricing in stable values. The line taken by the RdI, however, was that "wages should be the last thing" to be calculated in stable values and that the "preconditions" for wages calculated in gold marks would have to be "the elimination of the controlled economy and longer hours of work."[135]

By implication, therefore, there was some contradiction between this national industrial policy of the RdI, which suggested a cautious conversion to calculation in gold marks in order to promote a downward pressure on wages and the implementation of its socioeconomic program, and the more narrowly conceived effort of the syndicates to calculate everything in stable values. The tendency of the syndicates to preempt the situation by taking decisions without reference to broader policy considerations provoked sharp criticism from Oscar Funcke, who pointed out that the general directors, "who have the

[135] Dr. Meissinger in the Wage Contract Committee of the VDA, August 8, 1923, *ibid.*, Nr. 300193024/3.

dominant influence on the economic policy of the great concerns," did not participate in Steel Federation meetings. Their subordinates were acting autonomously and paying no attention to the delicate negotiations being conducted with the trade union leaders in the *Zentralarbeitsgemeinschaft* and to the dangerous implications of the Steel Federation's "elimination of our legal currency" for the development of wages and the general political situation.[136] Naturally, the trade union leaders were no less aware of the contradictions in industrialist policy, and this intensified the debates at ZAG meetings, where union leaders asked how employers could at once call for decontrol of the economy and then defend the cartels.[137]

The Pig Iron Syndicate achieved particular notoriety in this connection because production costs in the unoccupied areas were extremely high as a result of the need to import coal, ores, and other needed materials, and the syndicate made regular demands for preferential treatment in receiving foreign exchange from its customers. By summer, the RWM was permitting the Pig Iron Syndicate to calculate a substantial portion of its price in gold, and relations between customers and the syndicate at times literally descended to the level of exchanging insults.[138] This did little to improve the popularity of the syndicate which, like all the syndicates at this time, was under heavy attack from consumers and trade unions, who were demanding public control of cartels and syndicates.

Increasingly, both the Pig Iron Syndicate and the Steel Federation asked for prepayment from customers as protection against the galloping inflation, and this caused more than a little tension with consumers and merchants.[139] The movement toward gold mark prices had been unmistakable since July, but it was resisted in part because of the wage problem mentioned earlier, in part because the Reichsbank remained resistant to the introduction of the gold accounts that were a necessary complement to gold prices, and in part because the RWM requested that the change be delayed while agreeing, at the end of July, to have the Steel Federation follow the lead of the Pig Iron Syndicate and set two-thirds of its price on each product in a stable value.[140]

Indeed, throughout the late summer the question of going over to

---

[136] Funcke to Poensgen, July 9, 1923, Krupp WA IV 1404. Poensgen admitted the validity of Funcke's charge about the nonpresence of the general directors at these meetings in a letter to Krupp of July 10, 1923, in *ibid.*

[137] ZAG Directors meeting, April 23, 1923, DZA Potsdam, ZAG, Nr. 31, Bl. 23.

[138] Minute by Director Wirtz, August 25, 1923, and related correspondence in Friedrich-Wilhelms-Hütte Archiv, Nr. 860/20.

[139] See the report in *Stahl und Eisen*, 43:2, September 6, 1923, p. 1185.

[140] Meeting of July 26, 1923, in HA/GHH, Nr. 300070/11.

pricing in a stable currency was actively discussed in industrial circles, where it was understood that the lead had to be taken by the primary industries. The change came in September. On September 1, the Pig Iron Syndicate introduced schilling prices, and the Steel Federation followed on September 11 with gold pricing. A week later, the Finance Ministry formally announced the separation of the Reichsbank from the state finances. The Reichsbank would no longer discount Reich Treasury notes, and it would serve as a gold note bank for the economy. Furthermore, the Reich Cabinet had set up a committee on August 30 to make plans for the creation of a new currency. The inflation was far from over, but if the worst months were yet to come, a distinct movement toward the end was in evidence.[141]

Pricing in gold and preparation for the issue of a new currency coexisted for the time being with the continued printing of money and government expenditure to support passive resistance, a policy Stresemann maintained for as long as he felt there was a chance of bringing the French to the negotiating table.[142] The tensions between producers and consumers in the Pig Iron Syndicate and Steel Federation continued, and the merchants actually quit the Steel Federation pricing committee in protest against the payment conditions set by the producers. However, the open conversion to pricing in stable values revealed for all to see the extent to which German prices had gone beyond world market levels. Producers could now argue with more passion than ever that they had to reduce prices, that they could only do this if they reduced costs, and that the reduction of costs required a return to free market conditions and longer hours of work. At the end of September, the producers put on a little demonstration of their concern for the export market by reducing the price of 30% of their sales to manufacturers as an "incentive to export."[143] It was an unmistakable reminder of the old prewar days when the Steel Works Association provided exporting manufacturers with rebates, and this gesture was accompanied by the reiteration of the proposition that the issue of the hour was maximum incentive to exporters and complete freedom for producers. The entire situation was one that strengthened the hand of industry and made its arguments appear more plausible

[141] In a note to Vögler of July 17, 1923, asking for a meeting on the transition to pricing in gold, Köttgen remarked that "In our circles we are fully conscious of the fact that we can only take up accounting in gold when the iron industry has gone over to it." SAA, Nachlass Köttgen, 11/Lf 265, and *Stahl und Eisen*, 43:2, October 11, 1923, pp. 1308–1309.

[142] Alfred E. Cornebise, "Gustav Stresemann and the Ruhr Occupation: The Making of a Statesman," *European Studies Review*, Vol. 2, No. 1 (January 1972), pp. 43–68.

[143] *Stahl und Eisen*, 43:2, October 11, 1923, p. 1309.

than ever. The Stresemann government—at least the non-Socialist elements in it—were sympathetic in any case, and his regime provided in many respects the transition from almost a decade of economic controls to a period in which government intervention in economic policy resumed more familiar and traditional forms.

The first victims of this transition were exports controls and the export levy, both of which no longer had any real justification because German goods were not competitive on world markets and because it could be argued that any export levy, instead of being "social," would only end up increasing unemployment and burdening export opportunities still further. Because exporters were now calculating in stable currencies, the danger of underpricing in a manner harmful to the economy, or at least underpricing for the purpose of securing an exchange profit, no longer seemed to exist. Consequently, on September 23, the Reich Economics Council, against union opposition, recommended the acceptance of the Raumer program of eliminating export controls except for coal and basic iron and steel products, which were in short supply, as well as the elimination of the export levy on all products except coal and potash. It recommended the creation of new agencies for the various branches of industry that would give employers and workers an opportunity to discuss economic problems. There is no reason to believe that Raumer was insincere about the latter plan, which remained an object of discussion in the RWM for some time, but it was clearly sop to labor. On the day the Reich Economics Council passed its resolution, Raumer issued a series of decrees putting the decontrol of exports and the elimination of the export levy into effect. It was an event of both symbolic and practical significance for which industry had waited a long time, and no less an industrial leader than C. F. von Siemens warmly praised Raumer's ministership for achieving "a great success which no one else has been able to manage: the elimination of export controls, which had developed into nothing more than a pointless burden for industry, but to which the Social Democrats had held on with extraordinary tenacity."[144]

It must be said that there was no justification for retaining the export controls and export levy as they existed, and that the Social Democratic attachment to these institutions of the war and inflation was a pitiful demonstration of their desperate effort to retain some influence on the economy in the approaching stabilization crisis. Such influence seemed all the more necessary to them because Raumer was so clearly favorable to industrial interests in his handling of a host of other issues. The elimination of export controls required the creation of new decrees

[144] Siemens to Sieg, October 5, 1923, SAA 4 Lf/724, and Dr. Hauschild, *Der Vorläufige Reichswirtschaftsrat 1920–1926* (Berlin, 1926), pp. 180–181.

controlling exchange received from exports, and exporters were now required to sell only for foreign currency and to surrender 30% of their foreign exchange derived from exports to the Reichsbank in return for German currency denominated in gold. Even Stresemann wondered if it was not appropriate to ask for more than 30% of the exchange and if businessmen could not be required to surrender their exchange in less than four weeks after receipt.[145] Although Raumer took steps to restrict raw materials imports and to tighten controls on illegally held exchange, the Socialists in the cabinet were unimpressed by Raumer's contention that industry only had "productive" foreign exchange. Former Economics Minister Schmidt, now Vice-Chancellor and Reconstruction Minister, thought industry was retaining a good deal of "unproductive" foreign exchange for future use and did not think that the vast amounts of illegally hoarded foreign exchange in Germany could be found only in sanatoria and hotels.[146] Insofar as Raumer was compelled to take or even contemplate measures that might be found unpleasant by industry, he insisted that one had to avoid "measures of great consequence which will not prove effective."[147] He demonstrated this not only in the matter of exchange controls, but also in his handling of a contemplated decree controlling cartels and syndicates, where he argued for the registration and state surveillance of cartels but opposed stronger measures. Insofar as he strongly supported a reduction of coal prices as a first step toward a general reduction of prices, he was in harmony with most of industry. Like the industrialists, he was steadfast in his opposition to the eight-hour day and in his insistence that the industry had to be relieved of limitations on its rights to dismiss workers.[148]

In the context of these RWM policies, there is something sad but by no means insignificant about a petition the EWB Vice President, the Christian metal trade union representative, Hermann Weimann, sent to the RWM on September 3 on behalf of the workers in the EWB.[149] In it, Weimann pointed out that Germany was threatened by an "economic anarchy" that could destroy the economic and political order. The breakdown of the currency and the calculation in gold marks had led to "price demands which cannot be related to actual costs." Consequently, he turned to the RWM with the request that the powers of the EWB be expanded to include ore and coal on the

[145] Cabinet meeting, September 10, 1923, 1748/D765624.

[146] Cabinet meeting, September 7, 1923, 1748/D765558–559.

[147] Cabinet meeting, September 4, 1923, 1748/D765507–508.

[148] Cabinet meeting, October 1, 1923, 1748/D765896ff.

[149] For the discussion and quotations see DZA Potsdam, RWM, Nr. 4612, Bl. 164–166.

grounds that these played so major a role in the pricing of iron and steel that the planning of production and the determination of costs and prices could scarcely be considered without their inclusion. In order to prevent unnecessary shutdowns and prevent unemployment, no factory within the province of the EWB was to be shut down without its consent, and guidelines were to be developed to determine the conditions under which shutdowns were to occur. Lastly, because of the immense differences in costs and prices among firms as a result of technological and locational differences, Weimann recommended that sales be centralized in a central agency and an equalization fund be established to keep prices under control.

Clearly Weimann was trying to save the EWB, the weaknesses of which he certainly must have been aware, and it is hard to believe that he did not have some sense of the futility of his effort to procure for labor some influence in "the coming severe crisis, of whose arrival all economic experts are convinced." Although agreeing with Raumer on the need to raise production, he could not accept the idea that this be done by eliminating all restraints on the ways in which labor was treated. Underlying Weimann's plea was the conviction that the coming hardships could best be dealt with on the basis of a planned and coordinated raw materials production and allocation policy rather than the pursuit of self-interest on the part of the concerns, be it individually or through the mechanisms of cartels and syndicates. Because labor was going to be called upon to make major sacrifices, it deserved a voice in the decisions.

Under the conditions then existing, such a program, however moderate in tone and intent, was utopian. The case for planning was far better than the instrumentalities and mechanisms being proposed, and Weimann overestimated the power of the trade unions at a time when they were in constant need of financial support from the government. It is difficult to imagine anything further from the minds of the heavy industrial leaders at this time than the notion that the dangers facing the economy could be warded off by any means other than their own self-help along with the requisite government backing. To be sure, they were happy to see the workers employed and kept quiet so long as the government bore the major costs, but they were in a truly ruthless mood in the last months of 1923. They were more prepared to challenge and even revenge themselves on the workers than to invite the assistance of labor leaders in the stabilization crisis and the rationalization of production.

This harsh mood was particularly evident in their response to the government's increasing efforts, even before the ending of passive resistance, to reduce its expenditure on unproductive wages as well as to reduce the Ruhr credits. They were extremely impatient with the government's inefficiency in providing them with the monies promised under the wage guarantee agreements, and noted with chagrin in mid-September that only one or two of the works were actually receiving more than two-thirds of their unproductive wage payments although they were all working at no more than 10–15% levels of productivity. The RWM was hastening to correct this situation, but the steel men were increasingly adamant in their refusal to pay any unproductive wages from their own resources on the grounds that they did not have the working capital to do so. Matters almost reached a critical point on September 13–15, when the question arose as to whether or not the government would begin reductions in its wage and credit allocations immediately. Stresemann was most anxious to continue full support for as long as possible in order to show the French that Germany was still capable of resistance as well as to allay reported French fears that the Ruhr would be pushed into chaos by a sudden termination of Reich support and passive resistance. Within the cabinet, Hilferding and the Food Minister, Luther, argued that credit restrictions and the beginning of a reduction in wage support payments were necessary, whereas the RAM and RWM joined with Stresemann in opposing reductions.[150]

Anxiously waiting upon these decisions was a small group of steel industry representatives from the major concerns and the VdESI assigned the task of negotiating with the government from week to week concerning the level of wage guarantee payments. During the previous week, they had received eight-ninths of their unproductive wage costs, but they wanted full recompense for the coming week. While threatening to begin laying off workers if they received anything less, the majority were willing to compromise on receiving eight-ninths if the government promised to pay the missing amount retroactively should a work be able to demonstrate 100% unproductivity. Only the GHH held out, threatening immediate lay-offs if the full amount was not paid. Whether the GHH was acting out of chagrin at the government or parsimony is difficult to say. Given Reusch's hostility toward the government and his later rigor in laying off workers, a combination of motives is likely. The majority of the industrialists, however, seemed to have been moved by the considerations presented by Director Sempell of Deutsch-Lux, who reported that Vögler had "asked that one act as strongly as possible against every form of defeatism in employer circles, and particularly that one make no difficulties for the Stresemann cabinet, which is acting purposefully in foreign affairs and is

[150] Imhoff to RAM, September 15, 1923, *ibid.*, Nr. 4620, Bl. 67–68, and Cabinet meeting, September 13–15, 1923, 1748/D765681ff.

pursuing the only possible path at present of direct negotiations with France."[151] While agreeing with Vögler as to the undesirability of "falling upon the government from the rear," however, the industrialists emphasized that "the disquiet in employer circles is primarily the result of the threat of Hilferding to close off credits to the Ruhr industry and one must absolutely impress upon the government that its Finance Minister must show more understanding for the situation in the large iron works of the occupied area and not express baseless and groundless suspicions." Nevertheless, the industrialists followed Vögler's advice for the moment because there continued to be real concern "that the government could not have any appearance of justification in shifting the blame for the ending of passive resistance to industry."

A precise evaluation of industry's role in the three developments of the final months of 1923 of particular concern here—the termination of passive resistance and negotiation of agreements with the French, the large-scale layoffs that accompanied the cessation of government wage supports and credits, and the undermining of the eight-hour day—is extremely difficult because of the interdependence of governmental and industrialist actions. There certainly had been some contacts between industrial leaders and French officials prior to the government's decision to terminate passive resistance. Such contacts were particularly easy in the Rhineland, where the occupation dated back to 1918, was sanctioned by the Treaty, and had necessitated contacts between businessmen and the authorities on a regular basis. As noted earlier, Otto Wolff had held discussions with Denvignes in late August, and there were reports of meetings between French officials and Wolff and Klöckner in mid-September. Furthermore, the French could always take advantage of pre-1923 relationships and open discussions with German industrialists such as General Director Pattberg of Phoenix's Rheinpreussen Mining Company, a man with whom they had been dealing for years in connection with Rhineland matters. At the same time, the French had created a less easygoing but highly effective basis for new relationships with leading industrialists by putting them in jail. In contrast to the harshly treated Krupp administrative officials jailed early in the year, a second set of higher-placed Krupp directors incarcerated at the end of August 1923 were kept in mild confinement, and this undoubtedly helped render the latter psychologically disposed as well as physically accessible for negotiation. Ultimately, however, the most effective means employed by the French in readying

---

[151] Meeting, September 14, 1923, HA/GHH, Nr. 300193024/3, for the quotations in this paragraph. Also, see the report of the arbitration court of October 2, 1923, sent by Syrup to Imhoff in DZA Potsdam, RWM, Nr. 4620, Bl. 97–99.

the German industrialists for negotiation was through the seizure of various mines and the confiscation of coal, iron, and steel stocks. A number of German coal mines, particularly those of Klöckner, and large quantities of stocks, particularly those belonging to Phoenix and Rheinstahl, had been seized by the French to cover unpaid coal taxes, reparations, and other charges, and it is no accident that many of the industrialists in the forefront of the subsequent negotiations were those who suffered most from these imprecations. Nevertheless, there is no evidence of any successful negotiations or "deals" with the French prior to the official termination of passive resistance by the government itself on September 26, 1923.[152]

There is rather more ambiguity about the negotiations that took place between industry and the French after the cessation of passive resistance. Although the accusations of industrialist "treason" bandied about at the time and subsequently were misplaced and misleading, the performance of the industrialists in October 1923 does not constitute a golden chapter in their history whether viewed from the standpoint of either their service to the nation or from that of their cohesion as a group. To understand why this is so, it is necessary to review briefly Stresemann's policy at the end of September. In terminating passive resistance, Stresemann was bowing to economic necessity but was still trying to steer a course between a total surrender to the French, which might endanger German sovereignty over occupied areas as well as the acceptance of impossible burdens, and a policy of desperation, such as that advocated by the Duisburg mayor, Karl Jarres, who hoped that through a unilateral declaration that the Versailles Treaty was null and void conditions of such difficulty and tension in Europe would be created as to call forth foreign intervention and more bearable conditions in the end. Reusch, and possibly Vögler, sympathized with this policy advocated by Jarres, but Stresemann and most businessmen considered it little more than a "ditching" policy (*Versackungspolitik*), which could cost Germany her richest provinces. Stresemann hoped that the termination of passive resistance would place the French on the moral and international defensive and force them to negotiate within a framework that retained German sovereignty, led to the release of prisoners and return of expellees, and allowed industry to revive in such a manner that Germany could fulfill her reparations obligations. Stresemann understood that the termination of wage supports and credits to industry meant that productive work would have to be taken up again, and he knew that this would

[152] See Wentzcke, *Ruhrkampf*, II, p. 179ff. and p. 457. On Pattberg, see the report of October 9, 1923, in HA/GHH, Nr. 300193008/16.

involve complicated negotiations with the French in which industrialists could hardly be uninvolved. Thus, at the cabinet meeting on September 26, Stresemann raised no principled objections to a telegram from the Lignite Syndicate or to statements made by Stinnes, Vögler, and Hasslacher that the industries would have to pay the coal tax and use French-controlled railroads if government wage supports ceased. What Stresemann was unwilling to do at this point was to authorize negotiations or make any statements about the timing of negotiations because he hoped that the French would discuss the basic questions pertaining to the resumption of productive work with an official representative of the German government. Raumer assumed that such an official negotiator would come from industry, and Stresemann does not appear to have opposed this suggestion. Furthermore, to gain time for such official negotiations and prevent chaos in the Ruhr, Stresemann resisted the idea of a total cessation of credits and wage supports even after the ending of passive resistance and promoted a fairly rapid but still gradual termination instead. Thus, on September 29, the Reichstag Committee voted to terminate Steel Finance credits by October 20 and wage supports by October 31 and gradually to scale down the latter during the ensuing weeks. Nevertheless, this was not much breathing space, and the termination of financial support in the Ruhr was clearly in sight.[153]

The situation was a challenge to the discipline of the heavy industrialists because they were caught between the need to resume productive work as rapidly as possible and their responsibility to avoid undermining the government's position by making agreements with the French inimical to official policy. The matter was all the more difficult because Stresemann's hope that the French would negotiate officially appears to have been an unrealistic one. Whatever Poincaré's ultimate intentions, he seems to have been intent on keeping his options open and dealing directly only with individual concerns and groups and local authorities. Thus, the French were as solicitous of the industrialists as they were cold to Berlin, and for the industrialists this presented at once the temptation to come to terms and the danger that they would be divided and conquered on terms very costly to themselves as well as to the economy. Also involved in the situation, albeit less clearly, was the temptation of trying to achieve certain domestic

---

[153] Favez, *Le Reich devant l'occupation*, p. 301ff.; Etienne Weill-Raynal, *Les Réparations Allemandes et la France*, 2 vols. (Paris, 1947), II, p. 458ff.; Karl Jarres, "Meine Beteiligung am Ruhrabwehrkampf und seine Liquidierung," BA, Nachlass Jarres, Nr. 49; Cabinet meeting, September 26, 1923, 1748/D756842f. Also, see Maier, *Recasting Bourgeois Europe*, p. 390ff.

goals, such as the abrogation of the eight-hour day, in direct negotiation with the French and in disregard of the wishes of the government in Berlin and the already inflammatory social situation in the Ruhr.

The most concerted, organized, and large-scale effort to prepare for the coming negotiations with the French was made by the Mining Association (*Zechenverband*) at its meetings at Unna-Königsborn and Bochum on September 30 and October 1, 1923. A decision was taken there to begin mining operations again even if the coal could not be transported or sold, and that only mines occupied by the French might be excused from this obligation. It was clear, however, that this decision would involve problems that could be solved only through negotiation with the French, because the new production could easily be confiscated. In contrast to previous confiscations, however, the Reich no longer promised compensation, and the Coal Finance Corporation had been denied the right to purchase new production. The French would be certain to demand payment of the coal tax to themselves for as long as that tax continued in existence, and they might demand a resumption of reparations deliveries even if the Reich made no provision for crediting these to the reparations account and thus compensating the industry. To take the lead in solving these many problems, therefore, a committee was set up, which became known as the Committee of Six, composed of Stinnes and Vögler, Klöckner, Director von Velsen of the state-owned Hibernia Mining Company, and Directors Herbig and Janus of the Coal Syndicate. In the negotiations during the coming weeks, the composition of the Committee was to vary, but its activities were initially dominated by Stinnes and then by Vögler, who acted as Stinnes' representative. Although there was every intention of having the Committee get into contact with the commander-in-chief in the Ruhr, General Degoutte, Stinnes and his colleagues had no intention of acting behind Stresemann's back, and it was clearly intended at the September 30–October 1 meetings that negotiations with Degoutte would only follow upon discussions with the government leadership in Berlin.[154]

While demonstrating a certain deference to the government in matters of foreign policy, however, the coal men demonstrated no such respect for its authority or delicacy about matters of procedure when it came to social questions. They were fully aware of the fact that the hours-of-work question was the most divisive issue facing the Stresemann regime, which was trying to hammer out an Enabling Act to

[154] Report by Nebelung, October 3, 1923, HA/GHH, Nr. 3001100/18. See also the well-informed but apologetic discussion of Hans Spethmann, *Zwölf Jahre Ruhrbergbau. Aus Seiner Geschichte vom Kriegsanfang bis zum Franzosenabmarsch, 1914–1925*, 5 vols. (Berlin, 1928–1931), III, p. 154ff.

meet the national crisis—a crisis that included not only the diplomatic uncertainties attendant upon the end of passive resistance, an inflation in which it took 28,809,524 paper marks to buy one gold mark on September 25 and 76,190,476 paper marks to buy one gold mark on October 2, and massive social unrest, violence, and separatism in the Ruhr, but also a growing crisis between the Reich and the left-wing government in Saxony and the right-wing government in Bavaria and a state of siege throughout the Reich. Although even the Social Democrats were fatalistic about the need to allow exceptions to the eight-hour day, the majority were unwilling to permit the government to change the existing hours-of-work regulations by decree under the projected Enabling Act, but were prepared to consider an hours-of-work bill that had been drawn up by Labor Minister Brauns which allowed for labor contracts that provided for a longer work day but which also protected workers in particularly strenuous or dangerous occupations from exploitation.[155] Apparently, the coal men were convinced that they could decide this question by unilateral action which did not even wait upon the passage of an Enabling Act satisfying their demands. Indeed, their decision in this matter was consciously political in intent and was taken in full awareness of the political implications involved because it was taken before the first Stresemann Great Coalition government split apart on October 2 and was designed to bring about that regime's collapse. The decision taken on the eight-hour day at Unna-Königsborn read:

> There is the intention of attaining the necessary increase of productivity in the mining industry by the elimination of the eight-hour day and the reintroduction of the prerevolutionary hours of work. A legislative regulation is not considered necessary in view of the fact that the eight-hour day had been introduced in an illegal manner. There is clarity concerning the effect of such an action upon the composition of the government.[156]

[155] See especially the October 1, 1923, Cabinet meeting, 1748/D756896ff.

[156] Nebelung report, October 3, 1923, HA/GHH, Nr. 3001100/18. This quotation demonstrates that Spethmann's interpretation of the decision as being taken with the understanding of various ministers and with the expectation of a government decree legitimizing the action falsifies the attitudes and motives of the industrialists. See Spethmann, *Ruhrbergbau*, III, pp. 186–187. As the quotation shows, they denied the legitimacy of existing legislation and sought to force the elimination of the SPD from the government, a goal also pursued by the DVP in its own declaration of October 2 with regard to the hours-of-work question. See Stresemann's meeting with the party leaders on October 2, where Scholz declared: "The present situation is impossible; every product costs one and a half times what

The intention of the coal men was to increase the working day underground from 7 to 8½ hours beginning October 8. It was a very remarkable action on their part because it was illegal in at least three respects. Even if one accepts the argument that the proclamation of the eight-hour day on November 12, 1918, by the Revolutionary government was at worst "illegal" and at best a mere statement of intention without force of law, no such claim could be made against the Demobilization Decree of November 23, 1918, regulating the hours of work, the Hours of Work Law for the Mining Industry of July 1922, which permitted exceptions to the seven-hour day in the industry only on the basis of agreement between the parties to the labor contracts in the industry, and the actual contract between the Mining Association and the trade unions.[157] The coal men certainly must have realized that they had broken the law and were guilty of breach of contract, and one of their number not in attendance at the meeting later frankly confessed to his colleagues that he was shaken when he heard the news of their decision for these reasons.[158] They could only excuse their actions by "necessity" and with the presumption that the regime in Berlin would change and legitimize their actions by decree. They did intend to go to Berlin with their *fait accompli* because they also wanted the coal tax reduced in the amount of the wage increase recently negotiated for the occupied areas and then eliminated totally. The increase of working hours combined with the elimination of the coal tax would permit them, they argued, to reduce coal prices to world market levels.[159] Apparently, the coal industrialists were confident that the government in Berlin—that is, the new government of the right they anticipated—would give them full support.

When a delegation from the Mining Association went to Stresemann on October 3 to secure permission to negotiate with Degoutte and support on the other issues at hand, however, they were first put off because the chancellor was at a cabinet meeting and then informed by

it costs abroad. Decisive actions must be taken here. In this respect, there must be no stopping in the matter of the hours of work under any circumstances. The German Peoples' Party will demand this very decisively. We cannot stop with the miners; other categories of workers must follow also." 1748/D756964.

[157] Preller, *Sozialpolitik*, pp. 274–275.

[158] At a meeting of coal mine directors on October 9, 1923, in Hamm, one of their number urged that the order extending the working day be rescinded "because of the illegality of our intended action; he had not participated in the decisions at Königsborn and was really shocked when he heard that it was decided there, however well considered the reasons, to ignore existing law and collective agreements. . . ." Bergbau Archiv, Bestand 15, Nr. 75.

[159] The decisions of Unna-Königsborn are reprinted in Spethmann, III, p. 378.

Stresemann that the government had just resigned and that he was not authorized to negotiate with them.[160] Stresemann, in fact, was caught between the intransigence of the SPD and the right wing of his own party. Raumer had resigned on October 2 without even consulting his own party caucus because of the "unbridgeable" differences in the cabinet as well as because he felt that Stresemann was using him as a "scapegoat."[161] Fundamentally, Stresemann agreed with Raumer and with his party about the need to use the projected Enabling Act to decree at least a temporary end to the eight-hour day. His views were shared by Labor Minister Brauns, who felt that the Socialists would inevitably support Communist amendments to his Hours of Work Bill and ruin it. At the same time, Brauns was not getting any support from industry for his bill because it was based on his conception of a "sanitary" working day, contained provisions for the protection of various categories of workers, and, as Stresemann noted, was less than the industrialists thought they could get under the circumstances. The Socialists would not enter a government that abrogated the eight-hour day, "the only thing that is left to the workers," by decree.[162] The DVP, strongly influenced by Stinnes and other heavy industrialists, was insisting that the hours of work be included in the Enabling Act and was inclined to support a right-wing government under Stresemann. The Nationalists, however, would not work with Stresemann. The industrialists would not give him practical assistance either. When he looked to industry for a replacement for Raumer, he found that neither the former Krupp director and Ambassador to Washington, Wiedfeldt, nor the former Stinnes concern director, Minoux, were prepared to deal with the existing Reichstag. Although there was constant talk of the need for a "finance dictator" to replace Hilferding and the need for dictatorial action, the basic posture of Stinnes and his colleagues was that the government should move to the right because of the economic necessities but that they had to act while leaving "politics to the politicians."[163]

Nevertheless, they were careful to cover themselves with some mantle of governmental authorization before accepting an "invitation" from General Degoutte to come to Düsseldorf on October 5 for unofficial and informal discussion of the situation. On the one hand, Vögler had

[160] Stresemann, *Vermächtnis*, I, p. 161.

[161] Siemens to Sieg, October 5, 1923, SAA 4 Lf/724 and Stresemann, *Vermächtnis*, I, p. 140ff.

[162] Cabinet meetings, October 3, 1923, 1748/D756896ff.

[163] Stresemann, *Vermächtnis*, I, p. 145, and Henry Turner, *Stresemann and the Politics of the Weimar Republic* (Princeton, 1963), pp. 122–123.

411

procured the authorization of the Mayor of Cologne, Konrad Adenauer, for the discussions, and Adenauer could give such authorization in his capacity as unofficial representative of the Reich government in the occupied areas. He had been so designated by Fuchs, the Minister for the Occupied Areas. On the other hand, Stinnes had telephoned Stresemann from Düsseldorf to inform him of the negotiations and ask that they not be obstructed. Thus, Stinnes and his colleagues on the "Committee of Six" had been careful to keep the political authorities informed.[164]

All this did not prevent a good deal of bungling and inappropriate action on their part, however, and they were encouraged in this by the care Degoutte had taken to make their trip comfortable, the respect they were shown, and Degoutte's tact in the handling of such painful subjects as the occupation of Klöckner's coal mines. Klöckner was very much taken with Degoutte's tasteful expression of sympathy with his problems as well as with the general's "military decisiveness, understanding of economic questions, and his general cultivation."[165] This favorable impression was strengthened undoubtedly by reports that Degoutte considered the "German workers to be completely demoralized and gone to the dogs (*verkommen und verlottert*)."[166] Originally, the committee seems to have anticipated discussing the hours-of-work question with Degoutte, but the majority felt that the matter should not be discussed when they planned their strategy just before the actual meeting with the Frenchman.[167] Apparently, they realized by then that the government in Berlin was not going to be as much to their liking as they had assumed on September 30–October 1, and they knew that the French had studiously avoided the violation of German social legislation. The heartwarming atmosphere provided by Degoutte and the latter's reputed attitude toward the workers, however, as well as the absence of a government in Berlin and a recent statement by Brauns supporting an increased working day all seemed to have undermined Klöckner's inhibitions as well as his willingness to abide by the desires of the rest of his colleagues.[168] Thus, he

[164] Erdmann, *Adenauer*, p. 111n10, and meeting between Brauns and the industrialists on October 9, 1923, Nachlass Stresemann, 3099/7118/H146008–9 and Cabinet meeting, October 10, 1923, 1749/D757042–43.

[165] Report by Woltmann, October 6, 1923, HA/GHH, Nr. 300193008/16.

[166] *Ibid.*, which confirms the report on the meeting with Degoutte in the Stresemann Nachlass, 3099/7188, H145990ff. The latter is reprinted in full in Spethmann, *Ruhrbergbau*, III, pp. 160–169.

[167] On the original intention, see the Nebelung report of the September 30–October 1 meetings at Unna-Königsborn in HA/GHH, Nr. 301100/18. For the change of plans see Blank to Reusch, October 9, 1923, *ibid.*, Nr. 300193024/3.

[168] This was related at a meeting of October 11, 1923, *ibid.*, Nr. 301100/18.

launched into a lengthy discourse to the effect that Germany had to increase production to supply her own needs as well as those of her neighbors, that German prices were too high to compete on world markets, and that the industrialists intended to correct the "mistake" of 1918 on the following Monday by reintroducing prewar working hours. Klöckner informed Degoutte that "industry is not in the position to carry out its intentions without the support of the occupying powers, and that is one of the reasons for their visit."[169] Degoutte interrupted Klöckner to remind him that since the beginning of the occupation the French had respected German laws, and "the eight-hour day is a German law." At this point, Klöckner, assisted by Stinnes, beat a rapid and clumsy retreat by indicating that they had no intention of asking the occupying powers to interfere in industry-labor relations and that "the request for support relates only to such points where the actions of the occupying powers prevent industry from carrying out its intentions"—that is, the sequestrations, confiscations, seizures, interruptions of railroad traffic, etc.

Stinnes, probably to the relief of all present, now took the lead in the discussions and turned to the practical questions of resuming productive work. He not only asked that the French cease the above-mentioned harmful activities, but also that they release the stocks of coal and particularly the stocks of iron and steel they had confiscated, because the iron industry needed these to start operating again and could not wait until coal and coke were being produced. Also, the stocks were needed to finance the resumption of operations. Degoutte responded that the confiscations and other unpleasant actions had been undertaken because of the violations of French orders, the refusal to develop a delivery program for coal and coke, and the unwillingness to pay the coal tax. Although he intended to maintain the occupation of the mines already seized as security for a final settlement and could not return coal or coke, he was prepared to return such stocks of iron and steel as had not already been sold provided that the back coal taxes were paid. He intended to retain control of the railroads, but he was prepared to consider setting up a joint company to manage the railroads with the Germans. He was rather less sympathetic with the financial plight of the industrialists, pointing out that although the Reich was poor, industry was not and had credit resources. To be sure, it was hard to get Anglo-American credits so long as the French were threatening confiscation, and France was unwilling to give money. However, Degoutte was certain that private domestic loans could be raised. Without going into details, Degoutte expressed the belief that only a part of the newly mined coal would have to be taken for rep-

[169] Spethmann, *Ruhrbergbau*, III, pp. 161–162.

arations, that the coal tax could and should be eliminated for future production, and that assistance could be given on the food supply question. Once a settlement was reached, he was prepared to be helpful with the release of prisoners and the return of expellees.[170]

Following these discussions, the committee returned to the Ruhr, leaving Vögler behind as liaison. Klöckner came back in an optimistic frame of mind about the October 5 discussions. If Degoutte had cut him off on the hours-of-work question, he had still been gentlemanly, open, and frank, and he seemed to respect private property and left the impression that the mines would be returned someday.[171] While Klöckner was conveying these glad tidings, however, Vögler was getting a less cheerful picture of what the French had in mind. First he had a discussion with Frantzen, the President of the *Mission Interalliée de Contrôle des Usines et des Mines* (Micum), the organization of engineers for whose protection and support the occupation had been ostensibly undertaken. Frantzen told Vögler that his organization, not Degoutte, would determine the conditions of any settlement. Degoutte, Frantzen informed Vögler, was only being kept on at his post because he had "won" the Ruhr occupation. Vögler gained the impression that the Micum was intended by the French to be "an exploitation society of the very worst sort," and he learned that the Micum wanted to collect the 40% coal taxes back to the last quarter of 1922 and that it was willing to deal only with individual firms and concerns and would treat him as a representative of the Stinnes concern and nothing more.[172]

Sunday, October 7, was a day filled with gloom for heavy industry. In addition to the bad news from Vögler, which dispelled the fantasies Klöckner had spread about so liberally, there was the enraging report that Stresemann had managed to form a new Great Coalition cabinet on the previous day. Such a cabinet would not support the unilateral abrogation of the eight-hour day openly proclaimed at various mines and scheduled to go into effect on October 8. The state-owned mines had already gone back on the decision to extend the working day, and the miners, agitated and enraged, were being made even more furious by leaflets thrown from French military autos throughout the day on October 7 declaring untrue rumors to the effect that Degoutte had supported a lengthening of the working day.[173]

[170] *Ibid.*, pp. 163–169.

[171] Woltmann report of meeting at Unna-Königsborn, October 6, 1923, HA/GHH, Nr. 300193008/16.

[172] Report on Mine Owners Association meeting, October 9, 1923, in *ibid.*, and Northwest Group meeting, October 11, 1923, in *ibid.*, and Nr. 3001100/18.

[173] *Ibid.*

414

The worst was yet to come for the industrialists, however. Clearly the continuation of negotiations with Degoutte, assistance in the handling of the financial burdens of any agreement with the Micum, and a solution to the hours-of-work question required some arrangement with the government unless the industrialists were prepared to take their chances and assume all the risks and burdens of concluding an agreement with the French on their own. This would leave them without any promise of government compensation and completely at the tender mercies of the Micum. Stinnes and those allied with him did not want this risk, and he met with Stresemann and Baron von Maltzan of the Foreign Office on October 7. Stinnes used this meeting to raise various "questions" connected with the French demands, and he also asked for a 150–200 million gold mark credit to help industry start up again. Stresemann asked that the "questions" be stated in writing, and they were sent to Stresemann and von Maltzan on the same day.[174] Basically, Stinnes wanted to know by Tuesday afternoon, October 9, if the government was going to settle matters with the French itself or if it was prepared to leave to the industrialists the creation of a "modus vivendi with the occupying powers in order to feed the population and assure as far as possible the survival of the works." If the latter were to be the case, then he raised ten questions. These fell into three categories. First, he sought specific approval for the continuation of negotiations by the committee that had met with Degoutte (7) as well as the right to determine which French agencies were, in fact, in a position to make agreements (8). Second, he wished to know if the Reich was prepared to compensate the industrialists in connection with agreements made concerning the confiscated stocks of coal, iron, and steel (1), payments of back and future coal taxes to the French (2), and deliveries of coal on the reparations account (4). Finally, he raised questions pertaining to domestic economic and social measures, specifically, the elimination of the coal tax (3), fulfillment of the French demand that priority in the delivery of coal be given to the occupied areas (5), elimination of legislation and agencies controlling the supply, distribution, and pricing of coal (6), permitting the railroads under French control to be transformed into a corporation under some form of joint Franco-German control (9), and last, but in no way least, the lengthening of the working day and the elimination of the demobilization decrees and special decrees issued to prevent or restrict the dismissal of workers (10).

[174] The letter on which the discussion and quotations below are based is reprinted in Spethmann, *Ruhrbergbau*, III, pp. 171–172. See also Stresemann, *Vermächtnis*, p. 158ff.

This confidential letter, as well as fulsome reports and commentary on the meeting with Degoutte of October 5 and Klöckner's disquisition on the eight-hour day, graced the pages of the liberal and Socialist press on October 9–10. Old critics of Stinnes, such as Georg Bernhard of the *Vossische Zeitung*, had a field day with articles about the "rebellion of the Grand Dukes," but the entire "Jewish Democratic press," as Reusch's lobbyist in Berlin, Martin Blank, reported, "agitated in the most hateful ways against the German negotiators." Blank suspected, as did Stinnes, that the "underground connections" between the Chancellery and the Ullstein press were responsible for the "monstrous indiscretion," although it later appeared that Rhenish journalists had access to industrialist materials and were responsible.[175] In any case, it was clear that great damage had been done, and subsequent clarifications by Stresemann and others could scarcely repair it. Furthermore, although it was possible to argue on firm grounds that Stinnes and his committee had kept the authorities informed of their actions and that Stinnes' letter contained "questions" and not demands, neither the government nor the industrialists themselves could condone what they chose to consider Klöckner's "mistake" in bringing up the hours-of-work question with Degoutte.[176] The retreat of the industrialists before the onslaught of criticism was most humiliatingly apparent when the Mine Owners Association decided on October 10 to go beyond Stinnes' proposal that the extension of the working day in the mines be put off by one day while awaiting a response from the government and simply withdraw the prominently displayed notifications to the workers. The despair and anger and the sense of humiliation were quite expressively stated by one of the many steel industrialists who was counting on the coal industry to take the lead in eliminating the eight-hour day when he declared that "German industry has not suffered such a disgrace in many years. When one makes such a decision, one must also hold out, even allow oneself to be beaten to death. Now everything is ruined for many years to come."[177]

The disorder and confusion in industrialist ranks did not end even here, however, for along with the publicity about Stinnes and his committee came news as disturbing to the government as it was to most of the industrialists themselves, namely, reports of separate negotia-

[175] Blank to Reusch, October 9, 1923, HA/GHH, Nr. 300193024/3. Reusch's papers demonstrate that although he certainly detested the liberal press, he did not share his subordinate's anti-Semitism. For the Bernhard article see Spethmann, *Ruhrbergbau*, III, pp. 375–377. Also, Stresemann, *Vermächtnis*, I, p. 162, and Stresemann's remarks at the October 10, 1923, Cabinet meeting, 1749/D757038.

[176] Reichert to Reusch, October 12, 1923, HA/GHH, Nr. 300193008/16.

[177] Director Grosse at the VdESI Northwest Group meeting, October 10, 1923, *ibid.*

416

tions and blossoming agreements between the Wolff group and the French. Wolff had been in contact with the French High Commissioner in the Rhineland, Tirard, in mid and late September, and it was reported that he had been accompanied by his Dutch banking friends. It was widely felt by informed circles and particularly by the new Finance Minister, Hans Luther, that Wolff, and more specifically the Rheinstahl and Phoenix concerns, were moved in the direction of separate agreement with the French by Dutch pressure. This is likely, although it cannot be conclusively proven, and it is extremely difficult to answer the more complicated and perhaps more interesting question of the weight that is to be attached to this influence as against other considerations that played an important role in the decisions of Wolff, Hasslacher, and Fahrenhorst. These considerations shed light on the complex differences among the various industrial leaders and concerns in heavy industry.[178]

To begin with, Wolff's own attitude was conditioned, as the well-informed *Kölnische Zeitung* noted, by the fact that he was more a merchant than an industrialist and could therefore "accept a heavy burdening of his industrial production more easily because he has the greater possibility of making up for it in his own province of marketing."[179] If Wolff, with his large marketing organization and connections, was able to sell, then he was able to make money, and the basic characteristic of the agreements with which he was associated was that they gave him the opportunity to handle products coming out of the Ruhr once again. Going one step further, however, Georg Bernhard also argued that Wolff was using the opportunity to free himself of some of the guidelines and pricing policies of the Coal Syndicate. Although certainly not of decisive importance, there can be no question about the fact that Wolff hated the syndicate, which he had fought for some time as inimical to his interests.[180] In any case, a leading role in the Wolff group negotiations was played by General Director Pattberg of the Phoenix controlled Rheinpreussen Mining Company, who was summoned to Düsseldorf by the Micum to receive terms on October 1—that is, four days before the Committee of Six held their first discussions with Degoutte. The coal industrialists at that time had found it "noteworthy" that Rheinpreussen was already operating at 50% of capacity at a time when the other mines were just

[178] Wentzcke, *Ruhrkampf*, II, p. 192ff., and Hans Luther, *Politiker ohne Partei* (Stuttgart, 1960), pp. 188–189, and the Bernhard article in Spethmann, *Ruhrbergbau*, III, p. 376.

[179] *Kölnische Zeitung*, November 6, 1923.

[180] Spethmann, *Ruhrbergbau*, III, p. 376, and Wolff to O. Krawehl, December 1, 1923, Rheinstahl Archiv, Nr. 920.

planning to resume production.[181] It was Rheinpreussen that signed the first agreement with the Micum on October 9, 1923, whereas the more important agreements with Phoenix and Rheinstahl, who signed jointly with the Micum, were not formally concluded until October 20. The basic details were worked out by October 6 and were shown to a surprised Stresemann by Wolff on October 10. The entire sequence of events suggests that the coal issue was secondary to Wolff and that the interests of the concerns with which he was associated were primarily connected with iron and steel.[182]

The concerns most closely associated with Wolff, namely Rheinstahl and Phoenix, had reasons to conclude an agreement with the French quite independently of Wolff's marketing interests and Dutch connections. Indeed, Fahrenhorst was to object to the references to a "Wolff Agreement" by the press and even by colleagues such as Reichert on the grounds that Wolff was only the third largest stockholder in Phoenix and handled only its foreign marketing.[183] It was somewhat misleading to speak of Wolff, as Stresemann did, as the "leader of the Phoenix concern,"[184] and the protracted negotiations from the end of September to October 20 are some evidence for the case that a variety of interests and considerations were involved. If Hasslacher and Fahrenhorst had good reasons to surrender to the French as quickly as possible even without Otto Wolff to encourage and help them to do so, however, it must be noted that he actively engaged in the negotiations and defended them to Stresemann. Both concerns were in serious financial difficulty. Hasslacher had ordered a cessation of all ore purchases on August 7 and was using up his Steel Finance credits to pay wages that were not paid rapidly enough by the government to spare his directors threats against their lives from the workers. The greatest menace, however, was presented by the French seizure of Rheinstahl plants and the confiscation of about 10,000 tons of rolled material and machines in Duisburg. In October, the French seemed about to seize the remaining plants and stocks, a matter that was particularly easy in the case of Rheinstahl because of its ready access to

---

[181] See the Mine Owners Association meeting at Unna-Königsborn, September 30–October 1, 1923, HA/GHH, Nr. 3001100/18, and the report on a discussion with Pattberg on October 14, 1923, *ibid.*, Nr. 300193008/16.

[182] For the sequence of the Micum agreements see Spethmann, *Ruhrbergbau*, III, pp. 390–392. The sequence of events leading to the Wolff agreements, as they were called, is narrated by Wolff himself in a letter to Stresemann of October 19, 1923, in BA, Nachlass Silverberg, Nr. 407, Bl. 8–11. The French newspapers reported that the agreements with Phoenix and Rheinstahl had already been signed on October 10. This was untrue, but it caused a sensation.

[183] Fahrenhorst to Reichert, October 30, 1923, HA/GHH, Nr. 3001900/4.

[184] Cabinet meeting, October 10, 1923, 1749/D757043.

waterways. The French had already sold the material from the Duis-burg works abroad, and Rheinstahl faced the prospect of losing every-thing.[185]

Phoenix was in a similar situation. In justifying his actions to Reich-ert, Fahrenhorst explained that the steel works were much more threat-ened by stock seizures than the coal mines because of the greater value of the steel. Unless these stocks of steel could be mobilized, Phoenix, which had used up its foreign exchange and mark resources, would have to let its 60,000 workers go.[186] Both Rheinstahl and Phoenix had been represented at the September 30–October 1 meetings where the Mining Association had appointed the Committee of Six, but by this time they had already been negotiating with the French concern-ing their iron and steel works. They did not think that the Committee was suitably organized to represent these interests, a fact they made clear at the time, but they also did not feel that they could negotiate about their iron and steel works without also bringing in their coal mines. In any case, Phoenix and Rheinstahl "danced out of line" be-cause they felt that their special interest required the protection of the iron and steel stocks from further confiscation. More generally, in the cases of Phoenix and Rheinstahl, as in the cases of the Stahlwerk Becker, which concluded a separate agreement on October 23, and Krupp, which concluded its separate agreement on October 31, iron and steel interests predominated over coal.

Initially, Stresemann was angrier at Wolff than he was at Stinnes and the Committee of Six because Wolff had crossed up his foreign policy effort to get the French to negotiate with an official German repre-sentative. This may have been all the more the case because Tirard, with whom Wolff had frequent contacts, appears to have been em-ployed by Poincaré to test the possibilities of encouraging the creation of a separate Rhenish state, whereas Degoutte seems to have been used to test the benefits of a more general agreement on reparations with the Reich. Although recognizing both privately and publicly that the Wolff agreements made no financial demands on the Reich, Strese-mann reproached Wolff for negotiating without authorization and placed the blame for Poincaré's refusal to deal with an official German negotiator on Wolff. This charge received some confirmation from Poincaré himself, who made specific reference to the negotiations with Wolff in announcing his refusal to engage in negotiations at the gov-ernment-to-government level. Wolff was not moved by Stresemann's argument and pointed out that it was necessary "to put his works into

[185] Hasslacher to Filius, August 7, 1923, and Hasslacher to Supervisory Board members, January 19, 1924, in Rheinstahl Archiv, Nr. 290 and 123.

[186] Fahrenhorst to Reichert, October 30, 1923, HA/GHH, Nr. 3001900/4.

order again. He must point out that he employs more than 100,000 workers."[187] When the RWM withheld remaining Steel Finance credits from Phoenix and when local authorities in Duisburg discriminated against emergency money issued by Rheinstahl and Phoenix, Wolff became infuriated because this was viewed as a punishment, a conclusion that seemed all the more logical because Stresemann had publicly criticized Wolff's action in a newspaper interview. Wolff demanded that all differentiation between his group and that of Stinnes be eliminated immediately. He did not care about the money itself, which he promised not to take, but rather about the "moral" side of the affair. Stresemann was warned by those who had discussed the matter with Wolff that the treatment of this industrial group in such a manner was politically unwise because of the effect it might have in the Rhineland, where the separatist danger was very great, and the RWM seems to have relented. Interestingly enough, Wolff does not seem to have bothered to consult with Hasslacher and Fahrenhorst before his *de facto* surrender of the credits, and the two general directors were quite annoyed to find themselves cut off from the credits when they applied for them at the end of October.[188]

In the last analysis, however, the demands of Stinnes and his colleagues were more consequential than the actions of the Wolff group because they involved major economic concessions by the Reich in the form of credits and compensation for coal tax and reparations payments as well as major sociopolitical demands with regard to hours of work. Stinnes, Vögler, and Silverberg held a preliminary discussion of these issues with Brauns and Luther on October 9. Brauns indicated that a return to pre-1914 labor conditions was out of the question, and Luther pointed out that the Reich simply did not have the money to give credits. Like Degoutte, Luther asked if the industrialists could not draw upon their resources in the unoccupied areas. The industrialists denied that such resources were available and warned that chaos would break out if they did not get financial help and then the French would attain their goal of ruling the Ruhr. When Brauns argued that if the real French goal was chaos and a takeover in the area, then there was no way the Reich could prevent this by temporary palliatives, Stinnes retorted with his now familiar argument that the "energetic implementation of the lengthened work day" would renew con-

[187] Cabinet meeting, October 10, 1923, 1749/D757044.

[188] Stresemann, *Vermächtnis*, I, pp. 161–162; report by Fahrenhorst, October 27, 1923, Rheinstahl Archiv, Nr. 920; Kalle of the Foreign Office Press Bureau to Stresemann, October 13, 1923, Nachlass Stresemann, 3091/7118/41460024ff. Although Stresemann publicly exonerated Hasslacher and Fahrenhorst, Wolff remained angry over the attacks upon himself and his colleagues. See his letter to Stresemann of October 19, 1923, in BA, Nachlass Silverberg, Nr. 407, Bl. 8–11.

fidence in Germany, encourage foreign loans, and make stabilization possible. Given this prospect, a "temporary" increase of the inflation seemed permissible.[189]

Luther and his cabinet colleagues were not convinced. Although the government was quite prepared to clear the industrialists of all accusations that they had negotiated improperly and to oppose Communist efforts in the Reichstag to charge them with treason, they were unprepared to endanger the intended currency reform or what was left of the economy and of the political stability of the country for the Rhine and Ruhr. Similarly, they were not going to let it appear that industry was dictating the hours-of-work question. The most extreme statement of this position was made by the new Economics Minister, Joseph Koeth, who once again took his familiar line that desperate situations required desperate decisions, warned against putting "another cent" into the Ruhr, and urged that the industrial groups be told to negotiate about economic but not about political questions.[190] Although not all members of the cabinet were as extreme in this posture as Koeth, there was a general consensus that the Ruhr could no longer be saved by the printing press but that the Reich could be destroyed by it.

On October 12, the government's position was made clear to Stinnes in a response by Stresemann to Stinnes' "questions." Stinnes was told that industry would receive no new credits from the government beyond the Coal and Steel Finance credits and the wage guarantee payments scheduled to run out that month. Stresemann also refused compensation for reparations coal and coal tax payments. Reparations could not be paid until the financial situation of the Reich made this possible, and it was impossible to guarantee that Stinnes and his friends would be repaid for what they delivered under this heading. The Reich would eliminate the coal tax if coal prices were reduced, and it was prepared to accept any arrangements the industrialists made with the French regarding coal distribution. However, the Reich insisted upon maintaining its formal sovereignty over the railroads in the occupied areas and, by implication, would not allow an arrangement with the French permitting Stinnes to realize his old plan of privatizing the German railroads. Finally, Stinnes was told that existing regulations covered hours of work in the Reich and that the fact that "a new legislative regulation of working hours in the very near future is being planned may be presumed to be known by you."[191]

Thus, the industrialists basically were thrown upon their own re-

[189] For the discussion see Nachlass Stresemann, 3099/7118/H146008ff.

[190] Cabinet meeting, October 10, 1923, 1749/D757048.

[191] Stresemann to Stinnes, October 12, 1923, reprinted in Spethmann, *Ruhrbergbau*, III, pp. 173–174.

sources and reminded to obey the law. This tough response reflected not only the financial and political problems of the Reich but also Stresemann's disgust with the arrogance of the industrialists and their open opposition to his efforts to retain a Great Coalition government. He openly reproached them for their loud attacks on the "failures" of parliamentary government in connection with the reconstitution of his cabinet, and he secretly sought to strengthen his position vis-à-vis Stinnes by planting articles in friendly newspapers attacking the notion that Stresemann was a tool of Stinnes and asserting that Stinnes had wanted to set up a right-wing dictatorship in order to get rid of the eight-hour day in line with the industrialist discussions with Degoutte.[192] At the same time, however, Stresemann had legitimized further industrialist negotiations with the Micum because there was no other choice if the government was to lay the groundwork for stabilization and create a new currency. On October 11 decrees were issued valorizing all taxes, and on October 15 the decree creating the Rentenbank, which was to begin operation on November 15, was issued. The Reichsbank could no longer discount treasury bills. The days of unrestricted credit giving to industry were over, and without such a hold on the industrialists one could not tell them to delay their negotiations with the French.

The industrialists had not been given a freedom they could relish, and their fortunes had reached their nadir in mid-October 1923. The road uphill was to be hard and tedious, and even the first milestone, the conclusion of the Micum agreements, was not reached until November 23, 1923. During much of the negotiations, Stinnes, Vögler, and their allies were undercut by the separate negotiations of the Wolff group and Krupp. Reichert had anticipated this danger even before Stinnes first met with Degoutte and had urged Stinnes and Klöckner to arrange a common front among the leading industrialists before talking with the French general.[193] Even then, it probably would have been too late given the speed with which Wolff and his associates were acting at the end of September and beginning of October. There were, however, very angry and demoralizing altercations in the Northwest Group on October 11, where the fear was expressed that all the concerns would start running individually to the Micum to be "butchered one after the

---

[192] For the industrialist attacks see the formal resolution of the VdESI of October 5, 1923, against a Great Coalition government in BA R 13 I/90, Bl. 26ff., and for Stresemann's campaign against Stinnes, see Stresemann to Rudolph Schneider, October 19, 1923, Nachlass Stresemann, 3105/7163/H154337–338.

[193] Reichert reported on this conversation with Stinnes, which probably took place on October 4, in a letter to Meyer, Reusch, and other industrial leaders of October 12, 1923, HA/GHH, Nr. 300193008/16.

other."[194] Dechamps of the Rombacher Hütte went so far as to refuse to talk about the discussions with the French in the presence of the Phoenix representatives, and the latter remained tight-lipped about their negotiations. Köngeter of Stumm seemed to have taken the lead in restoring a measure of cohesion among the industrialists by putting an end to the quarrels and threats. He stressed the futility of the latter and emphasized the importance of working together as much as possible and drawing up guidelines for the negotiations. A decision was made to invite Thyssen to join the Committee of Six in order to prevent yet another major group from straying.

Briefly, in mid-October it even seemed as if the Wolff group might have returned to the fold because of reports that its negotiations had run into difficulties. This hope was shattered when the Wolff agreements were formally signed on October 20. The terms imposed on Phoenix and Rheinstahl were harsh. They had to agree to pay back coal taxes, to accept restrictions on their exports, and, most onerously, to pay 16–17% of their production as reparations coal and, additionally, to pay the 40% coal tax to the French. Like Vögler and his colleagues, the Phoenix-Rheinstahl negotiators argued that this was a financial impossibility but finally felt compelled to agree to the "experiment" of paying reparations coal and the coal tax for one month.[195] The French, of course, made the most of such concessions. When Frantzen of the Micum informed Vögler that such "outstanding representatives" of heavy industry as Otto Wolff had agreed to pay a 40% tax on new production, Vögler could only reply that "the mines could under no circumstances make such contributions."[196] The French did not omit to influence trade union opinion also. Degoutte told German trade union representatives that the industrialists were not justified in claiming that they could not pay both reparations coal and a tax on new production by pointing out that Phoenix "and many other" concerns had signed on such terms and that they

> . . . told us that the taxes placed on them by us are bearable. It would be possible to rebuild industry again under these conditions. In general, I would add that there is perhaps the intention to pass the burdens on to you in that one pays you lower wages. But that is something we must leave to you and you must defend yourselves. What we want is a tax on capital, and the employers, who have earned a great deal before, must now accept a smaller profit in the future.[197]

[194] Meeting, October 11, 1923, *ibid.*, Nr. 3001100/18.

[195] *Kölnische Zeitung*, October 18, 1923, and Fahrenhorst to Reichert, October 30, 1923, HA/GHH, Nr. 30019000/4.

[196] Meeting, October 22, 1923, *ibid.*, Nr. 300193008/16.

[197] DMV report on its meeting with Degoutte, October 24, 1923, in *ibid.*

The concerns in the Wolff group did not consider the Micum burdens in any way bearable, but telling such fables to the trade unionists was a splendid way of increasing the pressures on Vögler and his friends. Although the actions of the Wolff group seem to have been viewed as the most deleterious to the efforts of the Committee of Six to get better terms, the Krupp agreement of October 31 was also viewed with alarm because, in addition to the coal tax and reparations burdens, Krupp also agreed to pay a 4% tax on exports abroad or to the unoccupied area. Before the terms of the Krupp agreement became known, Reusch had the distinct impression that the French would yield on these demands, and he did not fail to point out to Krupp that the negotiations with the French would be prejudiced by Krupp's concessions. Reusch considered "unbearable" the combination of coal tax, export taxes, and need to chase after permission to export from the "lazy good-for-nothings" (*Faulnetzer*) who would inevitably staff a large French apparatus and that would have a vested interest in keeping their jobs and unlimited opportunities for harassment and chicanery. Obviously, export controls and levies imposed in the French manner would be even more onerous than the German, and Reusch seems to have had Krupp as well as Wolff in mind when he referred to the separate negotiations as a "crime against the fatherland."[198]

Reusch and other critics of these concerns did have reason to be angry, for even if there was a measure of poetic justice in the industrialists discovering for themselves what German governmental leaders had experienced every time industry refused to cooperate in a crisis, it nevertheless was extremely dangerous for the industrialists to fail to stick together. The French were using the negotiations to create obligations and agencies that would involve the Rhine and Ruhr as closely with France in an economic and administrative sense as possible, and the concessions of the Wolff and Krupp agreements could only strengthen this tendency. Rheinstahl and Krupp directors, for example, were quite aware of discussions between some of their industrial colleagues in the Ruhr and a prominent Frenchman at which the latter declared that although France had no intention of annexing the Rhine and Ruhr, "the French government would regard it as a success if the Rhine and Ruhr territory were separated from the State of Prussia and would form an independent state with its own administration in the federation of the German Reich."[199] Their concessions, there-

[198] Reusch to Baron von Wilmowski (Gustav Krupp von Bohlen und Halbach's son-in-law), October 31, 1923, *ibid.*, Nr. 300193008/15, and to Karl Haniel, October 31, 1923, *ibid.*, Nr. 300193008/18.

[199] Report of Goldschmidt of the Darmstädter Bank on a discussion with Bernhard Desouches in Paris on October 18, 1923, and discussion with Schäffer

fore, particularly on the export control and customs boundary questions, had political as well as economic implications. At the same time, industry had a particular interest in receiving compensation or at least the promise of compensation from the Reich for its burdens under any arrangements with the Micum. The separate agreements, which undertook obligations without compensation or promise of compensation, only served to encourage the French in their charges that the rest of industry was able but unwilling to make sacrifices.

After October 12, from the viewpoint of Stinnes and Vögler, the major problem was to reverse Stresemann's complete refusal to promise compensation for the obligations that might arise from an agreement with the Micum. To accomplish this, Stinnes proposed that industry offer to provide from 16 to 18% of its coal production as reparations payment until April 1, 1924, on its own account and that the Reich obligate itself to repay the costs as soon as its finances were in order through the mechanism of tax remissions. The mine workers unions joined Stinnes in making this proposal to the government and warned that a refusal by the Reich to promise compensation for reparations coal payments would lead to chaos and the separation of the industrial regions from the Reich. Clearly, Stinnes' suggestion had great risks for the employers because the obligation to supply reparations coal without immediate compensation would be both onerous because of the low level of production and speculative because the future prospects of the Reich were far from sanguine. Under the circumstances, however, the gamble had real advantages: cessation of confiscations, resumption of production, possibility of export, and tax relief at a time when taxes were again levied on the basis of real values. Enormous pressure was thus put on Stresemann and the cabinet by Vögler, who bluntly told the government on October 19 that if it continued to take the view that it could not pay reparations, then it had the obligation to declare openly that it was "giving up the population and the industry of the Rhine and Ruhr,"[200] and thereby relieving industry of all responsibility. On the following day, despite some objection in the cabinet from Koeth, who felt that they were only putting off the inevitable separation of the industrial region from the Reich, Stresemann and Luther decided to accept the basic proposition that the government would assume an obligation to compensate the industrialists because there would be no immediate costs and the en-

(Krupp), Rabbinowitz (Simon Hirschland), and Rechlin (Essen Chamber of Commerce) in Essen on October 19, 1923, Rheinstahl Archiv, Nr. 920.

[200] Blank report on talk with Reichert, October 19, 1923, HA/GHH, Nr. 300-193024/3, and, more generally, Charles Maier, *Recasting Bourgeois Europe*, p. 392ff.

tire arrangement presupposed that the economy would recover first. Initially, Stresemann refused to promise compensation for payment of the coal tax, although he relented on this issue as well by November 1. At the same time, however, Stresemann instructed Stinnes that he would accept no customs boundary between the occupied and unoccupied areas, and the Chancellor reaffirmed the sovereignty of the Reich.[201]

The agreement of the government to the principle of compensation was an important achievement on Stinnes and Vögler's parts, but it did not put an end to the difficulties with the Micum. In early November the French increased their demands, probably in part as a consequence of the Wolff and Krupp concessions. A more serious crisis developed on November 14, when the French suddenly demanded that the coal deliveries be credited, not to the reparations account, but rather to a special "guarantee" fund from which occupation costs were to be paid before the balance would be charged against reparations. On the one hand, this reflected the French desire to distinguish between "pledges" for reparations and the reparations themselves. On the other hand, it was a device to keep control of the deliveries which, as reparations, would have to be reported to the other reparations claimants and divided accordingly. Significantly, the French had not fulfilled this requirement with regard to the deliveries promised under the Wolff agreements. Ultimately, however, the French gave way by accepting a complicated compromise under which coal tax payments went into the "guarantee" fund and the reparations deliveries were credited to the reparations fund. The compromise reflected the growing pressure on France to settle. Poincaré feared diplomatic isolation, financial and political pressures within France for a settlement were increasing, and the other reparations claimants had no intention of being denied their due via a "pledge" fund. On November 23, the Micum agreements were signed. The coal mines promised to pay up to fifteen million dollars in back coal taxes for the period to November 1, 1923 within six months, to pay ten francs per ton for all new production after October 1, to deliver 18% of their new coal and 35% of their new coke to France and Belgium on the reparations account while yielding rights to all coal and coke previously sequestered, to supply all coal needed by the occupation authorities free of charge, and to accept control and duties on the export of iron and steel stocks returned or newly produced. The agreements were to remain in force until April 15, 1924.[202]

[201] Cabinet meetings, October 20–November 1, 1923, 1749/D757259ff., and Spethmann, *Ruhrbergbau*, III, p. 205.

[202] *Kölnische Zeitung*, November 18, 1923; Bergmann, *History of Reparations*, p. 214ff.

The industrialists entered into this agreement most unwillingly and with little faith that it could be carried out. They did so because they had reached a dead end and wished to prevent complete collapse. If German industry had fought to usurp the Berlin government's role in negotiations with the allies, it had not been to make agreements requiring a 27% surrender of their production! Furthermore, the Micum demands would have to be met under conditions where credits of all kinds were being cut off or severely reduced and where the fulfillment of the government's promise of compensation seemed very far off. The immediate prospect was for an enormous demand for productivity and a serious liquidity crisis. The "miracle" of the Rentenmark, which was introduced on November 15, was not yet in evidence, but the less edifying "miracle" of a paper currency pegged at 4.2 trillion marks to the dollar on November 20, of vast amounts of emergency money, some of it issued by concerns without cover, and the spectre of continued mass unemployment and unrest were plainly in evidence. It was impossible for industrialists not to be skeptical and quite primitive in their thinking. As Reusch put it, "I don't think much of the new money. So long as we do not change our economic and social legislation from the bottom up and make sure that we work more than in the prewar period, every new currency that we create will depreciate."[203]

As may be noted from the above comments, the currency reform and the terms of the Micum agreements, the basic outlines of which were already quite clear by early October, only heightened the importance of an increase in the hours of work for the industrialists. Their first initiatives on the hours of work question, like those taken with regard to opening negotiations with the French, had produced very inglorious results, and here, too, it took some time to move forward again. It was to prove easier to handle the workers than the French, but they did recognize by early October that they would have to move more cautiously and pay attention to what was happening in Berlin. It would not do to violate the law, presume that Berlin would sanction anything they did, and provoke the workers unnecessarily or prematurely.

Paradoxically, but in complete keeping with the Malthusian mentality of the heavy industrialists, they anticipated breaking down worker resistance to longer hours through unemployment and low wages as well as through exerting influence in Berlin. In this connection, the intended cutting off of government wage support funds played into their hands. Thus, at the very time when the mine owners

[203] Paul Reusch to Hermann Reusch, October 31, 1923, HA/GHH, Nr. 40010-1298/37.

were announcing their intention to convert to a longer work day, the other plants in the major concerns were announcing on October 5–6 that they were planning to reduce the working week to thirty hours beginning October 8 because of the government's intention to cut wage supports to 60%.[204] At the same time, the reduction of hours was coupled with dismissals wherever permitted by the various laws and ordinances, and although the unions complained to the arbitration boards about this, Director Woltmann of the GHH had the "pleasure" of reporting to Reusch on October 5 that these complaints had been rejected.[205] More generally, the employers could always take the view that whatever the barriers to layoffs and dismissals, no law could be imposed on those physically unable to fulfill it. The mining industry intended its revocation of the extended hours of work to be "temporary," therefore, and although there was every intention of negotiating with trade unions and government agencies to achieve the goal and avoiding fiascoes and difficulties, there was also the anticipation, expressed quite bluntly by Köngeter of Stumm, that "through shortage of work we will come to a prolonged working day."[206] For this reason, as well as for the obvious economic ones, the employers continuously pressed for relief from the demobilization decrees regulating their right to shut down their plants and dismiss their workers as well as for immediate relief from the Decree of July 17, 1923, which had been issued in connection with the wage guarantee payments by the government and which restricted the right of dismissal. In brief, dismissals, plant shutdowns, layoffs, reduced working days, and mass unemployment would demonstrate to the workers and the government that only through a level of productivity that permitted a financial return could the works keep their doors open and make possible a recovery that would increase employment once again.

Mass unemployment, of course, was a tricky business, and there were major disturbances in the Ruhr cities in the first weeks of October as the works began to reduce hours and uncertainty grew as to the extent and length of continued wage payments by the government. The employers themselves were unclear about the government's intentions because the government yielded somewhat to worker pressure in the scaling down of its supports during the last weeks of October. To clarify things, Arbeno decided to "shake into wakefulness" the government's "sense of responsibility" by asking it to make its intentions

[204] Meetings of October 5–6, 1923, *ibid.*, Nr. 3001100/18.

[205] Woltmann to Reusch, October 5, 1923, *ibid.*, Nr. 300193003/8.

[206] Meeting of October 11, *ibid.*, Nr. 300193008/16, and meeting of October 10, 1923, Bergbau Archiv, Bestand 15, Nr. 73.

clear and reminding it that it would have "to take full responsibility for the consequences" of a decision to shut off funds and leave the works with no choice but to send their workers out on relief.[207] On October 18–19, an agreement was reached with Berlin under which workers would be paid whole or partial unemployment welfare support, depending on the amount of work that could be offered them. Because the communal agencies were not technically in a position to pay welfare, it was to be handled by the works, and the government promised to compensate the works for costs as well as supply the needed money on time.[208]

Although it was contradictory at once to seek to prevent unemployment by appealing for continued government support and to seek to promote it by eliminating unproductive labor and threatening complete shutdown, there were strong motives for both policies, and this was not the most logical of times or situations. Slowing the pace of unemployment was useful in maintaining some measure of order and, at times, strengthening the hand of the industrialists in their dealings with the unions and the French. Speeding the pace of unemployment and using the threat of shutdown, however, was no less useful because it threatened disorganization and chaos. The government in Berlin was in no less contradictory a situation. On the one hand, it had an obvious interest in preventing unemployment, particularly on a scale, as anticipated by Koeth, of two to three million at the end of October. To control the situation, it had issued a new decree on October 15 providing for some continued barriers against the arbitrary dismissal of workers as well as for the continued payment of dismissed workers for a brief period after notice had been given. On the other hand, the government was also committed to maximum productivity, and Koeth made his priorities quite clear when he declared that "The question of unemployment is the problem of the coming winter. The most pressing question at present is the regulation of working hours. A further delaying of the issue is unbearable. It must be made possible for industry to bring out the unproductive elements. The factories can no longer be places of social welfare; they must become places of real production again."[209] It was in this spirit that Koeth and Brauns decided to grant an Arbeno petition of late October permitting industry to release workers and shut down plants to the extent that they were unproductive. This was not complete freedom to lay off and dismiss

[207] Arbeno meeting, October 17, 1923, HA/GHH, Nr. 300193008/16.

[208] Report of October 17, 1923, *ibid.*

[209] Cabinet meeting, November 9, 1923, 1749/D757702–3 and October 24 meeting, *ibid.*, D757309.

workers at will, but it was strong government support in that direction.[210]

Satisfying the demands of the employers with regard to the hours of work law was a much more difficult proposition, however, and the government continued to be caught between the demands of the trade unions and those of the employers. Consequently, a decision was made on October 27 to extend the Demobilization Decree pertaining to the eight-hour day yet once more until November 17, 1923. The press and all concerned were told, however, that this extension was temporary and that the government was committed to a change in the existing regulations. The government wanted to permit extended working hours on the basis of contract negotiations between labor and management and temporary exceptions to restrictions on hours in times of emergency or heavy demand through special dispensation of the industrial inspectors. From the standpoint of the iron and steel industrialists, however, these were inadequate changes in the existing circumstances. The supreme goal of the iron and steel men was to have legislation or a decree permitting a return to the two-shift system—that is, a twelve-hour shift that would include two hours of pauses and ten hours of working time. Labor Minister Brauns' proposed Hours of Work Bill was not intended to provide for a two-shift system but only for a longer working day of nine hours. Consequently, the iron and steel men were demanding that the bill be changed to allow explicitly for the reintroduction of the old two-shift system. Additionally, the industrialists wanted greater discretionary power in making extensions of the working day for prolonged periods in times of emergency in the noncontinuous plants. Although confident by the end of October that some kind of law would be passed giving them most of what they wanted, their expectations about exerting sufficient influence to attain all the changes they desired oscillated with the political situation. At the end of October they were pessimistic about their maximum program and viewed the bill as a compromise filled with concessions to the left-wing parties that would not be alterable. In early November, they were heartened by the departure of the Social Democrats from the government because of the government's discriminatory handling of the crises in Saxony and Bavaria.[211]

The industrialists knew, however, that the outcome would not de-

[210] Arbeno to RAM, October 23, 1923, and RWM to Government Presidents, October 23, 1923, in HA/GHH, Nr. 3001100/18.

[211] See Labor Minister Brauns' remarks at a meeting of December 12, 1923, *ibid.*, Nr. 300141/17; VdESI to member groups, October 25, 1923, BA R 13 I/202, Bl. 191–194, and Borsig to German Chamber of Commerce, BA R 11/1248. Cabinet meeting, October 27, 1923, 1748/D757443.

430

pend entirely on what happened in Berlin alone. They recognized that "the danger to a contractual establishment of longer working time lies less in the law itself than in the lack of unity among the employers. For example, one cannot expect that a blast furnace or rolling mill worker will agree to a longer working time if the mining industry considers the eight-hour day sufficient for the cokeries."[212] There was the constant danger that the mining industry would look after its own interests and accept an extension of the working day under ground while sacrificing an increase above ground commensurate with the goals of the iron and steel industry. Similarly, there was the danger that individual concerns or even individual plants within a concern would make concessions that would prejudice the interests of the industry as a whole. When Raabe of Thyssen suggested in early November that they threaten the unions with a refusal to sign the Micum agreements unless the two-shift system was accepted, a colleague pointed out that this was really "inopportune" when 25% of the works had already signed Micum agreements. It was difficult to make the Socialist Metal Workers Union leader in the Ruhr, Karl Wolff, see "reason" on the two-shift system when the latter was able to report that Degoutte had told him that the industrialists who had signed separate agreements did not believe that they needed to go beyond the eight-hour day to fulfill the terms of the agreements. The claim seemed confirmed by the fact that Phoenix-Ruhrort had reopened two of its blast furnaces on the eight-hour shift.[213]

Even without Degoutte's efforts to increase discord between industry and the trade unions, relations with the latter were extraordinarily tense. The Metal Workers Union had given Arbeno notice on its general labor contract, and the latter expired on October 1. A new contract had to be negotiated, therefore, and the two sides were completely at odds. Naturally, the main goal of the employers was to get union agreement to the reintroduction of prewar hours. Unhappily, they did not have much to offer the workers in return. They could not offer the wages in stable values the unions were demanding because they did not have sufficient stable currency on hand to do so. They were resolved, however, only to pay a "gold wage for gold performance," i.e., for productivity measured in real values, and they were intent on paying a gold wage, when they finally did, that was below the prewar rate because of the condition of the economy and their finances. Although convinced that the workers were psychologically prepared to accept longer hours, the attitude of the unions suggested that the

[212] Meeting in Essen Chamber of Commerce, November 6, 1923, HA/GHH Nr. 30011100/18, and Arbeno negotiations, November 7, 1923, *ibid.*, Nr. 30140/10.
[213] Arbeno negotiations, November 7, 1923, *ibid.*

threat of unemployment would be more useful than persuasion and that "the shut down of the plants makes possible the declaration of the employers that the reopening will only follow with the old working hours."[214] The problem was that there was not enough real suffering from the unemployment because "the state welfare support permits an idle existence." The arguments the steel men used in their discussions with the trade union people were something less than a triumph of social psychology:

> . . . We know that the lengthening of the working day will increase unemployment at first. But that is only a transitory phase that we must overcome, after which there will be an increase in production and increased work opportunity through cost reduction. For the unemployed in the unoccupied area there is still work available, especially through more intensive soil cultivation, a counterweight against industrialization that should have been used long ago to eliminate unproductive welfare support. What we demand is not a demand of ours but of economic life which makes inescapable requirements. . . .[215]

The union leaders, however, found it difficult to fathom why they should ask their men to work ten hours when industry could not find enough work to employ them for eight. They rejected the notion that the worker could be treated like a machine, and they were not enthusiastic about the proposed return to the alleged joys of nonindustrial life.

The industrialists did not want "to step forward as despisers of the law, as dictators," but if the trade unions would not cooperate, then they felt compelled "to turn to the legislator and force him to do what the economic necessities require."[216] In sheer desperation they even looked to the despised Hours of Work Decree of November 23, 1918, and attempted to employ its provision permitting the Demobilization Commissars to extend hours of work in cases where the public interest and especially the prevention of unemployment so required by claiming that they could not keep their plants open and fulfill the pending Micum agreements unless there was a return to prewar hours in their industry. This effort to employ the hated decree as the mechanism for its circumvention was never really tested because Berlin unexpectedly came to their rescue with a decision to end the stalemate in the Reichstag and force a settlement of the hours-of-work question by simply allowing the demobilization decree in question to lapse as scheduled

[214] Ibid., and VDA memorandum of October 25, 1923, BA R 11/1248.
[215] Arbeno negotiations, November 7, 1923, HA/GHH, Nr. 30140/10.
[216] Ibid.

on November 17. Although Brauns, Koeth, and Stresemann would have liked to issue a new decree in the form of Brauns' Hours of Work Bill, this would not have been in keeping with the Enabling Act of October 13. Consequently, as of November 17, the only noncontractual constraints on hours of work were those of the old prewar Industrial Code and the law governing hours of work in the mines of July 1922.[217]

On November 14, Reichert confidentially informed the industrialists that "the way is now open for a prolongation of the hours of work insofar as no contractual constraints exist."[218] These tidings of joy were extraordinarily welcome to the steel men. The contract had been terminated by the unions, and they were free, therefore, to negotiate on any terms they wished. At the same time, they were at their wits' end with their colleagues in the mining industry, who were supposed to take the lead in extending the working day. Arbeno had appointed a committee to coordinate policy on working hours with the Mining Association, but the latter had refused to permit Arbeno to participate in the negotiations with the mine worker unions. In contrast to the iron and steel industry, the general wage and hours contract in the mining industry remained in force, and the mining industry felt extremely vulnerable in both a legal and a practical sense. Before teaming up with the more extreme steel men, therefore, the mining association wished to see if it could not come to an agreement with its union on its own, an attitude that provoked "unanimous outrage" among the steel men.[219]

With the lapse of the Hours of Work Decree of 1918, however, the iron industry was free to take the lead and no longer had to wait upon either the mining industry or the permission of some official to change the hours of work. They had the right to determine the conditions of labor by making new contracts on an individual or collective basis, although they recognized that legal barriers to such a termination of existing contracts remained in the form of the Decrees of July 17, 1923, and of October 15, 1923, regulating the dismissal of workers. Still, they were now in a stronger negotiating position with the unions and, if negotiations failed, they could tell their workers that they would only reopen closed plants with workers prepared to work a double shift and only continue the operation of existing plants if the workers agreed to begin working the new hours within two weeks. Needless to say, the implementation of this plan would require discipline among the steel firms, and it was a bad sign that the assembled directors had to berate Director

[217] Arbeno to Düsseldorf Demobilization Commissar, *ibid.*, Nr. 3001100/18, and Cabinet meeting, November 15, 1923, 1750/D757763ff.

[218] Reichert to VdESI groups, November 14, 1923, BA R 13 I/202, Bl. 166.

[219] Arbeno meeting, November 17, 1923, HA/GHH, Nr. 3001100/18.

Esser, who behaved like the soul of innocence when it was pointed out that Rheinstahl had dared to pay new workers overtime for the additional hours. A more serious problem, however, was that the French feared that mass lockouts would cause unrest, and General Degoutte issued an order on November 18 seeking at once to counter industrialist threats in the Micum negotiations that they would shut down and the officially planned shutdown scheduled by the Mining Association for November 30. Degoutte threatened imprisonment and fines to industrialists who released all their workers or any portion of their workers in conformity with a decision taken by an employer association.[220]

A ban on collusive lockouts, however, was not a ban on "individual" actions by employers who might release workers who would not work a prolonged day. On November 30, Reusch implemented the ten-hour working day and two-shift system at his plants, and he fired workers who left after eight hours. At the GHH, as well as at other plants in the Ruhr, the employers and workers privately agreed to the extension of the eight-hour day as a precondition for their return to work, and although there was some violence against workers who accepted these conditions by radical elements, some trade union people were telling the men in early December that they should work the new hours, which were to be viewed as "temporary." The reality was that the trade unions were in horrendous financial condition and largely dependent on the government for survival. They now lacked the support of the 1918 Decrees on the hours of work, and were convinced that some extension of the hours of work would be required by the Micum agreements. The one significant exception was the Socialist Metal Workers Union, but the other important unions had been truly weakened in their stand, and there is good reason to believe that the workers, ill paid and ill fed, had been sufficiently ravaged to accept the new terms of employment with sullen resignation.[221]

On November 29, 1923, an agreement was reached in Berlin between the coal mining industry and the unions to extend the working day underground from seven to eight hours inclusive of entry and departure into the mine, and to extend from eight to nine hours the working day for workers above ground directly involved in the actual coal mining operations. The agreement was to run from December 5 to May 1, 1924, during which time it was to be reviewed by the interested parties to determine if peacetime productivity had been reattained and, if not, how it might be. The coal men had wanted an 8½

[220] Spethmann, *Ruhrbergbau*, III, p. 397.
[221] Reusch to his directors, November 17, 1923, HA/GHH, Nr. 300193008/10, and reports in *ibid.*, Nr. 300193008/11 and 300140/15. Also, Cabinet meeting, November 19, 1923, 1750/D757823ff.

day shift underground, but they were compelled to compromise because Thyssen and Krupp had granted their miners eight hours and thus ruined the united front of the coal men.[222] From the standpoint of the iron and steel industry, the most favorable aspect of the agreement was that no provision had been made for the cokeries and other mining industry operations not directly related to coal mining itself. The agreement provided that the hours of work in these plants were to be determined in collaboration with the iron industry because of the need for uniformity of labor conditions in heavy industry as a whole. Naturally, the steel men welcomed an opportunity to control the decisions of the coal men and prevent a prejudicing of their effort to restore the two-shift system. It was all the more important at the end of November because of the strong resistance the Metal Workers Union was putting up to a return to the two-shift system in continuously operating plants.

On November 27, Arbeno had again sought to persuade the DMV to accept its proposals by presenting a written declaration to the effect that although a change to a two-shift system would be undertaken where economically necessary and "technically feasible," they would not "exploit the physical strength of the individual worker" and would not reintroduce the old 24-hour Sunday shift "under any circumstances." To this presumably conciliatory effort on the part of the employer representatives, the trade union leader Karl Wolff gave the "shattering" response that the unions refused to give up the eight-hour day and that "the mood among the workers is such that they would rather emigrate and work nine hours for the Americans or ten hours for the French."[223] They were prepared to work overtime for overtime pay in plants where there were normal temperature and working conditions, and they refused to consider a double shift in plants where there was extreme heat or other difficult working conditions.

When the Krupp director Klönne, who was the chief negotiator for Arbeno, reported his experience to his colleagues on November 30, he and his fellow negotiators were criticized for even mentioning the elimination of the 24-hour Sunday shift and the nonexploitation of workers and for even implying that there might be technical conditions under which the two-shift system could not be reintroduced. A decision was taken to put an end to the dilatory handling of the unions. It was believed that the recent negotiations in the mining industry would cause a change in the position of the Metal Workers Union, and the steel men were resolved to force the issue and either have their

[222] Report of December 3, 1923, HA/GHH, Nr. 30193008/11, and Preller, *Sozialpolitik*, p. 305.
[223] Report of November 28, 1923, HA/GHH, Nr. 300141/17.

way or stop negotiating. Now the union negotiators were handed a new declaration which promised to avoid the 24-hour Sunday shift "wherever possible" and said nothing about the nonexploitation of the workers. The union men were shocked by the harsh tone of the employers. They were prepared to concede an extra hour of work in all plants, but they insisted that the two-shift system only be introduced after the employers satisfactorily demonstrated that they could not make do without it. Arbeno rejected these proposals, and negotiations were broken off on November 30.[224]

The steel men now moved to solidify their own stand. On December 5, representatives of the Mining Association and Arbeno agreed to collaborate on hours and wage questions—that is, to reintroduce the twelve-hour shift in cokeries and other appropriate mining plants and to follow a common policy on maintaining certain wage levels and reintroducing skill and age differentials of a more pronounced character.[225] On December 7–8, the Arbeno Board of Directors and other specially invited iron and steel men met in Essen to decide on future policy, and they signed an agreement, the violation of any terms of which would be penalized by a fine of five gold marks per worker in the offending firm as of January 11, 1923. The first provision of the agreement was that they would engage in no negotiations with the unions or appear before any arbitration board. The object of this provision was not to end all negotiations with unions, but rather to force the unions to accept the two-shift system in principle as the price of continued discussion, be such discussion direct, be it before the mediator in Düsseldorf, or be it even before the Labor Minister in Berlin. A second provision of the agreement was to limit wages for the period December 10–17 to 350 million times the wage paid on March 1, 1923, a compromise made after lengthy debate which, however, constituted a deliberate effort to reduce wages.[226] The next provision of the agreement was that no plant was to reopen except on the basis of the prewar workday, and that those that had reopened with the eight-hour day were to convert to the ten-hour work day and twelve-hour shift within four weeks. The time limit was set as a means of pressure on concerns such as Krupp, whose representative, when asked how soon Krupp intended to go off the eight-hour day, irritated his colleagues by "blissfully" declaring that "he cannot yet say when it would be convenient for him."[227] He now knew. Indeed, such plants were urged to give

[224] Report on meeting of November 30, 1923, and related documents in *ibid*.

[225] Meeting of December 5, 1923, in *ibid*.

[226] Report on December 8, 1923, meeting, dated December 10 in *ibid*.

[227] *Ibid*.

436

workers on the eight-hour shift an hour and a half pause between morning and afternoon so that the workers would get used to a longer shift even when on the short one. A similar effort to make sure that there were no false impressions or dangerous precedents was reflected in the final provision of the Arbeno agreement, which stipulated that plants not able to introduce the full prewar hours were under no circumstances to employ workers on the eight-hour shift. This problem had provoked much debate among the industrialists because they were anxious to produce again and to "reduce the army of the unemployed before the French exercised compulsion in this direction," but many of them feared that temporarily employing workers for less than ten working hours would make the transition to the prewar hours more difficult and be costly in wages. The majority, however, felt that employment of workers on a shift of six hours would be satisfactory if no more such workers were hired than would be necessary to staff regular work on the double shift once full operation was possible. Indeed, the only break in this otherwise relentless effort to ensure the return to prewar working conditions was the willingness of the steel men finally to surrender the 24-hour Sunday shift.

If the steel men were assuming a very aggressive posture, however, it was not without a goodly sense of anxiety. There were disturbances among the unemployed workers, threats of violence against workers who accepted employer terms, and a seething resentment that alternated with the fatalistic and sullen acceptance of the overt shifting of the balance of social and economic power so strongly in favor of the heavy industrialists. It was easier for the industrialists to have their way in the Ruhr than in Berlin, where political considerations tended to prevail and weaken the impact of their demands and reduce their effectiveness. That is why less conciliatory Ruhr coal industry leaders such as Otto Wiskott and the steel industrialists had been pleased that the regulation of hours of work for overground workers in the mining industry was to be settled in common with the iron industry on its home base in the Ruhr.[228] Nevertheless, the coal men had been effective in Berlin in getting Brauns to take a tough stand toward the miners. Brauns had accepted industry's claim that it could not get credits without an increase in the working day under and above ground, and he had put great pressure on the miners. Similarly, in the first days of December he forced the miner unions to maintain their contract with the industry despite disagreements over wages by threatening to abolish the Hours of Work Law for the Mining Industry of 1922 by

[228] Meeting of December 5, 1923, and report by Klönne on December 7, 1923, meeting in *ibid.*

decree.[229] Industry really could not simply forget about Berlin, where laws could be made and unmade and where the central authority of the Reich continued to dispose of military power, financial resources, and authority. To rule the Ruhr, heavy industry ultimately needed the backing of Berlin, and the prospect of such backing became more likely when the bourgeois government led by the Centrist Wilhelm Marx replaced the Stresemann government on December 1.

It also became more necessary for a variety of other reasons. First, the Socialist newspaper *Vorwärts* was claiming that the eight-hour day was law in Germany by the proclamation of the Council of People's Delegates of November 12, 1918, and that this had precedence over the lapsed November 23 Decree. The point could be argued on both sides, but it alarmed Vögler and Sempell of Deutsch-Lux, who were facing strong worker opposition and serious incidents at their plants. Furthermore, Sempell and Vögler were under great pressure from Stinnes, who "had the leaders of his concern told that they should come to an agreement with the worker representatives under all circumstances, since he is informed that if work is not taken up again on Monday, the French will take the matter up themselves, if necessary with the retention of the eight-hour day."[230] Consequently, Sempell called the VdESI headquarters in Berlin on December 8 and informed it that "he, as well as Dr. Vögler, consider it absolutely essential, particularly in view of the conditions in the occupied area, that a decree of the government appear expressly stating that the hours of work can be set for longer than eight hours by contract between the work and the individual worker in free agreement even when the factory work code, etc., contradicts this and, above all, that those willing to work should be granted protection."[231] Similarly, the industrialists remained anxious to eliminate the law of July 17, 1923, limiting their right to dismiss workers. They argued, with some justification, that the law had the specific purpose of supporting passive resistance and represented an employer obligation undertaken in return for the lapsed wage guarantee for unproductive work. Under the circumstances it was obsolete. The major reason for their turning to Berlin, however, was their desire to secure government sanction for a return to the twelve-hour shift. A decree to this effect now seemed possible

[229] See the negotiations of November 28–29, 1923, in DZA Potsdam, RAM, Nr. 29, Bl. 42–43, and Cabinet meeting of December 3, 1923, in Günter Abramowski, ed., *Die Kabinette Marx I und II. 30. November 1923 bis 3 Juni 1924. 3 Juni 1924 bis 15. Januar 1925. Akten der Reichskanzlei. Weimarer Republik*, 2 vols. (Boppard am Rhein, 1973), I, p. 22.

[230] Reported at meetings of December 13–14, 1923, HA/GHH, Nr. 300141/16.

[231] Bülow to Hoff of Arbeno, December 8, 1923, *ibid.*, Nr. 30041/17.

because the Reichstag had passed a new Enabling Act on December 8 that did not preclude the right to issue decrees on working hours, although all decrees required the approval of a Reichstag committee. Such a decree would obviously strengthen the hand of the employers in bringing the trade unions and workers to terms.

When Brauns met with the steel industry representatives on December 12, he was either under the impression or pretended to believe that they had come to discuss the repeal of the Decree of July 17, a request that had the sympathy of the Labor Ministry, and he seemed taken aback when Klönne gave a lengthy speech pointing out that the eight-hour day was ruinous to their industry, which before the French invasion had employed 100% more workers than in 1914 but had only attained the same level of productivity as before the war. The workers were "not interested in work, but in idleness and pleasure." The pressures of the Micum agreements, mass unemployment, and the occupation required a return to productive labor, but they had negotiated for weeks with the unions to no effect. In this situation, the "employers have had to take recourse to the government and now ask for information as to what the government intends to do to see to it that work is resumed again."[232] Brauns responded to this seemingly unanticipated interpellation by pointing out that he was not in complete agreement with the steel men. He did not think it possible to simply "spring over from the eight-hour to the twelve-hour day" and that some exception had to be made for workers exposed to great heat (*Feuerarbeiter*) because they had received special treatment even before the war and received such treatment abroad. Furthermore, Brauns reminded the steel men that the workers were getting "hunger wages." In his view, the difficulties of industry came from having too many unproductive workers, but he was not aware of the fact that the Micum agreements burdened the iron and steel industry so badly. He indicated, however, that he was prepared to help the steel men to get a longer working day just as he had mediated such a change for the mining industry. The kind of help that Brauns seemed to be offering and that he had offered all along, however, was a limited extension of the hours of work that stopped short of the two-shift system for continuously operating plants and that gave special protection to workers in the most arduous and strenuous categories. His "sanitary" working day seemed to be a very elastic concept, and it was attacked as impractical and insufficient.

Fundamentally, however, the iron and steel men were insisting that their economic situation had to be given primacy over other considerations, and Brauns found it "difficult to place solely economic interest

232 The quotations and discussions are based on the protocol in *ibid.*

in place of sanitary and social interests." He had been told by a representative of the mining industry that the iron and steel industry could easily afford to retain the eight-hour day in many areas, and Brauns believed that the iron and steel industry, like the mining industry, would have to make some concessions before prewar hours were generally introduced. Under the difficult circumstances, however, he was prepared to play the "honest broker" and mediate an agreement between Arbeno and the Metal Workers Union. In the meantime, he asked the industrialists to provide him with material proving that the Micum agreements were truly as burdensome to their industry as they claimed. Under these circumstances, the steel men were apparently willing to drop their refusal to negotiate with the DMV in the presence of the Labor Minister, and the stage was set for the final negotiation on the hours-of-work question.

By the time Brauns met with the management and labor leaders on December 13, he seemed convinced that the iron and steel industry was burdened by the Micum agreements to the point where the industry could not be competitive without an increase of hours of work and its accompanying cost reductions. He openly stated that "he did not feel bound by the eight-hour day," and that an increased work day was "imperative." He hoped that the trade unions would cooperate. Significantly, however, he made no overt commitment to the double-shift system. It was Klönne, as might be expected, who made this demand. He argued that the Micum agreements added 26 gold marks to each ton of iron so that, for example, German billets cost 160 gold marks as against 130 gold marks for the English product. The pre-Ruhr occupation prosperity of the industry had been nothing more than an apparent one, and "The only way out seems to be reducing the cost of production, reintroducing the double shift and thereby saving 50% on wages."[233] He asked the unions to collaborate and promised that the terms would be eased as the effects of the change could be evaluated by both sides. As in the coal industry, he suggested that an investigation be made by April 1, 1924, with a view toward new negotiations. The trade unions argued that the investigation should precede rather than follow the introduction of so major a departure from the eight-hour day and that they were prepared to work overtime to get the plants moving again if they were finally paid in gold wages.

Following lengthy separate negotiations with both sides, however, an agreement was reached that was distinctly favorable to the employers because it allowed for the two-shift system. For the moment, at least, Brauns seems to have decided to give way to the employer

[233] For the negotiations of December 13–14, 1923, see *ibid.*, Nr. 300141/16, and DZA Potsdam, RAM, Nr. 290, Bl. 117–119.

position, perhaps because of the immediacy of the Micum burdens. Under the agreement, the double shift and ten hours effective working time were to be reintroduced in all areas where they had existed before the war. The work week for regular workers was to be 60 hours on the night shift and 58 hours on the day shift, but certain categories of workers doing very difficult work were to work a 54-hour week. The Sunday double shift was to be eliminated, and there was to be a shortened work day on Saturday. Investigations were to be conducted to determine which categories of workers should be entitled to alleviations from the full return to prewar working conditions. Similar arrangements were to be made for work above ground in the cokeries and related plants in the mining industry.[234]

The credit for the reversion to the two-shift system in the continuously operating plants of heavy industry as well as for the relentless extension of the hours of work in mining and finishing must go to the iron and steel industrialists. Wherever possible, they stiffened the backs of the coal men, who periodically seemed more willing to compromise. Similarly, every effort was made to press the manufacturing industries into extending their working day, even when such extensions went beyond what had been customary in the industry before the war and were not justified by market demand. Heavy industry insisted that the manufacturing industries would benefit from the extended hours in heavy industry in the form of reduced prices for coal, iron, and steel. In short, manufacturing had to extend its hours of work, not only because it would benefit from the cost reductions involved, but even more because it had to be done for the sake of heavy industry. Thus, Köttgen of Siemens fought for a ten-hour day in the Berlin metal industry, where 8¾ hours had been the average before the war, with the argument that "we must support the efforts of the raw materials producers by making such a demand."[235]

Tactically, this pressure to increase hours throughout industry was understandable, but underlying the entire effort was an insensitivity toward the workers and an ingratitude for their loyalty in the Ruhr struggle that is difficult to comprehend and impossible to excuse. Thus, when at the GHH, the worker representatives were informed of the Berlin agreements of December 13–14, the workers accepted their fate but complained that since the ending of the Ruhr struggle, their supervisors and foremen had taken a very harsh tone. To this the directors replied that "the behavior of the workers in the factories

---

[234] For the agreement and interpretation, see BA R 13 I/202, Bl. 121.

[235] See the revealing letters of Hoff to Köttgen, March 22, 1924, Sempell to Köttgen, March 26, 1924, and Köttgen to Sempell, April 12, 1924, in SAA, Nachlass Köttgen, 11/Lf 129.

441

since the beginning of the Ruhr struggle has been a much less satisfactory one than before," and that "the *Schlamperei* must stop."[236]

The elimination of the eight-hour day was not the only victory that
heavy industry won by the end of 1923. The yearned-for decontrol of
the coal, iron, and steel industry took place as well. On December 3,
the Steel Federation declared itself in dissolution after Rheinstahl had
taken its now traditional lead in these matters by announcing its withdrawal from the organization. Under the existing poor market conditions in which prices were being reduced, it was believed that each
work could best deal with its customers alone and that selling would
have to be done at a sacrifice for the time being in any case. The works
agreed to continue meeting informally from time to time and to invite
the manufacturing interests to join in when deemed appropriate. The
EWB was informed that the Steel Federation would no longer contribute to pricing discussions in the EWB.[237] Naturally, producers were
most anxious to eliminate the EWB, and they certainly could argue
that it had long ceased to be an effective organization and that it was
regarded with distaste by both the producers and the consumers. Since
November 1923 it had ceased to function in pricing altogether, and
prices were being determined by direct negotiations between producers and manufacturers.[238] The move to disband the EWB was opposed
by the Federation of Iron Consumers, however. With the possible exception of the energetic new VDMA business manager, Baron von Buttlar, they had no affection for the organization, but they did argue that
it should not be eliminated "since one does not know if it will have to
start functioning again sometime. It can suspend its activity to be sure,
but one should keep it in reserve."[239] It was kept "in reserve" throughout the Weimar Republic as yet one of a number of zombie-like institutions inherited from the days of inflation. For all intents and purposes,
the decontrol of the iron and steel industry was a reality.

The major threat to producer interests now came from traditional
sources and problems, namely, the consumer interests who were, above
all, resisting existing tariffs and demands for higher ones. In November
1923 there had been an open rebellion in the VDMA by members who
felt that the organization was not doing enough to fight the tariff
policies and plans of heavy industry, and although heavy industry was

[236] Discussions with GHH worker leaders, December 27, 1923, HA/GHH, Nr.
300141/16.

[237] Discussion in Hagen, December 3, 1923, Nr. 3000035/3b.

[238] Steel Federation to RWM, January 18, 1924, and related correspondence
DZA Potsdam, RWM, Nr. 4459.

[239] Reported by Reichert to Heinson, January 25, 1924, BA R 13 I/349, Bl. 25.

able to take its revenge on Baron von Buttlar by having him thrown out of office in 1924 with the usual threat that the GHH and other concerns would otherwise resign their membership, there was a much broader sense among manufacturers that heavy industry did not deserve the protection it was getting and demanding. The machine construction industry accounted for 20–25% of Germany's exports in 1922 as contrasted with 14.3% in 1912.[240] Its importance to the economy had thus grown enormously, and it felt entitled to demand a full and cheap supply of the raw materials it needed. Although heavy industry was reducing its prices at the end of 1923, those prices were still considered too high by the consumers. Yet there was a strong belief in consumer circles that the well-being of the manufacturing industries depended on Germany possessing a strong primary production sector, and there could be no denying that heavy industry had special problems because of the Micum burdens. On December 8, therefore, the two sides reached an agreement to momentarily avoid public discussion of the tariff issue until the economic situation cleared and there was an opportunity to test the effects of the price reductions being undertaken as well as the cost reductions anticipated through increased hours, freight rate reductions, layoffs, and the like. As always, heavy industry was anxious to "carry out its fight peacefully, in that we try to learn the interests of the other side, so that we stand as a closed front against the government and parliament."[241]

Indeed, heavy industry had already worked out its basic program for the future by early 1924:

Insofar as the production statistics are concerned, we were already producing 88% of the 1913–1914 production in 1922. This production was achieved despite substantial shortages of coke, despite the eight-hour day, despite the lack of tariffs for imports from France and Lorraine. New blast furnaces have been finished in the meantime. If we work at full capacity, then we have a productive capacity that in no small measure exceeds that of 1913–1914. The excess demand for semifinished material could be imported duty-free from Lorraine and France if France could be persuaded to allow an equivalent amount of finished products in duty-free. But it will naturally turn this down. The Lorraine works do have too much semifinished production. Furthermore, we might think of a system of export rebates, which naturally can only be granted under the precondition of well-established syndicates. If we could grant export premiums through

[240] See the discussion for 1923–1924 in "Deutscher Maschinenbau."
[241] Meeting of December 8, 1923, in BA R 13 I/202, Bl. 133. The quotation is from a meeting of March 28, 1924, in *ibid.*, 350, Bl. 41.

the Coal Syndicate, the Pig Iron Syndicate, and eventually a new steel works association, then we could build substantial bridges to the iron consuming industry.[242]

Here, in March 1924, Bruhn was already anticipating the development of a host of new syndicates and cartels, agreements between heavy industry and manufacturing, and trade treaties that were to constitute much of the economic and organizational activity of the coming years. The path to it had been paved by the inflation, and, as Bruhn noted, it had been done despite the allegedly disastrous eight-hour day and absence of tariffs against France.

The situation of heavy industry was anything but good at the end of 1923. The Micum agreements were a great burden, and the shortage of working capital was serious whereas the future prospects for international loans were still unclear. Nor could heavy industry find full satisfaction in its recent victories over labor. Work was resuming slowly, but there was much labor unrest. Even more worrisome was that the government had taken new initiatives that promised difficulties over the long run. Brauns had issued an Hours of Work Decree on December 21, 1923, that was a modified version of his Hours of Work Bill. Industry strongly opposed the decree because paragraph 7 provided for exemptions from a prolonged working day for categories of workers yet to be determined whose labor was too strenuous or dangerous not to receive special consideration. Here was to be the stuff of future controversy and an erosion of some of industry's gains from the return to the two-shift system. Similarly, Braun's Decree on Arbitration of October 30, 1923, was to form the basis of a system of binding arbitration by the government that was to provide no end of irritation to industry in the coming years.[243] Lastly, there were the unresolved controversies with the manufacturing industries over prices and tariffs that could pose grave threats to the future. As in 1918–1919, however, so in 1923–1924 there was some value in having low production, financial difficulty, and burdens about which one could complain bitterly and forcefully and which one could blame for the untoward circumstances. So long as heavy industry could continue to persuade its customers and Berlin that its problems and its welfare were more significant than those of other groups in the society and had to be given priority, it could retain the advantageous "point of departure" it had so skillfully capitalized upon throughout the inflation.

[242] Meeting of March 27, 1924, in *ibid.*, Bl. 56ff.
[243] Preller, *Sozialpolitik*, pp. 275, 313–314.

Epilogue

In the winter of 1923–1924, German heavy industry seemed to be at the nadir of its fortunes. Production of coal, pig iron, and crude steel in 1923 had fallen even below the levels of 1919, and the Herculean efforts of heavy industry to restore its domestic and international position and redress the losses brought about by the defeat of 1918 hung in the balance. The Micum burdens seemed to leave room only for the slowest of recoveries, and even then for a recovery that would serve the interests of Germany's major continental competitors. Hopefully, however, this study of the iron and steel industry in the inflation will have served to dispel unwarranted anxiety about the recuperative power of German heavy industry.

Attentive contemporary observers well understood that the basis for recovery in 1924 was a different and better one than that of 1918:

> Out of the riot of post-war finance there has grown up in Germany a new industrial unit directed with the utmost skill and foresight, supreme in its adaptability. The position in respect to its capitalisation charges is thoroughly obscure, the benefits it derived at the expense of the State equally indeterminate. With a characteristic prescience for its welfare it has forced the introduction of longer working hours and low wages. Left alone it enjoys a very favorable position; coerced it will be prepared to make terms. . . .[1]

C. J. Kavanagh, the perceptive British Commercial Secretary in Cologne who penned these lines, feared that the German steel industry would respond to French coercion by coming to terms with the French through a series of international agreements designed to terminate the Micum burdens and create a continental iron and steel producing bloc inimical to British interests. The anxiety was not unfounded. In late 1923 and early 1924, Stinnes, Vögler, Rhenish banking and business circles led by J. H. von Stein, Louis Hagen, and Paul Silverberg, and the Mayor of Cologne, Konrad Adenauer, had been working toward an accommodation with France that involved cooperation between the industries of the two nations, the establishment of a gold discount bank in the Rhineland based on joint Franco-German funding, and the separation of the Rhineland from Prussia with a view toward estab-

[1] J. W. F. Thelwall and C. J. Kavanagh, *Report on the Economic and Financial Conditions in Germany, Revised to April, 1924* (Board of Overseas Trade) (London, 1924), p. 124.

*So that it will not be so easy for the workers to bear
the huge tax burdens, reparations, etc., we landlords
have decided to reoccupy our cherished place. Now
the proletarians will have their hands free for the 10
hour work day. From* Vorwärts, *January 6, 1924.*

lishing a separate Rhenish state within the Reich. Such an arrangement would at once relieve immediate economic difficulties, set a limit on the separatist danger, and provide the bridge leading to conciliation with France. Adenauer's goals were political, and the proposed economic and political arrangements were seen by him as instrumentalities for the achievement of a Franco-German rapprochement that would relieve the Rhineland of having to bear the brunt of past and present tension between the two nations and make it the linchpin of future collaboration and prosperity.[2]

As might be expected, the goals of Stinnes and Vögler were largely economic, and it was no accident that Stinnes had picked up where he had left off with the Stinnes-Lubersac Agreement of 1922. The end of the inflation threatened to bring down his overblown and chaotic empire, and the Micum Agreements had a particularly punishing effect on the less well-founded concerns. Stinnes was desperate for credit, and the projected Rhenish Gold Discount Bank and French participation in German industrial enterprises promised rapidly to create new sources of liquidity. In December 1923 he asked for relief from the fusion tax so that he might consolidate the GBAG, Deutsch-Lux, and the Bochumer Verein into one corporation centered in Berlin. On the one hand, the basing of these enterprises outside the Ruhr seemed imperative to protect their holdings abroad and in the unoccupied areas of Germany from French imprecations. For the same reasons, Reusch, for example, had moved the seat of the GHH to Nürnberg in November 1923. On the other hand, and here the similarity with Reusch ceases, Stinnes argued that a fusion was necessary to give his German works the counterweight they would need in any negotiations with French industry aimed at establishing a community of interest and restoring the prewar exchanges of ore, pig iron, and semis from Lorraine in return for coke and finished products from the Ruhr.[3]

During the first three months of 1924, Stinnes and his agents did negotiate with French industrial leaders to create such an industrial community of interest. The final result was a four-point plan presented by the French to Director Osius of the Stinnes concern in February under which (1) the French would be given ownership of German mines sufficient to supply Lorraine's coke needs, the value of these mines to be credited against reparations, (2) a long-term agreement

[2] Erdmann, *Rheinlandpolitik*, p. 156ff.

[3] Maier, *Recasting Bourgeois Europe*, p. 387ff. *Kabinette Marx*, I, pp. 101–103; Maschke, *Konzern*, pp. 187–188. It is interesting to note that the plan to move the seat of the GHH to Nürnberg was devised and approved in the spring of 1921 and was to be carried out "when the occupation of the Ruhr has taken place or is certain to occur."

would be concluded for the exchange of coke needed by the remainder of French heavy industry in return for minette, (3) Germany would permit the import of French pig iron duty-free, and (4) negotiations would be taken up for the reconstruction of the prewar international rails agreement (IRMA) as a first step toward a series of international agreements cartelizing steel production. Stinnes and Vögler, previously so fanatical in their insistence that all participation schemes between France and Germany had to be based on mutuality, were prepared to negotiate on the basis of this proposal. Apparently, they expected that it would eventually lead to a more mutual interpenetration of German and French heavy industry, and they argued that it was the only way to keep the Rhineland German.[4]

In reality, it was the desperate attempt of a dying man to keep his empire together and continue to operate in the style to which he had become accustomed, just as it was the last political misjudgment of a man notoriously incapable of comprehending the limits of economic rationality. Stinnes' day was over, both literally and figuratively. He died on April 10, 1924, late enough to see the impending collapse of his life's work in the offing, but early enough to leave the full brunt of the experience to fall on his heirs. His final program was as doomed to failure as his economic constructions. Stinnes had always rejected the ideas of the maverick potash industrialist, Arnold Rechberg, whose anti-Bolshevism had driven him to advocate a one-sided French participation in German industry as a means of promoting a western alliance. In this attitude toward Rechberg's schemes, Stinnes had been at one with his industrial colleagues in the Ruhr, and the latter were not prepared to abandon their opposition in 1924 and join with Stinnes in gambling on French goodwill. Thus, Otto Wolff, who looked toward the creation of a Franco-German customs union, and Peter Klöckner, who was a strong advocate of mutual participation schemes, refused to go along with Stinnes in early 1924, whereas Reusch, who took a hard line toward France and regretted the termination of passive resistance, continued to regard such ideas as treasonous.[5]

[4] Erdmann, *Rheinlandpolitik*, pp. 173–174 and 377–378.

[5] On Rechberg, see Eberhard von Vietsch, *Arnold Rechberg und das Problem der politischen West-Orientierung Deutschlands nach dem 1. Weltkrieg* (Koblenz, 1958), p. 73ff.; Erdmann, *Rheinlandpolitik*, pp. 183–184. Reusch stated his views with the usual extreme formulation in a letter to Cossmann of the *Süddeutsche Monatshefte* on February 17, 1923: "If an industrialist in the Ruhr would today find himself ready to permit the French to participate in his enterprises, he would be justly beaten to death by the local population and the workers. But hopefully, as in the past, so also in the future, there will be no one who would enter into such a shameless business." HA/GHH, Nr. 30019390/6. If there was a virtue Reusch had, it was that of consistency, and his views certainly had not changed by 1924.

Their posture strengthened the hand of Stresemann, who sought to block the plans of Adenauer, Hagen, and Stinnes at every turn. The Foreign Minister warned Chancellor Marx on January 16 that Stinnes, Vögler, and Silverberg were not speaking for the RdI, for the Krupp and Haniel concerns, or for the chemical industry, and that Stinnes' private negotiations with the French simply strengthened claims by the political opposition that the Weimar Republic had been transformed into a "Stinnes Republic." Stresemann's policy of putting off and delaying decisions was appropriate to the conclusion of the Ruhr controversy because, for a change, time was on the side of Germany in an international conflict. The costs of the prolonged Ruhr occupation were devastating French finances. As the franc depreciated, so did the political support for Poincaré, who became increasingly dependent on Anglo-American help for a solution. Stresemann, therefore, could veto any Franco-German industrial accord that was not contingent on French acceptance of the findings of the Dawes Committee that had been set up to determine Germany's capacity to pay, whereas Poincaré knew that the English would take a particularly negative view of French interests if a Franco-German heavy industrial bloc were formed. Thus, once again, French industry found itself restricted by the political leadership in Paris, while in Germany, where industry was far more influential, Stresemann was acting in conformity with most of the industrialists against the desperate plans of an isolated Stinnes.[6]

To be sure, the industrialists shared many of Stinnes' difficulties but not his desperation and willingness to gamble. Their financial problems were much more restricted in scope, and they were more prepared to press the government for aid and wait upon the arrival of international loans following the acceptance of a reparations plan than to engage in politically risky ventures and arrangements. The tone of German business practice was no longer to be set by Stinnes but rather by the new head of the Reichsbank, Hjalmar Schacht, as well as by more sober and conservative heavy industrialists, the Thyssens, Vögler, and Reusch. Between the issuance of the Rentenmark and April 1924, it did not seem that there was much of a difference in the banking practices of the late Havenstein and Schacht, because the Reichsbank pursued an easy credit policy that threatened to renew the inflation and that encouraged currency speculation. At the beginning of April 1924, however, Schacht reversed this policy, the only mistaken one he ever admitted to, and imposed severe credit restrictions. But these restrictions were practically coincident with the creation of a Gold Discount Bank subscribed to by the great German banks on the basis of a Bank of England loan, as well as the issuance

---

[6] Erdmann, *Rheinlandpolitik*, pp. 184ff. and 361–365.

449

of the Dawes Committee Report that opened up the prospect of large-scale American lending to Germany. Designed to counter the Rhenish Gold Discount Bank plan, the new institution was to become Schacht's instrument for granting and controlling industrial credits, as well as for strongly influencing the financial policies of the government.[7]

The credit restrictions of April 1924 did cause a crisis for the industrialists which was compounded by the renewal of the Micum Agreements in April and June and a four-week lockout and strike in the mining industry arising from industry's efforts to transfer the costs of the Micum Agreements to the workers. The problems were much alleviated by the government, however, which retreated from its plan of waiting upon the complete stabilization of its finances to begin covering the costs of the Micum burdens, and instead proceeded to cover the costs by surreptitious means. At the same time, the government not only provided heavy industry relief in the spring of 1924 by repaying the Micum coal deliveries at artificially high prices, supplying credits to "overcome strike damages," and granting tax reprieves or ordering liberal tax assessments, but it also began in the fall of 1924 to pay compensation for damages incurred during the Ruhr occupation. The payments, made on the basis of industry claims without real investigation or parliamentary surveillance, later became the subject of an inconclusive Reichstag investigation. Although it was known that the payments had been excessive, it was impossible to determine how excessive they were because even Reichert was refused concrete information supporting the claims by the concerns involved. These payments, which naturally were viewed as insufficient by the industrialists, supplied much needed relief to heavy industry between the stabilization and the influx of foreign loans to German industry, as illustrated by the SRSU, where it was reported on October 9, 1924, that "the situation of the heavy industry group has particularly improved because of the repayments from the Reich."[8]

Such financial relief, however, was no solution to the structural crisis faced by heavy industry, which was becoming increasingly aware of its overcapacity and poor competitive position and which was facing the inevitable *Sanierung* once orderly political and economic conditions were restored. The age of Stinnes was, indeed, over. The broader significance of Stinnes' death was perhaps most tellingly stated by Emil Kirdorf, for it was only after that event that Kirdorf fully appreciated "what extraordinary influence" Stinnes "exercised through his remarkable qualities and how blindly I followed him." Kirdorf had

[7] Claus-Dieter Krohn, *Stabilisierung und ökonomische Interessen. Die Finanzpolitik des Deutschen Reiches 1923–1927* (Düsseldorf, 1974), p. 54ff.

[8] *Ibid.*, p. 102ff., and the Freund study of the SRSU, SAA 54/Lm 123.

to confess "a feeling of being freed from a paralyzing pressure" with the necessity of having to think and speak for himself once again, and this made him suspect that "Hugo Stinnes, despite his remarkable qualities, was driven by a false conception of German political and economic conditions." Stinnes apparently had been convinced that Germany's reconstruction had to take place in collaboration with the Socialists and Centrists, as was reflected in his efforts to ally with labor in the ZAG, and Kirdorf easily reverted to his old position that collaboration with these "fatherlandless rascals" (*vaterlandslosen Gesellen*) was impossible. Kirdorf became no less skeptical about Stinnes' economic judgments:

> . . . he had until his end believed in the continuation of the lively demand for coal and iron and thereby promoted plant construction and measures which caused us severe financial and economic problems afterward. Here one may also doubt that this important and otherwise far-sighted man recognized his mistake in time and would have sought effective remedy such as we were compelled to seek without his help.[9]

The truth was that Kirdorf, the worshipper of Bismarck, the "responsible administrator of the property of others," the general director and syndicate builder, was far closer to the essential character and spirit of German heavy industry than the experimental, expansive Stinnes, who constantly sought to break out of a political, social, and economic reality he correctly sensed as having been drawn too rigidly by contemporary theory and practice. His successors in the leadership of heavy industry had never really been "at home" in the inflation from which they had also profited and, in most cases, had never really come to honest terms with the new sociopolitical order either. Within heavy industry, the mantle of leadership now passed to the securely based and economically well-prepared August and Fritz Thyssen, the technocratic rationalizer finally liberated from his bondage to Stinnes' speculative venturesomeness, Albert Vögler, and the overbearing, ingenious conservative organizer, Paul Reusch.

Discipline and organization became the order of the day, and heavy industry prepared for its impending crisis and sought to steer its structural crisis by putting an end to the "cartel-less period" and organizing with unparalleled intensity. On November 1, 1924, the entire German steel industry entered into the Crude Steel Cartel (*Rohstahlgemeinschaft*), which served as a parent quota cartel for a host of tightly organized A and B product syndicates that were to be

[9] Emil Kirdorf's unpublished "Erinnerungen 1847–1930," pp. 39–40, in GBAG Archiv, Nr. 200/01/3.

established during the ensuing months to encompass 90% of the industry's production as against the 43% that had been so organized in the prewar period. The lead in this particular organizational effort was taken by the Thyssens, whose reversal of position on the syndicalization of the industry was indicative of the changes wrought by war and inflation, as well as of the particular conditions existing in 1924–1925. The loss of the works in Lorraine and Luxemburg, as well as most of the works in Silesia, had made cartel formation simpler, just as the concentration process had led to the absorption of most of the independent works that had caused such difficulties before the war. At the same time, the concentration process had also attained a point of temporary relative balance among the concerns in which even the most modern and aggressive, such as Thyssen, lacked the capital to expand further or combine with other enterprises and were discouraged from ruthless competition by the poor market and the increasingly evident overcapacity of the industry. After a decade of war, inflation, and expansionary reorganization, the psychological disposition of the industrialists was geared toward stabilization in every sense, as well as toward a defensive posture, and this attitude was further inspired by the impending battle over iron tariffs, the severe competition anticipated from other steel producing nations, and the special and altogether too well understood advantages available to the French in 1924–1925 as a consequence of the depreciation of the franc.[10]

The same conditions that drove the iron and steel industry toward the creation of a rigid cartel structure for its own industry also drove it to seek some stable accommodation with the manufacturing industries. Stabilization set limits on the advantages heavy industry had been enjoying in its dealings with the manufacturers. Coal, iron, and steel were no longer scarce raw materials, and heavy industry had ceased to enjoy the same measure of large capital resources that exploitation of scarcity had brought with it. It needed to reserve the domestic market for its own use because of the increased international competition, and it would have to make concessions if it were to receive the political support necessary to institute high iron tariffs. The return to the *Solidarprotektionismus* of the prewar period was less simple in 1924 than in 1913 because, although an alliance with big agriculture could be and was eventually made by heavy industry, the political and economic power of the agrarians had seriously declined. Support from manufacturing was necessary, and why should the manufacturing industries support the iron tariff when heavy industry's portion of Ger-

[10] Paul Berkenkopf, *Die Neuorganisation der deutschen Grosseisenindustrie seit der Währungsstabilisierung* (Essen, 1928), pp. 11–48.

man exports had fallen from 22% in 1913 to 14.1% in 1922, while that of the manufacturing industries had risen from 66% to 82% during the same period.[11] There were powerful forces within the manufacturing industries that argued against strong tariff support for the iron industry on these grounds, and the French sought to play upon such differences in the Franco-German negotiations at the end of 1924.

The French efforts failed, however, just as had the German government's efforts to play upon the split between raw materials producers and manufacturers in 1919–1920. In the last analysis, the failure of the government to control heavy industry effectually in the revolution and inflation and its bungling and stumbling efforts at consumer protection had strengthened the tendencies toward mutual accommodation among the German producers and primary consumers at the expense of the "final consumers"—i.e., the real income of the German people. To be sure, vertical concentration and the penetration of the manufacturing trade associations had tamed the latter somewhat, and critics of the VDMA could well be satisfied with the dismissal of Frölich and Buttlar in early 1924, as well as with the severe reduction in the organizational apparatus and income of the VDMA brought about by the elimination of export control boards. However, the benefits of collective action by the manufacturers in the EWB had not been forgotten, and the loose Federation of Iron Consumers set up to represent the manufacturing interests in the EWB had an even more formidable successor in the Working Community of the Iron Finishing Industry (*Arbeitsgemeinschaft der Eisenverarbeitenden Industrie*—AVI) organized in March 1924. Furthermore, the new leading Business Manager of the VDMA, Karl Lange, understood the necessity of playing to the anti-heavy industrial constituency in the VDMA to maintain its membership and to inspire support for the renewal of his yearly contract.[12]

Although Lange, Raumer, Schrey, Funcke, and other manufacturing industry leaders supported friendly collaboration with heavy industry, therefore, they made it understood that such collaboration had to be purchased. Heavy industry appears also to have learned its own lessons, and the consequence was a series of agreements beginning at the end of 1924 that regulated the relations between the two sides until

[11] *Industrielles System*, p. 972. On the return to *Solidarprotektionismus*, see Dirk Stegmann, "Deutsche Zoll- und Handelspolitik 1924/25–1929 unter Berücksichtigung agrarischer und industrieller Interessen" in *ibid.*, pp. 499–513.

[12] See Ulrich Nocken, "Inter-Industrial Conflicts and Alliances as Exemplified by the AVI-Agreement" in *ibid.*, pp. 693–703, and the unpublished doctoral dissertation now being completed by the same author on the history of the AVI Agreement.

453

1941, the so-called AVI Agreements. In return for support of the iron tariff desired by heavy industry, the manufacturers were promised a rebate on iron used in manufacture for export that amounted to the difference between the world and the domestic price. These arrangements enabled both German industrial groups to bargain and support one another's efforts to procure concessions in the trade negotiations with the French in 1925–1926. The AVI Agreements brought to new heights the autonomous power of industry in the Weimar Republic, whose fundamental economic policies were being determined on the basis of interindustrial agreements, as well as direct international negotiations among industrialists largely independent of government interference and strongly supported by a large contingent of deputies in the Reichstag financed and influenced by industry. The agreements at once reflected and preserved the power of heavy industry in the Weimar Republic, which had the backing of the organized manufacturing interests.

Such backing was extremely useful when heavy industry was spurred on to attempt a solution of some of its structural problems by the stabilization crisis in the second half of 1925. This stabilization crisis struck the iron and steel industry with particular intensity for a variety of reasons. The industry gained little immediate advantage from the cartels and syndicates it had recently created or from the termination of the low tariff against Franco-Belgian imports because customers had stocked up in anticipation of the new domestic prices, demand was low in any case, and the international competition derived special advantages from inflation. The industry could expect little relief from government contracts because a return to the large prewar military contracts was out of the question, and the railroads and shipyards had overbuilt during the inflation. In 1924, Germany had more locomotives and railway cars than she had before the war, despite the wearing out of equipment and the heavy delivery of rolling stock to the Allies. Now, the government was reducing its procurement to a minimum, and heavy industry confronted the overcapacities and irrationalities produced by its hot-housed reconstruction during the inflation.[13]

Not surprisingly, the stabilization crisis brought down overextended empires built up during the inflation, the most famous of which was that of the deceased Hugo Stinnes, and it caused a limited turning away from vertical to horizontal concentration. The problems of the heavy industrial side of the SRSU, however, did not derive from the peculiar difficulties of Stinnes' own concern, although the SRSU and spokesmen for industry generally had a difficult time trying to prove to anxious foreign creditors that conditions within the Stinnes concern

[13] Berkenkopf, *Neuorganisation*, pp. 77–78; Krohn, *Stabilisierung*, p. 21.

were not "symptomatic" of conditions in heavy industry as a whole.[14] The new gold mark balances set up after the inflation indicated that German heavy industry had increased its capital when compared to 1913, although it is difficult to discover the extent to which this merely reflected absorption of smaller firms, elimination of debts, and a certain overstatement of capital in order to increase depreciation claims. Whatever the case, the ratios of nominal capital in 1913 to nominal capital in 1924 were 100:134 in the iron and steel industry, 100:136 in mining, and 100:130 in machine building. The gain, such as it was, was significantly less than that of the chemical industry, 100:227, but it demonstrated that it was not heavy industry that had lost out in the inflation. Rather, it was banking and trade, whose ratio of nominal capital in 1913 to that of 1924 was 100:30, and the host of small and medium-sized businesses that went into bankruptcy in 1924–1925 that bore the most serious consequences of war and inflation.[15]

The SRSU provides a good illustration of the situation. Between 1913 and 1925, the nominal capital of the heavy industrial member corporations had decreased from 400 to 367 million marks, but the reduction of capital is almost entirely accounted for by the GBAG, whose nominal capital had declined from 268 to 140 million marks. This decline would have been much greater had it not been for the inflation, however, because the GBAG was able to compensate somewhat for the diminution of its assets from 180 to 130 million marks resulting from losses under the Treaty because the value of its mortgages and loans had decreased from 74 to 13 million marks. Thanks to such debt reduction as well as new acquisitions and construction, therefore, the Rhein-Elbe Union had held its own through the inflation, although its relative position vis-à-vis its electrotechnical partners had declined, as evidenced in part by the fact that the capital of the Siemens group had increased from 177 million marks before the war to 273 million marks in 1925.[16]

If the SRSU did not survive the first years of stabilization, this was not because of the collapse of the Stinnes empire, but rather because the transitory conditions that had caused its creation no longer existed and other long-term tendencies were reasserting themselves. The Ruhr occupation hastened the dissolution of the partnership by "loosening

[14] See the attacks on Georg Bernhard by C. F. von Siemens of June–July 1925 in SAA 4/Lf 635/3 and Kastl to Vögler, July 8, 1925, in *ibid.*, Nachlass Köttgen, 11/Lf 131.

[15] Krohn, *Stabilisierung*, p. 21, Bresciani-Turroni, *Economics of Inflation*, pp. 282–283; Franz Eulenburg, "Die sozialen Wirkungen der Währungsverhältnisse," *Jahrbücher für Nationalökonomie und Statistik*, III, 67 (1924), pp. 748–794; Richard Lewinsohn, *Die Umschichtung der europäischen Vermögen* (Berlin, 1925).

[16] Bresciani-Turroni, *Economics of Inflation*, pp. 278–279, 283.

business relationships to an extraordinarily high degree" between the Ruhr firms and their electrotechnical partners in the SRSU.[17] Business conditions in 1925 did little to improve the situation, because heavy industry had too much to sell and manufacturing too little to buy. At the same time, the Siemens group had nothing more to gain from its heavy industrial partners in the continuing search for working capital. Indeed, the reverse was the case. The heavy industrial side benefitted greatly from Siemens' international connections, and it was Director Haller of Siemens who made the first connections between the American banking house of Dillon, Read, and Co. and the heavy industrial members of the SRSU that culminated in a 25 million dollar loan at the end of 1925. Increasingly, however, the two sides went their separate ways in negotiating with the Americans. This drifting apart was promoted by the increasingly evident sense of the inviability of the profit-pooling arrangements, as well as by the fact that the balance of interests and power that these arrangements were meant to fix were doomed to disruption by Rhein-Elbe's engagement in the massive trustification that culminated in the creation of the United Steel Works (*Vereinigte Stahlwerke*—Vestag) in April 1926. C. F. von Siemens understood the need for trustification in heavy industry and supported the establishment of the Vestag, which brought together the Rhein-Elbe group, Thyssen, Phoenix, and Rheinstahl, but he had no intention of seeing his own group become an "appendage" (*Anhängsel*) of heavy industry. Consequently, the SRSU was dissolved.[18]

The stabilization crisis of 1925, therefore, triggered but did not create the conditions leading to the founding of the Vestag and the dismantling of the SRSU. Furthermore, the turn from vertical to horizontal concentration after the inflation should not be exaggerated, because the SRSU was simply an extreme form of vertical concentration that in no way typified the more viable forms of vertical concentration that began before the war and continue in various forms in German heavy industry to this day. The major iron and steel concerns that suffered the most and effectively collapsed in 1925, Stumm and Rombach, were not victims of excessive vertical concentration but rather of an irrational, helter-skelter reconstruction of their holdings following their wartime losses and of mistaken financial policies. The same fate did not overtake the skillfully reconstructed empire of Klöckner, which exhibited significant vertical tendencies, nor the vertically organized

[17] Vögler to Köttgen, February 21, 1925, SAA, Nachlass Köttgen, 11/Lf 130.

[18] Siemens to Salomonsohn et al., October 26, 1925, *ibid.*, Ld/241 and Siemens to Vögler, December 27, 1925, *ibid.*, 4/Lf 635, and the Freund study in *ibid.*, 54/Lm 123.

GHH.[19] If there seemed to be a somewhat dramatic turn from vertical to horizontal concentration, it was above all one that had strong continuity with the past, as witnessed by the sentiment for trustification on the part of Thyssen as early as 1905, the Vögler-Beukenberg proposals during the war, Vögler's trustification and rationalization proposals of 1918 and 1920, and even Hasslacher's recognition in 1920 that a time would come when the great concerns would join together voluntarily because of economic rather than political necessities.

Hasslacher, Vögler, and Thyssen played leading roles in the negotiations that began in the summer of 1925 and culminated in the creation of the Vestag. They knew that rationalization was necessary if the German iron and steel industry was to restore its competitive position, and they recognized that the trustification effort would be necessary to attract the large credits needed for rationalization. Stabilization had restored some of the influence of the banks, who resumed their traditional role of promoting restraints on competition and concentration in heavy industry and who acted as intermediaries for the more powerful American financial interests investing in German industry. The involved industrialists well understood that "the creation of a new community of enterprises, which would probably lower costs quite a few Reichsmarks on the ton would, in the view of the great Berlin banks, create a creditor which would be viewed with confidence abroad so that it would be possible in any case to finance the further operation of the factories in the future."[20]

When establishing the Vestag, the involved heavy industrialists managed once again to make their cause that of the manufacturers and the state. A major difficulty in forming the Vestag was the fusion tax and other corporate taxes that Stinnes had tried to escape in his own efforts to form a single corporation out of his heavy industrial works. What had been denied Stinnes was granted those who founded the Vestag, and their success appears to have owed much to the background of friendly cooperation with manufacturing interests signalized by the AVI Agreements. In fact, the influential Hans von Raumer pushed Vögler in the fall of 1925 to be "firm" with the government and place the government "before the alternative of making the fusion

[19] Berkenkopf, *Neuorganisation*, p. 67ff.

[20] Report on the meeting of July 11, 1925, summoned by Hasslacher, Rheinstahl Archiv, Nr. 170/1/2/1. See also Berkenkopf, *Neuorganisation*, p. 86ff.; Kurt Gossweiler, "Die Vereinigten Stahlwerke und die Grossbanken. Eine Studie über das Verhältnis von Bank und Industriekapital in der Weimarer Republik und unter der faschistischen Diktatur (1926 bis 1936)" in *Jahrbuch für Wirtschaftsgeschichte* (1965), pp. 11–53; Manfred Nussbaum, "Unternehmenskonzentration und Investstrategie nach dem ersten Weltkrieg," *ibid.* (1974), pp. 51–75.

possible by tax relief or preventing it by lack of cooperation."[21] Raumer was convinced that the industries he represented had a great stake in rationalization as a means of lowering prices, and he performed notable services for heavy industry by lobbying with the government and winning over Social Democrats such as Rudolf Hilferding, for whom giant trusts such as IG Farben, also being created in its ultimate form at this time, and the Vestag were path-breaking exemplars of the "organized capitalism" that was paving the way for the evolution of Socialism. Heavy industry had every reason to follow Raumer's wise tactical suggestions: "The iron producing industry should not conduct the battle, because it will appear in the struggle solely as a financially interested party. The battle can only be led by the iron consuming industry, which is pressing for measures reducing the cost of its primary products. . . ."[22]

Quite naturally, Raumer and his colleagues did hope for cost and price reductions through the Vestag and its rationalization programs. Furthermore, the iron consumers were alarmed by the creation of an iron and steel trust second only to U.S. Steel, and the Vestag did conclude an agreement with the AVI not to expand further into manufacturing. Nevertheless, it is important to note that the public was being asked to pay the costs of correcting heavy industry's overexpansion during the war and inflation, as well as for the irrationalities of that overexpansion, and that the manufacturing industries stood behind heavy industry in this demand. Indeed, in their direct petitions to the government, Hasslacher and his colleagues, in a most familiar manner, shifted the responsibility for the condition of their industry entirely from their own shoulders to conditions, institutions, and groups for which they claimed no responsibility. "We are not to blame for the straits in which we find ourselves," Hasslacher told the Finance Minister. The lost war, the losses in Lorraine, the "false hours-of-work policy," the "excessive social burdens, taxes, and freight rates," the Ruhr occupation, Micum Agreements, and the "so-called Reich compensation," which he considered "totally inadequate," had made it impossible for heavy industry to make a profit. After the war, the Reich had required them to use the funds received as compensation to rebuild the lost capacities, as well as to house the workers required to bring coal, iron, and steel production back to the old levels. They had done their job, and "today it is clear that the productive possibilities in the West German coal and iron industry are not only sufficient

[21] Raumer to Vögler, September 12, 1925, Rheinstahl Archiv, Nr. 170/1/2/1.

[22] Raumer to Hasslacher, October 2, 1925, *ibid.*, Nr. 170, and R. Hilferding, *Die Aufgaben der Sozialdemokratie in der Republik. Hilferding auf dem Parteitag zu Kiel. Mai 1927* (Berlin, 1927), pp. 2–4.

to cover the entire domestic need of Germany and a large amount of export in addition, but that it is far too great to be operated in the old way." If they were not to collapse under the weight of their over-capacity and the "dead capital" invested in worker housing, and if the workers were to remain employed, then the government would have to support their trustification and rationalization in every possible way.[23]

When one considers these claims, it is difficult not to conclude that heavy industry's capacity for disingenuousness had kept pace with its capacity for overproduction. There was more than a little hypocrisy in the claim that the industry bore no responsibility for its circum-stances. The disaster of 1918 certainly bore some relationship to Ger-many's pursuit of unattainable war aims, not the least prominent of which was the annexation of Briey-Longwy, and it was heavy industry that had hammered into the government and public mind the notion that the ores of that region were essential for the well-being of the German iron industry. The reconstruction of the German iron and steel industry after 1918 proved that this was nonsense, and there is no bet-ter demonstration than Paul Reusch's commentary on his opposition to negotiations with French industry in June 1924: "These negotiations can only have the result of the French compelling us to take their ore and their semis. We need neither the one nor the other! The fairy tale that we are dependent upon minette must finally be knocked out of the heads of German officialdom."[24] Similarly, it was more than mildly hypocritical even to imply that the peculiarities of heavy industry's postwar reconstruction were the product of government pressures, and that heavy industry had not been free to propose alternatives. The reality was that heavy industry rejected an accommodation with its French counterpart on politically viable terms, encouraged the Ger-man intransigence that led to the Ruhr occupation, and then sup-ported the passive resistance policy in its most radical forms. At no time did heavy industry complain that it was creating the basis for future overproduction, and throughout the inflation its leaders empha-sized their accomplishments in restoring Germany's self-sufficiency in coal, iron, and steel. Although there was some recognition that ration-alization would be necessary one day, both government requests for a rationalization program, such as that made by Undersecretary Hirsch in September 1919, and those proposed by Vögler, were rejected.

[23] Hasslacher to the RFM, November 27, 1925, Rheinstahl Archiv, Nr. 170.

[24] Reusch to Reichert, June 15, 1924, HA/GHH, Nr. 400101222/7. The neces-sity of annexing Briey-Longwy had been hammered into the heads of the wartime German government by the VdESI in its *Zur Einverleibung der französisch-loth-ringischen Erzbecken in das deutsche Reichsgebiet* (Berlin, 1917).

459

Fundamentally, each concern was permitted to go its own way and place itself in as favorable a position as possible for the time when cartel, syndicate, and trust building would once again require organization among the concerns. The aggregate effect, however, was to enable the German iron and steel industry to rebuild itself along purely national lines and to reconstitute itself as the leader on the European continent, a position formally recognized in the quota arrangements of the International Steel Cartel created in September 1926.[25] Whether this restoration to supremacy was conducive to the well-being of Germany or Europe is, of course, another question, but it does show that German heavy industry had little justification for its constant claims to ill treatment and externally imposed inhibitions.

Furthermore, the available evidence does not suggest that the cartelization, trustification, and rationalization of the postinflationary period marked as significant a break with the anarchic conditions of the preceding period as might appear on the surface. To be sure, the twelve corporations of which the Vestag was eventually composed represented an unparalleled concentration of heavy industrial enterprises, and by the end of the 1920s its plants accounted for 50% of German pig iron production, 43% of crude steel production, and 40% of rolling mill production.[26] Although the present state of research does not permit definitive conclusions, there can be little doubt that the Vestag and the other concerns in heavy industry made major advances in rationalization in the late 1920s through the shutting down of old and unprofitable plants and a program of concentration of production and specialization that reduced duplication of effort, simplified administration and marketing, and thus achieved one of the major goals of rationalization—the reduction of fixed costs. However, the rationalization of the Vestag or the rationalization of other concerns did not constitute the rationalization of the industry. Just as the concerns duplicated one another's concern building efforts during the inflation, so they duplicated one another's rationalization efforts during the ensuing period. Although Hoesch and Krupp were involved in the first negotiations leading to the formation of the Vestag, the former was unwilling to provide confidential information about the return on its plants and dropped out of the negotiations, whereas the latter decided to maintain its independence and family character and turn to the Reich and the banks for financial succor.[27] Krupp played upon its special relationship to the government and threatened to sell 50% of its capital

[25] Bariéty in *Industrielles System*, pp. 552–568.

[26] Brady, *Rationalization*, p. 108. See also Ottfried Dascher, "Probleme der Konzernorganisation" in *Industrielles System*, pp. 127–134.

[27] Treue, *A-T-H*, p. 237ff.

stock to the English. Mannesmann, Klöckner, and Stumm also sought government subventions of various types, and only the Stumm group proved incapable of maintaining its independence of the Vestag.[28] The GHH maintained its independence throughout. Reusch opposed all direct government subventions, as distinct from high compensation for various losses arising from political circumstances, tax breaks, and government contracts, on the grounds that direct subventions "only lead to further wage and salary increases, quite aside from the fact that we thereby give up our independence."[29] As usual, Reusch could afford his virtue, a matter Klöckner did not omit to point out to him, because his coal mines were of such limited number and high quality as to permit the GHH to produce at low cost. Similarly, the GHH's transportation advantages made it secure enough to stay out of the Vestag, which Reusch viewed as an overcapitalized and excessively indebted trust that the GHH "does not need to fear."[30] The Vestag's rationalization efforts, therefore, were paralleled by those of its great competitors in the oligopolistic German steel industry, and there seems little reason to question Robert Brady's conclusion that the rationalization of the iron and steel industry involved "no such thing as planning for the industry" and that "as an industry, it is without plan, systematic organization or group objectives other than those common to all narrowly organized capitalistic enterprises."[31]

In fact, the evidence suggests that the organizations that did bind the various concerns to one another, namely, the cartels and syndicates, were peculiarly dysfunctional in taking advantage of the relative prosperity triggered by the English coal strike in the second half of 1926 and in responding to the slump that began in mid-1928 and was followed by the Great Depression of the ensuing years. When the cartels and syndicates were reestablished in 1924–1925, special consideration had to be shown to the large marketing organizations of the various concerns that had been built up during the inflation, and a consequence of this favoritism which manifested itself in rebates was that independent iron merchants were forced into dependence on the so-called

[28] Krohn, *Stabilisierung*, p. 212ff. Indeed, the Krupp firm jeopardized Stresemann's Locarno policy through its dealings with the English and thus forced the Reich to come to terms and thereby save it from absorption into the Vestag. See Karl Pohl, "Die Finanzkrise bei Krupp und die Sicherheitspolitik Stresemanns" in *Vierteljahrschrift für sozial- und Wirtschaftsgeschichte*, Vol. 61, No. 4 (1974), pp. 505–525.

[29] Reusch to Klöckner, November 27, 1925, HA/GHH, Nr. 400101290/45; see also the correspondence with Julius Curtius of December 1925 in *ibid.*, Nr. 400-1012000/15.

[30] Reusch to Richard Haniel, January 27, 1926, *ibid.*, Nr. 400101200/7.

[31] Brady, *Rationalization*, p. 138.

works or cartel merchants in such a manner that all the iron and steel merchants lost much of their capacity to respond to market conditions and thus fulfill their primary economic function. Instead, they "pressed the consumers into a rigid price system through differing classifications, premiums or price surcharge schedules."[32] During the boom of 1926–1928, the industrialists cried that the boom was purely quantitative and that the rationalization taking place had not progressed sufficiently to cover the losses incurred through high wages, social burdens, and taxes. Looking back at the situation in 1931, however, there was some admission that the Labor Ministry was not the only source of the "profitless prosperity" of the late 1920s and that "we ought not to forget the other side. In 1926, 1927, and 1928 we produced ourselves to exhaustion, but we only benefited quantitatively from the boom, not in terms of prices. If we had a more flexible price system at that time, it would have gone better with us and we would have made money."[33] As in boom, so in bust, the rigid cartel and syndicate pricing structure made things worse. Insofar as it did not break down business morality by encouraging merchants to receive and give bribes in order to sell and buy at reduced prices, it served to depress still further an already depressed market. As one director candidly asked in connection with the discussions among the industrialists in 1931 concerning the need to restore a measure of flexibility to the iron market: "Is it not unfortunate that one can hardly speak of the marketing (*Handeln*) of iron any more, but only of that regulation (*Bewirtschaftung*) which we otherwise detest so much?"[34] The historian might go further in his questioning. Was the Crude Steel Syndicate any more or less harmful and any more or less of a control of the iron trades than the Iron Trades Federation, and had the industrialists justified the freedom from controls they had won back after the inflation?

Naturally, the heavy industrialists did not discuss their mistakes much in public, and they certainly discouraged such discussion on the part of others. Furthermore, the historian must be cautious when criticizing their decisions not to take excessive advantage of hindsight or to treat the German heavy industrialists entirely in isolation from the general interwar economic situation. As was noted at the beginning of this study, the steel industry was hit particularly hard by the relative economic stagnation of the interwar period and, in the last analysis, the problems of the industry were international in character. The behavior of the German branch of the industry was not very different

[32] See the memorandum by Director Klemme of July 30, 1931, in HA/GHH, Nr. 400001/11.

[33] Meeting of September 10, 1931, in *ibid.*, Nr. 4001012003/18.

[34] Memorandum of July 30, 1931, *ibid.*, Nr. 400001/11.

from that of its counterparts in other major producing countries.[35] Furthermore, if the present European Coal and Steel Community marks a major improvement in the atmosphere and some of the practices relating to the organization of European heavy industry, it must also be recognized that these industries continue to remain fundamentally national in character and that overcapacity continues to be a problem. Prosperity and real economic growth over a sustained period following the World War II have provided the industry with advantages it never enjoyed in the interwar period.[36] The industrialists never had enough time during the Weimar period to benefit fully from the rationalization measures they undertook nor to assimilate fully to new economic and sociopolitical doctrines in the manner of their successors after 1945. These very considerations, however, would also make it anachronistic to argue that their adaptability during the inflation, their support of high employment policies, and their economic expansionism were anything more than economic opportunism designed to procure the most favorable advantages for themselves and political opportunism designed to hold back the forces of revolution until they could be dealt with under calmer circumstances. Fundamentally, they were no different than their counterparts in Europe and America, who took their stabilization, depression, and high unemployment in 1920–1921, while the Germans, for specific and very good economic and political reasons, took theirs in 1924–1925. The governmental and industrial supporters of the German inflation, if one leaves aside truly speculative personalities such as Stinnes, whose willingness to try anything was a model only for what his colleagues were prepared to do in sheer desperation, would be more at home with the economic policies of Brüning and Hoover than with those of Keynes, Roosevelt, or even the early Hitler.

Although it is possible to understand this incapacity of the German heavy industrialists to leap over their own economic and sociopolitical shadows or transcend the conditions under which they operated, however, it is necessary to record and contemplate the pernicious consequences of their success in retaining their economic power and strengthening it during the inflation in such a manner that they persisted in dominating the industrial politics of the Weimar Republic. Just as they had led and directed the periodic mobilizations of industry against liberal economic and social policies before the war and during the war, so had they organized the doctrinal mobilization and the prac-

[35] Brady, *Rationalization*, p. 127, and Svennilson, *Growth and Stagnation*, pp. 136–139.

[36] See J. E. S. Hayward, "Steel" in Raymond Vernon, ed., *Big Business and the State. Changing Relations in Western Europe* (Cambridge, Mass., 1974), chap. 12.

tical attack on the more progressive socioeconomic policies of the Weimar Republic that was truly launched with the deliberations of an economic program in the RdI in 1922 and that persisted year in and year out until the Republic succumbed to its many enemies in 1933. Before the war, the heavy industrialists had yielded to the agrarian Junkers in claiming exceptional political status, but after 1918, heavy industry laid claim to political primacy for *die Wirtschaft* and assumed a role in diplomatic negotiations, domestic political affairs, and administrative functions that has no real parallel in other capitalist societies of the period despite efforts to characterize it as a part of the "Americanization" of German life. Ernst Troeltsch was mistaken in thinking that there was a parallel in the way in which American business influenced American political life because he did not understand the consensus on the role of business in American life nor the different character of the "State" in America, but he well understood the very peculiar quality of German industry's political claims. As he wrote in 1922:

> The industrial leaders, among whom one should certainly not think of Stinnes alone, step forward today as those who, with their private credit, their organizational skill, their leadership ability, and their ability to command, can alone remedy the emergency. They wish the actual power and command alongside a powerless phantom democratic government. The state shall be constructed upon and dissolved into nothing more than private contractual relationships. In its tendency, it is comparable with the birth of the feudal and corporate limitations upon the princes, conceived not in the medieval, but rather in the ultramodern American sense. . . .[37]

The heavy industrialists were, indeed, the worthy successors of their sometime agrarian allies, and just as the Junkers had translated the structural crisis of German agriculture into one of the most fundamental and determining factors of German politics after 1873, so heavy industry made its structural crisis the stuff of German politics in the Weimar Republic. Both groups shared the same "feudal" tendencies, which were spelled out with regard to heavy industry in economic terms by the liberal economist Moritz Bonn in 1926:

> The more the technical development of modern industry compels it to an increasing tying of its capital in fixed plant, the more its situation, and with it also its notions of political economy, resemble the ways of thinking of the large landowners with a purely feudal past. The coal barons and iron and steel magnates seek to apply the same

[37] Troeltsch, *Spektator-Briefe*, p. 241.

authoritarian feudalism to their workers with which the landowners approached their small holders in the past. . . .

. . . influential groups in capitalism return in their modes of thought to the medieval system of the just price. They assume that an enterprise has the moral right to earn its costs, since the expenditure and employment of a specific amount of capital carries with it the right to a fixed, unchangeable and irreducible profit. If the profit diminishes then either the powers of the state are called upon or the attempt is made to shift the reduced earnings to wages without seeking to repair the losses through changes in the operation of the plant. This kind of capitalism considers there to be a right to a constant return as the self-understood principle of the economic order, while at the same time it rejects the right to a social wage with righteous indignation.[38]

Just as the agrarian Junkers had understood how to organize, agitate, and use pseudodemocratic techniques to achieve their goals, so the heavy industrialists again proved worthy successors in their influence of the press and mass media, infiltration of political parties, and support of paramilitary and other mass organizations in the effort to achieve their goals. Although it is perfectly true that economic power does not easily or automatically translate itself into political influence and did not do so in the Weimar Republic, it is misleading to stop at this point without recognizing that heavy industry was at the very least a crucial veto group in the Weimar Republic, as well as a major destabilizing force politically.

Throughout the period between 1924 and 1933, heavy industry systematically agitated against social reform, particularly the eight-hour day, and the trade unions, and promoted political movements designed to move the Weimar Republic in a more authoritarian direction. Just as Thyssen had taken the lead in cartel formation and Vögler in rationalization programs, so Reusch took the initiative beginning in December 1923 in the organization of heavy industry's interest group operations. In 1924, he inspired a regrouping of the various heavy industrial interest organizations which, if it did not eliminate the organizational irrationalities and duplication of effort that the industrialists found so insupportable in the government, nevertheless magnified the voice of heavy industry in the Ruhr and Germany. The chosen instrument for this purpose was a revitalized *Langnamverein* with Reusch as its chairman and the notoriously conservative Max Schlenker, who was imported from the Saar to be its business manager and supplement the activities of Reichert in the VdESI. Even this

[38] Moritz Bonn, *Schicksal*, pp. 78–79.

465

formidable concentration of heavy industrial influence was insufficient in Reusch's view, however, and at the turn of 1927–1928, he created the *Ruhrlade*, an exclusive club of twelve leading industrialists which met in formal attire once a month to discuss the major problems facing industry, coordinate their efforts, and, wherever possible, define the position they would take in the industrial interest groups and organizations.[39]

It was Reusch and Vögler who persistently claimed to speak for industry after 1924, and they did so in the manner described by Moritz Bonn. At the very height of the boom in 1926–1927, Reusch demanded pessimism from his colleagues with the slogans that "wage increases, taxes and social burdens eat up all the improvements that have been made in the course of time," and that "It is really no pleasure to be in industry in the German fatherland these days."[40] When Peter Klöckner conveyed different sentiments in an optimistic speech in 1926, Reusch and Vögler were outraged by Klöckner's incapacity to take into account the "sociopolitical burdens which stand before us in the very near future" and his indirect encouragement of the left to think that it could raise demands because of the improved business conditions.[41] They launched such a severe attack on Klöckner that the latter resigned from the *Langnamverein*. Similarly, Reusch, Vögler, Vielhaber, and other like-minded heavy industrialists raised more polite but no less strong opposition to Paul Silverberg's famous speech of September 4, 1926, at the RdI meeting in Dresden in which Silverberg advocated support for the Republic and a settlement of differences between industry and organized labor through a renewal of the *Arbeitsgemeinschaft*. Silverberg, like Klöckner, shared most of the views of their fellow heavy industrialists on the eight-hour day and other "social burdens," but they were prepared to take their chances with a more conciliatory posture such as that widely advocated by the newer

[39] Bernd Weisbrod, "Zur Form schwerindustrieller Interessenvertretung in der zweiten Hälfte der Weimarar Republik" in *Industrielles System*, pp. 674–692, and Henry Turner, "The *Ruhrlade*: Secret Cabinet of Heavy Industry in the Weimar Republic," *Central European History*, 3 (September 1970), pp. 195–228. The predecessor of the *Ruhrlade* was the so-called *Montagsgesellschaft* Reusch had set up after the war following a model provided by Kurt Sorge in Magdeburg. Reusch let the admissions policy of the earlier organization get out of hand, however, and he found himself with a group of some forty-five people which proved unwieldy for his purposes. He let the organization lapse in 1923.

[40] Report to the GHH Stockholders, November 1, 1927, HA/GHH, Nr. 400101-2002/1.

[41] See the Reusch-Vögler correspondence of November 1926 in *ibid.*, Nr. 40010-1290/27.

and less structurally troubled industries. Thanks to the counterattack by Reusch and Vögler, however, such promise as was present in Silverberg's conversion to a far less belligerent stance than the one he had taken in 1922 was never realized.[42]

Reusch and Vögler in fact sought battle with the trade unions. The former had always opposed the *Arbeitsgemeinschaft* and the latter, like Kirdorf, had been liberated to pursue his technocratic inclinations by Stinnes' death. They became strong advocates of the *Werksgemeinschaft* idea, a reconstitution of the old company union and nonstriking union policy of heavy industry along more modern lines, and Vögler sought to tie the old yellow union principle with the new rationalization efforts by assuming leadership of the Institute for Technical Labor Training (*Deutsches Institut für Technische Arbeitsschulung—DINTA*).[43] More important, beginning in late 1927, they organized and launched a major offensive against organized labor and the political left, ostensibly over the usual wage and hours-of-work questions, but actually with the broader object of breaking the system of compulsory arbitration and the political and social policies with which it was connected. This mobilization, comparable to that of the employers in 1922–1923, culminated in the worst labor conflict in the history of the Republic, the Great Lockout of 250,000 workers in the Ruhr in the fall of 1928. In this struggle, as in October 1923, heavy industry challenged the basic social legislation of the Republic and achieved results, again at times violating the law, in which they accomplished their goals sufficiently well to procure new advantages and with sufficient limitations to have continued cause for complaint. As in the brief "prosperity," so in the Great Depression, the basic posture of heavy industry was that labor had to bear the costs of reduced profitability and the burdens of economic disaster. Just as they locked labor out in 1928 to prevent it from implementing the goal of raising the wages of labor, so they broke with Brüning in December 1931 when this once-favored Chancellor sought to reduce prices as well as wages.[44]

The precise contribution of heavy industry to the rise of Hitler in

[42] Dirk Stegmann, "Die Silverberg Kontroverse 1926. Unternehmerpolitik zwischen Reform und Restauration" in Hans-Ulrich Wehler, ed., *Sozialgeschichte Heute. Festschrift für Hans Rosenberg zum 70. Geburtstag* (Göttingen, 1974), pp. 594–611.

[43] On the DINTA, see Brady, *Rationalization*, p. 120.

[44] On the lockout, see Preller, *Sozialpolitik*, pp. 403–406; Ernst Fraenkel, "Der Ruhreisenstreit 1928–1929 in historisch-politischer Sicht" in *Staat, Wirtschaft und Politik in der Weimarer Republik. Festschrift für Heinrich Bruning* (Berlin, 1967), pp. 97–117. The Reusch papers in the GHH contain voluminous material from which one can trace in detail the course of the employer offensive of 1927–1928.

both financial and political terms remains hotly debated and need not be discussed here.[45] No responsible historian, however, would argue against the proposition that heavy industry, by and large, supported the conservative opposition to the Republic throughout most of its final crisis and that, at the very least, it favored an authoritarian reconstruction of the constitution. Insofar as it supported or came to terms with Hitler, it undoubtedly received a good deal more authoritarianism than it bargained for. The harmful role played by heavy industry in the political and socioeconomic history of the Weimar Republic, however, and its domination of industrial politics despite its relative diminution of economic power as compared to that of the newer industrial branches would not have been possible had it not been for the advantages it derived from the war and inflation and the unwillingness and inability of the revolutionary and postrevolutionary regimes to challenge the pretended omniscience of the heavy industrialists, to take advantage of the conflicts within German industry as a whole, and to shift the balance in favor of more progressive elements. The heavy industrialists were correct when they accused the Weimar regimes of lacking authority.

Times have changed, of course. The successors of the iron and steel industrialists discussed in this book seem to have accepted political democracy and free labor unions as permanent fixtures, just as there is a general recognition of the necessity of government interference in the economic process and regulation. Assuming, however, that one does not support the view that the problems of capitalism are best cured by its elimination, and this writer does not, then there is a need to confront certain problems in the functioning of contemporary capitalism that are distressingly similar to those raised in connection with the historical situation discussed in this book. Quite aside from the fact that, whatever the advances in the theoretical understanding of inflation, we are unable to control it or to find ways out of it that do not involve depression and high unemployment, there is also the repeated experience, albeit in very different ways, of producers of scarce raw materials being in a position to maximize their advantages to the detriment of the general welfare and the persistent difficulty, as in the case of the oil companies, of forming an accurate picture of their financial position. At the same time, the German heavy industrialists certainly were not the last industrialist group to claim a "just" return on capital falsely and inefficiently invested, and it is difficult not to think that their "feudal" behavior was peculiarly modern in the light

[45] See Henry A. Turner, Jr., *Faschismus und Kapitalismus in Deutschland* (Göttingen, 1972), pp. 9–32, and Dirk Stegmann, "Zum Verhältnis von Grossindustrie und Nationalsozialismus 1930–1933," *Archiv für Sozialgeschichte*, 13 (1973), pp. 399–482.

of subsequent developments, which have hardly been limited to Germany. If there has been a major change, it is that now industry and labor often collaborate in passing the costs on to the general public rather than industry seeking to place the burdens almost exclusively on labor. The *Arbeitsgemeinschaft* has become much less formal and much more real. Finally, the Weimar experience raised in extreme form persistent problems of the economic activity of the state in pluralistic democracies, namely those of finding modes of regulation that do not persistently grant the wishes of those being regulated and of exercising authority without becoming authoritarian.

APPENDIXES

APPENDIX ONE

Dollar Exchange Rate of the Paper Mark and the Gold Mark in Berlin, 1914–1923
(In monthly averages)

1. *Paper Marks*

	1914	1915	1916	1917	1918	1919	1920	1921	1922	1923
January	4,21	4,61	5,35	5,79	5,21	8,20	64,80	64,91	191,81	17,972
February	4,20	4,71	5,38	5,87	5,27	9,13	99,11	61,31	207,82	27,918
March	4,20	4,82	5,55	5,82	5,21	10,39	83,89	62,45	284,19	21,190
April	4,20	4,86	5,45	6,48	5,11	12,61	59,64	63,53	291,00	24,457
May	4,20	4,84	5,22	6,55	5,14	12,85	46,48	62,30	290,11	47,670
June	4,19	4,88	5,31	7,11	5,36	14,01	39,13	69,36	317,14	109,966
July	4,20	4,91	5,49	7,14	5,79	15,08	39,48	76,67	493,22	353,412
August	4,19	4,92	5,57	7,14	6,10	18,83	47,74	84,31	1,134,56	4,620,455
September	4,17	4,85	5,74	7,21	6,59	24,05	57,98	104,91	1,465,87	98,860[a]
October	4,38	4,85	5,70	7,29	6,61	26,83	68,17	150,20	3,180,96	25,260[b]
November	4,61	4,95	5,78	6,64	7,43	38,31	77,24	262,96	7,183,10	2,193,600[b]
December	4,50	5,16	5,72	5,67	8,28	46,77	73,00	191,93	7,589,27	4,200,000[b]
Average	4,28	4,86	5,52	6,58	6,01	19,76	63,06	104,57	1,885,78	534,914[b]

2. Gold Marks (4.198 GM = $1.00)

	1914	1915	1916	1917	1918	1919	1920	1921	1922	1923
January	1,002	1,10	1,27	1,38	1,24	1,95	15,43	15,46	45,69	4,281
February	1,001	1,12	1,28	1,40	1,26	2,17	23,60	14,60	49,51	6,650
March	1,000	1,15	1,32	1,39	1,24	2,48	19,97	14,87	67,70	5,048
April	0,999	1,16	1,30	1,54	1,22	3,00	14,20	15,13	69,32	5,826
May	0,999	1,15	1,24	1,56	1,22	3,06	11,07	14,83	69,11	11,355
June	0,998	1,16	1,26	1,69	1,28	3,34	9,32	16,51	75,62	26,202
July	0,999	1,17	1,31	1,70	1,38	3,59	9,40	18,26	117,49	84,186
August	0,998	1,17	1,33	1,70	1,45	4,48	11,37	20,07	270,26	1,100,632
September	0,997	1,16	1,37	1,72	1,57	5,73	13,81	24,98	349,18	23,549[a]
October	1,043	1,16	1,36	1,74	1,57	6,39	16,23	35,76	757,73	6,017[b]
November	1,097	1,18	1,38	1,65	1,77	9,12	18,39	62,64	1,711,08	522,286[b]
December	1,072	1,23	1,36	1,35	1,97	11,14	17,38	45,72	1,807,83	1,000,000[b]
Average	1,017	1,16	1,32	1,57	1,43	4,70	15,01	24,91	449,21	127,360[b]

[a] In thousands.
[b] In millions.

Source: Statistisches Reichsamt, *Wirtschaft und Statistik. Sonderheft. Zahlen zur Geldentwertung in Deutschland 1914 bis 1923* (Berlin, 1925), p. 10.

Production of Coal, Pig Iron, and Crude Steel in Germany,
Great Britain, France, and Belgium, 1913–1929
(In thousands of tons)

A. Coal

Year	Germany[a]	Percentage Produced by the Ruhr[b]	Great Britain	France	Belgium
1913	190,109	60.1	292,044	40,051	22,842
1914	161,385	60.8	269,908	26,841	16,714
1915	146,868	58.9	257,270	18,856	14,178
1916	159,170	59.2	260,490	20,542	16,863
1917	167,747	59.0	252,488	27,757	14,931
1918	160,822	59.5	231,404	24,941	13,891
1919	116,707	60.7	233,467	21,546	18,483
1920	140,766	62.6	233,106	24,293	22,389
1921	145,826	64.4	165,782	28,212	21,750
1922	141,205	68.5	253,613	31,141	21,209
1923	71,508	58.5	280,431	37,679	22,922
1924	132,801	70.9	271,405	44,019	23,362
1925	145,612	71.7	247,079	47,097	23,097
1926	158,977	70.6	128,305	51,392	25,260
1927	167,195	70.6	255,264	51,792	27,551
1928	163,968	69.9	241,283	51,365	27,578
1929	177,020	69.8	262,046	53,780	26,940

B. Pig Iron

Year	Germany[a]	Percentage Produced by the Ruhr[b]	Great Britain	France	Belgium
1913	19,309	42.5	10,482	4,207	2,485
1914	14,390	45.9	9,006	2,691	1,454
1915	11,529	44.8	8,794	5,586	68
1916	13,314	43.2	9,194	1,489	128
1917	13,142	45.1	9,572	1,735	8
1918	11,755	49.5	9,185	1,307	—
1919	6,284	61.9	7,517	2,412	250
1920	7,044	63.4	8,137	3,468	1,113
1921	7,845	71.9	2,616	3,308	863
1922	9,396	75.9	4,902	5,147	1,588
1923	4,941	59.2	7,560	5,468	2,148
1924	7,833	80.0	7,425	7,693	2,844
1925	10,089	79.3	6,362	8,505	2,543
1926	9,636	80.6	2,498	9,430	3,368
1927	13,089	79.1	7,410	9,326	3,709
1928	11,804	77.7	6,716	10,072	3,857
1929	13,239	83.0	7,711	10,362	4,041

C. Crude Steel

Year	Germany[a]	Percentage Produced by the Ruhr[b]	Great Britain	France	Belgium
1913	17,148	59.0	7,787	4,687	2,467
1914	15,620	53.9	7,918	2,656	1,396
1915	13,288	57.5	8,688	1,088	99
1916	16,183	56.6	9,345	1,952	98
1917	15,288	61.2	9,717	2,196	9
1918	13,871	62.6	9,539	1,780	10
1919	7,021	75.7	7,894	—	328
1920	8,404	73.3	9,067	—	1,233
1921	9,840	76.6	3,703	—	776
1922	11,531	79.8	5,881	—	1,540
1923	6,208	63.1	8,618	5,302	2,297
1924	9,703	83.1	8,333	6,670	2,875
1925	12,051	82.1	7,504	7,464	2,549
1926	12,226	80.8	3,654	8,617	3,339
1927	16,123	80.5	9,243	8,306	3,680
1928	14,318	80.1	8,656	9,479	3,905
1929	16,023	82.2	9,791	9,716	4,110

[a] Until 1918 including Alsace-Lorraine, until 1919 including Upper-Silesia.
[b] Rhineland and Westphalia excluding the Saarland, Siegerland, and the Dill region.

Source: Paul Wiel, *Wirtschaftsgeschichte des Ruhrgebietes. Tatsachen und Zahlen* (Essen, 1970), pp. 127, 227, 238.

Bibliography

UNPUBLISHED SOURCES

No attempt will be made here to list by number and title all the volumes of documents employed in this study or even to list all the collections employed in any given archive. Instead, the major collections will be cited or generally indicated.

State Archives

1. Badisches Generallandesarchiv Karlsruhe
   Rep. 237 Finanzministerium
2. Bayerisches Hauptstaatsarchiv München, Abt. I. Geheimes Staatsarchiv
   Wirtschaftsministerium (MWi)
   Handelsministerium (MH)
3. Bayerisches Hauptstaatsarchiv München, Abt. IV. Kriegsarchiv.
   Important materials on the demobilization in the collection on the Bavarian Kriegsamt.
4. Bundesarchiv Koblenz (BA)
   R 2 Reichsfinanzministerium
   R 11 Deutscher Industrie und Handelstag
   R 13/I Verein deutscher Eisen- und Stahlindustrieller (VdESI)
   R 38 Reichsminister für Wiederaufbau
   R 43 Reichskanzlei
   R 85 Handelspolitische Abteilung des Auswärtigen Amtes
   Nachlässe:
   Karl Jarres
   Günter von Le Suire
   Wichard von Moellendorff
   Alexander Rüstow
   Friedrich Saemisch
   Paul Silverberg
5. Deutsches Zentralarchiv Potsdam (DZA Potsdam)
   Reichswirtschaftsministerium (RWM)
   Reichsarbeitsministerium (RAM)
   Reichswirtschaftsrat (RWR)
   Zentralarbeitsgemeinschaft der industriellen und gewerblichen Arbeitgeber und Arbeitnehmer Deutschlands (ZAG)

477

6. Doe Library, Berkeley
   Nachlass Gustav Stresemann (Microfilm)
   Reichskabinettsprotokolle (Microfilm)
7. Geheimes Staatsarchiv (Stiftung Preussischer Kulturbesitz) in Berlin-Dahlem
   Rep. 300. Reports of Arndt von Holtzendorff to the Hapag (now in the BA)

Private Archives

8. Archiv und Bibliothek des Vereins deutscher Maschinenbauanstalten, Frankfurt am Main
   Its most important unpublished holding is "Der Deutsche Maschinenbau 1890–1923," to which are appended important protocols and documents pertaining to the VDMA.
9. Archiv und Bibliothek, Zentralverband der Elektrotechnischen Industrie e.V., Frankfurt am Main
   M. Frese, "Annalen zur Geschichte des Zentralverbandes der deutschen elektrotechnischen Industrie und der Wirtschaftsgruppe Elektroindustrie" (unpublished history of the Zendei).
10. August-Bebel Institut, Berlin
    ADGB-Restakten
11. August-Thyssen-Hütte AG, Duisburg-Hamborn (A.T.H. Archiv)
    A small collection of documents from the Fritz Thyssen Sekretariat and useful volumes on the Stahlwerksverband, the Swedish ore question, and other isolated but important matters.
12. Bergbau Archiv und Museum, Bochum (Bergbau Archiv)
    Bestand 13   Verein für die bergbaulichen Interessen
    Bestand 15   Fachgruppe Bergbau
13. Brinckmann, Wirtz & Co., Hamburg
    Max Warburg Papers
14. Deutsche Bank Archiv, Frankfurt am Main
    A small and scattered selection which nevertheless contains some very illuminating material on the banks and major concerns.
15. Deutsches Industrie-Institut, Köln
    Nachlass Oscar Funcke
    Papers pertaining to the RdI and other industrial organizations.
16. Friedrich-Wilhelms-Hütte Archiv, Mülheim Ruhr
    A very important collection of papers that includes significant materials on the Deutsch-Lux concern, the Pig Iron Syndicate, the EWB, and the SRSU.
17. Gelsenberg AG, Essen (GBAG Archiv)
    Restnachlass Emil Kirdorf, his unpublished memoirs and papers pertaining to the GBAG.

18. Hapag-Lloyd AG, Hamburg (Hapag Archiv)
    Nachlass Wilhelm Cuno
19. Historisches Archiv der Gutehoffnungshütte Oberhausen (HA/GHH)
    Nachlass Paul Reusch
    A vast collection of company papers dealing with its own affairs as well as with the concern, industrial and interest group organizations, and political affairs.
20. MAN Werksarchiv Augsburg
    Nachlass Emil Guggenheimer
    Papers pertaining to the MAN as well as to industrial organizations such as the RdI and the VDMA.
21. MAN Werksarchiv Nürnberg
    Papers pertaining to the activities of Anton von Rieppel as well as to the firm and various industrial organizations.
22. Metallgesellschaft AG, Historisches Archiv, Frankfurt am Main
    Privatbriefe Richard Merton
23. Rheinstahl Archiv, Essen
    A small but illuminating collection of documents pertaining to Rheinstahl itself, the activities of Hasslacher, and Otto Wolff.
24. Werksarchiv Bayer-Leverkusen
    Autographensammlung Carl Duisberg
25. Werksarchiv Krupp, Essen (WA Krupp)
    Nachlass Otto Wiedfeldt
    Papers pertaining to Krupp and various industrial organizations.
26. Werner von Siemens Institut für Geschichte des Hauses Siemens, München (SAA)
    Nachlässe: Carl Friedrich von Siemens, Arnold Köttgen, Max Haller
    Major collections pertaining to the SRSU, Zendei, and industrial and political organizations and problems.

PUBLISHED SOURCE MATERIALS, REFERENCE WORKS, NEWSPAPERS, AND PERIODICALS

Published Source Materials and Reference Works

Akten der Reichskanzlei. Weimarer Republik. Das Kabinett Scheidemann 13. Februar bis 20. Juni 1919. ed. Hagen Schulze (Boppard am Rhein, 1971).

Das Kabinett Müller I. 27. März 1920 bis 21. Juni 1920. ed. Martin Vogt (Boppard am Rhein, 1971).

Das Kabinett Fehrenbach. 25. Juni 1920 bis 4. Mai 1921. ed. Peter Wulf (Boppard am Rhein, 1972).

Die Kabinette Wirth I und II. 10. Mai 1921 bis 26. Oktober 1921. 26. Oktober 1921 bis 22. November 1922. ed. Ingrid Schulze-Bidlingmaier, 2 vols. (Boppard am Rhein, 1973).

Das Kabinett Cuno. 22. November 1922 bis 12. August 1923. ed. Karl Heinz Harbeck (Boppard am Rhein, 1968).

Die Kabinette Marx I und II. 30. November 1923 bis 3. Juni 1924, 3. Juni 1924 bis 15. Januar 1925. ed. Günter Abramowski (Boppard am Rhein, 1973).

Handbuch der Politik. ed. Gerhard Anschütz *et al.*, 3rd ed. (Munich, 1921ff.).

Michaelis, Herbert, Ernst Schraepler, und Günter Scheel, *Ursachen und Folgen. Vom deutschen Zusammenbruch 1918 und 1945 bis zur staatlichen Neuordnung Deutschlands in der Gegenwart*, 7 vols., (Berlin, 1961ff.).

Nekrologe aus dem Rheinisch-Westfälischen Industriegebiet Jahrgang 1939–1951 (Schriften der Volks- und Betriebswirtschaftlichen Vereinigung im Rheinisch-Westfälischen Industriegebiet) (Düsseldorf, 1955).

Reichsgesetzblatt, 1916ff.

Rheinisch Westfälische Wirtschaftsbiographien, ed. Provinzialinstitut für Westfälische Landes- und Volkskunde, Historische Kommission, Vol. 1ff. (Münster, 1937–1967).

Schulthess' Europäischer Geschichtskalender (Munich, 1918ff.).

Statistik des Deutschen Reiches. Reichsamt für Statistik (Berlin, 1914ff.).

Verhandlungen und Berichte. Ausschuss zur Untersuchung der Erzeugungs- und Absatzbedingungen der Deutschen Wirtschaft (15. April 1926 bis 1. Oktober 1930) (Berlin, 1927ff.).

Verhandlungen der Verfassungsgebenden Deutschen Nationalversammlung, Vols. 1–18 (Berlin, 1919ff.).

Verhandlungen des Reichstags. 1. Wahlperiode ff., Stenographische Berichte, Vol. 344ff. (Berlin, 1920ff.).

Newspapers and Periodicals

Archiv für Sozialwissenschaft
Bank Archiv
Deutsche Bergwerks-Zeitung
Deutsche Metallarbeiterzeitung
Frankfurter Zeitung
Kölnische Zeitung
Metall und Erz
Mitteilungen des Kriegsausschusses der deutschen Industrie
Mitteilungen des Reichsverbandes der deutschen Industrie

Schmollers Jahrbuch für Gesetzgebung, Wirtschaft und Verwaltung
Stahl und Eisen
Veröffentlichungen des Reichsverbandes der deutschen Industrie
Vossische Zeitung
Weltwirtschaftliches Archiv
Zeitschrift für das Berg-, Hütten- und Salinenwesen

PUBLISHED LITERATURE

Albertin, Lothar, *Liberalismus und Demokratie am Anfang der Weimarer Republik. Eine vergleichende Analyse der DDP und der DVP* (Beiträge zur Geschichte des Parlamentarismus und der politischen Parteien, Vol. 45) (Düsseldorf, 1972).

Albertin, Lothar, "Die Verantwortung der liberalen Parteien für das Scheitern der Grossen Koalition im Herbst 1921. Ökonomische und ideologische Einflüsse auf die Funktionsfähigkeit der parteienstaatlichen Demokratie," *Historische Zeitschrift*, 205 (1967), pp. 566–627.

Ausschuss zur Untersuchung der Erzeugungs- und Absatzbedingungen der deutschen Wirtschaft. Verhandlungen und Berichte des Unterausschusses für allgemeine Wirtschaftsstruktur. (I. Unterausschuss) 3. Arbeitsgruppe. *Wandlungen in den wirtschaftlichen Organisationsformen. Erster Teil. Wandlungen in den Rechtsformen der Einzelunternehmungen und Konzerne* (Berlin, 1928).

Bariéty, Jacques, "Das Zustandekommen der Internationalen Rohstahlgemeinschaft (1926) als Alternative zum misslungenen "Schwerindustriellen Projekt" des Versailler Vertrages," *Industrielles System und politische Entwicklung in der Weimarer Republik: Verhandlungen des Internationalen Symposiums in Bochum vom 12.–17. Juni 1973*, ed. Hans Mommsen, Dietmar Petzina, Bernd Weisbrod (Düsseldorf, 1974) (= *Industrielles System*), pp. 552–568.

Bariéty, Jacques, "Les Réparations Allemandes après la Première Guerre Mondiale: Objet ou Pretexte à une Politique Rhénane de la France (1919–1924)," *Bulletin de la Société d'Histoire Moderne*, 5th series, No. 6 (1973), pp. 20–33.

Baumont, Maurice, *La Faillité de la Paix (1918–1939)*, 2 vols., 3rd ed. (Paris, 1951).

Beckerath, Herbert von, *Grossindustrie und Gesellschaftsordnung. Industrielle und politische Dynamik* (Tübingen and Zürich, 1954).

Beckerath, Herbert von, *Kräfte, Ziele und Gestaltungen in der deutschen Industrie* (Jena, 1922).

Beckerath, Herbert von, *Modern Industrial Organization. An Economic Interpretation* (New York and London, 1933).

481

Benham, Frederic, *The Iron and Steel Industry of Germany, France, Belgium, Luxembourg and the Saar* (London, 1934).

Berg, Peter, *Deutschland und Amerika 1918–1929* (Lübeck and Hamburg, 1963).

Bergmann, Carl, *The History of Reparations* (Boston and New York, 1927).

Berkenkopf, Paul, *Die Neuorganisation der deutschen Grosseisenindustrie seit der Währungsstabilisierung* (Essen, 1928).

Blaich, Fritz, *Kartell- und Monopolpolitik im kaiserlichen Deutschland* (Düsseldorf, 1973).

Bogner, H., *Die Wandlungen in der Organisation der deutschen Stahlindustrie und ihre Ursachen* (Diss. Phil.) (Heidelberg, 1929).

Böhme, Helmut, "Emil Kirdorf, Überlegungen zu einer Unternehmerbiographie," *Tradition, Zeitschrift für Firmengeschichte und Unternehmerbiographie*, 13 (December 1968), pp. 282–300.

Bonn, Moritz J., *Das Schicksal des deutschen Kapitalismus* (Berlin, 1926).

Bonn, Moritz J., *So macht man Geschichte. Bilanz eines Lebens* (Munich, 1953).

Bracher, Karl Dietrich, *Die Auflösung der Weimarer Republik*, 2nd ed. (Stuttgart and Düsseldorf, 1957).

Brady, Robert, *The Rationalization of German Industry. A Study in the Evolution of Economic Planning* (Berkeley, Calif., 1933).

Brecht, Arnold, *Aus nächster Nähe* (Stuttgart, 1966).

Brecht, Arnold, *The Political Education of Arnold Brecht. An Autobiography 1884–1970* (Princeton, 1970).

Bresciani-Turroni, Costantino, *The Economics of Inflation. A Study of Currency Depreciation in Post-War Germany, 1914–1923* (London, 1968) (1st ed. 1937).

Bry, Gerhard, *Wages in Germany, 1871–1945* (Princeton, 1960).

Buchner, Fritz, *Hundert Jahre Geschichte der Maschinenfabrik Augsburg-Nürnberg* (n.p., 1940).

Die bürgerlichen Parteien in Deutschland. Handbuch der Geschichte der bürgerlichen Parteien und anderer bürgerlicher Interessenorganisationen vom Vormärz bis zum Jahre 1945. ed. Dieter Fricke et al., 2 vols. (Leipzig 1968 and 1970).

Burn, D. L., *The Economic History of Steelmaking* (Cambridge, 1940).

Cecil, Lamar, *Albert Ballin* (Princeton, 1967).

Clausing, Gustav, *Die wirtschaftlichen Wechsellagen von 1919–1932* (Jena, 1933).

Cornebise, Alfred E., "Gustav Stresemann and the Ruhr Occupation:

The Making of a Statesman," *European Studies Review*, Vol. 2, No. 1 (January 1972), pp. 43–68.

Curth, Hermann, ed., *Wichard von Moellendorff, Konservativer Sozialismus* (Hamburg, 1932).

Czada, Peter, "Grosse Inflation und Wirtschaftswachstum," *Industrielles System*, pp. 386–394.

Czada, Peter, "Ursachen und Folgen der grossen Inflation," Harold Winkel, ed., *Finanz- und wirtschaftspolitische Fragen der Zwischenkriegszeit* (Schriften der Vereins für Sozialpolitik, Vol. 73) (Berlin, 1973), pp. 9–43.

Dalberg, Rudolf, *Valuta-Dumping* (Berlin, 1921).

Degenfeld-Schönberg, Ferdinand Graf von, "Die Unternehmerpersönlichkeit in der modernen Volkswirtschaft," *Schmollers Jahrbuch für Gesetzgebung Verwaltung und Volkswirtschaft im Deutschen Reich*. 55 (1929), pp. 55–75.

Deutscher Metallarbeiterverband, ed., *Konzerne der Metallindustrie. Eine Darstellung der Entwicklung und des gegenwärtigen Standes der grossen Konzerne der deutschen Metallindustrie* (Stuttgart, 1923).

Döhn, Lothar, *Politik und Interesse. Die Interessenstruktur der Deutschen Volkspartei* (Meisenheim, 1970).

Elben, Wolfgang, *Das Problem der Kontinuität in der deutschen Revolution* (Beiträge zur Geschichte des Parlamentarismus und der politischen Parteien, Vol. 31) (Düsseldorf, 1969).

Ellis, Howard S., *German Monetary Theory 1905–1933* (Cambridge, 1937).

Elster, Karl, *Von der Mark zur Reichsmark. Die Geschichte der deutschen Währung in den Jahren 1914–1924* (Jena, 1928).

Embacher, Georg, *Periodische Wandlungen im Zusammenschluss der deutschen Industrie* (Diss. Phil.) (Dessau, 1928).

Epstein, Klaus, *Matthias Erzberger und das Dilemma der deutschen Demokratie* (Berlin and Frankfurt, 1962).

Erdmann, Karl-Dietrich, *Adenauer in der Rheinlandpolitik nach dem Ersten Weltkrieg* (Stuttgart, 1966).

Eulenberg, Franz, "Die sozialen Wirkungen der Währungsverhältnisse," *Jahrbücher für Nationalökonomie und Statistik*, III, 67 (1924).

Eyck, Erich, *A History of the Weimar Republic*, 2 vols. (Cambridge, 1962).

Favez, Jean-Claude, *Le Reich devant l'occupation franco-belge de la Ruhr en 1923* (Geneva, 1969).

Feldman, Gerald D., *Army, Industry, and Labor in Germany 1914–1918* (Princeton, 1966).

Feldman, Gerald D., "Big Business and the Kapp Putsch," *Central European History*, IV, 2 (June 1971), pp. 99–130.

Feldman, Gerald D., "Fondements sociaux de la mobilisation économique en Allemagne (1914–1916)," *Annales. Économies. Sociétés. Civilisations*, 24, 1 (January–February 1969), pp. 102–127.

Feldman, Gerald D., "German Business Between War and Revolution: The Origins of the Stinnes-Legien Agreement," Gerhard A. Ritter, ed., *Entstehung und Wandel der modernen Gesellschaft. Festschrift für Hans Rosenberg zum 65. Geburtstag* (Berlin, 1970), pp. 312–341.

Feldman, Gerald D., "The Social and Economic Policies of German Big Business 1918–1929," *American Historical Review*, LXXV, 1 (October 1969), pp. 47–55.

Feldman, Gerald D., "The Origins of the Stinnes-Legien Agreement: A Documentation," *Internationale wissenschaftliche Korrespondenz zur Geschichte der Deutschen Arbeiterbewegung*, 19/20 (December 1972), pp. 45–102.

Feldman, Gerald D., "Wirtschafts- und sozialpolitische Probleme der deutschen Demobilmachung 1918/19," *Industrielles System*, pp. 618–636.

Feldman, Gerald D., "The Collapse of the Steel Works Association, 1912–1919," *Sozialgeschichte Heute. Festschrift für Hans Rosenberg zum 70. Geburtstag*. Hans-Ulrich Wehler, ed. (Göttingen, 1974), pp. 575–593.

Feldman, Gerald D., Eberhard Kolb, and Reinhard Rürup, "Die Massenbewegungen der Arbeiterschaft in Deutschland am Ende des Ersten Weltkrieges (1917–1920)," *Politische Vierteljahresschrift 13* (1972), pp. 84–105.

Felix, David, *Walther Rathenau and the Weimar Republic. The Politics of Reparations* (Baltimore and London, 1971).

Fischart, Johannes, "Hans von Raumer," *Die Weltbühne*, 20 (October 23, 1924), pp. 622–624.

Fischer, Fritz, *Griff nach der Weltmacht* (Düsseldorf, 1961).

Fischer, Wolfram, "Konjunkturen und Krisen im Ruhrgebiet seit 1840 und die wirtschaftspolitische Willensbildung der Unternehmer," *Wirtschaft und Gesellschaft im Zeitalter der Industrialisierung. Aufsätze, Studien, Vorträge* (Göttingen, 1972).

Fischer, Wolfram, "Staatsverwaltung und Interessenverbände im deutschen Reich 1871–1914," *Wirtschaft und Gesellschaft*, pp. 194–223.

Fischer, Wolfram, "Die Weimarer Republik unter den weltwirtschaftlichen Bedingungen der Zwischenkriegszeit," *Industrielles System*, pp. 26–30.

Fischer, Wolfram, and Peter Czada, "Wandlungen in der deutschen Industriestruktur im 20. Jahrhundert," Gerhard A. Ritter, ed., *Entstehung und Wandel*, pp. 116–165.

Flink, Salomon, *The German Reichsbank and Economic Germany* (New York, 1930).

Fraenkel, Ernst, "Der Ruhreisenstreit 1928–1929 in historisch-politischer Sicht," *Staat, Wirtschaft und Politik in der Weimarer Republik. Festschrift für Heinrich Brüning* (Berlin, 1967), pp. 97–117.

Friedensburg, Ferdinand, *Kohle und Eisen im Weltkriege und in den Friedensschlüssen* (Munich and Berlin, 1934).

Gatzke, Hans, *Germany's Drive to the West. A Study of German War Aims During the First World War* (Baltimore, 1950).

Gehr, M., *Das Verhältnis zwischen Banken und Industrie in Deutschland seit der Mitte des 19. Jahrhunderts* (Diss. Phil.) (Stuttgart, 1959).

Geiger, Theodor, *Die Klassengesellschaft im Schmelztiegel* (Cologne, 1949).

Geyer, Curt, *Drei Verderber Deutschlands. Ein Beitrag zur Geschichte Deutschlands und der Reparationsfrage von 1920–1924* (Berlin, 1924).

Gossweiler, Kurt, "Die Vereinigten Stahlwerke und die Grossbanken. Eine Studie über das Verhältnis von Banken und Industriekapital in der Weimarer Republik und unter der faschistischen Diktatur (1926–1936)," *Jahrbuch für Wirtschaftsgeschichte* (1965), pp. 11–53.

Graham, Frank D., *Exchange, Prices and Production in Hyper-Inflation: Germany 1920–1923* (Princeton, 1930).

Greer, Guy, *The Ruhr-Lorraine Industrial Problem. A Study of the Two Regions and their Relation to the Reparation Question* (New York, 1925).

Hachenburg, Max, *Lebenserinnerungen eines Rechtsanwalts.* (Düsseldorf, 1927).

Hagemann, W., *Das Verhältnis der deutschen Grossbanken zur Industrie* (Berlin, 1931).

Hallgarten, George F., *Hitler, Reichswehr und Industrie* (Frankfurt, 1955).

Halperin, S. William, *Germany Tried Democracy. A Political History of the Reich from 1918 to 1933* (New York, 1946).

Hartmann, Heinz, *Authority and Organization in German Management* (Princeton, 1959).

Hartwich, Hans-Hermann, *Arbeitsmarkt, Verbände und Staat 1918–1933. Die öffentliche Bindung unternehmerischer Funktionen in der Weimarer Republik* (Berlin, 1967).

Hauenstein, Fritz, et al., *Der Weg zum industriellen Spitzenverband* (Frankfurt a.M., 1956).

Dr. Hauschild, *Der Vorläufige Reichswirtschaftsrat 1920–1926* (Berlin, 1926).

Helfer, Christian, "Über militärische Einflüsse auf die Industrielle Entwicklung in Deutschland," *Schmollers Jahrbuch für Gesetzgebung, Verwaltung und Wirtschaft*, 83 (1963), pp. 597–609.

Hennig, Eike, "Materialien zur Diskussion der Monopolgruppentheorie," *Neue Politische Literatur* (April–June 1973), pp. 170–193.

Hermann, Walther, "Otto Wolff," *Rheinisch- Westfälische Wirtschaftsbiographien*, Vol. 8 (Münster, 1962), pp. 123–156.

Herzog, Bodo, "Die Freundschaft zwischen Oswald Spengler und Paul Reusch," Anton Kontanek, ed., *Spengler-Studien. Festgabe für Manfred Schröter zum 85. Geburtstag* (Munich, 1965).

Heymann, H. G., *Die gemischten Werke im deutschen Grosseisengewerbe* (Stuttgart and Berlin, 1904).

Hilferding, Rudolf, *Die Aufgaben der Sozialdemokratie in der Republik. Hilferding auf dem Parteitag zu Kiel.* Mai 1927 (Berlin, 1927).

Hirsch, Julius, *Die deutsche Währungsfrage* (Jena, 1924).

Hirsch, Julius, *Der moderne Handel, seine Organisation und Formen und die staatliche Binnenhandelspolitik.* Grundriss der Sozialökonomie V. Abteilung. Handel. Transportwesen. Bankwesen. II. Teil, 2nd ed. (Tübingen, 1925).

Hoffmann, Walther G., "Die unverteilten Gewinne der Aktiengesellschaften in Deutschland 1871–1957. Trend, Konjunkturverlauf und branchenmässige Unterschiede," *Zeitschrift für die gesamte Staatswissenschaft*, 115 (1959), pp. 271–291.

Hoffmann, Walther G., *Das Wachstum der deutschen Wirtschaft seit der Mitte des 19. Jahrhunderts* (Berlin, Heidelberg, New York, 1965).

Holborn, Hajo, *A History of Modern Germany 1840–1945* (New York, 1969).

Holzschuher, Veit, *Soziale und ökonomische Hintergründe der Kartellbewegung* (Diss. Phil.) (Erlangen, 1962).

Honhart, Michael W., "The Incomplete Revolution. The Social Democrats' Failure to Transform the German Economy, 1918–1920," Ph.D. Diss. (Duke, 1972).

Hortzschansky, Günter, *Der nationale Verrat der deutschen Monopolherren während des Ruhrkompfes 1923* (Berlin, 1961).

Huber, Ernst-Rudolf, *Deutsche Verfassungsgeschichte seit 1789*, Vol. 3 (Stuttgart, 1963).

"L'Industrie du Fer dans la Ruhr," ed. Mission Interalliée de Contrôle des Usines et des Mines, *1914–1924. Dix Ans du Développement Industriel Allemand*, 10 vols. (Brusssels, November 1924).

Industrielles System und politische Entwicklung in der Weimarer Republik: Verhandlungen des Internationalen Symposiums in Bochum vom 12.–17. Juni 1973, ed. Hans Mommsen, Dietmar Petzina, Bernd Weisbrod (Düsseldorf, 1974).

Jaeger, Hans, *Unternehmer in der deutschen Politik (1890–1918)* (Bonner Historische Forschungen, Vol. 30) (Bonn, 1967).

Jeidels, O., *Das Verhältnis der deutschen Grossbanken zur Industrie mit besonderer Berücksichtigung der Eisenindustrie* (Leipzig, 1905).

Kaelble, Helmut, *Industrielle Interessenpolitik in der Wilhelminischen Gesellschaft. Centralverband Deutscher Industrieller 1895–1914* (Berlin, 1967).

Kaun, Heinrich, *Die Geschichte der Zentralarbeitsgemeinschaft der industriellen und gewerblichen Arbeitgeber und Arbeitnehmer Deutschlands* (Jena, 1938).

Kessler, Harry Graf, *Walther Rathenau. Sein Leben und sein Werk* (Berlin, 1928).

Kessler, Harry Graf, *Tagebücher 1918–1937* (Frankfurt a.M., 1961).

Klass, Gert von, *Hugo Stinnes* (Tübingen, 1958).

Klass, Gert von. *Albert Vögler. Einer der Grossen des Reviers* (Tübingen, 1957).

Klotzbach, Arthur, *Der Roheisen-Verband. Ein geschichtlicher Rückblick auf die Zusammenschlussbestrebungen in der deutschen Hochofenindustrie* (Düsseldorf, 1926).

Kocka, Jürgen, "Industrielles Management. Konzeptionen und Modell in Deutschland vor 1914," *Vierteljahrschrift für Sozial- und Wirtschaftsgeschichte*, 56 (1969), pp. 332–372.

Kocka, Jürgen, *Klassengesellschaft im Krieg 1914–1918* (Kritische Studien zur Geschichtswissenschaft, Vol. 8) (Göttingen, 1973).

Kocka, Jürgen, *Unternehmensverwaltung und Angestelltenschaft am Beispiel Siemens 1874–1914. Zum Verhältnis von Kapitalismus und Bürokratie in der deutschen Industrialisierung* (Stuttgart, 1969).

Kocka, Jürgen, *Unternehmer in der deutschen Industrialisierung* (Göttingen, 1975).

Krämer, Georg, *Die deutsche Aussenhandelskontrolle in der Nachkriegszeit.* (Wirtschafts- und Sozialwissenschaft. Diss.) (Frankfurt a.M., 1926).

Krohn, Claus-Dieter, *Stabilisierung und ökonomische Interessen. Die Finanzpolitik des Deutschen Reiches 1923–1927* (Düsseldorf, 1974).

Krüger, Peter, "Die Rolle der Banken und der Industrie in den deutschen reparationspolitischen Entscheidungen nach dem Ersten Weltkrieg," *Industrielles System*, pp. 568–582.

Krüger, Peter, *Deutschland und die Reparationen 1918/19. Die Genesis des Reparationsproblems in Deutschland zwischen Waffenstillstand und Versailler Friedensschluss* (Stuttgart, 1973).

Kuznets, Simon, "Retardation of Economic Growth," *Journal of Economic and Business History*, 1 (August 1929), pp. 534–600.

Lamert, Franz, *Das Verhältnis zwischen eisenschaffender und eisenverarbeitender Industrie seit dem 1. Weltkrieg* (Cologne, 1960).

Landes, David, *The Unbound Prometheus. Technological Change and Industrial Development in Western Europe from 1750 to the Present* (Cambridge, 1969).

Lansburgh, Alfred, *Die Politik der Reichsbank und die Reichsschatzanweisungen nach dem Krieg* (Schriften des Vereins für Sozialpolitik, Vol. 166, Part II) (Munich and Leipzig, 1924).

Laubach, Ernst, *Die Politik der Kabinette Wirth 1921/22* (Lübeck and Hamburg, 1968).

Laursen, Karsten and Jørgen Pedersen, *The German Inflation 1918–1923* (Amsterdam, 1964).

Leckebusch, Günter, *Die Beziehungen der deutschen Seeschiffswerften zur Eisenindustrie an der Ruhr in der Zeit von 1850–1930* (Schriften zur Rheinisch-Westfälischen Wirtschaftsgeschichte, Vol. 8) (Cologne, 1963).

Levy, Hermann, *Industrial Germany. A Study of Its Monopoly Organization and Their Control by the State* (Cambridge, 1935).

Lewinsohn, Richard, *Das Geld in der Politik* (Berlin, 1930).

Lewinsohn, Richard, *Die Umschichtung der europäischen Vermögen* (Berlin, 1925).

Liefmann, Robert, *Die Kartelle in und nach dem Kriege* (Berlin, 1918).

Liefmann, Robert, *Cartels, Concerns and Trusts* (London, 1932).

Luther, Hans, *Politiker ohne Partei* (Stuttgart, 1960).

McDougall, Walter A., "French Rhineland Policy and the Struggle for European Stabilization: Reparations, Security, and Rhenish Separatism, 1918–1924," Ph.D. Diss. (Chicago, 1974).

Maier, Charles, "Coal and Economic Power in the Weimar Republic: The Effects of the Coal Crisis of 1920," *Industrielles System*, pp. 530–542.

Maier, Charles, *Recasting Bourgeois Europe: Stabilization in France, Germany and Italy in the Decade after World War I* (Princeton, 1975).

Mariaux, Paul, ed., *Paul Silverberg. Reden und Schriften* (Cologne, 1951).

Maschke, Erich, *Es entsteht ein Konzern. Paul Reusch und die GHH* (Tübingen, 1969).

Maschke, Erich, *Grundzüge der deutschen Kartellgeschichte bis 1914* (Dortmund, 1964).

Meissner, Otto, *Staatssekretär unter Ebert-Hindenburg-Hitler*, 3rd ed. (Hamburg, 1950).

Müller, Alfred, *Die deutsche Rohstoffbewirtschaftung im Dienst des deutschen Monopolkapitals* (Berlin, 1955).

Neuloh, Otto, *Die deutsche Betriebsverfassung und ihre Sozialformen bis zur Mitbestimmung* (Tübingen, 1956).

Nocken, Ulrich, "Inter-Industrial Conflicts and Alliances as Exemplified by the AVI Agreement," *Industrielles System*, pp. 693–703.

Nussbaum, Helga, *Unternehmer gegen Monopole. Über Struktur und Aktionen antimonopolistischer bürgerlicher Gruppen zu Beginn des 20. Jahrhunderts* (Berlin, 1966).

Nussbaum, Manfred, "Unternehmenskonzentration und Investstrategie nach dem Ersten Weltkrieg," *Jahrbuch für Wirtschaftsgeschichte* (1974), pp. 51–75.

Oertzen, Peter von, *Betriebsräte in der Novemberrevolution. Eine politikwissenschaftliche Untersuchung über Ideengehalt und Struktur der betrieblichen und wirtschaftlichen Arbeiterräte in der deutschen Revolution 1918/19* (Beiträge zur Geschichte des Parlamentarismus und der politischen Parteien, Vol. 25) (Düsseldorf, 1962).

Offe, Klaus, *Strukturprobleme des kapitalistischen Staates* (Frankfurt a.M., 1973).

Ogger, Günter, *Friedrich Flick der Grosse* (Bern, Munich, Vienna, 1971).

Parker, William N., "Coal and Steel Output Movements in Western Europe," *Explorations in Entrepreneurial History*, 9 (April 1957), pp. 214–230.

Parker, William, "Entrepreneurship, Industrial Organization, and Economic Growth: A German Example," *Journal of Economic History*, 14 (1954), pp. 380–400.

Petzina, Dieter, und Werner Abelshauser, "Zum Problem der relativen Stagnation der deutschen Wirtschaft in den zwanziger Jahren," *Industrielles System*, pp. 57–76.

Pinner, Felix (= Frank Fassland), "Hugo Stinnes," *Deutsche Wirtschaftsführer* (Berlin, 1924).

Pinson, Koppel, *Modern Germany. Its History and Civilisation*, 2nd ed. (New York, 1966).

Polysius, Otto, *Verbandsbestrebungen im deutschen Maschinenbau* (Diss. Phil.) (Dessau, 1921).

Pounds, Norman, and William N. Parker, *Coal and Steel in Western Europe. The Influence of Resources and Techniques on Production* (Bloomington, Ind., 1957).

Preller, Ludwig, *Sozialpolitik in der Weimarer Republik* (Stuttgart, 1949).

Raumer, Hans von, "Walther Rathenau," *Deutsche Rundschau*, 78 (1952).

Redlich, Fritz, "German Economic Planning for War and Peace," *Review of Politics*, VI (July 1944), pp. 319–326.

Reichert, Jakob, *Die Arbeitsgemeinschaft der industriellen Arbeitgeber und Arbeitnehmer Deutschlands—Ein Faktor unserer Wirtschaftspolitik* (Berlin, 1919).

Reichert, Jakob, *Rettung aus der Valutanot* (Berlin, 1919).

Reichert, Jakob, "Peter Klöckner," *Rheinisch-Westfälische Wirtschaftsbiographien* (Münster, 1960), pp. 85–104.

Riesser, E., *Die deutschen Grossbanken und ihre Konzentration* (Jena, 1910).

Ringer, Fritz, *The German Inflation of 1923* (Problems of European History: A Documentary Collection) (New York, London, Toronto, 1969).

Roesler, Konrad, *Die Finanzpolitik des deutschen Reiches im Ersten Weltkrieg* (Untersuchungen über das Spar-, Giro- und Kreditwesen. Schriften des Instituts für das Spar-, Giro- und Kreditwesen an der Universität Bonn, Vol. 37) (Bonn, 1967).

Rosenberg, Arthur, *Geschichte der Weimarer Republik* (Stuttgart, 1961).

Rosenberg, Hans, *Bureaucracy, Aristocracy, and Autocracy. The Prussian Experience 1660–1815* (Cambridge, Mass., 1958).

Rosenberg, Hans, *Grosse Depression und Bismarckzeit. Wirtschaftsablauf, Gesellschaft und Politik in Mitteleuropa* (Berlin, 1967).

Rupieper, Hermann J., "Industrie und Reparationen: Einige Aspekte des Reparationsproblems 1922–1924," *Industrielles System*, pp. 582–592.

Rupieper, Hermann J., "Politics and Economics: The Cuno Government and Reparations, 1922–1923," Ph.D. Diss. (Stanford, Calif., 1974).

Rürup, Reinhard, *Probleme der Revolution in Deutschland* (Institut für Europäische Geschichte, Vorträge, No. 50) (Wiesbaden, 1968).

Sachtler, Heinz, *Wandlungen des industriellen Unternehmers in Deutschland seit Beginn des 19. Jahrhunderts. Ein Versuch zur Typologie des Unternehmers* (Diss. Phil.) (Halle, 1938).

Saul, Klaus, *Staat, Industrie, Arbeiterbewegung im Kaiserreich. Zur Innen- und Sozialpolitik des Wilhelminischen Deutschland 1903–1914* (Düsseldorf, 1974).

Schacht, Hjalmar, *76 Jahre meines Lebens* (Bad Wörishofen, 1953).

Schacht, Hjalmar, *Die Stabilisierung der Mark* (Stuttgart, Berlin, Leipzig, 1927).

Schieck, Hans, *Der Kampf um die deutsche Wirtschaftspolitik nach dem Novemberumsturz 1918* (Diss. Phil.) (Heidelberg, 1958).

Schiffer, Eugen, *Ein Leben für den Liberalismus* (Berlin, 1951).

Schlaghecke, Alfons, *Die Preissteigerung, Absatzorganisation und Bewirtschaftung des Eisens 1914–1920* (Diss. Phil.) (Giessen, 1920).

Schneider, Hans J., "Zur Analyse des Eisenmarktes," *Vierteljahreshefte zur Konjunkturforschung*, Sonderheft 1 (Berlin, 1927).

Schneider, Hans J., *Der Wiederaufbau der Grosseisenindustrie an Rhein und Ruhr* (Berlin, 1930).

Schröder, Ernst, *Otto Wiedfeldt. Eine Biographie* (Beiträge zur Geschichte von Stadt und Stift Essen, Vol. 80) (Essen, 1964).

Schrödter, Emil, "25 Jahre deutsche Eisenindustrie," *Stahl und Eisen*, 24 (May 1, 1904), pp. 490–500.

Schulz, Gerhard, *Zwischen Demokratie und Diktatur, Vol. I: Die Periode der Konsolidierung und der Revision des Bismarckschen Reichsaufbaus. 1919–1930* (Berlin, 1963).

Schumpeter, Joseph, *Business Cycles*, 2 vols. (New York and London, 1939).

Schumpeter, Joseph, *Kapitalismus, Sozialismus und Demokratie*. 2nd rev. ed. (Bern, 1950).

Schumpeter, Joseph, "Sozialistische Möglichkeiten von Heute," *Archiv für Sozialwissenschaft*, 48 (1920–1921), pp. 305–360.

Schumpeter, Joseph, "Der Unternehmer in der Volkswirtschaft von Heute," Bernhard Harms, ed., *Strukturwandlungen der deutschen Wirtschaft*, 2 vols. (Berlin, 1928).

Soutou, Georges, "Der Einfluss der Schwerindustrie auf die Gestaltung der Frankreichpolitik Deutschlands 1919–1921," *Industrielles System*, pp. 543–552.

Spencer, Elaine, Glovka, "West German Coal, Iron and Steel Industrialists as Employers, 1896–1914," Ph.D. Diss. (Berkeley, Calif., 1970).

Spethmann, Hans, *Zwölf Jahre Ruhrbergbau. Aus seiner Geschichte vom Kriegsanfang bis zum Franzosenabmarsch, 1914–1925*, 5 vols. (Berlin, 1928–1931).

Stegmann, Dirk, "Deutsche Zoll- und Handelspolitik 1924/25–1929 unter Berücksichtigung agrarischer und industrieller Interessen," *Industrielles System*, pp. 499–513.

Stegmann, Dirk, "Die Silverberg Kontroverse 1926. Unternehmerpolitik zwischen Reform und Restauration," Hans-Ulrich Wehler, ed., *Sozialgeschichte Heute. Festschrift für Hans Rosenberg zum 70. Geburtstag* (Göttingen, 1974), pp. 594–611.

Stegmann, Dirk, "Zum Verhältnis von Grossindustrie und Nationalsozialismus 1930–1933," *Archiv für Sozialgeschichte*, 13 (1973), pp. 399–482.

Stinnes, Hugo, *Mark-Stabilisierung und Arbeitsleistung. Rede von Hugo Stinnes gehalten am 9. November 1922 im Reichswirtschaftsrat* (Berlin, 1922).

Stockder, Archibald H., *History of the Trade Associations of the German Coal Industry Under Private and State Control* (New York, 1924).

Stockhausen, Max von, *6 Jahre Reichskanzlei. Von Rapallo nach Locarno* (ed. Walter Görlitz) (Bonn, 1954).

Stolper, Gustav, Karl Häuser, and Knut Bochardt, *The German Economy. 1870 to the Present* (London, 1967).

Stresemann, Gustav, *Vermächtnis. Der Nachlass in drei Bänden*, ed. Henry Bernhard, 3 vols. (Berlin, 1932).

Svennilson, Ingvar, *Growth and Stagnation in the European Economy* (Geneva, 1954).

Thelwall, J. W. F., and C. J. Kavanagh, *Report on the Economic and Financial Conditions in Germany to March, 1922* (Board of Overseas Trade) (London, 1922).

Thelwall, J. W. F., and C. J. Kavanagh, *Report on the Economic and Financial Conditions in Germany, Revised to April, 1924* (Board of Overseas Trade) (London, 1924).

Todsal, H. R., "The German Steel Syndicate," *Quarterly Journal of Economics*, 32 (1917), pp. 259–306.

Trachtenberg, Marc, "French Reparation Policy, 1918–1921," Ph.D. Diss. (Berkeley, Calif., 1974).

Trendelenburg, Ernst, *Weltwirtschaftskrise und Aussenhandel. Vortrag gehalten am 26. Januar 1921 in der Deutschen Hochschule für Politik in Berlin* (Berlin, 1921).

Treue, Wilhelm, "Carl Duisbergs Denkschrift von 1915 zur Gründung der 'kleinen IG,'" *Tradition*, 8 (October 1963), pp. 193–227.

Treue, Wilhelm, *Die Feuer verlöschen nie. August Thyssen Hütte 1890–1926* (Düsseldorf and Vienna, 1966).

Troeltsch, Ernst, *Spektator-Briefe. Aufsätze über die deutsche Revolution und die Weltpolitik 1918/1922* (Tübingen, 1924).

Tross, Arnold, *Der Aufbau der eisenerzeugenden und eisenverarbeitenden Industrie-Konzerne Deutschlands* (Berlin, 1923).

Tübben, Willi, *Die nationale und internationale Verbandspolitik der Schwerindustrie vor und nach dem Kriege* (Diss. Phil.) (Heidelberg, 1930).

Turner, Henry A., *Stresemann and the Politics of the Weimar Republic* (Princeton, 1963).

Turner, Henry A., "The Ruhrlade: Secret Cabinet of Heavy Industry in the Weimar Republic," *Central European History*, 3 (September 1970), pp. 195–228.

Turner, Henry A., *Faschismus und Kapitalismus in Deutschland* (Göttingen, 1972).

Ufermann, Paul, *Könige der Inflation* (Berlin, 1924).

Ufermann, Paul, and Carl Hüglin, *Stinnes und seine Konzerne* (Berlin, 1924).

Verbindungsstelle Eisen für Schrifttum und Presse, Düsseldorf, Stahlhof, 1941: *Ernst Poensgen—Die Ehrung im Stahlhof am 17. Oktober 1941.*

Verein Deutscher Eisen- und Stahlindustrieller, *Zur Einverleibung der französisch-lothringischen Erzbecken in das deutsche Reichsgebiet* (Berlin, 1917).

Verein Deutscher Eisenhüttenleute, *Gemeinfassliche Darstellung des Eisenhüttenwesens* (Düsseldorf, 1918).

Vernon, Raymond, ed., *Big Business and the State. Changing Relations in Western Europe* (Cambridge, Mass., 1974).

Vietsch, Eberhard von, *Arnold Rechberg und das Problem der politischen West-Orientierung Deutschlands nach dem Ersten Weltkrieg* (Koblenz, 1958).

Wagenführ, Rolf, *Die Industriewirtschaft. Entwicklungstendenzen der deutschen und internationalen Industrieproduktion 1860 bis 1932* (Vierteljahrshefte zur Konjunkturforschung, Sonderheft 31) (Berlin, 1933).

Warburg, Max M., *Aus meinen Aufzeichnungen* (New York, 1952).

Warriner, D., *Combines and Rationalization in Germany, 1924–1928* (London, 1931).

Weill-Raynal, Étienne, *Les Reparations Allemandes et la France*, 2 vols. (Paris, 1947).

Weisbrod, Bernd, "Zur Form schwerindustrieller Interessenvertretung in der zweiten Hälfte der Weimarer Republik," *Industrielles System*, pp. 674–692.

Wentzcke, Paul, *Ruhrkampf. Einbruch und Abwehr im rheinisch-westfälischen Industriegebiet*, 2 vols. (Berlin, 1930–1932).

Wenzel, Georg, *Deutsche Wirtschaftsführer. Lebensgänge deutscher Wirtschaftspersönlichkeiten. Ein Nachschlagebuch über 1300 Wirtschaftspersönlichkeiten unserer Zeit* (Hamburg, Berlin, Leipzig, 1929).

Whale, Barrett P., *Joint Stock Banking in Germany. A Study of German Credit Banks Before and After the War* (London, 1930).

Wiedenfeld, Kurt, *Ein Jahrhundert rheinischer Montanindustrie 1815–1915* (Bonn, 1916).

Wiedenfeld, Kurt, *Das Persönliche im modernden Unternehmertum*, 2nd ed. (Munich, 1920).

Wiedenfeld, Kurt, *Zwischen Wirtschaft und Staat* (Berlin, 1960).

Wiel, Paul, *Wirtschaftsgeschichte des Ruhrgebietes. Tatsachen und Zahlen* (Essen, 1970).

Williamson, John G., *Karl Helfferich 1872–1924. Economist, Financier, Politician* (Princeton, 1971).

Wilmowsky, Tilo Frh. von, *Rückblickend möchte ich sagen . . .* (Oldenburg and Hamburg, 1961).

Winkler, Heinrich A., ed., *Organisierter Kapitalismus. Voraussetzungen und Anfänge* (Kritische Studien zur Geschichtswissenschaft, Vol. 9) (Göttingen, 1974).

Wiskott, Otto, *Eisenschaffende und eisenverarbeitende Industrie. Eine Untersuchung über die Verschiedenartigkeit ihrer Struktur und über ihr gegenseitiges Verhältnis* (Bonner Staatswissenschaftliche Untersuchungen, Vol. 16) (Bonn and Leipzig, 1929).

Witt, Peter-Christian, "Finanzpolitik und sozialer Wandel in Krieg und Inflation 1918–1924," *Industrielles System*, pp. 394–425.

Wolff, Otto, *Die Geschäfte des Herrn Ouvrard. Aus dem Leben eines genialen Spekulanten* (Frankfurt a.M., 1932).

Wulf, Peter, "Regierung, Parteien, Wirtschaftsverbände und die Sozialisierung des Kohlenbergbaus 1920–1921," *Industrielles System*, pp. 647–657.

Zapf, Wolfgang, *Wandlungen der deutschen Elite. Ein Zirkulationsmodell deutscher Führungsgruppen 1919–1961* (Munich, 1965).

Zimmermann, Ludwig, *Deutsche Aussenpolitik in der Ära der Weimarer Republik* (Göttingen and Berlin, 1958).

Zorn, Wolfgang, "Typen und Entwicklungskräfte deutschen Unternehmertums im 19. Jahrhundert," *Vierteljahrschrift für Sozial- und Wirtschaftsgeschichte*, 44 (March 1957), pp. 57–77.

Zunkel, Friedrich, "Die Gewichtung der Industriegruppen bei der Etablierung des Reichsverbandes der deutschen Industrie," *Industrielles System*, pp. 637–646.

Zunkel, Friedrich, *Der Rheinisch-Westfälische Unternehmer 1834–1879* (Cologne, 1962).

Zunkel, Friedrich, *Industrie und Staatssozialismus. Der Kampf um die Wirtschaftsordunung in Deutschland 1914–1918* (Düsseldorf, 1974).

INDEX

A products, 58, 60, 64, 65n, 67, 147;
export bans on, 60, 86; price in-
creases of, 96, 99; syndicalization of,
30–32
AEG, *see* Allgemeine Elektrizitätsge-
sellschaft
A. G. Hugo Stinnes für Seeschiffahrt
und Überseehandel, 267
Aachener Hüttenverein, 21
Adenauer, Konrad, 412, 445, 447, 449
Adlerwerke, 273
admiralty, 181
agriculture, 452, 464
airplane industry, 70
Aktiengesellschaft für Hoch- und
Tiefbau, 329
Aktieselskabet Sydvaranger, 267
Albert, Heinrich, 392
Allgemeine Elektrizitätsgesellschaft
(AEG), 46, 72, 74, 79, 134, 155–56,
190, 220, 226, 246–47, 249, 252, 272,
274, 276, 278
Allied governments and Allies, 141,
170, 192–93, 207, 228, 228n, 314,
335, 388, 391, 454. *See also* Entente
Alpine Montangesellschaft, 219, 319,
383
Altona, 137
America, Americans, *see* United States
"Americanization," 464
Anglo-American credits, 413
annexationists, 15
anti-Semitism, 416n
Arbeitsgemeinschaft, or *Zentralarbeitsgemeinschaft* (ZAG, Central Working Community of the German Commercial and Industrial Employers
and Employees), 99–100, 326, 344,
394, 399, 451, 469; founding of, 82,
94, 156, 223, 226; in demobilization,
83, 89, 91; criticized by manufacturers, 98, 138; and Moellendorff program, 102, 104–106; and export
controls and levies, 163, 190–92,
195–97, 196n; and EWB, 153, 167,
168n, 176–77, 207; proposed rejuve-
nation, 466–67
Arbeno (Employer Association of the
Northwest Group of the Association
of German Iron and Steel Industrialists), 343, 371, 375, 428–29, 431,
433, 435–37, 440. *See also* Associa-

tion of German Iron and Steel
Industrialists, Northwest Group
arbitration and arbitration boards (for
labor disputes), 252, 257, 324, 336,
343, 389, 428, 436, 467
Arenberg mining group, 251
armistice, 86, 94, 115
army, 41, 51, 53, 56–57, 61–62
assets, 257
Association of Bavarian Metal Industrialists, 75
Association of Employers of Medium-
Sized and Small Factories of the
Iron Industry, 138
Association of German Engineers, 226
Association of German Foundry Engineers, 36n, 46, 259
Association of German Iron and Steel
Industrialists (VdESI), 49n, 81, 104,
107–108, 152, 161, 343, 352–53,
372, 404, 459n; organization, 43–45,
48; discussions between producers
and manufacturers, 78, 96, 132, 138,
145; and export controls and levies,
60, 189–90, 196, 198–99, 201–202,
207, 307; and hours of work, 339f,
438. *See also* Northwest group, Arbeno, heavy industry, producers, iron
and steel industry
Association of German Machine Builders (VDMA), 78, 80, 86f, 95, 108,
139, 149–51, 328, 342, 355, 369;
organization and internal conflicts,
46–48, 72, 74f, 155f, 174, 301f, 442,
453; attack on export levy, 194–96,
196n. *See also* manufacturers, consumers
Association of German Machine Tool
Manufacturers, 75
Association of German Railroad Car
Manufacturers, 151, 137, 175
Association of German Shipbuilders, 43
Association of German Shipyard Works,
98n
August Thyssen Hütte, *see* Thyssen
concern
Austria, 219, 270, 283
authoritarianism, 468f
automotive industry, 70, 271, 273–75
Auxiliary Service Law, 68, 87
AVI Agreements, 454, 457f

495

Library of Congress Cataloging in Publication Data

Feldman, Gerald D
  Iron and steel in the German inflation, 1916–1923.

  Bibliography: p.
  1. Iron industry and trade—Germany—History.
2. Steel industry and trade—Germany—History.
3. Trusts, Industrial—Germany—History. 4. Industry and state—
Germany—History. 5. Inflation (Finance)—Germany—History.
I. Title.
HD9523.5.F44   338.4'7'66910943   76-41900
ISBN 0-691-04215-2